A Bibliographical Guide to the History of

Indian-White Relations

in the United States

A Bibliographical Guide to the History of

Indian-White Relations

in the United States

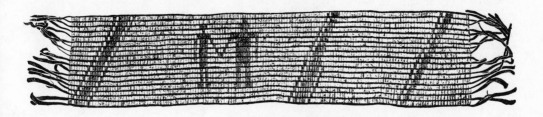

Francis Paul Prucha

A Publication of the
Center for the History of the American Indian
of the Newberry Library

The University of Chicago Press

Chicago and London

FRANCIS PAUL PRUCHA, S.J., is professor of
history at Marquette University, where he
has taught since 1960. Among his numerous
publications are *Broadax and Bayonet: The
Role of the United States Army in the Development of the Northwest, 1815-1860;
American Indian Policy in the Formative
Years: The Indian Trade and Intercourse
Acts, 1790-1834; The Sword of the Republic:
The United States Army on the Frontier,
1783-1845;* and *American Indian Policy in
Crisis: Christian Reformers and the Indian,
1865-1900.*

The University of Chicago Press, Chicago
  60637
The University of Chicago Press, Ltd,
  London

Library of Congress Cataloging in Publication Data

Prucha, Francis Paul.
  A bibliographical guide to the history of Indian-
white relations in the United States.

  "A Publication of the Center for the History of the
American Indian of the Newberry Library."
  Includes index.
  1. Indians of North America--Government relations--
Bibliography. I. Title.
Z1209.2.U5P67   [E93]   016.3231'19'7073 76-16045
ISBN 0-226-68476-8 (clothbound); 0-226-68477-6 (paper)

Contents

PART TWO

CLASSIFIED BIBLIOGRAPHY OF PUBLISHED WORKS

Chapter 15

Social and Economic Developments

Chapter 16

Indians and Indian Groups

Chapter 17

Special Topics

Preface

This bibliographic guide is intended as a tool for persons interested in the history of Indian-white relations in the United States. Part One lists the important guides and other reference works that will direct readers to valuable materials on Indian affairs--in government archives and publications, in manuscript collections, in newspapers and periodicals, and in other categories of sources not limited to Indian-white relations only. Part Two gives lists of books, articles, and other published works dealing with a wide variety of Indian-white relations. This bibliography is classified according to subject, and the chapters and subdivisions are introduced by brief remarks. Since each work is entered in the bibliography only once, use of the index is necessary to locate all items that touch on a given topic.

The number of publications on Indian-white relations is greater, of course, than could be included in this single volume, and some hard decisions had to be made about excluding certain categories and omitting individual items within the categories that were selected. Unpublished master's theses, although many of them contain valuable material, were excluded. Reports and studies originating in agencies of the federal government have not been listed except in some special cases; catalogs of government documents, however, are given in Part One. Anthropological works have in general been omitted unless they give essential background or in some other way pertain to Indian-white relations. The line, of course, has been very difficult to draw, and absolute consistency has not been possible. Mimeographed material for the most part has been excluded. No attempt has been made to indicate all recent reprints of books or other studies; these have proliferated greatly in recent years and can usually be easily located if the original publication is known. It should be noted that the classification is not primarily by tribal groups. Thus items on Cherokee education, for example, will be found in the chapter on education, not in the section on Cherokee Indians.

Although most of the works listed were written by historians--amateur or professional--and provide historical narrative and analysis or biographical treatment, some reminiscences and similar accounts have been included. And many of the works, of course, on health, education, law, and similar specialized subjects have been written by experts in those fields. There are also sections labeled "Current Comment," in which are listed comments on Indian affairs period by period. These writings give a good indication of the thought and attitudes on Indian matters at different times in our past.

Emphasis is on United States history, but British colonial Indian affairs have been included. By and large, Canadian items have been excluded, and no attempt has been made to provide material dealing with Spanish-Indian relations in what is now the United States. These topics warrant full bibliographies of their own.

The bibliography contains items published through 1974, but a few works published later have been included.

A bibliographic guide of this scope has depended upon the assistance of many persons. I have been helped in gathering, verifying, and classifying titles by a series of capable student research assistants: Gerald R. Toner at the Charles Warren Center, Harvard University; Patricia Hosey, John A. Langellier, and Helen M. Wanken at Marquette University. A special debt of gratitude is due Phillip M. Runkel, who served as a research assistant during the final five months of concentrated work on the project and who did much of the work in checking materials in the libraries in Chicago and in the Library of Congress. Georgia R. Crawford expertly typed many of the bibliography cards and the manuscript.

The staffs of many libraries have generously given help. Work on the bibliography was done in the following libraries: Library of Congress, the libraries of Harvard University, Marquette University, University of Chicago, Northwestern University, University of Wisconsin--Madison, University of Wisconsin--Milwaukee, University of Illinois--Chicago Circle, Loyola University of Chicago, State Historical Society of Wisconsin, and Medical College of Wisconsin, and in the public libraries of Milwaukee and Chicago. The final work on the bibliography was done at the Newberry Library, Chicago, whose holdings on Indian subjects were of special value and whose staff greatly aided the project.

The completion of the project was made possible by a research grant from the National Endowment for the Humanities.

Problems of selection and classification arose at many points in the preparation of this volume. It is too much to hope that they were all solved in a way that will satisfy everyone. But I do hope that the bibliography will prove useful to many.

Part One
Guides to Sources

1
Materials in the National Archives

Because the federal government conducted the official relations with the American Indian groups, the largest and most important source of records for the history of Indian-white relations in the United States is the National Archives, Washington, D.C.

These archival records are organized by originating agency and classified by Record Group. An understanding of the arrangement and general contents of the Record Groups can be gained from the following guide.

1. Guide to the National Archives of the United States. Washington: National Archives and Records Service, 1974.

RECORDS OF THE BUREAU OF INDIAN AFFAIRS

The most important collection of records is that of the Bureau of Indian Affairs (Record Group 75), which is described in detail in the following publication.

2. Hill, Edward E. Preliminary Inventories, no. 163: Records of the Bureau of Indian Affairs. 2 volumes. Washington: National Archives, 1965.

"The records described in this inventory," Hill says, "are those of the Bureau of Indian Affairs that were in the National Archives on March 31, 1965. They amount to 10,328 cubic feet and are designated Record Group 75, Records of the Bureau of Indian Affairs. Included are records of the Office of the Secretary of War relating to Indian Affairs, 1800-1824, that were separated from the records of the Office of the Secretary and transferred to the Bureau; records of the Office of Indian Trade; general records of the Bureau; records of most of the divisions of the Bureau that existed before 1940; records of some of the field offices; and records of the Board of Indian Commissioners and of the Indian Arts and Crafts Board--units not part of the Bureau but closely connected with it. Also included are photographic and cartographic materials maintained apart from the textual records." (p. 9)

RELATED INDIAN RECORDS

Since Indian affairs touched upon the activities of many federal offices and agencies, valuable material exists in other Record Groups. A brief account of these records is provided by Hill.

"For the pre-Federal period there are records concerning Indian affairs in Record Group 360, Records of the Continental Congress and the Constitutional Convention. In Record Group 107, Records of the Office of the Secretary of War, there are records for both the period until 1824, when the Secretary had immediate responsibility for Indian affairs, and the period from 1824 until 1849, when the Secretary had supervisory control over the Bureau. Also in Record Group 107 are records concerning military activities throughout the 19th Century. Other War Department records relating to Indian affairs are in Record Group 92, Records of the Office of the Quartermaster General; Record Group 94, Records of the Adjutant General's Office; Record Group 98, Records of United States Army Commands, [now classified as Record Group 393, Records of the United States Army Continental Commands]; and Record Group 192, Records of the Office of the Commissary General of Subsistence.

"In Record Group 48, Records of the Office of the Secretary of the Interior, there are records reflecting the Secretary's supervisory role in Indian affairs. These records are chiefly among those of the Indian Division and the Indian Territory Division of the Secretary's Office. The records of the Appointments Division are also useful, especially for information on personnel matters.

"Of the records of other agencies under the Department of the Interior, those of the General Land Office--now part of Record Group 49, Records of the Bureau of Land Management--are the most important. They contain much information concerning Indian lands and the public domain. In Record Group 115, Records of the Bureau of Reclamation, there are records concerning reclamation projects on Indian lands.

"In Record Group 11, United States Government Documents Having General Legal Effect, are the originals of most ratified Indian treaties. There are other records concerning treaties in Record Group 46, Records of the United States Senate; and there are records concerning Indian legislation in this same record group and in Record Group 233, Records of the United States House of Representatives. There are records concerning claims of and against Indians in Record Group 123, Records of the United States Court of Claims; Record Group 205, Records of the Court of Claims Section (Justice); and Record Group 279, Records of the Indian Claims Commission. Fiscal records concerning Indian administration are in Record Group 39, Records of the Bureau of Accounts (Treasury), and in Record Group 217, Records of the United States General Accounting Office.

"Records relating to programs conducted in cooperation with other agencies are in the following record groups: Record Group 33, Records of the Federal Extension Service; Record Group 35, Records of the Civilian Conservation Corps; Record Group 69, Records of the Work Projects Administration; Record Group 90, Records of the Public Health Service; Record Group 95, Records of the Forest Service; Record Group 96, Records of the Farmers Home Administration; Record Group 114, Records of the Soil Conservation Service; Record Group 135, Records of the Public Works Administration; and Record Group 187, Records of the National Resources Planning Board." (Pre-liminary Inventories, no. 163, pp. 9-10)

There are Preliminary Inventories for many of these Record Groups.

The following special guides to Indian materials in the National Archives were prepared by staff members of the National Archives for the National Archives Conference on Research in the History of Indian-White Relations, June 1972. These preliminary guides were distributed only to the participants in the Conference, but they are available for use at the National Archives. They will be superseded by a new guide to records in the National Archives relating to American Indians, now in preparation.

3. Audiovisual Records Relating to Indians in the United States. Compiled by Joe Dean Thomas.

4. Guide to Records in the Civil Archives Division Pertaining to Indian-White Relations. Compiled by Richard C. Crawford and Charles E. South.

5. Guide to Records in the Military Archives Division Pertaining to Indian-White Relations. Compiled by Marie Bouknight, Robert Gruber, Maida Lescher, Richard Meyers, and Geraldine Phillips.

6. Records in the General Archives Division Relating to American Indians. Compiled by Edward E. Hill.

7. Records Pertaining to Indians in Records of the Continental and Confederation Congresses and the Constitutional Convention (Record Group 360): A Preliminary Guide. Compiled by Howard H. Wehmann.

CARTOGRAPHIC RESOURCES

The extensive cartographic holdings of the National Archives contain valuable Indian materials. These are described in the following guides.

8. Kelsay, Laura E. Cartographic Records in the National Archives Relating to Indians in the United States. Preliminary draft prepared for the Conference on the National Archives and Research in Historical Geography, 1971.

9. _____. List of Cartographic Records of the Bureau of Indian Affairs. Special List no. 13. Washington: National Archives, 1954.

REGIONAL BRANCHES OF THE NATIONAL ARCHIVES

In addition to the National Archives in Washington, D.C., there are eleven archives branches (located at the Federal Records Centers). The branches in Atlanta, Chicago, Kansas City, Fort Worth, Denver, San Francisco, Los Angeles, and Seattle contain records of the Bureau of Indian Affairs. These depositories hold records of the field activities of the Bureau--reports, administrative and correspondence files, vital statistics records, tribal census rolls, and school records. Most of these records date from mid-nineteenth century to 1952, although there are later materials for some Indian agencies and other administrative units. These records are described in the following preliminary guide, prepared for the National Archives Conference on Research in the History of Indian-White Relations, 1972.

10. Guide to the Records of the Bureau of Indian Affairs in the Archives Branches of the Federal Records Centers. Compiled by the staffs of the Archives Branches.

MICROFILM PUBLICATIONS

A great many of the Indian records of the National Archives are available in the microfilm publications of the National Archives. This is especially true of the records before 1880. The following publications indicate the microfilmed records.

4

11. The American Indian: Select Catalog of National Archives Microfilm Publications. Washington: National Archives and Records Service, 1972.

12. Catalog of National Archives Microfilm Publications. Washington: National Archives and Records Service, 1974. This booklet indicates only the microcopy number; the reel numbers can be found in pamphlets provided for each microcopy number.

The archives branches in the Federal Records Centers are depositories for copies of National Archives microfilm publications and will lend the reels on interlibrary loan.

OTHER PUBLICATIONS RELATING TO NATIONAL ARCHIVES MATERIAL

13. Hill, Edward E. The Office of Indian Affairs, 1824-1880: Historical Sketches. New York: Clearwater Publishing Company, 1974. Brief histories of agencies and superintendencies, with lists of agents and superintendents, geared to organization of letters received by the Office of Indian Affairs, 1824-1880 (Microcopy 234).

14. Jackson, W. Turrentine. "Materials for Western History in the Department of the Interior Archives." Mississippi Valley Historical Review 35 (June 1948): 61-76.

15. Litton, Gaston. "The Resources of the National Archives for the Study of the American Indian." Ethnohistory 2 (Summer 1955): 191-208.

16. Martin, John H., comp. List of Documents Concerning the Negotiation of Ratified Indian Treaties, 1801-1869. Special List no. 6. Washington: National Archives, 1949.

17. Ryan, Carmelita S. "The Written Record and the American Indian: The Archives of the United States." Western Historical Quarterly 6 (April 1975): 163-173.

18. Schusky, Mary Sue, and Ernest L. Schusky. "A Center of Primary Sources for Plains Indian History." Plains Anthropologist 15 (May 1970): 104-108.

2

Documents of the Federal Government

Because the federal government was charged under the Articles of Confederation and the Constitution with direction of Indian affairs, the federal records are the most important source for the history of official Indian-white relations. The National Archives records discussed above are the fullest documentary source, but printed federal government records are of tremendous extent and absolutely essential for research in almost all aspects of Indian relations. Individual documents are too numerous to be listed here. What follows is a description of the most important printed compilations, catalogs, indexes, and guides, which will enable a student to locate material of interest. A number of these works have been reprinted in recent years.

GUIDES TO GOVERNMENT PUBLICATIONS

19. Schmeckebier, Laurence F., and Roy B. Eastin. Government Publications and Their Use. 2d revised edition. Washington: Brookings Institution, 1969. The most useful guide; full details on the various publications and their idiosyncrasies.

20. Boyd, Anne Morris, and Rae Elizabeth Rips. United States Government Publications. 3d revised edition. New York: H. W. Wilson Company, 1949. A useful general survey.

GENERAL CATALOGS AND INDEXES

Comprehensive indexes or checklists to government publications are necessary for locating Indian materials. Items should be checked under names of individual tribes as well as under "Indian" or "Indians."

21. Poore, Benjamin Perley. A Descriptive Catalogue of the Government Publications of the United States, September 5, 1774-- March 4, 1881. Washington: Government Printing Office, 1885. Also issued as Senate Miscellaneous Document no. 67, 48th Congress, 2d session, serial 2268. Catalog entries are listed chronologically,

with a subject index at the end of the volume. Because of vague or incomplete citations it needs to be used with the Checklist of United States Public Documents (25).

22. Greely, A. W. Public Documents of the First Fourteen Congresses, 1789-1817-- Papers Relating to Early Congressional Documents. Issued as Senate Document no. 428, 56th Congress, 1st session, serial 3879. A supplement, "Public Documents of the First Fourteen Congresses," appeared in Annual Report of the American Historical Association for the Year 1903, 1: 343-406, and was issued also as House Document no. 745, 58th Congress, 2d session, serial 4735. A chronological catalog.

23. Ames, John G. Comprehensive Index to the Publications of the United States Government, 1881-1893. 2 volumes. Washington: Government Printing Office, 1905. Issued as House Document no. 754, 58th Congress, 2d session, serials 4745-4746.

24. Tables of and Annotated Index to the Congressional Series of United States Public Documents. Washington: Government Printing Office, 1902. A selected list of Congressional documents from the 15th to the 52d Congress (1817-1893).

25. Checklist of United States Public Documents, 1789-1909; Congressional: To Close of Sixtieth Congress; Departmental: To End of the Calendar Year 1909. 3d revised and enlarged edition. Washington: Government Printing Office, 1911. Especially useful for finding the serial numbers of documents.

26. Catalogue of the Public Documents . . . of the Government of the United States. 25 volumes. Washington: Government Printing Office, 1896-1945. Generally one volume for each Congress; runs from the 53d Congress (1893-1895) through the 76th Congress (1939-1941).

27. Monthly Catalog of United States Government Publications. Washington: Government Printing Office, 1895--. Title varies. For indexes, see Decennial Cumu-

lative Index, 1941-1950 (Washington: Government Printing Office, 1954) and Decennial Cumulative Index, 1951-1960 (Washington: Government Printing Office, 1968). A new comprehensive index is Cumulative Subject Index to the Monthly Catalog of United States Government Publications, 1900-1971, 15 volumes (Washington: Carrollton Press, 1973-1975).

28. Numerical Lists and Schedule of Volumes of the Reports and Documents of . . . Congress. Washington: Government Printing Office, 1934--. Used to obtain serial numbers for Congressional reports and documents, which since 1941 have been listed in the Monthly Catalog without serial numbers.

CONGRESSIONAL PUBLICATIONS

Proceedings

Indian affairs have received much attention in Congress. The legislative history of the bills dealing with Indian matters can be traced in the official journals of proceedings.

29. Journals of the Continental Congress, 1774-1789. Edited by Worthington Chauncey Ford and others. 34 volumes. Washington: Government Printing Office, 1904-1937. This comprehensive publication supersedes the contemporary printings and early reprints. The journals include a great many reports and other documents as well as the strict account of official proceedings.

Legislative Journals. The journals of the first thirteen Congresses (1789-1815) were reprinted in the following publications.

30. Journal of the Senate. 5 volumes. Washington: Gales and Seaton, 1820-1821.

31. Journal of the House of Representatives. 9 volumes. Washington: Gales and Seaton, 1826.

Beginning with the 15th Congress, the House Journal and the Senate Journal for each session appear in the Serial Set of Congressional Documents. Each volume is indexed separately by both subject matter and bill number. General indexes to the journals of the first sixteen Congresses are the following.

32. Ordway, Albert. General Index of the Journals of Congress, from the First to Tenth Congress Inclusive: Being a Synoptical Subject-Index of the Proceedings of Congress on All Public Business from 1789 to 1809, with References to the Debates, Documents, and Statutes Connected Therewith. Washington: Government Print-

ing Office, 1880. Issued as House Report no. 1776, 46th Congress, 2d session, serial 1939.

33. _____. General Index of the Journals of Congress, from the Eleventh to Sixteenth Congress Inclusive: Being a Synoptical Subject-Index of the Proceedings of Congress on All Public Business from 1809 to 1821, with References to the Debates, Documents, and Statutes Connected Therewith. Washington: Government Printing Office, 1883. Issued as House Report no. 1559, 47th Congress, 1st session, serial 2071.

The regular Senate Journal does not include proceedings dealing with the ratification of Indian treaties. The journal of executive proceedings was printed by special authorization from time to time.

34. Journal of the Executive Proceedings of the Senate of the United States. Volumes 1-3, Washington: Duff Green, 1828; volumes 4--, Washington: Government Printing Office, 1887--.

Debates

Reports of debates in Congress offer much material on Indian affairs in the debates on Indian bills. The debates appear in four series.

35. Annals of Congress. [Full title: The Debates and Proceedings in the Congress of the United States with an Appendix Containing Important State Papers and Public Documents and All the Laws of a Public Nature, with a Copious Index.] 42 volumes. Washington: Gales and Seaton, 1834-1856. Covers the period 1789 to 1824. Not verbatim debates but abstracts compiled later from newspaper and other sources. Each volume has a separate index for Senate and House. The Annals of Congress are also indexed to 1821 in Ordway's indexes (32-33).

36. Register of Debates in Congress. 14 volumes. Washington: Gales and Seaton, 1825-1837. Covers the period 1824 to 1837. Published contemporaneously with the proceedings but not a verbatim account. Each volume has separate indexes for Senate and House.

37. The Congressional Globe. 46 volumes. Washington: Globe Office, 1834-1873. Covers the period 1833 to 1873, thus overlapping with the Register of Debates. At first an abstract of debates but later close to a verbatim report. Separate Senate and House indexes for each session.

38. Congressional Record. Washington: Government Printing Office, 1874--. Bound volumes indexed by session.

Documents and Reports

Items ordered to be printed by the Senate or House are considered Congressional documents. They may be reports of Congressional committees, reports of special investigations, or memorials submitted to Congress, for example. They also include extensive material originating in the executive branch of the government, such as messages of the President to Congress, annual reports of cabinet members (often including the reports of their subordinates), and reports on a great variety of topics submitted in response to resolutions of the Senate or House. There is much material relating to Indian affairs in these documents and reports. This is the most convenient place to find the nineteenth century reports of the Commissioner of Indian Affairs, the Secretary of War, and the Secretary of the Interior, all of which are important for the history of Indian relations. Congressional documents are published in the following series.

39. American State Papers: Documents, Legislative and Executive of the Congress of the United States. 38 volumes. Washington: Gales and Seaton, 1832-1861. These are arranged in ten classes. The most important for Indian affairs is Class 2: Indian Affairs, 2 volumes (Washington, 1832-1834), which covers material from May 25, 1789, to March 1, 1827. Other material relating to Indians can be found in Class 5: Military Affairs, 7 volumes; Class 8: Public Lands, 8 volumes; and Class 10: Miscellaneous, 2 volumes. Each volume in the American State Papers is indexed separately.

40. Serial Set of Congressional Documents. In most libraries Congressional documents beginning with the 15th Congress, 1817, are shelved by serial numbers, assigned consecutively to volumes of documents produced by each session of Congress. The material in the Serial Set is indexed in the catalogs and indexes listed above.

The following special indexes may be of use in locating Indian materials.

41. Index to the Executive Communications Made to the House of Representatives from the Commencement of the Present Form of Government until the End of the Fourteenth Congress, Inclusive . . . also, An Index to All the Printed Committee Reports [1789-1817]. Washington: Gales and Seaton, 1824. House Document no. 163, 18th Congress, 1st session, serial 104.

42. Index to the Executive Communications and Reports of Committees Made to the House of Representatives from December 3d, 1817, to March 3d, 1823, 15th, 16th, & 17th Congress. Washington: Gales and Seaton, 1823. Unnumbered document, 17th Congress, 2d session, serial 85, part 2.

43. Digested Index to the Executive Documents, and Reports of Committees, of the House of Representatives, from the Eighteenth to the Twenty-First Congress, Both Included [1823-1831]. Washington: Duff Green, 1832. Unnumbered document, 21st Congress, 2d session, serial 209, part 2.

44. Index to the Executive Documents and Reports of Committees of the House of Representatives, from the Twenty-Second to the Twenty-Fifth Congress, Both Included, Commencing December 1831, and Ending March 1839. Washington: S. D. Langtree, n.d. Unnumbered document, 25th Congress, 3d session, serial 350.

45. Consolidated Index of the Reports of the Committees of the House of Representatives, from the Twenty-Sixth to the Fortieth Congress, Inclusive [1839-1869]. Prepared under the direction of Edward McPherson. Washington: Government Printing Office, 1869. Unnumbered document, 40th Congress, 3d session, serial 1386.

46. Consolidated Index of the Executive Documents of the House of Representatives, from the Twenty-Sixth to the Fortieth Congress, Inclusive [1839-1869]. Prepared under the direction of Edward McPherson. Washington: Government Printing Office, 1870. Unnumbered document, 40th Congress, 3d session, serial 1387.

47. McKee, T. H., comp. "Index to Reports of Committee on Indian Affairs, United States Senate, from January 3, 1820, to March 4, 1887, Inclusive," and "Index to Reports of Committee on Indian Affairs, House of Representatives, from December 17, 1821, to March 4, 1887, Inclusive." McKee collected printed committee reports of the Senate and House for the 14th to the 49th Congress, 1815-1887, and bound them together in 94 collections (a separate collection for each committee), a total of 515 volumes. There was a separate index for the reports of each committee. Although the compilations themselves are not generally available, the indexes were published separately, one volume for the House and another for the Senate, with varying titles.

Bills and Resolutions

To trace legislation on Indian or other matters it is often necessary to consult the various bills introduced in their original form. The bills and resolutions are numbered in series, beginning with each Congress. The bills, especially for earlier

Congresses, are not readily available in printed form, but they have all been micro-filmed by the Library of Congress and are available in that form.

Hearings

Important material on Indian affairs is found in transcripts of hearings before Senate and House committees. Some of this material appears in documents or reports published in the Serial Set of Congressional Documents, but in more recent times hearings are printed outside the regular series of Congressional documents. They are identified by the name of the committee, the session of Congress, and the number of the bill on which the hearings are held. The following indexes to hearings are useful.

48. Index of Congressional Committee Hearings (Not Confidential in Character) Prior to January 3, 1935, in the United States Senate Library. Washington: Government Printing Office, 1935.

49. Index to Congressional Committee Hearings in the Library of the United States House of Representatives Prior to January 1, 1951. Washington: Government Printing Office, 1954.

50. Cumulative Index of Congressional Committee Hearings (Not Confidential in Character) from Seventy-Fourth Congress (January 3, 1935) through Eighty-Fifth Congress (January 3, 1959) in the United States Senate Library. Washington: Government Printing Office, 1959. Quadrennial supplements to this index were published in 1963, 1967, and 1971.

51. Thomen, Harold O., comp. Checklist of Hearings before Congressional Committees through the Sixty-Seventh Congress. Washington: Library of Congress, 1959. Published in nine parts. The House Committee on Indian Affairs is in part 4, pp. 105-117; the Senate Committee on Indian Affairs is in part 7, pp. 127-129.

FEDERAL LAWS AND TREATIES

Laws and Resolutions

Congressional legislation on Indian affairs can be found in the following chronological compilation of laws enacted by Congress. This series includes all laws, whether or not they are still in force, and thus provides essential information for historical study.

52. United States Statutes at Large. Volumes 1-17, Boston: Little, Brown and Company, 1845-1873; volumes 18--, Washington: Government Printing Office, 1875--. Volume

5 has an index to volumes 1-5; volume 8 has an index to volumes 1-8. Later volumes have separate indexes.

Codifications of United States laws contain general and permanent laws in force at time of publication.

53. Revised Statutes of the United States, Passed at the First Session of the Forty-Third Congress, 1873-1874: Embracing the Statutes of the United States, General and Permanent in Their Nature, in Force December 1, 1873. 2d edition. Washington: Government Printing Office, 1878. Supplements were published in 1891 and 1901.

54. United States Code. [Full title: The Code of the Laws of the United States . . . of a General and Permanent Character in Force December 1, 1925, and Appendix with Laws to December 6, 1926 . . . Volume 44-Part 1 of the United States Statutes at Large.] Washington: Government Printing Office, 1926. Supplements and new editions have been published from time to time.

Indian material in the statutes can be located in the following cumulative indexes.

55. A Synoptical Index to the Laws and Treaties of the United States of America, from March 4, 1789, to March 3, 1851. Boston: Charles C. Little and James Brown, 1852.

56. Index Analysis of the Federal Statutes (General and Permanent Law) 1789-1873. Compiled by Middleton G. Beaman and A. K. McNamara. Washington: Government Printing Office, 1911.

57. Index Analysis of the Federal Statutes . . . (1873-1907): General and Permanent Law in the Revised Statutes of 1873 and the Statutes at Large 1873-1907 (Vols. 18-34). Compiled by George W. Scott and Middleton G. Beaman. Washington: Government Printing Office, 1908.

58. Index to the Federal Statutes 1874-1931, General and Permanent Law Contained in the Revised Statutes of 1874 and Volumes 18-46 of the Statutes at Large. Compiled by Walter H. McClenon and Wilfred C. Gilbert. Washington: Government Printing Office, 1933. A revision of the Scott and Beaman Index Analysis (57).

Indian Laws and Treaties

The most important compilation of treaties, laws, executive orders, and proclamations pertaining to Indian affairs is the following five-volume series.

59. Kappler, Charles J., comp. Indian

Affairs: Laws and Treaties. 5 volumes.
Washington: Government Printing Office,
1904-1941.
Volume 1 (Laws). 1904. Senate Document
no. 319, 58th Centress, 2d session, serial 4623. Compiled to December 1, 1902.
Volume 2 (Treaties). 1904. Senate Document no. 319, 58th Congress, 2d session,
serial 4624. An earlier edition of volumes 1 and 2 was issued as Senate Document no. 452, 57th Congress, 1st session,
serials 4253-4254.
Volume 3 (Laws). 1913. Senate Document
no. 719, 62d Congress, 2d session, serial
6166. Compiled to December 1, 1913.
Volume 4 (Laws). 1929. Senate Document
no. 53, 70th Congress, 1st session, serial
8849. Compiled to March 4, 1927. Includes text of unratified Indian treaties
and discussion of Indian legal matters--
power of Congress, federal jurisdiction,
citizenship, and Indian rights to land.
Reprints Title 25 (Indians) of the United
States Code. Contains separate indexes
for volumes 1-4.
Volume 5 (Laws). 1941. Senate Document
no. 194, 76th Congress, 3d session, serial 10458. Compiled from December 22,
1927, to June 29, 1938.

The Civil Rights Act of 1968, Title VII,
authorized and directed the Secretary of
the Interior to "have the document entitled
'Indian Affairs, Laws and Treaties' (Senate
Document Numbered 319, volumes 1 and 2,
Fifty-eighth Congress), revised and extended to include all treaties, laws, executive orders, and regulations relating to
Indian affairs in force on September 1,
1967, and to have such revised document
printed at the Government Printing Office,"
and to "take such action as may be necessary to keep such document . . . current on
an annual basis."

There are a number of other compilations
of Indian treaties, which have some value
because of special arrangement, notes, or
annotations.

60. United States Statutes at Large. Volume 7: Treaties between the United States
and the Indian Tribes. Edited by Richard
Peters. Boston: Charles C. Little and
James Brown, 1848. Prints treaties up to
October 1842. A few treaties are included in later volumes.

61. Indian Treaties, and Laws and Regula-
tions Relating to Indian Affairs: To
Which Is Added an Appendix, Containing
the Proceedings of the Old Congress, and
Other Important State Papers, in Relation
to Indian Affairs. Washington: Way and
Gideon, 1826. Compiled by Samuel S.
Hamilton.

62. Treaties between the United States of
America and the Several Indian Tribes,

from 1778 to 1837. New edition. Washington: Langtree and O'Sullivan, 1837.
Compiled under the supervision of the Commissioner of Indian Affairs.

63. A Compilation of All the Treaties between the United States and the Indian
Tribes, Now in Force as Laws. Washington:
Government Printing Office, 1873. Treaties arranged alphabetically by tribes.

There are two recent series of compilations of the texts of treaties and related
documents. One is edited by George E. Fay
and published as Occasional Papers, Miscellaneous Series or Ethnology Series,
of the Museum of Anthropology, University
of Northern Colorado, Greeley, Colorado.
The other, The American Indian Treaty
Series, is published by the Institute for
the Development of Indian Law, Washington,
D.C. In both series the treaties are arranged by tribe.

The following items also may be useful in
studying Indian laws and Indian treaties.

64. "Digest of Indian Treaties Affecting
Titles to the Public Lands." In House
Miscellaneous Document no. 45, part 3,
47th Congress, 2d session, serial 2157,
pp. 1185-1226.

65. Cohen, Felix S. "Annotated Table of
Statutes and Treaties." In Handbook of
Federal Indian Law, pp. 485-608. Wash-
ington: Government Printing Office, 1942.
Lists laws and treaties pertaining to
Indians chronologically as they appear in
each volume of United States Statutes at
Large, volumes 1-52.

A synopsis of treaties pertaining to various tribes is given in Alice C. Fletcher,
Indian Education and Civilization (5997),
and an abstract of the land cession provisions of each treaty appears in Charles
C. Royce, Indian Land Cessions in the
United States (3089).

MATERIAL FROM THE EXECUTIVE BRANCH

Presidential Documents

Annual messages and many special messages
of the President are printed in the Serial
Set of Congressional Documents. In addition there are compilations of presidential messages and papers, which contain
the basic public statements of the Presidents on Indian affairs.

66. Richardson, James D., comp. A Compilation of the Messages and Papers of the
Presidents, 1789-1897. 10 volumes. Washington: Government Printing Office, 1896-
1899. Also issued as House Miscellaneous

Document no. 210, 53d Congress, 2d session, serial 3265, parts 1-10. Later editions were published commercially in sets of 10, 11, and 20 volumes. The ultimate volumes carry the documents through the Coolidge administration. Some of the editions are paginated continuously throughout the whole set of volumes.

67. Inaugural Addresses of the Presidents of the United States from George Washington 1789 to Richard Milhous Nixon 1969. Washington: Government Printing Office, 1969. House Document no. 142, 91st Congress, 1st session, serial 12852-3.

68. Public Papers of the Presidents of the United States: Containing the Public Messages, Speeches, and Statements of the President. Washington: Government Printing Office, 1961--. This series begins with Harry S. Truman.

69. Weekly Compilation of Presidential Documents. Washington: National Archives and Records Service, 1965--.

70. Israel, Fred L., ed. The State of the Union Messages of the Presidents, 1790-1966. 3 volumes. New York: Chelsea House, 1966. Indian material is indicated in the index.

Material on Indian matters is also found in presidential executive orders. These are printed in Charles J. Kappler, Indian Affairs: Laws and Treaties (59), but see also the following.

71. Lord, Clifford L., ed. Presidential Executive Orders, Numbered 1-8030, 1862-1938. 2 volumes. New York: Archives Publishing Company, 1944. Volume 1 gives a list of orders in chronological order; volume 2 is a subject index to the list.

72. Executive Orders Relating to Indian Reservations from May 5, 1855, to July 1, 1912. Washington: Government Printing Office, 1912.

73. Executive Orders Relating to Indian Reservations from July 1, 1912, to July 1, 1922. Washington: Government Printing Office, 1922.

For a large number of Presidents and other public figures there are comprehensive publication projects of papers completed or under way. Many of these contain valuable material on Indian affairs.

Reports of Executive Departments and Bureaus

The annual reports of the departments and bureaus concerned with Indian affairs are very rich in information, especially when they append reports from subordinate officials. Most important for the development of Indian policy are the annual reports of the Secretary of War, the Secretary of the Interior, and the Commissioner of Indian Affairs.

74. Secretary of War. Annual Reports, 1789-1848. Until 1849 the War Department was responsible for Indian affairs. The reports for that period can be found in the Serial Set of Congressional Documents (40). Serial numbers are shown in the Checklist (25). For the years 1824-1848 these reports include the annual reports of the Commissioner of Indian Affairs. Later reports of the Secretary of War have material on military relations with the Indians.

75. Secretary of the Interior. Annual Reports, 1849--. With the establishment of the Department of the Interior in 1849, Indian affairs were transferred to that department. Until 1920 these reports were printed in the Serial Set of Congressional Documents (40). They also appear in a separate series.

76. Commissioner of Indian Affairs. Annual Reports, 1824--. In 1824 an Indian Office was created in the War Department; in 1832 Congress established the position of Commissioner of Indian Affairs; and in 1834 the present Bureau of Indian Affairs was established.

Annual reports from the head of the Indian Office and the Commissioner of Indian Affairs are a key source for the history of Indian relations. The reports form part of the Annual Reports of the Secretary of War (to 1848) and of the Secretary of the Interior (since 1849). They have also appeared in a separate edition, not always with the same pagination.

Until 1906 inclusive, these annual reports included the reports of Indian superintendents and agents, and these subordinate reports are an extensive and rich source of information. After 1920 the Commissioner's report no longer appears in the Serial Set.

For 1927 and 1928 the annual reports of the Bureau of Indian Affairs, along with those of some other bureaus, were discontinued, and the only report available is the section on Indian affairs in the report of the Secretary of the Interior. The appropriate pages from these reports have been reprinted with independent pagination as follows.

77. Extracts from the Annual Report of the Secretary of the Interior, Fiscal Year, 1927, Relating to the Bureau of Indian Affairs. Washington: Government Printing Office, 1927.

78. Extracts from the Annual Report of the Secretary of the Interior, Fiscal Year, 1928, Relating to the Bureau of Indian

Affairs. Washington: Government Printing Office, 1928.

From 1929 to 1932 the reports were again issued as separate reports; but from 1933 to 1963 they appear only as part of the annual reports of the Secretary of the Interior.

Beginning in 1964, the reports, in very brief form, were issued under the following title.

79. Indian Affairs 1964 [--date] : A Progress Report from the Commissioner of Indian Affairs. Washington: Government Printing Office, 1964--.

A helpful checklist and guide to the annual reports of the Commissioner of Indian Affairs is the following article.

80. Jones, J. A. "Key to the Annual Reports of the United States Commissioner of Indian Affairs." Ethnohistory 2 (Winter 1955): 58-64.

Bureau of American Ethnology

Ethnological information, which can often be of use to the historian of Indian affairs, is contained in two series of publications of the Bureau of American Ethnology, Smithsonian Institution. There is an index to each series.

81. Bureau of American Ethnology. Annual Reports, 1-48, 1879-1880 to 1930-1931. Washington: Government Printing Office, 1881-1933.

82. Bonnerjea, Biren, comp. "General Index, Reports of the Bureau of American Ethnology, Vols. 1 to 48 (1879 to 1931)." In Forty-Eighth Annual Report of the Bureau of American Ethnology, 1930-1931, pp. 25-1220. Washington: Government Printing Office, 1933.

83. Bureau of American Ethnology. Bulletin. Washington: Government Printing Office, 1887--.

84. Bonnerjea, Biren, comp. Index to Bulletins 1-100 of the Bureau of American Ethnology, with Index to Contributions to North American Ethnology, Introductions, and Miscellaneous Publications. Bureau of American Ethnology, Bulletin 178. Washington: Government Printing Office, 1963.

85. Judd, Neil M. The Bureau of American Ethnology: A Partial History. Norman: University of Oklahoma Press, 1967.

COURT DECISIONS

Cases in federal courts concerning Indian affairs are an important part of the history of Indian-white relations. Decisions of the Supreme Court and of lesser federal courts are found in United States Reports, Federal Cases, Cases Decided in the Court of Claims of the United States, and the like. For Indian matters see the following.

86. Cohen, Felix S. "Table of Federal Cases." In Handbook of Federal Indian Law, pp. 609-627. Washington: Government Printing Office, 1942. An alphabetical list of cases dealing with Indians, in all federal courts.

87. Murchison, Kenneth S. Digest of Decisions Relating to Indian Affairs. Washington: Government Printing Office, 1901. House Document no. 538, 56th Congress, 2d session, serial 4190.

SPECIAL PUBLICATIONS

A number of other publications contain government document materials related to Indian affairs.

88. Carter, Clarence E., ed. The Territorial Papers of the United States. 26 volumes. Washington: Government Printing Office, 1934-1956; National Archives, 1958-1962. Continued by John Porter Bloom, ed., volume 27--. Washington: National Archives, 1969--. These transcripts of territorial records from the National Archives are rich in material on Indian relations, even though Indian affairs were not a topic of special emphasis in the volumes.

89. The New American State Papers: Indian Affairs. Introduction by Loring B. Priest. 13 volumes. Wilmington, Delaware: Scholarly Resources, 1972. Covers the period to 1860. Chiefly photographic reproduction of Congressional documents.

90. Washburn, Wilcomb E., ed. The American Indian and the United States: A Documentary History. 4 volumes. New York: Random House, 1973. Reprints selected documents from five classes: Reports of the Commissioner of Indian Affairs; Congressional debates on Indian affairs; laws, acts, and ordinances; major peace treaties; and judicial decisions affecting the Indians.

91. Prucha, Francis Paul, ed. Documents of United States Indian Policy. Lincoln: University of Nebraska Press, 1975.

3
Guides to Manuscripts

There is no comprehensive catalog listing manuscripts relating to Indians. It is necessary, therefore, to extract pertinent material from general catalogs of manuscript collections and from special guides, checklists, and descriptive articles that deal with particular collections.

GENERAL GUIDES TO MANUSCRIPTS

92. The National Union Catalog of Manuscript Collections. 1959-1961 Ann Arbor: J. W. Edwards; 1962 Hamden, Connecticut: Shoe String Press; 1963-1964 and later volumes Washington: Library of Congress. This work lists important collections in all depositories in the United States. Indexes to the various volumes are detailed; Indian topics are broken down by place, subject, and tribe, with extensive cross references.

93. Hamer, Philip M. A Guide to Archives and Manuscripts in the United States. New Haven: Yale University Press, 1961. An expertly edited guide--not a complete catalog--which indicates important collections. It is well indexed and points to a great many Indian materials.

BIBLIOGRAPHIES OF MANUSCRIPT GUIDES

94. Billington, Ray Allen. "Guides to American History Manuscript Collections in Libraries of the United States." Mississippi Valley Historical Review 38 (December 1951): 467-496. Also published separately, New York: Peter Smith, 1952. Although prepared before the publication of the National Union Catalog of Manuscript Collections, when it was necessary to consult local and regional guides, it is still a useful tool.

95. "Guides to Manuscript Collections." In Harvard Guide to American History, edited by Frank Freidel, pp. 105-107. Revised edition. 2 volumes. Cambridge: Harvard University Press, 1974. See also the more complete "Guides to Manuscript Mate-

rials," in Harvard Guide to American History, edited by Oscar Handlin and others, pp. 79-87. Cambridge: Harvard University Press, 1954.

96. "Manuscripts." In Bibliographies in American History: Guide to Materials for Research, compiled by Henry Putney Beers, pp. 84-88. New York: H. W. Wilson Company, 1942.

GUIDES TO SPECIAL DEPOSITORIES OR COLLECTIONS

Since Indian affairs were so pervasive in much of American history, a great many collections of historical manuscripts contain some Indian material. Most of the guides are indexed, and items can be found under "Indians" or under the names of individual tribes.

A large number of state guides to depositories of manuscript collections were prepared by the Historical Records Survey of the Work Projects Administration and reproduced in mimeographed form. These guides, as well as guides to particular depositories prepared by the Survey, are still useful. Most of the state guides show Indian materials in the indexes. The following bibliography is the most comprehensive list of the completed surveys.

97. Child, Sargent B., and Dorothy P. Holmes. Bibliography of Research Projects Reports: Check List of Historical Records Survey Publications. W. P. A. Technical Series, Research and Records Bibliography, no. 7. Washington: Federal Works Agency, Work Projects Administration, 1943. Reprinted Baltimore: Genealogical Publishing Company, 1969.

In addition to the guides prepared by the Historical Records Survey and the other guides listed in such bibliographies as those of Beers, Billington, and the Harvard Guide, the following selected publications may prove useful. They are, for the most part, general catalogs of manuscript material for a given collection, depository, or area, with extensive indexes that list Indian subjects.

American Philosophical Society

98. Bell, Whitfield J., Jr., and Murphy D. Smith. Guide to the Archives and Manuscript Collections of the American Philosophical Society. Philadelphia: American Philosophical Society, 1966.

99. Freeman, John F. A Guide to Manuscripts Relating to the American Indian in the Library of the American Philosophical Society. Philadelphia: American Philosophical Society, 1966.

Arizona Historical Society

100. Colley, Charles C. Documents of Southwestern History: A Guide to the Manuscript Collections of the Arizona Historical Society. Tucson: Arizona Historical Society, 1972.

Bancroft Library, University of California

101. Morgan, Dale L., and George P. Hammond. A Guide to the Manuscript Collections of the Bancroft Library. Volume 1: Pacific and Western Manuscripts (Except California). Berkeley: University of California Press, 1963.

Clements Library, University of Michigan

102. Peckham, Howard H. Guide to the Manuscript Collections in the William L. Clements Library. Ann Arbor: University of Michigan Press, 1942.

103. Ewing, William S. Guide to the Manuscript Collections in the William L. Clements Library. 2d edition. Ann Arbor: Clements Library, 1953.

Duke University

104. Tilley, Nannie M., and Noma Lee Goodwin. Guide to the Manuscript Collections in the Duke University Library. Durham, North Carolina: Duke University Press, 1947.

Eleutherian Mills Historical Library

105. Riggs, John Beverley. A Guide to the Manuscripts in the Eleutherian Mills Historical Library: Accessions through the Year 1965. Greenville, Delaware: Eleutherian Mills Historical Library, 1970.

Gilcrease Institute

106. Keene, Mrs. H. H. A Guidebook to Manuscripts in the Library of the Thomas Gilcrease Institute of American History and

Art. Tulsa: Thomas Gilcrease Institute of American History and Art, 1969.

Iowa, State Historical Society of

107. Harris, Katherine. Guide to Manuscripts. Iowa City: State Historical Society of Iowa, 1973.

Kentucky Historical Society

108. Clift, G. Glenn. Guide to the Manuscripts of the Kentucky Historical Society. Frankfort: Kentucky Historical Society, 1955.

Maine

109. Ring, Elizabeth. A Reference List of Manuscripts Relating to the History of Maine. Part I: Maine Bulletin 41 (August 1938); Part II: Maine Bulletin 42 (August 1939); Part II, Index: Maine Bulletin 43 (February 20, 1941).

Maryland Historical Society

110. Pedley, Avril J. M. The Manuscript Collections of the Maryland Historical Society. Baltimore: Maryland Historical Society, 1968.

Massachusetts Historical Society

111. Catalog of Manuscripts of the Massachusetts Historical Society. 7 volumes. Boston: G. K. Hall and Company, 1969.

Michigan, University of

112. Warner, Robert M., and Ida C. Brown. Guide to Manuscripts in the Michigan Historical Collections of the University of Michigan. Ann Arbor, 1963.

Minnesota Historical Society

113. Nute, Grace Lee, and Gertrude W. Ackermann. Guide to the Personal Papers in the Manuscript Collections of the Minnesota Historical Society. St. Paul: Minnesota Historical Society, 1935.

114. Kane, Lucile M., and Kathryn A. Johnson. Manuscript Collections of the Minnesota Historical Society: Guide Number 2. St. Paul: Minnesota Historical Society, 1955.

Missouri, University of

115. Guide to the Western Historical Manuscripts Collection. University of Missouri Bulletin, volume 53, no. 33 (Western Historical Manuscripts Collection Bulletin no. 6), November 8, 1952.

116. Galloway, John A. Guide to the Western

Historical Manuscripts Collection. University of Missouri Bulletin, volume 58, no. 13 (Western Historical Manuscripts Collection Bulletin no. 7), April 1, 1957. Supplement to Bulletin no. 6.

National Anthropological Archives, Smithsonian Institution

117. Catalog to Manuscripts at the National Anthropological Archives. 4 volumes. Boston: G. K. Hall and Company, 1975.

Nebraska State Historical Society

118. A Guide to the Archives and Manuscripts of the Nebraska State Historical Society. Bulletin Number One (compiled by William F. Schmidt, June 1965); Bulletin Number Two (compiled by William F. Schmidt and Harold E. Kemble, Jr., June 1966); Bulletin Number Three (compiled by Douglas A. Bakken, Duane J. Reed, and Harold E. Kemble, June 1967). Lincoln: Nebraska State Historical Society.

Nevada

119. Armstrong, Robert D. A Preliminary Union Catalog of Nevada Manuscripts. Reno: University of Nevada Library and Nevada Library Association, 1967.

Newberry Library

120. Butler, Ruth Lapham. A Check List of Manuscripts in the Edward E. Ayer Collection. Chicago: Newberry Library, 1937.

New Mexico, University of

121. Diaz, Albert James. Manuscripts and Records in the University of New Mexico Library. Albuquerque: University of New Mexico Library, 1957.

New-York Historical Society

122. Breton, Arthur J. A Guide to the Manuscript Collections of the New-York Historical Society. 2 volumes. Westport, Connecticut: Greenwood Press, 1972.

New York Public Library

123. Dictionary Catalog of the Manuscript Division. 2 volumes. Boston: G. K. Hall and Company, 1967.

North Carolina Historical Commission

124. Guide to the Manuscript Collections in the Archives of the North Carolina Historical Commission. Raleigh: North Carolina Historical Commission, 1942.

North Carolina State Archives

125. Crabtree, Beth G. Guide to Private Manuscript Collections in the North Carolina State Archives. Raleigh: State Department of Archives and History, 1964.

North Carolina, University of

126. Blosser, Susan Sokol, and Clyde Norman Wilson, Jr. The Southern Historical Collection: A Guide to Manuscripts. Chapel Hill: University of North Carolina Library, 1970.

Ohio Historical Society

127. Lentz, Andrea D., and Sara S. Fuller. A Guide to Manuscripts at the Ohio Historical Society. Columbus: Ohio Historical Society, 1972.

Oklahoma, University of

128. Gibson, A. M. A Guide to Regional Manuscript Collections in the Division of Manuscripts, University of Oklahoma Library. Norman: University of Oklahoma Press, 1960.

Oregon Historical Society

129. Oregon Historical Society Manuscripts Collections. Portland: Oregon Historical Society, 1971. See also Supplement to the Guide to the Manuscript Collections, March 1973.

Oregon, University of

130. Schmitt, Martin. Catalogue of Manuscripts in the University of Oregon Library. Eugene: University of Oregon, 1971.

Pennsylvania

131. Richman, Irwin. Historical Manuscript Depositories in Pennsylvania. Harrisburg: Pennsylvania Historical and Museum Commission, 1965.

Pennsylvania Historical and Museum Commission

132. Preliminary Guide to the Research Materials of the Pennsylvania Historical and Museum Commission. Harrisburg: Pennsylvania Historical and Museum Commission, 1959.

Pennsylvania, Historical Society of

133. Guide to the Manuscript Collections of the Historical Society of Pennsylvania. 2d edition. Philadelphia: Historical Society of Pennsylvania, 1949.

Tennessee Historical Society

134. Owsley, Harriet Chappell. Guide to the Processed Manuscripts of the Tennessee Historical Society. Nashville: Tennessee Historical Commission, .Tennessee Historical Society, and Tennessee State Library and Archives, 1969.

Texas, University of

135. Kielman, Chester V. The University of Texas Archives: A Guide to the Historical Manuscripts Collections in the University of Texas Library. Austin: University of Texas Press, 1967.

United States Army Military History Research Collection

136. Sommers, Richard J. Manuscript Holdings of the Military History Research Collection. Carlisle Barracks, Pennsylvania: U.S. Army Military Research Collection, 1972.

United States Military Academy

137. Russell, J. Thomas. Preliminary Guide to the Manuscript Collection of the U.S. Military Academy Library. West Point, New York: U.S. Military Academy, 1968.

Utah State University

138. Washington, Mary. An Annotated Bibliography of Western Manuscripts in the Merrill Library at Utah State University, Logan, Utah. Logan: Utah State University Press, 1971.

Western Reserve Historical Society

139. Pike, Kermit J. A Guide to the Manuscripts and Archives of the Western Reserve Historical Society. Cleveland: Western Reserve Historical Society, 1972.

West Virginia University

140. Shetler, Charles. Guide to Manuscripts and Archives in the West Virginia Collection. Morgantown: West Virginia University Library, 1958.

141. Ham, F. Gerald. Guide to Manuscripts and Archives in the West Virginia Collection--Number II, 1958-1962. Morgantown: West Virginia University Library, 1965.

Wisconsin, State Historical Society of

142. Thwaites, Reuben Gold. Descriptive List of Manuscript Collections of the State Historical Society of Wisconsin, Together with Reports on Other Collections of Manuscript Material for American History in Adjacent States. Madison: State Historical Society of Wisconsin, 1906.

143. Smith, Alice E. Guide to the Manuscripts of the Wisconsin Historical Society. Madison: State Historical Society of Wisconsin, 1944.

144. Harper, Josephine L., and Sharon C. Smith. Guide to the Manuscripts of the State Historical Society of Wisconsin: Supplement Number One. Madison: State Historical Society of Wisconsin, 1957.

145. Harper, Josephine L. Guide to the Manuscripts of the State Historical Society of Wisconsin: Supplement Number Two. Madison: State Historical Society of Wisconsin, 1966.

Yale University

146. Goddard, Jeanne M., and Charles Kritzler. A Catalogue of the Frederick W. and Carrie S. Beinecke Collection of Western Americana. Volume 1: Manuscripts. New Haven: Yale University Press, 1965.

147. Withington, Mary C. A Catalogue of Manuscripts in the Collection of Western Americana Founded by William Robertson Coe, Yale University Library. New Haven: Yale University Press, 1952.

4
Guides to Other Sources

A great many kinds of sources contain valuable information on Indian-white relations. Listed here are the essential finding aids for periodicals and newspapers, printed library catalogs, general bibliographies on Indian affairs, and guides to other materials.

PERIODICAL INDEXES AND ABSTRACTS

Both historical studies and current or contemporary articles on the American Indian appear in a wide variety of magazines and journals, scholarly and popular. A large number of these articles are listed in this volume, but by no means all. For a more exhaustive compilation on Indian-related subjects, use the following periodical indexes. The general bibliographies (241 to 283), of course, also include many items from periodicals, as well as books and other published materials.

General Periodical Indexes

148. Poole's Index to Periodical Literature, 1802-1881. Compiled by William Frederick Poole. Revised edition. Boston: Houghton Mifflin and Company, 1891. Five supplements carry the index through 1906. This is a subject index only. For authors see Cumulative Author Index for Poole's Index to Periodical Literature, 1802-1906. Compiled by C. Edward Wall. Ann Arbor: Pierian Press, 1971.

149. Nineteenth Century Readers' Guide to Periodical Literature, 1890-1899. 2 volumes. New York: H. W. Wilson Company, 1944. An author-subject index to some fifty general periodicals, for the decade before the start of the Readers' Guide.

150. Readers' Guide to Periodical Literature, 1900--. New York: H. W. Wilson Company, 1905--. Author-subject index and by title as necessary. General, rather than scholarly, periodicals.

151. Social Sciences and Humanities Index, 1907--. New York: H. W. Wilson Company. Formerly International Index to Periodi-

cals (1916-1965). Beginning in June 1974 this index is divided into two separate indexes: Humanities Index and Social Sciences Index. Covers more scholarly journals than the Readers' Guide.

152. Annual Magazine Subject Index, 1907-1949. 43 volumes. Boston: F. W. Faxon Company, 1908-1952. Subject index; includes many historical journals.

153. Cumulated Magazine Subject Index 1907-1949. 2 volumes. Boston: G. K. Hall and Company, 1964. Reproduces in one alphabetical sequence all items from the 43 volumes of the Annual Magazine Subject Index.

154. Index to Early American Periodicals to 1850. Edited by Nelson F. Adkins. New York: Readex Microprint Corporation. A microform publication of a card file index to early magazines compiled by the WPA at New York University.

Special Periodical Indexes

155. Alternative Press Index, 1969--. Northfield, Minnesota: Radical Research Center, 1970--. Indexes radical magazines and papers. Numerous Indian items.

156. Catholic Periodical Index, 1930--. Published by the Catholic Library Association. Combined with Guide to Catholic Literature in 1967 and title changed to Catholic Periodical and Literature Index. Includes articles on Indians in Catholic journals.

157. Index to Religious Periodical Literature, 1949--. Published by the American Theological Library Association.

Other special periodical indexes, such as those for law, health, and education, will be found under appropriate subject headings.

Abstracts

158. America: History and Life, a Guide to Periodical Literature, 1964--. Santa Barbara, California: American Bibliographical Center--Clio Press, 1965--.

Classified abstracts of periodical articles.

159. Smith, Dwight L., ed. Indians of the United States and Canada: A Bibliography. Santa Barbara, California: American Bibliographical Center--Clio Press, 1973. Contains 1,771 abstracts of scholarly periodical literature, reprinted from America: History and Life.

Lists of Articles

Lists of current articles appearing in scholarly historical journals are printed regularly in the American Historical Review, the Journal of American History, and the Western Historical Quarterly. The latter two journals have subdivisions in their lists for Indian-related articles.

NEWSPAPERS

Newspapers, both weekly and daily, are an indispensable source of information on Indian-white relations. During some periods of American history coverage on Indian matters was considerable. Newspaper accounts must be used with great caution, of course, for the facts often are not accurate, and sectional and other biases are sometimes strong. But newspapers can be a valuable source of white attitudes toward Indians and of reaction to Indian-related events.

Union Lists

Union lists give the names of the newspapers and the inclusive dates of their publication. They list papers by state and city and indicate the depositories that contain runs of issues.

160. Brigham, Clarence S. History and Bibliography of American Newspapers, 1690-1820. 2 volumes. Worcester, Massachusetts: American Antiquarian Society, 1947.

161. _____. Additions and Corrections to History and Bibliography of American Newspapers, 1690-1820. Worcester, Massachusetts: American Antiquarian Society, 1961. Reprinted from the Proceedings of the American Antiquarian Society for April 1961.

162. Gregory, Winifred, ed. American Newspapers, 1821-1936: A Union List of Files Available in the United States and Canada. New York: H. W. Wilson Company, 1937.

163. Library of Congress, Catalog Publication Division. Newspapers in Microform: United States, 1948-1972. Washington: Library of Congress, 1973. Supersedes earlier lists of newspapers on microfilm, edited by George A. Schwegmann.

Indexes

Only a few newspapers have printed indexes. The most important is that of the New York Times, which can serve also as a guide to information in other papers, since events are reported by date. A good deal of Indian material appears. National papers which have begun indexes in recent years are valuable sources for recent and contemporary Indian affairs.

164. The New York Times Index, 1851--. New York: New York Times, 1913--. Older indexes from the beginning of the newspaper in 1851 are being published by the R. R. Bowker Company, New York, 1966--.

165. Index to the Christian Science Monitor, 1958--. Compiled by Helen M. Cropsey. Distributed by University Microfilms, Ann Arbor, Michigan.

166. The National Observer Index, 1969--. Semi-annual volumes, June 1969 to June 1970, Flint, Michigan: Newspaper Indexing Center. Annual volumes, 1971--, Princeton, New Jersey: Dow Jones Books, 1972.

167. The Wall Street Journal Index, 1958--. New York: Dow Jones and Company, 1959--. A good many Indian items appear in the section, "General News."

Colonial Indian affairs can be traced in the following index to a colonial newspaper.

168. Cappon, Lester J., and Stella F. Duff. Virginia Gazette Index, 1736-1780. 2 volumes. Williamsburg, Virginia: Institute of Early American History and Culture, 1950.

Some newspapers have unprinted indexes, usually in 3 x 5 card files, maintained in local libraries or other depositories. A large number of these were the result of WPA projects, and they vary in quality and length of period covered. One such index is that for the Milwaukee Sentinel, 1837-1880, in the Milwaukee Public Library. For a guide to these indexes, see the following list.

169. Brayer, Herbert O. "Preliminary Guide to Indexed Newspapers in the United States, 1850-1900." Mississippi Valley Historical Review 33 (September 1946): 237-258.

Reprinted News Articles

170. Wax, Murray L., and Robert W. Buchanan, eds. Solving "the Indian Problem": The White Man's Burdensome Business. New York: New Viewpoints, 1975. Reprints

news stories and essays from the New
York Times on the Modoc War, the New
Deal for Indians, termination, economic
activity, and pan-Indianism.

LIBRARY CATALOGS

Many publications on Indian affairs can
be located in the printed catalogs of libraries or collections having large holdings
on Indians. The following catalogs are particularly useful.

171. The Bancroft Library, University of
California, Berkeley: Catalog of Printed
Books. 22 volumes. Boston: G. K. Hall
and Company, 1964. First Supplement. 6
volumes. 1969.
Second Supplement. 6 volumes. 1974.

172. Denver Public Library. Catalog of the
Western History Department. 7 volumes.
Boston: G. K. Hall and Company, 1970.
First Supplement. 1 volume. 1975.

173. Harvard University. Author and Subject Catalogues of the Library of the
Peabody Museum of Archaeology and Ethnology. 54 volumes, including Index to Subject Headings. Boston: G. K. Hall and
Company, 1963. First Supplement. 12
volumes. 1970. Second Supplement. 6
volumes. 1971.

174. Library of Congress Catalog: Books:
Subjects. Ann Arbor: J. W. Edwards,
1955--. This multi-volume catalog begins
with 1950. Indian materials are listed
under appropriate subject headings.

175. Newberry Library. Dictionary Catalog
of the Edward E. Ayer Collection of Americana and American Indians in the Newberry
Library. 16 volumes. Boston: G. K. Hall
and Company, 1961. First Supplement. 3
volumes. 1970.

176. New York Public Library. Dictionary
Catalog of the History of the Americas
Collection. 28 volumes. Boston: G. K.
Hall and Company, 1961. First Supplement.
9 volumes. 1974.

177. United States Department of the Interior. Biographical and Historical
Index of American Indians and Persons Involved in Indian Affairs. 8 volumes.
Boston: G. K. Hall and Company, 1966. Not
a library catalog but a card index to published materials, developed in the library
of the Bureau of Indian Affairs.

178. _____. Dictionary Catalog of the
Department Library, United States Depart-
ment of the Interior. 37 volumes.
Boston: G. K. Hall and Company, 1967.
First Supplement. 4 volumes. 1968. Sec-
ond Supplement. 2 volumes. 1971. Third
Supplement. 4 volumes. 1973.

179. Wisconsin, State Historical Society
Library. Subject Catalog. 23 volumes.
Westport, Connecticut: Greenwood Publish-
ing Corporation, 1971.

180. Yale University. Catalog of the Yale
Collection of Western Americana. 4 volumes. Boston: G. K. Hall and Company,
1961.

ORAL HISTORY

Oral history projects and collections
dealing with Indians can be located in the
following guides.

181. Meckler, Alan M., and Ruth McMullin,
eds. Oral History Collections. New
York: R. R. Bowker Company, 1975. A name
and subject index to collections.

182. Shumway, Gary L. Oral History in the
United States: A Directory. New York:
Oral History Association, 1971.

Listed here are descriptions of Indian
oral history projects, a book that provides
transcriptions of interviews, and articles
on oral tradition.

183. Cash, Joseph H. "A New Dimension in
Indian History." In Western American
History in the Seventies: Selected Pa-
pers Presented to the First Western His-
tory Conference, Colorado State Univer-
sity, August 10-12, 1972, edited by
Daniel Tyler, pp. 46-49. Fort Collins:
Robinson Press for Educational Media and
Information Systems, 1973.

184. Cash, Joseph H., and Herbert T. Hoover,
eds. To Be an Indian: An Oral History.
New York: Holt, Rinehart and Winston,
1971. Selected transcriptions from an
Indian oral history project.

185. Day, Gordon M. "Oral Tradition as
Complement." Ethnohistory 19 (Spring
1972): 99-108.

186. Ellis, Richard N. "The Duke Indian
Oral History Collection at the University of New Mexico." New Mexico Historical Review 48 (July 1973): 259-263.

187. Fontana, Bernard L. "American Indian
Oral History: An Anthropologist's Note."
History and Theory 8 (1969): 366-370.

188. Jordan, Julia A. "Oklahoma's Oral
History Collection: New Source for Indian
History." Chronicles of Oklahoma 49
(Summer 1971): 150-172.

189. Lowie, Robert H. "Oral Tradition and
History." In Lowie's Selected Papers in
Anthropology, edited by Cora DuBois,
pp. 202-210. Berkeley: University of
California Press, 1960.

190. Ortiz, Alfonso. "A Uniquely American Legacy." Princeton University Library Chronicle 30 (Spring 1969): 147-157. Princeton oral history project on Pueblo Indian culture.

GUIDES TO MAPS

Maps showing Indian data are a useful source of information on Indian-white relations. Maps are often difficult to find, but the following general catalogs and indexes can be used to locate Indian materials.

191. American Geographical Society of New York, Map Department. Index to Maps in Books and Periodicals. 10 volumes. Boston: G. K. Hall and Company, 1968. First Supplement. 1 volume. 1971.

192. The Bancroft Library, University of California, Berkeley: Index to Printed Maps. Boston: G. K. Hall and·Company, 1964. First Supplement. 1975.

193. Claussen, Martin P., and Herman R. Friis. Descriptive Catalog of Maps Published by Congress 1817-1843. Washington, 1941. A list of maps published in the Serial Set of Congressional Documents.

194. Map Collections in the United States and Canada: A Directory. New York: Special Libraries Association, 1954.

195. New York Public Library. Dictionary Catalog of the Map Division. 10 volumes. Boston: G. K. Hall and Company, 1971.

196. Phillips, P. Lee. List of Maps of America in the Library of Congress. Washington: Government Printing Office, 1901. Arranged by geographical locations, not by subject matter.

197. Research Catalog of Maps of America to 1860 in the William L. Clements Library, University of Michigan. 4 volumes. Boston: G. K. Hall and Company, 1972.

Maps on Indian reservations and Indian population are published currently by the federal government. See also the guides to cartographic records in the National Archives (8 and 9) and the maps in Royce, Indian Land Cessions (3089).

TRAVEL ACCOUNTS

Travelers, both foreign and American, had much to say about Indians. Those who moved on or near the frontier could not escape contact with the Indians or reports about them. The accounts written by travelers, therefore, are important contemporary sources on the Indian communities and on Indian-white relations.

Published reports are very numerous, and individual titles are not listed here. Three kinds of works are given below: bibliographies that list and annotate travel accounts, works of analysis and commentary dealing with travelers and their observations, and collections of travel accounts that contain substantial Indian material. The indexes in all these works will direct the researcher to Indian-related materials.

Bibliographies

198. Clark, Thomas D., ed. Travels in the Old South: A Bibliography. 3 volumes. Norman: University of Oklahoma Press, 1956-1959. Volume 1, The Formative Years, 1527-1783: From the Spanish Exploration through the American Revolution. Volume 2, The Expanding South, 1750-1825: The Ohio Valley and the Cotton Frontier. Volume 3, The Ante Bellum South, 1825-1860: Cotton, Slavery, and Conflict. There is a separate index to each volume.

199. _____. Travels in the New South: A Bibliography. 2 volumes. Norman: University of Oklahoma Press, 1962. Volume 1, The Postwar South, 1865-1900: An Era of Reconstruction and Readjustment. Volume 2, The Twentieth-Century South, 1900-1955: An Era of Change, Depression, and Emergence.

200. Coulter, E. Merton, ed. Travels in the Confederate States: A Bibliography. Norman: University of Oklahoma Press, 1948.

201. Hubach, Robert R., ed. Early Midwestern Travel Narratives: An Annotated Bibliography, 1634-1850. Detroit: Wayne State University Press, 1961.

202. _____. "Unpublished Travel Narratives on the Early Midwest, 1720-1850: A Preliminary Bibliography." Mississippi Valley Historical Review 42 (December 1955): 525-548.

203. Monaghan, Frank. French Travellers in the United States, 1765-1932: A Bibliography. Supplement by Samuel J. Marino. New York: Antiquarian Press, 1961. First published in 1933 by the New York Public Library.

204. Wagner, Henry R., ed. The Plains and the Rockies: A Bibliography of Original Narratives of Travel and Adventure, 1800-1865. 3d revised edition by Charles L. Camp. Columbus, Ohio: Long's College Book Company, 1953.

Analysis and Commentary

205. Athearn, Robert G. Westward the Briton. New York: Charles Scribner's Sons, 1953. Includes a chapter on the Indians.

206. McDermott, John Francis, ed. Travelers on the Western Frontier. Urbana: University of Illinois Press, 1970. Analyses of types of traveler accounts and related sources.

207. Miner, Donald D. "Western Travelers in Quest of the Indian." In Travelers on the Western Frontier, edited by John Francis McDermott, pp. 267-289. Urbana: University of Illinois Press, 1970.

208. Randolph, J. Ralph. British Travelers among the Southern Indians, 1660-1763. Norman: University of Oklahoma Press, 1973.

209. Sibley, Marilyn M. Travelers in Texas, 1761-1860. Austin: University of Texas Press, 1967. Includes a chapter on Indians.

210. Stein, Gary C. "'And the Strife Never Ends': Indian-White Hostility as Seen by European Travelers in America, 1800-1860." Ethnohistory 20 (Spring 1973): 173-187.

Collections of Travel Accounts

211. Bieber, Ralph P., and LeRoy R. Hafen, eds. The Southwest Historical Series. 12 volumes. Glendale, California: Arthur H. Clark Company, 1932-1943. Volume 12 is an Analytical Index to the whole series, with numerous Indian entries.

212. Hafen, LeRoy R., and Ann W. Hafen, eds. The Far West and the Rockies Historical Series, 1820-1875. 15 volumes. Glendale, California: Arthur H. Clark Company, 1954-1961. Volume 15 contains a General Analytical Index to the whole series.

213. Handlin, Oscar, ed. This Was America: True Accounts of People and Places, Manners and Customs, as Recorded by European Travelers to the Western Shore in the Eighteenth, Nineteenth, and Twentieth Centuries. Cambridge: Harvard University Press, 1949.

214. Morgan, Dale L., ed. Overland in 1846: Diaries and Letters of the California-Oregon Trail. 2 volumes. Georgetown, California: Talisman Press, 1963.

215. Thwaites, Reuben Gold, ed. Early Western Travels, 1748-1846. 32 volumes. Cleveland: Arthur H. Clark Company, 1904-1907. Volumes 31 and 32 contain an Analytical Index.

216. Williams, Samuel Cole, ed. Early Travels in the Tennessee Country, 1540-1800. Johnson City, Tennessee: Watauga Press, 1928.

REPORTS ON SPECIAL COLLECTIONS

Listed here are a number of reports on

collections of archival or manuscript materials that contain items pertaining to Indian affairs. Included also are calendars of papers. Some other similar items are listed under appropriate subject headings.

217. Alden, John R. "The Eighteenth Century Cherokee Archives." American Archivist 5 (October 1942): 240-244.

218. Ault, Nelson A. The Papers of Lucullus Virgil McWhorter. Pullman: Friends of the Library, State College of Washington, 1959. A calendar of papers.

219. Ballenger, T. L. "The Andrew Nave Letters: New Cherokee Source Material at Northeastern State College." Chronicles of Oklahoma 30 (Spring 1952): 2-5.

220. Bannon, John Francis. "The St. Louis University Collection of Jesuitica Americana." Hispanic American Historical Review 37 (February 1957): 82-88.

221. Brann, Harrison A. "Bibliography of Sheldon Jackson Collection in the Presbyterian Historical Society." Journal of the Presbyterian Historical Society 30 (September 1952): 139-164.

222. Brugge, David M. Navajos in the Catholic Church Records of New Mexico, 1694-1875. Window Rock, Arizona: Research Section, Parks and Recreation Department, Navajo Tribe, 1968.

223. Burrus, Ernest J. "The Bandelier Collection in the Vatican Library." Manuscripta 10 (July 1966): 67-84.

224. Calendar of the American Fur Company's Papers. 2 volumes. Washington: Government Printing Office, 1945. Also issued as Annual Report of the American Historical Association for the Year 1944, volumes 2 and 3. Directed by Grace Lee Nute.

225. Cosgrove, Elizabeth Williams. "The Grant Foreman Papers: Indian and Pioneer History." Chronicles of Oklahoma 37 (Winter 1959-1960): 507-510.

226. Foreman, Grant. "A Survey of Tribal Records in the Archives of the United States Government in Oklahoma." Chronicles of Oklahoma 11 (March 1933): 625-634.

227. Freeman, John Finley. "The American Indian in Manuscript: Preparing a Guide to Holdings in the Library of the American Philosophical Society." Ethnohistory 8 (Spring 1961): 156-178.

228. Freeze, Alys H. "The Western History Collection of the Denver Public Library." Great Plains Journal 11 (Spring 1972): 101-115.

229. Hamilton, Kenneth G. "The Moravian

Archives at Bethlehem, Pennsylvania."
American Archivist 24 (October 1961):
415-423.

230. _____. "The Resources of the Moravian Church Archives." Pennsylvania
History 27 (July 1960): 263-272.

231. Hanna, Archibald. "The Richard Henry
Pratt Papers." Yale University Library
Gazette 34 (July 1959): 38-42.

232. Jones, William K. "General Guide to
Documents on the Five Civilized Tribes
in the University of Oklahoma Library Division of Manuscripts." Ethnohistory 14
(Winter-Spring 1967): 47-76.

233. Nute, Grace Lee. "The Papers of the
American Fur Company: A Brief Estimate of
Their Significance." American Historical
Review 32 (April 1927): 519-538.

234. Ruoss, G. Martin. "The Archives in
the Special Collection of the Zimmerman
Library." Great Plains Journal 11
(Spring 1972): 116-124.

235. Snyderman, George S. "The Manuscript
Collections of the Philadelphia Yearly
Meeting of Friends Pertaining to the American Indian." Proceedings of the American Philosophical Society 102 (December
1958): 613-620.

236. _____. "A Preliminary Survey of
American Indian Manuscripts in Reposi-
tories of the Philadelphia Area." Proceedings of the American Philosophical
Society 97 (October 1953): 596-610.

237. Turcheneske, John A., Jr. "The Southwest in La Follette Land: The Carlos
Montezuma Papers." Manuscripts 25 (Summer 1973): 202-207.

238. Walker, Mary Alden. "The Archives of
the American Board for Foreign Missions."
Harvard Library Bulletin 4 (Winter 1952):
52-68.

239. Wallace, Paul A. W. "The John Heckewelder Papers." Pennsylvania History 27
(July 1960): 249-262.

240. Weaks, Mabel Clare. Calendar of the
Kentucky Papers of the Draper Collection
of Manuscripts. Madison: State Historical Society of Wisconsin, 1925.

BIBLIOGRAPHIES OF INDIAN MATERIALS

Bibliographies have been published on
many aspects of Indian history and Indian-
white relations. Listed here are a variety
of such works, including bibliographies of
bibliographies, general bibliographies
(anthropological as well as historical),
and a number of bibliographies on special
aspects of the subject, designed for special
readers, or representing particular

libraries. Other bibliographies--for example, on Indian health or Indian educa-
tion--are listed under appropriate headings.

241. Abler, Thomas S., and Sally M. Weaver.
A Canadian Indian Bibliography, 1960-
1970. Toronto: University of Toronto
Press, 1974. Includes Case Law Digest
prepared by Douglas E. Sanders.

242. The American Indian, a Bibliography:
A List of Books about American Indians,
Located in the Belk Library, Appalachian
State University. Boone, North Carolina:
Belk Library, Appalachian State Univer-
sity, 1973.

243. American Indians: An Annotated Bibliography of Selected Library Resources.
Will Antell, Project Director. Minneapolis: Library Services Institute for
Minnesota Indians, University of Minnesota, 1970. Primarily materials for
elementary and high school students.

244. "Bibliography on Iowa Indians."
Palimpsest 50 (April 1969): 271-272.

245. Butterfield, Lyman H., Wilcomb E. Washburn, and William N. Fenton. "Bibliography." In American Indian and White
Relations to 1830: Needs and Opportunities
for Study, pp. 31-122. Chapel Hill:
University of North Carolina Press, 1957.

246. Carlson, Alvar W. "A Bibliography of
the Geographical Literature on the
American Indian." Professional Geographers 24 (August 1972): 258-263.

247. Clancy, James Thomas. Native American
References: A Cross-Indexed Bibliography
of Seventeenth-Century American Imprints
Pertaining to American Indians. Worcester, Massachusetts: American Antiquarian
Society, 1974. Reprinted from Proceedings of the American Antiquarian Society
83 (1973): 287-341. Lists items pertaining to Indians in Charles Evans,
American Bibliography and supplements, up
to 1700. Arranged chronologically, by
tribe, and by state.

248. Edwards, Everett E., and Wayne D.
Rasmussen. A Bibliography on the Agri-
culture of the American Indians. United
States Department of Agriculture Miscel-
laneous Publication no. 447. Washington:
Government Printing Office, 1942.

249. Fay, George E. Bibliography of the
Indians of Wisconsin. Museum of Anthropology, Miscellaneous Series, no. 2.
Oshkosh: Museum of Anthropology, Wisconsin State University--Oshkosh, 1965.

250. Field, Thomas W. An Essay towards an
Indian Bibliography: Being a Catalogue
of Books, Relating to the History, Antiquities, Languages, Customs, Religion,
Wars, Literature, and Origin of the

American Indians, in the Library of Thomas W. Field. New York: Scribner, Armstrong and Company, 1873.

251. Gibson, Gordon D. "A Bibliography of Anthropological Bibliographies: The Americas." Current Anthropology 1 (January 1960): 61-75.

252. Griffin, Appleton Prentiss Clark. Bibliography of American Historical Societies (the United States and the Dominion of Canada). Annual Report of the American Historical Association for the Year 1905, volume 2. Washington: Government Printing Office, 1907. A listing of items in the collections and other publications of historical societies. There is a detailed index, showing much material pertaining to Indians.

253. Hargrett, Lester. The Gilcrease-Hargrett Catalogue of Imprints. Norman: University of Oklahoma Press, 1972. Emphasis on materials pertaining to the Five Civilized Tribes.

254. Heizer, Robert F., Karen M. Nissen, and Edward D. Castillo. California Indian History: A Classified and Annotated Guide to Source Materials. Ramona, California: Ballena Press, 1975.

255. Hewlett, Leroy. Indians of Oregon: A Bibliography of Materials in the Oregon State Library. Salem: Oregon State Library, 1969.

256. Hirschfelder, Arlene B. American Indian and Eskimo Authors: A Comprehensive Bibliography. New York: Association on American Indian Affairs, 1973.

257. Hodge, William H. A Bibliography of Contemporary North American Indians: Selected and Partially Annotated with Study Guides. New York: Interland Publishing, 1976.

258. Icolari, Dan. "Bibliography." In Reference Encyclopedia of the American Indian, edited by Barry T. Klein and Dan Icolari. 1:319-537. 2d edition. 2 volumes. Rye, New York: Todd Publications, 1973.

259. Index to Literature on the American Indian, 1970. San Francisco: Indian Historian Press, 1972. A comprehensive bibliography, arranged alphabetically by author and by subject categories.

260. Index to Literature on the American Indian, 1971. San Francisco: Indian Historian Press, 1972.

261. Index to Literature on the American Indian, 1972. Edited by Jeannette Henry. San Francisco: Indian Historian Press, 1974.

262. Jaquith, James R. "Bibliography of Anthropological Bibliographies of the Americas." America Indigena 30 (April 1970): 419-469.

263. Jullson, Willard Rouse. A Selected Bibliography on the American Indian Historic and Prehistoric in Kentucky. Frankfort, Kentucky: Roberts Printing Company, 1964.

264. Kaiser, Ernest. "American Indians and Mexican Americans: A Selected Bibliography." Freedomways: A Quarterly Review of the Freedom Movement 9 (Fourth Quarter 1969): 298-327. Bibliography has an emphasis on black-Indian relations and some Marxist articles, not found in other bibliographies.

265. Marken, Jack W. The Indians and Eskimos of North America: A Bibliography of Books in Print through 1972. Vermillion, South Dakota: Dakota Press, 1973.

266. _____. The Literatures and Languages of the North American Indian. Northbrook, Illinois: AHM Publishing Corporation, forthcoming.

267. Murdock, George Peter. Ethnographic Bibliography of North America. 3d edition. New Haven, Connecticut: Human Relations Area Files, 1960. Arranged by tribes.

268. North American Indians: A Comprehensive Annotated Bibliography for the Secondary Teacher. Tempe: Indian Education Center, Arizona State University, 1973.

269. Perkins, David, and Norman Tanis. Native Americans of North America: A Bibliography Based on Collections in the Libraries of California State University, Northridge. Northridge: California State University, 1975.

270. Rader, Jesse Lee. South of Forty, from the Mississippi to the Rio Grande: A Bibliography. Norman: University of Oklahoma Press, 1947.

271. Ray, Roger B. The Indians of Maine: A Bibliographical Guide. Portland: Maine Historical Society, 1972.

272. Spofford, Ainsworth R. "Rare Books Relating to the American Indians." American Anthropologist, new series 3 (April-June 1901): 270-286.

273. Stensland, Anna Lee. Literature by and about the American Indian: An Annotated Bibliography for Junior and Senior High School Students. Urbana, Illinois: National Council of Teachers of English, 1973.

274. Storm, Colton. A Catalogue of the Everett D. Graff Collection of Western Americana. Chicago: University of Chicago Press, 1968. A collection in the Newberry Library with many Indian items.

275. Torrans, Thomas. "General Works on the American Indian: A Descriptive Bibliography." <u>Arizona and the West</u> 2 (Spring 1960): 79-103.

276. Vail, R. W. G. "A Bibliography of North American Frontier Literature, 1542-1800." In <u>The Voice of the Old Frontier</u>, pp. 84-492. Philadelphia: University of Pennsylvania Press, 1949. A detailed chronological checklist with many Indian items.

277. Whiteford, Andrew Hunter. "North American Indians: 1492-1969." <u>Choice</u> 6 (February 1970): 1709-1719.

278. Whiteside, Don. <u>Aboriginal People: A Selected Bibliography Concerning Canada's First People</u>. Ottawa: National Indian Brotherhood, 1973. Includes some United States material.

Dissertations on Indian subjects can be located in the following general and specialized bibliographies.

279. <u>Comprehensive Dissertation Index, 1861-1972</u>. 37 volumes. Ann Arbor: Xerox University Microfilms, 1973. A subject and author index.

280. Dockstader, Frederick J. <u>The American Indian in Graduate Studies: A Bibliography of Theses and Dissertations</u>. New York: Museum of the American Indian, Heye Foundation, 1957. Period 1890-1955.

281. Dockstader, Frederick J., and Alice W. Dockstader. <u>The American Indian in Graduate Studies: A Bibliography of Theses and Dissertations</u>. New York: Museum of the American Indian, Heye Foundation, 1974. Period 1955-1970.

282. Kuehl, Warren F. <u>Dissertations in History: An Index to Dissertations Completed in History Departments of United States and Canadian Universities, 1873-1960</u>. Lexington: University of Kentucky Press, 1965.

283. _____. <u>Dissertations in History: An Index to Dissertations Completed in History Departments of United States and Canadian Universities, 1961-June 1970</u>. Lexington: University Press of Kentucky, 1972.

The new handbook on North American Indians, in preparation at the Smithsonian Institution, will include a comprehensive bibliography.

INDIAN PERIODICALS

Periodicals published by Indians or by organizations interested in Indian affairs are a fruitful source of information on Indian-white relations. Many of the publications, however, had only a short existence and are difficult to locate in full series. The following are bibliographies of Indian periodicals.

284. Bush, Alfred L., and Robert S. Fraser. <u>American Indian Periodicals in the Princeton University Library: A Preliminary List</u>. Princeton: Princeton University Library, 1970.

285. Center for the Study of Man, Smithsonian Institution. "Current North American Indian Periodicals." <u>Social Education</u> 36 (May 1972): 494-500.

286. "Magazines and Periodicals." In <u>Reference Encyclopedia of the American Indian</u>, edited by Barry T. Klein and Dan Icolari, 1:301-317. 2d edition. 2 volumes. Rye, New York: Todd Publications, 1973.

287. "Native American Publications." In <u>Index to Literature on the American Indian, 1970</u>, pp. 139-177. San Francisco: Indian Historian Press, 1972. A similar list appears in the <u>Index to Literature</u>, 1971.

The following are some valuable periodicals no longer being published. Others are listed under appropriate subject headings.

288. <u>The American Indian</u>. 1926-1931. Published at Tulsa, Oklahoma.

289. <u>The American Indian</u>. 1943-1959. Published by the Association on American Indian Affairs, New York.

290. <u>American Indian Life</u>. 1925-1936. Published by the American Indian Defense Association, Washington.

291. <u>American Indian Magazine</u>. 1913-1920. Called <u>Quarterly Journal</u>, 1913-1915. Published by the Society of American Indians, Washington.

292. <u>Indian Voices</u>. 1962-1968. Edited by Robert K. Thomas, University of Chicago.

Currently published periodicals include the following:

293. <u>Akwesasne Notes</u>. Published by the Mohawk Nation, Rooseveltown, New York.

294. <u>American Indian Culture and Research Journal</u>. Published by the American Indian Culture and Research Center, University of California--Los Angeles. Supersedes the <u>American Indian Culture Center Journal</u>.

295. <u>American Indian Quarterly: A Journal of Anthropology, History, and Literature</u>. Published by the Southwestern American Indian Society, Hurst, Texas.

296. Americans Before Columbus. Published by the National Indian Youth Council, Albuquerque, New Mexico.

297. The Amerindian: American Indian Review. Published by Marion E. Gridley, Chicago.

298. Indian Affairs. Published by the Association on American Indian Affairs, New York.

299. The Indian Historian. Published by the American Indian Historical Society, San Francisco.

300. The Sentinel. Published by the National Congress of American Indians, Washington.

301. Wassaja. Published by the American Indian Historical Society, San Francisco. A newspaper.

REFERENCE WORKS

The following are general reference works on the American Indians.

302. Encyclopedia of Indians of the Americas. Keith Irvine, general editor. St. Clair Shores, Michigan: Scholarly Press, 1974--.

303. Hodge, Frederick Webb, ed. Handbook of American Indians North of Mexico. 2 volumes. Washington: Government Printing Office, 1907-1910. A standard work; to be superseded by the new handbook being prepared at the Smithsonian Institution.

304. Klein, Barry T., and Dan Icolari, eds. Reference Encyclopedia of the American Indian. 2d edition. 2 volumes. Rye, New York: Todd Publications, 1973.

305. Marquis, Arnold. A Guide to America's Indians: Ceremonials, Reservations, and Museums. Norman: University of Oklahoma Press, 1974.

306. Swanton, John R. The Indian Tribes of North America. Bureau of American Ethnology Bulletin 145. Washington: Government Printing Office, 1952.

Part Two
Classified Bibliography of Published Works

5
Indian Affairs/Indian Policy

Much of the writing about Indians in the United States has dealt with what might be called the political status of the Indians. In this general category fall such topics as the policy of the federal government, humanitarian reform movements directed toward the Indians, and public concern over Indian affairs. Listed here are historical studies and also items of current comment, in a chronological arrangement of topics.

GENERAL WORKS ON INDIAN-WHITE RELATIONS

Comprehensive Accounts

A number of authors have written general histories of Indian policy or Indian affairs in the United States, covering the whole period of Indian-white contact or some major portion of it. The books vary greatly in scope and purpose, and some of them contain a good deal of ethnological information.

307. American Heritage Book of Indians. Editor in charge, Alvin M. Josephy, Jr. Narrative by William Brandon. New York: American Heritage Publishing Company, 1961. Text only published New York: Dell Publishing Company, 1964.

308. Brandon, William. The Last Americans: The Indian in American Culture. New York: McGraw-Hill Book Company, 1974.

309. Collier, John. The Indians of the Americas. New York: W. W. Norton and Company, 1947.

310. Debo, Angie. A History of the Indians of the United States. Norman: University of Oklahoma Press, 1970.

311. Ellis, George E. The Red Man and the White Man in North America from Its Discovery to the Present Time. Boston: Little Brown and Company, 1882.

312. Fey, Harold E., and D'Arcy McNickle. Indians and Other Americans: Two Ways of Life Meet. New York: Harper and Brothers, 1959.

313. Gabriel, Ralph Henry. The Lure of the Frontier: A Story of Race Conflict. New Haven: Yale University Press, 1929.

314. Georgakas, Dan. The Broken Hoop: The History of Native Americans from 1600 to 1890, from the Atlantic Coast to the Plains. Garden City, New York: Doubleday and Company, 1973.

315. _____. Red Shadows: The History of Native Americans from 1600 to 1900, from the Desert to the Pacific Coast. Garden City, New York: Doubleday and Company, 1973.

316. Hagan, William T. American Indians. Chicago: University of Chicago Press, 1961.

317. Humphrey, Seth K. The Indian Dispossessed. Boston: Little, Brown and Company, 1905.

318. La Farge, Oliver. As Long as the Grass Shall Grow. New York: Alliance Book Corporation, Longmans, Green and Company, 1940.

319. _____. A Pictorial History of the American Indians. New York: Crown Publishers, 1956. Revised by Alvin M. Josephy, Jr., 1974.

320. Leupp, Francis E. In Red Man's Land: A Study of the American Indian. New York: Fleming H. Revell Company, 1914.

321. Lindquist, G. E. E., with the collaboration of Erna Gunther, John H. Holst, and Flora Warren Seymour. The Indian in American Life. New York: Friendship Press, 1944.

322. MacLeod, William C. The American Indian Frontier. New York: Alfred A. Knopf, 1928.

323. McNickle, D'Arcy. Native American Tribalism: Indian Survivals and Renewals. New York: Oxford University Press, 1973.

324. _____. They Came Here First: The Epic of the American Indian. Philadelphia: J. B. Lippincott Company, 1949.

325. McNicol, Donald M. The Amerindians: From Acuera to Sitting Bull, from Donnacona to Big Bear. New York: Frederick A.

Stokes Company, 1937.

326. Moorehead, Warren K. The American Indian in the United States, Period 1850-1914. Andover, Massachusetts: Andover Press, 1914.

327. Peithmann, Irvin M. Broken Peace Pipes: A Four-Hundred-Year History of the American Indian. Springfield, Illinois: Charles C. Thomas, 1964.

328. Seymour, Flora Warren. The Story of the Red Man. New York: Longmans, Green and Company, 1929.

329. _____. We Called Them Indians. New York: D. Appleton-Century Company, 1940.

330. Spicer, Edward H. A Short History of the Indians of the United States. New York: Van Nostrand-Reinhold Company, 1969.

331. Thomas, Cyrus. The Indians of North America in Historic Times. Philadelphia: George Barrie's Sons, 1903.

332. Tyler, S. Lyman. A History of Indian Policy. Washington: Department of the Interior, Bureau of Indian Affairs, 1973.

333. _____. Indian Affairs: A Study of the Changes in Policy of the United States toward the Indians. Provo, Utah: Institute of American Indian Studies, Brigham Young University, 1964.

334. Washburn, Wilcomb E. The Indian in America. New York: Harper and Row, 1975.

335. _____. Red Man's Land/White Man's Law: A Study of the Past and Present Status of the American Indian. New York: Charles Scribner's Sons, 1971.

336. Wise, Jennings C. The Red Man in the New World Drama: A Politico-Legal Study with a Pageantry of American History. Washington: W. F. Roberts Company, 1931. Revised edition, with six chapters added by Vine Deloria, Jr. New York: Macmillan Company, 1971.

Brief or Specialized Accounts

337. Abel, Annie Heloise. "Proposals for an Indian State, 1778-1878." Annual Report of the American Historical Association for the Year 1907, 1:87-104.

338. Baker, Donald G. "Color, Culture and Power: Indian-White Relations in Canada and America." Canadian Review of American Studies 3 (Spring 1972): 3-20.

339. Berthrong, Donald J. The American Indian: From Pacifism to Activism. St. Louis: Forum Press, 1973.

340. Costo, Rupert. "Presidents of the United States in American Indian History." Indian Historian 1 (Fall 1968): 4-13.

341. Flickinger, Samuel J. "The American Indian." Proceedings of the Annual Meeting of the Order of Indian Wars of the United States, February 18, 1939, pp. 21-31.

342. Haas, Theodore H. "The Legal Aspects of Indian Affairs from 1887 to 1957." Annals of the American Academy of Political and Social Science 311 (May 1957): 12-22.

343. Haines, Francis. "Problems of Indian Policy." Pacific Northwest Quarterly 41 (July 1950): 203-212.

344. Hoopes, Alban W. "Some Thoughts upon the American Indian." General Magazine and Historical Chronicle 39 (July 1937): 385-395.

345. Jackson, Kathleen O'Brien. "A Study of Changes in Authority Relations between American Indians and Government." Ph.D. dissertation, University of Oregon, 1971.

346. Jacobs, Wilbur R. "The Fatal Confrontation: Early Native-White Relations on the Frontiers of Australia, New Guinea, and America--A Comparative Study." Pacific Historical Review 40 (August 1971): 283-309.

347. Kelly, William H. "Indian Adjustment and the History of Indian Affairs." Arizona Law Review 10 (Winter 1968): 559-577.

348. Lurie, Nancy Oestreich. "Historical Background." In The American Indian Today. edited by Stuart Levine and Nancy Oestreich Lurie, pp. 25-45. Deland, Florida: Everett/Edwards, 1968.

349. McNickle, D'Arcy. "Indian and European: Indian-White Relations from Discovery to 1887." Annals of the American Academy of Political and Social Science 311 (May 1957): 1-11.

350. Metcalf, P. Richard. "Who Should Rule at Home? Native American Politics and Indian-White Relations." Journal of American History 61 (December 1974): 651-665.

351. Munkres, Robert L. "Indian-White Contact before 1870: Cultural Factors in Conflict." Journal of the West 10 (July 1971): 439-473.

352. Officer, James E. "The American Indian and Federal Indian Policy." In The American Indian in Urban Society, edited by Jack O. Waddell and O. Michael Watson, pp. 8-65. Boston: Little, Brown and Company, 1971.

353. Price, A. Grenfell. White Settlers and Native Peoples: An Historical Study of Racial Contacts between English-Speaking Whites and Aboriginal Peoples in the United States, Canada, Australia and New Zealand. Melbourne: Georgian House, 1949.

354. Schifter, Richard. "Trends in Federal Indian Administration." South Dakota Law Review 15 (Winter 1970): 1-21.

355. Sheehan, Bernard W. "The American Indian as Victim." Alternative: An American Spectator 8 (January 1975): 5-8.

356. Spicer, Edward H. "Indigenismo in the United States." America Indigena 24 (October 1964): 349-363.

357. Stewart, Omer C. "Federal vs. Local Treatment of Indians." Delphian Quarterly 42 (Winter 1959): 27-35.

358. Strong, Esther B. "Wardship in American Indian Administration: A Political Instrumentality for Social Change." Ph.D. dissertation, Yale University, 1941.

359. Taylor, Theodore W. "American Indians and Their Government." Current History 67 (December 1974): 254-258, 275-277.

Collected Articles

Listed here are a number of publications that contain articles on Indian affairs by various authors. Some of them are collections of original papers, others of reprinted materials. In most cases the individual articles are listed separately under appropriate headings in the sections that follow.

360. Baerreis, David A., ed. The Indian in Modern America. Madison: State Historical Society of Wisconsin, 1956.

361. Bahr, Howard M., Bruce A. Chadwick, and Robert C. Day, eds. Native Americans Today: Sociological Perspectives. New York: Harper and Row, 1972.

362. Daniels, Walter M., ed. American Indians. The Reference Shelf, volume 29, no. 4. New York: H. W. Wilson Company, 1957.

363. Ellis, Richard N., ed. The Western American Indian: Case Studies in Tribal History. Lincoln: University of Nebraska Press, 1972.

364. Indian Voices: The First Convocation of American Indian Scholars. San Francisco: Indian Historian Press, 1970.

365. Indian Voices: The Native American Today. San Francisco: Indian Historian Press, 1974. The Second Convocation of American Indian Scholars. Transcriptions of panel discussions on water rights, education, land use, health professions, museums, and the Indian Claims Commission.

366. Jones, Charles, ed. Look to the Mountain Top. San Jose, California: Gousha Publications, 1972. Articles by contemporary authors, Indian and non-Indian.

367. La Farge, Oliver, ed. The Changing Indian. Norman: University of Oklahoma Press, 1942.

368. Leacock, Eleanor Burke, and Nancy Oestreich Lurie, eds. North American Indians in Historical Perspective. New York: Random House, 1971.

369. Levine, Stuart, and Nancy Oestreich Lurie, eds. The American Indian Today. Deland, Florida: Everett/Edwards, 1968.

370. Marx, Herbert L., Jr., ed. The American Indian: A Rising Ethnic Force. The Reference Shelf, volume 45, no. 5. New York: H. W. Wilson Company, 1973.

371. Nichols, Roger L., and George R. Adams, eds. The American Indian: Past and Present. Waltham, Massachusetts: Xerox College Publishing, 1971.

372. Prucha, Francis Paul, ed. The Indian in American History. New York: Holt, Rinehart and Winston, 1971.

373. Roe, Melvin W., ed. Readings in the History of the American Indian. New York: MSS Information Corporation, 1971.

374. Walker, Deward E., Jr., ed. The Emergent Native Americans: A Reader in Culture Contact. Boston: Little, Brown and Company, 1972.

Collected Documents

Increased interest in Indian affairs has stimulated the publication of books containing a variety of source materials pertaining to Indian-white relations. Some of these are listed here.

375. Council on Interracial Books for Children. Chronicles of American Indian Protest. Greenwich, Connecticut: Fawcett Publications, 1971.

376. Deloria, Vine, Jr., ed. Of Utmost Good Faith. San Francisco: Straight Arrow Books, 1971.

377. Forbes, Jack D., ed. The Indian in America's Past. Englewood Cliffs, New Jersey: Prentice-Hall, 1964.

378. Vogel, Virgil J., ed. This Country Was Ours: A Documentary History of the American Indian. New York: Harper and Row, 1972.

379. Washburn, Wilcomb E., ed. The Indian and the White Man. Garden City, New York: Doubleday and Company, 1964.

380. Wrone, David R., and Russell S. Nelson, Jr., eds. Who's the Savage? A Documentary History of the Mistreatment of the Native North Americans. Greenwich, Connecticut: Fawcett Publications, 1973.

COLONIAL INDIAN AFFAIRS

British Indian Policy: General

Relations between the British colonists and the Indians were largely left to the individual colonies, but after the middle of the eighteenth century some imperial control was attempted. Listed here are studies of those plans and of general relations between Indians and whites in the colonial period. Other works are listed below according to region.

381. Alden, John R. "The Albany Congress and the Creation of the Indian Superintendencies." Mississippi Valley Historical Review 27 (September 1940): 193-210.

382. Alvord, Clarence Walworth. "The Genesis of the Proclamation of 1763." Collections and Researches Made by the Michigan Pioneer and Historical Society 36 (1908): 20-52.

383. _____. The Mississippi Valley in British Politics: A Study of the Trade, Land Speculation, and Experiments in Imperialism Culminating in the American Revolution. Cleveland: Arthur H. Clark Company, 1917.

384. Axtell, James L. Through a Glass Darkly: Colonial Attitudes toward the Native Americans. Essays from Sarah Lawrence Faculty, volume 2, no. 1. Bronxville, New York: Sarah Lawrence College, 1973.

385. Beer, David F. "Anti-Indian Sentiment in Early Colonial Literature." Indian Historian 2 (Spring 1969): 29-33, 48.

386. Bishop, Morris. "Four Indian Kings in London." American Heritage 23 (December 1971): 62-65.

387. Bond, Richmond P. Queen Anne's American Kings. Oxford: Oxford University Press, 1952.

388. Carter, Clarence E. "The Significance of the Military Office in America, 1763-1775." American Historical Review 28 (April 1923): 475-488.

389. Carter, Clarence E., ed. "Observations of Superintendent John Stuart and Governor James Grant of East Florida on the Proposed Plan of 1764 for the Future Management of Indian Affairs." American Historical Review 20 (July 1915): 815-831.

390. Crane, Ellery B. "The Treatment of the Indians by the Colonists." Proceedings of the Worcester Society of Antiquity 20 (1904): 220-248.

391. Edmunds, R. David. "Pickawillany: French Military Power versus British Economics." Western Pennsylvania Historical Magazine 58 (April 1975): 169-184.

392. Ellis, George E. "The Red Indian of North America in Contact with the French and English." In Narrative and Critical History of America, edited by Justin Winsor, 1:283-328. 8 volumes. Boston: Houghton, Mifflin and Company, 1884-1889.

393. Farrand, Max. "The Indian Boundary Line." American Historical Review 10 (July 1905): 782-791.

394. Garratt, John G. "The Four Indian Kings." History Today 18 (February 1968): 93-101.

395. Hammerer, John Daniel. An Account of a Plan for Civilizing the North American Indians, Proposed in the Eighteenth Century. Edited by Paul Leicester Ford. Brooklyn: Historical Printing Club, 1890. Originally published in 1765.

396. Humphreys, R. A. "Lord Shelburne and the Proclamation of 1763." English Historical Review 49 (April 1934): 241-258.

397. Humphreys, R. A., ed. "Governor Murray's Views on the Plan of 1764 for the Management of Indian Affairs." Canadian Historical Review 16 (June 1935): 162-169.

398. Jacobs, Wilbur R. "British-Colonial Attitudes and Policies toward the Indian in the American Colonies." In Attitudes of Colonial Powers toward the American Indian, edited by Howard Peckham and Charles Gibson, pp. 81-106. Salt Lake City: University of Utah Press, 1969.

399. _____. Diplomacy and Indian Gifts: Anglo-French Rivalry along the Ohio and Northwest Frontiers, 1748-1763. Stanford, California: Stanford Universtiy Press, 1950. Republished as The Northern Colonial Frontier, 1748-1763: Wilderness Politics and Indian Gifts. Lincoln: University of Nebraska Press, 1966.

400. _____. Dispossessing the American Indian: Indians and Whites on the Colonial Frontier. New York: Charles Scribner's Sons, 1972. Revisions of earlier essays.

401. _____. "Edmond Atkin's Plan for Imperial Indian Control." Journal of Southern History 19 (August 1953): 311-320.

402. _____. "The Indian Frontier of 1763." Western Pennsylvania Historical Magazine 34 (September 1951): 185-198.

403. _____. "Presents to Indians along the French Frontiers in the Old Northwest, 1748-1763." Indiana Magazine of History 44 (September 1948): 245-256.

404. _____. "Wampum, the Protocol of Indian Diplomacy." William and Mary Quarterly, 3d series 6 (October 1949): 596-604.

405. James, James Alton. "English Institutions and the American Indian." Johns Hopkins University Studies in Historical and Political Science 12 (1894): 460-519.

406. Jennings, Francis. "Virgin Land and Savage People." American Quarterly 23 (October 1971): 519-541.

407. Kellogg, Louise Phelps. The British Regime in Wisconsin and the Northwest. Madison: State Historical Society of Wisconsin, 1935. Carries the story to 1815.

408. _____. The French Regime in Wisconsin and the Northwest. Madison: State Historical Society of Wisconsin, 1925.

409. Kimmey, Fred M. "Christianity and Indian Lands." Ethnohistory 7 (Winter 1960): 44-60.

410. Leach, Douglas Edward. The Northern Colonial Frontier, 1607-1763. New York: Holt, Rinehart and Winston, 1966.

411. Lurie, Nancy Oestreich. "Indian Intellectual Adjustment to European Civilization." In Seventeenth-Century America: Essays in Colonial History, edited by James Morton Smith, pp. 33-60. Chapel Hill: University of North Carolina Press, 1959.

412. MacLeod, William Christie. "Big Business and the North American Indian." American Journal of Sociology 34 (November 1928): 480-491.

413. Marshall, Peter. "Colonial Protest and Imperial Retrenchment: Indian Policy, 1764-8." Journal of American Studies 5 (April 1971): 1-17.

414. _____. "Imperial Regulation of American Indian Affairs, 1763-1774." Ph.D. dissertation, Yale University, 1960.

415. Nash, Gary B. Red, White and Black: The Peoples of Early America. Englewood Cliffs, New Jersey: Prentice-Hall, 1974.

416. Peckham, Howard, and Charles Gibson, eds. Attitudes of Colonial Powers toward the American Indian. Salt Lake City: University of Utah Press, 1969.

417. Sauer, Carl Ortwin. Sixteenth Century North America: The Land and the People as Seen by Europeans. Berkeley: University of California Press, 1971.

418. Sosin, Jack M. Whitehall and the Wilderness: The Middle West in British Colonial Policy, 1760-1775. Lincoln: University of Nebraska Press, 1961.

419. Thomson, Charles. An Enquiry into the Causes of the Alienation of the Delaware and Shawanese Indians from the British Interest, and into the Measures Taken for Recovering Their Friendship. St. Clair Shores, Michigan: Scholarly Press, 1970. Originally published in London, 1759.

420. Tootle, James Roger. "Anglo-Indian Relations in the Northern Theatre of the French and Indian War, 1748-1761." Ph.D. dissertation, Ohio State University, 1972.

421. Washburn, Wilcomb E. "The Moral and Legal Justifications for Dispossessing the Indians." In Seventeenth-Century America: Essays in Colonial History, edited by James Morton Smith, pp. 15-32. Chapel Hill: University of North Carolina Press, 1959.

See also studies on colonial Indian wars, on colonial treaties, and on colonial Indian trade.

Colonial New England

The Puritans of New England were much concerned about the Indians, and historians have investigated and evaluated those relationships.

422. Adolf, Leonard A. "Squanto's Role in Pilgrim Diplomacy." Ethnohistory 11 (Summer 1964): 247-261.

423. Axtell, James. "The Scholastic Philosophy of the Wilderness." William and Mary Quarterly, 3d series 29 (July 1972): 335-366.

424. Blackmon, Joab L., Jr. "Judge Samuel Sewall's Efforts in Behalf of the First Americans." Ethnohistory 16 (Spring 1969): 165-176.

425. Bushnell, David. "The Treatment of the Indians in Plymouth Colony." New England Quarterly 26 (June 1953): 193-218.

426. Clark, J. S. "Did the Pilgrims Wrong the Indians?" Congregational Quarterly 1 (April 1859): 129-135.

427. Davis, Jack L. "Roger Williams among the Narragansett Indians." New England Quarterly 43 (December 1970): 593-604.

428. Day, Gordon M. "English-Indian Contacts in New England." Ethnohistory 9 (Winter 1962): 24-40.

429. Eisinger, Chester E. "The Puritans' Justification for Taking the Land." Essex Institute Historical Collections 84 (April 1948): 131-143.

430. Eno, Joel N. "The Puritans and the Indian Lands." Magazine of History with

Notes and Queries 4 (November 1906): 274-281.

431. H. L. R. "Puritan Treatment of the American Indians." American Catholic Quarterly Review 12 (January 1887): 157-168.

432. Hansen, Chadwick. "The Metamorphosis of Tituba; or, Why American Intellectuals Can't Tell an Indian Witch from a Negro." New England Quarterly 47 (March 1974): 3-12.

433. Kawashima, Yasuhide. "Indians and the Law in Colonial Massachusetts, 1689-1763." Ph.D. dissertation, University of California, Santa Barbara, 1968.

434. _____. "Jurisdiction of the Colonial Courts over the Indians in Massachusetts, 1689-1763." New England Quarterly 42 (December 1969): 532-550.

435. _____. "Legal Origins of the Indian Reservation in Colonial Massachusetts." American Journal of Legal History 13 (January 1969): 42-56.

436. Lewis, Guy Loran. "Daniel Gookin, Superintendent and Historian of the New England Indians: A Historiographical Study." Ph.D. dissertation, University of Illinois, 1973.

437. MacCulloch, Susan L. "A Tripartite Political System among Christian Indians of Early Massachusetts." Kroeber Anthropological Society Papers no. 34 (Spring 1966): 63-73.

438. MacFarlane, Ronald O. "Indian Relations in New England, 1620-1760: A Study of a Regulated Frontier." Ph.D. dissertation, Harvard University, 1933.

439. Martin, Calvin. "The European Impact on the Culture of a Northeastern Algonquian Tribe: An Ecological Interpretation." William and Mary Quarterly 31 (January 1974): 3-26.

440. Ronda, James P. "Red and White at the Bench: Indians and the Law in Plymouth Colony, 1620-1691." Essex Institute Historical Collections 110 (July 1974): 200-215.

441. Salisbury, Neal Emerson. "Conquest of the 'Savage': Puritans, Puritan Missionaries, and Indians, 1620-1680." Ph.D. dissertation, University of California, Los Angeles, 1972.

442. Thomas, G. E. "Puritans, Indians, and the Concept of Race." New England Quarterly 48 (March 1975): 3-27.

443. Trask, William Blake, ed. Letters of Colonel Thomas Westbrook and Others Relative to Indian Affairs in Maine, 1722-1726. Boston: George E. Littlefield, 1901.

444. Vaughan, Alden T. New England Frontier: Puritans and Indians, 1620-1675. Boston: Little, Brown, and Company, 1965.

445. _____. "A Test of Puritan Justice." New England Quarterly 38 (September 1965): 331-339.

446. Warner, Robert Austin. "The Southern New England Indians to 1725: A Study in Culture Contact." Ph.D. dissertation, Yale University, 1935.

447. Weeden, William B. Indian Money as a Factor in New England Civilization. Johns Hopkins University Studies in Historical and Political Science, 2d series 8-9. Baltimore: Johns Hopkins University, 1884.

See also studies on the Indian wars in New England and on Puritan missionary efforts.

The Middle Colonies

Indian-white relations in the middle colonies have received considerable historical treatment, especially those with the Iroquois and with the Indians in Pennsylvania.

448. Borkowski, Joseph A. "Polish-Born Pennsylvania Pioneer." Polish-American Studies 20 (July-December 1963): 81-86. Christian Frederick Post and the Indians of Pennsylvania.

449. Brock, R. Alonzo, ed. "Journal of William Black, 1744, Secretary of the Commissioners Appointed . . . to Treat with the Iroquois." Pennsylvania Magazine of History and Biography 1 (1877): 117-132, 233-249, 404-419.

450. Colley, Charles C. "Indians in Colonial Pennsylvania: Historical Interpretations." Indian Historian 7 (Winter 1974): 2-5.

451. Cribbs, George Arthur. "The Frontier Policy of Pennsylvania." Western Pennsylvania Historical Magazine 2 (January 1919): 5-35; (April 1919): 72-106; (July 1919): 174-198.

452. De Valinger, Leon, Jr. "Indian Land Sales in Delaware." Bulletin of the Archaeological Society of Delaware 3 (February 1940): 29-32; (February 1941): 25-33.

453. Everett, Edward G. "Pennsylvania's Indian Diplomacy, 1747-1753." Western Pennsylvania Historical Magazine 44 (September 1961): 241-256.

454. Fleming, Thomas J. "G. Washington Meets a Test." American Heritage 14 (February 1963): 56-59, 79-81.

455. Gamble, Anna Dill. "Col. James Smith and the Caughnawaga Indians." Records of the American Catholic Historical Society of Philadelphia 49 (March 1938): 1-26.

456. Handlin, Oscar, and Irving Mark, eds. "Chief Nimham v. Roger Morris, Beverly Robinson, and Philip Philipse--an Indian Land Case in Colonial New York, 1765-1767." Ethnohistory 11 (Summer 1964): 193-246.

457. Heckewelder, John. "Indian Tradition of the First Arrival of the Dutch at Manhattan Island, Now New-York." Collections of the New-York Historical Society, 2d series 1 (1841): 69-74.

458. Hunter, William A. "Provincial Negotiations with the Western Indians, 1754-58." Pennsylvania History 18 (July 1951): 213-219.

459. Hyde, John Alden Lloyd. The Relations between the Early Dutch and Indians as Affecting the Subsequent Development of the Colony of New York. Society of Colonial Wars in the State of New York Publication no. 34. New York, 1924.

460. Jennings, Francis. "The Delaware Interregnum." Pennsylvania Magazine of History and Biography 89 (April 1965): 174-198.

461. _____. "Glory, Death, and Transfiguration: The Susquehannock Indians in the Seventeenth Century." Proceedings of the American Philosophical Society 112 (February 15, 1968): 15-53.

462. _____. "Incident at Tulpehocken." Pennsylvania History 35 (October 1968): 335-355.

463. _____. "Miquon's Passing: Indian-European Relations in Colonial Pennsylvania, 1674 to 1755." Ph.D. dissertation, University of Pennsylvania, 1965.

464. _____. "The Scandalous Indian Policy of William Penn's Sons: Deeds and Documents of the Walking Purchase." Pennsylvania History 37 (January 1970): 19-39.

465. Johnson, Frederick C . "Count Zinzendorf and the Moravian and Indian Occupancy of the Wyoming Valley, 1742-1763." Proceedings and Collections of the Wyoming Historical and Geological Society 8 (1902-1903): 119-182.

466. Lee, Francis B. "Some Aspects of the Legal Status of Indians, and, Incidentally, of Negroes in Colonial New Jersey." New Jersey Law Journal 15 (April 1892): 103-109.

467. Nammack, Georgiana C. Fraud, Politics, and the Dispossession of the Indians: The Iroquois Land Frontier in the Colonial Period. Norman: University of Oklahoma Press, 1969.

468. Rankin, Edward S. "The Purchase of Newark from the Indians." Proceedings of the New Jersey Historical Society, new series 12 (October 1927): 442-445.

469. Sahli, John R. "The Growth of British Influence among the Seneca to 1768." Western Pennsylvania Historical Magazine 49 (April 1966): 127-139.

470. Trelease, Allen W. "Dutch Treatment of the American Indian, with Particular Reference to New Netherland." In Attitudes of Colonial Powers toward the American Indian, edited by Howard Peckham and Charles Gibson, pp. 47-59. Salt Lake City: University of Utah Press, 1969.

471. _____. Indian Affairs in Colonial New York: The Seventeenth Century. Ithaca: Cornell University Press, 1960.

472. _____. "Indian-White Contacts in Eastern North America: The Dutch in New Netherland." Ethnohistory 9 (Spring 1962): 137-146.

473. Trigger, Bruce G. "The Mohawk-Mahican War (1624-28): The Establishment of a Pattern" Canadian Historical Review 52 (September 1971): 276-286.

474. Uhler, Sherman P. Pennsylvania's Indian Relations to 1754. Allentown, Pennsylvania, 1951.

475. Wallace, Anthony F. C. "Origins of Iroquois Neutrality: The Grand Settlement of 1701." Pennsylvania History 24 (July 1957): 223-235.

476. Walton, Joseph S. Conrad Weiser and the Indian Policy of Colonial Pennsylvania. Philadelphia: George W. Jacob and Company, 1900.

477. Weiser, Frederick S. "Conrad Weiser, Peacemaker of Colonial Pennsylvania." Historical Review of Berks County 25 (Summer 1960): 83-97.

478. Wraxall, Peter. An Abridgement of the Indian Affairs Contained in Four Folio Volumes, Transacted in the Colony of New York, from the Year 1678 to the Year 1751. Edited by Charles H. McIlwain. Cambridge: Harvard University Press, 1915.

See also studies on the Iroquois.

The Southern Colonies

British Indian affairs in the South were especially important because of the presence of strong tribes such as the Cherokees and the Creeks and international rivalry for their support.

479. Alden, John Richard. John Stuart and the Southern Colonial Frontier: A Study of Indian Relations, War, Trade, and Land Problems in the Southern Wilderness, 1754-1775. Ann Arbor: University of

of Michigan Press, 1944.

480. Barbour, Philip L. "Captain Newport Meets Opechancanough." Virginia Caval-cade 17 (Winter 1968): 42-47.

481. _____. Pocahontas and Her World: A Chronicle of America's First Settle-ment. Boston: Houghton Mifflin Company, 1970.

482. Bronner, Edwin B. "Indian Deed for Petty's Island, 1678." Pennsylvania Magazine of History and Biography 89 (January 1965): 111-114.

483. Carter, Clarence E. "British Policy towards the American Indians in the South, 1763-8." English Historical Review 33 (January 1918): 37-56.

484. Corkran, David H. The Creek Frontier, 1540-1783. Norman: University of Okla-homa Press, 1967.

485. _____. The Cherokee Frontier: Con-flict and Survival, 1740-1762. Norman: University of Oklahoma Press, 1962.

486. Corry, John Pitts. Indian Affairs in Georgia, 1732-1756. Philadelphia, 1936.

487. Covington, James. "English Gifts to the Indians, 1765-1766." Florida Anthro-pologist 13 (September 1960): 71-75.

488. Covington, James W., ed. The British Meet the Seminoles: Negotiations between British Authorities in East Florida and the Indians: 1763-68. Gainesville: Uni-versity of Florida, 1961.

489. Crane, Verner W. "The Southern Fron-tier in Queen Anne's War." American Historical Review 24 (April 1919): 379-395.

490. _____. The Southern Frontier, 1670-1732. Ann Arbor: University of Michigan Press, 1929.

491. Craven, Wesley Frank. "Indian Policy in Early Virginia." William and Mary Quarterly, 3d series 1 (January 1944): 65-82.

492. _____. White, Red, and Black: The Seventeenth-Century Virginian. Char-lottesville: University Press of Virginia, 1971.

493. DeVorsey, Louis, Jr. "Indian Bound-aries in Colonial Georgia." Georgia Historical Quarterly 54 (Spring 1970): 63-78.

494. _____. The Indian Boundary in the Southern Colonies, 1763-1775. Chapel Hill: University of North Carolina Press, 1966.

495. Forbes, Gerald. "The International Conflict for the Lands of Creek Confed-eracy." Chronicles of Oklahoma 14 (De-cember 1936): 478-498.

496. Glenn, Keith. "Captain John Smith and the Indians." Virginia Magazine of History and Biography 52 (October 1944): 228-248.

497. Gold, Robert L. "The East Florida In-dians under Spanish and English Control, 1763-1765." Florida Historical Quarterly 44 (July-October 1965): 105-120.

498. Hamer, Philip M. "Anglo-French Rivalry in the Cherokee Country, 1754-1757." North Carolina Historical Review 2 (July 1925): 303-322.

499. Hawes, Lilla Mills, ed. "The Frontiers of Georgia in the Late Eighteenth Century: Jonas Fauche to Joseph Vallance Bevan." Georgia Historical Quarterly 47 (March 1963): 84-95.

500. Henry, Jane. "The Choptank Indians of Maryland under the Proprietary Govern-ment." Maryland Historical Magazine 65 (Summer 1970): 171-180.

501. Jacobs, Wilbur R., ed. Indians of the Southern Colonial Frontier: The Edmond Atkin Report and Plan of 1755. Columbia: University of South Carolina Press, 1954.

502. Kawashima, Yasuhide. "Indians and Southern Colonial Statutes." Indian Historian 7 (Winter 1974): 10-16.

503. Kinnaird, Lawrence. "International Rivalry in the Creek Country." Florida Historical Society Quarterly 10 (Octo-ber 1931): 59-85.

504. Koontz, Louis K. The Virginia Fron-tier, 1754-1763. Johns Hopkins Univer-sity Studies in Historical and Political Science, 43d series 2. Baltimore: Johns Hopkins Press, 1925.

505. Lofton, John M., Jr. "White, Indian, and Negro Contacts in Colonial South Carolina." Southern Indian Studies 1 (April 1949): 3-12.

506. McCary, Ben Clyde. Indians in Seven-teenth Century Virginia. Virginia 350th Anniversary Historical Booklet no. 18. Williamsburg: Virginia 350th Anniversary Celebration Corporation, 1957.

507. McDowell, William L., Jr., ed. Docu-ments Relating to Indian Affairs, May 21, 1750--August 7, 1754. Colonial Records of South Carolina, series 2. Columbia: South Carolina Archives Department, 1958.

508. _____. Documents Relating to Indian Affairs, 1754-1765. Colonial Records of South Carolina, series 2. Columbia: South Carolina Archives Department, 1969.

509. _____. Journals of the Commission-ers of the Indian Trade, September 20, 1710--August 29, 1718. Colonial Records of South Carolina, series 2. Columbia: South Carolina Archives Department, 1955.

510. O'Donnell, James H. III. "The Southern

Indians in the War for American Independence, 1775-1783." In Four Centuries of Southern Indians, edited by Charles M. Hudson, pp. 46-64. Athens: University of Georgia Press, 1975.

511. Osborn, George C. "Relations with the Indians in West Florida during the Administration of Governor Peter Chester, 1770-1781." Florida Historical Quarterly 31 (April 1953): 239-272.

512. Parish, John C. "John Stuart and the Cartography of the Indian Boundary Line." In The Persistence of the Westward Movement and Other Essays, pp. 131-146. Berkeley: University of California Press, 1943.

513. Phelps, Dawson A. "The Chickasaw, the English, and the French, 1699-1744." Tennessee Historical Quarterly 16 (June 1957): 117-133.

514. Rand, James Hall. "The Indians of North Carolina and Their Relations with the Settlers." James Sprunt Historical Publications 12 (1913): 3-41.

515. Robinson, W. Stitt. "The Legal Status of the Indian in Colonial Virginia." Virginia Magazine of History and Biography 61 (July 1953): 247-259.

516. _____. "Tributary Indians in Colonial Virginia." Virginia Magazine of History and Biography 67 (January 1959): 49-64.

517. _____. "Virginia and the Cherokees: Indian Policy from Spotswood to Dinwiddie." In The Old Dominion: Essays for Thomas Perkins Abernethy, edited by Darrett B. Rutman, pp. 21-40. Charlottesville: University Press of Virginia, 1964.

518. Rountree, Helen Clark. "Indian Land Loss in Virginia: A Prototype of U.S. Federal Indian Policy." Ph.D. dissertation, University of Wisconsin--Milwaukee, 1973.

519. Shaw, Helen Louise. British Administration of the Southern Indians, 1756-1783. Lancaster, Pennsylvania: Lancaster Press, 1931.

520. Smith, Hale G. The European and the Indian: European-Indian Contacts in Georgia and Florida. Florida Anthropological Society Publications, no. 4. Gainesville, Florida, 1956.

521. Sonderegger, Richard P. "The Southern Frontier from the Founding of Georgia to the End of King George's War." Ph.D. dissertation, University of Michigan, 1964.

522. Sturtevant, William C. "Spanish-Indian Relations in Southeastern North America." Ethnohistory 9 (Winter 1962): 41-94.

523. Trimble, David B. "Christopher Gist

and the Indian Service in Virginia, 1757-1759." Virginia Magazine of History and Biography 64 (April 1956): 143-165.

524. Woodward, Isaiah A. "The Influence of the Bosomworth Family on Anglo-Indian Relations in Colonial Georgia, 1745-1759." Quarterly Review of Higher Education among Negroes 16 (April 1948): 83-89.

Colonial Indian Superintendents

The British government in the mid-eighteenth century appointed superintendents to handle Indian affairs in the colonies. The most important of these men was Sir William Johnson.

525. Bryce, Peter H. "Sir John Johnson, Baronet: Superintendent-General of Indian Affairs, 1743-1830." New York State Historical Association Quarterly Journal 9 (July 1928): 233-271.

526. _____. "Sir William Johnson, Bart.: The Great Diplomat of the British-French Frontier." New York State Historical Association Quarterly Journal 8 (October 1927): 352-373.

527. Day, Richard E., ed. Calendar of Sir William Johnson Manuscripts in the New York State Library. Albany: University of the State of New York, 1909.

528. Downes, Randolph C. "George Morgan, Indian Agent Extraordinary, 1776-1779." Pennsylvania History 1 (October 1934): 202-216.

529. Flexner, James T. Mohawk Baronet: Sir William Johnson of New York. New York: Harper, 1959.

530. Hamilton, Milton W. "Myths and Legends of Sir William Johnson." New York History 34 (January 1953): 3-26.

531. _____. "Sir William Johnson and Pennsylvania." Pennsylvania History 19 (January 1952): 52-74.

532. _____. "Sir William Johnson: Interpreter of the Iroquois." Ethnohistory 10 (Summer 1963): 270-286.

533. Hamilton, Milton W., ed. "Guy Johnson's Opinions on the American Indian." Pennsylvania Magazine of History and Biography 77 (July 1953): 311-327.

534. Inouye, Frank T. "Sir William Johnson and the Administration of the Northern Indian Department." Ph.D. dissertation, University of Southern California, 1951.

535. Jackson, George B. "John Stuart: Superintendent of Indian Affairs for the Southern District." Tennessee Historical Magazine 3 (September 1917): 165-191.

536. Johnson, William. The Papers of Sir William Johnson. Edited by James Sullivan, and others. 14 volumes. Albany: University of the State of New York, 1921-1965.

537. Marshall, Peter. "Sir William Johnson and the Treaty of Fort Stanwix, 1768." Journal of American Studies 1 (1967): 149-179.

538. Mishoff, Willard Oral. "The Indian Policy of Sir William Johnson." Ph.D. dissertation, University of Iowa, 1933.

539. Murray, Eleanor M. "Sir William Johnson, Bart.: A Compendium of His Life and Career." Bulletin of the Fort Ticonderoga Museum 6 (July 1941): 42-61.

540. Parish, John Carl. "Edmond Atkin, British Superintendent of Indian Affairs." In The Persistence of the Westward Movement and Other Essays, pp. 147-160. Berkeley: University of California Press, 1943.

541. Pound, Arthur, and Richard E. Day. Johnson of the Mohawks: A Biography of Sir William Johnson, Irish Immigrant, Mohawk War Chief, American Soldier, Empire Builder. New York: Macmillan Company, 1930.

542. Russell, Francis. "Father to the Six Nations." American Heritage 10 (April 1959): 46-51, 81-85. Concerns Sir William Johnson.

543. Seymour, Flora Warren. Lords of the Valley: Sir William Johnson and His Mohawk Brothers. New York: Longmans, Green and Company, 1930.

544. Stone, William L. The Life and Times of Sir William Johnson, Bart. 2 volumes. Albany, New York: Joel Munsell, 1865.

INDIAN POLICY DURING THE REVOLUTION

Indian military participation in the Revolutionary War was an essential part of Indian-white relations, but there have been studies as well on Indian policy during that period. Such works are listed here, together with broader studies in which Indian affairs play a part.

545. Bast, Homer. "Creek Indian Affairs, 1775-1778." Georgia Historical Quarterly 33 (March 1949): 1-25.

546. Ganyard, Robert L. "Threat from the West: North Carolina and the Cherokee, 1776-1778." North Carolina Historical Review 45 (January 1968): 47-66.

547. Graymont, Barbara. The Iroquois in the American Revolution. Syracuse: Syracuse University Press, 1972.

548. Hamer, Philip M. "John Stuart's Indian Policy during the Early Months of the American Revolution." Mississippi Valley Historical Review 17 (December 1930): 351-366.

549. _____. "The Wataugans and the Cherokee Indians in 1776." East Tennessee Historical Society's Publications no. 3 (January 1931): 108-126.

550. James, James Alton. "Indian Diplomacy and the Opening of the Revolution in the West." Proceedings of the State Historical Society of Wisconsin, 1909, pp. 125-142.

551. _____. "The Significance of the Attack on St. Louis, 1780." Proceedings of the Mississippi Valley Historical Association 2 (1908-1909): 199-217.

552. Kellogg, Louise Phelps. "Indian Diplomacy during the Revolution in the West." Transactions of the Illinois State Historical Society, 1929, pp. 47-57.

553. Kellogg, Louise Phelps, ed. Frontier Advance on the Upper Ohio, 1778-1779. Madison: State Historical Society of Wisconsin, 1916.

554. _____. Frontier Retreat on the Upper Ohio, 1779-1781. Madison: State Historical Society of Wisconsin, 1917.

555. Mohr, Walter H. Federal Indian Relations, 1774-1788. Philadelphia: University of Pennsylvania Press, 1933.

556. Nasatir, Abraham P. "The Anglo-Spanish Frontier in the Illinois Country during the American Revolution, 1778-1783." Journal of the Illinois State Historical Society 21 (October 1928): 291-358.

557. Notestein, Wallace. "The Western Indians in the Revolution." Ohio Archaeological and Historical Quarterly 16 (July 1907): 269-291.

558. O'Donnell, James H. III. Southern Indians in the American Revolution. Knoxville: University of Tennessee Press, 1973.

559. Pastore, Ralph T. "The Board of Commissioners for Indian Affairs in the Northern Department and the Iroquois Indians, 1775-1778." Ph.D. dissertation, University of Notre Dame, 1972.

560. _____. "Congress and the Six Nations, 1775-1778." Niagara Frontier 20 (Winter 1973): 80-95.

561. Prucha, Francis Paul. "The American Indians and the Revolution." Historical Messenger of the Milwaukee County Historical Society 30 (Summer 1974): 42-54.

562. Rossie, Jonathan G. "The Northern Indian Department and the American Revolution." Niagara Frontier 20 (Autumn 1973): 52-65.

563. Russell, Nelson Vance. "The Indian Policy of Henry Hamilton: A Re-evaluation." Canadian Historical Review 11 (March 1930): 20-37.

564. Sosin, Jack M. The Revolutionary Frontier, 1763-1783. New York: Holt, Rinehart and Winston, 1967.

565. Stanley, George F. G. "The Six Nations and the American Revolution." Ontario History 56 (December 1964): 217-232.

566. Thwaites, Reuben Gold, and Louise Phelps Kellogg, eds. Frontier Defense on the Upper Ohio, 1777-1778. Madison: State Historical Society of Wisconsin, 1912.

567. _____. The Revolution on the Upper Ohio, 1775-1777. Madison: State Historical Society of Wisconsin, 1908.

568. Vivian, James F., and Jean H. Vivian. "Congressional Indian Policy during the War for Independence: The Northern Department." Maryland Historical Magazine 63 (September 1968): 241-274.

See also studies of military relations between Indians and whites during the Revolution (3350 to 3371).

INDIAN AFFAIRS, 1780-1815

Formation of a policy for dealing with the Indians was an important task for the new federal government after the Revolutionary War, both in the Old Northwest, where British influence was strong, and in the South.

569. Abbott, Martin. "Indian Policy and Management in the Mississippi Territory, 1798-1817." Journal of Mississippi History 14 (July 1952): 153-169.

570. Adams, Mary P. "Jefferson's Military Policy with Special Reference to the Frontier, 1805-1809." Ph.D. dissertation, University of Virginia, 1958.

571. Barce, Elmore. The Land of the Miamis: An Account of the Struggle to Secure Possession of the Northwest from the End of the Revolution until 1812. Fowler, Indiana: Benton Review Shop, 1922.

572. _____. "Tecumseh's Confederacy." Indiana Magazine of History 12 (June 1916): 161-174; 13 (March 1917): 67-91.

573. Berkhofer, Robert F., Jr. "Barrier to Settlement: British Indian Policy in the Old Northwest, 1783-1794." In The Frontier in American Development: Essays in Honor of Paul Wallace Gates, edited by David M. Ellis, pp. 249-276. Ithaca: Cornell University Press, 1969.

574. Berry, Jane M. "The Indian Policy of Spain in the Southwest, 1783-1795." Mississippi Valley Historical Review 3 (March 1917): 462-477.

575. Bradley, Jared W. "William C. C. Claiborne: The Old Southwest and the Development of American Indian Policy." Tennessee Historical Quarterly 33 (Fall 1974): 265-278.

576. Burt, A. L. "A New Approach to the Problem of the Western Posts." Report of the Annual Meeting of the Canadian Historical Association, 1931, pp. 61-75.

577. Caughey, John W. "Alexander McGillivray and the Creek Crisis, 1783-1784." In New Spain and the Anglo-American West: Historical Contributions Presented to Herbert Eugene Bolton, edited by George P. Hammond, 1:263-288. 2 volumes. Lancaster, Pennsylvania: Lancaster Press, 1932.

578. Chalou, George Clifford. "The Red Pawns Go to War: British-American Indian Relations, 1810-1815." Ph.D. dissertation, Indiana University, 1971.

579. Coe, Stephen H. "Indian Affairs in Pennsylvania and New York, 1783-1794." Ph.D. dissertation, American University, 1968.

580. Coleman, Kenneth. "Federal Indian Relations in the South, 1781-1789." Chronicles of Oklahoma 35 (Winter 1957-1958): 435-458.

581. Cotterill, R. S. "Federal Indian Management in the South, 1789-1825." Mississippi Valley Historical Review 20 (December 1933): 333-352.

582. Cox, Isaac J. "The Indian as a Diplomatic Factor in the History of the Old Northwest." Ohio Archaeological and Historical Quarterly 18 (October 1909): 542-565.

583. De Rosier, Arthur H., Jr. "Thomas Jefferson and the Removal of the Choctaw Indians." Southern Quarterly 1 (October 1962): 52-62.

584. Downes, Randolph C. "Cherokee-American Relations in the Upper Tennessee Valley, 1776-1791." East Tennessee Historical Society's Publications 8 (1936): 35-53.

585. _____. Council Fires on the Upper Ohio: A Narrative of Indian Affairs in the Upper Ohio Valley until 1795. Pittsburgh: University of Pittsburgh Press, 1940.

586. _____. "Creek-American Relations,

1782-1790." Georgia Historical Quarterly 21 (June 1937): 142-184.

587. _____. "Creek-American Relations, 1790-1795." Journal of Southern History 8 (August 1942): 350-373.

588. _____. "Indian Affairs in the Southwest Territory, 1790-1796." Tennessee Historical Magazine, 2d series 3 (January 1937): 240-268.

589. Duran, Elizabeth C., and James Duran, Jr. "Indian Rights in the Jay Treaty." Indian Historian 6 (Winter 1973): 33-37.

590. Dyer, Weston Albert. "The Influence of Henry Knox on the Formation of American Indian Policy in the Northern Department, 1786-1795." Ed.D. dissertation, Ball State University, 1970.

591. Ewers, John C. "Plains Indians' Reactions to the Lewis and Clark Expedition." Montana, the Magazine of Western History 16 (January 1966): 2-11.

592. Ferguson, Clyde R. "Andrew Pickens and U.S. Policy toward the Creek Nation, 1789-1793." Kansas Quarterly 3 (Fall 1971): 21-28.

593. Godward, Wilhelmina. "The Decline of British Control on the Middle Northwest, 1783-1815." Ph.D. dissertation, University of California, 1930.

594. Graham, G. S., ed. "The Indian Menace and the Retention of the Western Posts." Canadian Historical Review 15 (March 1934): 46-48.

595. Hamer, Philip M., ed. "The British in Canada and the Southern Indians, 1790-1794." East Tennessee Historical Society's Publications 2 (1930): 107-134.

596. Hatfield, Joseph T. "Governor William Charles Cole Claiborne, Indians, and Outlaws in Frontier Mississippi, 1801-1803." Journal of Mississippi History 27 (November 1965): 323-350.

597. Hatheway, G. G. "The Neutral Indian Barrier State: A Project in British North American Policy, 1754-1815." Ph.D. dissertation, University of Minnesota, 1957.

598. Hillbruner, Anthony. "Word and Deed: Jefferson's Addresses to the Indians." Speech Monographs 30 (November 1963): 328-334.

599. Holmes, Jack D. L. "The Southern Boundary Commission, the Chattahoochee River, and the Florida Seminoles, 1799." Florida Historical Quarterly 44 (April 1966): 312-341.

600. _____. "Spanish Policy toward the Southern Indians in the 1790s." In Four Centuries of Southern Indians, edited by Charles M. Hudson, pp. 65-82.

Athens: University of Georgia Press, 1975.

601. Horsman, Reginald. "American Indian Policy and the Origins of Manifest Destiny." University of Birmingham Historical Journal 11 (December 1968): 128-140.

602. _____. "American Indian Policy in the Old Northwest, 1783-1812." William and Mary Quarterly 18 (January 1961): 35-53.

603. _____. "The British Indian Department and the Abortive Treaty of Lower Sandusky, 1793." Ohio Historical Quarterly 70 (July 1961): 189-213.

604. _____. "British Indian Policy in the Northwest, 1807-1812." Mississippi Valley Historical Review 45 (June 1958): 51-66.

605. _____. Expansion and American Indian Policy, 1783-1812. East Lansing: Michigan State University Press, 1967.

606. Hough, Franklin B., ed. Proceedings of the Commissioners of Indian Affairs, Appointed by Law for the Extinguishment of Indian Titles in the State of New York. Albany: Albany Institute, 1861. Also published as volumes 9-10 in Munsell's Historical Series. Albany: Joel Munsell, 1861.

607. Leavitt, Orpha E. "British Policy on the Canadian Frontier, 1782-1792: Mediation and an Indian Barrier State." Wisconsin Historical Society Proceedings 63 (1916): 151-185.

608. McDaniel, Mary Jane. "Relations between the Creek Indians, Georgia, and the United States, 1783-1797." Ph.D. dissertation, Mississippi State University, 1971.

609. McMurray, Donald L. "The Indian Policy of the Federal Government and the Economic Development of the Southwest, 1789-1801." Tennessee Historical Magazine 1 (March 1915): 21-39; (June 1915): 106-119.

610. Meriwether, Colyer, ed. "General Joseph Martin and the Cherokees." Publications of the Southern History Association 8 (November 1904): 443-450; 9 (January 1905): 27-41.

611. Miller, Otis Louis. "Indian-White Relations in the Illinois Country, 1789 to 1818." Ph.D. dissertation, Saint Louis University, 1972.

612. Montgomery, Samuel. "A Journey through the Indian Country beyond the Ohio, 1785," edited by David I. Bushnell. Mississippi Valley Historical Review 2 (September 1915): 261-273.

613. Parsons, Joseph A., Jr. "Civilizing

the Indians of the Old Northwest, 1800-1810." Indiana Magazine of History 56 (September 1960): 195-216.

614. Pate, James P. "The Chickamauga: A Forgotten Segment of Indian Resistance on the Southern Frontier." Ph.D. dissertation, Mississippi State University, 1969.

615. Phillips, Edward Hake. "Timothy Pickering at His Best: Indian Commissioner, 1790-1794." Essex Institute Historical Collections 102 (July 1966): 163-202.

616. Severance, Frank H. "The Niagara Peace Mission of Ephraim Douglas in 1783." Buffalo Historical Society Publications 18 (1914): 115-142.

617. Sheehan, Bernard W. Seeds of Extinction: Jeffersonian Philanthropy and the American Indian. Chapel Hill: University of North Carolina Press, 1973.

618. Smith, Daniel M. "James Seagrove and the Mission to Tuckaubatchee, 1793." Georgia Historical Quarterly 44 (March 1960): 41-55.

619. Thomason, Hugh M. "Governor Peter Early and the Creek Indian Frontier, 1813-1815." Georgia Historical Quarterly 45 (September 1961): 223-237.

620. Whitaker, Arthur Preston. "Spain and the Cherokee Indians, 1783-1798." North Carolina Historical Review 4 (July 1927): 252-269.

See the studies by George D. Harmon (650-652) and Francis Paul Prucha (681), which deal in part with this period. Works on the factory system (705 to 717), on Indian wars, 1780-1812 (3372 to 3436), and on the War of 1812 (3437 to 3470) should also be consulted.

FROM THE WAR OF 1812 TO THE CIVIL WAR

Indian Affairs, 1815-1860: General

Between the War of 1812 and the Civil War the United States expanded rapidly across the continent. This mass movement of white population pushed the Indians westward and then on to reservations. Old policies were extended over new regions, and new policies were adopted. Studies on two specific aspects of Indian affairs in this period--the factory system and the removal of the eastern Indians to the West--are listed under separate headings below.

621. Abel, Annie Heloise, ed. "Indian Affairs in New Mexico under the Administration of William Carr Lane, from the Journal of John Ward." New Mexico Historical Review 16 (April 1941): 206-232; (July 1941): 328-358.

622. Barbour, George W. "The Journal of George W. Barbour, May 1, to October 4, 1851," edited by Alban W. Hoopes. Southwestern Historical Quarterly 40 (October 1936): 145-153; (January 1937): 247-261.

623. Biesele, R. L. "The Relations between the German Settlers and the Indians in Texas, 1844-1860." Southwestern Historical Quarterly 31 (October 1927): 116-129.

624. Blackburn, George M. "George Johnston and the Sioux-Chippewa Boundary Survey." Michigan History 51 (Winter 1967): 313-322.

625. Bowker, Mabel Edna. "The Indian Policy of the United States, 1789-1841." Ph.D. dissertation, Boston University, 1926.

626. Briggs, John Ely. "Indian Affairs." Palimpsest 21 (September 1940): 261-277. Sacs and Foxes in Iowa.

627. Brown, Elizabeth Gaspar. "Lewis Cass and the American Indian." Michigan History 37 (September 1953): 286-298.

628. Brown, Lizzie M. "The Pacification of the Indians of Illinois after the War of 1812." Journal of the Illinois State Historical Society 7 (January 1916): 550-558.

629. Chambers, John. "Letters of Governor John Chambers on Indian Affairs, 1845." Iowa Journal of History and Politics 19 (April 1921): 246-286.

630. Coan, C. F. "The Adoption of the Reservation Policy in Pacific Northwest, 1853-1855." Oregon Historical Society Quarterly 23 (March 1922): 1-38.

631. _____. "The Federal Indian Policy in the Pacific Northwest, 1849-1870." Ph.D. dissertation, University of California, 1920.

632. _____. "The First Stage of the Federal Indian Policy in the Pacific Northwest, 1849-1852." Oregon Historical Society Quarterly 22 (March 1921): 46-89.

633. Colgrove, Kenneth W. "The Attitude of Congress toward the Pioneers of the West, 1820-1850: I, Relations between the Pioneers and the Indians." Iowa Journal of History and Politics 9 (March 1911): 196-302.

634. Comfort, Benjamin F. Lewis Cass and the Indian Treaties: A Monograph on the Indian Relations of the Northwest Territory from 1813 to 1831. Detroit: Charles F. May Company, 1923.

635. Covington, James W. "The Armed Occupation Act of 1842." Florida Historical Quarterly 40 (July 1961): 41-52.

636. _____. "Federal Relations with the Apalachicola Indians, 1823-1838." *Florida Historical Quarterly* 42 (October 1963): 125-141.

637. Crimmins, Martin L., ed. "Colonel George Croghan and the Indian Situation in Texas in 1847." *Southwestern Historical Quarterly* 56 (January 1953): 455-457.

638. Crouter, Richard E., and Andrew F. Rolle. "Edward Fitzgerald Beale and the Indian Peace Commissioners in California, 1851-1854." *Historical Society of Southern California Quarterly* 42 (June 1960): 107-132.

639. Ellison, William H. "The Federal Indian Policy in California, 1846-1860." *Mississippi Valley Historical Review* 9 (June 1922): 37-67.

640. _____. "The Federal Indian Policy in California, 1846-1860." Ph.D. dissertation, University of California, 1919.

641. Estep, Raymond, ed. "Lieutenant Wm. E. Burnett: Notes on Removal of Indians from Texas to Indian Territory." *Chronicles of Oklahoma* 38 (Autumn 1960): 274-309; (Winter 1960): 369-396; 39 (Spring 1961): 15-41.

642. Faust, Richard H. "William Medill: Commissioner of Indian Affairs, 1845-1849." *Old Northwest* 1 (June 1975): 129-140.

643. Foreman, Grant. *Advancing the Frontier, 1830-1860.* Norman: University of Oklahoma Press, 1933.

644. _____. *Indians and Pioneers: The Story of the American Southwest before 1830.* Revised edition. Norman: University of Oklahoma Press, 1936. First published in 1930.

645. Foreman, Grant, ed. "In Search of the Comanches (the Journal of J. C. Eldredge)." *Panhandle-Plains Historical Review* 7 (1934): 7-41.

646. _____. "The Journal of Elijah Hicks." *Chronicles of Oklahoma* 13 (March 1935): 68-99.

647. Gittinger, Roy. "The Separation of Nebraska and Kansas from the Indian Territory." *Chronicles of Oklahoma* 1 (January 1921): 9-29.

648. _____. "The Separation of Nebraska and Kansas from the Indian Territory." *Mississippi Valley Historical Review* 3 (March 1917): 442-461.

649. Green, Michael David. "Federal-State Conflict in the Administration of Indian Policy: Georgia, Alabama, and the Creeks, 1824-1834." Ph.D. dissertation, University of Iowa, 1973.

650. Harmon, George Dewey. *The Indian Trust Funds, 1797-1865.* Bethlehem, Pennsylvania: Lehigh University, 1934.

651. _____. "The Indian Trust Funds, 1797-1865." *Mississippi Valley Historical Review* 21 (June 1934): 23-30.

652. _____. *Sixty Years of Indian Affairs, Political, Economic, and Diplomatic, 1789-1850.* Chapel Hill: University of North Carolina Press, 1941.

653. _____. "The United States Indian Policy in Texas, 1845-1860." *Mississippi Valley Historical Review* 17 (December 1930): 377-403.

654. Hitchcock, Ethan Allen. *A Traveler in Indian Territory: The Journal of Ethan Allen Hitchcock, Late Major-General in the United States Army.* Edited by Grant Foreman. Cedar Rapids, Iowa: Torch Press, 1930.

655. Hoopes, Alban W. *Indian Affairs and Their Administration, with Special Reference to the Far West, 1849-1860.* Philadelphia: University of Pennsylvania Press, 1932.

656. "Indian Affairs of the Iowa Region, 1827-1830." *Annals of Iowa*, 3d series 16 (July 1927): 25-42.

657. "Indian Affairs in Iowa Territory, 1839-'43." *Annals of Iowa*, 3d series 5 (July 1902): 459-464; (October 1902): 524-527. Letters of Governors Robert Lucas and John Chambers.

658. Jack, Theodore H. "Alabama and the Federal Government: The Creek Indian Controversy." *Mississippi Valley Historical Review* 3 (December 1916): 301-317.

659. Jackson, Andrew. "Letter of Andrew Jackson to Governor John Reynolds of Illinois." *Journal of the Illinois State Historical Society* 7 (October 1914): 224.

660. James, Rhett S., ed. "Brigham Young-Chief Washakie Indian Farm Negotiations." *Annals of Wyoming* 39 (October 1967): 245-256.

661. Koch, Lena Clara. "The Federal Indian Policy in Texas, 1845-1860." *Southwestern Historical Quarterly* 28 (January 1925): 223-234; (April 1925): 259-286; 29 (July 1925): 19-35; (October 1925): 98-127.

662. Lane, Jack. "Federal-Quapaw Relations, 1800-1833." *Arkansas Historical Quarterly* 19 (Spring 1960): 61-74.

663. Lerner, Ralph. "Reds and Whites: Rights and Wrongs." *Supreme Court Review*, 1971, pp. 201-240.

664. Litton, Gaston. "The Peace Commission to the Indian Territory, 1832-1834." Ph.D. dissertation, Georgetown University, 1942.

665. Lollar, Wayne B. "Seminole-United States Financial Relations, 1823-1866." Chronicles of Oklahoma 50 (Summer 1972): 190-198.

666. Lucas, Robert. "Indian Affairs of Iowa in 1840." Annals of Iowa, 3d series 15 (April 1926): 255-280. Report of the territorial governor.

667. McKenney, Thomas L. Memoirs, Official and Personal: With Sketches of Travels among the Northern and Southern Indians. New York: Paine and Burgess, 1846. Reprinted, Lincoln: University of Nebraska Press, 1973.

668. McLaughlin, A. C. "The Influence of Governor Cass on the Development of the Northwest." Papers of the American Historical Association 3 (1888): 311-327.

669. McPhail, Leonard. "The Diary of Assistant Surgeon Leonard McPhail on His Journey to the Southwest in 1835," edited by Harold W. Jones. Chronicles of Oklahoma 18 (September 1940): 281-292.

670. Malin, James C. Indian Policy and Westward Expansion. Bulletin of the University of Kansas Humanistic Studies, volume 2, no. 3. Lawrence: University of Kansas, 1921.

671. Mattison, Ray H. "The Indian Frontier on the Upper Missouri to 1865." Nebraska History 39 (September 1958): 241-266.

672. Miriani, Ronald Gregory. "Lewis Cass and Indian Administration in the Old Northwest, 1815-1836." Ph.D. dissertation, University of Michigan, 1974.

673. Morgan, Dale L. "The Administration of Indian Affairs in Utah, 1851-1858." Pacific Historical Review 17 (November 1948): 383-409.

674. Morse, Jedidiah. A Report to the Secretary of War of the United States, on Indian Affairs, Comprising a Narrative of a Tour Performed in the Summer of 1820 . . . for the Purpose of Ascertaining, for the Use of the Government, the Actual State of the Indian Tribes in Our Country. New Haven: S. Converse, 1822.

675. Muckleroy, Anna. "The Indian Policy of the Republic of Texas." Southwestern Historical Quarterly 25 (April 1922): 229-260; 26 (July 1922): 1-29; (October 1922): 128-148; (January 1923): 184-206.

676. Neighbours, Kenneth F. Indian Exodus: Texas Indian Affairs, 1835-1859. N.p.: Nortex Offset Publications, 1973.

677. Park, Joseph F. "The Apaches in Mexican-American Relations, 1846-1861: A Footnote to the Gadsden Treaty." Arizona and the West 3 (Summer 1961): 129-146.

678. Parsons, Lynn Hudson. "'A Perpetual Harrow upon My Feelings': John Quincy Adams and the American Indian." New England Quarterly 46 (September 1973): 339-379.

679. Paulson, Howard W. "Federal Indian Policy and the Dakota Indians: 1800-1840." South Dakota History 3 (Summer 1973): 285-309.

680. Prucha, Francis Paul. "American Indian Policy in the 1840s: Visions of Reform." In The Frontier Challenge: Responses to the Trans-Mississippi West, edited by John G. Clark, pp. 81-110. Lawrence: University Press of Kansas, 1971.

681. _____. American Indian Policy in the Formative Years: The Indian Trade and Intercourse Acts, 1790-1834. Cambridge: Harvard University Press, 1962.

682. _____. Lewis Cass and American Indian Policy. Detroit: Wayne State University Press, 1967.

683. Prucha, Francis Paul, and Donald F. Carmony, eds. "A Memorandum of Lewis Cass Concerning a System for the Regulation of Indian Affairs." Wisconsin Magazine of History 52 (Autumn 1968): 35-50.

684. Reeve, Frank D. "The Government and the Navaho, 1846-1858." New Mexico Historical Review 14 (January 1939): 82-114.

685. Reid, John Phillip. "Conflict and Injustice: A Discussion of Francis Paul Prucha's 'American Indian Policy in the Formative Years.'" North Dakota Law Review 39 (January 1963): 50-70.

686. Rippy, J. Fred. "The Indians of the Southwest in the Diplomacy of the United States and Mexico, 1848-1853." Hispanic American Historical Review 2 (August 1919): 363-396.

687. Rister, Carl Coke. "A Federal Experiment in Southern Plains Indian Relations, 1835-1845." Chronicles of Oklahoma 14 (December 1936): 434-455.

688. Rogin, Michael Paul. Fathers and Children: Andrew Jackson and the Subjugation of the American Indian. New York: Alfred A. Knopf, 1975.

689. _____. "Liberal Society and the Indian Question." Politics and Society 1 (May 1971): 269-312.

690. Satz, Ronald N. American Indian Policy in the Jacksonian Era. Lincoln: University of Nebraska Press, 1975.

691. Shields, Lillian B. "Relations with the Cheyennes and Arapahoes in Colorado to 1861." Colorado Magazine 4 (August 1927): 145-154.

692. Smith, Ralph A. "Indians in American-Mexican Relations before the War of 1846." Hispanic American Historical Review 43 (February 1963): 34-64.

693. _____. "Mexican and Anglo-Saxon Trade in Scalps, Slaves and Livestock, 1835-1841." West Texas Historical Association Yearbook 36 (October 1960): 98-115.

694. Street, Ida M. "The Simon Cameron Indian Commission of 1838." Annals of Iowa, 3d series 7 (July 1905): 115-139; (October 1905): 172-195.

695. Todd, Ronald, ed. "Letters of Governor Isaac I. Stevens, 1857-1858." Pacific Northwest Quarterly 31 (October 1940): 403-459.

696. Trennert, Robert A., Jr. Alternative to Extinction: Federal Indian Policy and the Beginnings of the Reservation System, 1846-51. Philadelphia: Temple University Press, 1975.

697. _____. "The Mormons and the Office of Indian Affairs: The Conflict over Winter Quarters, 1846-1848." Nebraska History 53 (Fall 1972): 381-400.

698. Unrau, William E. "United States 'Diplomacy' with the Dhegiha-Siouan Kansa, 1815-1825." Kansas Quarterly 3 (Fall 1971): 39-46.

699. Viola, Herman J. Thomas L. McKenney: Architect of America's Early Indian Policy, 1816-1830. Chicago: Swallow Press, 1974.

700. Warner, Mildred. "Indians Challenge the Nebraska Territorial Government." Great Plains Journal 9 (Spring 1970): 53-58.

701. Warrick, W. Sheridan. "The American Indian Policy in the Upper Old Northwest Following the War of 1812." Ethnohistory 3 (Spring 1956): 109-125.

702. White, Lonnie L. "Arkansas Territorial Indian Affairs." Arkansas Historical Quarterly 21 (Autumn 1962): 193-212.

703. Wirt, William. An Opinion on the Claims for Improvements by the State of Georgia on the Cherokee Nation under the Treaties of 1817 and 1828. New Echota: Office of Cherokee Phoenix and Indians' Advocate, 1830.

704. Worley, Ted R. "Arkansas and the 'Hostile' Indians, 1835-1838." Arkansas Historical Quarterly 6 (Summer 1947): 155-164.

See also studies on the factory system (705 to 717), on Indian removal (718 to 832), and on Indian wars of the period. Contemporary discussion on Indian matters is found in the section on current comment, 1815-1860.

United States Factory System

From 1795 to 1822 the federal government managed its own system of trading houses (factories), in the hope that peace with the Indians would be promoted by eliminating the fraud and abuses of private fur traders. Studies of individual factories and of the system as a whole are listed here.

705. Chambers, Nella J. "The Creek Indian Factory at Fort Mitchell." Alabama Historical Quarterly 21 (1959): 15-53.

706. Coman, Katherine. "Government Factories: An Attempt to Control Competition in the Fur Trade." Bulletin of the American Economic Association, 4th series no. 2 (April 1911): 368-388.

707. Harmon, George D. "Benjamin Hawkins and the Federal Factory System." North Carolina Historical Review 9 (April 1932): 138-153.

708. James, J. A. "Indian Trading House or Factory System." National Magazine 16 (May 1892): 32-37.

709. Montagno, George L. "Matthew Lyon's Last Frontier." Arkansas Historical Quarterly 16 (Spring 1957): 46-53.

710. Morris, Wayne. "Traders and Factories on the Arkansas Frontier, 1805-1822." Arkansas Historical Quarterly 28 (Spring 1969): 28-48.

711. Peake, Ora Brooks. A History of the United States Indian Factory System, 1795-1822. Denver: Sage Books, 1954.

712. Plaisance, Aloysius. "The Arkansas Factory, 1805-1810." Arkansas Historical Quarterly 11 (Autumn 1952): 184-200.

713. _____. "The Choctaw Trading House--1803-1822." Alabama Historical Quarterly 16 (Fall-Winter 1954): 393-423.

714. _____. "The United States Government Factory System, 1796-1822." Ph.D. dissertation, Saint Louis University, 1954.

715. Quaife, Milo M. "An Experiment of the Fathers in State Socialism." Wisconsin Magazine of History 3 (January 1920): 277-290.

716. Way, Royal B. "The United States Factory System for Trading with the Indians, 1796-1822." Mississippi Valley Historical Review 6 (September 1919): 220-235.

717. Wesley, Edgar B. "The Government Factory System among the Indians, 1795-1822." Journal of Economic and Business History 4 (May 1932): 487-511.

See also general studies of Indian policy

during the period, especially Herman J. Viola's Thomas L. McKenney (699).

Indian Removal

In the 1820s the United States adopted a policy of exchanging eastern Indian lands for lands west of the Mississippi. The desire of white planters for lands in Georgia, Alabama, and Mississippi put special pressure on the southern Indians, and it was argued that removal of the Indians would free their lands, reduce disputes between the federal government and the states about jurisdiction over Indian lands, and allow the Indians to proceed at their own pace toward civilization. Andrew Jackson's aggressive enforcement of removal won him enmity at the time and criticism from many historians since. Listed here are studies and other writings on the removal policy, on the actual emigration of both southern and northern Indians, and on the legal cases that resulted.

718. Abel, Annie H. "The History of Events Resulting in Indian Consolidation West of the Mississippi." Annual Report of the American Historical Association for the Year 1906, 1:233-450.

719. Adams, Robert H. Speech of Mr. Adams, of Mississippi, on the Bill to Remove the Indians West of the Mississippi, Delivered in the Senate of the United States, April, 1830. Washington: Duff Green, 1830.

720. Anson, Bert. "Chief Francis Lafontaine and the Miami Emigration from Indiana." Indiana Magazine of History 60 (September 1964): 241-268.

721. _____. "Variations of the Indian Conflict: The Effects of the Emigrant Indian Removal Policy, 1830-1854." Missouri Historical Review 59 (October 1964): 64-89.

722. Baird, W. David. "The Reduction of a People: The Quapaw Removal, 1824-1834." Red River Valley Historical Review 1 (Spring 1974): 21-36.

723. Barnes, Lela, ed. "Journal of Isaac McCoy for the Exploring Expedition of 1828." Kansas Historical Quarterly 5 (August 1936): 227-277.

724. _____. "Journal of Isaac McCoy for the Exploring Expedition of 1830." Kansas Historical Quarterly 5 (November 1936): 339-377.

725. Bass, Althea. "Tsali of the Cherokees." Sewanee Review 50 (January 1942): 5-14.

726. Bauman, Robert F. "The Removal of the Indians from the Maumee Valley." Northwest Ohio Quarterly 30 (Winter 1957-1958): 10-25.

727. Berthrong, Donald J. "John Beach and the Removal of the Sauk and Fox from Iowa." Iowa Journal of History 54 (October 1956): 313-334.

728. Blunt, Joseph. Brief Examination of the Relations between the Cherokees and the Government of the United States. New York: Clayton and Van Norden, 1832.

729. Boudinot, Elias. Documents in Relation to the Validity of the Cherokee Treaty of 1835: Letters and Other Papers Relating to Cherokee Affairs, Being a Reply to Sundry Publications Authorized by John Ross. Washington: Blair and Rives, 1838.

730. _____. Letters and Other Papers Relating to Cherokee Affairs: Being in Reply to Sundry Publications Authorized by John Ross. Athens, Georgia: Southern Banner, 1837.

731. Brannon, Peter A. "Creek Indian War, 1836-37." Alabama Historical Quarterly 13 (1951): 156-158.

732. _____. "Removal of the Indians from Alabama." Alabama Historical Quarterly 12 (1950): 91-117.

733. Brown, John P. "Cherokee Removal, an Unnecessary Tragedy." East Tennessee Historical Society's Publications 11 (1939): 11-19.

734. Burke, Joseph C. "The Cherokee Cases: A Study in Law, Politics, and Morality." Stanford Law Review 21 (February 1969): 500-531.

735. "Centennial of Removal of the Potawatomi." Indiana History Bulletin 15 (August 1938): 285-286.

736. Chroust, Anton-Hermann. "Did President Jackson Actually Threaten the Supreme Court of the United States with the Nonenforcement of Its Injunction against the State of Georgia?" American Journal of Legal History 4 (January 1960): 76-78.

737. Copway, George. Organization of a New Indian Territory East of the Missouri River: Arguments and Reasons Submitted to the Honorable the Members of the Senate and House of Representatives of the 31st Congress of the United States, by the Indian Chief Kah-ge-ga-gah-bouh, or Geo. Copway. New York: S. W. Benedict, 1850.

738. Corn, James Franklin. "Removal of the Cherokees from the East." Filson Club Historical Quarterly 27 (January 1953): 36-51.

739. Covington, James Warren, ed. "Proposed Catawba Indian Removal, 1848." South Carolina Historical Magazine 55 (January 1954): 42-47.

740. Davis, Katharine Murdoch. "The Trail of Tears." Delphian Quarterly 34 (October 1951): 39-43.

741. Davis, Kenneth Penn. "The Cherokee Removal, 1835-1838." Tennessee Historical Quarterly 32 (Winter 1973): 311-331.

742. DeRosier, Arthur H., Jr. "Andrew Jackson and Negotiations for the Removal of the Choctaw Indians." Historian 29 (May 1967): 343-362.

743. _____. "The Choctaw Removal of 1831: A Civilian Effort." Journal of the West 6 (April 1967): 237-247.

744. _____. "John C. Calhoun and the Removal of the Choctaw Indians." Proceedings of the South Carolina Historical Association, 1957, pp. 33-45.

745. _____. "Myths and Realities in Indian Westward Removal: The Choctaw Example." In Four Centuries of Southern Indians, edited by Charles M. Hudson, pp. 83-100. Athens: University of Georgia Press, 1975.

746. _____. "Negotiations for the Removal of the Choctaw." Chronicles of Oklahoma 38 (Spring 1960): 85-100.

747. _____. The Removal of the Choctaw Indians. Knoxville: University of Tennessee Press, 1970.

748. Documents and Proceedings Relating to the Formation and Progress of a Board in the City of New York, for the Emigration, Preservation, and Improvement, of the Aborigines of America. New York: Vanderpool and Cole, 1829.

749. Edmunds, R. David. "The Prairie Potawatomi Removal of 1833." Indiana Magazine of History 68 (September 1972): 240-253.

750. Ellis, Albert G. "Advent of the New York Indians into Wisconsin." Collections of the State Historical Society of Wisconsin 2 (1855): 415-449.

751. Evarts, Jeremiah. Essays on the Present Crisis in the Condition of the American Indians: First Published in the National Intelligencer, under the Signature of William Penn. Boston: Perkins and Marvin, 1829.

752. Evarts, Jeremiah, ed. Speeches on the Passage of the Bill for the Removal of the Indians, Delivered in the Congress of the United States, April and May, 1830. Boston: Perkins and Marvin, 1830.

753. Everett, Edward. Speech of Mr. Everett, of Massachusetts, on the Bill for Removing the Indians from the East to the West Side of the Mississippi: Delivered in the House of Representatives on the 19th May, 1830. Washington: Gales and Seaton, 1830.

754. Faben, W. W. "Indians of the Tri-State Area: The Potowatomis, the Removal." Northwest Ohio Quarterly 40 (Spring 1968): 68-84.

755. Fensten, Joseph J. "Indian Removal." Chronicles of Oklahoma 11 (December 1933): 1073-1083.

756. Filler, Louis, and Allen Guttmann, eds. The Removal of the Cherokee Nation: Manifest Destiny or National Dishonor? Boston: D. C. Heath, 1962. A book of readings.

757. Foreman, Grant. Indian Removal: The Emigration of the Five Civilized Tribes of Indians. Norman: University of Oklahoma Press, 1932.

758. _____. The Last Trek of the Indians. Chicago: University of Chicago Press, 1946.

759. Foreman, Grant, ed. "Journey of a Party of Cherokee Emigrants." Mississippi Valley Historical Review 18 (September 1931): 232-245.

760. Frelinghuysen, Theodore. Speech of Mr. Frelinghuysen, of New Jersey, Delivered in the Senate of the United States, April 6, 1830, on the Bill for an Exchange of Lands with the Indians Residing in Any of the States or Territories, and for Their Removal West of the Mississippi. Washington: National Journal, 1830.

761. Godecker, Mary Salesia, ed. "Documents: Correspondence on Indian Removal, Indiana, 1835-1838." Mid-America 15 (January 1933): 177-192.

762. Gordon, Leon M., II. "The Red Man's Retreat from Northern Indiana." Indiana Magazine of History 46 (March 1950): 39-60.

763. Guttmann, Allen, ed. States' Rights and Indian Removal: The Cherokee Nation v. the State of Georgia. Boston: D. C. Heath and Company, 1965. A selection of documents for secondary school students.

764. Head, Sylvia, ed. "Old Letters." Georgia Review 14 (Summer 1960): 126-129. Concerning the murder of Creek Chief William McIntosh.

765. Hoffman, William S. "Andrew Jackson, State Rightest: The Case of the Georgia Indians." Tennessee Historical Quarterly 11 (December 1952): 329-345.

766. Hoole, William Stanley, ed. "Echoes from the 'Trail of Tears,' 1837." Alabama Review 6 (April 1953): 135-152; (July 1953): 222-232.

767. Horsman, Reginald. The Origins of Indian Removal, 1815-1824. East Lansing:

Michigan State University Press, 1970.

768. Jones, Dorothy V. "A Preface to the Settlement of Kansas." Kansas Historical Quarterly 29 (Summer 1963): 122-136. Removal of Eastern Indian to the Kansas region.

769. "Journal of an Emigrating Party of Pottawattomie Indians, 1838." Indiana Magazine of History 21 (December 1925): 315-336.

770. Kellogg, Louise Phelps. "The Removal of the Winnebago." Transactions of the Wisconsin Academy of Sciences, Arts and Letters 21 (1924): 23-29.

771. Klopfenstein, Carl G. "The Removal of the Indians from Ohio, 1820-1843." Ph.D. dissertation, Western Reserve University, 1956.

772. _____. "The Removal of the Wyandots from Ohio." Ohio Historical Quarterly 66 (April 1957): 119-136.

773. _____. "Westward Ho: Removal of Ohio Shawnees, 1832-1833." Bulletin of the Historical and Philosophical Society of Ohio 15 (January 1957): 3-31.

774. Knight, Oliver. "Cherokee Society under the Stress of Removal, 1820-1846." Chronicles of Oklahoma 32 (Winter 1954-1955): 414-428.

775. Kutsche, Paul. "The Tsali Legend: Culture Heroes and Historiography." Ethnohistory 10 (Fall 1963): 329-357.

776. Lamar, H. G. Speech of Mr. H. G. Lamar, of Georgia, on the Bill to Remove the Indians West of the Mississippi; Delivered in the House of Representatives of the United States, May, 1830. Washington: Duff Green, 1830.

777. Lightfoot, B. B. "The Cherokee Emigrants in Missouri, 1837-1839." Missouri Historical Review 56 (January 1962): 156-167.

778. Litton, Gaston, ed. "The Journal of a Party of Emigrating Creek Indians, 1835-1836." Journal of Southern History 7 (May 1941): 225-242.

779. Longaker, Richard. "Andrew Jackson and the Judiciary." Political Science Quarterly 71 (September 1956): 341-364.

780. Lumpkin, Wilson. The Removal of the Cherokee Indians from Georgia. 2 volumes. Wormsloe, Georgia, 1907; New York: Dodd, Mead and Company, 1907.

781. _____. Speech of Mr. Wilson Lumpkin, of Georgia, on the Bill Providing for the Removal of the Indians. Washington: Duff Green, 1830.

782. Lyons, Emory J. Isaac McCoy: His Plan of and Work for Indian Colonization. Fort Hays Kansas State College Studies, History Series, no. 1. Topeka, 1945.

783. McCoy, Isaac. Remarks on the Practicability of Indian Reform, Embracing Their Colonization, with an Appendix. 2d edition. New York: Gray and Bunce, 1829.

784. McDermott, John Francis, ed. "Isaac McCoy's Second Exploring Trip in 1828." Kansas Historical Quarterly 13 (August 1945): 400-462.

785. McDonald, Daniel. Removal of the Pottawatomie Indians from Northern Indiana. Plymouth, Indiana: D. McDonald and Company, 1899.

786. McKee, Irving. "The Centennial of 'The Trail of Death.'" Indiana Magazine of History 35 (March 1939): 27-41.

787. Mahan, Bruce E. "Moving the Winnebago." Palimpsest 3 (February 1922): 33-52.

788. Meserve, John Bartlett. "The Indian Removal Message of President Jackson." Chronicles of Oklahoma 13 (March 1935): 63-67.

789. _____. "The Removal of the Creeks." National Republic 19 (March 1932): 26-27, 40.

790. Miles, Edwin A. "After John Marshall's Decision: Worcester v. Georgia and the Nullification Crisis." Journal of Southern History 39 (November 1973): 519-544.

791. Miles, William. "'Enamoured with Colonization': Isaac McCoy's Plan of Indian Reform." Kansas Historical Quarterly 38 (Autumn 1972): 268-286.

792. Neumeyer, Elizabeth. "Michigan Indians Battle against Removal." Michigan History 55 (Winter 1971): 275-288.

793. Oliphant, J. Orin, ed. "Report of the Wyandot Exploring Delegation, 1831." Kansas Historical Quarterly 15 (August 1947): 248-262.

794. Owsley, Frank L., Jr. "Francis Scott Key's Mission to Alabama in 1833." Alabama Review 23 (July 1970): 181-192.

795. Parsons, John E., ed. "Letters on the Chickasaw Removal of 1837." New-York Historical Society Quarterly 37 (July 1953): 272-283.

796. Payne, John Howard. "The Captivity of John Howard Payne by the Georgia Guard." North American Quarterly Magazine 7 (January 1836): 107-124.

797. Peters, Richard. The Case of the Cherokee Nation against the State of Georgia. Philadelphia: John Grigg, 1831.

798. Petersen, William J., ed. "Moving the Winnebago into Iowa." Iowa Journal of History 58 (October 1960): 357-376.

799. Prucha, Francis Paul. "Andrew Jackson's Indian Policy: A Reassessment." Journal of American History 56 (December 1969): 527-539.

800. _____. "Indian Removal and the Great American Desert." Indiana Magazine of History 59 (December 1963): 299-322.

801. _____. "Thomas L. McKenney and the New York Indian Board." Mississippi Valley Historical Review 48 (March 1962): 635-655.

802. Ramage, B. J. "Georgia and the Cherokees." American Historical Magazine 7 (July 1902): 199-208.

803. "Removal of Indians from Ohio: Dunihue Correspondence of 1832." Indiana Magazine of History 35 (December 1939): 408-426.

804. Ross, John. Letter from John Ross, Principal Chief of the Cherokee Nation of Indians, in Answer to Inquiries from a Friend Regarding the Cherokee Affairs with the United States: Followed by a Copy of the Protest of the Cherokee Delegation Laid before the Senate and House of Representatives at the City of Washington, June 21, 1836. Philadelphia, 1836.

805. _____. Letter from John Ross, the Principal Chief of the Cherokee Nation, to a Gentleman of Philadelphia. Philadelphia, 1837.

806. Ross, John, and others. Memorial of John Ross and Others, Representatives of the Cherokee Nation of Indians, on the Subject of the Existing Difficulties in That Nation, and Their Relations with the United States. Washington: Ritchie and Heiss, 1846.

807. Shoemaker, Floyd Calvin. "The Cherokee 'Trail of Tears' across Missouri." Missouri Historical Review 47 (January 1953): 124-130.

808. Silver, James W. "A Counter-Proposal to the Indian Removal Policy of Andrew Jackson." Journal of Mississippi History 4 (October 1942): 207-215.

809. _____. "General Gaines Meets Governor Troup: A State-Federal Clash in 1825." Georgia Historical Quarterly 27 (September 1943): 248-270.

810. Sioussat, St. George L. "Tennessee and the Removal of the Cherokees." Sewanee Review 16 (July 1908): 337-344.

811. Smith, Dwight L., ed. "The Attempted Potawatomi Emigration of 1839." Indiana Magazine of History 45 (March 1949): 51-80.

812. _____. "A Continuation of the Journal of an Emigrating Party of Potawatomi Indians, 1838, and Ten William Polke Manuscripts." Indiana Magazine of History 44 (December 1948): 393-408.

813. _____. "Jacob Hull's Detachment of the Potawatomi Emigration of 1838." Indiana Magazine of History 45 (September 1949): 285-288.

814. Sprague, Peleg. Speech of Mr. Sprague, of Maine: Delivered in the Senate of the United States, 16th April, 1830, in Reply to Messrs. White, McKinley, and Forsyth, upon the Subject of the Removal of the Indians. Washington: National Journal, 1830.

815. Stein, Gary C. "Indian Removal as Seen by European Travelers in America." Chronicles of Oklahoma 51 (Winter 1973-1974): 399-410.

816. Steiner, Bernard E. "Jackson and the Missionaries." American Historical Review 29 (July 1924): 722-723.

817. Storrs, Henry. Speech of Mr. Storrs, of New York, on the Bill for the Removal of the Indians West of the Mississippi. Utica, New York: Northway and Porter, 1830.

818. Stuart, Benjamin F. "The Deportation of Menominee and His Tribe of the Pottawattomie Indians." Indiana Magazine of History 18 (September 1922): 255-265.

819. Syndergaard, Rex. "The Final Move of the Choctaws, 1825-1830." Chronicles of Oklahoma 52 (Summer 1974): 207-219.

820. Thoburn, Joseph B. "Centennial of the Chickasaw Migration." Chronicles of Oklahoma 15 (December 1937): 387-391.

821. Treacy, Kenneth W. "Another View on Wirt in Cherokee Nation." American Journal of Legal History 5 (October 1961): 385-388.

822. Van Every, Dale. Disinherited: The Lost Birthright of the American Indian. New York: Morrow, 1966.

823. Van Hoeven, James William. "Salvation and Indian Removal: The Career Biography of the Rev. John Freeman Schermerhorn, Indian Commissioner." Ph.D. dissertation, Vanderbilt University, 1972.

824. Wade, John Williams. "The Removal of the Mississippi Choctaws." Publications of the Mississippi Historical Society 8 (1904): 397-426.

825. Washburn, Wilcomb E. "Indian Removal Policy: Administrative, Historical and Moral Criteria for Judging Its Success or Failure." Ethnohistory 12 (Summer 1965): 274-278.

826. Wilde, Richard Henry. Speech of Mr. Wilde, of Georgia, on the Bill for Removing the Indians from the East to the West Side of the Mississippi: Delivered

in the House of Representatives on the 20th May, 1830. Washington: Gales and Seaton, 1830.

827. Wilkins, Thurman. *Cherokee Tragedy: The Story of the Ridge Family and the Decimation of a People.* New York: Macmillan Company, 1970.

828. Wirt, William. *Opinion on the Right of the State of Georgia to Extend Her Laws over the Cherokee Nation.* Baltimore: F. Lucas, Jr., 1830.

829. "'Worcester vs. State of Georgia.'" *Chronicles of Oklahoma* 28 (Spring 1950): 109-113. Letters of Samuel A. Worcester and Ann Worcester.

830. Wright, Muriel H. "The Removal of the Choctaws to the Indian Territory, 1830-1833." *Chronicles of Oklahoma* 6 (June 1928): 103-128.

831. Young, Mary E. "Indian Removal and Land Allotment: The Civilized Tribes and Jacksonian Justice." *American Historical Review* 64 (October 1958): 31-45.

832. _____. *Redskins, Ruffleshirts, and Rednecks: Indian Allotments in Alabama and Mississippi, 1830-1860.* Norman: University of Oklahoma Press, 1961.

See also writings under Indian policy, 1815-1860, and under current comment, 1815-1860, as well as studies of the Black Hawk War and the Second Seminole War.

Current Comment, 1815-1860

Indian affairs interested the public as well as the federal officials and others concerned directly with the Indians, and magazines of the day carried Indian items. This was especially true regarding the controversy over Indian removal. Some of the writings are listed here.

833. "Administration of Indian Affairs." *United States Magazine and Democratic Review* 18 (May 1845): 333-336.

834. Alexander, A. "Indian Affairs." *Biblical Repertory and Princeton Review* 10 (October 1838): 513-535.

835. "The American Indians." *Commercial Review of the South and West* 5 (March 1848): 272-274.

836. "The American Indians." *Commercial Review of the South and West* 6 (August 1848): 100-106.

837. Beeson, John. *Are We Not Men and Brethren? An Address to the People of the United States.* New York: National Indian Aid Office, 1859.

838. _____. *A Plea for the Indians, with Facts and Features of the Late War*

in Oregon. New York, 1857. Republished with revisions, 1858.

839. Cass, Lewis. "Indians of North America." *North American Review*, new series 13 (January 1826): 53-119.

840. _____. *Inquiries, Respecting the History, Traditions, Languages, Manners, Customs, Religion, &c. of the Indians, Living within the United States.* Detroit: Sheldon and Reed, 1823.

841. _____. *Remarks on the Policy and Practice of the United States and Great Britain in Their Treatment of the Indians.* Boston: Frederick T. Gray, 1827. Reprinted from *North American Review* 24 (April 1827): 365-442.

842. _____. "Removal of the Indians." *North American Review* 30 (January 1830): 62-121.

843. "The Cherokee Case." *American Annual Register* 7 (1831-1832): 364-380.

844. "Cherokee Case." *American Quarterly Review* 11 (March 1832): 1-30.

845. Clark, Aaron. *An Oration: A Project for the Civilization of the Indians of North America.* Albany: Packard and Van Benthuysen, 1819.

846. "Condition of the American Indians." *Eclectic Review* 52 (July 1830): 77-86.

847. "Creek Controversy." *American Annual Register* 1 (1825-1826): 42-48.

848. Darneille, J. *Discourse or Lecture on the Subject of Civilizing the Indians, in Which Is Exhibited a New Plan to Effect Their Civilization and to Meliorate Their Condition.* Washington: F. S. Myer, 1826.

849. Evarts, Jeremiah. "Indian Affairs." *American Annual Register* 5 (1829-1830): 43-61.

850. Everett, A. H. "The Cherokee Case." *North American Review* 33 (July 1831): 136-153.

851. "Georgia Controversy." *Southern Review* 2 (November 1828): 541-582.

852. Head, T. B. "The Red Man." *Quarterly Review* 65 (March 1840): 384-419.

853. Humphrey, Heman. *Indian Rights and Our Duties: An Address Delivered at Amherst, Hartford, etc., December, 1829.* Amherst: J. S. and C. Adams and Company, 1830. Reprinted as "An 1829 Defense of the American Indian." *Chronicles of Oklahoma* 34 (Winter 1956-1957): 491-502.

854. Hunter, J. D. *Reflections of the Different States and Conditions of Society: With the Outlines of a Plan to Ameliorate the Circumstances of the In-*

dians of North America__. London: J. R. Lake, 1823.

855. "Indian Affairs." American Annual Register 2 (1827-1829): 69-85.

856. "Indian Affairs." American Annual Register 6 (1830-1831): 26-38.

857. "The Indians, and Our Relations with Them." Boston Quarterly Review 2 (April 1839): 229-259.

858. "The Indians of the United States-- Their Past, Their Present, and Their Future." De Bow's Review 16 (February 1854): 143-149.

859. Kah-Ge-Ga-Gah-Bouh [George Copway]. "The American Indians." American Review: A Whig Journal, Devoted to Politics and Literature 9 (June 1849): 631-637.

860. "North American Indians." Penny Magazine 4 (January 31, 1835): 38-40.

861. "The North American Indians." Penny Magazine 4 (February 7, 1835): 53-55.

862. "The North American Review for January 1830: Article III." Spirit of the Pilgrims 3 (March 1830): 141-161.

863. "Our Indian Policy." United States Magazine and Democratic Review 14 (February 1844): 169-184.

864. "Past and Present of the Indian Tribes." American Review: A Whig Journal of Politics, Literature, Art and Science 1 (May 1845): 502-510.

865. The Removal of the Indians: An Article from the American Monthly Magazine: An Examination of an Article in the North American Review, and an Exhibition of the Advancement of the Southern Tribes, in Civilization and Christianity. Boston: Peirce and Williams, 1830.

866. Review of an Article in the North American for January 1830, on the Present Relations of the Indians. N.p., n.d.

867. "Reviews: The Case of the Cherokee Nation against the State of Georgia." Spirit of the Pilgrims 4 (August 1831): 492-513.

868. Riggs, Stephen P. "The Indian Question." New Englander 15 (May 1857): 250-273.

869. "Rights of the Aborigines of Our Country." Western Review and Miscellaneous Magazine 4 (June 1821): 292-300.

870. Sewell, S. C. "Indian Controversy." Christian Examiner and General Review 9 (September 1830): 107-160.

871. "Speeches on the Indian Bill." Spirit of the Pilgrims 3 (September 1830): 492-500.

872. A Statement of the Indian Relations: With a Reply to the Article in the Sixty-Sixth Number of the North American Review, on the Removal of the Indians. New York, 1830.

873. Tyson, Job R. Discourse on the Surviving Remnant of the Indian Race in the United States. Philadelphia: A. Waldie, 1836.

The journals of the period are indexed in Poole's Index (148) and in the Index to Early American Periodicals (154). Of special value is Niles' Weekly Register, published from 1811 to 1849, which carried a great deal of news and documentation on Indian affairs.

THE CIVIL WAR

Indian Affairs during the Civil War: General

The Civil War did not entirely end concern for Indian affairs, and reservation policy especially developed. A few studies treat of the Indian policy of Lincoln and his Commissioner of Indian Affairs. Listed here also are miscellaneous writings dealing with the period.

874. Blegen, Theodore, ed. Lincoln's Secretary Goes West: Two Reports, by John G. Nicolay, on Frontier Indian Troubles, 1862. La Crosse, Wisconsin: Sumac Press, 1965.

875. Colton, Ray C. The Civil War in the Western Territories: Arizona, Colorado, New Mexico, and Utah. Norman: University of Oklahoma Press, 1959.

876. Covington, James W. "Federal Relations with the Colorado Utes, 1861-1865." Colorado Magazine 28 (October 1951): 257-265.

877. Danziger, Edmund J., Jr. "Civil War Problems in the Central and Dakota Superintendencies: A Case Study." Nebraska History 51 (Winter 1970): 411-424.

878. _____. "The Indian Office during the Civil War: Impotence in Indian Affairs." South Dakota History 5 (Winter 1974): 52-72.

879. _____. Indians and Bureaucrats: Administering the Reservation Policy during the Civil War. Urbana: University of Illinois Press, 1974.

880. _____. "The Steck-Carleton Controversy in Civil War New Mexico." Southwestern Historical Quarterly 74 (October 1970): 189-203.

881. Ellis, Richard N. "Civilians, the Army, and the Indian Problem on the Northern Plains, 1862-1866." North Dakota

History 37 (Winter 1970): 20-39.

882. _____. "Political Pressures and Army Policies on the Northern Plains, 1862-1865." Minnesota History 42 (Summer 1970): 43-53.

883. Hofsommer, Donovan L. "William Palmer Dole, Commissioner of Indian Affairs, 1861-1865." Lincoln Herald 75 (Fall 1973): 97-114.

884. Kelsey, Harry. "William P. Dole and Mr. Lincoln's Indian Policy." Journal of the West 10 (July 1971): 484-492.

885. Kibby, Leo P. "California, the Civil War, and the Indian Problem." Journal of the West 4 (April 1965): 183-210; (July 1965): 377-410.

886. Morgan, Lewis Henry. "An Unknown Letter from Lewis H. Morgan to Abraham Lincoln," edited by Paul Kosok. University of Rochester Library Bulletin 6 (Winter 1951): 34-40.

887. Moulton, Gary E. "John Ross and W. P. Dole: A Case Study of Lincoln's Indian Policy." Journal of the West 12 (July 1973): 414-423.

888. Nichols, David A. "The Other Civil War: Lincoln and the Indians." Minnesota History 44 (Spring 1974): 2-15.

889. Sievers, Michael A. "The Administration of Indian Affairs on the Upper Missouri, 1858-1865." North Dakota History 38 (Summer 1971): 367-394.

890. Tate, Michael L. "The Frontier of Northwest Texas during the Civil War." Chronicles of Oklahoma 50 (Summer 1972): 177-189.

891. Warner, Mildred. "The Attitude of the Nebraska Territorial Government towards the Indians." Great Plains Journal 9 (Spring 1970): 59-66.

See also studies on Indian wars of the period, especially those with the Sioux and with the Navajos, and the following section on the Civil War in the Indian Territory.

Civil War and Reconstruction in the Indian Territory

The Indians in the Indian Territory were deeply affected by the Civil War. Many of them were slaveholders and sympathized with the South, and the Five Civilized Tribes and some others formally joined the Confederacy, although there were significant Union elements among them. The Civil War brought ruin to much of Indian Territory, and the readjustment and reconstruction after the war were painful events.

892. Abel, Annie Heloise. The American Indian as Slaveholder and Secessionist: An Omitted Chapter in the Diplomatic History of the Southern Confederacy. Volume 1 of The Slaveholding Indians. Cleveland: Arthur H. Clark Company, 1915.

893. _____. The American Indian as Participant in the Civil War. Volume 2 of The Slaveholding Indians. Cleveland: Arthur H. Clark Company, 1919.

894. _____. The American Indian under Reconstruction. Volume 3 of The Slaveholding Indians. Cleveland: Arthur H. Clark Company, 1925.

895. _____. "The Indians in the Civil War." American Historical Review 15 (January 1910): 281-296.

896. Andrews, Thomas F. "Freedmen in Indian Territory: A Post-Civil War Dilemma." Journal of the West 4 (July 1965): 367-376.

897. Ashcraft, Allan C. "Confederate Indian Department Conditions in August, 1864." Chronicles of Oklahoma 41 (Autumn 1963): 270-285.

898. _____. "Confederate Indian Territory Conditions in 1865." Chronicles of Oklahoma 42 (Winter 1964-1965): 421-428.

899. _____. "Confederate Indian Troop Conditions in 1864." Chronicles of Oklahoma 41 (Winter 1963-1964): 442-449.

900. Bailey, M. Thomas. Reconstruction in Indian Territory: A Story of Avarice, Discrimination, and Opportunism. Port Washington, New York: Kennikat Press, 1972.

901. Banks, Dean. "Civil War Refugees from Indian Territory in the North, 1861-1864." Chronicles of Oklahoma 41 (Autumn 1963): 286-298.

902. Bearss, Edwin C. "The Civil War Comes to Indian Territory, 1861: The Flight of Opothleyoholo." Journal of the West 11 (January 1972): 9-42.

903. _____. "General Cooper's CSA Indians Threaten Fort Smith." Arkansas Historical Quarterly 26 (Autumn 1967): 257-284.

904. Britton, Wiley. "Some Reminiscences of the Cherokee People, Returning to Their Homes the Exiles of a Nation." Chronicles of Oklahoma 6 (June 1928): 163-177.

905. _____. The Union Indian Brigade in the Civil War. Kansas City, Missouri: Franklin Hudson Publishing Company, 1922.

906. Brown, Gayle Ann. "Confederate Surrenders in Indian Territory." Journal of the West 12 (July 1973): 455-461.

51

907. Buice, Sammy D. "The Civil War and the Five Civilized Tribes: A Study in Federal-Indian Relations." Ph.D. dissertation, University of Oklahoma, 1970.

908. Coffman, Edward M., ed. "Ben McCulloch Letters." Southwestern Historical Quarterly 60 (July 1956): 118-122.

909. Coleman, R. B. "Indian Tribes in the Confederacy." Confederate Veteran 24 (November 1916): 509.

910. Cubage, Annie Rosser. "Engagement at Cabin Creek, Indian Territory, July 1 and 2, 1863." Chronicles of Oklahoma 10 (March 1932): 44-51.

911. Cunningham, Frank. General Stand Watie's Confederate Indians. San Antonio: Naylor Company, 1959.

912. Currin, Jean McCulley. "Why Indian Territory Joined the Confederacy." Lincoln Herald 69 (Summer 1967): 83-91.

913. Dale, Edward Everett. "Arkansas and the Cherokees." Arkansas Historical Quarterly 8 (Summer 1949): 95-114.

914. _____. "The Cherokees in the Confederacy." Journal of Southern History 13 (May 1947): 159-185.

915. Danziger, Edmund J., Jr. "The Office of Indian Affairs and the Problem of Civil War Indian Refugees in Kansas." Kansas Historical Quarterly 35 (Autumn 1969): 257-275.

916. Debo, Angie. "The Location of the Battle of Round Mountains." Chronicles of Oklahoma 41 (Spring 1963): 70-104.

917. _____. "Southern Refugees of the Cherokee Nation." Southwestern Historical Quarterly 35 (April 1932): 255-266.

918. Demorse, Charles. "Indians for the Confederacy." Chronicles of Oklahoma 50 (Winter 1972-1973): 474-478.

919. Fischer, LeRoy H., ed. The Civil War Era in Indian Territory. Los Angeles: Lorrin L. Morrison, 1974. Reprint of articles from Journal of the West 12 (July 1973).

920. Fischer, LeRoy H., and Kenny A. Franks. "Confederate Victory at Chusto-Talasah." Chronicles of Oklahoma 49 (Winter 1971-1972): 452-476.

921. Foreman, Grant. "Fort Davis." Chronicles of Oklahoma 17 (June 1939): 147-150.

922. Franks, Kenny A. "The Confederate States and the Five Civilized Tribes: A Breakdown of Relations." Journal of the West 12 (July 1973): 439-454.

923. _____. "Operations against Opothleyahola, 1861." Military History of Texas and the Southwest 10 (1972): 187-196.

924. Freeman, Charles R. "The Battle of Honey Springs." Chronicles of Oklahoma 13 (June 1935): 154-168.

925. Gibson, Arrell M. "Confederates on the Plains: The Pike Mission to Wichita Agency." Great Plains Journal 4 (Fall 1964): 7-16.

926. Hall, Martin Hardwick. "Planter vs. Frontiersman: Conflict in Confederate Indian Policy." In Essays on the American Civil War, edited by William F. Holmes and Harold M. Hollingsworth, pp. 45-72. Austin: University of Texas Press, 1968.

927. Hancock, Marvin J. "The Second Battle of Cabin Creek, 1864." Chronicles of Oklahoma 39 (Winter 1961-1962): 414-426.

928. Heath, Gary N. "The First Federal Invasion of the Indian Territory." Chronicles of Oklahoma 44 (Winter 1966-1967): 409-419.

929. Hood, Fred. "Twilight of the Confederacy in Indian Territory." Chronicles of Oklahoma 41 (Winter 1963-1964): 425-441.

930. Horton, L. W. "General Sam Bell Maxey: His Defense of North Texas and the Indian Territory." Southwestern Historical Quarterly 74 (April 1971): 507-524.

931. James, Parthena Louise. "Reconstruction in the Chickasaw Nation: The Freedman Problem." Chronicles of Oklahoma 45 (Spring 1967): 44-57.

932. Kensell, Lewis Anthony. "Phases of Reconstruction in the Choctaw Nation, 1865-1870." Chronicles of Oklahoma 47 (Summer 1969): 138-153.

933. Lemley, Harry J. "Historic Letters of General Ben McCulloch and Chief John Ross in the Civil War." Chronicles of Oklahoma 40 (Autumn 1962): 286-294.

934. _____. "Letters of Henry M. Rector and J. R. Kannaday to John Ross of the Cherokee Nation." Chronicles of Oklahoma 42 (Autumn 1964): 320-329.

935. Martin, Howard N. "Texas Redskins in Confederate Gray." Southwestern Historical Quarterly 70 (April 1967): 586-592.

936. Moore, Jessie Randolph. "The Five Great Indian Nations: Cherokee, Choctaw, Chickasaw, Seminole and Creek: The Part they Played in Behalf of the Confederacy in the War between the States." Chronicles of Oklahoma 29 (Autumn 1951): 324-336.

937. Morton, Ohland. "Confederate Government Relations with the Five Civilized Tribes." Chronicles of Oklahoma 31

(Summer 1953): 189-204; (Autumn 1953): 299-322.

938. _____. "Reconstruction in the Creek Nation." *Chronicles of Oklahoma* 9 (June 1931): 171-179.

939. Pool, William C. "The Battle of Dove Creek." *Southwestern Historical Quarterly* 53 (April 1950): 367-385.

940. Rampp, Lary C. "Civil War Battle of Barren Creek, Indian Territory, 1863." *Chronicles of Oklahoma* 48 (Spring 1970): 74-82.

941. _____. "Confederate Indian Sinking of the J. R. Williams." *Journal of the West* 11 (January 1972): 43-50.

942. Rampp, Lary C., and Donald L. Rampp. *The Civil War in the Indian Territory.* Austin, Texas: Presidial Press, 1975.

943. _____. "The Civil War in the Indian Territory: The Confederate Advantage, 1861-1862." *Military History of Texas and the Southwest* 10 (1972): 29-41.

944. _____. "The Civil War in the Indian Territory: The Union Counter, 1862-1863." *Military History of Texas and the Southwest* 10 (1972): 93-114.

945. _____. "The Civil War in the Indian Territory: Blunt's Pursuit." *Military History of Texas and the Southwest* 10 (1972): 249-272.

946. _____. "The Civil War in the Indian Territory: The Phillips' Expedition and Stalemate." *Military History of Texas and the Southwest* 11 (1973): 77-108.

947. _____. "The Civil War in the Indian Territory: Confederate Guerilla Operations Intensify." *Military History of Texas and the Southwest* 11 (1973): 173-195.

948. _____. "The Civil War in the Indian Territory: Confederate Guerilla Operations End and Conclusions." *Military History of Texas and the Southwest* 11 (1973): 251-280.

949. Ream, Robert L. "A Nearly Forgotten Fragment of Local History." *Chronicles of Oklahoma* 4 (March 1926): 34-44.

950. Shirk, George H. "The Place of the Indian Territory in the Command Structure of the Civil War." *Chronicles of Oklahoma* 45 (Winter 1967-1968): 464-471.

951. Shoemaker, Arthur. "The Battle of Chustenahlah." *Chronicles of Oklahoma* 38 (Summer 1960): 180-184.

952. Thoburn, Joseph B., ed. "The Cherokee Question." *Chronicles of Oklahoma* 2 (June 1924): 141-242. Reprint of pamphlet by Commissioner of Indian Affairs

Dennis N. Cooley.

953. Trees, May. "Socioeconomic Reconstruction in the Seminole Nation, 1865-1870." *Journal of the West* 12 (July 1973): 490-498.

954. Trickett, Dean. "The Civil War in the Indian Territory, 1861." *Chronicles of Oklahoma* 17 (September 1939): 315-327; (December 1939): 401-412; 18 (June 1940): 142-153; (September 1940): 266-280.

955. _____. "Civil War in the Indian Territory: 1862." *Chronicles of Oklahoma* 19 (March 1941): 55-69; (December 1941): 381-396.

956. Warren, Hanna R. "Reconstruction in the Cherokee Nation." *Chronicles of Oklahoma* 45 (Summer 1967): 180-189.

957. West, Larry L. "Douglas H. Cooper, Confederate General." *Lincoln Herald* 71 (Summer 1969): 69-76.

958. Willey, William J. "The Second Federal Invasion of Indian Territory." *Chronicles of Oklahoma* 44 (Winter 1966-1967): 420-430.

959. Willson, Walt. "Freedmen in Indian Territory during Reconstruction." *Chronicles of Oklahoma* 49 (Summer 1971): 230-244.

960. Wrone, David R., ed. "The Cherokee Act of Emancipation." *Journal of Ethnic Studies* 1 (Fall 1973): 87-90.

961. Wright, Muriel H. "General Douglas H. Cooper, C.S.A." *Chronicles of Oklahoma* 32 (Summer 1954): 142-184.

962. Wright, Muriel H., and LeRoy H. Fischer. "Civil War Sites in Oklahoma." *Chronicles of Oklahoma* 44 (Summer 1966): 158-215.

See also the studies on Negro slavery among the Indians in the section on Indians and blacks, general studies on the Indian Territory, and studies of pertinent treaties.

INDIAN AFFAIRS, 1865-1900

General and Miscellaneous Studies, 1865-1900

There are a few general histories of United States Indian policy in the period between the Civil War and 1900. These treat of the reform movements that attempted to end tribalism and bring the Indians into the mainstream of white society.

963. Fritz, Henry E. *The Movement for Indian Assimilation, 1860-1890.* Philadelphia: University of Pennsylvania Press, 1963.

964. Mardock, Robert Winston. *The Reformers*

and the American Indian. Columbia: University of Missouri Press, 1971.

965. Priest, Loring Benson. Uncle Sam's Stepchildren: The Reformation of United States Indian Policy, 1865-1887. New Brunswick: Rutgers University Press, 1942.

966. Prucha, Francis Paul. American Indian Policy in Crisis: Christian Reformers and the Indian, 1865-1900. Norman: University of Oklahoma Press, 1976.

Other studies deal with a wide variety of topics. Separate headings are provided below for those of special importance. Listed here are miscellaneous studies that fall into the period.

967. Berthrong, Donald J. "Federal Indian Policy and the Southern Cheyennes and Arapahoes, 1887-1907." Ethnohistory 3 (Spring 1956): 138-153.

968. _____. "White Neighbors Come among the Southern Cheyenne and Arapaho." Kansas Quarterly 3 (Fall 1971): 105-115.

969. Buntin, Martha. "Difficulties Encountered in Issuing Cheyenne and Arapaho Subsistence 1861-1870." Chronicles of Oklahoma 13 (March 1935): 37-45.

970. Chaput, Donald. "Generals, Indian Agents, Politicians: The Doolittle Survey of 1865." Western Historical Quarterly 3 (July 1972): 269-282.

971. Condition of the Indian Tribes: Report of the Joint Special Committee, Appointed under Joint Resolution of March 3, 1865, with an Appendix. Washington: Government Printing Office, 1867. Report of the Doolittle Committee. Also issued as Senate Report no. 156, 39th Congress, 2d session, serial 1279.

972. Cornish, Dudley Taylor. "The First Five Years of Colorado's Statehood: Indian Trouble." Colorado Magazine 25 (September 1948): 220-232.

973. Davison, Kenneth E. "President Hayes and the Reform of American Indian Policy." Ohio History 82 (Summer-Autumn 1973): 205-214.

974. D'Elia, Donald J. "The Argument over Civilian or Military Indian Control, 1865-1880." Historian 24 (February 1962): 207-225.

975. Deutsch, Herman J. "Indian and White in the Inland Empire: The Contest for the Land, 1880-1912." Pacific Northwest Quarterly 47 (April 1956): 44-51.

976. Ekland, Roy E. "The 'Indian Problem': Pacific Northwest, 1879." Oregon Historical Quarterly 70 (June 1969): 101-137.

977. Ellis, Richard N. "General Pope's Report on the West, 1866." Kansas Historical Quarterly 35 (Winter 1969): 345-372.

978. Ellis, Richard N., ed. "Bent, Carson, and the Indians, 1865." Colorado Magazine 46 (Winter 1969): 55-68.

979. Fritz, Henry E. "George W. Manypenny and Our Indian Wards." Kansas Quarterly 3 (Fall 1971): 100-104.

980. Garfield, Marvin H. "The Indian Question in Congress and in Kansas." Kansas Historical Quarterly 2 (February 1933): 29-44.

981. Gressley, Gene M., ed. "A Cattleman Views Indian Policy--1875." Montana, the Magazine of Western History 17 (January 1967): 2-11. Views of William Sturgis of Wyoming.

982. Hauptman, Laurence M. "Governor Theodore Roosevelt and the Indians of New York State." Proceedings of the American Philosophical Society 119 (February 21, 1975): 1-7.

983. Jackson, W. Turrentine. "Indian Affairs and Politics in Idaho Territory, 1863-1870." Pacific Historical Review 14 (September 1945): 311-325.

984. Joyner, Christopher C. "The Hegira of Sitting Bull to Canada: Diplomatic Realpolitik, 1876-1881." Journal of the West 13 (April 1974): 6-18.

985. Kelsey, Harry. "The Doolittle Report of 1867: Its Preparation and Shortcomings." Arizona and the West 17 (Summer 1975): 107-120.

986. Lass, William E. "The Removal from Minnesota of the Sioux and Winnebago Indians." Minnesota History 38 (December 1963): 353-364.

987. Littlefield, Daniel F., Jr., and Lonnie E. Underhill. "Renaming the American Indian, 1890-1913." American Studies 12 (Fall 1971): 33-45.

988. McNeal, T. A. "The Indians Agree to Abandon Kansas." Transactions of the Kansas State Historical Society 6 (1897-1900): 344-346.

989. Mardock, Robert Winston. "The Anti-Slavery Humanitarians and Indian Policy Reform." Western Humanities Review 12 (Spring 1958): 131-146.

990. Martin, Douglas D. "Indian-White Relations on the Pacific Slope, 1850-1890." Ph.D. dissertation, University of Washington, 1969.

991. Monahan, Forrest D., Jr. "Kiowa-Federal Relations in Kansas, 1865-1868." Chronicles of Oklahoma 49 (Winter 1971-1972): 477-491.

992. Ogle, Ralph H. "The Apache and the Government--1870's." New Mexico Histori-

cal Review 33 (April 1958): 81-102.

993. Olson, James C. Red Cloud and the Sioux Problem. Lincoln: University of Nebraska Press, 1965.

994. Reeve, Frank D. "The Federal Indian Policy in New Mexico, 1858-1880." New Mexico Historical Review 12 (July 1937): 218-269; 13 (January 1938): 14-62; (April 1938): 146-191; (July 1938): 261-313.

995. _____. "The Government and the Navajo, 1878-1883." New Mexico Historical Review 16 (July 1941): 275-312.

996. _____. "The Government and the Navajo, 1883-1888." New Mexico Historical Review 18 (January 1943): 17-51.

997. "Report of the Sioux Commission." Nebraska History Magazine 22 (January-March 1941): 110-112.

998. Rister, Carl Coke, ed. "Documents Relating to General W. T. Sherman Southern Plains Indian Policy, 1871-1875." Panhandle-Plains Historical Review 9 (1936): 7-28; 10 (1937): 48-63.

999. Roberts, Gary L. "Condition of the Tribes, 1865: The Report of General McCook." Montana, the Magazine of Western History 24 (December 1974): 14-25.

1000. Rubenstein, Bruce Alan. "Justice Denied: An Analysis of American Indian-White Relations in Michigan, 1855-1889." Ph.D. dissertation, Michigan State University, 1974.

1001. Small, John. "Trip of Col. James McLaughlin, Indian Inspector, to the Big Horn Hot Springs, Wyoming." Annals of Wyoming 8 (July 1932): 489-491.

1002. Smith, Duane A. "Gold, Silver, and the Red Man." Journal of the West 5 (January 1966): 114-121.

1003. Taylor, Lloyd C., Jr. "Lydia Maria Child and the Indians." Boston Public Library Quarterly 12 (January 1960): 51-56.

1004. Textor, Lucy E. Official Relations between the United States and the Sioux Indians. Leland Stanford Junior University Publications, History and Economics, no. 2. Palo Alto, California, 1896.

1005. Trennert, Robert A., Jr. "A Grand Failure: The Centennial Indian Exhibition of 1876." Prologue: The Journal of the National Archives 6 (Summer 1974): 118-129.

1006. Trimble, W. J. "American and British Treatment of the Indians in the Pacific Northwest." Washington Historical Quarterly 5 (January 1914): 32-54.

1007. Vestal, Stanley. Warpath and Council Fire: The Plains Indians' Struggle for Survival in War and in Diplomacy, 1851-1891. New York: Random House, 1948.

1008. Waltmann, Henry G. "The Interior Department, War Department and Indian Policy, 1865-1887." Ph.D. dissertation, University of Nebraska, 1962.

See also the sections immediately below and studies on the Indian wars of the period.

Grant's Peace Policy

The administration of President Ulysses S. Grant was noted for remarkable changes in Indian policy: the appointment of a Board of Indian Commissioners to help in the administration of Indian affairs and especially the assignment of Indian agencies to various religious denominations. Particular studies of this "peace policy" are listed here.

1009. Address of the Catholic Clergy of the Province of Oregon, to the Catholics of the United States, on President Grant's Indian Policy, in Its Bearings upon Catholic Interests at Large. Portland, Oregon: Catholic Sentinel Publication Company, 1874.

1010. Arnold, S. G. "President Grant's Indian Policy." Methodist Quarterly Review 59 (July 1877): 409-430.

1011. Beaver, R. Pierce. "The Churches and President Grant's Peace Policy." Journal of Church and State 4 (November 1962): 174-190.

1012. Ewing, Charles. Circular of the Catholic Commissioner for Indian Missions, to the Catholics of the United States. Baltimore: John Murphy and Company, 1874. Catholic complaints about the peace policy.

1013. Fritz, Henry E. "The Making of Grant's Peace Policy." Chronicles of Oklahoma 37 (Winter 1959-1960): 411-432.

1014. Illick, Joseph E. "'Some of Our Best Indians Are Friends. . .': Quaker Attitudes and Actions Regarding the Western Indians during the Grant Administration." Western Historical Quarterly 2 (July 1971): 283-294.

1015. Keller, Robert H., Jr. "The Protestant Churches and Grant's Peace Policy: A Study in Church-State Relations, 1869-1881." Ph.D. dissertation, University of Chicago, 1967.

1016. Mardock, Robert Winston. "Alfred H. Love, Indian Peace Policy, and the Universal Peace Union." Kansas Quarterly 3 (Fall 1971): 64-71.

1017. _____. "The Plains Frontier and the Indian Peace Policy, 1865-1880." Nebraska History 49 (Summer 1968): 187-201.

1018. "Quaker Report on Indian Agencies in Nebraska, 1869." Nebraska History 54 (Summer 1973): 151-219.

1019. Rahill, Peter James. The Catholic Indian Missions and Grant's Peace Policy, 1870-1884. Washington: Catholic University of America Press, 1953.

1020. Rushmore, Elsie Mitchell. The Indian Policy during Grant's Administrations. Jamaica, New York: Marion Press, 1914.

1021. Steele, Aubrey L. "The Beginning of Quaker Administration of Indian Affairs in Oklahoma." Chronicles of Oklahoma 17 (December 1939): 364-392.

1022. Tatum, Lawrie. Our Red Brothers and the Peace Policy of Ulysses S. Grant. Philadelphia: John C. Winston and Company, 1899.

1023. Utley, Robert M. "The Celebrated Peace Policy of General Grant." North Dakota History 20 (July 1953): 121-142.

1024. Waltmann, Henry G. "Circumstantial Reformer: President Grant and the Indian Problem." Arizona and the West 13 (Winter 1971): 323-342.

1025. Weber, Francis J., ed. "Grant's Peace Policy: A Catholic Dissenter." Montana, the Magazine of Western History 19 (January 1969): 56-63. John Baptist Camillus Imoda, S.J.

1026. White, Barclay. The Friends and the Indians: Report of Barclay White, Late Superintendent of Indian Affairs in the Northern Superintendency, Nebraska, Exhibiting the Progress in Civilization of the Various Tribes of Indians Whilst under the Care of Friends as Agents. Oxford, Pennsylvania, 1886.

1027. Whitner, Robert L. "Grant's Indian Peace Policy on the Yakima Reservation, 1870-1882." Pacific Northwest Quarterly 50 (October 1959): 135-142.

1028. _____. "The Methodist Episcopal Church and Grant's Peace Policy: A Study of the Methodist Agencies, 1870-1882." Ph.D. dissertation, University of Minnesota, 1959.

General studies on Indian relations in the post-Civil War period (963 to 966) also include much material on the peace policy.

Ponca Affair

A celebrated case in the Indian reform movement was the removal of the Ponca Indians from Dakota to Oklahoma and the agitation that arose when some of them fled back to their homelands in 1879. Reformers seized upon the issue and laid the blame at the door of Secretary of the Interior Carl Schurz, with whom they had extensive verbal battles.

1029. Clark, J. Stanley. "The Killing of Big Snake." Chronicles of Oklahoma 49 (Autumn 1971): 302-314.

1030. _____. "Ponca Publicity." Mississippi Valley Historical Review 29 (March 1943): 495-516.

1031. Goddard, M. LeB. "The Story of the Poncas." International Review 9 (October 1880): 388-404.

1032. Hayter, Earl W. "The Ponca Removal." North Dakota Historical Review 6 (July 1932): 262-275.

1033. The Indian Question: Report of the Committee Appointed by Hon. John D. Long, Governor of Massachusetts. Boston: Frank Wood, 1880.

1034. King, James T. "'A Better Way': General George Crook and the Ponca Indians." Nebraska History 50 (Fall 1969): 239-257.

1035. Schurz, Carl. An Open Letter in Answer to a Speech of Hon. H. L. Dawes, United States Senate, on the Case of Big Snake, by Hon. Carl Schurz, Secretary of the Interior. Washington, 1881.

1036. _____. Removal of the Ponca Indians: Open Letter to Hon. John D. Long, Governor of Massachusetts, by Hon. Carl Schurz, Secretary of the Interior. Washington, 1880.

1037. _____. "The Removal of the Poncas." Independent 32 (January 1, 1880): 1.

1038. "The Schurz Mystery." Nation 32 (February 24, 1881): 125-126.

1039. Secretary Schurz: Reply of the Boston Committee, Governor John D. Long, Chairman: Misrepresentations Corrected and Important Facts Presented. Boston: Frank Wood, 1881.

1040. Tibbles, Thomas Henry. Buckskin and Blanket Days. Garden City, New York: Doubleday, 1957. Autobiographical account written in 1905.

1041. _____. The Ponca Chiefs: An Indian's Attempt to Appeal from the Tomahawk to the Courts: A Full History of the Robbery of the Ponca Tribe of Indians, with All the Papers Filed and Evidence Taken in the Standing Bear Habeas Corpus Case, and Full Text of Judge Dundy's Celebrated Decision, with Some Suggestions towards a Solution of the Indian Question. Boston: Lockwood, Brooks and Company, 1880. Published under the pseudonym

Zylyff. Reprinted, edited with an introduction by Kay Graber, under the title
The Ponca Chiefs: An Account of the Trial
of Standing Bear. Lincoln: University of
Nebraska Press, 1972.

1042. _____. Western Men Defended:
Speech of Mr. T. H. Tibbles in Tremont
Temple, Boston, Mass., December, 1880.
Boston: Lockwood, Brooks and Company,
1880.

Schurz's correspondence on the subject is
also found in the published edition of his
speeches and papers, edited by Frederic
Bancroft (1913).

Indian Affairs in the Indian Territory

Developments in the Indian Territory between the Civil War and the admission of
Oklahoma to the Union in 1907 were an important part of Indian relations. The concentration of western tribes in the area
and the political struggles of the Five
Tribes to maintain their autonomy marked the
period.

General and Miscellaneous Accounts

Included here are historical studies,
contemporary accounts, and recent histories
of Oklahoma (which include a good deal of
information on Indian affairs).

1043. Abbott, L. J. "The Race Question
in the Forty-Sixth State." Independent
63 (July 25, 1907): 206-211.

1044. Adair, William Penn. "The Indian
Territory in 1878." Chronicles of Oklahoma 4 (September 1926): 255-274.

1045. Allen, C. M. The "Sequoyah" Movement. Oklahoma City: Harlow Publishing
Company, 1925.

1046. Applen, Allen G. "An Attempted Indian State Government: The Okmulgee Constitution in Indian Territory, 1870-1876."
Kansas Quarterly 3 (Fall 1971): 89-99.

1047. Balyeat, Frank A. "Education of
White Children in the Indian Territory."
Chronicles of Oklahoma 15 (June 1937):
191-197.

1048. Bass, Althea. "The Cheyenne Transporter." Chronicles of Oklahoma 46 (Summer 1968): 127-140. Indian Territory
newspaper, 1879-1886.

1049. Boudinot, Elias Cornelius. "The Indian Territory and Its Inhabitants."
Geographical Magazine 1 (June 1874): 92-
95.

1050. Brown, Henry S. "The Indians and
Oklahoma." Outlook 85 (January 19, 1907):
115-118.

1051. Buck, Solon J. "The Settlement of

Oklahoma." Transactions of the Wisconsin
Academy of Sciences, Letters and Arts 15
(September 1907): 325-380.

1052. Chapman, Berlin B. "The Enid 'Railroad War': An Archival Study." Chronicles
of Oklahoma 43 (Summer 1965): 126-197.

1053. _____. "The Legal Sooners of 1889
in Oklahoma." Chronicles of Oklahoma 35
(Winter 1957-1958): 382-415.

1054. _____. "Opening of the Cherokee
Outlet: An Archival Study." Chronicles
of Oklahoma 40 (Summer 1962): 158-181;
(Autumn 1962): 253-285.

1055. Clark, Ira G., Jr. "The Railroads
and Tribal Lands: Indian Territory, 1838-
1890." Ph.D. dissertation, University of
California, 1947.

1056. Condra, G. E. "Opening of the Indian
Territory." Bulletin of the American
Geographical Society of New York 39
(1907): 321-340.

1057. Dale, Edward Everett, and Morris L.
Wardell. History of Oklahoma. New York:
Prentice-Hall, 1948.

1058. Dawes, Anna Laurens. "An Unknown Nation." Harper's New Monthly Magazine 76
(March 1888): 598-605. Cherokees of Indian Territory.

1059. Dawes, Henry L. "The Indian Territory." Independent 52 (October 25,
1900): 2561-2565.

1060. Downing, A. "The Cherokee Indians
and Their Neighbors." American Antiquarian 17 (November 1895): 307-316.

1061. Draper, W. R. "The Reconstruction
of the Indian Territory." Outlook 68
(June 22, 1901): 444-447.

1062. Duncan, D. W. C. "The Cherokee Outlet." Andover Review 16 (October 1891):
342-351.

1063. _____. "The Cherokee Outlet."
Lend a Hand 7 (October 1891): 257-258.

1064. Eggleston, George Cary. "The Historical Status of the Indian Territory."
Magazine of American History 9 (June
1883): 440-451.

1065. Ellinger, Charles Wayne. "The Drive
for Statehood in Oklahoma, 1889-1906."
Chronicles of Oklahoma 41 (Spring 1963):
15-37.

1066. _____. "Political Obstacles Bar-
ring Oklahoma's Admission to Statehood,
1890-1906." Great Plains Journal 3
(Spring 1964): 60-83.

1067. "The End of the Civilized Tribes."
Independent 60 (May 10, 1906): 1110-1111.

1068. "Exeunt the Five Civilized Tribes."
Independent 54 (October 9, 1902): 2431-
2432.

1069. Fishback, W. M. "The Failure of Government in the Indian Territory." American Magazine of Civics 6 (January 1895): 96-98.

1070. Flynt, Josiah. "Town Life in the Indian Territory." Cosmopolitan 39 (June 1905): 137-144.

1071. Foreman, Carolyn Thomas. "The Light-Horse in the Indian Territory." Chronicles of Oklahoma 34 (Spring 1956): 17-43.

1072. Foreman, Carolyn Thomas, ed. "An Open Letter from Too-Qua-Stee to Congressman Charles Curtis, 1898." Chronicles of Oklahoma 47 (Autumn 1969): 298-311. A letter of DeWitt Clinton Duncan.

1073. Foreman, Grant. A History of Oklahoma. Norman: University of Oklahoma Press, 1942.

1074. _____. "The Home of the Red Man in Statehood." Overland Monthly 54 (October 1909): 368-374.

1075. _____. "The Last of the Five Tribes." Overland Monthly 49 (March 1907): 196-198.

1076. _____. "Oklahoma and the Indian Territory." Outlook 82 (March 10, 1906): 550-552.

1077. Gage, Duane. "Oklahoma: A Resettlement Area for Indians." Chronicles of Oklahoma 47 (Autumn 1969): 282-297.

1078. Gannett, Henry. Indian Territory. New York: Charles Scribner's Sons, 1881.

1079. _____. "Survey and Subdivision of Indian Territory." National Geographic Magazine 7 (March 1896): 112-115.

1080. Gibson, Arrell M. Oklahoma: A History of Five Centuries. Norman, Oklahoma: Harlow Publishing Corporation, 1965.

1081. Gideon, D. C. Indian Territory, Descriptive, Biographical and Genealogical . . . with a General History of the Territory. New York: Lewis Publishing Company, 1901.

1082. Gittinger, Roy. The Formation of the State of Oklahoma (1803-1906). Berkeley: University of California Press, 1917. New edition, Norman: University of Oklahoma Press, 1939.

1083. Graham, William. "Lost among the Choctaws during a Tour in the Indian Territory, 1845." Chronicles of Oklahoma 50 (Summer 1972): 226-233.

1084. Hamilton, Gail. "Prisoner among the Indians." North American Review 146 (January 1888): 55-66.

1085. Harger, Charles Moreau. "The Indian's Last Stand." Outlook 70 (January 25,

1902): 217-222.

1086. _____. "The Next Commonwealth: Oklahoma." Outlook 67 (February 2, 1901): 273-281.

1087. _____. "Oklahoma and the Indian Territory as They Are Today." American Monthly Review of Reviews 25 (February 1902): 177-181.

1088. Harvey, Charles M. "The Red Man's Last Roll-Call." Atlantic Monthly 97 (March 1906): 323-330.

1089. Hendricks, Allen. "The Land of the Five Tribes." Lippincott's Monthly Magazine 58 (November 1896): 670-676.

1090. Hinton, Richard J. "The Indian Territory--Its Status, Development, and Future." American Monthly Review of Reviews 23 (April 1901): 451-458.

1091. Hollon, W. Eugene. "Rushing for Land: Oklahoma 1889." American West 3 (Fall 1966): 4-15, 69-71.

1092. Humphrey, Seth K. "Rushing the Cherokee Strip." Atlantic Monthly 147 (May 1931): 566-577.

1093. James, Parthena Louise. "The White Threat in the Chickasaw Nation." Chronicles of Oklahoma 46 (Spring 1968): 73-85.

1094. Jenness, Theodora R. "Indian Territory." Atlantic Monthly 43 (April 1879): 444-452.

1095. Johnson, W. H. "The Saloon in Indian Territory." North American Review 146 (March 1888): 340-341.

1096. "Journal of the Adjourned Session of First General Council of the Indian Territory." Chronicles of Oklahoma 3 (June 1925): 120-136.

1097. "Journal of the General Council of the Indian Territory." Chronicles of Oklahoma 3 (April 1925): 33-44.

1098. King, Henry. "The Indian Country." Century Magazine 30 (August 1885): 599-606.

1099. "Land Scandal in Indian Territory." Independent 55 (August 20, 1903): 1951.

1100. Littlefield, Daniel F., Jr., and Lonnie E. Underhill. "Negro Marshals in the Indian Territory." Journal of Negro History 56 (April 1971): 77-87.

1101. McAdam, Rezin W. "An Indian Commonwealth." Harper's New Monthly Magazine 87·(November 1893): 884-897.

1102. McReynolds, Edwin C. Oklahoma: A History of the Sooner State. Norman: University of Oklahoma Press, 1956.

1103. Maxwell, Amos. "The Sequoyah Convention." Chronicles of Oklahoma 28 (Summer 1950): 161-192; (Autumn 1950):

299-340.

1104. Meserve, John Bartlett. "The Plea of Crazy Snake (Chitto Harjo)." Chronicles of Oklahoma 11 (September 1933): 899-911.

1105. Miller, Nyle H., ed. "The Cherokee Strip Run: From Cameron and Bluff City, Harper County, Kansas." Kansas Historical Quarterly 39 (Spring 1973): 161-187.

1106. Miner, Craig. "Border Frontier: The Missouri River, Fort Scott and Gulf Railroad in the Cherokee Neutral Lands, 1868-1870." Kansas Historical Quarterly 35 (Summer 1969): 105-129.

1107. Moore, J. H. The Political Condition of the Indians and the Resources of the Indian Territory. St. Louis: Southwestern Book and Publishing Company, 1874.

1108. Moore, Junius B. "The Survey of Indian Territory, 1894-1907." Chronicles of Oklahoma 28 (Winter 1950-1951): 445-451.

1109. Mothershead, Harmon. "The Journal of Ado Hunnius, Indian Territory, 1876." Chronicles of Oklahoma 51 (Winter 1973-1974): 451-472.

1110. Painter, Charles C. The Oklahoma Bill, and Oklahoma. Philadelphia: Indian Rights Association, 1889.

1111. Peery, Dan W. "Oklahoma, a Foreordained Commonwealth." Chronicles of Oklahoma 14 (March 1936): 22-48.

1112. Platt, Orville H. "Problems in the Indian Territory." North American Review 160 (February 1895): 195-202.

1113. Posey, Alexander Lawrence. "Journal of Creek Enrollment Field Party,1905." Chronicles of Oklahoma 46 (Summer 1968): 2-19.

1114. Prettyman, William S. Indian Territory: A Frontier Photographic Record. Edited by Robert E. Cunningham. Norman: University of Oklahoma Press, 1957.

1115. Rainey, George. The Cherokee Strip. Guthrie, Oklahoma: Co-operative Publishing Company, 1933.

1116. _____. The Cherokee Strip: Its History. Enid, Oklahoma, 1925.

1117. "Reaching for Indian Lands." Nation 82 (April 26, 1906): 336-337.

1118. "Report on the Five Civilized Tribes: 1897." Chronicles of Oklahoma 48 (Winter 1970-1971): 416-430. Report of the Kansas City Star.

1119. Reynolds, Milton W. "The Indian Territory." Western Monthly 4 (November 1870): 260-266.

1120. Rister, Carl Coke. Land Hunger: David L. Payne and the Oklahoma Boomers. Norman: University of Oklahoma Press, 1942.

1121. Savage, W. Sherman. "The Role of Negro Soldiers in Protecting the Indian Territory from Intruders." Journal of Negro History 36 (January 1951): 25-34.

1122. Savage, William W., Jr. "Intruders at Chilocco." Chronicles of Oklahoma 50 (Summer 1972): 199-204.

1123. _____. "The Rock Falls Raid: An Analysis of the Documentary Evidence." Chronicles of Oklahoma 49 (Spring 1971): 75-82.

1124. Self, Nancy Hope. "The Building of the Railroads in the Cherokee Nation." Chronicles of Oklahoma 49 (Summer 1971): 180-205.

1125. Sherman, Caroline B., ed. "A Young Army Officer's Experiences in Indian Territory." Chronicles of Oklahoma 13 (June 1935): 146-153. Letters of Henry E. Alvord.

1126. Stewart, Dora Ann. Government and Development of Oklahoma Territory. Oklahoma City: Harlow Publishing Company, 1933.

1127. Toler, Sally F. "A Glimpse of the New Country." Era Magazine 12 (October 1903): 313-317. Comanche and Kiowa Reservation.

1128. Whelpley, J. D. "The Passing of the Five Tribes." Harper's Weekly 45 (April 27, 1901): 444-445.

1129. Williams, A. M. "A Grand Council at Okmulgee." Lippincott's Magazine 24 (September 1879): 371-375.

1130. Wright, Muriel H. "The Indian International Fair at Muskogee." Chronicles of Oklahoma 49 (Spring 1971): 14-51.

1131. Wright, Muriel H., ed. "A Report to the General Council of the Indian Territory Meeting at Okmulgee in 1873." Chronicles of Oklahoma 34 (Spring 1956): 7-16.

1132. Yancey, David W. "Need of a Better Government in the Indian Territory." Forum 28 (February 1900): 737-740.

1133. Young, Claiborne Addison. "A Walking Tour in the Indian Territory, 1874." Chronicles of Oklahoma 36 (Summer 1958): 167-180.

See also the sections on Political Pamphlets (1134 to 1180) and on the Cherokee Commission and Dawes Commission (1181 to 1195).

Political Pamphlets

The Five Civilized Tribes in the Indian Territory after the Civil War were under great pressure from the federal government to organize a regular territorial government and to divide their tribal lands in severalty. Opposition to these measures was strong, and the views on both sides were set forth at length in pamphlets published by the interested parties.

1134. Adair, William P. Protest of W. P. Adair, Chairman Cherokee Delegation, against the Right Claimed by the United States Government to Exact Licenses from Adopted Cherokees, under the Intercourse Act of 1834, to Trade in the Indian Country, and for Other Purposes. Washington: Joseph L. Pearson, 1870.

1135. _____. Remarks of W. P. Adair, Cherokee Delegate, in Relation to the Expediency and Legality of Organizing the Indian Country into a Territory of the United States, to Be Called the Territory of "Ok-la-ho-ma," Made before the Committee on Territories of the House of Representatives of the United States, January 31, 1876. N.p., 1876.

1136. Boudinot, Elias Cornelius. Division of Lands, United States Courts, a Delegate in Congress for the Civilized Indians of the Indian Territory: Speech of Elias C. Boudinot, of the Cherokee Nation, Delivered at Vinita, Indian Territory, August 29th, 1874. St. Louis: Barns and Beynon, 1874.

1137. _____. Indian Territory: Argument of Elias C. Boudinot, Submitted to the Senate Committee on Territories, January 17, 1879. Washington: Thomas McGill and Company, 1879.

1138. _____. Oklahoma: An Argument by E. C. Boudinot, of the Cherokee Nation, Delivered before the House Committee on Territories, February 3, 1876. Washington: McGill and Witherow, 1876.

1139. _____. Oklahoma: Argument of Col. E. C. Boudinot before the Committee on Territories, January 29, 1878. Alexandria, Virginia: G. H. Ramey and Son, 1878.

1140. _____. Remarks of Elias C. Boudinot, of the Cherokee Nation, in Behalf of the Bill to Organize the Territory of Oklahoma, before the House Committee on Territories, May 13, 1874. Washington: McGill and Witherow, 1874.

1141. _____. Reply of the Southern Cherokees to the Memorial of Certain Delegates from the Cherokee Nation, Together with the Message of John Ross, Ex-Chief of the Cherokees, and Proceedings of the Council of the "Loyal Cherokees," Relative to the Alliance with the So-Called Confederate States. Washington: McGill and Witherow, 1866.

1142. _____. Speech of Elias C. Boudinot, a Cherokee Indian, Delivered before the House Committee on Territories, February 7, 1872, in Behalf of a Territorial Government for the Indian Territory, in Reply to Wm. P. Ross, a Cherokee Delegate, in His Argument against Any Congressional Action upon the Subject. Washington: McGill and Witherow, 1872.

1143. _____. Speech of Elias C. Boudinot, a Cherokee Indian, on the Indian Question, Delivered at Vinita, Cherokee Nation, the Junction of the Atlantic and Pacific, and the Missouri, Kansas, and Texas Railroads, September 21, 1871. Washington: McGill and Witherow, 1872.

1144. _____. Speech of Elias C. Boudinot, of the Cherokee Nation, Delivered before the House Committee on Territories, March 5, 1872, on the Question of a Territorial Government for the Indian Territory, in Reply to the Second Argument of the Indian Delegations in Opposition to Such Proposed Government. Washington: McGill and Witherow, 1872.

1145. _____. A Territorial Government for the Civilized Indians of the Indian Territory: If They Must Be Subjected to the Responsibilities of Citizens of the United States, They Should Have Their Privileges Also. N.p., 1874.

1146. Boudinot, Elias C., and William P. Adair. Reply of the Southern Cherokees to the Memorial of Certain Delegates from the Cherokee Nation, Together with the Message of John Ross, Ex-Chief of the Cherokees, and Proceedings of the Council of the "Loyal Cherokees," Relative to the Alliance with the So-Called Confederate States. Washington: McGill and Witherow, 1866.

1147. Communication of the Delegation of the Cherokee Nation to the President of the United States, Submitting the Memorial of Their National Council, with the Correspondence between John Ross, Principal Chief, and Certain Officers of the Rebellious States. Washington: Gibson Brothers, 1866.

1148. Cooley, Dennis N. The Cherokee Question: Report of the Commissioner of Indian Affairs to the President of the United States, June 15, 1866: Being Supplementary to the Report of the Commissioners Appointed by the President to Treat with the Indians South of Kansas, and Which Assembled at Fort Smith, Arkansas, in September, 1865. Washington: Government Printing Office, 1866. Reprinted in Chronicles of Oklahoma 2 (June

1924): 141-242, edited by Joseph B.
Thoburn.

1149. Denial of Indians to Charges of
Dawes Commission. Washington: Gibson
Brothers, 1894.

1150. Harkins, George W. Argument of George
W. Harkins, Delegate of the Chickasaw
Nation, in Opposition to the Bill Introduced by Mr. Springer to Provide for the
Organization of the Territory of Oklahoma,
and for Other Purposes. Washington: Gibson Brothers, 1888.

1151. Hodge, D. M. Remarks of D. M. Hodge,
Delegate of the Muscogee Nation of Indians, against the Establishment by Congress of a United States Government over
the Indian Country without the Consent
of the Indians. Washington: John L.
Ginck, 1876.

1152. The Indians Opposed to the Transfer
Bill: United Action of the Delegations
of the Cherokee, Creek, Seminole, Chickasaw, and Choctaw Nations in Opposition to
the Measure: They Protest against It, and
Give Their Reasons for So Doing. Washington: Gibson Brothers, 1878.

1153. Memorial of Indian Delegates, Remon-
strating against the Passage of an Act
Providing for the Organization of a United
States Territorial Government over the
Indian Country. Washington, 1880.

1154. Memorial of the Delegates of the Cherokee, Creek and Choctaw Nations of Indians, Remonstrating against the Passage
of the Bill to Organize the Territory of
Oklahoma, Consolidate the Indian Tribes
under a Territorial Government, and Carry
Out Provisions of the Treaties of 1866
with Certain Indian Tribes. Washington,
1870.

1155. Memorial of the Delegates of the
Cherokee Nation to the President of the
United States and the House of Representatives in Congress. Washington: Washington Chronicle Print, 1866.

1156. Memorial of the Indian Delegates
against the Passage by Congress of Any
Act Providing for the Organization of a
United States Territorial Government over
the Indian Country: No Territorial Government of the United States Can Be Organized over the Indian Country without the
Express Consent of the Indian Nations to
Be Affected: Nor Can Their Lands Be Allotted Except by Their Consent As Provided by Treaty Stipulation. Washington:
John L. Ginck, 1880.

1157. Memorial of the Indian Delegates to
Congress, Asking the Repeal of So Much
of Certain Railroad Charters as Grant
Conditional Grants of Indian Lands to
Railroads. N.p., 1874.

1158. Message of the Chief of the Muskogees,
and Reply of the National Council in
Extraordinary Session April 4, 1894, to
the Dawes Commission. Eufaula, Indian
Territory, 1894.

1159. Morris, Isaac N. Argument of Hon.
Isaac N. Morris, of Illinois, of Counsel
for the Cherokee Indians, before the House
Committee on Indian Affairs, against the
Bill Proposing to Establish a Territorial
Government over the Indians: Submitted
February 2, 1870. Washington: Chronicle
Print, 1870.

1160. Objections of the Delegates of the
Chickasaw, Cherokee and Creek Nations
to the Bill (S. 54) Entitled "An Act for
the Allotment of Lands in Severalty to
Indians on the Various Reservations, and
to Extend the Protection of the Laws of
the United States and of the Territories
over the Indians, and for Other Purposes,"
Now Pending in the Senate of the United
States. Washington: Gibson Brothers,
1887.

1161. "Oklahoma," and the Rights of the
Five Tribes of the Indian Territory: Submitted to Congress by the Cherokee Delegation. Washington: Gray and Clarkson,
1888.

1162. Pitchlynn, Peter P. Argument Submitted by P. P. Pitchlynn, Choctaw Delegate,
to the Judiciary Committee of the U.S.
Senate, upon the Question Whether the
People of the Choctaw Nation Have Become
Citizens of the United States by Virtue
of the Fourteenth Amendment to the Constitution. Washington: Cunningham and
McIntosh, 1870.

1163. _____. Letter of P. P. Pitch-
lynn to the People of the Choctaw and
Chickasaw Nations upon the Question of
Sectionizing and Dividing Their Lands in
Severalty. Washington, 1870.

1164. _____. Report of the Choctaw
Delegation. Washington: G. S. Gideon,
1856.

1165. _____. To His Excellency the
Principal Chief and General Council of
the Choctaw Nation. Washington: McGill
and Witherow, 1868.

1166. Pitchlynn, Peter P., and Winchester
Colbert. Address by P. P. Pitchlynne,
Principal Chief of the Choctaw Nation,
and Winchester Colbert, Governor of the
Chickasaw Nation, to the Choctaws and
Chickasaws: Explanatory of the Circum-
stances under Which the Treaty with the
United States, Concluded April 28, 1866,
Was Negotiated, and of the More Important
Stipulations Contained Therein, with Sug-
gestions as to the Policy Proper to Be
Pursued Hereafter by the Two Nations.
Washington: Joseph L. Pearson, 1866.

1167. Protest of Indian Delegates against Organization of Territorial Government over the Indian Country: Protest of the Delegates from the Cherokee, Creek, and Choctaw Nations, against the Organization of a United States Territorial Government over the Indian Territory. Washington, 1879.

1168. Protest of the Indian Delegation against the Establishment by Congress of a Territorial Government of the United States over the Indian Territory. Washington, 1875.

1169. Protest of the Lawful Delegates of the Civilized Nations of Indians of the Indian Territory (Herein Named) on Their Behalf and on Behalf of the Indian Race against the Passage of a Law by Congress Transferring Them and Their Property to Military Control. Washington: Gibson Brothers, 1876.

1170. Remonstrance of the Cherokee, Creek, Choctaw and Seminole Delegations against the Organization of the Indian Territory into a Territory of the United States: It Is Unlawful, and Destructive to the Rights of the Citizen Population of Said Territory. Washington: John L. Ginck, 1876.

1171. Reply of the Cherokee National Council to the Propositions of the Dawes Commission in Regard to Change of Government for the Cherokee Nation. Washington: Gibson Brothers, 1894.

1172. Reply of the Delegates of the Cherokee Nation to the Pamphlet of the Commissioner of Indian Affairs. Washington, 1866.

1173. Report of the Cherokee Delegation of Their Mission to Washington, in 1868 and 1869. N.p., 1869.

1174. Ridge, John R., and others. Comments on the Objections of Certain Cherokee Delegates to the Proposition of the Government to Separate Hostile Parties of the Cherokee Nation. Washington: Intelligencer Printing House, 1866.

1175. Ross, William P. The Indian Territory: Arguments of William P. Ross, of the Cherokee Delegation, Delivered before the Committee on Territories of the House of Representatives, in Opposition to Bills before the Committee to Establish the Territory of Oklahoma, on the 1st Day of February and the 5th Day of March, 1872. Washington: Chronicle Publishing Company, 1872.

1176. _____. Indian Territory: Remarks in Opposition to Bills to Organize the Territory of Oklahoma, by Wm. P. Ross, of the Cherokee Nation, before the Committee on Indian Affairs of the House of Representatives, Wednesday, March 8th,

1876. Washington: Gibson Brothers, 1876.

1177. _____. Indian Territory: Remarks in Opposition to the Bill to Organize the Territory of Oklahoma, by Wm. P. Ross, Principal Chief of the Cherokee Nation, before the Committee on Territories of the House of Representatives, Monday, February 9th, 1874. Washington: Gibson Brothers, 1874.

1178. _____. Indian Territory: Remarks of William P. Ross, of the Cherokee Delegation, before the Committee on Territories of the United States Senate, on the Subjects Referred to in the Resolutions of Mr. Voorhees, as Delivered in Part January 17, 1879, and Submitted in Full January 23, 1879. Washington: Gibson Brothers, 1879.

1179. Taliaferro, T. D. Report of the Dawes Commission Analyzed and Statement Sharply Controverted. Washington: Gibson Brothers, 1895.

1180. Taylor, James L. Speech of James L. Taylor, in Behalf of the Cherokee Nation, in Opposition to the Bill Introduced by Mr. Springer to Provide for the Organization of the Territory of Oklahoma, and for Other Purposes. Washington: Grimsely, Printer, 1888.

Many of these pamphlets are listed in The Gilcrease-Hargrett Catalogue of Imprints (253). Other similar materials can be found in memorials sent to Congress by the tribes and printed in the Serial Set of Congressional Documents.

Cherokee Commission and Dawes Commission

The intention of the United States to force the Indians in the Indian Territory to allot their lands in severalty and to dispose of surplus lands led to the formation by Congress of two special commissions. The first was the Cherokee Commission (also called the Jerome Commission), appointed in 1889, which dealt with the Cherokees for the Outlet and with the western tribes of the Territory. The second was the Commission to the Five Civilized Tribes (the Dawes Commission), appointed in 1893 to treat with the Five Civilized Tribes for allotment and for ultimate formation of a territorial government. The Dawes Commission was dissolved in 1905, but its work was continued by a Commissioner to the Five Civilized Tribes.

1181. Brown, Loren Nunn. "The Appraisal of the Lands of the Choctaws and Chickasaws by the Dawes Commission." Chronicles of Oklahoma 22 (Summer 1944): 177-191.

1182. _____. "The Choctaw-Chickasaw Court Citizens." Chronicles of Oklahoma 16 (December 1938): 425-443.

1183. _____. "The Dawes Commission." Chronicles of Oklahoma 9 (March 1931): 70-105.

1184. _____. "The Establishment of the Dawes Commission for Indian Territory." Chronicles of Oklahoma 18 (June 1940): 171-181.

1185. _____. "The Work of the Dawes Commission among the Choctaw and Chickasaw Indians." Ph.D. dissertation, University of Oklahoma, 1937.

1186. Chapman, Berlin B. "The Cherokee Commission at Kickapoo Village." Chronicles of Oklahoma 17 (March 1939): 62-74.

1187. _____. "The Cherokee Commission, 1889-1893." Indiana Magazine of History 42 (June 1946): 177-190.

1188. _____. "Final Report of the Cherokee Commission." Chronicles of Oklahoma 19 (December 1941): 356-367.

1189. _____. "How the Cherokees Acquired and Disposed of the Outlet: Part Three--The Fairchild Failure." Chronicles of Oklahoma 15 (September 1937): 291-321.

1190. _____. "How the Cherokees Acquired and Disposed of the Outlet: Part Five--The Cherokees Concede to a Contract." Chronicles of Oklahoma 16 (June 1938): 135-162.

1191. _____. "Secret 'Instructions and Suggestions' to the Cherokee Commission, 1889-1890." Chronicles of Oklahoma 26 (Winter 1948-1949): 449-458.

1192. Meserve, Charles F. The Dawes Commission and the Five Civilized Tribes of Indian Territory. Philadelphia: Indian Rights Association, 1896.

1193. U.S. Commission to the Five Civilized Tribes. Annual Reports, 1893-1894--1919-1920. Washington: Government Printing Office, 1894-1920. Issued by the Commission, then by the Commissioner to the Five Civilized Tribes, and finally by the Superintendent for the Five Civilized Tribes. See also Index to the Annual Reports of the Commission to the Five Civilized Tribes for the Years 1894 to 1905, Inclusive. Washington: Government Printing Office, 1906.

1194. U.S. Commissioner to the Five Civilized Tribes. Laws, Decisions, and Regulations Affecting the Work of the Commissioner to the Five Civilized Tribes, 1893-1906, Together with Maps Showing Classification of Lands in the Chickasaw, Choctaw, Cherokee, Creek, and Seminole Nations, and Recording Districts, Railroads, and Principal Towns of the Indian Territory. Washington: Government Printing Office, 1906.

1195. Williams, Robert L. "Tams Bixby." Chronicles of Oklahoma 19 (September

1941): 205-212. Commissioner to the Five Civilized Tribes.

Reformers and Reform Organizations

Board of Indian Commissioners

The Board of Indian Commissioners was a semi-official body of philanthropists appointed by the President, which played an important role in Indian reform. It was established in 1869 and lasted until 1933.

1196. Annual Report of the Board of Indian Commissioners. 1869-1932. Included report of the annual meeting of the Board with representatives of religious societies and annual report of the Lake Mohonk Conference.

1197. Journal of the Second Annual Conference of the Board of Indian Commissioners with the Representatives of the Religious Societies Cooperating with the Government, and Reports of Their Work among the Indians. Washington: Government Printing Office, 1873. This was the only report of the annual meeting with the missionary societies that was not included in the Annual Report of the Board.

1198. Acts of Congress Relating to the Board of Indian Commissioners, and By-Laws of the Board. Washington: Government Printing Office, 1875.

Reports on Indian conditions made by members of the Board are listed under appropriate subject headings. For lives of members of the Board of Indian Commissioners, see the biographies of Bonaparte (9613), Brunot (9633), Dodge (9608 and 9622), Fisk (9618), Moorehead (9638), and Stuart (9634).

Helen Hunt Jackson

Helen Hunt Jackson, a minor literary figure, became interested in Indian reform in 1879 at the time of the Ponca affair and devoted the remaining six years of her life to Indian affairs. Her A Century of Dishonor was a severe indictment of federal Indian policy and brought her to the attention of government officials, who sent her to investigate the condition of the Mission Indians in California. Listed here are works about Mrs. Jackson; her own writings are listed elsewhere under appropriate subject headings.

1199. Byers, John R., Jr. "Helen Hunt Jackson (1830-1885)." American Literary Realism 1870-1910 2 (Summer 1969): 143-148.

1200. Byers, John R., Jr., and Elizabeth S. Byers. "Helen Hunt Jackson (1830-1885):

A Critical Bibliography of Secondary Comment." American Literary Realism 1870-1910 6 (Summer 1973): 197-241.

1201. Davis, Carlyle Channing, and William A. Alderson. The True Story of "Ramona," Its Facts and Fictions, Inspiration and Purpose. New York: Dodge Publishing Company, 1914.

1202. Dobie, J. Frank. "Helen Hunt Jackson and Ramona." Southwest Review 44 (Spring 1959): 93-98.

1203. Goddard, M. LeB. "A Century of Dishonor." Atlantic 47 (April 1881): 572-575.

1204. Higginson, Thomas Wentworth. "Mrs. Helen Jackson ('H. H.')." Century Illustrated Monthly Magazine 31 (December 1885): 251-257.

1205. _____. "Helen Jackson ('H. H.')." In Contemporaries, pp. 142-167. Boston: Houghton, Mifflin and Company, 1899.

1206. McConnell, Virginia. "'H. H.,' Colorado, and the Indian Problem." Journal of the West 12 (April 1973): 272-280.

1207. Martin, Minerva L. "Helen Hunt Jackson in Relation to Her Time." Ph.D. dissertation, Louisiana State University, 1940.

1208. Nevins, Allan. "Helen Hunt Jackson, Sentimentalist vs. Realist." American Scholar 10 (Summer 1941): 269-285.

1209. Odell, Ruth. Helen Hunt Jackson (H. H.). New York: D. Appleton-Century Company, 1939. Includes an exhaustive bibliography of Mrs. Jackson's writings.

Women's National Indian Association (National Indian Association)

Founded in 1879 as the Central Indian Committee and soon called the Indian Treaty-Keeping and Protective Association, the organization took the name Women's National Indian Association in 1883 and in 1901 changed to the National Indian Association. Its work can be studied in the following reports and other publications of and about the Association.

1210. Annual Reports. Volumes 1-58. 1881-1937. Title varies.

1211. Christian Civilization and Missionary Work of the Women's National Indian Association. Philadelphia, 1887.

1212. Dewey, Mary E. Historical Sketch of the Formation and Achievements of the Women's National Indian Association in the United States. Philadelphia: Women's National Indian Association, 1900.

1213. Dickinson, Mrs. J. B. Address of the President, Mrs. J. B. Dickinson, at the Annual Meeting of the Women's National Indian Association, Philadelphia, November 17, 1885. Philadelphia, 1885.

1214. A Few Facts for Workers of the Indian Treaty-Keeping and Protective Association. Philadelphia, 1881.

1215. Foote, Kate. The Indian Legislation of 1888. Philadelphia, n.d.

1216. Johnson, Ellen Terry. Historical Sketch of the Connecticut Indian Association from 1881 to 1888. Hartford: Fowler and Miller Company, 1888.

1217. Missionary Work of the Women's National Indian Association, and Letters of Missionaries. Philadelphia, 1885.

1218. Our Work--What? How? Why? Philadelphia, 1893.

1219. Proceedings on the Occasion of the Presentation of the Petition of the Women's National Indian Association, by Hon. H. L. Dawes, of Massachusetts, in the Senate of the United States, February 21, 1882. Washington, 1882.

1220. Prucha, Francis Paul. "A 'Friend of the Indian' in Milwaukee: Mrs. O. J. Hiles and the Wisconsin Indian Association." Historical Messenger of the Milwaukee County Historical Society 29 (Autumn 1973): 78-95.

1221. Quinton, Amelia S. "Care of the Indian." In Woman's Work in America, edited by Annie Nathan Meyer, pp. 373-391. New York: Henry Holt and Company, 1891.

1222. _____. "The Indian." In The Literature of Philanthropy, edited by Frances A. Goodale, pp. 116-128. New York: Harper and Brothers, 1893.

1223. _____. Indians and Their Helpers. N.p., n.d.

1224. Report on Indian Home Building. Philadelphia, 1888.

1225. Sketch and Plan of the Indian Treaty-Keeping and Protective Association. Philadelphia, 1881.

1226. Sketches of Delightful Work. Philadelphia, 1893.

1227. A Thrilling Record. Philadelphia, 1880.

In 1888 the Association began publication of a monthly paper, chiefly to keep its own membership informed. After the annual reports ceased to be published separately, they were printed in the journal.

1228. The Indian's Friend. 1888-1951. Reports of local auxiliaries of the Association as well as other news of the Association's work can be found from time to time in the periodical Lend a Hand.

Indian Rights Association

The most important of the late nineteenth- and early twentieth-century organizations was the Indian Rights Association, founded in 1882. It carried on an extensive publication program, lobbied in Washington for measures it advocated, and otherwise publicized Indian problems, both through the parent organization and through its branches.

1229. Annual Report of the Executive Committee of the Indian Rights Association. 1883-1934. Title varies. Some of the reports form part of the Association's publications series.

1230. Indian Truth. 1924--. A monthly newsletter published by the Association.

The extensive collection of materials of the Indian Rights Association at the Historical Society of Pennsylvania has been issued on microfilm.

1231. Papers of the Indian Rights Association, 1864 (1882-1968) 1973. Glen Rock, New Jersey: Microfilming Corporation of America, 1973. Contains incoming and outgoing correspondence, organizational matter, Herbert Welsh papers (1877-1934), photographs, and printed annual reports and publications. Also includes papers of the Council on Indian Affairs, 1943-1968. The publisher has issued a Guide to the Microfilm Edition (1975).

The Association issued two series of publications, usually brief pamphlets written by its officers or agents or reprints of pertinent material from newspapers or other sources. Many of these are listed under appropriate subject headings. Those that describe the work of the Association are listed here.

1232. Objects of the Indian Rights Association. Philadelphia: Indian Rights Association, 1884.

1233. Protects Poor Lo: Something about the Indian Rights Association. Philadelphia: Indian Rights Association, 1903.

1234. Sniffen, Matthew K. The Record of Thirty Years: A Brief Statement of the Indian Rights Association, Its Objects, Methods, and Achievements. Philadelphia: Indian Rights Association, 1912.

1235. Welsh, Herbert. A Brief Statement of the Objects, Achievements and Needs of the Indian Rights Association. Philadelphia: Indian Rights Association, 1887.

1236. Why the Work of the Indian Rights Association Should Be Supported. Philadelphia: Indian Rights Association, 1895.

Lake Mohonk Conference

A Quaker member of the Board of Indian Commissioners, Albert K. Smiley, annually invited men and women interested in Indian affairs to his resort hotel at Lake Mohonk, New York. From 1883 to 1916 these Lake Mohonk Conferences of Friends of the Indian served as an important forum for Indian reform proposals. A final meeting was held in 1929.

1237. Proceedings of the . . . Annual Meeting of the Lake Mohonk Conference of Friends of the Indian. 1883-1916, 1929. Title varies. These were published separately by the Conference and were also printed in the annual reports of the Board of Indian Commissioners. The full series has been issued on microfilm by Clearwater Publishing Company, New York.

The following publications tell about the work of the Lake Mohonk Conference.

1238. Abbott, Lyman. "Albert K. Smiley." Outlook 102 (December 14, 1912): 801-803.

1239. Burgess, Larry E. "The Lake Mohonk Conferences on the Indian, 1883-1916." Ph.D. dissertation, Claremont Graduate School, 1972.

1239a. _____. "'We'll Discuss It at Mohonk.'" Quaker History: The Bulletin of Friends Historical Association 40 (Spring 1971): 14-28.

1240. Gates, Merrill E. "Mohonk Indian Conferences." In Handbook of American Indians North of Mexico, edited by Frederick W. Hodge, 1:928-929. 2 volumes. Washington: Government Printing Office, 1907-1910.

1241. "Mohonk and Its Conferences." New England Magazine 16 (June 1897): 447-464.

1242. Partington, Frederick E. The Story of Mohonk. Fulton, New York: Morrill Press, 1911. 2d edition, 1932, contains a second part compiled by Daniel Smiley, Jr., and Albert K. Smiley, Jr., which covers the period 1911-1931.

Other Reformers

Another aspect of the reform movement in the late nineteenth century was the work of Alfred B. Meacham and Dr. Thomas A Bland.

1243. Bland, T. A. Life of Alfred B. Meacham: Together with His Lecture, the Tragedy of the Lava Beds. Washington: T. A. and M. C. Bland, 1883.

1244. National Indian Defence Association. Preamble, Platform, and Constitution of the National Indian Defence Association. Philadelphia: Rufus H. Darby, 1885. Reprinted in Americanizing the American Indians, edited by Francis Paul Prucha, pp. 141-145. Cambridge: Harvard University Press, 1973. Organization directed by Thomas A. Bland.

1245. Phinney, Edward Sterl. "Alfred B. Meacham, Promoter of Indian Reform." Ph.D. dissertation, University of Oregon, 1963.

The following was an important journal devoted to Indian reform. It was founded by Meacham and continued by Bland.

1246. The Council Fire. 1878-1889.

Civil Service Reform

The Indian Rights Association and other reform groups were vitally interested in improving the administration of Indian affairs. One of their chief goals was to bring all Indian department personnel under Civil Service regulations.

1247. Extract, Report of the Special Committee of the National Civil-Service Reform League upon the Present Condition of the Reform Movement and the Relations to It of the National, State, and Municipal Administrations. Philadelphia: Indian Rights Association, 1887.

1248. A Hideous System. Philadelphia: Indian Rights Association, 1890.

1249. Leupp, Francis E. Civil Service Reform Essential to a Successful Indian Administration. Philadelphia: Indian Rights Association, 1895.

1250. _____. Indian School Management: Reply to Attacks by Captain Pratt upon the Introduction of Civil Service Reform Methods. Philadelphia: Indian Rights Association, 1897.

1251. _____. "The Spoilsmen and the Indian Agencies." Nation 65 (October 28, 1897): 333-334.

1252. _____. "The Spoils System and the Indian Service." Public Opinion 18 (May 23, 1895): 570-571.

1253. The Question of Indian Commissioner Oberly's Retention. Philadelphia: Indian Rights Association, 1889.

1254. Welsh, Herbert. "Civil Service Reform in the Indian Service." Good Government 13 (October 15, 1893): 41-43.

1255. _____. A Dangerous Assault upon the Integrity of the Civil Service Law in the Indian Service. Philadelphia: Indian Rights Association, 1893.

1256. _____. "Indian Affairs under the Present Administration." Civil-Service Reformer 4 (August 1888): 90-92.

Mission Indians of California

The plight of the Mission Indians was one of the concerns of the reformers in the late nineteenth century. Helen Hunt Jackson took a special interest in the problem, and the Indian Rights Association followed up on her work.

1257. DuBois, Constance Goddard. The Condition of the Mission Indians of Southern California. Philadelphia: Indian Rights Association, 1901.

1258. Indian Rights Association. The Case of the Mission Indians in Southern California, and the Action of the Indian Rights Association in Supporting the Defense of Their Legal Rights. Philadelphia: Indian Rights Association, 1886.

1259. Jackson, Helen Hunt. "The Present Condition of the Mission Indians in Southern California." Century 26 (August 1883): 511-529.

1260. Jackson, Helen Hunt, and Abbot Kinney. Report of Mrs. Helen Hunt Jackson and Abbot Kinney on the Mission Indians in 1883. Boston: Stanley and Usher, 1887. An abbreviation of the official government report.

1261. _____. Report on the Condition and Needs of the Mission Indians of California, Made by Special Agents Helen Jackson and Abbot Kinney, to the Commissioner of Indian Affairs. Washington: Government Printing Office, 1883.

1262. Painter, Charles C. The Condition of Affairs in Indian Territory and California. Philadelphia: Indian Rights Association, 1888.

1263. _____. A Visit to the Mission Indians of California. Philadelphia: Indian Rights Association, 1887.

1264. _____. A Visit to the Mission Indians of Southern California, and Other Western Tribes. Philadelphia: Indian Rights Association, 1886.

Wild West Shows

One contact of the Indians with the whites in the late nineteenth and early twentieth centuries was their participation in Wild West shows.

1265. Gibson, Arrell M. "Medicine Show." American West 4 (February 1967): 34-39, 74-79.

1266. Gohl, E. H. "The Effect of Wild Westing." Quarterly Journal of the Society of American Indians 2 (July-

September 1914): 226-228.

1267. McNamara, Brooks. "The Indian Medicine Show." Educational Theatre Journal 23 (December 1971): 431-449.

1268. Ralph, Julian. "Behind the 'Wild West' Scenes." Harper's Weekly 38 (August 18, 1894): 775-776.

1269. Russell, Don. "Cody, Kings, and Coronets." American West 7 (July 1970): 4-10, 62.

1270. _____. The Wild West: A History of the Wild West Shows. Fort Worth, Texas: Amon Carter Museum of Western Art, 1970.

1271. Salsbury, Nate. "The Origin of the Wild West Show." Colorado Magazine 32 (July 1955): 205-214.

1272. Sell, Henry Blackman, and Victor Weybright. Buffalo Bill and the Wild West. New York: Oxford University Press, 1955.

1273. Yellow Robe, Chauncey. "The Menace of the Wild West Show." Quarterly Journal of the Society of American Indians 2 (July-September 1914): 224-225.

Current Comment, 1865-1880

Indian affairs in the post-Civil War years were much in the public press, as the policies of peace and war, of civilizing and Christianizing the Indians, and of transfer of the Indian Bureau to the War Department were discussed and debated. The following are representative examples of such writings.

1274. Ainslie, George. "The Indian Question." Presbyterian Quarterly and Princeton Review, new series 4 (July 1875): 438-447.

1275. Bond, Henry F. "The Proposed Indian Policy." Unitarian Review and Religious Magazine 7 (June 1877): 639-655.

1276. Brown, George LeR. "How to Civilize the Indians." Nation 28 (January 9, 1879): 31.

1277. Butler, E. "A Glance at the Indian Question." Catholic World 26 (November 1877): 195-203.

1278. Carrington, Henry B. "The Decotah Tribes: Their Beliefs, and Our Duty to Them Outlined." Proceedings of the American Association for the Advancement of Science 29 (1880): 689-692.

1279. _____. The Indian Question: An Address . . . before the Geographical and Biological Sections of the British Association for the Advancement of Science, at Their Forty-Fifth Meeting, at Bristol, 1875. Boston: Charles H. Whiting, 1884.

1280. Child, Lydia Maria. An Appeal for the Indians. New York: William P. Tomlinson, n.d.

1281. Colyer, Vincent. "Notes among the Indians." Putnam's Magazine 4 (October 1869): 474-480.

1282. _____. Peace with the Apaches of New Mexico and Arizona: Report of Vincent Colyer, Member of the Board of Indian Commissioners, 1871. Washington: Government Printing Office, 1872.

1283. _____. "Shall the Red-Men Be Exterminated? Notes of Tours among the Wilder Tribes of Arizona, New Mexico, Montana, Colorado, and the Indian Territory." Putnam's Magazine 4 (September 1869): 367-374.

1284. Condict, J. Elliot. "Our Indians and the Duty of the Presbyterian Church to Them." Presbyterian Quarterly and Princeton Review, new series 5 (January 1876): 76-93.

1285. Coues, Elliott. "The Western Sphinx: An Analysis of Indian Traits and Tendencies." Penn Monthly 10 (March 1879): 180-193.

1286. Cox, Jacob D. "The Army and Indians." Nation 30 (April 15, 1880): 291-292.

1287. _____. "The Indian Question." International Review 6 (June 1879): 617-634.

1288. Davis, A. C. Frauds of the Indian Office: Argument of A. C. Davis before the Committee on Indian Affairs of the House of Representatives, January 12, 1867. Washington: Intelligencer Printing House, 1867.

1289. Dudley, L. Edwin. "How to Treat the Indians." Scribner's Monthly 10 (August 1875): 484-487.

1290. Girard, P. "Our New Indian Policy and Religious Liberty." Catholic World 26 (October 1877): 90-108.

1291. Gray, W. H. The Moral and Religious Aspect of the Indian Question. Astoria, Oregon: Astorian Book and Job Print, 1879. An anti-Catholic tract.

1292. Gwyther, George. "An Indian Reservation." Overland Monthly 10 (February 1873): 123-134.

1293. Head, Frank H. "Our Ishmaelites." Overland Monthly 4 (February 1870): 105-111.

1294. Hibbetts, J. H. The Indian Problem: Peace, Civilization and Citizenship. Topeka, Kansas: George W. Martin, Kansas Publishing House, 1877. Speech in Kansas State House of Representatives, February 22, 1877.

1295. Hinton, Richard Josiah. "Our Indian

Policy." Nation 2 (January 25, 1866): 102-103.

1296. Holmes, Oliver W., ed. "Peregrinations of a Politician: James A. Garfield's Diary of a Trip to Montana in 1872." Montana, the Magazine of Western History 6 (October 1956): 34-45.

1297. Howard, Guy. "A Practical View of the Indian Problem." Californian 1 (June 1880): 494-498.

1298. "The Indian Bureau Transfer." Nation 28 (January 2, 1879): 7-8.

1299. "Indian Citizenship." Every Saturday 11 (December 30, 1871): 627.

1300. "The Indian Difficulty." Nation 7 (December 31, 1868): 544-546.

1301. "Indian Extermination or Civilization." Republic 2 (May 1874): 308-316.

1302. "The Indian Question." Penn Monthly 5 (November 1874): 828-832.

1303. "The Indian System." North American Review 99 (October 1864): 449-464.

1304. Jackson, Helen Hunt. "The Wards of the United States Government." Scribner's Monthly 19 (March 1880): 775-782.

1305. Joseph, Chief. "An Indian's View of Indian Affairs." North American Review 128 (April 1879): 412-433. Reprinted North American Review 6 (Spring 1969): 56-64.

1306. Kellogg, D. O. "The New Indian Question." American 14 (May 28, 1877): 88-89.

1307. Koch, P. "The Crow Indians and Their Neighbors." Nation 28 (February 13, 1879): 116-117.

1308. Linn, J. M. "The Relation of the Church to the Indian Question." Presbyterian Review 1 (October 1880): 677-693.

1309. Lossing, Benson J. "Our Barbarian Brethren." Harper's New Monthly Magazine 40 (May 1870): 793-811.

1310. Lowe, Charles. "The President's New Indian Policy." Old and New 3 (April 1871): 497-504.

1311. Lowrie, John C. "Our Indian Affairs." Presbyterian Quarterly and Princeton Review, new series 3 (January 1874): 5-22.

1312. MacMahon, Richard Randolph. The Anglo-Saxon and the North American Indian. Baltimore: Kelly, Piet and Company, 1876.

1313. Mallery, Garrick. "The Indian Systems of Canada and the United States." Nation 25 (September 6, 1877): 147-149.

1314. _____. "Otis's Indian Question."

Nation 27 (July 4, 1878): 13-14.

1315. _____. "Our New 'Hostiles.'" Nation 25 (July 12, 1877): 20-21.

1316. "The Management of the Indians." National Quarterly Review 40 (January 1880): 27-40.

1317. Manypenny, George W. Our Indian Wards. Cincinnati: Robert Clarke and Company, 1880.

1318. _____. A Word About Indians. Columbus, Ohio, 1867.

1319. Meacham, Alfred B. "North American Indians." In The Great West: Its Attractions and Resources, pp. 431-444. Bloomington, Illinois: Charles R. Brodix, 1880.

1320. Miles, Nelson A. "The Indian Problem." North American Review 128 (March 1879): 304-314.

1321. Millroy, R. H. "Our Indian Policy Further Considered." Presbyterian Quarterly and Princeton Review, new series 5 (October 1876): 624-628.

1322. Morgan, Lewis Henry. "Factory System for Indian Reservations." Nation 23 (July 27, 1876): 58-59.

1323. _____. "The Hue and Cry against the Indians." Nation 23 (July 20, 1876): 40-41.

1324. _____. "The Indian Question." Nation 27 (November 28, 1878): 332-333.

1325. Neill, Edward D. Effort and Failure to Civilize the Aborigines: Letter to Hon. N. G. Taylor, Commissioner of Indian Affairs, from Edward D. Neill. Washington: Government Printing Office, 1868.

1326. "The New Indian Hostilities." Nation 4 (January 17, 1867): 51-52.

1327. "New Negotiations with the Indians." Merchant's Magazine and Commercial Review 53 (October 1865): 299-304.

1328. New York City Indian Peace Commission. A Thorough Digest of the Indian Question with Suggestions for the Proper Management of the Indians. New York, n.d.

1329. "On the War-Path." Cornhill Magazine 20 (September 1869): 313-326.

1330. Otis, Elwell S. The Indian Question. New York: Sheldon and Company, 1878.

1331. "Our Indian Policy." Nation 2 (January 25, 1866): 102-103; (February 1, 1866): 134-135.

1332. "Our Indian Tribes." Boston Review 2 (September 1862): 517-525.

1333. "Our Indian Wards." Nation 23 (July 13, 1876): 21-22.

1334. Patterson, Robert. "Our Indian

Policy." Overland Monthly 11 (September 1873): 201-214.

1335. The Political Status of the American Indian. N.p., n.d.

1336. Preuss, H. Clay. Columbus Crockett to General Grant on the Indian Policy. Washington: J. Bradley Adams, 1873. A poem.

1337. Pumphrey, Stanley. Indian Civilization: A Lecture by Stanley Pumphrey of England. Philadelphia: Bible and Tract Distributing Society, 1877.

1338. "The Recent Change in the Indian Bureau." Nation 13 (August 17, 1871): 100-101.

1339. "The Red Men of To-Day." Chamber's Journal 49 (November 16, 1872): 721-726.

1340. Reynolds, Grindall. "Our Bedouins: What Can We Do with Them?" Unitarian Review and Religious Magazine 8 (August 1877): 139-162.

1341. Riggs, Alfred L. "What Shall We Do with the Indians?" Nation 5 (October 31, 1867): 356.

1342. Risher, D. W., ed. The Indian and White Man or the Indian in Self-Defense. Indianapolis: Carlon and Hollenbeck, 1880.

1343. Sturgis, Thomas. Common Sense View of the Sioux War, with True Method of Treatment, as Opposed to both the Exterminative and the Sentimental Policy. Waltham, Massachusetts: Hasting's Sentinel Office, 1877.

1344. Trask, J. N. "Indian Affairs." Old and New 8 (August 1873): 232-239.

1345. United States Indian Commission. A Specific Plan for the Treatment of the Indian Question. New York, 1870.

1346. "The Ute Matter." Lippincott's Magazine 25 (March 1880): 373-378.

1347. Walker, Francis A. "The Indian Question." North American Review 116 (April 1873): 329-388. Reprinted in The Indian Question. Boston, 1874.

1348. _____. The Indian Question. Boston: James R. Osgood and Company, 1874.

1349. Welsh, William. Indian Office: Wrongs Doing and Reforms Needed: An Open Letter to President Grant. Philadelphia, 1874.

1350. _____. Report of a Visit to the Sioux and Ponka Indians on the Missouri River, Made by Wm. Welsh to the Secretary of the Interior. Philadelphia: McCalla and Stavely, 1872.

1351. _____. Sales of Indians' Pine Timber. Philadelphia, 1874.

1352. _____. Sioux and Ponca Indians: Reports to the Missionary Organizations of the Protestant Episcopal Church and to the Secretary of the Interior, on Indian Civilization. Philadelphia: McCalla and Stavely, 1870.

1353. _____. Summing up of Evidence before a Committee of the House of Representatives, Charged with the Investigation of Misconduct in the Indian Office. Washington: H. Polkinhorn and Company, 1871.

1354. _____. Taopi and His Friends, or the Indians' Wrongs and Rights. Philadelphia: Claxton, Remsen and Haffelfinger, 1869.

1355. "What Shall Be Done with the Indians?" Pennsylvania School Journal 28 (February 1880): 327-329.

1356. "What Shall We Do with the Indians?" Catholic World 6 (December 1867): 403-407.

1357. What the Government and the Churches Are Doing for the Indians. Washington: Government Printing Office, 1874. A report based on information gathered by the Board of Indian Commissioners.

1358. Williamson, T. S. "The Indian Tribes, and the Duty of the Government to Them." American Presbyterian and Theological Review 13 (October 1864): 587-611.

1359. Williamson, Thomas. "The Indian Question." Presbyterian Quarterly and Princeton Review, new series 5 (October 1876): 608-624.

1360. Woodhull, Alfred Alexander. "One of the Indian Outbreaks." Nation 19 (August 6, 1874): 85-86.

More material in the form of articles, editorials, and book reviews can be located in Poole's Index (148).

Current Comment, 1881-1900

The appearance of new Indian reform organizations after 1880 was an indication of new interest in Indian matters. Pamphlets of the Indian Rights Association and its members and contributions of the reformers to the popular press swelled the output of comment on current Indian affairs.

1361. Abbott, Lyman. "Our Indian Problem." North American Review 167 (December 1898): 719-728.

1362. "The Approaching End of the Indian Problem." Independent 52 (October 25, 1900): 2586-2587.

1363. Armstrong, Samuel C. The Indian

Question. Hampton, Virginia: Normal School Steam Press, 1883.

1364. _____. Report of a Trip Made in Behalf of the Indian Rights Association to Some Indian Reservations of the Southwest. Philadelphia: Indian Rights Association, 1884.

1365. Aubrey, Dr. "The Immediate Future of the North American Indians." Leisure Hour 39 (1890): 449-452.

1366. Bandelier, Adolph F. A. "The Apache Outbreak." Nation 41 (July 2, 1885): 8-9.

1367. _____. "Must We Have Another Indian War?" Nation 42 (May 13, 1886): 397-398.

1368. _____. "Removal of the Apaches from Arizona." Nation 43 (September 9, 1886): 208-209.

1369. Barrows, William. The Indian's Side of the Indian Question. Boston: D. Lothrop Company, 1887.

1370. Bebok, Horace M. "The First Continental Congress of North American Indians." Midland Monthly 11 (February 1899): 102-111.

1371. Bishop, Joseph Bucklin. "Cost of Our Latest Indian War." Nation 52 (January 22, 1891): 63-64.

1372. Bland, T. A. "The New Indian Policy: Land in Severalty." American 14 (May 31, 1887): 73-74.

1373. Bond, H. F. "Exodus of the Utes." Lend a Hand 8 (April 1892): 230-235.

1374. Bradley, A. G. "The Red Man and the White." Macmillan's Magazine 63 (March 1891): 381-391.

1375. Butler, Edward. Essay on Our Indian Question. Chicago: A. B. Sherwood, 1882.

1376. _____. "Our Indian Question." Journal of the Military Service Institution of the United States 2 (1881): 183-221.

1377. Canfield, George F. "Carl Schurz on the Indian Problem." Nation 32 (June 30, 1881): 457-458.

1378. Carson, Charles. "The Indians as They Are." Catholic World 68 (November 1898): 146-160.

1379. Catholic Grievances in Relation to the Administration of Indian Affairs, Being a Report Presented to the Catholic Young Men's National Union, at Its Annual Convention, Held in Boston, Massachusetts, May 10th and 11th, 1882. Richmond, Virginia: Catholic Visitor Print, 1882.

1380. Colyar, A. S. "Indians: Whether They Have Been Justly Dealt with by Our Government." Proceedings of the Bar Association of Tennessee, 1895, pp. 144-160.

1381. Cook, Jessie W. "The Representative Indian." Outlook 65 (May 5, 1900): 80-83.

1382. Cook, Joseph. Frontier Savages, White and Red. Philadelphia: Indian Rights Association, 1885.

1383. _____. "Rights and Wrongs of the Red Men." Our Day 7 (May 1891): 351-360.

1384. Crane, Alice Rollins. "Why the Indians Break Out." Arena 20 (October 1898): 491-498.

1385. Crook, George. Letter from General Crook on Giving the Ballot to the Indians. Philadelphia: Indian Rights Association, 1885.

1386. Crow Creek Reservation, Dakota: Action of the Indian Rights Association, and Opinion of the Press, West and East, Regarding Its Recent Occupation by White Settlers, Together with the Proclamation of the President Commanding the Removal of the Settlers and Restoring the Land to the Indians. Philadelphia: Indian Rights Association, 1885.

1387. Cummings, Lincoln. "The Probable Future of the Indian." Education 10 (December 1889): 234-238.

1388. Cutcheon, Byron M. Indian Civilization. N.p., n.d. Speech delivered in the House of Representatives, March 1886.

1389. Davis, Jefferson. "The Indian Policy of the United States." North American Review 143 (November 1886): 436-446.

1390. Dawes, Henry L. The Case of McGillicuddy: Senator Dawes Explains the Trouble at the Sioux Agencies. Philadelphia: Indian Rights Association, 1884. Reprinted from the Springfield Republican, August 7, 1884.

1391. _____. "Have We Failed with the Indian?" Atlantic Monthly 84 (August 1899): 280-285.

1392. _____. "The Present Crisis." Lend a Hand 11 (November 1893): 346-352.

1393. Day, Sherman. "Civilizing the Indians of California." Overland Monthly, new series 2 (December 1883): 575-581.

1394. Dewey, Mary E. "The Indian Need." Lend a Hand 9 (August 1892): 77-81.

1395. _____. "Present Status of the Indians." Lend a Hand 8 (April 1892): 225-229.

1396. Dodge, Richard Irving. A Living Issue. Washington: Francis B. Mohun, 1882.

1397. _____. Our Wild Indians: Thirty-Three Years' Personal Experience among the Red Men of the Great West. Hartford, Connecticut: A. D. Worthington and Company, 1882.

1398. Eagle, Philip Beresford. "Indian Reservations." Eclectic Magazine of Foreign Literature, Science and Art 130 (March 1898): 303-310.

1399. _____. "Indian Reservations." Gentleman's Magazine 284 (January 1898): 51-63.

1400. Eastman, Elaine Goodale. "The Indian--a Woman among the Indians." In The Literature of Philanthropy, edited by Frances A. Goodale, pp. 129-140. New York: Harper and Brothers, 1893.

1401. Ellis, Charles. "Our Future Indian Policy." Nation 42 (March 11, 1886): 215-216.

1402. Evans, Robert K. "The Indian Question in Arizona." Atlantic Monthly 58 (August 1886): 167-176.

1403. Fletcher, Alice C. "Preparation of the Indian for Citizenship." Lend a Hand 9 (September 1892): 190-198.

1404. Franks, Kenny A., ed. "Among the Plains Tribes in Oklahoma with Frederic Remington." Chronicles of Oklahoma 52 (Winter 1974-1975): 419-438. Reprint of Remington articles from 1889.

1405. "A Fresh Phase of the Indian Problem." Nation 69 (November 16, 1899): 367-368.

1406. A Further Report to the Indian Rights Association on the Proposed Removal of the Southern Utes. Philadelphia: Indian Rights Association, 1892. Report of Francis Fisher Kane and Frank M. Riter.

1407. Galpin, S. A. "Some Administrative Difficulties of the Indian Problem." New Englander and Yale Review 46 (April 1887): 305-318.

1408. Garrett, Philip C. "Change of Administration of the Indian Service." Lend a Hand 11 (November 1893): 328-337.

1409. Gates, Merrill E. "Land and Law as Agents in Educating Indians." Journal of Social Science 21 (September 1886): 113-146.

1410. Gibbon, John. "Our Indian Question." Journal of the Military Service Institution of the United States 2 (1881): 101-120.

1411. _____. "The Transfer of the Indian Bureau to the War Department." American Catholic Quarterly Review 19 (April 1894): 244-259.

1412. "Glimpses of Indian Life at the Omaha Exposition." American Monthly Review of Reviews 18 (October 1898): 436-443.

1413. Godkin, Edwin Lawrence. "A Good Field for Reform." Nation 46 (March 15, 1888): 210-211.

1414. Goodale, Elaine. "How to Americanize the Indian." New Englander and Yale Review 52 (May 1890): 452-455.

1415. _____. "Plain Words on the Indian Question." New England Magazine 2 (April 1890): 146-148.

1416. _____. "A Woman's View of the Indian Troubles." Chautauquan 12 (March 1891): 786-789.

1417. Greene, J. Evarts. "Our Dealings with the Indians." Lend a Hand 17 (August 1896): 128-135.

1418. _____. "Our Dealings with the Indians." Proceedings of the American Antiquarian Society, new series 11 (1896-1897): 23-42.

1419. Greene, Lewis D. "The Army and the Indian." Harper's Weekly 38 (May 19, 1894): 471.

1420. Grinnell, George Bird. The Enforcement of Liquor Laws a Necessary Protection to the Indians. Philadelphia: Indian Rights Association, 1893.

1421. _____. Held Up by the Senate: Indian Service Said to Be Suffering from Petty Politics. Philadelphia: Indian Rights Association, 1896.

1422. _____. "The Indian on the Reservation." Atlantic Monthly 83 (February 1899): 255-267.

1423. _____. The Indians of To-Day. Chicago: Herbert S. Stone and Company, 1900.

1424. _____. "The North American Indian of Today." Cosmopolitan 26 (March 1889): 537-548.

1425. Hamilton, Gail. "The Lion's Side of the Lion Question." North American Review 146 (March 1888): 294-309.

1426. Harriman, Mary Alice. "The Congress of American Aborigines at the Omaha Exposition." Overland Monthly, new series 33 (June 1899): 505-512.

1427. _____. "The Indian in Transition." Overland Monthly, new series 35 (January 1900): 33-39.

1428. Harrison, J. B. "The Indians of the United States." Chautauquan 9 (December 1888): 140-142; (January 1889): 208-210.

1429. Harsha, William Justin. "The Indian Question in the United States." Catholic

Presbyterian 5 (April 1881): 248-256.

1430. _____. "What Next for the Indian?" Lend a Hand 1 (September 1886): 530-532.

1431. Heineman, A. H. "The Indian Question." Open Court 12 (December 1898): 756-760.

1432. Huggins, E. L. "A Suggestion on the Indian Question." Overland Monthly, new series 6 (December 1885): 569-572.

1433. Huntington, C. A. "The Indian Question." Overland Monthly, new series 22 (November 1893): 516-519.

1434. "An Indian Policy." Independent 52 (December 20, 1900): 3058-3059.

1435. Indian Rights Association. The Action of Congress in Regard to the Piegan Indians of Montana. Philadelphia: Indian Rights Association, 1885.

1436. _____. The Attorney-General and Seven Indian Policemen of Cheyenne River Agency--a Case Where to Serve Faithfully Came Near Meaning the Gallows. Philadelphia: Indian Rights Association, 1895.

1437. _____. A Crisis in Indian Affairs. Philadelphia: Indian Rights Association, 1891.

1438. _____. Facts Regarding the Recent Opening to White Settlement of Crow Creek Reservation in Dakota. Philadelphia: Indian Rights Association, n.d.

1439. _____. Friendship That Asks for Pay: Pretended Friends of the Indians and Their Methods. Philadelphia: Indian Rights Association, 1887.

1440. _____. The Honorable Commissioner of Indian Affairs and the Census at Pine Ridge Indian Agency, Dakota. Philadelphia: Indian Rights Association, 1886.

1441. _____. Protest by the Executive Committee of the Indian Rights Association against the Passage of Senator Pettigrew's Bill for the Removal of the Lower Brule Indians to the Rosebud Reserve. Philadelphia: Indian Rights Association, 1893.

1442. Ingersoll, Ernest. "The Red Man in a New Light." Gentleman's Magazine 257 (August 1884): 138-144.

1443. "Is the United States Government a Nuisance to Be Abated?" Catholic World 34 (October 1881): 62-69.

1444. Jackson, Helen Hunt. A Century of Dishonor: A Sketch of the United States Government's Dealings with Some of the Indian Tribes. New York: Harper and Brothers, 1881.

1445. Jacques. "The Indian Question."

Nation 38 (March 20, 1884): 254-255.

1446. Kercheval, George Truman. "The Wrongs of the Ute Indians." Forum 8 (January 1890): 578-585.

1447. La Flesche, Francis. "An Indian Allotment." Independent 52 (November 8, 1900): 2686-2688.

1448. Larned, William Trowbridge. "Effacing the Frontier." Lippincott's Monthly Magazine 55 (May 1895): 647-657.

1449. Leupp, Francis E. "Civilization's" Lesson to "Barbarism": A Dastardly Outrage upon Inoffensive Navajos--Can the Great Father Afford to Ignore It? Philadelphia: Indian Rights Association, 1897.

1450. _____. "A Fresh Phase of the Indian Problem." Nation 69 (November 16, 1899): 367-368.

1451. _____. Notes of a Summer Tour among the Indians of the Southwest. Philadelphia: Indian Rights Association, 1897.

1452. _____. "The Protest of the Pillager Indian." Forum 26 (December 1898): 471-484.

1453. Linn, William Alexander. "The Indians and the Government." Nation 43 (December 23, 1886): 517.

1454. _____. "The Indian's Last Stand." Nation 42 (January 7, 1886): 7.

1455. McNaughton, J. H. "The Red Man." Nineteenth Century 17 (May 1885): 819-826.

1456. Manley, D. "The Catholic Church and the Indian." Catholic World 55 (July 1892): 473-481.

1457. Martin, Sam. "Laws for the Indians." Penn Monthly 11 (October 1890): 808-814.

1458. Marty, Martin. "The Indian Problem and the Catholic Church." Catholic World 48 (February 1889): 577-584.

1459. Mays, Thomas J. "The Future of the American Indian." Popular Science Monthly 33 (May 1888): 104-108.

1460. Meserve, Charles F. A Tour of Observation among Indians and Indian Schools in Arizona, New Mexico, Oklahoma, and Kansas. Philadelphia: Indian Rights Association, 1894.

1461. Miles, Nelson A. "The Future of the Indian Question." North American Review 152 (January 1891): 1-10.

1462. _____. "Our Indian Question." Journal of the Military Service Institution of the United States 2 (1881): 278-292.

1463. Mooney, James. "The Indian Congress at Omaha." American Anthropologist, new series 1 (January 1899): 126-149.

1464. Morgan, Thomas J. "Columbus and the Indians." Independent 44 (June 2, 1892): 754.

1465. _____. The Present Phase of the Indian Question: Also a Memorial on the Extension of Law to the Indians, by the Boston Indian Citizenship Committee. Boston: Boston Indian Citizenship Committee, 1891.

1466. Newlin, James W. M. Proposed Indian Policy. Philadelphia, 1881.

1467. Newlin, Sarah. "Indian Treaties and National Honor." New Princeton Review 2 (September 1886): 223-233.

1468. Oates, James Wyatt. "The Indian Problem--Mr. Schurz Reviewed." Californian 4 (September 1881): 202-212.

1469. "Our Indian Problem and How We Are Solving It." Review of Reviews 5 (June 1892): 551-557.

1470. Owen, G. W. The Indian Question. N.p., 1881.

1471. Painter, Charles C. Cheyennes and Arapahoes Revisited and a Statement of Their Agreement and Contract with Attorneys. Philadelphia: Indian Rights Association, 1893.

1472. _____. Civilization by Removal! The Southern Utes. Philadelphia: Indian Rights Association, 1889.

1473. _____. "An Indian Circumlocution Office." Lend a Hand 1 (January 1886): 86-88.

1474. _____. Oleomargarine versus the Indian. Philadelphia: Indian Rights Association, 1886.

1475. _____. The Proposed Removal of Indians to Oklahoma. Philadelphia: Indian Rights Association, 1887.

1476. _____. "Removal of the Southern Utes." Lend a Hand 5 (April 1890): 258-269.

1477. Pancoast, Henry S. Impressions of the Sioux Tribes in 1882, with Some First Principles in the Indian Question. Philadelphia: Franklin Printing House, 1883.

1478. Peabody, Elizabeth P. Sarah Winnemucca's Practical Solution of the Indian Problem: A Letter to Dr. Lyman Abbott of the "Christian Union." Cambridge, Massachusetts: John Wilson and Son, 1886.

1479. "A Plea for the Indian." Catholic World 42 (March 1886): 848-853.

1480. Pokagon, Simon. "The Future of the Red Man." Forum 23 (August 1897): 698-708.

1481. _____. "An Indian on the Problems of His Race." Review of Reviews 12 (December 1895): 694-695.

1482. Powell, John Wesley. "Are Our Indians Becoming Extinct?" Forum 15 (May 1893): 343-354.

1483. _____. "Proper Training and the Future of the Indians." Forum 18 (January 1895): 622-629.

1484. Powell, William H. "The Indian as a Soldier." United Service: A Monthly Review of Military and Naval Affairs, new series 3 (March 1890): 229-238.

1485. _____. "The Indian Problem." United Service: A Monthly Review of Military and Naval Affairs, new series 5 (April 1891): 329-338.

1486. _____. "Soldier or Granger?" United Service: A Monthly Review of Military and Naval Affairs, new series 2 (November 1889): 445-453.

1487. Pratt, Richard Henry. "Violated Principles the Cause of Failure in Indian Civilization." Journal of the Military Service Institution of the United States 7 (March 1886): 46-60.

1488. Price, Hiram. "The Government and the Indians." Forum 10 (February 1891): 708-715.

1489. Prucha, Francis Paul, ed. Americanizing the American Indians: Writings by the "Friends of the Indian" 1880-1900. Cambridge: Harvard University Press, 1973.

1490. Reed, Joseph P. "In Darkest America." Cosmopolitan 10 (March 1891): 539-548.

1491. Rhoads, James E. "The Indian Question in the Concrete." Lend a Hand 1 (March 1886): 135-139.

1492. _____. Our Next Duty to the Indians. Philadelphia: Indian Rights Association, 1887.

1493. Riggs, Alfred L. "Some Difficulties of the Indian Problem." New Englander and Yale Review 54 (April 1891): 325-334.

1494. "The Rights of the Red Men." Our Day 2 (November 1888): 391-394.

1495. Roosevelt, Theodore. Report of Hon. Theodore Roosevelt Made to the United States Civil Service Commission, upon a Visit to Certain Indian Reservations and Indian Schools in South Dakota, Nebraska, and Kansas. Philadelphia: Indian Rights Association, 1893.

1496. Sanford, George Bliss. "'Thou Art the Man': An Address on the Indian Question in 1892 by Colonel George Bliss Sanford," edited by E. R. Hagemann. Journal of Arizona History 9 (Spring 1968): 30-38.

1497. Schurz, Carl. "Present Aspects of the Indian Problem." North American Review 133 (July 1881): 1-24.

1498. Shea, John Gilmary. "What Right Has the Federal Government to Mismanage the Indians." American Catholic Quarterly Review 6 (July 1881): 520-541.

1499. Smith, Hoke. "Indian Service." Lend a Hand 14 (March 1895): 170-173.

1500. "Some Causes of Indian Wars." Nebraska History 22 (January-March 1941): 103-105. Letter written after Wounded Knee.

1501. Sparhawk, Frances C. "The Indian Question." Education 7 (September 1886): 50-54.

1502. Stimson, F. J. "Law for the Indian." Lend a Hand 8 (January 1892): 5-10.

1503. Sumner, William G. "The Indians in 1887." Forum 3 (May 1887): 254-262.

1504. Terry, Frank. "Naming the Indians." Review of Reviews 15 (March 1897): 301-307.

1505. Thanet, Octave. "The Trans-Mississippi Exposition." Cosmopolitan 25 (October 1898): 598-614.

1506. Thayer, James B. Remarks Made at a Meeting in Cambridge, Mass., Called by the Women's Indian Association of That City, May 3, 1886. N.p., n.d.

1507. _____. Remarks Made before the Worcester Indian Association at Worcester, Mass., February 13, 1887. N.p., n.d.

1508. Tibbles, Susette (Bright Eyes). "Perils and Promises of Indian Citizenship." Our Day 5 (June 1890): 460-471.

1509. Tibbles, Thomas Henry. "A New Government for Indians." Our Day 7 (May 1891): 341-345.

1510. Trant, William. "The Treatment of the Canadian Indians." Westminster Review 144 (November 1895): 506-527.

1511. Welsh, Herbert. Civilization among the Sioux Indians: Report of a Visit to Some of the Sioux Reservations of South Dakota and Nebraska. Philadelphia: Indian Rights Association, 1893.

1512. _____. Four Weeks among Some of the Sioux Tribes of Dakota and Nebraska, Together with a Brief Consideration of the Indian Problem. Germantown, Pennsylvania: Horace F. McCann, 1882.

1513. _____. "The Incoming Administration and the Indian." Lend a Hand 10 (February 1893): 112-118.

1514. _____. "Indian Agents, What Shall We Do with Them?" Lend a Hand 17 (December 1896): 430-436.

1515. _____. The Indian Problem: Secretary Welsh of the Indian Rights Association Reviews and Criticises Dr. Bland's Recent Statements--Dr. Sunderland a Self-Confessed Novice. Philadelphia: Indian Rights Association, 1886.

1516. _____. "The Indian Question Past and Present." New England Magazine, new series 3 (October 1890): 257-266.

1517. _____. The Murrain of Spoils in the Indian Service. New York: National Civil Service Reform League, 1898.

1518. _____. "Partisanship and the Indian." Lend a Hand 1 (March 1886): 130-133.

1519. _____. "Reform for the Indian Service." Lend a Hand 3 (May 1888): 276-278.

1520. _____. Report of a Visit to the Great Sioux Reserve, Dakota, Made during the Months of May and June, 1883, in Behalf of the Indian Rights Association. Philadelphia: Indian Rights Association, 1883.

1521. _____. Report of a Visit to the Navajo, Pueblo, and Hualapais Indians of New Mexico and Arizona. Philadelphia: Indian Rights Association, 1885.

1522. _____. "Some Phases of the Indian Problem." Public Opinion 18 (April 18, 1895): 408-409.

1523. Wickersham, James. "The Indian as a Citizen." American Antiquarian 17 (November 1895): 329-334.

1524. Wilson, George S. "How Shall the American Savage Be Civilized?" Atlantic Monthly 50 (November 1882): 596-607.

1525. Wilson, Ida. "Civilization of the Indians." American Antiquarian 22 (January 1900): 25-31.

1526. Wood, C. E. S. "Our Indian Question." Journal of the Military Service Institution of the United States 2 (1881): 123-181.

1527. Woodruff, Thomas M. "Our Indian Question." Journal of the Military Service Institution of the United States 2 (1881): 293-303.

Other material in the form of articles,

editorials, and book reviews can be located in Poole's Index (148) and in the Nineteenth Century Reader's Guide (149).

INDIAN AFFAIRS, 1901-1932

Current Comment, 1901-1920

The first two decades of the twentieth century were a period of considerable interest in Indian matters--a continuation of the reform agitation of the late nineteenth century. Journals of opinion like the Independent, the Outlook, and the Nation carried numerous articles and editorials on Indian affairs. A good many of these, as well as those from other journals, are listed here, together with other current writings on Indian problems.

1528. Abbott, Lyman. "The Rights of Man, a Study in Twentieth Century Problems: X--American Domestic Problems." Outlook 68 (June 8, 1901): 349-355.

1529. Boas, Franz. "Making the Red Faces White." World Outlook 4 (January 1918): 6.

1530. Brosius, S. M. A New Indian Policy-- the Red Man's Rights in Jeopardy. Philadelphia: Indian Rights Association, 1902.

1531. _____. "Turning the Indian Loose." Case and Comment 23 (February 1917): 739-741.

1532. "Can the Indian Problem Be Settled?" Outlook 83 (June 9, 1906): 305.

1533. Chapman, Arthur. "Indian Lands for the White Men." World To-Day 9 (September 1905): 980-983.

1534. Clark, Howard A. "Conditions among the Navajo Indians." Missionary Review of the World 40 (December 1917): 917-922.

1535. Cole, Evangeline. "The Red Man's Burden." World Outlook 4 (January 1918): 14.

1536. "Commissioner Leupp's Service." Independent 67 (July 8, 1909): 98-99.

1537. Crissey, Forrest. "Renaming the Indians." World To-Day 10 (January 1906): 84-90.

1538. Curtis, Edward S. "The Vanishing Red Man: Inhumanity of the White Man toward the North American Indian." Hampton Magazine 28 (May 1912): 245-253, 308.

1539. "Dealing with Indians Individually." Independent 59 (December 15, 1905): 1419-1420.

1540. Decker, A. "Making the Warrior a Worker." Munsey's Magazine 26 (October

1901): 88-95.

1541. Dixon, Joseph K. "The Indian." Case and Comment 23 (February 1917): 712-716.

1542. _____. The Vanishing Race: The Last Great Indian Council. Garden City, New York: Doubleday, Page and Company, 1913.

1543. Donehoo, George P. "The Real Indian of the Past and the Real Indian of the Present." Red Man 5 (February 1913): 227-232.

1544. Draper, William R. "The Indian as a Farmer." Harper's Weekly 45 (July 20, 1901): 725.

1545. _____. "The Indians as Farmers." Current History and Modern Culture 12 (March 1902): 199-202.

1546. Eastman, Charles A. "The Indian and the Moral Code." Outlook 97 (January 7, 1911): 30-34.

1547. _____. "The Indian as a Citizen." Lippincott's 95 (January 1915): 70-76.

1548. _____. The Indian To-Day: The Past and Future of the First American. Garden City, New York: Doubleday, Page and Company, 1915.

1549. Eliot, Samuel A., and William H. Ketcham. Report on Conditions among the Papago Indians. Washington, 1914.

1550. Forbes-Lindsay, C. H. "The North American Indian as a Laborer: His Value as a Worker and a Citizen." Craftsman 14 (May 1908): 146-157.

1551. Foreman, Grant. "Plight of the Full Blood Indians." Overland Monthly 63 (March 1914): 240-243.

1552. Frank, Glenn. "A Vanishing Race Comes Back." Century Magazine 99 (April 1920): 800-801.

1553. "'Friends of the Indian.'" Nation 81 (October 26, 1905): 332-333.

1554. Funsten, James Bowen. "The Indian as a Worker." Outlook 81 (December 9, 1905): 875-878.

1555. Garland, Hamlin. "The Red Man's Present Needs." North American Review 174 (April 1902): 476-488.

1556. Gilmore, Melvin R. "The Victory Dance of the Dakota Indians at Fort Yates on the Standing Rock Reservation in November, 1918." Papers of the Michigan Academy of Science, Arts and Letters 18 (1933): 23-30.

1557. "The Gospel of Work for the Indians." Nation 79 (October 6, 1904): 273.

1558. Harvey, Charles M. "The Epic of the Indian." Atlantic Monthly 111 (January 1913): 118-128.

1559. _____. "The Indian of To-Day and To-Morrow." American Monthly Review of Reviews 33 (June 1906): 696-705.

1560. _____. "The Last Race Rally of Indians." World's Work 8 (May 1904): 4803-4809.

1561. Henshaw, Henry W. "Popular Fallacies Respecting the Indian." American Anthropologist 7 (January-March 1905): 104-113.

1562. Hough, Emerson. "The Last Stand of the Indian: The Nation's Wards and What the Nation Has Done to Them--the Agency System--Reservations--Present Status in Oklahoma." Hampton's Magazine 22 (April 1909): 515-526.

1563. Hrdlicka, Ales. "The Vanishing Indian." Science 46 (September 14, 1917): 266-267.

1564. "The Indian Lands Investigation." Outlook 95 (August 20, 1910): 852-853.

1565. "The Indian Question." Outlook 75 (September 19, 1903): 149-151.

1566. Indian Rights Association. Chippewa Indians Threatened. Philadelphia: Indian Rights Association, 1916.

1567. _____. Imprisonment without Trial. Philadelphia: Indian Rights Association, 1909.

1568. _____. The Johnson Bill. Philadelphia: Indian Rights Association, 1916.

1569. _____. The Present Situation of Indian Affairs. Philadelphia: Indian Rights Association, 1912.

1570. _____. Responsibility for Indian Management. Philadelphia: Indian Rights Association, 1914.

1571. _____. A Threatened Raid on the Crow Indian Lands. Philadelphia: Indian Rights Association, 1916.

1572. _____. What We Should Do for the Indian: Recommendations of the Conference of the Friends of the Indian, Held at Philadelphia, January 22-23, 1919. Philadelphia: Indian Rights Association, 1919.

1573. "Indians as Wards." Independent 64 (February 13, 1908): 380-381.

1574. "The Indian Warehouses." Nation 90 (February 24, 1910): 178-179.

1575. "Interior Department and the Indians." Outlook 76 (March 19, 1904): 679-680.

1576. Jackson, Joseph. "The Upward March of the Indian." Southern Workman 39 (April 1910): 242-245.

1577. Jacob, Harvey D. "Uncle Sam--the Great White Father." Case and Comment 23 (February 1917): 703-709.

1578. Jones, William A. "A New Indian Policy." World's Work 3 (March 1902): 1838-1840.

1579. Kennan, George. "Have Reservation Indians Any Vested Rights?" Outlook 70 (March 29, 1902): 759-765.

1580. _____. "Have the Standing Rock Indians Been Fairly Treated?: A Reply to Commissioner Jones's Letter." Outlook 71 (May 3, 1902): 90-96.

1581. _____. "Indian Lands and Fair Play." Outlook 76 (February 27, 1904): 498-501.

1582. _____. "Settlement of the Standing Rock Indian Case." Outlook 72 (December 13, 1902): 907-908.

1583. Lane, Franklin K. "From the War-Path to the Plow." National Geographic Magazine 27 (January 1915): 73-87.

1584. Leupp, Francis E. "Back to Nature for the Indian." Charities and the Commons 20 (June 6, 1908): 336-340.

1585. _____. "The Failure of the Educated American Indian." Appleton's Booklover's Magazine 7 (May 1906): 594-602.

1586. _____. "The Gospel of Work for the Indians." Nation 79 (October 6, 1904): 273.

1587. _____. The Indian and His Problem. New York: Charles Scribner's Sons, 1910.

1588. _____. "Indian Lands: Their Administration with Reference to Present and Future Use." Annals of the American Academy of Political and Social Science 33 (May 1909): 620-630.

1589. _____. "The Indian Land Troubles and How to Solve Them." American Review of Reviews 42 (October 1910): 468-472.

1590. _____. "Is Uncle Sam a Good Indian Chief?" World Outlook 4 (January 1918): 8.

1591. _____. "'Law or No Law' in Indian Administration." Outlook 91 (January 30, 1909): 261-263. Reply of Carl E. Grammer (March 20, 1909): 629-630.

1592. _____. "The New Indian." Nation 79 (July 21, 1904): 47-48.

1593. _____. "Our 'New Policy' with the Red Brother." Nation 79 (September 15, 1904): 211-212.

1594. _____. "Outlines of an Indian Policy." Outlook 79 (April 15,

1905): 946-950.

1595. _____. "The Story of Four Strenuous Years." Outlook 92 (June 5, 1909): 328-331.

1596. _____. "Woman in the Indian Service." Delineator 75 (June 1910): 484-485, 550-551.

1597. Lindquist, G. E. E. "Urgent Needs of American Indians." Missionary Review of the World 43 (November 1920): 988-994.

1598. Lummis, Charles F. Bullying the Moqui. Edited with an introduction by Robert Easton and Mackenzie Brown. Prescott, Arizona: Prescott College Press, 1968. A collection of pieces written by Lummis for Out West, April to October 1903.

1599. _____. "The Indian of Commerce." Nation 72 (April 18, 1901): 319-320.

1600. _____. "A New Indian Policy." Land of Sunshine 15 (December 1901): 457-464.

1601. McKenzie, Fayette Avery. "The American Indian of Today and Tomorrow." Journal of Race Development 3 (October 1912): 135-155.

1602. _____. "The Indian and His Problem." Dial 49 (October 1, 1910): 228-230.

1603. _____. The Indian in Relation to the White Population of the United States. Columbus, Ohio, 1908.

1604. Millard, Thomas F. "The Passing of the American Indian." Forum 34 (January-March 1903): 466-480.

1605. Moffett, Thomas C. "Americanizing the First American." World Outlook 4 (October 1918): 15-17.

1606. "Mohonk Conference and the Vreeland Bill." Outlook 72 (November 8, 1902): 569-570.

1607. Mooney, James. "The Passing of the Indian." Proceedings of the Second Pan American Scientific Congress, Washington, U.S.A., Monday, December 27, 1915, to Saturday, January 8, 1916: Section 1, Anthropology, 1:174-179.

1608. "Mr. Leupp and Mr. Valentine." Outlook 92 (June 26, 1909): 421.

1609. "The Nation's Wards." Independent 61 (October 25, 1906): 1007-1009.

1610. "The Navajo Reservation." Nation 95 (August 1, 1912): 96-97.

1611. "A New Indian Question: Can the State Protect the Indians." Outlook 108 (September 9, 1914): 62-63.

1612. "A New Step in Our Indian Policy."

Outlook 116 (May 23, 1917): 136.

1613. Oskison, John N. "In Governing the Indian, Use the Indian!" Case and Comment 23 (February 1917): 722-726.

1614. _____. "Making an Individual of the Indian." Everybody's Magazine 16 (June 1907): 723-733.

1615. _____. "Remaining Causes of Indian Discontent." North American Review 184 (March 1, 1907): 486-493.

1616. "Our New Policy with the Red Brother." Nation 79 (September 15, 1904): 211-212.

1617. "Our 'Subject' Races." Outlook 75 (October 31, 1903): 482-484.

1618. Parker, Arthur C. "The Social Elements of the Indian Problem." American Journal of Sociology 22 (September 1916): 252-267.

1619. "The Passing of Rations." Independent 54 (December 11, 1902): 2976-2977.

1620. "Personal Equation in Indian Legislation." Independent 54 (April 17, 1902): 944-945.

1621. Pratt, Richard Henry. "The Indian No Problem." Missionary Review of the World 33 (November 1910): 851-856.

1622. _____. "Our Indian Policy." Journal of Education 83 (February 24, 1916): 203-204.

1623. _____. Why Most of Our Indians Are Dependent and Non-Citizen. N.p., n.d. Paper read at Lake Mohonk Conference, October 16, 1914.

1624. "The Redskin as Laborer and Agriculturist." American Review of Reviews 37 (June 1908): 728-729.

1625. Roe, Walter C. "The Mohonk Lodge: An Experience in Indian Work." Outlook 68 (May 18, 1901): 176-178.

1626. Scoville, Annie Beecher. "The Field Matron's Mission." Outlook 68 (August 24, 1901): 975-978.

1627. "Self-Help for Indians." Outlook 84 (December 1, 1906): 798-799.

1628. Seton, William. "The Indians since the Revolution." Catholic World 73 (August 1901): 641-651.

1629. "Shall the Indian Be Made a Citizen?" Chautauquan 34 (January 1902): 360-361.

1630. Sniffen, Matthew K. The Meaning of the Ute "War." Philadelphia: Indian Rights Association, 1915.

1631. _____. Observation among the Sioux. Philadelphia: Indian Rights Association, 1906.

1632. _____. A Problem "Over Here."
Philadelphia: Indian Rights Association,
1919.

1633. Sparhawk, Frances Campbell. "The
Indian's Yoke." North American Review
182 (January 1906): 50-61.

1634. Sweet, Evander M. "Richest People in
the World." World To-Day 5 (November
1903): 1454-1458. Osage Indians.

1635. "A Trust Not Trustworthy." Independent 56 (February 25, 1904): 450-451.

1636. Valentine, Robert G. "Making Good
Indians." Sunset 24 (June 1910): 598-
611.

1637. Welsh, Herbert. Vicious Indian Legislation: A Brief Analysis of Bills Now
Pending in Congress That Ought to Be Defeated. Philadelphia: Indian Rights
Association, 1916.

1638. Wood, Frank. "The Evils of the Reservation System." Outlook 75 (September 19, 1903): 164-166.

Indian Affairs in the 1920s

Considering the dramatic attack made upon
federal Indian policy and administration in
the 1920s, surprisingly little historical
work has been done on the period. Included
here is the famous Meriam report of 1928.

1639. Downes, Randolph C. "A Crusade for
Indian Reform, 1922-1934." Mississippi
Valley Historical Review 32 (December
1945): 331-354.

1640. Meriam, Lewis, and others. The Problem of Indian Administration. Institute
for Government Research, Studies in Administration. Baltimore: Johns Hopkins
Press, 1928.

1641. Philp, Kenneth R. "Albert B. Fall
and the Protest from the Pueblos, 1921-
23." Arizona and the West 12 (Autumn
1970): 237-254.

1642. _____. "Herbert Hoover's New Era:
A False Dawn for the American Indian,
1929-1932." Rocky Mountain Social
Science Journal 9 (April 1972): 53-60.

1643. _____. "John Collier and the
Crusade to Protect Indian Religious Free-
dom, 1920-1926." Journal of Ethnic
Studies 1 (Spring 1973): 22-38.

1644. Quinten, B. T. "Oklahoma Tribes, the
Great Depression and the Indian Bureau."
Mid-America 49 (January 1967): 29-43.

1645. Szasz, Margaret Garretson. "Indian
Reform in a Decade of Prosperity."
Montana, the Magazine of Western History
20 (Winter 1970): 16-27.

For an appreciation of the enthusiasm for
reform in Indian policy in this period, see
the items listed under Current Comment,
1921-1932.

Current Comment, 1921-1932

The attempt of the government to support land claims of white settlers on
Pueblo lands touched off a new wave of agitation for Indian rights. Led by John
Collier, the reformers filled popular
magazines with attacks upon the Indian
Bureau and with support of the Pueblos.
These writings and other current comment
during the 1920s are listed here.

1646. "The Administration of Indian Affairs." School and Society 29 (January
19, 1929): 80-81.

1647. "Are the Pueblo Indians to Be Robbed
of Their Heritage?" Current Opinion 74
(February 1923): 213-214.

1648. Atwood, Stella M. "The Case for the
Indian." Survey 49 (October 1922):
7-11, 57.

1649. _____. "The S.O.S. of the Pimas:
They Must Have Water for Their Crops to
Avoid Starvation and Beggary." Sunset
Magazine 50 (April 1923): 24.

1650. Austin, Mary. "Our Indian Problem:
The Folly of the Officials." Forum 71
(March 1924): 281-288.

1651. _____. "Why Americanize the Indian?" Forum 82 (September 1929): 167-173.

1652. Black, Ruby A. "A New Deal for
the Red Man." Nation 130 (April 2,
1930): 388-390.

1653. Blanchard, Frances A. "The De-
plorable State of Our Indians." Current
History 18 (July 1923): 630-636.

1654. Bonnin, Gertrude, Charles H. Fabens,
and Matthew K. Sniffen. Oklahoma's
Poor Rich Indians: Legalized Robbery,
an Orgy of Graft and Exploitation of the
Five Civilized Tribes. Philadelphia:
Indian Rights Association, 1924.

1655. Brickman, Helen M. "The American
Indian Moves Ahead." Missionary Review
of the World 54 (October 1931): 778-780.

1656. _____. "A New Day for the American Indian." Missionary Review of the
World 52 (July 1929): 551-554.

1657. Brown, John R. "Citizens--and
Wards Too." Survey 54 (April 15, 1925):
95-97.

1658. Burke, Charles H. "Indians Making
Progress in Learning the White Man's
Way." School Life 9 (June 1924): 239-
242.

1659. Burleson, Hugh L. "Our Predecessor, the Indian." Missionary Review of the World 55 (July-August 1932): 391-394.

1660. Bynner, Witter. "'From Him That Hath Not.'" Outlook 133 (January 17, 1923): 125-127.

1661. Cole, Fay-Cooper. "The Relation of Anthropology to Indian and Immigrant Affairs." Science 71 (March 7, 1930): 249-253.

1662. Collett, Frederick G. "Undelivered Pottage." Survey 48 (April 29, 1922): 135-139.

1663. Collier, John. "'The Accursed System.'" Sunset 52 (June 1924): 15-16, 80-82.

1664. _____. "The American Congo." Survey 50 (August 1923): 467-476.

1665. _____. "America's Treatment of Her Indians." Current History 18 (August 1923): 771-781.

1666. _____. "Are We Making Red Slaves?" Survey 57 (January 1, 1927): 453-455, 474-480.

1667. _____. "Do Indians Have Rights of Conscience?" Christian Century 42 (March 12, 1925): 346-349.

1668. _____. "The Fate of the Navajos." Sunset 52 (January 1924): 11-13, 60-62, 73-74.

1669. _____. "The Flathead Water Power Lease." New Republic 64 (August 20, 1930): 20-21.

1670. _____. "Hammering at the Prison Door." Survey 60 (July 1, 1928): 389, 402-405.

1671. _____. "Helping the Indian." Forum 82 (October 1929): li-lii.

1672. _____. "The Indian Bureau's Record." Nation 135 (October 5, 1932): 303-305.

1673. _____. "Monopoly in Montana." New Freeman 1 (May 3, 1930): 178-180.

1674. _____. "Navajos." Survey 51 (January 1, 1924): 333-338, 363, 365.

1675. _____. "Needs in Administration of Indian Property." Proceedings of the National Conference of Social Work, 1932, pp. 627-639.

1676. _____. "'No Trespassing.'" Sunset 50 (May 1923): 14-15, 58-60.

1677. _____. "Our Indian Policy." Sunset 50 (March 1923): 13-15, 89-93.

1678. _____. "Persecuting the Pueblos." Sunset 53 (July 1924): 50, 92-93.

1679. _____. "Plundering the Pueblo Indians." Sunset 50 (January 1923): 21-25, 56.

1680. _____. "The Pueblos' Land Problem." Sunset 51 (November 1923): 15, 101.

1681. _____. "The Pueblos' Last Stand." Sunset 50 (February 1923): 19-22, 65-66.

1682. _____. "The Red Atlantis." Survey 48 (October 1922): 15-20, 63, 66.

1683. _____. "The Red Slaves of Oklahoma." Sunset 52 (March 1924): 9-11, 94-100.

1684. _____. "Senators and Indians." Survey Graphic 61 (January 1, 1929): 425-428, 457.

1685. _____. "The Vanquished Indian." Nation 126 (January 11, 1928): 38-41.

1686. Connolly, Vera L. "The Cry of a Broken People." Good Housekeeping 88 (February 1929): 30-31+.

1687. _____. "The End of the Road." Good Housekeeping 88 (May 1929): 44-45+.

1688. _____. "We Still Get Robbed." Good Housekeeping 88 (March 1929): 34-35+.

1689. Corey, Herbert. "He Carries the White Man's Burden." Collier's 71 (May 12, 1923): 13. Commissioner of Indian Affairs Charles H. Burke.

1690. Cornelison, J. M. "American Indians Yesterday and Today." Missionary Review of the World 51 (September 1928): 713-716.

1691. Dare, Helen. "Justice or Jujubes." Survey 48 (May 20, 1922): 269-288.

1692. DuPuy, William Atherton. "New Policy of Aiding the American Indian." Current History 32 (September 1930): 1138-1143.

1693. Eastman, Elaine Goodale. "Our New-Old Indian Policy." Christian Century 46 (November 27, 1929): 1471-1473.

1694. Fergusson, Erna. "Senators Investigate Indians." American Mercury 23 (August 1931): 464-468.

1695. Fergusson, Harvey. "The Cult of the Indian." Scribner's Magazine 88 (August 1930): 129-133.

1696. Gessner, Robert. Massacre: A Survey of Today's American Indian. New York: Jonathan Cope and Harrison Smith, 1931.

1697. Harlow, Rex F. "American Indians Facing a New Era." Current History 23 (January 1926): 512-517.

1698. Henderson, Alice Corbin. "The Death of the Pueblos." New Republic 33 (November 22, 1922): 11-13.

1699. Hermilt, John, and Louis Judge. "Wenatchee Indians Ask Justice." Washington Historical Quarterly 16 (January 1925): 20-28.

1700. Hulbert, Winifred. Indian Americans. New York: Friendship Press, 1932.

1701. Ickes, Harold. "The Federal Senate and Indian Affairs." Illinois Law Review 24 (January 1930): 570-578. Reply by John H. Wigmore, pp. 578-579.

1702. "Improper Guardianship." Nation 134 (February 3, 1932): 132.

1703. Johnson, William E. "Those Sacred Indian Ceremonials." Native American 24 (September 20, 1924): 173-177.

1704. "Justice for the Pueblo Indians." Science 56 (December 8, 1922): 665-666.

1705. Kane, Francis Fisher. "East and West: The Atlantic City Conference on the American Indian." Survey 61 (January 15, 1929): 472-474.

1706. Kelly, M. Clyde. "The Indian and His Master." Sunset 49 (December 1922): 17-18, 66.

1707. Lansdale, Robert T. "The Place of the Social Worker in the Indian Service Program." Proceedings of the National Conference of Social Work, 1932, pp. 609-616.

1708. Littell, Robert. "Indian Agency." Forum 86 (December 1931): 367-373.

1709. Moffett, Thomas C. "Live Issues in Indian Affairs." Missionary Review of the World 49 (August 1926): 634-636.

1711. "Our Duty to the Indian." Forum 71 (April 1924): 551-557.

1712. Owl, W. David. "Remaking the American Indian." Religious Education 26 (February 1931): 115-118.

1713. Parker, Arthur C. "The Attitude of the American Indian to American Life." Religious Education 26 (February 1931): 111-114.

1714. "The Pueblos Plea for Justice." Literary Digest 76 (February 17, 1923): 17.

1715. "The Red Man's Burden." New Republic 52 (October 19, 1927): 226-227.

1716. Reilly, Louis W. "The Indians of To-Day." Catholic World 125 (September 1927): 763-770.

1717. Renehan, A. B. The Pueblo Indians and Their Land Grants. Albuquerque: T. Hughes, 1923.

1718. Rhoads, Charles J. "The General Administration of Indian Affairs." Proceedings of the National Conference of Social Work, 1932, pp. 602-608.

1719. _____. "Report of the Commissioner of Indian Affairs." School and Society 32 (August 16, 1930): 221-222.

1720. Ross, Mary. "The New Indian Administration." Survey 64 (June 15, 1930): 268-269.

1721. Schultze, James Willard. "America's Red Armenians." Sunset 49 (November 1922): 17-19, 70-74.

1722. Scott, Hugh L. "The Paiute 'Uprising': The Indian Bureau Is Responsible for the Fighting between White and Red Men in Southern Utah." Sunset 50 (June 1923): 38-39, 118.

1723. Sergeant, Elizabeth Shepley. "Christmas in the Pueblos." Survey 51 (December 1, 1923): 252-256, 288-290, 294.

1724. _____. "Plight of the Pueblos." New Republic 37 (December 26, 1923): 121-122.

1725. _____. "The Red Man's Burden." New Republic 37 (January 16, 1924): 199-201.

1726. Seymour, Flora Warren. "Let My People Go." Outlook 141 (November 18, 1925): 441-444.

1727. _____. "Our Indian Problem: The Delusion of the Sentimentalists." Forum 71 (March 1924): 273-280.

1728. _____. "Red Man and White." Religious Education 26 (February 1931): 104-110.

1729. Sniffen, Matthew K. "Out of Thine Own Mouth," An Analysis of the House Subcommittee Report Denying and Confirming the Looting of Oklahoma's "Poor Rich Indians." Philadelphia: Indian Rights Association, 1925.

1730. Spinden, Herbert J. "What about the Indian?" World's Work 47 (February 1924): 377-388.

1731. Villard, Oswald Garrison. "For the Indian's Sake." Nation 117 (December 26, 1923): 734-735.

1732. Ward, Alice May. "Red Tragedies: The Experiences of a Field Matron on the Cheyenne Reservation of Montana." Sunset 50 (April 1923): 22-23, 80-81.

1733. White, Amelia E. "The Pueblo Titles." Survey 55 (March 15, 1926): 702-704. Includes reply by John Collier.

1734. White, Stewart Edward. "Our Treatment of the Indians." Sunset 49 (November 1922): 16

1735. Wigmore, John H. "The Federal Senate as a Fifth Wheel." Illinois Law Review 24 (May 1929): 89-96.

1736. Wilbur, Ray Lyman. "The Indian Problem Approaches Solution." Missionary Review of the World 55 (July-August 1932): 399-400.

1737. _____. "A New Day for the Indian." New York Herald Tribune Magazine, May 24, 1931, pp. 1-2, 12. This article also appeared in other newspapers.

1738. Wilbur, Ray Lyman, as told to W. A. DuPuy. "Uncle Sam Has a New Indian Policy." Saturday Evening Post 201 (June 8, 1929): 5, 136-137.

1739. Woehlke, Walter V. "The Filipino and the Indian." Sunset 50 (April 1923): 25, 87-88.

1740. _____. "Hope for the Blackfeet." Sunset 51 (December 1923): 9-11, 97-100.

1741. _____. "'Let 'em Die!'" Sunset 51 (July 1923): 14-15.

1742. _____. "Poisoning the Navajos with Oil." Sunset 51 (August 1923): 11, 91-92.

1743. Work, Hubert. "Our American Indians." Saturday Evening Post 196 (May 31, 1924): 27, 92-98.

1744. Yard, Robert Sterling. "Parks and Indians." Outlook 133 (January 17, 1923): 124-125.

Other material for the period can be located in the Readers' Guide (150).

INDIAN AFFAIRS, 1933-1945

The Indian New Deal

The dissatisfaction with Indian conditions that was so clearly seen in the 1920s culminated in a radical new Indian policy in the 1930s. Led by John Collier, Commissioner of Indian Affairs from 1933 to 1945, the federal government inaugurated a "New Deal" for the Indians, of which the Wheeler-Howard Act of May 15, 1934, was the essential piece of legislation. Because of John Collier's dominant role as architect of the new policies and programs, works about him are placed here, although much of his work for the Indian cause antedated his appointment as commissioner.

1745. Bach, Arthur L. "Administration of Indian Resources in the United States, 1933-1941." Ph.D. dissertation, University of Iowa, 1942.

1746. Brown, Ray A. "The United States of America's New Departure in Dealing with

Its Native Indian Population." Journal of Comparative Legislation and International Law 18 (February 1936): 129-132.

1747. Collier, John. "Collier Replies to Mekeel." American Anthropologist 46 (July-September 1944): 422-426.

1748. _____. From Every Zenith: A Memoir and Some Essays on Life and Thought. Denver: Sage Books, 1963. An autobiographical account.

1749. _____. "The Genesis and Philosophy of the Indian Reorganization Act." In Indian Affairs and the Indian Reorganization Act: The Twenty Year Record, edited by William H. Kelly, pp. 2-8. Tucson: University of Arizona, 1954.

1750. Dobyns, Henry F. "The Indian Reorganization Act and Federal Withdrawal." Applied Anthropology 7 (Spring 1948): 35-44.

1751. _____. "Therapeutic Experience of Responsible Democracy." In The American Indian Today, edited by Stuart Levine and Nancy Oestreich Lurie, pp. 171-185. Deland, Florida: Everett/Edwards, 1968. This appeared originally in Midcontinent American Studies Journal 6 (Fall 1965): 171-186. An evaluation of John Collier's program.

1752. Foley, Rudolph X. "The Origins of the Indian Reorganization Act of 1934." Ph.D. dissertation, Fordham University, 1937.

1753. Garry, Joseph R. "The Indian Reorganization Act and the Withdrawal Program." In Indian Affairs and the Indian Reorganization Act: The Twenty Year Record, edited by William H. Kelly, pp. 35-37. Tucson: University of Arizona, 1954.

1754. Gower, Calvin W. "The CCC Indian Division: Aid for Depressed Americans, 1933-1942." Minnesota History 43 (Spring 1972): 3-13.

1755. Haas, Theodore H. "The Indian Reorganization Act in Historical Perspective." In Indian Affairs and the Indian Reorganization Act: The Twenty Year Record, edited by William H. Kelly, pp. 9-25. Tucson: University of Arizona, 1954.

1756. Kelly, Lawrence C. "Choosing the New Deal Indian Commissioner: Ickes vs. Collier." New Mexico Historical Review 49 (October 1974): 269-288.

1757. Kelly, William H., ed. Indian Affairs and the Indian Reorganization Act: The Twenty Year Record. Tucson: University of Arizona, 1954. From a symposium held in conjunction with the meeting of the American Anthropological Association, December 30, 1953.

1758. Kinney, J. P. "E. C. W. on Indian Reservations." Journal of Forestry 31 (December 1933): 911-913. Indian Emergency Conservation Work.

1759. _____. Facing Indian Facts. Laurens, New York: Press of the Village Printer, 1973. A bitter attack on Collier's policies written in 1954.

1760. Kluckhohn, Clyde, and Robert Hackenberg. "Social Science Principles and the Indian Reorganization Act." In Indian Affairs and the Indian Reorganization Act: The Twenty Year Record, edited by William H. Kelly, pp. 29-34. Tucson: University of Arizona, 1954.

1761. Kunitz, Stephen J. "The Social Philosophy of John Collier." Ethnohistory 18 (Summer 1971): 213-229.

1762. Mekeel, Scudder. "An Appraisal of the Indian Reorganization Act." American Anthropologist 46 (April-June 1944): 209-217.

1763. Parman, Donald L. "The Indian and the Civilian Conservation Corps." Pacific Historical Review 40 (February 1971): 39-57.

1764. _____. "The Indian Civilian Conservation Corps." Ph.D. dissertation, University of Oklahoma, 1967.

1765. Philp, Kenneth R. "John Collier and the American Indian, 1920-1945." Ph.D. dissertation, Michigan State University, 1968. A revision in book form is forthcoming.

1766. _____. "John Collier and the American Indian, 1920-1945." In Essays on Radicalism in Contemporary America, edited by Leon Borden Blair, pp. 63-80. Austin: University of Texas Press, 1972.

1767. Smith, Michael T. "The Wheeler-Howard Act of 1934: The Indian New Deal." Journal of the West 10 (July 1971): 521-534.

1768. Taylor, Graham D. "Anthropologists, Reformers, and the Indian New Deal." Prologue: The Journal of the National Archives 7 (Fall 1975): 151-162.

1769. _____. "The Tribal Alternative to Bureaucracy: The Indian's New Deal, 1933-1945." Journal of the West 13 (January 1974): 128-142.

1770. "Tribal Self-Government and the Indian Reorganization Act of 1934." Michigan Law Review 70 (April 1972): 955-986.

1771. Wesley, Clarence. "Tribal Self-Government under the IRA." In Indian Affairs and the Indian Reorganization Act: The Twenty Year Record, edited by William H. Kelly, pp. 26-28. Tucson:

University of Arizona, 1954.

1772. Wright, Peter M. "John Collier and the Oklahoma Indian Welfare Act of 1936." Chronicles of Oklahoma 50 (Autumn 1972): 347-371.

1773. Young, Donald. Research Memorandum on Minority Peoples in the Depression. Social Science Research Council Bulletin 31. New York: Social Science Research Council, 1937.

1774. Zimmerman, William, Jr. "The Role of the Bureau of Indian Affairs since 1933." Annals of the American Academy of Political and Social Science 311 (May 1957): 31-40.

Extensive commentary on the new policies will be found in the section, Current Comment, 1933-1945. Indians at Work, a newsletter published by the Bureau of Indian Affairs from 1933 to 1945, is an excellent place to trace the operations of the Indian New Deal.

Indians and World War II

The part played by the Indians in World War II and the problems of the returning veterans are treated in a number of current writings and scientific studies.

1775. Adair, John. "The Navajo and Pueblo Veteran: A Force for Culture Change." American Indian 4, no. 1 (1947): 5-11.

1776. _____. "A Study of Culture Resistance: The Veterans of World War II at Zuni Pueblo." Ph.D. dissertation, University of New Mexico, 1948.

1777. Adair, John, and Evon Vogt. "Navaho and Zuni Veterans: A Study of Contrasting Modes of Culture Change." American Anthropologist 51 (October-December 1949): 547-561.

1778. Collier, John. "The Indian in a Wartime Nation." Annals of the American Academy of Political and Social Science 223 (September 1942): 29-35.

1779. Eells, Walter Crosby. "Educational Opportunities for the Indian Veteran." American Indian 2 (Fall 1945): 17-21.

1780. Howard, James H. "The Dakota Indian Victory Dance, World War II." North Dakota History 18 (January 1951): 31-40.

1781. Ickes, Harold L. "Indians Have a Name for Hitler." Collier's 113 (January 15, 1944): 58.

1782. Johnston, Philip. "Indian Jargon Won Our Battles." Masterkey 38 (October-December 1964): 130-137.

1783. La Farge, Oliver. "They Were Good

Enough for the Army." Harper's Magazine 195 (November 1947): 444-449.

1784. Neuberger, Richard L. "The American Indian Enlists." Asia and the Americas 42 (November 1942): 628-631.

1785. _____. "On the Warpath." Saturday Evening Post 215 (October 24, 1942): 79.

1786. Paul, Doris A. The Navajo Code Talkers. Philadelphia: Dorrance and Company, 1973.

1787. Ritzenthaler, Robert. "The Impact of War on an Indian Community." American Anthropologist 45 (April-June 1943): 325-326.

1788. Sergeant, Elizabeth Shepley. "The Indian Goes to War." New Republic 107 (November 30, 1942): 708-709.

1789. Useem, John, Gordon Macgregor, and Ruth Hill Useem. "Wartime Employment and Cultural Adjustments of the Rosebud Sioux." Applied Anthropology 2 (January-March 1943): 1-9.

1790. Vestal, Stanley. "The Plains Indian and the War." Saturday Review of Literature 25 (May 16, 1942): 9-10.

1791. Vogt, Evon Z. "Between Two Worlds: Case Study of a Navajo Veteran." American Indian 5, no. 1 (1949): 13-21.

Current Comment, 1933-1945

The Indian New Deal occasioned a good deal of controversy, for it reversed policies of long standing. Comment on current affairs touched on this conflict of views as well as on other matters.

1792. "Anthropologists and the Federal Indian Program." Science 81 (February 15, 1935): 170-171

1793. Armstrong, O. K. "Set the American Indians Free!" Reader's Digest 47 (August 1945): 47-52.

1794. Beatty, Willard W. "Preparation of Indians for Leadership." In The Changing Indian, edited by Oliver La Farge, pp. 139-143. Norman: University of Oklahoma Press, 1942.

1795. Beatty, Willard W., ed. Indians Yesterday and Today. Information Pamphlet no. 1. Washington: Education Division, U.S. Office of Indian Affairs, 1941.

1796. Beecher, George A. "Why Remember the Indian?" Nebraska History Magazine 21 (October-December 1940): 277-279.

1797. "C. C. C. Activities for Indians." Monthly Labor Review 49 (July 1939): 94-95.

1798. "Civilizing the Indian." Nation 138 (January 10, 1934): 33-34.

1799. Cloud, Henry Roe. "Culture and Progress," Southern Workman 66 (December 1937): 381-387.

1800. Cohen, Felix S. "Anthropology and the Problems of Indian Administration." Southwest Social Science Quarterly 18 (September 1937): 171-180.

1801. _____. "Indians Are Citizens!" American Indian 1 (Summer 1944): 12-22.

1802. Collier, John. "Does the Government Welcome the Indian Arts." American Magazine of Art (Supplement) 27 (September 1934): 10-11.

1803. _____. "Indians at Work." Survey Graphic 23 (June 1934): 261-265, 297, 299-302.

1804. _____. "Indians Come Alive: New Hope for Native Americans." Atlantic Monthly 170 (September 1942): 75-81.

1805. _____. "A Lift for the Forgotten Red Man, Too." New York Times Magazine, May 6, 1934, pp. 10-11.

1806. _____. "The Policies of the Indian Bureau." School and Society 37 (May 6, 1933): 585-586.

1807. _____. "A Reply to Mrs. Eastman." Christian Century 51 (August 8, 1934): 1018-1020.

1808. _____. "United States Indian Administration as a Laboratory of Ethnic Relations." Social Research 12 (September 1945): 265-303.

1809. Connolly, Vera. "The End of a Long, Long Trail." Good Housekeeping 98 (April 1934): 50-51 +.

1810. Corey, Herbert. "Lo, the Poor Indian Bureau." Nation's Business 33 (February 1945): 31-32, 69-70.

1811. Crichton, Kyle. "Storm over Alaska." Collier's 115 (March 31, 1945): 20, 74-75.

1812. Downes, Randolph C. "The American Indians Can Be Free." American Indian 2 (Fall 1945): 8-11.

1813. Eastman, Elaine Goodale. "Does Uncle Sam Foster Paganism?" Christian Century 51 (August 8, 1934): 1016-1018. Discussion was carried on in subsequent issues of the magazine in letters to the editor. See items under John Collier and J. C. Morgan.

1814. Emerson, Haven. "Freedom or Exploitation! Is Mr. O. K. Armstrong's Recent Solution of the American Indian Problem Sound?" American Indian 2 (Fall

1945): 3-7. Refutation of article by O. K. Armstrong, Reader's Digest, August 1945.

1815. Fergusson, Erna. "Crusade from Santa Fe." North American Review 242 (Winter 1936-1937): 376-387.

1816. Green, Elizabeth. "Indian Minorities under the American New Deal." Pacific Affairs 8 (December 1935): 420-427.

1817. Hassrick, Royal B. "The American Indian in Tomorrow's America." American Indian 2 (Winter 1944-1945): 3-13.

1818. Hughes, William. "Indians on a New Trail: Howard Wheeler Bill." Catholic World 139 (July 1934): 461-470.

1819. "Indians in C. C. C. Camps." Missionary Review of the World 56 (December 1933): 611.

1820. Kelly, Eugene. "Justice for the Alaska Indians: Shall We Play the White Man's Game Once More?" American Indian 1 (Summer 1944): 3-11.

1821. La Farge, Oliver. "The American Indian's Revenge." Current History 40 (May 1934): 163-168.

1822. _____. "The Changing Indian." Saturday Review of Literature 25 (May 16, 1942): 8.

1823. _____. "New Concepts in Indian Affairs." In The Changing Indian, edited by Oliver La Farge, pp. 166-174. Norman: University of Oklahoma Press, 1942.

1824. _____. "Revolutions with Reservations." New Republic 84 (October 9, 1935): 232-234.

1825. Lindquist, G. E. E. "The Government's New Indian Policy: Proposed Revival of Tribalism, Seen from the Missionary Angle." Missionary Review of the World 57 (April 1934): 182-184.

1826. Lindquist, G. E. E., ed. "The Outlook for the American Indian: Symposium." Missionary Review of the World 62 (November 1939): 501-507.

1827. Lips, Julius E. "Ethnopolitics and the Indians." Commonweal 21 (March 15, 1935): 562-564.

1828. Macgregor, Frances Cooke. Twentieth Century Indians. New York: G. P. Putnam's Sons, 1941. Photographs and brief text.

1829. McNickle, D'Arcy. "The American Indian Today." Missouri Archaeologist 5 (September 1939): 1-10.

1830. Mekeel, Scudder. "The American Indian as a Minority Group Problem." American Indian 2 (Fall 1944): 3-11.

1831. Merrill, Arch. "Have They Kept That Pledge?" American Indian 1 (November 1943): 4-14. Seneca Indians in New York.

1832. _____. "Salamanca Lease Settlement." American Indian 1 (Spring 1944): 3-8. Seneca lands in New York.

1833. Morgan, J. C. "A Navajo Dissenter." Christian Century 51 (October 31, 1934): 1379-1380. Discussion by John Collier, William R. Moody, and Elaine Goodale Eastman; (November 14, 1934): 1459-1460; (November 28, 1934): 1523-1524.

1834. Nash, Jay B., ed. The New Day for the Indians: A Survey of the Working of the Indian Reorganization Act of 1934. New York: Academy Press, 1938.

1835. Neuberger, Richard L. "Unhappy Fishing Ground." Collier's 104 (October 21, 1939): 19, 46, 48.

1836. "The 'New Deal' for Indians." Missionary Review of the World 57 (September 1934): 389-390.

1837. Orians, G. H. The Cult of the Vanishing American: A Century View, 1834-1934. Toledo: H. J. Chittenden Company, 1934.

1838. Ryan, W. Carson, Jr. "Social and Educational Implications of the Navajo Program." Proceedings of the National Conference of Social Work, 1934, pp. 557-563.

1839. Schroeder, Louis C. "Indian Conservation Camps." Recreation 28 (August 1934): 249-252.

1840. Sergeant, Elizabeth Shepley. "Crisis in Sia Pueblo." Scribner's Magazine 98 (July 1935): 27-32.

1841. _____. "A New Deal for the Indian." New Republic 95 (June 15, 1938): 151-154.

1842. Seymour, Flora Warren. "A Desert Domain--among the Indians." Missionary Review of the World 62 (October 1939): 448-450. Navajo Reservation.

1843. _____. "Federal Favor for Fetishism." Missionary Review of the World 58 (September 1935): 397-400.

1844. _____. "Thunder over the Southwest." Saturday Evening Post 211 (April 1, 1939): 23, 71-72, 74, 76.

1845. _____. "Trying It on the Indian." New Outlook 163 (May 1934): 22-25.

1846. Shepard, Ward. "Land and Self-Government for Indians." Proceedings of National Conference of Social Work, 1934, pp. 539-547.

1847. Stevens, Alden. "Once They Were Nomads." Survey Graphic 30 (February 1941): 62-67.

1848. _____. "Whither the American Indian?" Survey Graphic 29 (March 1940): 168-177.

1849. Swing, Raymond Gram. "The Fight on the New Indian Policy." Nation 140 (April 24, 1935): 479-480.

1850. Villard, Oswald Garrison. "Wardship and the Indian." Christian Century 61 (March 29, 1944): 397-398.

1851. White, Owen P. "Red Men and White." Collier's 92 (March 17, 1934): 10-11.

1852. _____. "Scalping the Indian." Collier's 92 (March 3, 1934): 10-11.

1853. Woehlke, Walter V. "The Battle for Grass." Saturday Evening Post 206 (November 25, 1933): 10-11, 79-81, 84. Navajo Reservation.

1854. _____. "The Economic Rehabilitation of the Navajos." Proceedings of the National Conference of Social Work, 1934, pp. 548-556.

The Readers' Guide (150) will be helpful in locating other popular writings of the period.

INDIAN AFFAIRS AFTER 1945

Indian Claims Commission

The Indian Claims Commission established in 1946 provided a means of rectifying injustices done the Indians in land cessions or other dealings with the United States government. Hundreds of cases have been heard and decisions handed down.

Commission Reports, Findings, and Testimony

The official work of the Indian Claims Commission can be studied in the following compilations and reports.

1855. Annual Report, Indian Claims Commission. The later reports give a summary of cases decided to date, a brief statement of cases pending, a list of all members of the Commission with dates of tenure, and a brief history of the Commission.

1856. Decisions of the Indian Claims Commission. Microfiche edition of official decisions. New York: Clearwater Publishing Company, 1973--.

1857. Indian Claims Commission Decisions. Boulder, Colorado: Native American Rights Fund, n.d. Bound volumes of reproductions of the official decisions. Series includes an Index to Indian Claims Commission Decisions, 1973.

1858. Expert Testimony before the Indian Claims Commission. Microfiche edition of written expert reports. New York: Clearwater Publishing Company, 1973. The same publisher has announced microfiche publication of transcripts of oral testimony, legal briefs in the cases, General Accounting Office reports, and a legislative history of the Indian Claims Commission.

1859. Ross, Norman A., ed. Index to the Decisions of the Indian Claims Commission. New York: Clearwater Publishing Company, 1973.

1860. _____. Index to the Expert Testimony before the Indian Claims Commission: The Written Reports. New York: Clearwater Publishing Company, 1973.

See also the materials in the American Indian Ethnohistory Series listed below.

General Studies on the Indian Claims Commission

The work of the Indian Claims Commission has been studied by historians, its implications discussed by lawyers, and some of the outcome treated in the popular press. Included here also are studies dealing with other aspects of Indian claims.

1861. Barker, Robert W. "The Indian Claims Commission--the Conscience of the Nation in Its Dealings with the Original American." Federal Bar Journal 20 (Summer 1960): 240-247.

1862. Barney, Ralph A. "Indian Claims, or the Historical Appraisal." Appraisal Journal 31 (April 1963): 169-177.

1863. _____. "Legal Problems Peculiar to Indian Claims Litigation." Ethnohistory 2 (Fall 1955): 315-325.

1864. _____. "Some Legal Problems under the Indian Claims Commission Act." Federal Bar Journal 20 (Summer 1960): 235-239.

1865. Chapman, Berlin B. "The Day in Court for the Kiowa, Commanche and Apache Tribes." Great Plains Journal 2 (Fall 1962): 1-21.

1866. Cohen, Felix S. "Indian Claims." American Indian 2 (Spring 1945): 3-11.

1867. Danforth, Sandra C. "Repaying Historical Debts: The Indian Claims Commission." North Dakota Law Review 49 (Winter 1973): 359-403.

1868. Downes, Randolph C. "The Indian Claims Commission Bill." American Indian 3 (Spring 1946): 1-8.

1869. Friedman, Howard M. "Interest on Indian Claims: Judicial Protection of the

FISC." Valparaiso University Law Review 5 (Fall 1970): 26-47.

1870. Gormley, Donald C. "The Role of the Expert Witness." Ethnohistory 2 (Fall 1955): 326-346.

1871. Guenzel, Robert C. "Indians--Claim for Lands Taken by the United States Based on Original Possession." Nebraska Law Review 26 (March 1947): 455-457.

1872. Haines, Francis. "The Nez Perce Tribe versus the United States." Idaho Yesterdays 8 (Spring 1964): 18-25.

1873. Hartley, William, and Ellen Hartley. "The Seminoles' Long Road to Victory." Reader's Digest 86 (February 1965): 199-200, 202-204.

1874. Jones, J. A. "Problems, Opportunities and Recommendations." Ethnohistory 2 (Fall 1955): 347-356.

1875. Kelly, James Michael. "Indians--Extent of the 'Fair and Honorable Dealings' Section of the Indian Claims Commission Act." Saint Louis University Law Journal 15 (Spring 1971): 491-507.

1876. Kennedy, Robert F. "Buying It Back from the Indians." Life 52 (March 23, 1962): 17, 19.

1877. Kroeber, Alfred L. "Nature of the Land-Holding Group." Ethnohistory 2 (Fall 1955): 303-314.

1878. LeDuc, Thomas. "The Work of the Indian Claims Commission under the Act of 1946." Pacific Historical Review 26 (February 1957): 1-16.

1879. Lurie, Nancy Oestreich. "The Indian Claims Commission Act." Annals of the American Academy of Political and Social Science 311 (May 1957): 56-70.

1880. _____. "Problems, Opportunities, and Recommendations." Ethnohistory 2 (Fall 1955): 357-375.

1881. _____. "A Reply to 'The Land Claims Cases: Anthropologists in Conflict.'" Ethnohistory 3 (Summer 1956): 256-279.

1882. Manners, Robert A. "The Land Claims Cases: Anthropologists in Conflict." Ethnohistory 3 (Winter 1956): 72-81.

1883. Moses, Marsha. "Administrative Law--the Indian Claims Commission's Jurisdiction to Hear Claims Based on Injuries to Tribal Structure." Wayne Law Review 20 (July 1974): 1097-1108.

1884. Nielsen, Richard Allen. "American Indian Land Claims: Land versus Money as a Remedy." University of Florida Law Review 25 (Winter 1973): 308-326.

1885. Ray, Verne F. "Introduction: Anthropology and Indian Claims Litigation."

Ethnohistory 2 (Fall 1955): 287-291.

1886. Selander, Kenneth J. "Section 2 of the Indian Claims Commission Act." George Washington Law Review 15 (June 1947): 388-425.

1887. Steward, Julian H. "Theory and Application in a Social Science." Ethnohistory 2 (Fall 1955): 292-302.

1888. Stewart, Omer C. "Anthropology and the Indian Claims." Delphian Quarterly 42 (Summer 1959): 8-12, 21.

1889. _____. "Chippewa Indian Claims." Delphian Quarterly 42 (Autumn 1959): 35-40.

1890. _____. "Claims of the Indians of California." Delphian Quarterly 42 (Spring 1959): 36-40.

1891. _____. "The First American and His Land: Background for American Indian Claims Cases." Delphian Quarterly 41 (Autumn 1958): 23-28, 38.

1892. _____. "Kroeber and the Indian Claims Commission Cases." Kroeber Anthropological Society Papers no. 25 (Fall 1961): 181-190.

1893. "Systematic Discrimination in the Indian Claims Commission: The Burden of Proof in Redressing Historical Wrongs." Iowa Law Review 57 (June 1972): 1300-1319.

1894. "Ute Indians Hit a $31.7 Million Jackpot." Life 29 (July 24, 1950): 37-40.

1895. Vance, John T. "The Congressional Mandate and the Indian Claims Commission." North Dakota Law Review 45 (Spring 1969): 325-336.

1896. Wilkinson, Glen A. "Indian Tribal Claims before the Court of Claims." Georgetown Law Journal 55 (December 1966): 511-528.

American Indian Ethnohistory Series

A large number of the ethnohistorical studies submitted as expert testimony to the Indian Claims Commission, as well as the findings of the Commission, have been published in book form by Garland Publishing, Inc. They have been compiled and edited by David Agee Horr. The volumes are divided into series on the basis of geographical areas and are given here in that order. Each series includes the following two brief introductory essays.

1897. Barney, Ralph A. "The Indian Claims Commission."

1898. Manners, Robert A. "Introduction to the Ethnohistorical Reports on the Land Claims Cases."

The individual studies and Commission findings included in the separate volumes are listed after the title of the volume. In some cases the volumes show different titles for the individual studies on the title page, in the table of contents. and on the first page of the study itself. The listing here follows the titles on the studies themselves unless some abbreviation or modification seemed essential for clarity.

North Central and Northeastern Indians

1899. Chippewa Indians I. New York: Garland Publishing, 1974.

1900. Wheeler-Voegelin, Erminie, and Harold Hickerson. "The Red Lake and Pembina Chippewa." Pp. 25-230.

1901. Chippewa Indians II. New York: Garland Publishing, 1974.

1902. Hickerson, Harold. "An Anthropological Report on the Indian Occupancy of Royce Area 357, Which Was Ceded to the United States by the Mississippi Bands, and the Pillager and Winnebigoshish Bands of Chippewa Indians under the Treaty of February 22, 1855." Pp. 9-317.

1903. Chippewa Indians III. New York: Garland Publishing, 1974.

1904. Hickerson, Harold. "An Anthropological Report on the Indian Use and Occupancy of Royce Area 332, Which Was Ceded to the United States by the Chippewa Indians of Lake Superior and the Mississippi under the Treaty of September 30, 1854." Pp. 9-180.

1905. Knuth, Helen E. "Economic and Historical Background of Northeastern Minnesota Lands Ceded by Chippewa Indians of Lake Superior September 30, 1854." Pp. 181-295.

1906. Chippewa Indians IV. New York: Garland Publishing, 1974.

1907. Hickerson, Harold. "An Anthropological Report on the Indian Occupancy of Area 242, Which Was Ceded to the United States by the Chippewa Nation of Indians under the Treaty of July 29, 1837." Pp. 9-253.

1908. Chippewa Indians V. New York: Garland Publishing, 1974.

1909. Wheeler-Voegelin, Erminie. "An Anthropological Report on Indian Use and Occupancy of Northern Michigan." Pp. 9-86.

1910. Stout, David B. "Ethnohistorical Report on Royce Area 111 (Michigan)." Pp. 87-132.

1911. Warner, Robert M. "Economic and

Historical Report on Royce Area 111." Pp. 133-318.

1912. Warner, Robert M., and Lois J. Groesbeck. "Historical Report on the Sault Ste. Marie Area." Pp. 319-345.

1913. Tanner, Helen Hornbeck. "The Chippewa of Eastern Lower Michigan." Pp. 347-377.

1914. Chippewa Indians VI. New York: Garland Publishing, 1974.

1915. Ewers, John C. "Ethnological Report on the Chippewa Cree Tribe of the Rocky Boy Reservation, Montana, and the Little Shell Band of Indians." Pp. 9-182.

1916. Sharrock, Floyd W., and Susan R. Sharrock. "A History of the Cree Indian Territorial Expansion from the Hudson Bay Area to the Interior Saskatchewan and Missouri Plains." Pp. 183-406.

1917. Chippewa Indians VII. New York: Garland Publishing, 1974.

1918. "Commission Findings on the Chippewa Indians." Pp. 9-548.

1919. Indians of Illinois and Indiana. New York: Garland Publishing, 1974.

1920. Jablow, Joseph. "Illinois, Kickapoo, and Potawatomi Indians: A Study of Indian Tribes in Royce Areas 48, 96-A, 110, 177, and 98, Illinois and Indiana, 1640-1832." Pp. 37-436.

1921. Indians of Illinois and Northwestern Indiana. New York: Garland Publishing, 1974.

1922. Wheeler-Voegelin, Erminie. "An Anthropological Report on the Indian Occupancy of Royce Area 117 Which Was Ceded to the United States by the 'Ottawa, Chippewa, and Pottawatamie Nations of Indians' under the Treaty Held at Chicago on August 29, 1821." Pp. 51-277.

1923. Stout, David B. "Report on Kickapoo, Illinois, and Potawatomi Indians." Pp. 279-414.

1924. Indians of Northeastern Illinois. New York: Garland Publishing, 1974.

1925. Baerreis, David A., Erminie Wheeler-Voegelin, and Remedios Wycoco-Moore. "An Anthropological Report on the Indian Occupancy of That Portion of Royce Area 148 East of the Fox River in Illinois Which Was Ceded to the United States by the United Nations of Chippewa, Ottawa, and Potawatomie Indians of the Waters of the Illinois, Milwaukee and Manitoouck Rivers under the Treaty of July 29, 1829." Pp. 51-246.

1926. _____. "The Identity of the Mascoutens." Pp. 247-344.

1927. Indians of Northern Indiana and South-

western Michigan. New York: Garland
Publishing, 1974.

1928. Berthrong, Donald J. "An Historical
Report on Indian Use and Occupancy of
Royce Areas 132, 133, 145, 146, 180 and
181 in Northern Indiana and Southwestern
Michigan as Related to the Treaties Held
at St. Mary's, October 2, 1818; Paradise
Springs, October 16, 23, 1826; Carey Mis-
sion, September 20, 1828; and Tippecanoe,
October 26, 27, 1832." Pp. 51-397.

1929. Indians of Northern Ohio and Southeastern Michigan. New York: Garland
Publishing, 1974.

1930. Wheeler-Voegelin, Erminie. "An
Ethnohistorical Report on the Indian
Use and Occupancy of Royce Area 53 . . .
and on the Indian Use and Occupancy of
Royce Area 54, Which Was Ceded to the
United States by the 'Wyandot, Ottawa,
Chipawa, Munsee and Delaware, Shawnanee,
and Pottawatima Nation' under the Treaty
Held 'at Fort Industry, on the Miami of
the Lake,' on July 4, 1805." Pp. 51-315.

1931. Tanner, Helen Hornbeck. "The Location of Indian Tribes in Southeastern
Michigan and Northern Ohio." Pp. 317-375.

1932. Indians of Northwest Ohio. New York:
Garland Publishing, 1974.

1933. Wheeler-Voegelin, Erminie. "An
Ethnohistorical Report on the Indian Use
and Occupancy of Royce Area 87 Ceded by
the 'Wyandot' Tribe of Indians and Royce
Area 88 Ceded by the 'Potawatomy, Ottawas
and Chippeway' Tribes of Indians to the
United States Pursuant to the Treaty Held
'at the Foot of the Rapids of the Miami of
Lake Erie' on September 29, 1817." Pp.
51-373.

1934. Indians of Ohio and Indiana Prior to
1795. 2 volumes. New York: Garland
Publishing, 1974.

1935. Tanner, Helen Hornbeck. "The Greenville Treaty, 1795." Pp. 1:51-128.

1936. Wheeler-Voegelin, Erminie. "An
Ethnohistorical Report on the Indian Use
and Occupancy of Royce Area 11, Ohio and
Indiana, Ceded . . . Pursuant to the
Treaty of Greenville on August 3, 1795."
Pp. 1:129-463; 2:7-468.

1937. Indians of Ohio, Indiana, Illinois,
Southern Michigan, and Southern Wisconsin. 3 volumes. New York: Garland Publishing, 1974.

1938. "Commission Findings." Pp. 1:51-334;
2:7-353; 3:7-448.

1939. Indians of Western Illinois and
Southern Wisconsin. New York: Garland
Publishing, 1974.

1940. Wheeler-Voegelin, Erminie, and Emily
J. Blasingham. "An Anthropological Report on the Indian Occupancy of Royce
Area 77 . . . and Royce Area 78, Which
Was Ceded . . . under the Treaty Held
at St. Louis on August 24, 1816." Pp.
51-299.

1941. Jones, J. A. "An Anthropological
Report on the Indian Occupancy of Royce
Area 187 Which Was Ceded to the United
States by 'the United Nation of the
Chippewa, Ottowa and Potawatamie Indians'
under the Treaty of September 26, 1833."
Pp. 301-386.

1942. Iroquois Indians I. New York: Garland
Publishing, 1974.

1943. Kent, Donald H. "Historical Report
on Pennsylvania's Purchases from the Indians in 1784, 1785 and 1789 and on
Indian Occupancy of the Areas Purchased."
Pp. 29-303.

1944. Iroquois Indians II. New York:
Garland Publishing, 1974.

1945. Kent, Donald H. "Historical Report
on the Niagara River and the Niagara
River Strip to 1759." Pp. 11-201.

1946. "Commission Findings on the Iroquois
Indians." Pp. 203-483.

1947. Miami, Wea, and Eel-River Indians of
Southern Indiana. New York: Garland
Publishing, 1974.

1948. Wheeler-Voegelin, Erminie, Emily J.
Blasingham and Dorothy R. Libby. "An
Anthropological Report on the History
of the Miamis, Weas, and Eel River Indians; on the Background of the Treaty
of Grouseland of August 21, 1805 and the
Treaty of Fort Wayne of September 30,
1809; on Native Use and Occupancy of
Royce Areas 56, 71, 72, 73 and 74; a History of the Mohican Claim to Lands in
Indiana." Pp. 27-494.

1949. Piankashaw and Kaskaskia Indians.
New York: Garland Publishing, 1974.

1950. Libby, Dorothy. "An Anthropological
Report on the Piankashaw Indians." Pp.
27-341.

1951. Stout, David B. "Report on the Piankashaw and Kaskaskia and the Treaty of
Greene Ville." Pp. 343-375.

1952. Sac, Fox, and Iowa Indians I. New
York: Garland Publishing, 1974.

1953. Gussow, Zachary. "An Anthropological
Report on Indian Use and Occupancy of
Royce Areas 69 and 120 Which Were Ceded
to the United States by the Sac, Fox, and
Iowa Indians under the Treaty of August
4, 1824." Pp. 29-120.

1954. _____. "An Ethnological Report
on the Historic Habitat of the Sauk, Fox,
and Iowa Indians." Pp. 121-184.

1955. Indian Claims Commission and others. "An Account of the Manners and Customs of the Sauk Nation of Indians." Pp. 185-236.

1956. Barlowe, Raleigh. "Spanish Land Grants in Royce's Cession 50 in Missouri." Pp. 237-381.

1957. Sac, Fox, and Iowa Indians II. New York: Garland Publishing, 1974.

1958. Stout, David B., Erminie Wheeler-Voegelin, and Emily J. Blasingham. "An Anthropological Report on the Indian Occupancy of Royce Area 50." Pp. 5-319.

1959. Sac, Fox, and Iowa Indians III. New York: Garland Publishing, 1974.

1960. "Commission Findings on the Sac, Fox, and Iowa Indians." Pp. 7-385.

1961. Winnebago Indians. New York: Garland Publishing, 1974.

1962. Jones, J. A. "An Anthropological Report on the Indian Occupancy of Royce Areas 149, 174 and 245 Which Were Ceded to the United States by the Winnebago Tribe." Pp. 25-223.

1963. Smith, Alice E., and Vernon Carstensen. "Report of Economic and Historical Background for the Winnebago Indian Claims (Royce Areas 149, 174, 245)." Pp. 225-453.

1964. "Commission Findings on the Winnebago Indians." Pp. 455-490.

Southern and Southeast Indians

1965. Alabama-Coushatta (Creek) Indians. New York: Garland Publishing, 1974.

1966. Jacobson, Daniel. "The Alabama-Coushatta Indians of Texas and the Coushatta Indians of Louisiana." Pp. 25-178.

1967. Martin, Howard N. "Ethnohistorical Analysis of Documents Relating to the Alabama and Coushatta Tribes of the State of Texas." Pp. 179-256.

1968. Marsh, Ralph Henry. "The History of Polk County, Texas, Indians." Pp. 257-361.

1969. Cherokee and Creek Indians. New York: Garland Publishing, 1974.

1970. Fairbanks, Charles H. "Ethnographic Report on Royce Area 79 Docket 275: Chickasaw, Cherokee, Creek." Pp. 31-285.

1971. Goff, John H. "Land Cessions of the Cherokee Nation in Tennessee, Mississippi, North Carolina, Georgia, Alabama, 1785-1835." Pp. 287-581.

1972. "Commission Findings." Pp. 583-639.

1973. Creek Indians. 2 volumes. New York: Garland Publishing, 1974.

1974. Doster, James F. "The Creek Indians and Their Florida Lands, 1740-1805." Pp. 1:27-296.

1975. _____. "The Creek Indians and Their Florida Lands, 1806-1823." Pp. 2:7-300.

1976. Florida Indians I. New York: Garland Publishing, 1974.

1977. Cline, Howard F. "Notes on Colonial Indians and Communities in Florida, 1700-1821." Pp. 23-287.

1978. _____. "Notes on the Treaty of Coweta." Pp. 289-303.

1979. Florida Indians II. New York: Garland Publishing, 1974.

1980. Cline, Howard F. "Provisional Historical Gazeteer with Locational Notes on Florida Colonial Communities, 1700-1823." Pp. 9-250.

1981. Florida Indians III. New York: Garland Publishing, 1974.

1982. Fairbanks, Charles H. "Ethnohistorical Report of the Florida Indians." Pp. 9-303.

1983. "Commission Findings on the Florida Indians." Pp. 305-582.

Plains Indians

1984. Arapaho-Cheyenne Indians. New York: Garland Publishing, 1974.

1985. Gussow, Zachary. "An Ethnological Report on Cheyenne and Arapaho: Aboriginal Occupation." Pp. 27-95.

1986. Hafen, LeRoy R. "Historical Background and Development of the Arapaho-Cheyenne Land Area." Pp. 97-173.

1987. Ekirch, Arthur A., Jr. "Cheyenne and Arapaho Indians vs. the United States: Historical Background." Pp. 175-225.

1988. "Commission Findings." Pp. 227-342.

1989. Blackfeet Indians. New York: Garland Publishing, 1974.

1990. Ewers, John C. "Ethnological Report on the Blackfeet and Gros Ventre Tribes of Indians: Lands in Northern Montana." Pp. 23-202.

1991. "Commission Findings on the Blackfeet Indians." Pp. 203-312.

1992. Caddoan Indians I. New York: Garland Publishing, 1974.

1993. Wyckoff, Donald G. "The Caddoan Cultural Area: An Archaeological Perspective." Pp. 25-279.

1994. Williams, Stephen. "The Aboriginal Location of the Kadohadacho and Related Indian Tribes." Pp. 281-330.

1995. Caddoan Indians II. New York: Garland Publishing, 1974.

1996. Neuman, Robert W. "Data Relative of the Historic Locations of Certain Caddoan Tribes." Pp. 9-158.

1997. Lange, Charles H. "A Report on Data Pertaining to the Caddo Treaty of July 1, 1835: The Historical and Anthropological Background and Aftermath." Pp. 159-322.

1998. Caddoan Indians III. New York: Garland Publishing, 1974.

1999. Hughes, Jack Thomas. "Prehistory of the Caddoan-Speaking Tribes." Pp. 9-435.

2000. Caddoan Indians IV. New York: Garland Publishing, 1974.

2001. Tanner, Helen Hornbeck. "The Territory of the Caddo Tribe of Oklahoma." Pp. 9-144.

2002. _____. "Rebuttal Statement . . . to Direct Evidence of Alabama Coushatta Indians, et al., and Direct Evidence of Wichita Tribe of Oklahoma, et al." Pp. 145-165.

2003. "Commission Findings." Pp. 167-218.

2004. Crow Indians. New York: Garland Publishing, 1974.

2005. Plummer, Norman B. "The Crow Tribe of Indians." Pp. 23-247.

2006. "Commission Findings on the Crow Indians." Pp. 249-317.

2007. Kiowa-Commanche Indians. 2 volumes. New York: Garland Publishing, 1974.

2008. "Transcript of Hearings of the Kiowa, Commanche, and Apache Indians vs. the United States of America." Pp. 1:27-219; 2:7-168.

2009. "Commission Findings on the Kiowa, Comanche, and Apache Tribes of Indians." Pp. 2:169-219.

2010. Omaha Indians. New York: Garland Publishing, 1974.

2011. Smith, G. Hubert. "Ethnohistorical Report on the Omaha People." Pp. 23-241.

2012. "Commission Findings on the Omaha Indians." Pp. 243-286.

2013. Osage Indians I. New York: Garland Publishing, 1974.

2014. Voget, Fred W. "Osage Research Report." Pp. 25-444.

2015. Osage Indians II. New York: Garland Publishing, 1974.

2016. Marriott, Alice. "Osage Research Report and Bibliography of Basic Research References." Pp. 9-270.

2017. Osage Indians III. New York: Garland Publishing, 1974.

2018. Chapman, Carl H. "The Origin of the Osage Indian Tribe: An Ethnographical, Historical, and Archaeological Study." Pp. 9-338.

2019. Osage Indians IV. New York: Garland Publishing, 1974.

2020. Chapman, Carl H. "A Preliminary Survey of Missouri Archaeology." Pp. 9-172.

2021. _____. "The Aboriginal Use and Occupancy of Lands West of the Mississippi River by the Osage Indian Tribe, and Village Locations and Hunting Territories of the Osage from Time Immemorial to 1808 A.D." Pp. 173-249.

2022. _____. "Location of Osage Indian Village Sites and Hunting Territory West of the Osage Line 1808 to 1825 A.D." Pp. 251-293.

2023. Henning, Dale R. "The Osage Nation: 1775-1818." Pp. 295-325.

2024. Osage Indians V. New York: Garland Publishing, 1974.

2025. "Commission Findings on the Osage Indians." Pp. 7-302.

2026. Oto and Missouri Indians. New York: Garland Publishing, 1974.

2027. "The Prehistoric and Historic Habitat of the Missouri and Oto Indians." Pp. 25-76.

2028. Chapman, Berlin B. "History of the Otoe and Missouria Lands." Pp. 77-226.

2029. "Commission Findings on the Oto and Missouri Indians." Pp. 227-379.

2030. Pawnee and Kansa (Kaw) Indians. New York: Garland Publishing, 1974.

2031. Champe, John L., and Franklin Fenenga. "Notes on the Pawnee." Pp. 23-169.

2032. Griffiths, Thomas M. "Historical and Economic Geography of the Pawnee Lands." Pp. 171-278.

2033. "Commission Findings on the Pawnee." Pp. 279-415.

2034. Wedel, Waldo R. "The Prehistoric and Historic Habitat of the Kansa Indians." Pp. 421-453.

2035. "Commission Findings on the Kaw Indians." Pp. 455-492.

2036. Ponca Indians. New York: Garland Publishing, 1974.

2037. Jablow, Joseph. "Ethnohistory of the Ponca with Reference to Their Claim to Certain Lands." Pp. 25-385.

2038. "Commission Findings on the Ponca Indians." Pp. 387-424.

2039. Sioux Indians I. New York: Garland Publishing, 1974.

2040. Hickerson, Harold. "Mdewakanton Band of Sioux Indians: An Anthropological Report on the Indian Occupancy of Area 243 and Area 289." Pp. 27-303.

2041. Sioux Indians II. New York: Garland Publishing, 1974.

2042. Hurt, Wesley R. "Anthropological Report on Indian Occupancy of Certain Territory Claimed by the Dakota Sioux Indians and by Rival Tribal Claimants." Pp. 9-264.

2043. Sioux Indians III. New York; Garland Publishing, 1974.

2044. Woolworth, Alan R. "Ethnohistorical Report on the Yankton Sioux." Pp. 9-245.

2045. Champe, John L. "Yankton Chronology." Pp. 247-274.

2046. Sioux Indians IV. New York: Garland Publishing, 1974.

2047. "Commission Findings on the Sioux Indians." Pp. 1-360.

2048. Wichita Indians. New York: Garland Publishing, 1974.

2049. Bell, Robert E., Edward B. Jelks, and W. W. Newcomb. "A Pilot Study of Wichita Indian Archeology and Ethnohistory." Pp. 25-434.

Indians of the Southwest

2050. Apache Indians I. New York: Garland Publishing, 1974.

2051. Schroeder, Albert H. "A Study of the Apache Indians: Part I, The Apaches and Their Neighbors, 1540-1700." Pp. 27-310.

2052. _____. "A Study of the Apache Indians: Part II, The Jicarilla Apaches." Pp. 311-469.

2053. _____. "A Study of the Apache Indians: Part III, The Mescalero Apaches." Pp. 471-583.

2054. Apache Indians II. New York: Garland Publishing, 1974.

2055. Bowden, Jocelyn J. "The Ascarate Grant." Pp. 9-214.

2056. Oppenheimer, Alan James. "An Ethnological Study of Tortugas, New Mexico." Pp. 215-361.

2057. Apache Indians III. New York: Garland Publishing, 1974.

2058. Gerald, Rex E. "Human Occupation of the Paso del Norte Area [Tigua, Manso, and Suma Indians]." Pp. 9-212.

2059. Jenkins, Myra Ellen. "History and Administration of the Tigua Indians of Ysleta del Sur during the Spanish Colonial Period." Pp. 213-276.

2060. Neighbours, Kenneth F. "An Ethnohistorical Report, Together with Supporting Exhibits Relating to the Cause of Action in the Lipan Apache Tribe, the Mescalero Apache Tribe, et al. . . . before the Indian Claims Commission." Pp. 277-358.

2061. Apache Indians IV. New York: Garland Publishing, 1974.

2062. Schroeder, Albert H. "A Study of the Apache Indians: Part IV, The Mogollon, Copper Mines, Mimbres, Warm Spring, and Chiricahua Apaches." Pp. 9-326.

2063. _____. "A Study of the Apache Indians: Part V, 'Tonto' and Western Apaches." Pp. 327-645.

2064. Apache Indians V. New York: Garland Publishing, 1974.

2065. Bender, Averam B. "A Study of Western Apache Indians, 1846-1886." Pp. 9-166.

2066. Aschmann, Homer. "Environment and Ecology in the 'Northern Tonto' Claim Area." Pp. 167-232.

2067. _____. "Terrain and Ecological Conditions in the Western Apache Range." Pp. 233-260.

2068. Apache Indians VI. New York: Garland Publishing, 1974.

2069. Gordon, B. L., and others. "Environment, Settlement, and Land Use in the Jicarilla Apache Claim Area." Pp. 9-244.

2070. Cutter, Donald C. "An Inquiry into Indian Land Rights in the American Southwest under Spain, Mexico, and the United States, with Particular Reference to the Jicarilla Apache Area of Northeastern New Mexico." Pp. 245-280.

2071. Apache Indians VII. New York: Garland Publishing, 1974.

2072. "Jicarilla Apache Tribe: Appendix to Brief of a Petitioner." Pp. 9-444.

2073. Apache Indians VIII. New York: Garland Publishing, 1974.

2074. Thomas, Alfred Barnaby. "The Jicarilla Apache Indians: A History, 1598-1888." Pp. 9-167.

2075. Nelson, Jean Ware. "Anthropological Material on Mode of Life and Aboriginal Tribal Lands of the Jicarilla Apaches." Pp. 171-185.

2076. Atwater, Elizabeth V. "Mode of Life and Tribal Lands of the Jicarilla Apaches during the Spanish-Mexican Period, 1601-1849." Pp. 189-269.

2077. Apache Indians IX. New York: Garland Publishing, 1974.

2078. Bénder, Averam B. "A Study of Jicarilla Apache Indians 1846-1887." Pp. 9-209.

2079. Apache Indians X. New York: Garland Publishing, 1974.

2080. Ray, Verne F. "Ethnohistorical Analysis of Documents Relating to the Apache Indians of Texas." Pp. 9-198.

2081. Opler, Morris E. "The Lipan and Mescalero Apache in Texas." Pp. 199-369.

2082. Apache Indians XI. New York: Garland Publishing, 1974.

2083. Thomas, Alfred B. "The Mescalero Apache 1653-1874." Pp. 9-60.

2084. Bender, Averam B. "A Study of Mescalero Apache Indians 1846-1880." Pp. 61-310.

2085. Apache Indians XII. New York: Garland Publishing, 1974.

2086. Basehart, Harry W. "Mescalero Apache Subsistence Patterns and Socio-Political Organization." Pp. 9-178.

2087. "Commission Findings on the Apache." Pp. 179-479.

2088. Havasupai Indians. New York: Garland Publishing, 1974.

2089. Manners, Robert A. "Havasupai Indians: An Ethnohistorical Report." Pp. 23-175.

2090. Dobyns, Henry F., and Robert C. Euler. "Aboriginal Socio-Political Structure and the Ethnic Group Concept of the Pai of Northwestern Arizona." Pp. 177-274.

2091. Euler, Robert C. "Havasupai Historical Data." Pp. 275-327.

2092. "Commission Findings on the Havasupai Indians." Pp. 329-356.

2093. Hopi Indians. New York: Garland Publishing, 1974.

2094. Ellis, Florence H. "The Hopi: Their History and Use of Lands." Pp. 25-277.

2095. Colton, Harold S. "Hopi History and Ethnobotany." Pp. 279-386.

2096. "Commission Findings on the Hopi Indians." Pp. 387-424.

2097. Hualapai Indians I. 3 volumes. New York: Garland Publishing, 1974.

2098. Dobyns, Henry F. "Prehistoric Indian Occupation within the Eastern Area of the Yuman Complex: A Study in Applied Archaeology." Pp. 1:23-318; 2:7-259; 3:7-254.

2099. Hualapai Indians II. New York: Garland Publishing, 1974.

2100. Manners, Robert A. "An Ethnological Report on the Hualapai (Walapai) Indians of Arizona." Pp. 9-191.

2101. "Commission Findings on the Hualapai Indians." Pp. 193-227.

2102. Navajo Indians I. New York: Garland Publishing, 1974.

2103. Ellis, Florence H. "An Anthropological Study of the Navajo Indians." Pp. 27-609.

2104. Navajo Indians II. New York: Garland Publishing, 1974.

2105. Jenkins, Myra Ellen, and Ward Alan Minge. "Record of Navajo Activities Affecting the Acoma-Laguna Area, 1746-1910." Pp. 9-234.

2106. Reeve, Frank D. "The Navajo Indians." Pp. 235-336.

2107. Navajo Indians III. New York: Garland Publishing, 1974.

2108. Van Valkenburgh, Richard F. "Navajo Sacred Places," edited by Clyde Kluckhohn. Pp. 9-199.

2109. _____. "A Short History of the Navajo People." Pp. 201-267.

2110. "Commission Findings on Navajo Indians." Pp. 269-303.

2111. Papago Indians I. New York: Garland Publishing, 1974.

2112. Hackenberg, Robert A. "Aboriginal Land Use and Occupancy of the Papago Indians." Pp. 23-308.

2113. Underhill, Ruth M. "Acculturation at the Papago Village of Santa Rosa." Pp. 309-348.

2114. Xavier, Gwyneth Harrington. "The Cattle Industry of the Southern Papago Districts with Some Information on the Reservation Cattle Industry as a Whole." Pp. 349-402.

2115. Papago Indians II. New York: Garland Publishing, 1974.

2116. King, William S., and Delmos J. Jones. "Papago Population Study." Pp. 9-349.

2117. Papago Indians III. New York: Garland Publishing, 1974.

2118. Kelly, William H. "The Papago Indians of Arizona: A Population and Economic Study." Pp. 9-149.

2119. Fontana, Bernard L. "The Papago Tribe of Arizona." Pp. 151-226.

2120. "Commission Findings on the Papago Indians." Pp. 227-273.

2121. Pima-Maricopa Indians. 2 volumes. New York: Garland Publishing, 1974.

2122. Hackenberg, Robert A. "Aboriginal Land Use and Occupancy of the Pima-Maricopa Indians." Pp. 1:25-350; 2:7-316.

2123. "Commission Findings on the Pima-Maricopa Indians." Pp. 2:317-366.

2124. Pueblo Indians I. New York: Garland Publishing, 1974.

2125. Ellis, Florence H. "Anthropological Data Pertaining to the Taos Land Claim." Pp. 29-150.

2126. Dunham, Harold H. "Spanish and Mexican Land Policies and Grants in the Taos Pueblo Region, New Mexico." Pp. 151-311.

2127. _____. "A Historical Study of Land Use Eastward of the Taos Indians' Pueblo Land Grant Prior to 1848." Pp. 313-343.

2128. "Commission Findings on the Pueblo Indians." Pp. 345-386.

2129. Pueblo Indians II. New York: Garland Publishing, 1974.

2130. Ellis, Florence H. "Archaeologic and Ethnologic Data Pertaining to Acoma and Laguna Land Claims, 1958-59." Pp. 9-330.

2131. Pueblo Indians III. New York: Garland Publishing, 1974.

2132. Ellis, Florence H. "Anthropology of Laguna Pueblo Land Claims." Pp. 9-120.

2133. Minge, Ward Alan. "Historical Treatise in Defense of the Pueblo of Acoma Land Claim." Pp. 121-210.

2134. Rands, Robert L. "Acoma Land Utilization: An Ethnohistorical Report." Pp. 211-407.

2135. Pueblo Indians IV. New York: Garland Publishing, 1974.

2136. Jenkins, Myra Ellen. "History of Laguna Pueblo Land Claims." Pp. 9-204.

2137. Rands, Robert L. "Laguna Land Utilization: An Ethnohistorical Report." Pp. 205-396.

2138. Pueblo Indians V. New York: Garland Publishing, 1974.

2139. "Commission Findings on the Pueblo Indians." Pp. 7-403.

2140. Yavapai Indians. New York: Garland Publishing, 1974.

2141. Schroeder, Albert H. "A Study of Yavapai History." Pp. 23-354.

2142. Thomas, Alfred B. "The Yavapai Indians, 1682-1848." Pp. 355-386.

2143. "Commission Findings on the Yavapai Indians." Pp. 387-439.

California and Basin-Plateau Indians

2144. California Indians I. 3 volumes. New York: Garland Publishing, 1974.

2145. Beals, Ralph L., and Joseph A. Hester, Jr. "Indian Land Use and Occupancy in California." Pp. 1:29-333; 2:7-388; 3:7-434.

2146. California Indians II. New York: Garland Publishing, 1974.

2147. Heizer, Robert F. "Indians of California: A Collection of Maps on Tribal Distribution." Pp. 7-95.

2148. Harvey, Herbert R. "The Luiseno: An Analysis of Change in Patterns of Land Tenure and Social Structure." Pp. 97-206.

2149. Willoughby, Nona Christensen. "Division of Labor among the Indians of California." Pp. 207-288.

2150. California Indians III. New York: Garland Publishing, 1974.

2151. Wheeler-Voegelin, Erminie. "An Ethnological Report on the Indians Living in the Northeastern Corner of the State of California with Special Reference to the Achomawi and Atsugewi, or So-Called 'Pitt River Indians of California.'" Pp. 9-184.

2152. Neasham, Ernest R. "Fall River Valley: A History." Pp. 185-362.

2153. California Indians IV. New York: Garland Publishing, 1974.

2154. Kroeber, A. L. "Basic Report on California Indian Land Holdings." Pp. 9-68.

2155. _____. "Excerpts from the Writings of A. L. Kroeber on Land Use and Political Organization of California Indians, with Comments by Harold E. Driver," prepared by Harold E. Driver. Pp. 69-199.

2156. Lounsbury, Ralph G. "Records of Mexican Land Claims in California." Pp. 201-297.

2157. California Indians V. New York: Garland Publishing, 1974.

2158. Davis, W. N., Jr. "Sagebrush Corner: The Opening of California's Northeast." Pp. 9-554.

2159. California Indians VI. New York: Garland Publishing, 1974.

2160. Beals, Ralph L., and Joseph A. Hester, Jr. "Indian Occupancy, Subsistence and Land Use Patterns in California." Pp. 9-264.

2161. "Commission Findings." Pp. 265-478.

2162. Mohave Indians. New York: Garland Publishing, 1974.

2163. Kroeber, Alfred L. "Report on Aboriginal Territory and Occupancy of the Mohave Tribe." Pp. 23-128.

2164. "Commission Findings on the Mohave Indians." Pp. 129-177.

2165. Paiute Indians I. New York: Garland Publishing, 1974.

2166. Manners, Robert A. "Southern Paiute and Chemehuevi: An Ethnohistorical Report." Pp. 29-300.

2167. Paiute Indians III. New York: Garland Publishing, 1974.

2168. Steward, Julian H., and Erminie Wheeler-Voegelin. "The Northern Paiute Indians." Pp. 9-328.

2169. Paiute Indians IV. New York: Garland Publishing, 1974.

2170. Grosscup, Gordon L. "Northern Paiute Archeology." Pp. 9-51.

2171. Train, Percy, James R. Henrichs, and W. Andrew Archer. "Medicinal Uses of Plants by Indian Tribes of Nevada." Pp. 53-257.

2172. Meacham, A. B., and others. "Notes on Snakes, Paiutes, Nez Perces at Malheur Reservation." Pp. 259-306. Letters and reports from the 1870s and 1880s.

2173. Paiute Indians V. New York: Garland Publishing, 1974.

2174. "Commission Findings on the Paiute Indians." Pp. 7-214.

2175. Shoshone Indians. New York: Garland Publishing, 1974.

2176. Malouf, Carling. "The Gosiute Indians." Pp. 25-172.

2177. Hultkrantz, Ake. "The Shoshones in the Rocky Mt. Area," translated by Arne Magnus. Pp. 173-214.

2178. _____. "The Indians in Yellowstone Park," translated by Astrid Liljeblad. Pp. 215-256.

2179. "Commission Findings on the Shoshone Indians." Pp. 257-320.

2180. Ute Indians I. New York: Garland Publishing, 1974.

2181. Steward, Julian H. "Aboriginal and Historical Groups of the Ute Indians of Utah: An Analysis." Pp. 25-103.

2182. _____. "Supplement: Native Components of the White River Ute Indians." Pp. 105-159.

2183. Ute Indians II. New York: Garland Publishing, 1974.

2184. Hart, Gerald T. "Appraisal: Confederated Ute Indian Lands in Southwestern Colorado Ceded to U.S. Government." Pp. 9-265.

2185. Hafen, LeRoy R. "Historical Summary of the Ute Indians and the San Juan Mining Region." Pp. 267-324.

2186. Smith, Anne M. "Cultural Differences and Similarities between Uintah and White River." Pp. 325-338.

2187. "Commission Findings." Pp. 339-411.

Indians of the Northwest

2188. Coast Salish and Western Washington Indians I. New York: Garland Publishing, 1974.

2189. Suttles, Wayne Prescott. "Economic Life of the Coast Salish of Haro and Rosario Straits." Pp. 41-570.

2190. Coast Salish and Western Washington Indians II. New York: Garland Publishing, 1974.

2191. Riley, Carroll L. "Ethnological Field Investigation and Analysis of Historical Material Relative to Group Distribution and Utilization of Natural Resources among Puget Sound Indians." Pp. 27-87.

2192. Collins, June McCormick. "The Influence of White Contact on Class Distinctions and Political Authority among the Indians of Northern Puget Sound." Pp. 89-204.

2193. "The Quileute Tribe of Indians: Ethnological and Historical Evidence." Pp. 205-400.

2194. Taylor, Herbert C., Jr. "Anthropological Investigation of the Medicine Creek Tribes Relative to Tribal Identity and Aboriginal Possession of Lands." Pp. 401-473.

2195. Tweddell, Colin Ellidge. "A Historical and Ethnological Study of the Snohomish Indian People: A Report Specifically Covering Their Aboriginal and Continued Existence, and Their Effective Occupation of a Definable Territory." Pp. 475-694.

2196. Coast Salish and Western Washington
Indians III. New York: Garland Publishing, 1974.

2197. Taylor, Herbert C., Jr. "Anthropological Investigation of the Makah Indians Relative to Tribal Identity and
Aboriginal Possession of Lands." Pp.
27-89.

2198. Gillis, Alix Jane. "History of the
Neah Bay Agency." Pp. 91-115.

2199. Taylor, Herbert C., Jr. "Anthropological Investigation of the Chehalis
Indians Relative to Tribal Identity and
Aboriginal Possession of Lands." Pp.
117-157.

2200. _____. "John Work on the Chehalis
Indians." Pp. 159-192.

2201. Fried, Jacob. "The Territorial Distribution of Some of the Aboriginal
Population of Western Washington State
and the Economic and Political Characteristics of Their Culture." Pp. 193-
243.

2202. Ray, Verne F. "Handbook of Cowlitz
Indians." Pp. 245-315.

2203. "Commission Findings." Pp. 317-422.

2204. Coast Salish and Western Washington
Indians IV. New York: Garland Publishing, 1974.

2205. Elmendorf, W. W. "The Structure of
Twana Culture." Pp. 27-618.

2206. Collins, June McCormick. "A Study
of Religious Change among the Skagit
Indians, Western Washington." Pp. 619-
763.

2207. Coast Salish and Western Washington
Indians V. New York: Garland Publishing, 1974.

2208. "Commission Findings on the Coast
Salish and Western Washington Indians."
Pp. 27-660.

2209. Interior Salish and Eastern Washington Indians I. New York: Garland Publishing, 1974.

2210. Chalfant, Stuart A. "Ethnological
Field Investigation and Analysis of
Historical Material Relative to Coeur
d'Alene Indian Aboriginal Distribution."
Pp. 37-196.

2211. Bischoff, William N. "The Coeur
d'Alene Country, 1805-1892: An Historical Sketch." Pp. 197-296.

2212. "Commission Findings on the Coeur
d'Alene Indians." Pp. 297-328.

2213. Interior Salish and Eastern Washing-

ton Indians II. New York: Garland Publishing, 1974.

2214. Chalfant, Stuart A. "Aboriginal
Territories of the Flathead, Pend
d'Oreille and Kutenai Indians of Western
Montana." Pp. 25-116.

2215. Malouf. Carling. "Economy and Land
Use by the Indians of Western Montana,
U.S.A." Pp. 117-178.

2216. Burlingame, Merrill G. "Historical
Report Concerning Lands Ceded to the
United States Government by the Flathead,
Pend d'Oreille and Kutenai Indians."
Pp. 179-288.

2217. Interior Salish and Eastern Washington Indians III. New York: Garland
Publishing, 1974.

2218. Fuller, E. O. "The Confederated
Salish and Kootenai Tribes of the Flathead Reservation, Montana." Pp. 25-
167.

2219. Chalfant, Stuart A. "Aboriginal
Territory of the Kalispel Indians." Pp.
169-231.

2220. Phillips, Paul C. "History of the
Confederated Salish and Kootenai Tribes
of the Flathead Reservation, Montana."
Pp. 233-305.

2221. Malouf, Carling, and Paul C. Phillips.
"Flathead, Kutenai, and Upper Pend
d'Oreille Genealogies." Pp. 307-328.

2222. "Commission Findings." Pp. 329-415.

2223. Interior Salish and Eastern Washington Indians IV. New York: Garland Publishing, 1974.

2224. Chalfant, Stuart A. "An Ethnohistorical Report on Aboriginal Land Use
and Occupancy by the Spokan Indians."
Pp. 25-142.

2225. Anastasio, Angelo. "Ethnohistory
of the Spokane Indians." Pp. 143-173.

2226. Chalfant, Stuart A. "Ethno-histori-
cal Report on Aboriginal Land Occupancy
and Utilization by the Palus Indians."
Pp. 175-227.

2227. _____. "A Report on Anthropological and Ethnohistorical Material Relative
to Aboriginal Land Use and Occupancy by
the Columbia Salish of Central Washington." Pp. 229-313.

2228. _____. "A Report on Anthropological and Ethnohistorical Material Relative to Aboriginal Land Use and Occupancy by the Wenatchi Salish of Central
Washington." Pp. 315-375.

2229. Ray, Verne F. "Ethnohistorical
Notes on the Columbia, Chelan, Entiat,
and Wenatchee Tribes." Pp. 377-435.

2230. "Commission Findings." Pp. 437-718.

2231. Nez Perce Indians. New York: Garland Publishing, 1974.

2232. Chalfant, Stuart A. "Aboriginal Territory of the Nez Perce Indians." Pp. 25-163.

2233. Ray, Verne F. "Ethnohistory of the Joseph Band of Nez Perce Indians: 1805-1905." Pp. 165-267.

2234. "Commission Findings on the Nez Perce Indians." Pp. 269-453.

2235. Oregon Indians I. New York: Garland Publishing, 1974.

2236. Taylor, Herbert C., Jr. "Anthropological Investigation of the Tillamook Indians Relative to Tribal Identity and Aboriginal Possession of Lands." Pp. 25-102.

2237. _____. "Anthropological Investigation of the Chinook Indians Relative to Tribal Identity and Aboriginal Possession of Lands." Pp. 103-165.

2238. Suphan, Robert J. "An Ethnological Report on the Identity and Localization of Certain Native Peoples of Northwestern Oregon." Pp. 167-256.

2239. "Commission Findings." Pp. 257-326.

2240. Oregon Indians II. New York: Garland Publishing, 1974.

2241. Suphan, Robert J. "Ethnological Report on the Wasco and Tenino Indians Relative to Socio-Political Organization and Land-Use." Pp. 9-84.

2242. _____. "Ethnological Report on the Umatilla, Walla Walla, and Cayuse Indians Relative to Socio-Political Organization and Land Use." Pp. 85-180.

2243. "Commission Findings." Pp. 181-534.

Termination

The reversal of policy in the 1950s, with emphasis on termination of federal responsibility for Indian tribes, did not work and created great antagonism among the Indians. Much of the writing has concerned the termination of the Menominee Indians in Wisconsin.

2244. Ames, David W., and Burton R. Fisher. "The Menominee Termination Crisis: Barriers in the Way of a Rapid Cultural Transition." Human Organization 18 (Fall 1959): 101-111.

2245. Currie, Anne H. "Bidwell Rancheria." California Historical Society Quarterly 36 (December 1957): 313-325.

2246. Debo, Angie. "Termination and the

Oklahoma Indians." American Indian 7 (Spring 1955): 17-23.

2247. Delorme, David P. "'Emancipation' and the Turtle Mountain Chippewas." American Indian 7 (Spring 1954): 11-20.

2248. Felsenthal, Steven A., and Joseph F. Preloznik. "The Menominee Struggle to Maintain Their Tribal Assets and Protect Their Treaty Rights Following Termination." North Dakota Law Review 51 (Fall 1974): 53-71.

2249. Hasse, Larry J. "Termination and Assimilation: Federal Indian Policy, 1943 to 1961." Ph.D. dissertation, Washington State University, 1974.

2250. Hood, Susan. "Termination of the Klamath Tribe in Oregon." Ethnohistory 19 (Fall 1972): 379-392.

2251. La Farge, Oliver. "Termination of Federal Supervision: Disintegration and the American Indians." Annals of the American Academy of Political and Social Science 311 (May 1957): 41-46.

2252. Lurie, Nancy Oestreich. "Menominee Termination; or, Can the White Man Ever Overcome a Cultural Lag and Learn to Progress with the Indians?" Indian Historian 4 (Winter 1971): 33-45.

2253. _____. "Menominee Termination: From Reservation to Colony." Human Organization 31 (Fall 1972): 257-270.

2254. Shames, Deborah, ed. Freedom with Reservation: The Menominee Struggle to Save Their Land and People. Madison, Wisconsin: National Committee to Save the Menominee People and Forests, 1972.

2255. Tyler, S. Lyman. Indian Affairs: A Work Paper on Termination, with an Attempt to Show Its Antecedents. Provo, Utah: Institute of American Indian Studies, Brigham Young University, 1964.

2256. Watkins, Arthur V. "Termination of Federal Supervision: The Removal of Restrictions over Indian Property and Person." Annals of the American Academy of Political and Social Science 311 (May 1957): 47-55.

See also the material listed under Current Comment.

Current Comment, 1946-1960

The changes in Indian policy after the Collier administration, especially the movement toward termination of federal status, called forth much discussion from both sides. Representative writings of the period are listed here.

2257. "Are Indians to Lose All Their Land?" Christian Century 72 (July 20, 1955): 835-836.

2258. Barnett, Milton L., and David A. Baer-
reis. "Some Problems Involved in the
Changing Status of the American Indian."
In The Indian in Modern America, edited by
David A. Baerreis, pp. 50-70. Madison:
State Historical Society of Wisconsin,
1956.

2259. Beatty, Willard W. "The Indian in
the Postwar Period." American Indian 3
(Winter 1946): 2-7

2260. Berry, Brewton. "The Myth of the
Vanishing Indian." Phylon 21 (Spring
1960): 51-57.

2261. Bohn, Dorothy. "'Liberating' the
Indian: Euphemism for a Land Grab."
Nation 178 (February 20, 1954): 150-151.

2262. Bronson, Ruth Muskrat. Indians Are
People, Too. New York: Friendship Press,
1944.

2263. _____. "Our National Honor and
the Indians of Alaska." American Indian
4, no. 2 (1947): 14-18.

2264. _____. "Plundering the Indians
of Alaska." Christian Century 64 (October 8, 1947): 1204. Reply by Lyle F.
Watts, 64 (December 24, 1947): 1587-1588.

2265. Brown, Alan A. "America Keeps a 165-
Year Old Promise." American Mercury 91
(September 1960): 113-115.

2266. Caldwell, Russell L. "Is There an
American Indian Policy?" Ethnohistory
3 (Spring 1956): 97-108.

2267. Carse, Mary Rowell. "Americans:
With Reservations." Commonweal 47
(March 5, 1948): 510-514.

2268. Cohen, Felix S. "Alaska's Nuremberg
Laws: Congress Sanctions Racial Discrimination." Commentary 6 (August
1948): 136-143.

2269. _____. "Colonialism: U.S. Style."
Progressive 15 (February 1951): 16-18.

2270. _____. "First Americans First."
New Leader 36 (January 26, 1953): 15-18.

2271. _____. "Indians and a National
F.E.P.C." American Indian 6 (Summer
1951): 26-32.

2272. _____. "Indian Self-Government."
American Indian 5, no. 2 (1949): 3-12.

2273. _____. "Our Country's Shame."
Progressive 13 (May 1949): 9-10.

2274. Collier, John. "Back to Dishonor?"
Christian Century 71 (May 12, 1954):
78-80.

2274a. _____. "The Beleaguered Indians." Nation 169 (September 17, 1949):
276-277.

2275. _____. "Humor and Facts." Nation
171 (October 21, 1950): 372-373.

2276. _____. "Indian Takeaway Betrayal
of a Trust." Nation 179 (October 2,
1954): 290-291.

2277. _____. "Letter to General Eisen-
hower." Nation 176 (January 10, 1953):
29-30.

2278. _____. "A Perspective on the
United States Indian Situation of 1952
in Its Hemispheric and World-wide Bear-
ing." America Indigena 13 (January
1953): 7-13.

2279. _____. "The Unfinished Indian
Wars." Nation 184 (May 25, 1957): 458-
459.

2280. _____. "The United States In-
dians." In Understanding Minority
Groups, edited by Joseph B. Gittler,
pp. 33-51. New York: John Wiley and
Sons, 1956. Commentary by Theodore H.
Haas, pp. 51-57.

2281. Connolly, Thomas E. "The Future of
the American Indian." Catholic World
181 (July 1955): 246-251.

2282. Dean, William. "Klamath Hearings in
Oregon." American Forests 63 (November
1957): 12, 65-67.

2283. Debo, Angie. "What Oklahoma Indians Need." American Indian 7 (Winter
1956): 13-21.

2284. Daniel, James. "He's Giving the
Indians a Chance." Reader's Digest 70
(March 1957): 164-167. Commissioner
of Indian Affairs Emmons.

2285. Ebersole, Charles D. "Not Quite
Too Late." Christian Century 74
(April 3, 1957): 426.

2286. Emmons, Glenn L. "A Quick Look
at Indian Affairs Today." Journal of the
American Association of University Women
48 (May 1955): 199-203.

2287. _____. "U.S. Aim: Give Indians a
Chance." Nations Business 43 (July
1955): 40-43, 51-53.

2288. Fey, Harold E. "The Cherokee Trail
of Tears." Christian Century 72 (June 8,
1955): 680-682.

2289. _____. "The Church and the Indian." Christian Century 72 (June 22,
1955): 728-730.

2290. _____. "Haunted by History."
Christian Century 73 (March 21, 1956):
363-365.

2291. _____. "The Indian and the Law."
Christian Century 72 (March 9, 1955):
297-299.

2292. _____. "Indians Help Each Other."
Christian Century 77 (March 2, 1960):
246-247.

2293. _____. "Indian Winter." Christian Century 72 (March 2, 1955): 265-267.

2294. _____. "Most Indians Are Poor."
Christian Century 72 (May 18, 1955):
592-594.

2295. _____. "Navaho Race with Tragedy."
Christian Century 72 (May 25, 1955):
617-619.

2296. _____. "Our National Indian
Policy." Christian Century 72 (March
30, 1955): 395-397.

2297. _____. "Our Neighbor the Indian." Christian Century 72 (March 23,
1955): 361-364.

2298. _____. "Why Care about Indians?"
Christian Century 73 (February 22, 1956):
236-238.

2299. Flickinger, Samuel L. "The American
Indian." Federal Bar Journal 20 (Summer
1960): 212-216.

2300. Freeman, John Leiper, Jr. "A Program
for Indian Affairs: Summary of the Report
of the Hoover Commission Task Force on Indian Affairs." American Indian 7 (Spring
1954): 48-62.

2301. "Good Faith with the Indians."
America 92 (November 27, 1954): 227.

2302. Haas, Theodore H. "Administration
and Self-Government." American Indian
5 (Spring 1950): 40-46.

2303. _____. "Plight of the American
Indians." Crisis 55 (July 1948): 202-
203, 220.

2304. Haas, Theodore H., and John E. Jay.
"Toward Effective Indian Government."
American Indian 6 (Summer 1951): 17-25.

2305. Hall, Albert G. "Washington Look-
out." American Forests 63 (June 1957):
9. Transfer of Klamath forest lands.

2306. Handlong, Margaret A. "Between Two
Worlds." Educational Outlook 31 (March
1957): 108-117.

2307. Harper, Allan G. "Economic Factors
in Self-Government." American Indian 5,
no. 2 (1949): 17-22.

2308. _____. "Ft. Berthold Indians
Hope for Justice." American Indian 5,
no. 1 (1949): 22-30.

2309. Hassrick, Royal. "Are the Buried
Hatchets Forgotten?" American Indian
3 (Spring 1946): 15-20.

2310. "Heap Bad Kluxers Armed with Gun,
Indian Angry, Paleface Run." Ebony 13
(April 1958): 25-26, 28.

2311. "Hold Up Sales of Indian Lands."
Christian Century 75 (June 18, 1958):
710.

2312. Ickes, Harold L. "The Indian Loses
Again." New Republic 125 (September 24,
1951): 16.

2313. _____. "'Justice' in a Deep
Freeze." New Republic 124 (May 21, 1951):
17.

2314. _____. "A New Low in Indian Legislation." New Republic 121 (October 24,
1949): 15-16.

2315. _____. "On Frisking the Alaska
Indians." New Republic 120 (May 9,
1949): 19-20.

2316. _____. "Representative Morris
Out of Bounds." New Republic 120 (June
27, 1949): 14.

2317. "Indian Reservations May Some Day
Run Out of Indians." Saturday Evening
Post 230 (November 23, 1957): 10.

2318. "Indians Still Losing Their Land."
Christian Century 75 (October 1, 1958):
1102-1103.

2319. Jenkins, Bill, and Robert W. Sawyer.
"Oregon Views Klamath Situation."
American Forests 64 (March 1958): 24-26,
46-47.

2320. Jenkins, Frank. "Klamath Editor
Speaks." American Forests 63 (November
1957): 12.

2321. Jennings, Joe. "Ill Wind in the
Cherokee Hills." Christian Century 76
(November 18, 1959): 1341-1343.

2322. Jones, Paul. "Report on Navajo
Progress." American Indian 7 (Winter
1956): 21-26.

2323. Kimball, Solon T. "The New Crisis in
Indian Affairs." American Indian 7
(Spring 1954): 21-28.

2324. Kinney, J. P. "Will the Indian Make
the Grade?" American Forests 60 (December 1954): 24-27, 52.

2325. Knurr, Ruth B. "Indian Students
Discuss Issues." Christian Century 74
(February 27, 1957): 274.

2326. Krutch, Joseph Wood. "Beside the
Point." Nation 171 (September 23,
1950): 268.

2327. La Farge, Oliver. "The Enduring
Indian." Scientific American 202
(February 1960): 37-45, 184.

2328. _____. "Freedom, Equality,
Brotherhood." American Indian 7 (Spring
1954): 4-11.

2329. _____. "The New Administration:
Indian Affairs in the Balance." American
Indian 6 (Summer 1953): 3-7.

2330. _____. "Not an Indian, but a
White-Man Problem." New York Times

Magazine, April 30, 1950, pp. 14, 66-67.

2331. _____. "A Plea for a Square Deal for the Indians." New York Times Magazine, June 27, 1948, pp. 14-16.

2332. _____. "To Be Free and Equal." American Indian 7 (Spring 1956): 5-14.

2333. _____. "To Set the Indians Free." New Republic 121 (October 3, 1949): 11-13.

2334. Lindley, Lawrence E. "Why Indians Need Land." Christian Century 74 (November 6, 1957): 1316-1318.

2335. McNickle, D'Arcy. "Basis for a National Indian Policy." American Indian 5, no. 1 (1949): 3-12.

2336. _____. "The Indian in American Society." In Social Welfare Forum, 1955, pp. 174-183. New York: Columbia University Press, 1955.

2337. _____. "It's Almost Never Too Late." Christian Century 74 (February 20, 1957): 227-229.

2338. _____. "Process or Compulsion: The Search for a Policy of Administration in Indian Affairs." America Indigena 17 (July 1957): 261-270.

2339. _____. "U.S. Indian Affairs--1953." America Indigena 13 (October 1953): 263-273.

2340. _____. "A U.S. Indian Speaks." Americas 6 (March 1954): 8-11, 27.

2341. McNickle, R. K. "Problems of the American Indian." Editorial Research Reports 1 (April 13, 1949): 253-269.

2342. Magnuson, Don. "How the Trick Was Turned." American Forests 64 (September 1958): 8. Klamath termination bill.

2343. Martin, Fredericka. "Wanted: A Pribilof Bill of Rights." American Indian 3 (Fall 1946): 15-25.

2344. Mirrielees, Edith R. "The Cloud of Mistrust." Atlantic Monthly 199 (February 1957): 55-59. Discussion (April 1957): 30; (May 1957): 25-26.

2345. Myer, Dillon S. "Indian Administration: Problems and Goals." Social Service Review 27 (June 1953): 193-200.

2346. Nader, Ralph. "American Indians: People without a Future." Harvard Law Record 22 (May 10, 1956): 1-4.

2347. Netboy, Anthony. "Uproar on Klamath Reservation." American Forests 63 (January 1957): 20-21, 61-62.

2348. Peterson, Helen L. "American Indian Political Participation." Annals of the American Academy of Political and Social Science 311 (May 1957): 116-126.

2349. Province, John, and others. "The American Indian in Transition." American Anthropologist 56 (June 1954): 387-394.

2350. "Racism a Factor in Future of Indians." Christian Century 65 (January 21, 1948): 69-70.

2351. "Raise the Indians to Full Citizenship." Christian Century 66 (July 20, 1949): 860-861.

2352. Reichert, Bert. "Wisconsin's New Indian County." American Mercury 90 (May 1960): 125-126.

2353. "The Relocated Indian." America 96 (January 12, 1957): 404.

2354. Rush, Dana Ann. "Our Debt to the American Indian." America 98 (February 1, 1958): 510-511.

2355. Russell, Charles. "Indian Arts in Tomorrow's America." American Indian 7 (Spring 1954): 29-36.

2356. Schermerhorn, R. A. "America's Disadvantaged Minorities: The American Indian." Journal of Negro Education 20 (Summer 1951): 290-300.

2357. "Seaton Outlines Klamath Indian Proposal to Congress." American Forests 64 (February 1958): 12-13, 38-39.

2358. "Shinnecock Pow-Wow: Mixed Offspring of Long Island Indians Cling to Heritage, Fight for Reservation." Ebony 14 (November 1958): 156-162.

2359. Stevens, Alden. "Voice of the Native." New York Times Magazine, November 2, 1952, p. 65.

2360. Talney, Mark A. "Question Validity of Klamath Plan." Christian Century 73 (July 25, 1956): 882-884. Reply of William A. Zimmerman, Jr. (September 5, 1956): 1027.

2361. Templin, Ralph T. "Indian Affairs: Brazil and the United States, Cultural Exploitation or Protection?" Journal of Human Relations 3 (Spring 1955): 46-62.

2362. "This Way Lies Freedom: A Statement of Policy of the Association on American Indian Affairs." American Indian 7 (Spring 1956): 1-4.

2363. Van de Mark, Dorothy. "The Raid on the Reservations." Harper's Magazine 212 (March 1956): 48-53. See discussion, 212 (May 1956): 4-10; 213 (July 1956): 8.

2364. Watson, Editha L. "Indian Progress." American Indian 3 (Winter 1946): 12-17.

2365. Weaver, Galen R. "Governmental Jurisdictions and the Indians." Journal of Religious Thought 7 (Spring-Summer 1950): 101-107.

2366. _____. "Indian Americans."
Social Action 21 (January 1955): 22-24.

2367. _____. "Indian Americans and the
84th Congress." Social Action 21 (June
1955): 6.

2368. Wesley, Clarence. "Arizona's Greatest Resource--the Indian People." Journal of Human Relations 6 (Winter 1958):
107-117.

2369. Wilson, Frank T. "Interview with
Dillon S. Myer, Commissioner of Indian
Affairs." Journal of Religious Thought
7 (Spring-Summer 1950): 93-100.

2370. Wright, Muriel H. "The American Indian Exposition in Oklahoma." Chronicles
of Oklahoma 24 (Summer 1946): 158-165.

2371. Yamada, George. "The Predatory White
Man." Crisis 59 (January 1952): 25-30,
63-65.

Other similar material can be located in
the Readers' Guide (150).

Current Comment, 1961-1970

The decade of the 1960s was one of growing agitation for Indian self-determination. Articulate Indians and white sup-
porters of the Indian cause were widely
read, and there was a new popular awareness of Indian problems. The following
writings indicate the development of the
"Red Power" movement.

2372. Bachrach, William B. "An Assault
in the Sixties." Humanist 27 (September-December 1967): 183-184.

2373. Barry, Lawrence E. "The Indian in a
Cultural Trap." America 112 (August
10, 1965): 482-484.

2374. Bennett, Robert L. "New Era for
the American Indian." Natural History
76 (February 1967): 6-11.

2375. _____. "Problems and Prospects
in Developing Indian Communities."
Arizona Law Review 10 (Winter 1968): 649-
659.

2376. Bigart, R. J. "American Indians in
the 'Melting Pot': Are Indian Communities Assimilating into White Society?"
Montana Business Quarterly 8 (Summer
1970): 27-30.

2377. Bims, Hamilton. "Indian Uprising
for Civil Rights." Ebony 22 (February
1967): 64-65, 68-70, 72. Fishing
rights.

2378. Bongartz, Roy. "Do These Indians
Really Own Florida?" Saturday Evening
Post 237 (February 1, 1964): 62-63, 65.
Seminole claims.

2379. _____. "The New Indian." Esquire
74 (August 1970): 107-109, 125-126.

2380. _____. "Who Am I? The Indian
Sickness: The White Hawk Case." Nation
210 (April 27, 1970): 496-498.

2381. Boyle, Kay. "A Day on Alcatraz
with the Indians." New Republic 162
(January 17, 1970): 10-11.

2382. Brandon, William. "American Indians:
The Alien Americans." Progressive 33
(December 1969): 13-17.

2383. _____. "American Indians: The
Real American Revolution." Progressive
34 (February 1970): 26-30.

2384. _____. "The American Indians:
The Un-Americans." Progressive 34 (January 1970): 35-39.

2385. Brightman, Lehman. "Red Power."
Black Politician 1 (Fall 1969): 37-39.

2386. Brophy, William A., and Sophie D.
Aberle. The Indian: America's Unfinished
Business: Report of the Commission on
the Rights, Liberties, and Responsibili-
ties of the American Indian. Norman:
University of Oklahoma Press, 1966.

2387. Cahn, Edgar S., ed. Our Brother's
Keeper: The Indian in White America.
New York: World Publishing Company, 1969.
Material assembled by the Citizens'
Advocate Center.

2388. Cass, James. "A Usable History for
the Red Man." Saturday Review 53 (May
16, 1970): 69.

2389. Clifton, James A. "Indian or American?" Delphian Quarterly 46 (Summer
1963): 1-5, 25-26.

2390. Cohen, Warren H., and Philip J.
Mause. "The Indian: The Forgotten
American." Harvard Law Review 81
(June 1968): 1818-1858.

2391. Coleman, John A. "Lords of the
Rock." America 122 (May 2, 1970): 465-
467. Alcatraz.

2392. Collier, John. "Comments on the
Essay of Robert A. Manners, 'Pluralism
and the American Indian.'" America
Indigena 22 (July 1962): 205-208.

2393. _____. "Final Reply of John
Collier." America Indigena 23 (January
1963): 76-77.

2394. _____. "The Indians' Heritage."
Americas 14 (September 1962): 34-38.

2395. _____. "Slow Recovery since
Wounded Knee." Saturday Review 46
(June 15, 1963): 31-32.

2396. Collier, Peter. "The Red Man's
Burden." Ramparts Magazine 8 (February
1970): 26-38.

2397. _____. "The Theft of a Nation: Apologies to the Cherokees." Ramparts Magazine 9 (September 1970): 35-45.

2398. Connolly, Thomas E. "A New Last Frontier." America 105 (June 10, 1961): 417. American Indian Chicago Conference.

2399. Cook, James. "An Indian Is As an Indian Does." Chicago Tribune Magazine, August 2, 1970, p. 44.

2400. Costo, Rupert. "The American Indian Today." Indian Historian 1 (Winter 1968): 4-8, 35.

2401. _____. "Forms and Uses of Tribal Government." In Indian Voices: The First Convocation of American Indian Scholars, pp. 283-290. San Francisco: Indian Historian Press, 1970.

2402. _____. "Moment of Truth for the American Indian." In Indian Voices: The First Convocation of American Indian Scholars, pp. 3-8. San Francisco: Indian Historian Press, 1970.

2403. Deloria, Vine, Jr. Custer Died for Your Sins: An Indian Manifesto. New York: Macmillan Company, 1969.

2404. _____. "This Country Was a Lot Better Off When the Indians Were Running It." New York Times Magazine, March 8, 1970, pp. 32-33 +.

2405. _____. "The War between the Redskins and the Feds." New York Times Magazine, December 7, 1969, pp. 47 +.

2406. _____. We Talk, You Listen: New Tribes, New Turf. New York: Macmillan Company, 1970.

2407. Dennis, Lloyd B. "American Indians: Neglected Minority." Editorial Research Reports 2 (1966): 623-640.

2408. Dorner, Peter. "Needed: A New Policy for the American Indians." Land Economics 37 (May 1961): 162-173.

2409. Emmons, Glenn L. "Readjustment with Security for the American Indian." In Toward Economic Development for Native American Communities, pp. 97-101. Washington: Government Printing Office, 1969. On ending trust relationships with the federal government.

2410. Ericson, Robert, and D. Rebecca Snow. "The Indian Battle for Self-Determination." California Law Review 58 (March 1970): 445-490.

2411. Farb, Peter. "The American Indians: A Portrait in Limbo." Saturday Review 51 (October 12, 1968): 26-29.

2412. Forbes, Jack D. "A Comprehensive Program for Tribal Development in the United States." Human Organization 24 (Summer 1965): 159-161.

2413. _____. "Who Speaks for the Indian?" Humanist 27 (September-December 1967): 174-176.

2414. Graymont, Barbara. "The American Indian in Today's Society." Journal of Religious Thought 19 (1962-1963): 19-33.

2415. Greenway, John. "Will the Indians Get Whitey?" National Review 21 (March 11, 1969): 223-228, 245.

2416. Hedgepeth, William. "Alcatraz: The Indian Uprising That Worked." Look 34 (June 2, 1970): 44-45.

2417. _____. "America's Indians: Reawakening of a Conquered People." Look 34 (June 2, 1970): 23-34.

2418. Henry, Jeannette. "The Indian Press: A Slow Development." Indian Historian 1 (Winter 1968): 15-16, 36.

2419. Hey, Nigel S. "The Not-So-Vanishing Americans." Interplay 3 (September 1969): 20-24.

2420. "Investiture Controversy." America 113 (July 24, 1965): 88-89.

2421. Josephy, Alvin M., Jr. "Indians in History." Atlantic Monthly 225 (June 1970): 67-72. Discussion, 226 (September 1970): 46-47.

2422. Kennedy, Edward M. "Let the Indians Run Indian Policy." Look 34 (June 2, 1970): 36, 38.

2423. "The 'Lake of Perfidy.'" Social Education 27 (October 1963): 293-333. Kinzua Dam controversy.

2424. Leon, Robert L. "Some Implications for a Preventive Program for American Indians." American Journal of Psychiatry 125 (August 1968): 232-236.

2425. "Less Termination, More Aid." America 105 (August 5, 1961): 579-580.

2426. Lesser, Alexander. "Who Speaks for the American Indians?" Midway, October 1961, pp. 3-17.

2427. Levine, Stuart. "Foreword: The Survival of Indian Identity." In The American Indian Today, edited by Stuart Levine and Nancy Oestreich Lurie, pp. 1-23. Deland, Florida: Everett/Edwards, 1968.

2428. _____. "The Indian as American: Some Observations from the Editor's Notebook." Midcontinent American Studies Journal 6 (Fall 1965): 3-22.

2429. _____. "Our Indian Minority." Colorado Quarterly 16 (Winter 1968): 297-320.

2430. Levy, Jerrold E. "The Older American

Indian." In Older Rural Americans: A Sociological Perspective, edited by E. Grant Youmans, pp. 221-238. Lexington: University of Kentucky Press, 1967.

2431. Lurie, Nancy Oestreich. "An American Indian Renascence?" In The American Indian Today, edited by Stuart Levine and Nancy Oestreich Lurie, pp. 187-208. Deland, Florida: Everett/Edwards, 1968. An earlier version appeared in Midcontinent American Studies Journal 6 (Fall 1965): 25-50.

2432. _____. "The Enduring Indian." Natural History 74 (November 1966): 10-22.

2433. _____. "The Voice of the American Indian: Report on the American Indian Chicago Conference." Current Anthropology 2 (December 1961): 478-500.

2434. _____. "What the Red Man Wants in the Land That Was His." Saturday Review 52 (October 4, 1969): 39-41, 80-81.

2435. McCloud, Janet. "The Continuing 'Last Indian War.'" Humanist 27 (September-December 1967): 177-179.

2436. McNickle, D'Arcy. "The Dead Horse Walks Again." Nation 205 (December 25, 1967): 677-678.

2437. _____. "The Indian Tests the Mainstream." Nation 203 (September 26, 1966): 275-279.

2438. _____. "Private Intervention." Human Organization 20 (Winter 1961-1962): 208-215.

2439. Mangel, Charles. "'Sometimes We Feel We're Already Dead': Arizona's Ruined Cocopah: Product of the White Man's Triumph." Look 34 (June 2, 1970): 39-43.

2440. Manners, Robert A. "Pluralism and the American Indian." America Indigena 22 (January 1962): 25-38.

2441. _____. "Robert Manners Answers John Collier's Comments on His Article." America Indigena 23 (January 1963): 71-75.

2442. Margolis, Richard J. "States of the Union: Whitewashing the Indians." New Leader 53 (December 28, 1970): 13-14.

2443. Maxey, David R. "Bureau of Indian Affairs: America's Colonial Service." Look 34 (June 2, 1970): 35.

2444. Medicine, Beatrice. "Red Power: Real or Potential?" In Indian Voices: The First Convocation of American Indian Scholars, pp. 299-307. San Francisco: Indian Historian Press, 1970.

2445. _____. "Responsibilities of Foundations in Native American Programs." In Indian Voices: The First Convocation of American Indian Scholars, pp. 357-361. San Francisco: Indian Historian Press, 1970.

2446. Miller, Robert A. "Indians: Better Dead than Red?" Southern California Law Review 42 (Fall 1968): 101-125.

2447. Morey, Sylvester M., ed. Can the Red Man Help the White Man? New York: Gilbert Church, 1970.

2448. Morris, Terry. "LaDonna Harris: A Woman Who Gives a Damn." Redbook 34 (February 1970): 75, 115, 117-118.

2449. Muskrat, Joseph C. "The Indians--an Analysis and Proposal." Legal Aid Brief Case 28 (May 1970): 187-195.

2450. Nabokov, Peter. "Our Most Silent Minority." Nation 210 (January 26, 1970): 86-88.

2451. Nader, Ralph. "'Lo, the Poor Indian.'" New Republic 158 (March 30, 1968): 14-15.

2452. Nash, Philleo. "Indian Administration in the United States: Address, December 6, 1962." Vital Speeches 29 (February 15, 1963): 278-283.

2453. "National Council Champions Taos Pueblo Indians." Christian Century 84 (July 19, 1967): 932.

2454. Nichols, Rosalie. "Right-Wing Rationale of Non-Recognition of Indian Rights." Indian Historian 3 (Spring 1970): 25-36, 65.

2455. "Notes and Comments on the American Indian." Civil Rights Digest 3 (Winter 1970): 19-21.

2456. Officer, James E. "Indian Unity." Journal of American Indian Education 3 (May 1964): 1-8.

2457. _____. "Informal Power Structures within Indian Communities." Journal of American Indian Education 3 (October 1963): 1-8.

2458. _____. "A New Image for the Great White Father?" Midcontinent American Studies Journal 11 (Spring 1970): 5-19.

2459. Old Person, Earl. "Indians as Human Beings." Integrated Education 5 (April-May 1967): 18-21.

2460. Ortiz, Alfonso. "American Indian Philosophy: Its Relation to the Modern World." In Indian Voices: The First Convocation of American Indian Scholars, pp. 9-17. San Francisco: Indian Historian Press, 1970.

2461. Owl, Frell M. "Who and What Is an American Indian?" Ethnohistory 9 (Summer 1962): 265-284.

2462. Pappalardo, Maria S. "American Indians--a Question of Survival." Journal of Intergroup Relations 5 (Autumn 1966): 86-93.

2463. Pratt, Wayne T. "Toward a Better Understanding of the Indian American." Journal of Intergroup Relations 3 (Autumn 1962): 364-373.

2464. "Proclamation: To the Great White Father and All His People." Journal of American Indian Education 9 (January 1970): 16-18. Alcatraz Island.

2465. Rachlin, Carol K. "Tight Shoe Night: Oklahoma Indians Today." In The American Indian Today, edited by Stuart Levine and Nancy Oestreich Lurie, pp. 99-114. Deland, Florida: Everett/Edwards, 1968. This appeared originally in Midcontinent American Studies Journal 6 (Fall 1965): 84-100.

2466. Richman, Robin. "Rediscovery of the Redman." Life 63 (December 1, 1967): 52-71.

2467. Ridgeway, James. "The Lost Indians." New Republic 153 (December 4, 1965): 17-20.

2468. _____. "More Lost Indians: A Trip to the Sioux Country." New Republic 153 (December 11, 1965): 19-22.

2469. Rosen, Sanford Jay. "Militancy Is Growing among Red Indians in the United States." Patterns of Prejudice 4 (May-June 1970): 13-16.

2470. Roucek, Joseph S. "The American Indian in Literature and Politics." Il Politico 27 (1962): 569-585.

2471. Sanchez, Abel. "The History of San Felipe Pueblo People." Integrated Education 6 (November-December 1968): 56-60.

2472. Schulz, Larold K. "The American Indian: A Contemporary Analysis." Social Action 32 (March 1966): 7-18.

2473. Schusky, Ernest L. "An Indian Dilemma." International Journal of Comparative Sociology 11 (March 1970): 58-66.

2474. _____. The Right to Be Indian. San Francisco: Indian Historian Press, 1970.

2475. Scullin, Michael. "Reviewing the Mass Media." Indian Historian 2 (Spring 1969): 49-50.

2476. "The Shame Is Ours." Social Education 26 (May 1962): 233, 268. Kinzua Dam Project.

2477. Sparks, Joe P. "The Indian Stronghold and the Spread of Urban America." Arizona Law Review 10 (Winter 1968): 706-724.

2478. Spicer, Edward H. "The Issues in Indian Affairs." Arizona Quarterly 21 (Winter 1965): 293-307.

2479. Spiker, LaRue. "Under the Indian Sign: A Blanket over Homicide." Nation 202 (April 25, 1966): 483-486.

2480. Steiner, Stan. "The American Indian: Ghettos in the Desert." Nation 198 (June 26, 1964): 624-627.

2481. _____. The New Indians. New York: Harper and Row, 1967.

2481a. Stewart, Omer C. "Background of American Indian Conference." Delphian Quarterly 44 (Autumn 1961): 22-25, 31.

2482. _____. "Group Assistance of American Indians." Delphian Quarterly 45 (Winter 1962): 15-18.

2483. _____. "The Indians in Chicago." Delphian Quarterly 45 (Spring 1962): 9-13, 37-38. Chicago Indian Conference.

2484. Strickland, Rennard, and Jack Gregory. "Nixon and the Indian: Is Dick Another Buffalo Bill?" Commonweal 92 (September 4, 1970): 432-436.

2485. Taylor, Walter. "The Treaty We Broke." Nation 193 (September 2, 1961): 120-121. Kinzua Dam controversy.

2486. Thomas, Robert K. "Colonialism: Classic and Internal." New University Thought 4 (Winter 1966-1967): 37-44.

2487. _____. "Powerless Politics." New University Thought 4 (Winter 1966-1967): 44-53. Pine Ridge Reservation.

2488. Udall, Stewart L. "The State of the Indian Nation--an Introduction." Arizona Law Review 10 (Winter 1968): 554-557.

2489. "Udall's Indians." New Republic 155 (October 15, 1966): 7-8.

2490. Vogel, Virgil J. "After 80 Years: The Indians Rise Again." New Politics 8 (Spring 1970): 62-72.

2491. Wahrhaftig, Albert. "Community and the Caretakers." New University Thought 4 (Winter 1966-1967): 54-76.

2492. Washburn, Wilcomb E. "Red Power." American West 6 (January 1969): 52-53.

2493. Wax, Rosalie H., and Robert K. Thomas. "American Indians and White People." Phylon 22 (Winter 1961): 305-317.

2494. Weaver, Galen. "Our Oldest Inhabitants: Indian-Americans and the Kennedy Administration." Interracial Review 36 (March 1963): 56-58.

2495. Welch, W. Bruce. "The American In-

dian (a Stifled Minority)." Journal of
Negro Education 38 (Summer 1969): 242-
246.

2496. Wells, Merle W. "An Indian Manifesto:
An Essay Review." Pacific Northwest
Quarterly 61 (July 1970): 162-164.

2497. Whatley, John T. "The Saga of Taos
Pueblo: The Blue Lake Controversy."
Indian Historian 2 (Fall 1969): 22-28.

2498. "Where the Real Poverty Is: Plight
of American Indians." U.S. News and
World Report 60 (April 25, 1966): 104-
108.

2499. White, Robert A. "American Indian
Crisis." Social Order 11 (May 1961):
201-211.

2500. Whitten, Edward. "Meanwhile, Back
at the Reservation." Commonweal 91
(February 6, 1970): 515-516.

2501. "Why No Integration for the American
Indian?" U.S. News and World Report 55
(September 2, 1963): 62-66.

2502. Willhelm, Sidney M. "Red Man, Black
Man and White America: The Constitutional
Approach to Genocide." Catalyst no. 4
(Spring 1969): 1-62.

2503. Witt, Shirley Hill. "Nationalistic
Trends among American Indians." In The
American Indian Today, edited by Stuart
Levine and Nancy Oestreich Lurie, pp. 53-
75. Deland, Florida: Everett/Edwards,
1968. An earlier version appeared in
Midcontinent American Studies Journal 6
(Fall 1965): 51-74.

2504. Young, Biloine D. "The American Indian: Citizen in Captivity." Saturday
Review 48 (December 11, 1965): 25-26.

Additional material can be located in the
Readers' Guide (150).

Current Comment, 1971--

The rise of Indian activism that began
in the 1960s continued unabated in the
1970s, occasioning much comment on Indian
affairs. The encounter at Wounded Knee
in 1973 was of special importance.

2505. Bahr, Howard M., and Bruce A. Chadwick. "Contemporary Perspectives on
Indian Americans: A Review Essay."
Social Science Quarterly 53 (December
1972): 606-618.

2506. Baines, Raymond. "Aliens in Our Own
Land." Engage/Social Action 1 (January
1973): 29-36.

2507. Barnes, Peter. "Bad Day at Black
Mesa." New Republic 165 (July 17, 1971):
23-24.

2508. _____. "Trinkets for the Navajos."
New Republic 165 (July 3, 1971): 15-16.

2509. Bauman, John F. "Forgotten Americans:
The Migrant and Indian Poor." Current
History 64 (June 1973): 264-267, 276-
278.

2510. Bell, Joseph N. "America's Oldest
Debt: Justice for the Indians." Good
Housekeeping 172 (January 1971): 78-79,
146-150.

2511. Bigjim, Frederick Seagayuk, and
James Ito-Adler. Letters to Howard: An
Interpretation of the Alaska Native Land
Claims. Anchorage: Alaska Methodist University Press, 1974. Letters originally
published in the Tundra Times, March,
1973.

2512. Bosmajian, Haig A. "Defining the
American Indian: A Case Study in the
Language of Suppression." Speech Teacher
22 (March 1973): 89-99.

2513. Bower, Donald E. "The Native American: A Changing Perspective." American
West 10 (July 1973): 48-63.

2514. Brown, Thomas M. "Native May Win
One: Great Alaskan Real-Estate Deal."
New York Times Magazine, October 17,
1971, pp. 42-43 +.

2515. Burnette, Robert, and John Koster.
The Road to Wounded Knee. New York:
Bantam Books, 1974.

2516. Castile, George P. "Federal In-
dian Policy and the Sustained Enclave:
An Anthropological Perspective." Human
Organization 33 (Fall 1974): 219-228.

2517. Coffeen, William R. "The Effects of
the Central Arizona Project on the Fort
McDowell Indian Community." Ethnohistory
19 (Fall 1972): 345-377.

2518. Collier, Peter. "Wounded Knee: The
New Indian War." Ramparts 11 (January
1973): 25-29, 56-59.

2519. Collins, Dabney Otis. "Battle for
Blue Lake: The Taos Indians Finally Re-
gain Their Sacred Land." American West
8 (September 1971): 32-37.

2520. Collins, Paul. "Showdown at Wounded
Knee: Black Artist Sketches Indian Confrontation." Ebony 28 (June 1973): 46-
48, 50, 52-54, 56.

2521. Conway, Thomas G. "Public Interest
in the Indian." Indian Historian 5
(Spring 1972): 37-43.

2522. Damio, Ward. "Twilight in the
House of Dawn." Media and Methods 7
(April 1971): 64-65, 70.

2523. Day, Robert C. "The Emergence of
Activism as a Social Movement." In

Native Americans Today; Sociological Perspectives, edited by Howard M. Bahr and others, pp. 506-532. New York: Harper and Row, 1972.

2524. Dean, S. Bobo. "The Consent of the Governed--a New Concept in Indian Affairs?" North Dakota Law Review 48 (Summer 1972): 533-550.

2525. "A Declaration of Apache Bill of Rights." Indian Historian 6 (Fall 1973): 55-56.

2526. Degler, Carl N. "Indians and Other Americans." Commentary 54 (November 1972): 68-72.

2527. Deloria, Vine, Jr. "The American Indian and His Commitments, Goals, Programs: A Need to Reconsider." Indian Historian 5 (Spring 1972): 5-10.

2528. _____. Behind the Trail of Broken Treaties: An Indian Declaration of Independence. New York: Delacorte Press, 1974.

2529. _____. God Is Red. New York: Grosset and Dunlap, 1973.

2530. _____. The Indian Affair. New York: Friendship Press, 1974.

2531. _____. "The Indian World Today." American Indian Culture Center Journal 4 (Winter 1973): 3-5.

2532. _____. "The Next Three Years: A Time for Change." Indian Historian 7 (Spring 1974): 25-27, 53.

2533. _____. "Religion and the Modern American Indian." Current History 67 (December 1974): 250-253.

2534. _____. "The Theological Dimension of the Indian Protest Movement." Christian Century 90 (September 19, 1973): 912-914.

2535. _____. "White Society Is Breaking Down Around Us . . . Even Its Myths--Like the Melting Pot--Are Dead." Mademoiselle 72 (April 1971): 202-204, 269. An interview edited by Peter Collier.

2536. Dilley, Russell. "NCC's Role at Wounded Knee." Christian Century 90 (April 4, 1973): 400-402. National Council of Churches.

2537. _____. "Standoff at Wounded Knee." Christian Century 90 (May 9, 1973): 527-528.

2538. Dollar, Clyde D. "Renaissance on the Reservation." American West 11 (January 1974): 6-9, 58-62.

2539. _____. "The Second Tragedy at Wounded Knee: A 1970s Confrontation and

Its Historical Roots." American West 10 (September 1973): 4-11, 58-61.

2540. Donnelly, James F. "Can Indians Trust Washington." America 127 (November 25, 1972): 445.

2541. Doyle, Barrie. "Bury My Tithe at Wounded Knee." Christianity Today 17 (June 8, 1973): 40-41.

2542. Ducheneaux, Franklin. "The American Indian: Beyond the Stereotypes." Today's Education 62 (May 1973): 22-24.

2543. Elbert, Ted. "Wounded Knee: A Struggle for Self-Determination." Christian Century 90 (March 28, 1973): 356-357.

2544. Faherty, Robert L. "The American Indian: An Overview." Current History 67 (December 1974): 241-244, 274.

2545. Farris, Charles E. "A White House Conference on the American Indian." Social Work 18 (January 1973): 80-86.

2546. Fenton, William N. "The New York State Wampum Collection: The Case for the Integrity of Cultural Treasures." Proceedings of the American Philosophical Society 115 (December 1971): 437-461.

2547. Fey, Harold E. "America's Most Oppressed Minority." Christian Century 88 (January 20, 1971): 65-68.

2548. Fishlow, David. "Reading the Riot Act." New Republic 169 (July 21, 1973): 11-12. Arrests after Wounded Knee.

2549. Forbes, Jack D. "The Americanization of Education in the United States." Indian Historian 7 (Spring 1974): 15-21.

2550. Fowler, Jo Ann V. "Threat to Grand Canyon." BioScience 24 (December 1974): 743. Havasupai Indian reservation expansion.

2551. Gold, Victor. "Of Fallen Trees and Wounded Knees." National Review 25 (April 27, 1973): 464-465, 482.

2552. Grumbach, Doris. "The Year of the Indian." New Republic 170 (May 18, 1974): 31-32.

2553. Hafdahl, Grayce. "Is Self-Determination an Answer to Problems of American Indians?" Delta Kappa Gamma Bulletin 37 (Winter 1971): 54-60.

2554. Hanlon, William T. "Whose Ox Was Gored at Wounded Knee?" America 130 (March 16, 1974): 190-192.

2555. Heath, G. Louis. "No Rock Is an Island." Phi Delta Kappan 52 (March 1971): 397-399. Alcatraz.

2556. Huck, Susan L. M. "Renegades: The

Second Battle of Wounded Knee." American Opinion 16 (May 1973): 1-14.

2557. "An Indian 'Nation' Is Gaining Unity, Respect--and Results." U.S. News and World Report 76 (February 25, 1974): 60-61.

2558. Indians of All Tribes. Alcatraz Is Not an Island. Edited by Peter Blue Cloud. Berkeley, California: Wingbow Press, 1972.

2559. Josephy, Alvin M., Jr. "Freedom for the American Indian." Critic 32 (September-October 1973): 18-27.

2560. _____. "Toward Freedom: The American Indian in the Twentieth Century." In American Indian Policy: Indiana Historical Society Lectures 1970-1971, pp. 38-65. Indianapolis: Indiana Historical Society, 1971.

2561. _____. "Wounded Knee and All That--What the Indians Want." New York Times Magazine, March 18, 1973, pp. 18-19 +.

2562. Josephy, Alvin M., Jr., ed. Red Power: The American Indians' Fight for Freedom. New York: American Heritage Press, 1971.

2563. King, Thomas F. "Archaeological Law and the American Indian." Indian Historian 5 (Fall 1972): 31-33.

2564. Koch, Walton Boston. "The Alaska Native Land Claims Bill: Pay Off or Rip Off?" Michigan Academician 6 (Winter 1974): 299-305.

2565. Langdon, Daniel. "The American Indian: Minority of Minorities." Community 46 (March-April 1971): 6-9, 11.

2566. Levitan, Sar A., and Barbara Hetrick. Big Brother's Indian Programs, with Reservations. New York: McGraw-Hill Book Company, 1971.

2567. Lurie, Nancy Oestreich. "The Contemporary American Indian Scene." In North American Indians in Historical Perspective, edited by Eleanor Burke Leacock and Nancy Oestreich Lurie, pp. 418-480. New York: Random House, 1971.

2568. _____. "Forked Tongue in Cheek; or, Life among the Noble Civilages." Indian Historian 7 (Spring 1974): 28-40, 52.

2569. Lynd, Staughton. "Wayne Kennedy Case: New Concept of Unionism." Nation 214 (January 24, 1972): 110-113.

2570. Marden, David. "Forgotten but Not Gone: A Case Study in the Persistence of Reform." Phylon 35 (March 1974): 108-119.

2571. Mathur, Mary E. Fleming. "The Case for Using Historical Data: Third Generation Tribal Nationalism." Indian Historian 6 (Fall 1973): 14-19.

2572. Medicine, Beatrice. "The Big Foot Trail to Wounded Knee." Indian Historian 6 (Fall 1973): 23-25.

2573. Meyer, Eugene I. "Bury My Heart on the Potomac: Indians at the B.I.A." Ramparts 11 (January 1973): 10-12.

2574. Meyer, William. Native Americans: The New Indian Resistance. New York: International Publishers, 1971.

2575. Morgan, Lael. And the Land Provides: Alaskan Natives in a Year of Transition. Garden City, New York: Doubleday and Company, 1974.

2576. Noble, Gaile P. "The Ganado Project: Any 'Change' for the Navajo Reservation?" Christian Century 88 (January 20, 1971): 78-80.

2577. Oakes, Richard. "Alcatraz Is Not an Island." Ramparts 11 (December 1972): 35-41.

2578. Ranck, Lee. "Siege at Wounded Knee." Engage/Social Action 1 (May 1973): 6-21.

2579. "The Real Goals of Restless Indians." U.S. News and World Report 74 (April 2, 1973): 26-30.

2580. Schonbach, Samuel. "What the Red Man Needs." Catholic World 214 (November 1971): 66-70.

2581. Schroeder, Richard C. "Preservation of Indian Culture." Editorial Research Reports 2 (November 8, 1972): 847-868.

2582. Schultz, Terri. "Bamboozle Me Not at Wounded Knee." Harper's Magazine 246 (June 1973): 46-48, 53-56.

2583. Shorris, Earl. The Death of the Great Spirit: An Elegy for the American Indian. New York: Simon and Schuster, 1971.

2584. Smith, Desmond. "Wounded Knee: The Media Coup d'Etat." Nation 216 (June 25, 1973): 806-809.

2585. Steiger, Brad. Medicine Power: The American Indian's Revival of His Spiritual Heritage and Its Relevance for Modern Man. Garden City, New York: Doubleday and Company, 1974.

2586. Stensland, Anna Lee. "American Indian Culture: Promises, Problems, and Possibilities." English Journal 60 (December 1971): 1195-1200.

2587. Svensson, Frances. The Ethnics in American Politics: American Indians.

Minneapolis: Burgess Publishing Company, 1973.

2588. Talbert, Carol. "Experiences at Wounded Knee." Human Organization 33 (Summer 1974): 215-217.

2589. Tilsen, Kenneth E. "U.S. Courts and Native Americans at Wounded Knee." Guild Practitioner 31 (Spring 1974): 61-69.

2590. Treisman, Eric. "Indian Giving: The White Man Still Speaks with a Lying Tongue." Harper's Magazine 246 (January 1973): 79-84.

2591. _____. "The Last Treaty." Harper's Magazine 250 (January 1975): 37-39. The Alaskan Native Claims Settlement Act of 1971.

2592. Trillin, Calvin. "U.S. Journal: Tesuque, N.M.: Some Facts about the Colonias Project, and Several Ways of Looking at Them." New Yorker, December 18, 1971, pp. 93-97. Resort development on Pueblo land.

2593. Trillin, Calvin, and Edward Koren. "A Reporter at Large (the Gallup Intertribal Indian Ceremonial)." New Yorker, August 5, 1972, pp. 32-37.

2594. Trotter, Robert J. "Indians and Sociologists: Science or Exploitation?" Science News 100 (October 2, 1971): 234.

2595. Wall, James M. "Indian Theology and the White Man's Laws." Christian Century 90 (September 19, 1973): 907-908.

2596. _____. "Wounded Knee Comes to Trial." Christian Century 91 (March 6, 1974): 251-252.

2597. Waters, Frank. "Crossroads: Indians and Whites." South Dakota Review 11 (Autumn 1973): 28-38.

2598. Watkins, T. H. "Ancient Wrongs and Public Rights." Sierra Club Bulletin 59 (September 1974): 15-16, 37-39.

2599. Westermeyer, Joseph J. "Indian Powerlessness in Minnesota." Society 10 (March-April 1973): 45-47, 50-52.

2600. Wieck, Paul R. "From Wards to Freemen: Indians on and off the Reservation." New Republic 168 (April 7, 1973): 16-19.

2601. Wilson, Paul E., and Elaine Oser Zingg. "What Is America's Heritage? Historic Preservation and American Indian Culture." University of Kansas Law Review 22 (Spring 1974): 413-453.

2602. Wolff, Anthony. "Showdown at Four Corners." Saturday Review of the Society 55 (June 3, 1972): 29-41.

2603. Zwerdling, Daniel. "Off the Reservation." Progressive 38 (April 1974): 45-47. Indians in Maine.

See the Readers' Guide (150) and newspaper indexes for further current materials.

6

The Indian Department

The Bureau of Indian Affairs and the Indian superintendencies and agencies, with their numerous personnel, made up what was often called the "Indian Department." The men in these offices carried out the Indian policy of the federal government and often helped to formulate it.

BUREAU OF INDIAN AFFAIRS

The top of the governmental bureaucracy devoted to Indian affairs is the Bureau of Indian Affairs (at one time called the Office of Indian Affairs), which was at first under the War Department and then transferred to the Department of the Interior in 1849. The only general study of the Bureau, now outdated, is the following.

2604. Schmeckebier, Laurence F. The Office of Indian Affairs: Its History, Activities, and Organization. Institute for Government Research, Service Monographs of the United States Government, no. 48. Baltimore: Johns Hopkins Press, 1927.

Much material on the Bureau, its subsidiaries, and its operations appears in official government publications (see the section on Documents of the Federal Government). The following compilations are useful references for various periods and contain many data on reservations, agencies, population, and the like.

2605. Report on Indians Taxed and Not Taxed in the United States (except Alaska) at the Eleventh Census: 1890. Issued by the Census Office, Department of the Interior. Washington: Government Printing Office, 1894. Also published as House Miscellaneous Document no. 340, part 15, 52d Congress, 1st session, serial 3016. A highly illustrated work, with descriptions of the condition of the Indians state by state and other valuable data.

2606. Investigation of the Bureau of Indian Affairs. Washington: Government Printing Office, 1953. House Report no. 2503, 82d Congress, 2d session, serial 11582.

A massive collection of data on Indian reservations, treaties, bureau organization, and the like.

2607. Federal and State Indian Reservations and Indian Trust Areas. New and revised edition. Washington: Government Printing Office, 1974. Lists reservations alphabetically by states; gives data on area, population, status, and facilities.

2608. Taylor, Theodore W. The States and Their Indian Citizens. Washington: U.S. Department of the Interior, Bureau of Indian Affairs, 1972.

The following works treat of the War Department and the Department of the Interior, of particular aspects of the operations of the Bureau of Indian Affairs, and of miscellaneous related topics.

2609. Alexander, Thomas G. "The Federal Frontier: Interior Department Financial Policy in Idaho, Utah, and Arizona, 1863-1896." Ph.D. dissertation, University of California, 1965.

2610. Bureau of Municipal Research. Administration of the Indian Office. Publication no. 65. New York: Bureau of Municipal Research, 1915.

2611. Burman, Barbara. "Mancari v. Morton: A Discussion of Preference." New Mexico Law Review 4 (May 1974): 283-296. On preferential hiring of Indians.

2612. Deloria, Vine, Jr. "The Bureau of Indian Affairs: My Brother's Keeper." Art in America 60 (July-August 1972): 110-115.

2613. Embree, John F. "The Indian Bureau and Self-Government." Human Organization 8 (Spring 1949): 11-14.

2614. Forness, Norman Olaf. "The Origins and Early History of the United States Department of the Interior." Ph.D. dissertation, Pennsylvania State University, 1964.

2615. Freeman, John Leiper, Jr. "The New Deal for Indians: A Study in Bureau-

Committee Relations in American Government." Ph.D. dissertation, Princeton University, 1952.

2616. Gamino, John. "Bureau of Indian Affairs: Should Indians Be Preferentially Employed?" American Indian Law Review 2 (Summer 1974): 111-118.

2617. Hebal, John James. "Field Administration of the Bureau of Indian Affairs in Minnesota and Wisconsin." Ph.D. dissertation, University of Minnesota, 1959.

2618. Leon, Robert L. "Maladaptive Interaction between Bureau of Indian Affairs Staff and Indian Clients." American Journal of Orthopsychiatry 35 (July 1965): 723-728.

2619. Mekeel, Scudder. "Comparative Notes on the 'Social Role of the Settlement House' As Contrasted with That of the United States Indian Service." Applied Anthropology: Problems of Human Organization 3 (October-December 1943): 5-8.

2620. Smith, Carlton B. "The United States War Department, 1815-1842." Ph.D. dissertation, University of Virginia, 1967.

2621. Taylor, Theodore Walter. "The Regional Organization of the Bureau of Indian Affairs." Ph.D. dissertation, Harvard University, 1960.

2622. Viola, Herman J. "Washington's First Museum: The Indian Office Collection of Thomas L. McKenney." Smithsonian Journal of History 3 (Fall 1968): 1-18.

2623. Ward, Harry M. The Department of War, 1781-1795. Pittsburgh: University of Pittsburgh Press, 1962.

AGENTS AND SUPERINTENDENTS

The men on the spot to deal with the Indians in the name of the United States were the Indian agents and superintendents. These men represented the Indians in Washington and were diplomatic agents of the government with the tribes. On them largely depended the success or failure of Indian relations. Included here are studies about the agents as well as writings by the agents themselves.

2624. Abel, Annie Heloise, ed. The Official Correspondence of James S. Calhoun while Indian Agent at Santa Fe and Superintendent of Indian Affairs in New Mexico. Washington: Government Printing Office, 1915.

2625. "All about Courtesy: In a Verbal War John P. Clum Has a Parting Shot." Arizoniana 4 (Summer 1963): 11-18.

2626. Anderson, Harry H., ed. "The Letters of Peter Wilson, First Resident Agent among the Teton Sioux." Nebraska History 42 (December 1961): 237-264.

2627. Arny, W. F. M. Indian Agent in New Mexico: The Journal of Special Agent W. F. M. Arny, 1870. Edited by Lawrence R. Murphy. Santa Fe: Stagecoach Press, 1967.

2628. Ashcraft, Ginger L. "Antoine Barraque and His Involvement in Indian Affairs of Southwest Arkansas, 1816-1832." Arkansas Historical Quarterly 32 (Autumn 1973): 226-240.

2629. Ayers, John. "A Soldier's Experience in New Mexico." New Mexico Historical Review 24 (October 1949): 259-266.

2630. Babcock, Willoughby M., Jr. "Major Lawrence Taliaferro, Indian Agent." Mississippi Valley Historical Review 11 (December 1924): 358-375.

2631. Barry, Louise, ed. "William Clark's Diary, May 1826--February 1831." Kansas Historical Quarterly 16 (February 1948): 1-36; (May 1948): 136-174; (August 1948): 274-305; (November 1948): 384-410.

2632. Blackburn, George M. "George Johnston: Indian Agent and Copper Hunter." Michigan History 54 (Summer 1970): 108-121.

2633. Bonsal, Stephen. Edward Fitzgerald Beale: A Pioneer in the Path of Empire, 1822-1903. New York: G. P. Putnam's Sons, 1912.

2634. Boyd, Joel D. "Creek Indian Agents, 1834-1874." Chronicles of Oklahoma 51 (Spring 1973): 37-58.

2635. Broemeling, Carol B. "Cherokee Indian Agents, 1830-1874." Chronicles of Oklahoma 50 (Winter 1972): 437-457.

2636. Brown, Thomas Elton. "Seminole Indian Agents, 1842-1874." Chronicles of Oklahoma 51 (Spring 1973): 59-83.

2637. Buntin, Martha. "The Quaker Indian Agents of the Kiowa, Comanche, and Wichita Indian Reservation." Chronicles of Oklahoma 10 (June 1932): 204-218.

2638. Chilcott, Winona Hunter. "Sylvester Witt Marston." Chronicles of Oklahoma 45 (Spring 1967): 68-72.

2639. Clum, Woodworth. Apache Agent: The Story of John P. Clum. Boston: Houghton Mifflin Company, 1936.

2640. Coe, Henry C. "An Indian Agent's Experience in the War of 1886." Oregon Historical Society Quarterly 14 (March 1913): 65-67.

2641. Cutler, Lee. "Lawrie Tatum and the

Kiowa Agency, 1869-1873." Arizona and the West 13 (Autumn 1971): 221-244.

2642. Davenport, T. W. "Recollections of an Indian Agent." Quarterly of the Oregon Historical Society 8 (March 1907): 1-41; (June 1907): 95-128; (September 1907): 231-264; (December 1907): 353-374.

2643. Dawson, Thomas F. "Major Thompson, Chief Ouray and the Utes." Colorado Magazine 7 (May 1930): 113-122.

2644. Egan, Ferol. "Warren Wasson, Model Indian Agent." Nevada Historical Society Quarterly 12 (Fall 1969): 3-26.

2645. Elliott, Richard Smith. Notes Taken in Sixty Years. St. Louis: R. P. Studley Company, 1883. Subagent at Council Bluffs, 1843-1845.

2646. Farb, Robert C. "Robert W. Furnas as Omaha Indian Agent, 1864-1866." Nebraska History 32 (September 1951): 186-203; (December 1951): 268-283.

2647. Fischer, LeRoy H. "United States Indian Agents to the Five Civilized Tribes." Chronicles of Oklahoma 50 (Winter 1972): 410-414.

2648. _____. "United States Indian Agents to the Five Civilized Tribes: Introduction." Chronicles of Oklahoma 51 (Spring 1973): 34-36.

2649. Foreman, Carolyn Thomas. "The Armstrongs of Indian Territory." Chronicles of Oklahoma 30 (Autumn 1952): 292-308; (Winter 1952-1953): 420-453; 31 (Spring 1953): 56-65.

2650. _____. "Dr. and Mrs. Richard Moore Crain." Chronicles of Oklahoma 35 (Spring 1957): 72-79. An agency physician.

2651. _____. "Dr. William Butler and George Butler, Cherokee Agents." Chronicles of Oklahoma 30 (Summer 1952): 160-172.

2652. _____. "Pierce Mason Butler." Chronicles of Oklahoma 30 (Spring 1952): 6-28. Cherokee agent, 1841-1847.

2653. Foreman, Grant. "J. George Wright: 1860-1941." Chronicles of Oklahoma 20 (1942): 120-123.

2654. Foster, William Omer. "The Career of Montfort Stokes in Oklahoma." Chronicles of Oklahoma 18 (March 1940): 35-52.

2655. Gaines, George S. "Notes on the Early Days of South Alabama." Alabama Historical Quarterly 26 (Fall-Winter 1964): 133-229. Reprint of articles published in 1872.

2656. Gallaher, Ruth A. "The Indian Agent in the United States before 1850."

Iowa Journal of History and Politics 14 (January 1916): 3-55.

2657. _____. "The Indian Agent in the United States since 1850." Iowa Journal of History and Politics 14 (April 1916): 173-238.

2658. _____. "Indian Agents in Iowa." Iowa Journal of History and Politics 14 (July 1916): 348-394; (October 1916): 559-596.

2659. Gates, Paul Wallace. "Introduction." In The John Tipton Papers, compiled by Glen A. Blackburn and edited by Nellie Armstrong Robertson and Dorothy Riker, pp. 1:3-53. 3 volumes. Indianapolis: Indiana Historical Bureau, 1942.

2660. Gilstrap, Harry B., Jr., ed. "Colonel Samuel Lee Patrick." Chronicles of Oklahoma 46 (Spring 1968): 58-63. Sac and Fox agent, 1889-1895.

2661. Green, Fletcher M. "James S. Calhoun: Pioneer Georgia Leader and First Governor of New Mexico." Georgia Historical Quarterly 39 (December 1955): 309-347.

2662. Greiner, John. "The Journal of John Greiner," edited by Annie Heloise Abel. Old Santa Fe 3 (July 1916): 189-243.

2663. Hafen, LeRoy R. Broken Hand: The Life of Thomas Fitzpatrick, Mountain Man, Guide and Indian Agent. Revised edition. Denver: Old West Publishing Company, 1973. First published in 1931.

2664. _____. "Thomas Fitzpatrick and the First Indian Agency in Colorado." Colorado Magazine 6 (March 1929): 53-62.

2665. _____. "Thomas Fitzpatrick and the First Indian Agency of the Upper Platte and Arkansas." Mississippi Valley Historical Review 15 (December 1928): 374-384.

2666. Hamilton, Doris H. "An Indian Agent in Indiana Territory." Hobbies 65 (September 1960): 110-111. John Johnston at Ft. Wayne.

2667. Harrison, Jeanne V. "Matthew Leeper, Confederate Agent at the Wichita Agency, Indian Territory." Chronicles of Oklahoma 47 (Autumn 1969): 242-258.

2668. Hawkins, Benjamin. Letters of Benjamin Hawkins, 1796-1806. Savannah: Georgia Historical Society, 1916.

2669. _____. A Sketch of the Creek Country, in the Years 1798 and 1799: And Letters of Benjamin Hawkins, 1796-1806. Spartanburg, South Carolina: Reprint Company, 1974. Reprint of works originally published in 1848 and 1916.

2670. Heaston, Michael D. "The Governor and the Indian Agent: 1855-1857." New Mexico Historical Review 45 (April 1970): 137-146. Governor David Meriwether and Agent Abraham G. Mayers.

2671. Hemperly, Marion R., ed. "Benjamin Hawkins' Trip across Western and Northern Georgia." Georgia Historical Quarterly 56 (Fall 1972): 415-431.

2672. Hiatt, Burritt M. "James M. Haworth, Quaker Indian Agent." Bulletin of Friends Historical Association 47 (Autumn 1958): 80-93.

2673. Hill, Burton S. "Thomas S. Twiss, Indian Agent." Great Plains Journal 6 (Spring 1967): 85-96.

2674. Hill, Leonard U. John Johnston and the Indians in the Land of the Three Miamis. Piqua, Ohio, 1957. Includes Johnston's Recollections of Sixty Years, pp. 147-192.

2675. Holman, Tom. "William G. Coffin, Lincoln's Superintendent of Indian Affairs for the Southern Superintendency." Kansas Historical Quarterly 39 (Winter 1973): 491-514.

2676. Hoopes, Alban W. "Thomas S. Twiss, Indian Agent on the Upper Platte, 1855-1861." Mississippi Valley Historical Review 20 (December 1933): 353-364.

2677. Hoopes, Alban W., ed. "Letters to and from Abraham G. Mayers, 1854-1857." New Mexico Historical Review 9 (July 1934): 290-335.

2678. Hoopes, Chad L. "Redick McKee and the Humboldt Bay Region, 1851-1852." California Historical Society Quarterly 49 (September 1970): 195-219.

2679. Howard, Helen Addison. "Indians and an Indian Agent: Chief Charlot and the Forged Document." Journal of the West 5 (July 1966): 379-397.

2680. Jackson, Donald. "William Ewing, Agricultural Agent to the Indians." Agricultural History 31 (April 1957): 3-7.

2681. Jones, Charles Thomas, Jr. "George Champlin Sibley: The Prairie Puritan (1782-1863)." Ph.D. dissertation, University of Missouri, 1969.

2682. Jones, Dorothy V. "John Dougherty and the Pawnee Rite of Human Sacrifice: April, 1827." Missouri Historical Review 63 (April 1969): 291-316.

2683. Kneale, Albert H. Indian Agent. Caldwell, Idaho: Caxton Printers, 1950.

2684. Lackman, Howard. "The Howard-Neighbors Controversy: A Cross-section in West Texas Indian Affairs." Panhandle-Plains Historical Review 25 (1952): 29-44.

2685. Le Van, Sandra W. "The Quaker Agents at Darlington." Chronicles of Oklahoma 51 (Spring 1973): 92-99.

2686. Lindley, Harlow. "William Clark--the Indian Agent." Proceedings of the Mississippi Valley Historical Association 2 (1908-1909): 63-75.

2687. Loos, John L. "William Clark, Indian Agent." Kansas Quarterly 3 (Fall 1971): 29-38.

2688. McGillycuddy, Julia B. McGillycuddy, Agent: A Biography of Dr. Valentine T. McGillycuddy. Stanford University, California: Stanford University Press, 1941.

2689. McLaughlin, James. My Friend the Indian. Boston: Houghton Mifflin Company, 1910.

2690. _____. My Friend the Indian; or, Three Heretofore Unpublished Chapters of the Book Published under the Title of My Friend the Indian. Edited by Usher L. Burdick. Baltimore: Proof Press, 1936.

2691. Malone, Henry T. "Return Jonathan Meigs--Indian Agent Extraordinary." East Tennessee Historical Society's Publications no. 28 (1956): 3-22.

2692. Marsden, Michael Thomas. "A Selected, Annotated Edition of Henry Rowe Schoolcraft's Personal Memoirs of a Residence of Thirty Years with the Indian Tribes on the American Frontiers." Ph.D. dissertation, Bowling Green State University, 1972.

2693. Meserve, John Bartlett. "Governor Montfort Stokes." Chronicles of Oklahoma 13 (September 1935): 338-340.

2694. Moody, Marshall D. "Kit Carson, Agent to the Indians in New Mexico 1853-1861." New Mexico Historical Review 28 (January 1953): 1-20.

2695. Morris, Cheryl Haun. "Choctaw and Chickasaw Indian Agents, 1831-1874." Chronicles of Oklahoma 50 (Winter 1972): 415-436.

2696. Murphy, Lawrence R. Frontier Crusader--William F. M. Arny. Tucson: University of Arizona Press, 1972.

2697. Neighbours, Kenneth F. "Robert S. Neighbors in Texas, 1836-1859: A Quarter Century of Frontier Problems." Ph.D. dissertation, University of Texas, 1955.

2698. Neil, William M. "The Territorial Governor as Indian Superintendent in the Trans-Mississippi West." Mississippi Valley Historical Review 43 (September

1956): 213-237.

2699. Owsley, Frank L., Jr. "Benjamin Hawkins, the First Modern Indian Agent." *Alabama Historical Quarterly* 30 (Summer 1968): 7-13.

2700. Paige, John C. "Wichita Indian Agents, 1857-1869." *Journal of the West* 12 (July 1973): 403-413.

2701. Pfaller, Louis. "The Forging of an Indian Agent." *North Dakota History* 34 (Winter 1967): 62-76. James McLaughlin, Sioux agent.

2702. Pickett, Ben Collins. "William L. McClellan, Choctaw Agent, West." *Chronicles of Oklahoma* 39 (Spring 1961): 42-53.

2703. Poole, D. C. *Among the Sioux of Dakota: Eighteen Months Experience as an Indian Agent.* New York: D. Van Nostrand, 1881.

2704. Pound, Merritt B. "Benjamin Hawkins, Indian Agent." *Georgia Historical Quarterly* 13 (December 1929): 392-409.

2705. _____. *Benjamin Hawkins--Indian Agent.* Athens: University of Georgia Press, 1951.

2706. _____. "Colonel Benjamin Hawkins--North Carolinian--Benefactor of the Southern Indians." *North Carolina Historical Review* 19 (January 1942): 1-21; (April 1942): 168-186.

2707. Ripich, Carol A. "Joseph W. Wham and the Red Cloud Agency, 1871." *Arizona and the West* 12 (Winter 1970): 325-338.

2708. Rosborough, Alex J. "A. M. Rosborough, Special Indian Agent." *California Historical Society Quarterly* 26 (September 1947): 201-207.

2709. Ryan, Pat M. "John P. Clum, 'Boss-with-the-White-Forehead.'" *Arizoniana* 5 (Fall 1964): 48-60.

2710. Scanlan, P. L. "Nicholas Boilvin, Indian Agent." *Wisconsin Magazine of History* 27 (December 1943): 145-169.

2711. Schoolcraft, Henry Rowe. *Personal Memoirs of a Residence of Thirty Years with the Indian Tribes on the American Frontiers.* Philadelphia: Lippincott, Grambo and Company, 1851.

2712. Seymour, Flora Warren. *Indian Agents of the Old Frontier.* New York: D. Appleton-Century Company, 1941.

2713. Sibley, George C. "Extracts from the Diary of Major Sibley." *Chronicles of Oklahoma* 5 (June 1927): 196-218.

2714. Sibley, John. *A Report from Natchitoches in 1807.* Edited by Annie Heloise Abel. New York: Museum of the American Indian, Heye Foundation, 1922.

2715. Smith, Robert E. "Indian Agent William Gay: A Victim of Bleeding Kansas." *Westport Historical Quarterly* 10 (December 1974): 74-85. Shawnee and Wyandot Agency.

2716. Spaid, Stanley S. "Joel Palmer and Indian Affairs in Oregon." Ph.D. dissertation, University of Oregon, 1950.

2717. Stauf, Margaret. "John Dougherty, Indian Agent." *Mid-America* 16 (January 1934): 135-146.

2718. Steele, Aubrey L. "Lawrie Tatum's Indian Policy." *Chronicles of Oklahoma* 22 (Spring 1944): 83-98.

2719. Steffen, Jerome O. "William Clark: Enlightenment Man on the Frontier." Ph.D. dissertation, University of Missouri, 1971.

2720. Stirling, Everett W. "Bishop Henry B. Whipple: Indian Agent Extraordinary." *Historical Magazine of the Protestant Episcopal Church* 26 (September 1957): 239-247.

2721. Street, Ida M. "Joseph M. Street's Last Fight with the Fur Traders." *Annals of Iowa*, 3d series 17 (October 1929): 105-148.

2722. Street, Joseph M. "Letters of General Joseph M. Street to Dr. Alexander Posey." *Annals of Iowa*, 3d series 12 (January 1921): 533-539.

2723. Sully, Langdon. "The Indian Agent: A Study in Corruption and Avarice." *American West* 10 (March 1973): 4-9. Concerns Walter M. Burleigh, Yankton agent.

2724. Taliaferro, Lawrence. "Auto-biography of Major Lawrence Taliaferro, Written in 1864." *Collections of the Minnesota Historical Society* 6 (1887-1894): 189-225.

2725. True, Clara D. "The Experiences of a Woman Indian Agent." *Outlook* 92 (June 5, 1909): 331-336.

2726. Tuggle, William Orrie. *Shem, Ham and Japheth: The Papers of W. O. Tuggle, Comprising His Indian Diary, Sketches and Observations, Myths and Washington Journal in the Territory and at the Capital, 1879-1882.* Edited by Eugene Current-Garcia, with Dorothy B. Hatfield. Athens: University of Georgia Press, 1973.

2727. Twiss, Thomas S. "Letter of Thomas S. Twiss, Indian Agent at Deer Creek, U.S. Indian Agency on the Upper Platte."

Annals of Wyoming 17 (July 1945): 148-152.

2728. Unger, Robert William. "Lewis Cass: Indian Superintendent of the Michigan Territory, 1813-1831: A Survey of Public Opinion As Reported by the Newspapers of the Old Northwest Territory." Ph.D. dissertation, Ball State University, 1967.

2729. Unrau, William E. "The Civilian as Indian Agent: Villain or Victim?" Western Historical Quarterly 3 (October 1972): 405-420.

2730. _____. "The Role of the Indian Agent in the Settlement of the South-Central Plains, 1861-1868." Ph.D. dissertation, University of Colorado, 1963.

2731. Wells, Merle W. "Caleb Lyon's Indian Policy." Pacific Northwest Quarterly 61 (October 1970): 193-200.

2732. Wilson, Peter. The Letters of Peter Wilson, Soldier, Explorer and Indian Agent West of the Mississippi River. Edited by Katherine Gideon Colt. Baltimore: Wirth Brothers, 1940.

2733. Wilson, Wesley C. "Doctor Walter A. Burleigh: Dakota Territorial Delegate to 39th and 40th Congress: Politician Extraordinary." North Dakota History 33 (Spring 1966): 93-104.

AGENCIES AND SUPERINTENDENCIES

Some studies have dealt with agencies and superintendencies rather than with particular men who administered them.

2734. Anderson, Harry H. "A History of the Cheyenne River Indian Agency and Its Military Post, Fort Bennett, 1868-1891." South Dakota Report and Historical Collections 28 (1956): 390-551.

2735. Bearss, Edwin C. "Fort Smith as the Agency for the Western Choctaws." Arkansas Historical Quarterly 27 (Spring 1968): 40-58.

2736. Brannon, Peter A. "Pole Cat Springs Agency." Arrow Points 10 (February 1925): 24-26.

2737. Clark, J. Stanley. "Irregularities at the Pawnee Agency." Kansas Historical Quarterly 12 (November 1943): 366-377.

2738. _____. "The Ponca Indian Agency." Ph.D. dissertation, University of Wisconsin, 1940.

2739. Clow, Richmond Lee. "The Brule Indian Agencies: 1868-1878." South Dakota Department of History Report and Historical Collections 36 (1972): 143-204.

2740. Cook, James H. "Sioux-Cheyenne Grievances at Pine Ridge Agency." Nebraska History Magazine 22 (January-March 1941): 68-72.

2741. Finney, Frank F., Sr. "The Kaw Indians and Their Indian Territory Agency." Chronicles of Oklahoma 35 (Winter 1957-1958): 416-424.

2742. _____. "The Osages and Their Agency during the Term of Isaac T. Gibson, Quaker Agent." Chronicles of Oklahoma 36 (Winter 1958-1959): 416-428.

2743. Guthrie, Chester L., and Leo L. Gerald. "Upper Missouri Agency: An Account of Indian Administration on the Frontier." Pacific Historical Review 10 (March 1941): 47-56.

2744. Harris, Frank H. "Neosho Agency, 1838-1871." Chronicles of Oklahoma 43 (Spring 1965): 35-57.

2745. _____. "Seneca Sub-Agency, 1832-1838." Chronicles of Oklahoma 42 (Summer 1964): 75-94.

2746. Hill, Edward E. "The Tucson Agency: The Use of Indian Records in the National Archives." Prologue: The Journal of the National Archives 4 (Summer 1972): 77-82.

2747. Hume, C. Ross. "Seventy-Fifth Anniversary of Wichita Agency." Chronicles of Oklahoma 12 (September 1934): 364-365.

2748. Jackson, W. H. "A Visit to the Los Pinos Indian Agency in 1874." Colorado Magazine 15 (November 1938): 201-209.

2749. "Kansas Agencies." Collections of the Kansas State Historical Society 16 (1923-1925): 773.

2750. Kayser, David. "The Southern Apache Agency." El Palacio 79 (1973): 16-23.

2751. Kellogg, Louise Phelps. "The Old Indian Agency House Association." Wisconsin Magazine of History 22 (March 1939): 280-285.

2752. Leggett, Richard C. "An Historic Indian Agency." Annals of Iowa 25 (April 1944): 257-274. Sac and Fox Agency.

2753. McCoy, Donald R. "The Special Indian Agency in Alaska, 1873-1874: Its Origins and Operation." Pacific Historical Review 25 (November 1956): 355-367.

2754. Masterson, James R. "The Records of the Washington Superintendency of Indian Affairs, 1853-1874." Pacific Northwest Quarterly 37 (January 1946): 31-57.

2755. "Old Choctaw Agency, Oldest Building in Oklahoma Burned in 1947." Chronicles of Oklahoma 26 (Spring 1948): 90-91.

2756. Phelps, Dawson A. "The Chickasaw Agency." Journal of Mississippi History 14 (April 1952): 119-137.

2757. Purser, Joyce. "The Administration of Indian Affairs in Louisiana, 1803-1820." Louisiana History 5 (Fall 1964): 401-419. Natchitoches Indian agency.

2758. "Quaker Report on Indian Agencies in Nebraska, 1869." Nebraska History 54 (Summer 1973): 150-219. Reprint of Society of Friends Delegation report.

2759. Schusky, Ernest L. "The Upper Missouri Indian Agency, 1819-1868." Missouri Historical Review 65 (April 1971): 249-269.

2760. Sievers, Michael A. "Malfeasance or Indirection? Administration of the California Indian Superintendency's Business Affairs." Southern California Quarterly 56 (Fall 1974): 273-294.

2761. Stacher, S. F. "Memories of Chief Ignacio and Old Navaho Springs Sub-Agency." Colorado Magazine 17 (November 1940): 212-221.

2762. Taylor, Joseph Henry. "Fort Berthold Agency in 1869." North Dakota Historical Quarterly 4 (July 1930): 220-226.

2763. Tidwell, H. M. "Uintah and Ouray Indian Agency, Fort Duchesne, Utah." Utah Historical Quarterly 4 (January 1931): 32.

2764. Tracy, Valerie. "The Indian in Transition: The Neosho Agency, 1850-1861." Chronicles of Oklahoma 48 (Summer 1970): 164-184.

2765. Umber, Harold. "Interdepartmental Conflict between Fort Yates and Standing Rock: Problems of Indian Administration, 1870-1881." North Dakota History 39 (Summer 1972): 4-13, 34.

2766. Unrau, William E. "Investigation or Probity? Investigations into the Affairs of the Kiowa-Comanche Indian Agency, 1867." Chronicles of Oklahoma 42 (Autumn 1964): 300-319.

See also Edward E. Hill's The Office of Indian Affairs (13), which gives brief historical sketches of individual agencies and superintendencies. Studies on agents (2624 to 2733) and on reservations (2767 to 2848) will also be pertinent.

INDIAN RESERVATIONS

The vast original land holdings of the Indians were steadily reduced, and restricted areas were set apart as reservations--by treaty, law, or executive order. Studies of single reservations or of groups of reservations are listed here.

2767. Abel, Annie Heloise. "Indian Reservations in Kansas and the Extinguishment of Their Title." Transactions of the Kansas State Historical Society 8 (1903-1904): 72-109.

2768. Amsden, Charles. "The Navaho Exile at Bosque Redondo." New Mexico Historical Review 8 (January 1933): 31-50.

2769. Ayer, Edward E. Report on Menominee Indian Reservation. Washington, 1914. Report of a member of the Board of Indian Commissioners.

2770. Bailey, Lynn R. Bosque Redondo: An American Concentration Camp. Pasadena, California: Socio-Technical Books, 1970.

2771. Ballas, Donald Joseph. "A Cultural Geography of Todd County, South Dakota, and the Rosebud Sioux Indian Reservation." Ph.D. dissertation, University of Nebraska, 1970.

2772. Baur, John E. "The Senator's Happy Thought: The Story of an Island, an Indian Tribe, and the Idle Speculations of a Comstock Millionaire." American West 10 (January 1973): 35-39, 62-63. James G. Fair's proposal to make Santa Catalina Island into an Indian Reservation.

2773. Blackburn, George M. "Foredoomed to Failure: The Manistee Indian Station." Michigan History 53 (Spring 1969): 37-50.

2774. Boulger, John V. "Indians--Reservations--Effect of Later Congressional Acts on Act Establishing Reservation Boundaries." North Dakota Law Review 49 (Winter 1973): 410-416.

2775. Bret Harte, John. "Conflict at San Carlos: The Military-Civilian Struggle for Control, 1882-1885." Arizona and the West 15 (Spring 1973): 27-44.

2776. _____. "The San Carlos Indian Reservation, 1872-1886: An Administrative History." Ph.D. dissertation, University of Arizona, 1972.

2778. Brockmann, Charles Thomas. "The Modern Social and Economic Organization of the Flathead Reservation." Ph.D. dissertation, University of Oregon, 1968.

2779. Bryce, J. Y. "Some Experiences in the Sac and Fox Reservation." Chronicles of Oklahoma 4 (December 1926): 307-311.

2780. Carleton, James H. "'To the People of New Mexico': General Carleton Defends the Bosque Redondo," edited by Gerald E. Thompson. Arizona and the West 14 (Winter 1972): 347-366.

2781. Chapman, Berlin B. "Charles Curtis and the Kaw Reservation." Kansas Historical Quarterly 15 (November 1947): 337-351.

2782. _____. "Dissolution of the Iowa Reservation." Chronicles of Oklahoma 14 (December 1936): 467-477.

2783. _____. "Dissolution of the Osage Reservation." Chronicles of Oklahoma 20 (September 1942): 244-254; (December 1942): 375-387; 21 (March 1943): 78-88; (June 1943): 171-182.

2784. _____. "Dissolution of the Wichita Reservation." Chronicles of Oklahoma 22 (Summer 1944): 192-209; (Autumn 1944): 300-314.

2785. _____. "Establishment of the Iowa Reservation." Chronicles of Oklahoma 21 (December 1943): 366-377.

2786. _____. "Establishment of the Wichita Reservation." Chronicles of Oklahoma 11 (December 1933): 1044-1055.

2787. _____. "The Nemaha Half-Breed Reservation." Nebraska History Magazine 38 (March 1957): 1-23.

2788. _____. "The Otoe and Missouria Reservation." Chronicles of Oklahoma 26 (Summer 1948): 132-158.

2789. _____. "The Pottawatomie and Absentee Shawnee Reservation." Chronicles of Oklahoma 24 (Autumn 1946): 293-305.

2790. Colson, Elizabeth. "Indian Reservations and the American Social System." Northwest Anthropological Research Notes 5 (Spring 1971): 7-11.

2791. Dale, Edward Everett. "The Cheyenne-Arapaho Country." Chronicles of Oklahoma 20 (December 1942): 360-371.

2792. Danziger, Edmund J., Jr. "The Crow Creek Experiment: An Aftermath of the Sioux War of 1862." North Dakota History 37 (Spring 1970): 104-123.

2793. Darton, N. H. "Opening of Shoshone Reservation." American Monthly Review of Reviews 34 (August 1906): 197-198.

2794. Deardorff, Merle H. "The Cornplanter Grant in Warren County." Western Pennsylvania Historical Magazine 24 (March 1941): 1-22.

2795. Dozier, Jack. "Coeur D'Alene Country: The Creation of the Coeur D'Alene

Reservation in Northern Idaho." Idaho Yesterdays 6 (Fall 1962): 2-7.

2796. Edwards, Thomas A. "Early Days in the C and A." Chronicles of Oklahoma 27 (Summer 1949): 148-161. Cheyenne-Arapaho Reservation.

2797. Embry, Carlos B. America's Concentration Camps: The Facts about Our Indian Reservations Today. New York: D. McKay Company, 1956.

2798. Fontana, Bernard L. "The Hopi-Navajo Colony on the Lower Colorado River: A Problem in Ethnohistorical Interpretation." Ethnohistory 10 (Spring 1963): 162-182.

2799. Foreman, Grant. "Historical Background of the Kiowa-Comanche Reservation." Chronicles of Oklahoma 19 (June 1941): 129-140.

2800. Galland, Isaac. "Dr. Galland's Account of the Half-Breed Tract." Annals of Iowa 10 (July 1912): 459-466.

2801. Green, Charles Lowell. "The Indian Reservation System of the Dakotas to 1889." South Dakota Historical Collections 14 (1928): 307-416.

2802. Hagan, William T. "Indian Policy after the Civil War: The Reservation Experience." In American Indian Policy: Indiana Historical Society Lectures 1970-1971, pp. 20-36. Indianapolis: Indiana Historical Society, 1971.

2803. _____. "Squaw Men on the Kiowa, Comanche, and Apache Reservation: Advance Agents of Civilization or Disturbers of the Peace?" In The Frontier Challenge: Responses to the Trans-Mississippi West, edited by John G. Clark, pp. 171-202. Lawrence: University Press of Kansas, 1971.

2804. Harrison, J. B. The Latest Studies on Indian Reservations. Philadelphia: Indian Rights Association, 1887.

2805. Hoffmeister, Harold. "The Consolidated Ute Indian Reservation." Geographical Review 35 (October 1945): 601-623.

2806. Houghton, Frederick. "The History of the Buffalo Creek Reservation." Publications of the Buffalo Historical Society 24 (1920): 4-181.

2807. Houghton, Ruth Edna Meserve. "Adaptive Strategies in an American Indian Reservation Community: The War on Poverty, 1965-1971." Ph.D. dissertation, University of Oregon, 1973.

2808. Hunt, Jack. "Land Tenure and Economic Development on the Warm Springs Indian Reservation." Journal of the

West 9 (January 1970): 93-109.

2809. Jones, Volney H. "The Establishment of the Hopi Reservation, and Some Later Developments concerning Hopi Lands." Plateau 23 (October 1950): 17-25.

2810. Karp, Walter. "Wounded Knee between the Wars." American Heritage 25 (December 1973): 34-35, 101. Pine Ridge Reservation, 1956.

2811. Ketcham, William H. Report upon the Conditions on the Flathead Indian Reservation. Washington, 1915. Report by a member of the Board of Indian Commissioners.

2812. _____. Report upon the Conditions on the Fort Peck Indian Reservation. Washington, 1915. Report by a member of the Board of Indian Commissioners. Report actually composed by F. H. Abbott.

2813. Kornweibel, Theodore, Jr. "The Occupation of Santa Catalina Island during the Civil War." California Historical Society Quarterly 46 (December 1967): 345-357.

2814. La Blanc, Rosella. "The Development of Turtle Mountain Indian Reservation." American Benedictine Review 21 (September 1970): 407-420.

2815. Levy, Jerrold E., and Stephen J. Kunitz. "Indian Reservations, Anomie, and Social Pathologies." Southwestern Journal of Anthropology 27 (Summer 1971): 97-128.

2816. Liljeblad, Sven. "Epilogue: Indian Policy and the Fort Hall Reservation." Idaho Yesterdays 2 (Summer 1958): 14-19.

2817. _____. "Some Observations on the Fort Hall Indian Reservation." Indian Historian 7 (Fall 1974): 9-13.

2818. McAlear, J. F., as told to Sharon Bergman. The Fabulous Flathead. Polson, Montana: Reservation Pioneers, 1962.

2819. Macgregor, Gordon. "Attitudes of the Fort Berthold Indians Regarding Removal from the Garrison Reservoir Site and Future Administration of Their Reservation." North Dakota History 16 (January 1949): 31-60.

2820. Meyer, Roy W. "The Establishment of the Santee Reservation, 1866-1869." Nebraska History 45 (March 1964): 59-98.

2821. _____. "Fort Berthold and the Garrison Dam." North Dakota History 35 (Summer and Fall 1968): 217-355.

2822. Monahan, Forrest D., Jr. "The Kiowa-Comanche Reservation in the 1890's." Chronicles of Oklahoma 45 (Winter 1967-1968): 451-463.

2823. O'Neil, Floyd A. "The Reluctant Suzerainty: The Uintah and Ouray Reservation." Utah Historical Quarterly 39 (Spring 1971): 129-144.

2824. "Opening of the Rosebud Indian Reservation, S.D., 1904." South Dakota Historical Collections 11 (1922): 519-563.

2825. Pennington, William David. "Government Policy and Farming on the Kiowa Reservation: 1869-1901." Ph.D. dissertation, University of Oklahoma, 1972.

2826. Reifel, Benjamin. "The Problem of Relocating Families on the Fort Berthold Indian Reservation." Journal of Farm Economics 32 (November 1950): 644-646.

2827. _____. "A Relocation Program for 300 Indian Families on the Fort Berthold Reservation, North Dakota." Ph.D. dissertation, Harvard University, 1952.

2828. Richardson, Rupert N. "The Comanche Reservation in Texas." West Texas Historical Association Year Book 5 (June 1929): 43-65.

2829. Ryer, Washington M. Islands as Indian Reservations. San Francisco: J. H. Carmany and Company, n.d.

2830. Sanchez, Jamie. "The Nisqually Indian Reservation." Indian Historian 5 (Spring 1972): 31-43.

2831. Sanders, Helen Fitzgerald. "The Opening of the Flathead Reservation." Overland Monthly 54 (August 1909): 120-140.

2832. Shane, Ralph M. "A Short History of the Fort Berthold Indian Reservation." North Dakota History 26 (Fall 1959): 181-214.

2833. Sherrill, Robert G. "The Lagoon of Excrement: Pine Ridge, an Impoverished Reservation in South Dakota." Nation 209 (November 10, 1969): 500-503.

2834. Shinkle, James D. Fort Sumner and the Bosque Redondo Indian Reservation. Roswell, New Mexico: Hall-Poorbaugh Press, 1965.

2835. Snow, C. O. "History of the Half-Breed Tract." Nebraska History Magazine 16 (January-March 1935): 36-48.

2836. Sterling, Everett W. "The Indian Reservation System on the North Central Plains." Montana, the Magazine of Western History 14 (April 1964): 92-100.

2837. Stern, Theodore, and James P. Boggs. "White and Indian Farmers on the Umatilla Indian Reservation." Northwest Anthropological Research Notes 5 (Spring 1971): 37-76.

2838. Swisher, J. A. "The Half-Breed Tract." Palimpsest 14 (February 1933): 69-76.

2839. Taylor, Eli F. "Indian Reservations in Utah." Utah Historical Quarterly 4 (January 1931): 29-31.

2840. Thompson, Gregory Coyne. Southern Ute Lands, 1848-1899: The Creation of a Reservation. Durango, Colorado: Fort Lewis College, 1972.

2841. "The Tribes and Reservations: A General Survey." Indian Historian 1 (Winter 1968): 9-11.

2842. Van der Zee, Jacob. "The Half-Breed Tract." Iowa Journal of History and Politics 13 (April 1915): 151-164.

2843. Voget, Fred. "The Reservation Community as an Interactional System." Northwest Anthropological Research Notes 5 (Spring 1971): 12-22.

2844. Walker, Deward E., Jr., ed. "An Exploration of the Reservation System in North America: A Special Issue." Northwest Anthropological Research Notes 5 (Spring 1971).

2845. Whicker, J. Wesley. "The Potawatomi Reservations in Benton, Fountain, Warren and Tippecanoe Counties." Indiana Magazine of History 22 (March 1926): 28-36.

2846. Wick, B. L. "The Struggle for the Half-Breed Tract." Annals of Iowa 7 (April 1905): 16-29.

2847. Will, George F. "On the Road to Civilization: A Visit to the Fort Berthold Reservation." North Dakota History 15 (January 1948): 5-13.

2848. Wissler, Clark. Indian Cavalcade; or, Life on the Old-Time Indian Reservations. New York: Sheridan House, 1938. Reissued as Red Man Reservations. New York: Macmillan Company, 1971. A series of articles by Wissler on reservation life appeared in Natural History, May 1937 to September 1938.

For data on reservations see numbers 2605 to 2608. Much material on modern reservations can be found in studies on economic development. See also the items listed under agents and under agencies.

INDIAN RESERVATIONS: GRAZING

White cattlemen were eager to graze their cattle on Indian reservations, especially in the Indian Territory. A number of studies deal with this particular problem of reservation administration. Works on the leasing of the Cherokee Outlet to cattlemen are also included here.

2849. Berthrong, Donald J. "Cattlemen on the Cheyenne-Arapaho Reservation, 1883-1885." Arizona and the West 13 (Spring 1971): 5-32.

2850. Buntin, Martha. "Beginning of the Leasing of the Surplus Grazing Lands on the Kiowa and Comanche Reservation." Chronicles of Oklahoma 10 (September 1932): 369-382.

2851. Burrill, Robert M. "The Establishment of Ranching on the Osage Indian Reservation." Geographical Review 62 (October 1972): 524-543.

2852. Dale, Edward Everett. "The Cherokee Strip Live Stock Association." Proceedings of the Fifth Annual Convention of the Southwestern Political and Social Science Association, 1924, pp. 97-115.

2853. _____. "Ranching on the Cheyenne-Arapaho Reservation 1880-1885." Chronicles of Oklahoma 6 (March 1928): 35-59.

2854. Hagan, William T. "Kiowas, Comanches, and Cattlemen, 1867-1906: A Case Study of the Failure of U.S. Reservation Policy." Pacific Historical Review 40 (August 1971): 333-355.

2855. Oliphant, J. Orin. "Encroachments of Cattlemen on Indian Reservations in the Pacific Northwest, 1870-1890." Agricultural History 24 (January 1950): 42-57.

2856. Poteet, Chrystabel Berrong. "On the Wichita-Caddo Range." Chronicles of Oklahoma 42 (Summer 1964): 55-61.

2857. Savage, William W., Jr. "Barbed Wire and Bureaucracy: The Formation of the Cherokee Strip Live Stock Association." Journal of the West 8 (July 1968): 405-414.

2858. _____. The Cherokee Strip Live Stock Association: Federal Regulation and the Cattleman's Last Frontier. Columbia: University of Missouri Press, 1973.

2859. _____. "Leasing the Cherokee Outlet: An Analysis of Indian Reaction, 1884-1885." Chronicles of Oklahoma 46 (Autumn 1968): 285-292.

INDIAN POLICE AND JUDGES

In the 1880s Indian police forces were established to aid agents in maintaining law and order on the reservations, and courts with Indian judges (courts of Indian offenses) were set up to try minor offenses.

2860. Clum, John P.   "The San Carlos Apache Police." New Mexico Historical Review 4 (July 1929): 203-219; 5 (January 1930): 67-92. Reprinted in Arizona Historical Review 3 (July 1930): 12-25; (October 1930): 21-43.

2861. Dunlap, H. E. "Clay Beauford--Welford C. Bridwell: Soldier under Two Flags, Captain of Apache Police, Arizona Legislator." Arizona Historical Review 3 (October 1930): 44-66.

2862. Hagan, William T. Indian Police and Judges: Experiments in Acculturation and Control. New Haven: Yale University Press, 1966.

2863. Jones, Oakah L., Jr. "The Origins of the Navajo Indian Police, 1872-1873." Arizona and the West 8 (Autumn 1966): 225-238.

2864. Robinson, Doane. "Sioux Indian Courts." South Dakota Historical Collections 5 (1910): 402-414.

See also legal studies dealing with jurisdiction of courts on Indian reservations.

7
Treaties and Councils

Until 1871 the United States dealt formally with Indian tribes by means of treaties, and after that date "agreements were made that were similar to the treaties. The treaties and the continuing obligations arising from them are at the heart of Indian-white relations.

COLONIAL INDIAN TREATIES

United States policy and practice in treaty-making with the Indian tribes followed colonial experience. The following works provide lists, texts, and summaries of colonial treaties.

2865. De Puy, Henry F. A Bibliography of the English Colonial Treaties with the American Indians, Including a Synopsis of Each Treaty. New York: Lenox Club, 1917.

2866. Boyd, Julian P., ed. Indian Treaties Printed by Benjamin Franklin, 1736-1762. Philadelphia: Historical Society of Pennsylvania, 1938. Included articles by Carl Van Doren and Julian P. Boyd.

Listed below are studies of specific treaties, including those made by individual colonies, as well as studies of the treaties as literature.

2867. Alvord, Clarence Walworth. "The British Ministry and the Treaty of Fort Stanwix." Proceedings of the State Historical Society of Wisconsin, 1908, pp. 165-183.

2868. Billington, Ray A. "The Fort Stanwix Treaty of 1768." New York History 25 (April 1944): 182-194.

2869. Cotterill, Robert S. "The Virginia-Chickasaw Treaty of 1783." Journal of Southern History 8 (November 1942): 483-496.

2870. Drummond, A. M., and Richard Moody. "Indian Treaties: The First American Dramas." Quarterly Journal of Speech 39 (February 1953): 15-24.

2871. Henderson, Archibald, ed. "The Treaty of Long Island of Holston, July, 1777."

North Carolina Historical Review 8 (January 1931): 55-116.

2872. Holmes, Jack D. L. "Spanish Treaties with West Florida Indians, 1784-1802." Florida Historical Quarterly 48 (October 1969): 140-154.

2873. Marshe, Witham. "Witham Marshe's Journal of the Treaty Held with the Six Nations by the Commissioners of Maryland, and Other Provinces, at Lancaster, in Pennsylvania, June, 1744." Collections of the Massachusetts Historical Society 7 (1800): 171-201.

2874. "Oglethorpe's Treaty with the Lower Creek Indians." Georgia Historical Quarterly 4 (March 1920): 3-16.

2875. Scott, Kenneth, and Charles E. Baker. "Renewals of Governor Nicholls' Treaty of 1665 with the Esopus Indians at Kingston, N.Y." New-York Historical Society Quarterly 37 (July 1953): 251-272.

2876. "Treaty between Col. Richard Nicolls, Governor of New York, and the Esopus Indians, 1665." Collections of the Ulster County Historical Society 1 (1860): 59-65.

2877. "Treaty between Virginia and the Catawbas and Cherokees, 1756." Virginia Magazine of History and Biography 13 (January 1906): 225-264.

2878. Van Loon, L. G. "Tawagonshi: Beginning of the Treaty Era." Indian Historian 1 (June 1968): 22-26. Treaty of 1613 between the Dutch and the Iroquois.

2879. Wroth, Lawrence C. "The Indian Treaty as Literature." Yale Review 17 (July 1928): 749-766.

UNITED STATES TREATIES AND COUNCILS

There have been numerous studies on individual treaties or groups of treaties but few general studies of treaties or the treaty-making process. The works listed here include those on councils, even though no treaty was signed, and on treaties concluded with the Indians by the Confederacy.

2880. Abel, Annie Heloise, ed. "The Cherokee Negotiations of 1822 and 1823." Smith

College Studies in History 1 (July 1916): 188-221.

2881. Abele, Charles A. "The Grand Indian Council and Treaty of Prairie du Chien, 1825." Ph.D. dissertation, Loyola University of Chicago, 1969.

2882. Abernethy, Alonzo. "Early Iowa Indian Treaties and Boundaries." Annals of Iowa, 3d series 11 (January 1914): 241-259; (April 1914): 358-380.

2883. Anderson, Harry H. "The Controversial Sioux Amendment to the Fort Laramie Treaty of 1851." Nebraska History 37 (September 1956): 201-220.

2884. _____. "A Sioux Pictorial Account of General Terry's Council at Fort Walsh, October 17, 1887." North Dakota History 22 (July 1955): 93-116.

2885. Arnold, John A. "Treaty of Traverse des Sioux." Red Man 8 (November 1915): 92-99.

2886. Atkinson, Henry. "Letter from General Atkinson to Colonel Hamilton." Nebraska History 5 (January-March 1922): 9-11. Negotiations with the Indians in 1825.

2887. Babcock, Willoughby M. "With Ramsey to Pembina: A Treaty-Making Trip in 1851." Minnesota History 38 (March 1962): 1-10.

2888. Balman, Gail. "The Creek Treaty of 1866." Chronicles of Oklahoma 48 (Summer 1970): 184-196.

2889. Barce, Elmore. "Governor Harrison and the Treaty of Fort Wayne, 1809." Indiana Magazine of History 11 (December 1915): 352-367.

2890. Barnes, Lela. "Isaac McCoy and the Treaty of 1821." Kansas Historical Quarterly 5 (May 1936): 122-142.

2891. Bischoff, William N., and Charles M. Gates, eds. "The Jesuits and the Coeur D'Alene Treaty of 1858." Pacific Northwest Quarterly 34 (April 1943): 169-181.

2892. Boyd, Mark F. "Horatio S. Dexter and Events Leading to the Treaty of Moultrie Creek with the Seminole Indians." Florida Anthropologist 11 (September 1958): 65-95.

2893. Brannon, Peter A. "Indian Treaties." Alabama Historical Quarterly 12 (1950): 242-250.

2894. Briggs, John Ely. "The Council on the Iowa." Palimpsest 9 (April 1928): 133-148. Sac and Fox Indians, 1832.

2895. "A British Journalist Reports the Medicine Lodge Peace Council of 1867." Kansas Historical Quarterly 33 (Autumn 1967): 249-320. Letters of Henry M. Stanley.

2896. Brugge, David M., and J. Lee Correll. The Story of the Navajo Treaties. Window Rock, Arizona: Research Section, Navajo Parks and Recreation Department, Navajo Tribe, 1971.

2897. Burns, Robert Ignatius. "The Jesuits and the Spokane Council of 1877." Pacific Historical Review 21 (February 1952): 65-73.

2898. Burns, Robert Ignatius, ed. "A Jesuit at the Hell Gate Treaty of 1855." Mid-America 34 (April 1952): 87-114. Report of Adrian Hoecken.

2899. "A Celebrated Indian Treaty." Annals of Iowa 4 (October 1900): 531-533.

2900. Chapman, Berlin B., ed. "Unratified Treaty with the Creeks, 1868." Chronicles of Oklahoma 16 (September 1938): 337-345.

2901. Connelley, William E. "The Treaty Held at Medicine Lodge, between the Peace Commission and the Comanche, Kiowa, Arapahoe, Cheyenne and Prairie Apache Tribes of Indians, in October 1867." Kansas State Historical Society Collections 17 (1926-1928): 601-606.

2902. "Council with the Sac and Fox Indians in 1840." Iowa Journal of History and Politics 15 (July 1917): 429-436.

2903. Danziger, Edmund J., Jr. "They Would Not Be Moved: The Chippewa Treaty of 1854." Minnesota History 43 (Spring 1973): 175-185.

2904. Dillard, Anthony Winston. "The Treaty of Dancing Rabbit Creek between the United States and the Choctaw Indians in 1830." Transactions of the Alabama Historical Society 3 (1898-1899): 99-106.

2905. Dolan, Thomas A. "Report of Council Proceedings with the Jicarilla Apache Indians, December, 1873." New Mexico Historical Review 4 (January 1929): 59-71. Creation of the Jicarilla Reservation.

2906. Drowne, Soloman. "Treaty at Fort Harmar, 1788-9, etc." Magazine of American History 9 (April 1883): 285-288.

2907. Dustin, Fred. The Saginaw Treaty of 1819 between General Lewis Cass and the Chippewa Indians. Saginaw, Michigan: Saginaw Publishing Company, 1919.

2908. _____. "The Treaty of Saginaw, 1819." Michigan History Magazine 4 (January 1920): 243-278.

2909. Ellison, W. H. "Rejection of California Indian Treaties: A Study in Local Influence on National Policy." Grizzly Bear 37 (May 1925): 4-5, 86; (June 1925): 4-5, Supplement 7; (July 1925): 6-7.

2910. "Ending the Outbreak." South Dakota

Historical Collections 9 (1918): 409-
469. Negotiations with the Sioux, 1865.

2911. Fenton, William N., ed. "The Journal
of James Emlen Kept on a Trip to Canan-
daigua, New York, September 15 to October
30, 1794, to Attend the Treaty between
the United States and the Six Nations."
Ethnohistory 12 (Fall 1965): 279-342.

2912. Fielder, Betty. "The Black Hawk
Treaty." Annals of Iowa 32 (January
1955): 535-540.

2913. Fisher, Robert L. "The Treaties of
Portage des Sioux." Mississippi Valley
Historical Review 19 (March 1933): 495-
508.

2914. Foreman, Carolyn Thomas. "The Lost
Cherokee Treaty." Chronicles of Oklahoma
33 (Summer 1955): 238-245.

2915. Foreman, Grant. "The Texas Comanche
Treaty of 1846." Southwestern Historical
Quarterly 51 (April 1948): 313-332.

2916. Foreman, Grant, ed. "The Journal of
the Proceedings at Our First Treaty with
the Wild Indians, 1835." Chronicles of
Oklahoma 14 (December 1936): 394-418.

2917. Franks, Kenny A. "An Analysis of the
Confederate Treaties with the Five Civi-
lized Tribes." Chronicles of Oklahoma 50
(Winter 1972-1973): 458-473.

2918. _____. "The Implementation of the
Confederate Treaties with the Five Civi-
lized Tribes." Chronicles of Oklahoma 51
(Spring 1973): 21-33.

2919. Frederick, Davis T. "The Seminole
Council, October 23-25, 1834." Florida
Historical Society Quarterly 7 (April
1929): 330-350.

2920. Gaines, George S. Dancing Rabbit
Creek Treaty. Historical and Patriotic
Series, no. 10. Birmingham: Alabama
State Department of Archives and History,
1928.

2921. Gates, Charles M., ed. "The Indian
Treaty of Point No Point." Pacific
Northwest Quarterly 46 (April 1955):
52-58.

2922. Gerwing, Anselm J. "The Chicago Indian
Treaty of 1833." Journal of the Illinois
State Historical Society 57 (Summer
1964): 117-142.

2923. Gibson, Arrell M. "An Indian Territory United Nations: The Creek Council
of 1845." Chronicles of Oklahoma 39
(Winter 1961-1962): 398-413.

2924. Grover, Frank R. "Indian Treaties Affecting Lands in the Present State of
Illinois." Journal of the Illinois State
Historical Society 8 (October 1915): 379-
419.

2925. Hagan, William T. "The Sauk and Fox
Treaty of 1804." Missouri Historical Review 51 (October 1956): 1-7.

2926. Halbert, Henry S. "Indian Treaties
Affecting Alabama." Arrow Points 7
(July 1923): 11-15.

2927. _____. "The Story of the Treaty
of Dancing Rabbit." Publications of the
Mississippi Historical Society 6 (1902):
373-402.

2928. Harmon, George D. "The North Carolina
Cherokees and the New Echota Treaty of
1835." North Carolina Historical Review
6 (July 1929): 237-253.

2929. Hawkinson, Ella. "The Old Crossing
Chippewa Treaty and Its Sequel." Minnesota History 15 (September 1934): 282-
300.

2930. Hayden, Ralston. The Senate and
Treaties, 1789-1817: The Development of
the Treaty-Making Functions of the United
States Senate during Their Formative Per-
iod. New York: Macmillan Company, 1920.
Includes material on Indian treaties.

2931. Heilbron, Bertha L. "Frank B.
Mayer and the Treaties of 1851." Minnesota History 22 (June 1941): 133-156.

2932. Heineman, John L. Twelve Mile Purchase: An Account of U.S. Treaty with Indians at Ft. Wayne, Indiana, September
30th, 1809. 2d edition. Connersville,
Indiana, 1929.

2933. Henslick, Harry. "The Seminole Treaty
of 1866." Chronicles of Oklahoma 48
(Autumn 1970): 280-294.

2934. Hill, Burton S. "The Great Indian
Treaty Council of 1851." Nebraska History 47 (March 1966): 85-110.

2935. Hryniewicki, Richard J. "The Creek
Treaty of November 15, 1827." Georgia
Historical Quarterly 52 (March 1968):
1-15.

2936. _____. "The Creek Treaty of
Washington, 1826." Georgia Historical
Quarterly 48 (December 1964): 425-441.

2937. Hughes, Thomas. "The Treaty of
Traverse des Sioux in 1851, under Gover-
nor Alexander Ramsey, with Notes of the
Former Treaty There, in 1841, under
Governor James D. Doty, of Wisconsin."
Collections of the Minnesota Historical
Society 10, part 1 (1900-1904): 101-129.

2938. Humphreys, A. Glen. "The Crow In-
dian Treaties of 1868: An Example of Power
Struggle and Confusion in United States
Indian Policy." Annals of Wyoming 43
(Spring 1971): 73-90.

2939. Hunt, Samuel F. "The Treaty of Greenville." Ohio Archaeological and Historical Quarterly 7 (January 1899): 218-240.

2940. Ibbotson, Joseph D. "Samuel Kirkland, the Treaty of 1792, and the Indian Barrier State." New York History 19 (October 1938): 374-391.

2941. "Indian Treaties and Councils Affecting Kansas: Dates and Places, Where Held, Names of Tribes, Commissioners and Indians Concluding Same." Collections of the Kansas State Historical Society 16 (1923-1925): 746-772.

2942. Jackson, Leroy F. "Sioux Land Treaties." Collections of the North Dakota State Historical Society 3 (1910): 498-528.

2943. Jones, Douglas C. "Medicine Lodge Revisited." Kansas Historical Quarterly 35 (Summer 1969): 130-142.

2944. _____. The Treaty of Medicine Lodge: The Story of the Great Treaty Council as Told by Eyewitnesses. Norman: University of Oklahoma Press, 1966.

2945. Josephy, Alvin M., Jr. "A Most Satisfactory Council." American Heritage 16 (October 1965): 26-31, 70-76. Council with Northwest tribes in 1855.

2946. Kane, Lucile M. "The Sioux Treaties and the Traders." Minnesota History 32 (June 1951): 65-80.

2947. Kellogg, Louise Phelps. "The Menominee Treaty at the Cedars, 1836." Transactions of the Wisconsin Academy of Sciences, Arts and Letters 26 (1931): 127-135.

2948. Kelsey, Harry. "The California Indian Treaty Myth." Southern California Quarterly 55 (Fall 1973): 225-238.

2949. Kingman, Samuel A. "Diary of Samuel A. Kingman at Indian Treaty in 1865." Kansas Historical Quarterly 1 (November 1932): 442-450.

2950. Kinnaird, Lucia Burk. "The Rock Landing Conference of 1789." North Carolina Historical Review 9 (October 1932): 349-365.

2951. Kip, Lawrence. The Indian Council in the Valley of the Walla Walla. San Francisco: Whitton, Towne and Company, 1855.

2952. Lambert, Paul F. "The Cherokee Reconstruction Treaty of 1866." Journal of the West 12 (July 1973): 471-489.

2953. Larson, Gustive O. "Uintah Dream: The Ute Treaty--Spanish Fork, 1865." Brigham Young University Studies 14 (Spring 1974): 361-381.

2954. Lea, John M. "Indian Treaties of Tennessee." American Historical Magazine 6 (October 1901): 367-380.

2955. Lewis, Anna. "Camp Napoleon." Chronicles of Oklahoma 9 (December 1931): 359-364. Signing of compact between tribes of Oklahoma, 1865.

2956. Lindquist, G. E. E. "Indian Treaty Making." Chronicles of Oklahoma 26 (Winter 1948-1949): 416-448.

2957. Litton, Gaston L., ed. "The Negotiations Leading to the Chickasaw-Choctaw Agreement, January 17, 1837." Chronicles of Oklahoma 17 (December 1939): 417-427.

2958. McCullar, Marion Ray. "The Choctaw-Chickasaw Reconstruction Treaty of 1866." Journal of the West 12 (July 1973): 462-470.

2959. McKenney, Thomas L. Sketches of a Tour to the Lakes, of the Character and Customs of the Chippeway Indians, and of Incidents Connected with the Treaty of Fond Du Lac. Baltimore: Fielding Lucas, Jr., 1827. Reprinted Barre, Massachusetts: Imprint Society, 1972.

2960. McNeil, Kenneth. "Confederate Treaties with the Tribes of Indian Territory." Chronicles of Oklahoma 42 (Winter 1964-1965): 408-420.

2961. Mahan, Bruce E. "The Great Council of 1825." Palimpsest 6 (September 1925): 305-318.

2962. _____. "Making the Treaty of 1842." Palimpsest 10 (May 1929): 174-180.

2963. Mahon, John K. "The Treaty of Moultrie Creek, 1823." Florida Historical Quarterly 40 (April 1962): 350-372.

2964. _____. "Two Seminole Treaties: Payne's Landing, 1832, and Ft. Gibson, 1833." Florida Historical Quarterly 41 (July 1962): 1-21.

2965. Manley, Henry S. "Buying Buffalo from the Indians." New York History 28 (July 1947): 313-329. Treaty with the Senecas.

2966. _____. The Treaty of Fort Stanwix, 1784. Rome, New York: Rome Sentinel Company, 1932.

2967. Morrison, T. F. "The Osage Treaty of 1865." Collections of the Kansas State Historical Society 17 (1926-1928): 692-708.

2968. Neighbours, Kenneth F. "The German-

Comanche Treaty of 1847." Texana 2 (Winter 1964): 311-322.

2969. Nesmith, James W., and Joseph Lane. "The Council of Table Rock, 1853." Quarterly of the Oregon Historical Society 7 (June 1906): 211-221.

2970. Parker, Arthur C. "The Pickering Treaty." Rochester Historical Society Publication Fund Series 3 (1924): 79-91.

2971. Partoll, Albert J., ed. "The Blackfoot Indian Peace Council." Frontier and Midland: A Magazine of the West 17 (Spring 1937): 199-207.

2972. _____. "The Flathead Indian Treaty Council of 1855." Pacific Northwest Quarterly 29 (July 1938): 283-314.

2973. Peters, Richard. "Indian Treaties." In United States Statutes at Large. Volume 7: Treaties between the United States and the Indian Tribes, pp. 1-11. Boston: Charles C. Little and James Brown, 1848.

2974. "Proceedings of a Council with the Chippewa Indians." Iowa Journal of History and Politics 9 (July 1911): 408-437.

2975. Quaife, Milo M., ed. "The Chicago Treaty of 1833." Wisconsin Magazine of History 1 (March 1918): 287-303.

2976. Raup, Hallock F., ed. "Journal of Griffith Evans, 1784-1785." Pennsylvania Magazine of History and Biography 65 (April 1941): 202-233. Treaty of Fort Stanwix, 1784.

2977. "The Rejected California Treaties." Indian Historian 6 (Winter 1973): 23-25.

2978. Rutland, Robert A. "Political Background of the Cherokee Treaty of New Echota." Chronicles of Oklahoma 27 (Winter 1949-1950): 389-406.

2979. "Sac and Fox Indian Council of 1841." Annals of Iowa 12 (July 1920): 321-331.

2980. "Sac and Fox Indian Council of 1842." Annals of Iowa 12 (July 1920): 331-345.

2981. "The Sac and Fox Indians and the Treaty of 1842." Iowa Journal of History and Politics 10 (April 1912): 261-265.

2982. Schifter, Richard. "Some Problems Relating to Indian Treaties: Problem of Congressional Abrogation of Treaties." In Proceedings of the Conference on Indian Tribes and Treaties, pp. 41-57. Minneapolis: Center for Continuation Study, University of Minnesota, 1955.

2983. Schultheis, Rose. "Harrison's Councils with Tecumseh." Indiana Magazine of History 27 (March 1931): 40-49.

2984. Silliman, Sue I. "The Chicago Indian Treaty of 1821." Michigan History Magazine 6 (1922): 194-197.

2985. Smith, Dwight L., ed. "William Wells and the Indian Council of 1793." Indiana Magazine of History 56 (September 1960): 217-226.

2986. Smith, Ralph A. "The Fantasy of a Treaty to End Treaties." Great Plains Journal 12 (Fall 1972): 26-51.

2987. Smith, William Rudolph. Incidents of a Journey from Pennsylvania to Wisconsin Territory, in 1837, Being the Journal of Gen. William Rudolph Smith, U.S. Commissioner for Treaty with the Chippewa Indians of the Upper Mississippi. Chicago: Wright Howes, 1927.

2988. Stern, Theodore. "The Klamath Indians and the Treaty of 1864." Oregon Historical Quarterly 57 (September 1956): 229-273.

2989. Taylor, Alfred A. "Medicine Lodge Peace Council." Chronicles of Oklahoma 2 (June 1924): 98-117.

2990. Unrau, William E. "Indian Agent vs. the Army: Some Background Notes on the Kiowa-Comanche Treaty of 1865." Kansas Historical Quarterly 30 (Summer 1964): 129-152.

2991. Watts, Charles W. "Colbert's Reserve and the Chickasaw Treaty of 1818." Alabama Review 12 (October 1959): 272-280.

2992. Webb, Walter Prescott. "The Last Treaty of the Republic of Texas." Southwestern Historical Quarterly 25 (January 1922): 151-173.

2993. Wilson, Frazer Ells. The Treaty of Greenville. Piqua, Ohio: Correspondent Press, 1894.

2994. Wilson, Richard H. "The Indian Treaty of April 1896." Annals of Wyoming 8 (October 1931): 539-545.

2995. Wright, J. Leitch, Jr. "Creek-American Treaty of 1790: Alexander McGillivray and the Diplomacy of the Old Southwest." Georgia Historical Quarterly 51 (December 1967): 379-400.

2996. Wright, Muriel H. "Notes on Events Leading to the Chickasaw Treaties of Franklin and Pontotoc, 1830 and 1832." Chronicles of Oklahoma 34 (Winter 1956-1957): 465-483.

Publications of the texts of United States Indian treaties and agreements are listed in the chapter on government documents (59 to 63).

8
Land and the Indians

One of the chief aspects of Indian-white relations--no doubt the most important in the nineteenth century--was land. The whites sought land as their population increased, and the transfer of land ownership and control from the Indian tribes to the federal government and then to white settlers was an essential part of American history. On the other hand, land as a basis of community is a necessary part of Indian tribal existence and development. The following guide is a thorough discussion of works on Indian land questions and includes an extensive bibliography.

2997. Sutton, Imre. Indian Land Tenure: Bibliographical Essays and a Guide to the Literature. New York: Clearwater Publishing Company, 1975.

LAND POLICY

A variety of studies and proposals have been made in regard to federal land policy as it concerned Indian lands, their acquisition, disposition, and protection.

2998. Bayard, Charles Judah. "The Development of the Public Land Policy, 1783-1820, with Special Reference to Indians." Ph.D. dissertation, Indiana University, 1956.

2999. Brayer, Herbert O. Pueblo Indian Land Grants of the "Rio Abajo," New Mexico. Albuquerque: University of New Mexico Press, 1938.

3000. Burney, Dudley H. "The Indian Policy of the United States Government from 1870 to 1906, with Particular Reference to Land Tenure." Ph.D. dissertation, Stanford University, 1937.

3001. Chambers, Reid Peyton, and Monroe E. Price. "Regulating Sovereignty: Secretarial Discretion and the Leasing of Indian Lands." Stanford Law Review 26 (May 1974): 1061-1096.

3002. Englund, Donald R. "Indians, Intruders, and the Federal Government." Journal of the West 13 (April 1974): 97-105.

3003. Gates, Paul Wallace. Fifty Million Acres: Conflicts over Kansas Land Policy, 1854-1890. Ithaca: Cornell University Press, 1954.

3004. Goding, M. Wilfred. "The Management of Tribal Lands." In Land: The Yearbook of Agriculture, pp. 96-102. Washington: Government Printing Office, 1958.

3005. Graebner, Norman Arthur. "The Public Land Policy of the Five Civilized Tribes." Chronicles of Oklahoma 23 (Summer 1945): 107-118.

3006. Gunther, Gerald. "Governmental Power and New York Indian Lands--a Reassessment of a Persistent Problem of Federal-State Relations." Buffalo Law Review 8 (1958): 1-26.

3007. Kelly, Lawrence C. "The Navajo Indians: Land and Oil." New Mexico Historical Review 38 (January 1963): 1-28.

3008. Kickingbird, Kirke, and Karen Ducheneaux. One Hundred Million Acres. New York: Macmillan Company, 1973.

3009. Kinney, J. P. A Continent Lost--a Civilization Won: Indian Land Tenure in America. Baltimore: Johns Hopkins Press, 1937.

3010. _____. Indian Forest and Range: A History of the Administration and Conservation of the Redman's Heritage. Washington: Forestry Enterprises, 1950.

3011. Laidlaw, Sally Jean. Federal Indian Land Policy and the Fort Hall Indians. Occasional Papers of the Idaho State College Museum, no. 3. Pocatello, Idaho, 1960.

3012. Langone, Stephen A. "The Heirship Land Problem and Its Effect on the Indian, the Tribe, and Effective Utilization." In Toward Economic Development for Native American Communities, pp. 519-548. Washington: Government Printing Office, 1969.

3013. McCoy, John C. "Survey of Kansas Indian Lands." Transactions of the Kansas

State Historical Society 4 (1886-1888): 298-311.

3014. Moore, Claire A. "The Preservation of Unallotted Tribal Lands: Concurrent Federal and Tribal Jurisdictions." Columbia Journal of Law and Social Problems 9 (Winter 1973): 279-307.

3015. Pomeroy, Kenneth B. "Unplanned Policies." American Forests 63 (May 1957): 24-27, 62-64.

3016. Province, John H. "Cultural Factors in Land Use Planning." In The Changing Indian, edited by Oliver La Farge, pp. 55-71. Norman: University of Oklahoma Press, 1942.

3017. Shepard, Ward. "Land Problems of an Expanding Population." In The Changing Indian, edited by Oliver La Farge, pp. 72-83. Norman: University of Oklahoma Press, 1942.

3018. Sorkin, Alan L. "Indian Trust Funds." In Toward Economic Development for Native American Communities, pp. 449-459. Washington: Government Printing Office, 1969.

3019. Sweeney, Marian Hopkins. "Indian Land Policy since 1887 with Special Reference to South Dakota." South Dakota Historical Collections 13 (1926): 250-283.

Because land touched many aspects of Indian-white relations, material on land policy can be found in many sections--especially those on general Indian policy, treaties, economic development, and current comment on Indian affairs.

LAND TENURE AND TITLES

Crucial problems in Indian-white relations arose out of the difficult questions of land tenure and land titles. The writings listed here deal with these topics. Some of them are recent legal studies.

3020. Arnold, W. C. Native Land Claims in Alaska. Anchorage, 1967.

3021. Bennett, J. E. The Law of Titles to Indian Lands. Oklahoma City: Harlow Publishing Company, 1917.

3022. Berger, Edward B. "Indian Lands--Minerals--Related Problems." Rocky Mountain Mineral Law Institute Proceedings 14 (1968): 89-122.

3023. Bledsoe, S. T. Indian Land Laws: Being a Treatise on Indian Land Titles in Oklahoma and under the General Allotment Act, Amendments and Legislation Supplemental Thereto, Including a Full Consideration of Conveyances of Lands of Minors, Descent, Dower, Curtesy, Taxation,

Easements in and Actions Affecting Title to Allotted Indian Lands. Kansas City: Vernon Law Book Company, 1913.

3024. Block, William E., Jr. "Alaska Native Claims." Natural Resources Lawyer 4 (April 1971): 223-250.

3025. Bodine, John J. "Blue Lake: A Struggle for Indian Rights." American Indian Law Review 1 (Winter 1973): 23-32.

3026. Cain, Gordon. "Indian Land Titles in Minnesota." Minnesota Law Review 2 (February 1918): 177-191.

3027. Chandler, Alfred N. Land Title Origins: A Tale of Force and Fraud. New York: Robert Schalkenbach Foundation, 1945.

3028. Cheadle, John Begg. Cases on Alienation and Descent of Indian Lands of the Five Civilized Tribes and the Osage Nation. Norman, Oklahoma, 1923.

3029. Clemmer, Richard O. "Land Use Patterns and Aboriginal Rights, Northern and Eastern Nevada: 1858-1971." Indian Historian 7 (Winter 1974): 24-41, 47-49.

3030. Cohen, Felix S. "Original Indian Title." Minnesota Law Review 32 (December 1947): 28-59.

3031. Colley, Charles C. "The Struggle of Nevada Indians to Hold Their Lands, 1847-1870." Indian Historian 6 (Summer 1973): 5-17.

3032. Cox, Bruce A. "Hopi Trouble Cases: Cultivation Rights and Homesteads." Plateau 39 (Spring 1967): 145-156.

3033. Dukelow, Gayle L., and Rosalyn S. Zakheim. "Recovering Indian Lands: The Land Patent Annulment Suit." Ecology Law Quarterly 2 (Winter 1972): 194-224.

3034. Edman, J. J. "Right to Condemn Indian Lands." Appraisal Journal 27 (April 1959): 265-266.

3035. Euler, Robert C., and Henry F. Dobyns. "Ethnic Group Land Rights in the Modern State: Three Case Studies." Human Organization 20 (Winter 1961-1962): 203-207.

3036. Fickinger, Paul L. "Delegations of Authority to Remove Restrictions and Other Acts Pertaining to Indian Lands." Oklahoma Bar Association Journal 26 (March 26, 1955): 455.

3037. Floren, Sigfrid E., Jr. "Indian Land Titles--Restriction on Alienation of Land Purchased with Mineral Royalties Derived from Allotment--Effective in Favor of Heir--Applicable to Sale on Execution." Oklahoma Bar Association Journal 13 (February 28, 1942): 71-73.

3038. Frison, Theodore H. "Acquisition of

Access Rights and Rights of Way on Fee, Public Domain, and Indian Lands." Rocky Mountain Mineral Law Institute Proceedings 10 (1965): 217-259.

3039. Frye, Roy. "Analysis of the Act of August 4, 1947, Removing Restrictions from Indian Land." Oklahoma Bar Association Journal 18 (December 27, 1947): 1902-1906.

3040. Gibbons, Francis M. "Examination of Indian Mineral Titles." Rocky Mountain Mineral Law Institute Proceedings 10 (1965): 73-105.

3041. Gilbert, William H., and John L. Taylor. "Indian Land Questions." Arizona Law Review 8 (Fall 1966): 102-131.

3042. Goldschmidt, Walter R., and Theodore H. Haas. Possessory Rights of the Natives of Southeastern Alaska. N.p., 1946.

3043. Goodman, Richard. "Charitable Donations under the Alaska Native Claims Settlement Act." UCLA-Alaska Law Review 3 (Fall 1973): 148-168.

3044. Grinnell, George Bird. "Tenure of Land among the Indians." American Anthropologist, new series 9 (January-March 1907): 1-11.

3045. Gross, Harold M. "Submarginal Lands: An Instance of How the Legislative Process Fails Native Americans." North Dakota Law Review 48 (Summer 1972): 561-591.

3046. Hodge, Ronald A. "Getting Back the Land: How Native Americans Can Acquire Excess and Surplus Federal Property." North Dakota Law Review 49 (Winter 1973): 333-341.

3047. Hogan, Thomas E. "City in a Quandary: Salamanca and the Allegany Leases." New York History 55 (January 1974): 79-101.

3048. Indian Land Tenure, Economic Status, and Population Trends. Part X of the Supplementary Report of the Land Planning Committee to the National Resources Board. Washington: Government Printing Office, 1935.

3049. "Indian Law--Occupancy Rights of Indians in Mexican Cession Area--What Constitutes Extinguishment of Occupancy." George Washington Law Review 10 (April 1942): 753-755.

3050. "Indians--Restrictions Imposed on Land Purchased for Indian by Secretary of the Interior." Harvard Law Review 39 (April 1926): 780.

3051. J. R. G. "Environmental Law--National Environmental Policy Act--Approval by Interior Department of Indian Lease Constitutes Major Federal Action." New York Law

Forum 19 (Fall 1973): 386-397.

3052. Linton, Ralph M. "Land Tenure in Aboriginal America." In The Changing Indian, edited by Oliver La Farge, pp. 42-54. Norman: University of Oklahoma Press, 1942.

3053. Lipps, Oscar H. Laws and Regulations Relating to Indians and Their Lands. Lewiston, Idaho: Lewiston Printing Company, 1913.

3054. Littlefield, Daniel F., Jr., and Lonnie E. Underhill. "The Cherokee Agency Reserve, 1828-1886." Arkansas Historical Quarterly 31 (Summer 1971): 166-180.

3055. Lysyk, Kenneth. "Approaches to Settlement of Indian Title Claims: The Alaskan Model." University of British Columbia Law Review 8 (1973): 321-342.

3056. McArthur, C. L. "Indian Land Law." Journal of the Oklahoma Bar Association 30 (December 26, 1959): 2168-2184.

3057. _____. "Oklahoma Indian Land Laws." Oklahoma Bar Association Journal 20 (July 30, 1949): 1165-1181.

3058. McCain, George A., Jr. "Real Property--Alaskan Indians--Right to Tribal Lands." Alabama Law Review 8 (Fall 1955): 170-174.

3059. McCluggage, Robert W. "The Senate and Indian Land Titles, 1800-1825." Western Historical Quarterly 1 (October 1970): 415-425.

3060. Manley, Henry S. "Indian Reservation Ownership in New York." New York State Bar Bulletin 32 (April 1960): 134-138.

3061. Mickenberg, Neil H. "Aboriginal Rights in Canada and the United States." Osgoode Hall Law Journal 9 (August 1971): 119-156.

3062. Mills, Lawrence. The Lands of the Five Civilized Tribes: A Treatise upon the Law Applicable to the Lands of the Five Civilized Tribes in Oklahoma. St. Louis: Thomas Law Book Company, 1919.

3063. _____. Oklahoma Indian Land Laws. St. Louis: Thomas Law Book Company, 1924.

3064. Notti, Emil. "Position with Respect to the Native Land Claims Issue." In Toward Economic Development for Native American Communities, pp. 442-447. Washington: Government Printing Office, 1969. Alaskan native land claims.

3065. Province, John. "Tenure Problems of the American Indian." In Land Tenure, edited by Kenneth H. Parsons, Raymond J. Penn, and Philip M. Raup, pp. 420-429. Madison: University of Wisconsin Press, 1956.

3066. Quail, Keith F. "The Tragic Story of Pueblo Indian Land Titles." Journal of the Bar Association of the State of Kansas 6 (November 1937): 158-163.

3067. Reeve, Frank D. "A Navajo Struggle for Land." New Mexico Historical Review 21 (January 1946): 1-21.

3068. Renehan, A. B. "Pueblo Lands Act." Report of Proceedings, New Mexico State Bar Association, 1927, pp. 33-72.

3069. "Res Judicata--Judgment in Suit between Navajo and Hopi Tribes Held to Estop Individual Navajo Indians Not Parties to the Prior Suit from Asserting Aboriginal Title Claim to Ancestral Lands." Rutgers Law Review 26 (Summer 1973): 909-928.

3070. Riley, Franklin L. "Choctaw Land Claims." Publications of the Mississippi Historical Society 8 (1904): 345-395.

3071. Rosser, M. E. "A New Acquisition As Applied to Inherited Lands of the Five Civilized Tribes." Proceedings of the Third Annual Meeting of the Oklahoma State Bar Association 3 (1910): 159-171.

3072. Schifter, Richard. "Indian Title to Land." American Indian 7 (Spring 1954): 37-47.

3073. Schifter, Richard, and W. Richard West, Jr. "Healing v. Jones: Mandate for Another Trail of Tears?" North Dakota Law Review 51 (Fall 1974): 73-106.

3074. Sells, Cato. "Land Tenure and the Organization of Agriculture on Indian Reservations in the United States." International Review of Agricultural Economics 77 (May 1917): 63-76.

3075. Seymour, Flora Warren. "Land Titles in the Pueblo Indian Country." American Bar Association Journal 10 (January 1924): 36-41.

3076. Sherman, Paschal. "Our Indian Land Law." Ph.D. dissertation, Catholic University of America, 1920.

3077. Speck, Frank G. "Basis of American Indian Ownership of the Land." In University of Pennsylvania, University Lectures Delivered by Members of the Faculty in the Free Public Lecture Course, 1914-1915, pp. 181-196. Philadelphia: University of Pennsylvania, 1915.

3078. Stone, Joseph C. "Present Status of Indian Land Law." Proceedings of the Thirteenth Annual Meeting of the Oklahoma State Bar Association 13 (1919): 72-102.

3079. Sutton, Imre. "Land Tenure and Changing Occupance on Indian Reservations in Southern California." Ph.D. dissertation,

University of California, Los Angeles, 1965.

3080. _____. "Private Property in Land among Reservation Indians in Southern California." Yearbook of the Association of American Geographers 29 (1967): 69-89.

3081. "Tribal Property Interests in Executive Order Reservations: A Compensable Indian Right." Yale Law Journal 69 (March 1960): 627-642.

3082. Twitchell, R. E. "Pueblo Indian Land Tenures in New Mexico and Arizona." El Palacio 12 (March 1, 1922): 31-33, 38-61.

3083. Tydings, Thomas J. "Rights of Indians on Public Lands." Case and Comment 23 (February 1917): 743-747.

3084. Whalen, Sue. "The Nez Perces' Relationship to Their Land." Indian Historian 4 (Fall 1971): 30-33.

3085. Williams, Ethel J. "Too Little Land, Too Many Heirs--the Indian Heirship Land Problem." Washington Law Review 46 (1971): 709-744.

3086. Wilson, Paul Burns. "Relationships of the Indian Reservation Land Tenure System to Land Use of the Wind River Indian Reservation." Annals of the Association of American Geographers 57 (December 1967): 809.

3087. Withington, W. R. "Kickapoo Titles in Oklahoma." Oklahoma Bar Association Journal 23 (October 25, 1952): 1751-1755.

3088. _____. "Land Titles in Oklahoma under the General Allotment Act." Journal of the Oklahoma Bar Association 31 (December 31, 1960): 2320-2328.

LAND CESSIONS

The essential work on Indian land cessions is the following compilation, which provides abstracts of treaty provisions and detailed maps (state by state) showing the cessions.

3089. Royce, Charles C., comp. Indian Land Cessions in the United States. Eighteenth Annual Report of the Bureau of American Ethnology, 1896-1897, part 2. Washington: Government Printing Office, 1899.

Listed here are general and special studies on land cessions and related matters.

3090. "The Acquisition of Iowa Lands from the Indians." Annals of Iowa, 3d series 7 (January 1906): 283-290.

3091. Aumann, F. R. "Dispossession of the

Tribes." <u>Palimpsest</u> 9 (February 1928): 56-61.

3092. Blumenthal, Walter Hart. <u>American Indians Dispossessed: Fraud in Land Cessions Forced upon the Tribes</u>. Philadelphia: G. S. MacManus Company, 1955.

3093. Brown, Taggart. "Wisconsin Indian Land Cessions." <u>Wisconsin Archeologist</u>, new series 16 (1936): 53-59.

3094. Cohen, Felix S. "How We Bought the United States." <u>Collier's</u> 117 (January 19, 1946): 22-23, 62.

3095. Cory, C. E. "The Osage Ceded Lands." <u>Transactions of the Kansas State Historical Society</u> 8 (1903-1904): 187-199.

3096. Crane, Katharine Elizabeth. "Some Basic Factors in Indian Land Cessions, with Especial Reference to the Old Northwest before 1811." Ph.D. dissertation, University of Chicago, 1930.

3097. Dart, Henry P., ed. "Louisiana Land Titles Derived from Indian Tribes." <u>Louisiana Historical Quarterly</u> 4 (January 1921): 134-144.

3098. Fay, George E., ed. <u>Land Cessions in Utah and Colorado by the Ute Indians, 1861-1899</u>. Museum of Anthropology Miscellaneous Series no. 13. Greeley: Museum of Anthropology, University of Northern Colorado, 1970.

3099. Gates, Paul Wallace. "A Fragment of Kansas Land History: The Disposal of the Christian Indian Tract." <u>Kansas Historical Quarterly</u> 6 (August 1937): 227-240.

3100. Halbert, Henry S. "Indian Land Cessions in Alabama." <u>Arrow Points</u> 7 (July 5, 1923): 6-10.

3101. Hilliard, Sam B. "Indian Land Cessions West of the Mississippi." <u>Journal of the West</u> 10 (July 1971): 493-510.

3102. McGinty, G. W. "Valuating the Caddo Land Cession of 1835." <u>Louisiana Studies</u> 2 (Summer 1963): 59-73.

3103. Neuhoff, Dorothy A. "The Platte Purchase." <u>Washington University Studies, Humanities Series</u> 11 (April 1924): 307-346.

3104. O'Callaghan, Jerry A. "Extinguishing Indian Titles on the Oregon Coast." <u>Oregon Historical Quarterly</u> 52 (September 1951): 139-144.

3105. Robbins, William G. "Extinguishing Indian Land Title in Western Oregon." <u>Indian Historian</u> 7 (Spring 1974): 10-14, 52.

3106. Royce, Charles C. "Cessions of Land by Indian Tribes to the United States:

Illustrated by Those in the State of Indiana." <u>First Annual Report of the Bureau of Ethnology</u>, 1879-1880, pp. 247-262. Washington: Government Printing Office, 1881.

3107. Silver, James W. "Land Speculation Profits in the Chickasaw Cession." <u>Journal of Southern History</u> 10 (February 1944): 84-92.

3108. Smith, Dwight L. "Indian Land Cession in Northern Ohio and Southeastern Michigan (1805-1808)." <u>Northwest Ohio Quarterly</u> 29 (Winter 1956-1957): 27-45.

3109. _____. "Indian Land Cessions in the Old Northwest, 1795-1809." Ph.D. dissertation, Indiana University, 1949.

3110. Smith, James F. <u>The Cherokee Land Lottery, Containing a Numerical List of the Names of the Fortunate Drawers in Said Lottery, with an Engraved Map of Each District</u>. New York: Harper and Brothers, 1838.

3111. Socolofsky, Homer E. "Wyandot Floats." <u>Kansas Historical Quarterly</u> 36 (Autumn 1970): 241-304.

3112. Stewart, William J. "Settler, Politician, and Speculator in the Sale of the Sioux Reserve." <u>Minnesota History</u> 39 (Fall 1964): 85-92.

3113. Thompson, Ray. <u>The Walking Purchase Hoax of 1737</u>. Fort Washington, Pennsylvania: Bicentennial Press, 1973.

3114. Thwaites, Reuben Gold. "Some Wisconsin Indian Conveyances, 1793-1836." <u>Collections of the State Historical Society of Wisconsin</u> 15 (1900): 1-24.

3115. Van der Zee, Jacob. "The Neutral Ground." <u>Iowa Journal of History and Politics</u> 13 (July 1915): 311-348.

3116. Wilms, Douglas C. "Georgia's Land Lottery of 1832." <u>Chronicles of Oklahoma</u> 52 (Spring 1974): 52-60.

See also studies on treaties, since many treaties provided for land cessions.

ALLOTMENT OF LAND IN SEVERALTY

Individual land holding was considered by white reformers to be essential for Indian advancement. A general law providing for allotment of reservation lands in severalty (Dawes Act) was passed in 1887. Included here are studies of that act and its results, together with contemporary writings about the act and writings about allotment before the Dawes Act.

3117. Brosius, S. M. <u>Need of Protecting In-</u>

dian Allotments. Philadelphia: Indian Rights Association, 1904.

3118. Cotroneo, Ross R., and Jack Dozier. "A Time of Disintegration: The Coeur d'Alene and the Dawes Act." Western Historical Quarterly 5 (October 1974): 405-419.

3119. Fletcher, Alice C. "Lands in Severalty to Indians Illustrated by Experience with the Omaha Tribe." Proceedings of the American Association for the Advancement of Science 33 (1884): 654-655.

3120. Gates, Paul W. "Indian Allotments Preceding the Dawes Act." In The Frontier Challenge: Responses to the Trans-Mississippi West, edited by John G. Clark, pp. 141-170. Lawrence: University Press of Kansas, 1971.

3121. Gay, E. J. "Experiences in Allotting Land." Lend a Hand 9 (October 1892): 241-251.

3122. Green, Elizabeth. The Indians of Southern California and Land Allotment. Long Beach, California, 1923.

3123. Hagan, William T. "Private Property: The Indian's Door to Civilization." Ethnohistory 3 (Spring 1956): 126-137.

3124. Harper, Allan G. "Salvaging the Wreckage of Indian Land Allotment." In The Changing Indian, edited by Oliver La Farge, pp. 84-102. Norman: University of Oklahoma Press, 1942.

3125. Holford, David M. "The Subversion of the Indian Land Allotment System, 1887-1934." Indian Historian 8 (Spring 1975): 11-21.

3126. Indian Land in Severalty, As Provided for by the Coke Bill. Philadelphia: Indian Rights Association, 1884.

3127. Johnston, Mary Antonio. Federal Relations with the Great Sioux Indians of South Dakota, 1887-1933, with Particular Reference to Land Policy under the Dawes Act. Washington: Catholic University of America Press, 1948.

3128. Meserve, Charles Francis. "The First Allotment of Lands in Severalty among the Oklahoma Cheyenne and Arapahoe Indians." Chronicles of Oklahoma 11 (December 1933): 1040-1043.

3129. Morrill, Allen C., and Eleanor D. Morrill. "The Measuring Woman and the Cook." Idaho Yesterdays 7 (Fall 1963): 2-15. Alice C. Fletcher and Jane Gay in the allotment of Nez Perce Lands.

3130. Nash, Douglas. "Remedy for a Breach of the Government-Indian Trust Duties." New Mexico Law Review 1 (January 1971): 321-334.

3131. Otis, D. S. The Dawes Act and the Allotment of Indian Lands. Edited by Francis Paul Prucha. Norman: University of Oklahoma Press, 1973.

3132. Painter, Charles C. The Dawes Land in Severalty Bill and Indian Emancipation. Philadelphia: Indian Rights Association, 1887.

3133. Paulson, Howard W. "The Allotment of Land in Severalty to the Dakota Indians before the Dawes Act." South Dakota History 1 (Spring 1971): 132-155.

3134. "Table of Land Values for Allotment of Lands in the Choctaw and Chickasaw Nations, 1902." Chronicles of Oklahoma 24 (Autumn 1946): 360-362.

3135. Thayer, James B. "The Dawes Bill and the Indians." Atlantic Monthly 61 (March 1888): 315-322.

3136. Washburn, Wilcomb E. The Assault on Indian Tribalism: The General Allotment Law (Dawes Act) of 1887. Philadelphia: J. B. Lippincott Company, 1975.

3137. Young, Mary E. "The Creek Frauds: A Study in Conscience and Corruption." Mississippi Valley Historical Review 42 (December 1955): 411-437.

See also the general histories of Indian policy in the post-Civil War period for discussion of the Dawes Act and the allotment policy.

9
Military Relations

Until the end of the nineteenth century military relations were an important part of Indian affairs. The resistance of the Indians to the encroachment of the whites and to the injustices that often arose from treaty arrangements led to hostilities and Indian wars. Historians have paid much attention to these events, and the literature on the Indian wars is almost overwhelming.

A reasonable bibliography that lists many useful books and articles is the following.

3138. Shiley, Harry A. "A Select Bibliography of Articles on Military and Indian Conflicts on the American Frontier." In Troopers West: Military and Indian Affairs on the American Frontier, edited by Ray Brandes, pp. 189-206. San Diego: Frontier Heritage Press, 1970.

GENERAL STUDIES

A number of works cover the whole field of Indian wars or major parts of it. There are listed here, in addition, studies about military policy, about the organization and techniques of the Indian-fighting army, about defense plans, about regional activities, and about military life on the frontier--topics that are broader than specific campaigns or engagements. Studies of particular wars and battles are listed later under appropriate headings.

3139. Andrist, Ralph K. The Long Death: The Last Days of the Plains Indians. New York: Macmillan Company, 1964.

3140. Arnold, R. Ross. Indian Wars of Idaho. Caldwell, Idaho: Caxton Printers, 1932.

3141. Athearn, Robert G. "The Firewagon Road." Montana, the Magazine of Western History 20 (April 1970): 2-19. Impact of railroads on military frontier.

3142. _____. "Frontier Critics of the Western Army." Montana, the Magazine of Western History 5 (Spring 1955): 16-28.

3143. _____. "War Paint against Brass: The Army and the Plains Indians." Montana, the Magazine of Western History 6 (July 1956): 11-22.

3144. Barsness, John, and William Dickinson. "Minutemen of Montana." Montana, the Magazine of Western History 10 (April 1960): 2-9.

3145. Barsness, Richard W. "John C. Calhoun and the Military Establishment, 1817-1825." Wisconsin Magazine of History 50 (Autumn 1966): 43-53.

3146. "Battles and Skirmishes in Wyoming Territory--1853-1882." Annals of Wyoming 14 (July 1942): 240-242.

3147. Beers, Henry Putney. The Western Military Frontier, 1815-1846. Philadelphia, 1935.

3148. Bender, Averam B. "The Soldier in the Far West, 1848-1860." Pacific Historical Review 8 (June 1939): 159-178.

3149. Blackburn, Forrest R. "Army Families in Frontier Forts." Military Review 49 (October 1969): 17-28.

3150. Brady, Cyrus Townsend. Indian Fights and Fighters: The Soldier and the Sioux. New York: McClure, Phillips and Company, 1904.

3151. Brady, Cyrus Townsend, comp. Northwestern Fights and Fighters. New York: McClure Company, 1907. Nez Perce and Modoc wars.

3152. Brandes, Ray, ed. Troopers West: Military and Indian Affairs on the American Frontier. San Diego: Frontier Heritage Press, 1970.

3153. Brown, Dee. Bury My Heart at Wounded Knee: An Indian History of the American West. New York: Holt, Rinehart and Winston, 1971.

3154. Burlingame, Merrill G. The Montana Frontier. Helena, Montana: State Publishing Company, 1942.

3155. Byrne, P. E. Soldiers of the Plains.

New York: Minton, Balch and Company, 1926.

3156. Carrington, Margaret Irvin. Ab-sa-ra-ka, Home of the Crows: Being the Experience of an Officer's Wife on the Plains. Philadelphia: J. B. Lippincott and Company, 1868. Later editions, under variant titles, include an Outline of Indian Operations and Conferences by Henry B. Carrington.

3157. Carroll, John M., ed. The Black Military Experience in the American West. New York: Liveright, 1971.

3158. _____. Buffalo Soldiers West. Fort Collins, Colorado: Old Army Press, 1971.

3159. Carter, Robert G. On the Border with Mackenzie; or, Winning West Texas from the Comanches. Washington: Eynon Printing Company, 1935.

3160. Coffman, Edward M. "Army Life on the Frontier, 1865-1898." Military Affairs 20 (Winter 1956): 193-201.

3161. Cook, James H. "The Art of Fighting Indians." American Mercury 23 (June 1931): 170-179.

3162. Croghan, George. Army Life on the Western Frontier: Selections from the Official Reports Made between 1826 and 1845. Edited by Francis Paul Prucha. Norman: University of Oklahoma Press, 1958.

3163. Deland, Charles Edmund. "The Sioux Wars: Minnesota Outbreak; Red Cloud and Other Wars of 1867; Little Big Horn; Wounded Knee." South Dakota Historical Collections 15 (1930): 9-724; 17 (1934): 177-551.

3164. De Shields, James T. Border Wars of Texas: Being an Authentic and Popular Account, in Chronological Order, of the Long and Bitter Conflict Waged between Savage Indian Tribes and the Pioneer Settlers of Texas. Tioga, Texas: Herald Company, 1912.

3165. Donnelly, Ralph W. "Proceedings of the Order of Indian Wars." Military Affairs 20 (Winter 1956): 229-230. Lists addresses published in the Proceedings, 1920-1941.

3166. Downey, Fairfax. The Buffalo Soldiers in the Indian Wars. New York: McGraw-Hill Book Company, 1969.

3167. _____. Indian-Fighting Army. New York: Charles Scribner's Sons, 1941.

3168. _____. Indian Wars of the U.S. Army, 1776-1865. Garden City, New York: Doubleday, 1963.

3169. _____. "Portrait of an Army."

Coast Artillery Journal 83 (July-August 1940): 320-327.

3170. Doyle, Cornelius J. "Indians and Indian Fighters." Journal of the Illinois State Historical Society 19 (October 1926-January 1927): 115-141.

3171. Dunn, Jacob Piatt. Massacres of the Mountains: A History of the Indian Wars of the Far West. New York: Harper and Brothers, 1886.

3172. Ellis, Edward S. The Indian Wars of the United States. New York: Cassell Publishing Company, 1892.

3173. Ewers, E. P. "The Military Service of Indians." Journal of the Military Service Institution of the United States 15 (November 1894): 1188-1192.

3174. Ewers, John C. "The Indian Wars of the West." In Great Western Indian Fights, pp. 19-25. Garden City, New York: Doubleday and Company, 1960.

3175. Faulk, Odie B. Crimson Desert: Indian Wars of the American Southwest. New York: Oxford University Press, 1974.

3176. Fay, George E., ed. Military Engagements between United States Troops and Plains Indians. 5 volumes. Occasional Publications of Anthropology, Ethnology Series, nos. 26-29. Greeley, Colorado: Museum of Anthropology, University of Northern Colorado, 1972-1973. Transcriptions of Congressional documents.

3177. Feaver, Eric. "Indian Soldiers, 1891-95: An Experiment on the Closing Frontier." Prologue: The Journal of the National Archives 7 (Summer 1975): 109-118.

3178. Flint, Timothy. Indian Wars of the West: Containing Biographical Sketches of Those Pioneers Who Headed the Western Settlers in Repelling the Attacks of the Savages, Together with a View of the Character, Manners, Monuments, and Antiquities of the Western Indians. Cincinnati: E. H. Flint, 1833.

3179. Frost, John [William V. Moore]. Indian Wars of the United States, from the Discovery to the Present Time. Philadelphia: R. W. Pomeroy, 1841. Also later editions.

3180. Fry, James Barnet. Army Sacrifices; or, Briefs from Official Pigeon-Holes: Sketches Based on Official Reports, Gathered Together for the Purpose of Illustrating the Services and Experiences of the Regular Army of the United States on the Indian Frontier. New York: D. Van Nostrand, 1879.

3181. Fowler, Arlen L. The Black Infantry in the West, 1869-1891. Westport,

Connecticut: Greenwood Publishing Corporation, 1971.

3182. Gallaher, Ruth A. "The Military-Indian Frontier, 1830-1835." Iowa Journal of History and Politics 15 (July 1917): 393-428.

3183. Glassley, Ray Hoard. Pacific Northwest Indians Wars: The Cayuse War of 1848, the Rogue River Wars of the '50s, the Yakima War, 1853-56, the Coeur d'Alene War, 1857, the Modoc War, 1873, the Nez Perce War, 1877, the Bannock War, 1878, the Sheepeater's War of 1879. Portland, Oregon: Binfords and Mort, 1953.

3184. Gottfredson, Peter. History of Indian Depredations in Utah. Salt Lake City: Skelton Publishing Company, 1919.

3185. Hadley, James Albert. "The Nineteenth Kansas Cavalry and the Conquest of the Plains Indians." Transactions of the Kansas State Historical Society 10 (1907-1908): 428-456.

3186. Holden, W. C. "Frontier Defense, 1846-1860." West Texas Historical Association Year Book 6 (June 1930): 35-64.

3187. _____. "Frontier Defense, 1865-1889." Panhandle-Plains Historical Review 2 (1929): 43-64.

3188. Hutchins, James S. "Mounted Riflemen: The Real Role of Cavalry in the Indian Wars." In Probing the American West: Papers from the Santa Fe Conference, edited by K. Ross Toole, and others, pp. 79-85. Santa Fe: Museum of New Mexico Press, 1962.

3189. Hyde, George E. Rangers and Regulars. The Old West Series, no. 1. Denver: John Van Male, 1933.

3190. Josselyn, Daniel W. "Indian Cavalry." Great Plains Journal 2 (Spring 1963): 77-79.

3191. King, James T. "Forgotten Pageant--the Indian Wars in Western Nebraska." Nebraska History 46 (September 1965): 177-192.

3192. Knight, Oliver. Following the Indian Wars: The Story of the Newspaper Correspondents among the Indian Campaigners. Norman: University of Oklahoma Press, 1960.

3193. _____. "A Revised Check List of Indian War Correspondents, 1866-91." Journalism Quarterly 68 (Winter 1961): 81-82.

3194. Leckie, William H. The Buffalo Soldiers: A Narrative of the Negro Cavalry in the West. Norman: University of Oklahoma Press, 1967.

3195. Leonard, Thomas C. "Red, White and the Army Blue: Empathy and Anger in the American West." American Quarterly 26 (May 1974): 176-190.

3196. McElroy, Harold L. "Mercurial Military: A Study of the Central Montana Frontier Army Policy." Montana Magazine of History 4 (Fall 1954): 9-23.

3197. Marshall, S. L. A. Crimsoned Prairie: The Wars between the United States and the Plains Indians during the Winning of the West. New York: Charles Scribner's Sons, 1972.

3198. Mattison, Ray H. "The Military Frontier on the Upper Missouri." Nebraska History 37 (September 1956): 159-182.

3199. Mayhall, Mildred P. Indian Wars of Texas. Waco, Texas: Texian Press, 1965.

3200. Moriarty, James Robert III. "The Congressional Medal of Honor during the Indian Wars." In Troopers West: Military and Indian Affairs on the American Frontier, edited by Ray Brandes, pp. 149-167. San Diego: Frontier Heritage Press, 1970.

3201. National Park Service. Soldier and Brave: Historical Places Associated with Indian Affairs and the Indian Wars in the Trans-Mississippi West. New edition. Washington: National Park Service, 1971. First edition, New York: Harper and Row, 1963.

3202. Nelson, Harold L. "Military Roads for War and Peace, 1791-1836." Military Affairs 19 (Spring 1955): 1-14.

3203. Nichols, Roger L. "The Army and the Indians, 1800-1830: A Reappraisal, the Missouri Valley Example." Pacific Historical Review 41 (May 1972): 151-168.

3204. Oliva, Leo E. "The Army and the Indian." Military Affairs 38 (October 1974): 117-119.

3205. Peters, Joseph P., comp. Indian Battles and Skirmishes on the American Frontier, 1790-1898. New York: Argonaut Press, 1966.

3206. Potomac Corral of the Westerners. Great Western Indian Fights. Garden City, New York: Doubleday and Company, 1960.

3207. Prucha, Francis Paul. Broadax and Bayonet: The Role of the United States Army in the Development of the Northwest, 1815-1860. Madison, Wisconsin: State Historical Society of Wisconsin, 1953.

3208. _____. The Sword of the Republic: The United States Army on the Frontier, 1783-1846. New York: Macmillan Company, 1969.

3209. Remington, Frederic. "Indians as Irregular Cavalry." Harper's Weekly 34 (December 27, 1890): 1004-1006.

3210. Richardson, Rupert Norval. The Comanche Barrier to South Plains Settlement: A Century and a Half of Savage Resistance to the Advancing White Frontier. Glendale, California: Arthur H. Clark Company, 1933.

3211. Rickey, Don, Jr. "'Bullets Buzzing like Bees.'" Montana, the Magazine of Western History 11 (July 1961): 2-10. Comments on problems in the Indian wars.

3212. _____. "The Enlisted Men of the Indian Wars." Military Affairs 23 (Summer 1959): 91-96.

3213. _____. Forty Miles a Day on Beans and Hay: The Enlisted Soldier Fighting the Indian Wars. Norman: University of Oklahoma Press, 1963.

3214. _____. War in the West: The Indian Campaigns. Crow Agency, Montana: Custer Battlefield Historical and Museum Association, 1956.

3215. _____. "Warrior-Soldiers: The All-Indian 'L' Troop, 6th U.S. Cavalry, in the Early 1890's." In Troopers West: Military and Indian Affairs on the American Frontier, edited by Ray Brandes, pp. 41-61. San Diego: Frontier Heritage Press, 1970. Indians enlisted in the U.S. Army.

3216. Rister, Carl Coke. The Southwestern Frontier, 1865-1881. Cleveland: Arthur H. Clark Company, 1928.

3217. Russell, Don. "How Many Indians Were Killed? White Man versus Red Man: The Facts and the Legend." American West 10 (July 1973): 42-47, 61-63.

3218. Schmitt, Martin F., and Dee Brown. Fighting Indians of the West. New York: Charles Scribner's Sons, 1948.

3219. Strong, Moses M. "The Indian Wars of Wisconsin." Report and Collections of the State Historical Society of Wisconsin 8 (1877-1879): 241-286.

3220. Tate, Michael L. "Soldiers of the Line: Apache Companies in the U.S. Army 1891-1897." Arizona and the West 16 (Winter 1974): 343-364.

3221. Tebbel, John. The Compact History of the Indian Wars. New York: Hawthorn Books, 1966.

3222. Tebbel, John, and Keith Jennison. The American Indian Wars. New York: Harper and Brothers, 1960.

3223. Temple, Frank M. "Federal Military Defense of the Trans-Pecos Region, 1850-1880." West Texas Historical Association Year Book 30 (October 1954): 40-60.

3224. Tuttle, Charles Richard. History of the Border Wars of Two Centuries, Embracing a Narrative of the Wars with the Indians from 1750 to 1874. Chicago: C. A. Wall and Company, 1874.

3225. Utley, Robert M. "Arizona Vanquished: Impressions and Reflections concerning the Quality of Life on a Military Frontier." American West 6 (November 1969): 16-21.

3226. _____. "A Chained Dog, the Indian-Fighting Army: Military Strategy on the Western Frontier." American West 10 (July 1973): 18-24, 61.

3227. _____. Frontier Regulars: The United States Army and the Indian, 1866-1891. New York: Macmillan Company, 1973.

3228. _____. Frontiersmen in Blue: The United States Army and the Indian, 1848-1865. New York: Macmillan Company, 1967.

3229. Vance, Z. B. "The Indian Soldier." Journal of the Military Service Institution of the United States 14 (November 1893): 1203-1207.

3230. Vaughn, J. W. Indian Fights: New Facts on Seven Encounters. Norman: University of Oklahoma Press, 1966.

3231. Watson, Elmo Scott. "The Indian Wars and the Press, 1866-1867." Journalism Quarterly 17 (December 1940): 301-312. Includes a checklist of Indian war correspondents.

3232. Webb, George W., comp. Chronological List of Engagements between the Regular Army of the United States and Various Tribes of Hostile Indians Which Occurred during the Years 1790 to 1898, Inclusive. St. Joseph, Missouri: Wing Printing and Publishing Company, 1939.

3233. Wellman, Paul I. Death in the Desert: The Fifty Years' War for the Great Southwest. New York: Macmillan Company, 1935.

3234. _____. Death on the Prairie: The Thirty Years' Struggle for the Western Plains. New York: Macmillan Company, 1934.

3235. _____. Death on Horseback: Seventy Years of War for the American West. Philadelphia: J. B. Lippincott Company, 1947. Combined edition of Death on the Prairie and Death in the Desert. Also published under the title of Indian Wars of the West. Garden City, New York: Doubleday, 1954.

3236. Welty, Raymond L. "The Frontier Army on the Missouri River, 1860-1870." North Dakota Historical Quarterly 2 (January 1928): 85-99.

3237. _____. "The Policing of the Frontier by the Army, 1860-1870." Kansas Historical Quarterly 7 (August 1938): 246-257.

3238. Wesley, Edgar B. Guarding the Frontier: A Study in Frontier Defense from 1815 to 1825. Minneapolis: University of Minnesota Press, 1935.

3239. White, Lonnie J. "Western Indian Battles and Campaigns: An Introduction." Journal of the West 11 (January 1972): 1-8.

3240. White, Lonnie J., ed. Hostiles and Horse Soldiers: Indian Battles and Campaigns in the West. Boulder, Colorado: Pruett Publishing Company, 1972. Reprint of articles from Journal of the West.

3241. White, William B. "The Military and the Melting Pot: The American Army and Minority Groups, 1865-1924." Ph.D. dissertation, University of Wisconsin, 1968.

3242. Wiltsey, Norman B. Brave Warriors. Caldwell, Idaho: Caxton Printers, 1964. Appeared in serial form in True West.

3243. Wood, Norman B. "Indian Wars and Warriors of Michigan." Michigan History Magazine 3 (October 1919): 547-563.

3244. Worcester, D. E. "The Weapons of American Indians." New Mexico Historical Review 20 (July 1945): 227-238.

COLONIAL PERIOD

Colonial Wars

The struggles between European nations for control of the New World had repercussions on Indian-white relations. The Indian nations often became involved in these wars, for their own political purposes or for those of the Europeans. The following general works will provide an introduction and guides for the study of this topic.

3245. Gipson, Lawrence Henry. The Great War for Empire. Volumes 6-7 The British Empire before the American Revolution. New York: Alfred A. Knopf, 1946-1949.

3246. Hamilton, Edward P. The French and Indian Wars: The Story of Battles and Forts in the Wilderness. Garden City, New York: Doubleday, 1962.

3247. Leach, Douglas Edward. Arms for Em-

pire: A Military History of the British Colonies in North America, 1607-1763. New York: Macmillan Company, 1973.

3248. Peckham, Howard H. The Colonial Wars, 1689-1762. Chicago: University of Chicago Press, 1964.

3249. _____. "Speculations on the Colonial Wars." William and Mary Quarterly, 3d series 17 (October 1960): 463-472.

Colonial Indian Wars

Frontier hostilities between whites and Indians marked much of colonial history. Some of the events, like the Pequot War, King Philip's War, Pontiac's Rebellion and Lord Dunmore's War, are formally designated as wars and studies on them are listed under separate headings.

3250. Adams, Paul K. "Colonel Henry Bouquet's Ohio Expedition in 1764." Pennsylvania History 40 (April 1973): 139-147.

3251. "Bacon's Rebellion: A Description of the Fight between the English and the Indians, in May 1676." William and Mary College Quarterly Historical Magazine 9 (July 1900): 1-10.

3252. Barnwell, John. "Journal of John Barnwell." Virginia Magazine of History and Biography 5 (April 1898): 391-402; 6 (July 1898): 42-55. Reprinted as "The Tuscarora Expedition: Letters of Colonel John Barnwell." South Carolina Historical and Genealogical Magazine 9 (January 1908): 28-54.

3253. Barnwell, Joseph W. "The Second Tuscarora Expedition." South Carolina Historical and Genealogical Magazine 10 (January 1909): 33-48. Queen Anne's War.

3254. Bedford, Denton R. "How to Start an Indian War." Indian Historian 6 (Spring 1973): 11-15.

3255. Caverly, Robert B. History of the Indian Wars of New England, with Eliot the Apostle Fifty Years in the Midst of Them. Boston: James H. Earle, 1882.

3256. Cook, Roy Bird. "Virginia Frontier Defenses, 1719-1795." West Virginia History 1 (January 1940): 119-130.

3257. Cummings, Hubertus M. "The Paxton Killings." Journal of Presbyterian History 44 (December 1966): 219-243.

3258. De Hass, Wills. History of the Early Settlement and Indian Wars of Western Virginia, Embracing an Account of the Various Expeditions in the West, Previous to 1795. Wheeling, West Virginia: H. Hoblitzell, 1851.

3259. Doddridge, Joseph. Notes on the Settlement and Indian Wars of the Western Parts of Virginia and Pennsylvania, from the Year 1763 until the Year 1783. Wellsburgh, Virginia, 1824.

3260. Drake, Samuel G. A Particular History of the Five Years French and Indian War in New England and Parts Adjacent. Boston: Samuel G. Drake, 1870.

3261. Dunbar, John R., ed. The Paxton Papers. The Hague: Martinus Nijoff, 1957.

3262. Eckstorm, Fannie H. "The Attack on Norridgewock: 1724." New England Quarterly 7 (September 1934): 541-578.

3263. Hamer, Philip M. "Fort Loudoun in the Cherokee War, 1758-1761." North Carolina Historical Review 2 (October 1925): 442-458.

3264. Hasse, Adelaide R., ed. A Narrative of an Attempt Made by the French of Canada upon the Mohaques Country. New York: Dodd, Mead and Company, 1903. Narrative of Nicholas Bayard and Charles Lodowick, first printed in 1693.

3265. Hindle, Brooke. "The March of the Paxton Boys." William and Mary Quarterly, 3d series 3 (October 1946): 461-486.

3266. Hoyt, Epaphras. Antiquarian Researches: Comprising a History of the Indian Wars in the Country Bordering Connecticut River and Parts Adjacent. Greenfield, Massachusetts: Ansel Phelps, 1824.

3267. Hunter, William A. "First Line of Defense, 1755-56." Pennsylvania History 22 (July 1955): 229-255.

3268. Jacobs, Wilbur R., ed. The Paxton Riots and the Frontier Theory. Chicago: Rand McNally, 1967.

3269. Johnson, Robert C., ed. "The Indian Massacre of 1622: Some Correspondence of the Reverend Joseph Mead." Virginia Magazine of History and Biography 71 (October 1963): 408-410.

3270. Larrabee, Edward Conyers M. "New Jersey and the Fortified Frontier System of the 1750's." Ph.D. dissertation, Columbia University, 1970.

3271. Lee, Enoch Lawrence. Indian Wars in North Carolina, 1663-1763. Raleigh, North Carolina: Carolina Charter Tercentenary Commission, 1963.

3272. Lincoln, Charles H., ed. Narratives of the Indian Wars, 1675-1699. New York: Charles Scribner's Sons, 1913. A collection of original narratives.

3273. Mahon, John K. "Anglo-American Methods of Indian Warfare, 1676-1794." Mississippi Valley Historical Review 45 (September 1958): 254-275.

3274. Malone, Patrick M. "Changing Military Technology among the Indians of Southern New England, 1600-1677." American Quarterly 25 (March 1973): 48-63.

3275. _____. "Indian and English Military Systems in New England in the Seventeenth Century." Ph.D. dissertation, Brown University, 1971.

3276. Mather, Increase. Early History of New England: Being a Relation of Hostile Passages between the Indians and European Voyagers and First Settlers. Edited by Samuel G. Drake. Albany, New York: Joel Munsell, 1864. First published in Boston, 1677.

3277. Morgan, William Thomas. "The Five Nations and Queen Anne." Mississippi Valley Historical Review 13 (September 1926): 169-189. Queen Anne's War.

3278. Morton, Louis. "The End of Formalized Warfare." American Heritage 6 (August 1955): 12-19, 95.

3279. Naroll, Raoul. "The Causes of the Fourth Iroquois War." Ethnohistory 16 (Winter 1969): 51-81.

3280. Patterson, Gerard A. "'. . . The Enemy Came in Like a Flood upon Us.'" American History Illustrated 1 (November 1966): 14-19.

3281. Penhallow, Samuel. "The History of the Wars of New-England with the Eastern Indians." Collections of the New-Hampshire Historical Society 1 (1824): 13-133. First published in Boston, 1726.

3282. Pennington, Edgar L. "The South Carolina Indian War of 1715, As Seen by the Clergymen." South Carolina Historical and Genealogical Magazine 32 (October 1931): 251-269.

3283. Powell, William S. "Aftermath of the Massacre: The First Indian War, 1622-1632." Virginia Magazine of History and Biography 66 (January 1958): 44-75.

3284. Reeve, J. C. "Henry Bouquet: His Indian Campaigns." Ohio Archaeological and Historical Quarterly 26 (October 1917): 489-506.

3285. Selden, George B., Jr. "The Expedition of the Marquis de Denonville against the Seneca Indians: 1687." Rochester Historical Society Publication Fund Series 4 (1925): 1-82.

3286. Sipe, C. Hale. The Indian Wars of Pennsylvania: An Account of the Indian

Events, in Pennsylvania, of the French
and Indian War, Pontiac's War, Lord Dun-
more's War, the Revolutionary War and the
Indian Uprising from 1789 to 1795.
Harrisburg, Pennsylvania: Telegraph
Press, 1929.

3287. Smoyer, Stanley C. "Indians as Allies
in the Intercolonial Wars." New York
History 17 (October 1936): 411-422.

3288. Snyderman, George S. "Behind the Tree
of Peace: A Sociological Analysis of
Iroquois Warfare." Pennsylvania Archaeologist 18 (Fall 1948): 2-93.

3289. Sylvester, Herbert Milton. Indian
Wars of New England. 3 volumes. Boston: W. B. Clarke Company, 1910.

3290. Trumbull, Benjamin. A Compendium of
the Indian Wars in New England, More
Particularly Such as the Colony of Connecticut Have Been Concerned and Active
In. Edited by Frederick B. Hartranft.
Hartford, Connecticut, 1926. First published in 1767.

3291. Wainwright, Nicholas B. "George
Croghan and the Indian Uprising of
1747." Pennsylvania History 21 (January
1954): 21-31.

3292. Williams, Edward G., ed. "The Orderly Book of Colonel Henry Bouquet's
Expedition against the Ohio Indians,
1764." Western Pennsylvania Historical
Magazine 42 (March 1959): 9-33; (June
1959): 179-200; (September 1959): 283-
302.

3293. _____. "Orderly Book I of Colonel
Henry Bouquet's Expedition against the
Ohio Indians, 1764 (Carlisle to Fort
Pitt)." Western Pennsylvania Historical
Magazine 56 (July 1973): 281-316; (Octo-
ber 1973): 383-428; 57 (January 1974):
51-106.

3294. Williams, Samuel C. "Fort Robinson
on the Holston." East Tennessee Historical Society's Publications no. 4
(January 1932): 22-31.

3295. Withers, Alexander S. Chronicles of
Border Warfare; or, A History of the Set-
tlement by the Whites, of North-Western
Virginia, and of the Indian Wars and
Massacres, in That Section of the State.
Clarksburg, Virginia: Joseph Israel,
1831.

Other information on border hostilities
can be found in captivity literature and in
studies on captivity narratives (9134 to
9162).

Pequot War

A war broke out in 1637 between the Pequot
Indians and the New England colonists, who
were joined by other Indian groups. The
Pequots were destroyed as a separate tribe.

3296. Bradstreet, Howard. The Story of the
War with the Pequots Re-Told. New Haven,
Connecticut: Yale University Press, 1933.

3297. Mason, John. "A Brief History of the
Pequot War." Collections of the Massachusetts Historical Society, 2d series 8
(1819): 120-153. Originally published in
Boston, 1736.

3298. Momaday, N. Scott. "The Morality of
Indian Hating." Ramparts 3 (Summer
1964): 29-40.

3299. Orr, Charles, ed. History of the
Pequot War: The Contemporary Accounts of
Mason, Underhill, Vincent and Gardener.
Cleveland: Helman-Taylor Company, 1897.

3300. Seiler, Grace. "The Destruction of
the Pequods." Social Studies 49
(January 1958): 27-29.

3301. Vaughan, Alden T. "Pequots and
Puritans: The Causes of the War of 1637."
William and Mary Quarterly, 3d series 21
(April 1964): 256-269.

3302. Vincent, Philip. "A True Relation
of the Late Battel Fought in New England,
between the English and the Pequet Sal-
vages." Collections of the Massachusetts
Historical Society, 3d series 6 (1837):
29-43. Originally published in London,
1637.

King Philip's War

A destructive war between the New England
colonists and Indians led by the Wampanoag
sachem, Philip, occurred in 1675-1676.
It ended Indian resistance in southern New
England.

3303. Bedford, Denton R. "The Great Swamp
Fight." Indian Historian 4 (Summer 1971):
27-41, 58.

3304. Bodge, George Madison. Soldiers in
King Philip's War. 3d edition. Boston,
1906.

3305. Burke, Charles T. Puritans at Bay:
The War against King Philip and the
Squaw Sachems. New York: Exposition
Press, 1967.

3306. Church, Thomas. The History of King
Philip's War. Edited by Henry Martyn
Dexter. Boston: John Kimball Wiggin,
1865. Originally published in Boston,
1716, under the title Entertaining Passages Relating to Philip's War.

3307. Drake, Samuel G., ed. The Old Indian Chronicle: Being a Collection of Ex-
ceeding Rare Tracts, Written and Published in the Time of King Philip's War,

by Persons Residing in the Country. Boston: Samuel A. Drake, 1867.

3308. Ellis, George W., and John E. Morris. King Philip's War. New York: Grafton Press, 1906.

3309. Gookin, Daniel. "An Historical Account of the Doings and Sufferings of the Christian Indians of New England, in the Years 1675, 1676, 1677," edited by Samuel G. Drake. Transactions and Collections of the American Antiquarian Society 2 (1836): 423-534.

3310. Greene, Welcome Arnold. "The Great Battle of the Narragansetts." Narragansett Historical Register 5 (December 1887): 331-343.

3311. Hale, Edward E. "Boston in Philip's War." In The Memorial History of Boston, edited by Justin Winsor, pp. 1:311-328. 4 volumes. Boston: James R. Osgood and Company, 1880.

3312. Hough, Franklin B., ed. A Narrative of the Causes Which Led to Philip's Indian War, of 1675 and 1676, by John Eaton, of Rhode Island, with Other Documents Concerning This Event in the Office of the Secretary of State of New York. Albany: Joel Munsell, 1858.

3313. Howe, George. "The Tragedy of King Philip and the Destruction of the New England Indians." American Heritage 10 (December 1958): 65-80.

3314. Hubbard, William. The History of the Indian Wars in New England from the First Settlement to the Termination of the War with King Philip, in 1677. Edited by Samuel G. Drake. Roxbury, Massachusetts: W. Elliot Woodward, 1865. Originally published in Boston, 1677, under the title A Narrative of the Troubles with the Indians in New-England.

3315. Leach, Douglas Edward. "Benjamin Batten and the London Gazette Report on King Philip's War." New England Quarterly 36 (December 1963): 502-517.

3316. _____. Flintlock and Tomahawk: New England in King Philip's War. New York: Macmillan Company, 1958.

3317. _____. "A New View of the Declaration of War against the Narragansetts, November 1675." Rhode Island History 15 (April 1956): 33-41.

3318. _____. "The Question of French Involvement in King Philip's War." Publications of the Colonial Society of Massachusetts 38 (1959): 414-421.

3319. Leach, Douglas Edward, ed. A Rhode Islander Reports on King Philip's War: The Second William Harris Letter of August

1676. Providence: Rhode Island Historical Society, 1963.

3320. Mather, Increase. The History of King Philip's War. Edited by Samuel G. Drake. Boston, 1862. Originally published in Boston, 1676, under the title A Brief History of the War with the Indians in New-England.

3321. Nelsen, Anne Kusener. "King Philip's War and the Hubbard-Mather Rivalry." William and Mary Quarterly, 3d series 27 (October 1970): 615-629.

3322. Reynolds, Grindall. "King Philip's War: With Special Reference to the Attack on Brookfield in August, 1675." Proceedings of the American Antiquarian Society, new series 5 (1887-1888): 77-95.

3323. Ronda, James P., and Jeanne Ronda. "The Death of John Sassamon: An Exploration in Writing New England Indian History." American Indian Quarterly 1 (Summer 1974): 91-102.

3324. Snook, George A. "Notes Concerning the Independent Companies in King Philip's War, 1675-1676." Military Collector and Historian 16 (Fall 1964): 74-76.

3325. Washburn, Wilcomb E. "Governor Berkeley and King Philip's War." New England Quarterly 30 (September 1957): 363-377.

Pontiac's Rebellion

Indian resentment continued after the fighting of the French and Indian War had ceased, and western Indians in 1763 attacked the western forts. Only Niagara, Fort Pitt, and Detroit withstood the assault. The principal Indian leader was the Ottawa chief, Pontiac, who directed the siege of Detroit in 1763-1764.

3326. Anderson, Niles. "Bushy Run, Decisive Battle in the Wilderness: Pennsylvania and the Indian Rebellion of 1763." Western Pennsylvania Historical Magazine 46 (July 1963): 211-245.

3327. Ellis, Edward S. The Life of Pontiac, the Conspirator, Chief of the Ottawas: Together with a Full Account of the Celebrated Siege of Detroit. New York: Beadle and Company, 1861.

3328. Grant, Charles S. "Pontiac's Rebellion and the British Troop Moves of 1763." Mississippi Valley Historical Review 40 (June 1953): 75-88.

3329. Hough, Franklin B., ed. Diary of the Siege of Detroit in the War with Pontiac: Also a Narrative of the Principal Events of the Siege, by Major Robert Rogers.

Albany: Joel Munsell, 1860.

3330. Jacobs, Wilbur R. "Presents to Indians as a Factor in the Conspiracy of
Pontiac." Michigan History 33 (December
1949): 314-322.

3331. _____. "Was the Pontiac Uprising
a Conspiracy?" Ohio Archaeological and
Historical Society Quarterly 59 (January
1950): 26-37.

3332. Kelsey, Harry. "The Amherst Plan:
A Factor in the Pontiac Uprising."
Ontario History 65 (September 1973): 149-
158.

3333. Knollenberg, Bernhard. "General Amherst and Germ Warfare." Mississippi
Valley Historical Review 41 (December
1954): 489-494. Rejoinder by Donald H.
Kent, 41 (March 1955): 762-763.

3334. Maxwell, Thomas J., Jr. "Pontiac before 1763." Ethnohistory 4 (Winter 1957):
41-46.

3335. Parkman, Francis. The Conspiracy of
Pontiac and the Indian War after the Conquest of Canada. 2 volumes. 6th edition
revised. Boston: Little, Brown and Company, 1870. Originally published in
1851 under the title, History of the Conspiracy of Pontiac.

3336. Peckham, Howard. Pontiac and the Indian Uprising. Princeton: Princeton
University Press, 1947.

3337. Platt, Myles M. "Detroit under Siege
1763." Michigan History 40 (December
1956): 465-497.

3338. Quaife, Milo M., ed. The Siege of
Detroit in 1763: The Journal of Pontiac's
Conspiracy, and John Rutherfurd's Narra-
tive of a Captivity. Chicago: R. R.
Donnelley and Sons, 1958.

3339. Randall, E. O. "Pontiac's Conspiracy." Ohio Archaeological and Historical
Quarterly 12 (October 1903): 410-437.

Dunmore's War

An attack by Virginia forces against the
Shawnee Indians along the Ohio in 1774 is
known as Dunmore's War, after the royal
governor of Virginia. The Indians were defeated in the battle of Point Pleasant at
the mouth of the Great Kanawha River on
October 10.

3340. Curry, Richard Orr. "Lord Dunmore
and the West: A Re-evaluation." West
Virginia History 19 (July 1958): 231-243.

3341. _____. "Lord Dunmore--Tool of
Land Jobbers or Realistic Champion of
Colonial 'Rights'? An Inquiry." West

Virginia History 24 (April 1963): 289-295.

3342. Downes, Randolph C. "Dunmore's War:
An Interpretation." Mississippi Valley
Historical Review 21 (December 1934): 311-
330.

3343. Fels, Elizabeth Meek. "The Battle of
Point Pleasant: Its Relation to the
American Revolution and to Tennessee."
Tennessee Historical Quarterly 33
(Winter 1974): 367-378.

3344. Kerby, Robert L. "The Other War in
1774: Dunmore's War." West Virginia
History 36 (October 1974): 1-16.

3345. Lewis, Virgil A. History of the Battle of Point Pleasant. Charleston, West
Virginia: Tribune Printing Company, 1909.

3346. MacDonald, Kenneth R., Jr. "The
Battle of Point Pleasant: First Battle
of the American Revolution." West Virginia History 36 (October 1974): 40-49.

3347. Sosin, Jack M. "The British Indian
Department and Dunmore's War, 1774."
Virginia Magazine of History and Bio-
graphy 74 (January 1966): 34-50.

3348. Thomas, William H. B., and Howard
McKnight Wilson. "The Battle of Point
Pleasant, 1774." Virginia Cavalcade 24
(Winter 1975): 100-107.

3349. Thwaites, Reuben Gold, and Louise
Phelps Kellogg, eds. Documentary History
of Dunmore's War, 1774. Madison: State
Historical Society of Wisconsin, 1905.

FROM THE REVOLUTION TO THE CIVIL WAR

Revolutionary War

Most of the Indians sided with the
British during the Revolutionary War, and
border conflicts between Indians and whites
continued throughout the war. Occasion-
ally, as in the attack upon the Cherokees
in 1776 or the Sullivan expedition against
the Iroquois in 1779, formalized warfare
occurred.

3350. Bertin, Eugene P. "Frontier Forts
on the Susquehanna." Now and Then 14
(July 1965): 376-393.

3351. Bishop, Morris. "The End of the
Iroquois." American Heritage 20 (October
1969): 28-33, 77-81. Sullivan's expedition, 1779.

3352. Bogert, Frederick W. "Marauders in
the Minnisink." Proceedings of the New
Jersey Historical Society 82 (October
1964): 271-282.

3353. Conover, George S., comp. Journals of

the Military Expedition of Major General John Sullivan against the Six Nations of Indians in 1779. Auburn, New York: Knapp, Peck and Thomson, 1887.

3354. Davis, Andrew McFarland. "The Employment of Indian Auxiliaries in the American War." English Historical Review 2 (October 1887): 709-728.

3355. _____. "The Indians and the Border Warfare of the Revolution." In Narrative and Critical History of America, edited by Justin Winsor, pp. 6:605-684. 8 volumes. Boston: Houghton, Mifflin and Company, 1884-1889.

3356. Downes, Randolph C. "Indian War on the Upper Ohio, 1779-1782." Western Pennsylvania Historical Magazine 17 (June 1934): 93-115.

3357. Flick, Alexander C. "New Sources on the Sullivan-Clinton Campaign in 1779." Quarterly Journal of the New York State Historical Association 10 (July 1929): 185-224; (October 1929): 265-317.

3358. Hamilton, J. G. de Roulhac, ed. "Revolutionary Diary of William Lenoir." Journal of Southern History 6 (May 1940): 247-259. Cherokee expedition, 1776.

3359. McAdams, Donald R. "The Sullivan Expedition: Success or Failure." New-York Historical Society Quarterly 54 (January 1970): 53-81.

3360. O'Donnell, James H. "The Virginia Expedition against the Overhill Cherokee, 1776." East Tennessee Historical Society's Publications no. 39 (1967): 13-25.

3361. Parker, Arthur C. "The Indian Interpretation of the Sullivan-Clinton Campaign." Rochester Historical Society Publication Fund Series 8 (1929): 45-59.

3362. Parker, Robert. "Journal of Lieutenant Robert Parker, of the Second Continental Artillery, 1779." Pennsylvania Magazine of History and Biography 27 (1903): 404-420; 28 (1904): 12-25.

3363. Rickey, Don, Jr. "The British-Indian Attack on St. Louis, May 26, 1780." Missouri Historical Review 55 (October 1960): 35-45.

3364. Rockwell, E. F., ed. "Parallel and Combined Expeditions against the Cherokee Indians in South and in North Carolina, in 1776." Historical Magazine 12 (October 1867): 212-220.

3365. Scott, John Albert. "Joseph Brant at Fort Stanwix and Oriskany." New York History 19 (October 1938): 399-406.

3366. Shimmell, Lewis Slifer. Border Warfare in Pennsylvania during the Revolution. Harrisburg, Pennsylvania: R. L. Myers and Company, 1901.

3367. Sosin, Jack M. "The Use of Indians in the War of the American Revolution: A Re-assessment of Responsibility." Canadian Historical Review 46 (June 1965): 101-121.

3368. The Sullivan-Clinton Campaign in 1779: Chronology and Selected Documents. Albany: University of the State of New York, 1929.

3369. Swiggett, Howard. War Out of Niagara: Walter Butler and the Tory Rangers. New York: Columbia University Press, 1933.

3370. Underwood, Wynn. "Indian and Tory Raids in the Otter Valley, 1777-1782." Vermont Quarterly, new series 15 (October 1947): 195-221.

3371. Williams, Richmond D., ed. "Col. Thomas Hartley's Expedition of 1778." Now and Then 12 (April 1960): 258-260.

For further information on the Indians in the Revolution, see the studies on frontier policy or Indian affairs of that period (545 to 568).

Indian Wars, 1780-1812

The end of the Revolutionary War brought peace with Great Britain but not with the Indians, who violently resisted white encroachments on their lands. Especially important were the campaigns against the confederated tribes north of the Ohio River from 1790 to 1794. Included here also are studies of army personnel and army life of the period.

3372. Adams, Randolph G. "The Harmar Expedition of 1790." Ohio State Archaeological and Historical Quarterly 50 (January-March 1941): 60-62.

3373. Adams, Randolph G., and Howard H. Peckham. Lexington to Fallen Timbers, 1775-1794. Ann Arbor: University of Michigan Press, 1942.

3374. Andrews, Joseph Gardner. A Surgeon's Mate at Fort Defiance: The Journal of Joseph Gardner Andrews for the Year 1795. Edited by Richard C. Knopf. Columbus: Ohio Historical Society, 1957.

3375. Bald, F. Clever. "Colonel John Francis Hamtramck." Indiana Magazine of History 44 (December 1948): 335-354.

3376. Beatty, Erkuries. "Diary of Major Erkuries Beatty, Paymaster of the Western Army, May 15, 1786, to June 5, 1787." Magazine of American History 1 (March

1877): 175-179; (April 1877): 235-243;
(May 1877): 309-315; (June 1877): 380-384;
(July 1877): 432-438.

3377. Bird, Harrison. War for the West,
1790-1813. New York: Oxford University
Press, 1971.

3378. Boyer, John. "Daily Journal of
Wayne's Campaign, from July 28th to November 2d, 1794, Including an Account of
the Memorable Battle of 20th August."
American Pioneer 1 (September 1842): 315-
322; (October 1842): 351-357. Reprinted
as A Journal of Wayne's Campaign, Cincinnati, 1866.

3379. Bradley, Daniel. Journal of Capt.
Daniel Bradley: An Epic of the Ohio Frontier. Edited by Frazer E. Wilson.
Greenville, Ohio: F. H. Jobes and Son,
1935.

3380. Brown, Alan S. "The Role of the Army
in Western Settlement: Josiah Harmar's
Command, 1785-1790." Pennsylvania Magazine of History and Biography 93 (April
1969): 161-178.

3381. Bunn, Matthew. A Journal of the Adventures of Matthew Bunn. Facsimile edition, Chicago: Stinehour Press, 1962.
First published in Providence, 1796.

3382. Burton, Clarence M. "Anthony Wayne
and the Battle of Fallen Timbers."
Collections and Researches Made by the
Michigan Pioneer and Historical Society
31 (1901): 472-489.

3383. Burton, Clarence M., ed. "General
Wayne's Orderly Book." Collections and
Researches Made by the Michigan Pioneer
and Historical Society 34 (1904): 341-733.

3384. Butterfield, Consul W., ed. Journal
of Capt. Jonathan Heart . . . [and] Dick-
inson-Harmar Correspondence of 1784-5.
Albany: J. Munsell's Sons, 1885.

3385. Caldwell, Norman W. "Civilian Personnel at the Frontier Military Post
(1790-1814)." Mid-America 38 (April
1956): 101-119.

3386. _____. "The Enlisted Soldier at
the Frontier Post, 1790-1814." Mid-
America 37 (October 1955): 195-204.

3387. _____. "The Frontier Army Officer,
1794-1814." Mid-America 37 (April 1955):
101-128.

3388. Chew, John. "The Diary of an Officer
in the Indian Country in 1794." American
Historical Magazine 3 (November 1908):
639-643; 4 (January 1909): 69-71.

3389. Connelly, Thomas Lawrence. "Indian
Warfare on the Tennessee Frontier, 1776-
1794: Strategy and Tactics." East
Tennessee Historical Society's Publica-

tions no. 36 (1964): 3-22.

3390. Cooke, John. "General Wayne's Campaign in 1794 and 1795: Captain John
Cooke's Journal." American Historical
Record 2 (July 1873): 311-316; (August
1873): 339-345.

3391. Denny, Ebenezer. "Military Journal
of Major Ebenezer Denny." Memoirs of the
Historical Society of Pennsylvania 7
(1860): 237-409.

3392. Edmunds, R. David. "Wea Participation
in the Northwest Indian Wars, 1790-1795."
Filson Club History Quarterly 46 (July
1972): 241-253.

3393. "General Wayne's Campaign of 1794
and the Battle of Fallen Timbers." Historical Society of Northwestern Ohio
Quarterly Bulletin 1 (April 1929): 9-16.

3394. Gifford, Jack Jule. "The Northwest
Indian War, 1784-1795." Ph.D. disserta-
tion, University of California, Los
Angeles, 1964.

3395. Goodpasture, Albert V. "Indian Wars
and Warriors of the Old Southwest, 1730-
1807." Tennessee Historical Magazine 4
(March 1918): 3-49; (June 1918): 106-145;
(September 1918): 161-210; (December
1918): 385-424.

3396. Guthman, William H. March to Massacre: A History of the First Seven Years
of the United States Army, 1784-1791.
New York: McGraw-Hill Book Company, 1975.

3397. Harmar, Josiah. "Letters of General
Josiah Harmar and Others." Memoirs of
the Historical Society of Pennsylvania
7 (1860): 413-477.

3398. Helderman, Leonard C. "The Northwest
Expedition of George Rogers Clark, 1786-
1787." Mississippi Valley Historical Review 25 (December 1938): 317-334.

3399. Horsman, Reginald. "The British In-
dian Department and the Resistance to
General Anthony Wayne, 1793-1795."
Mississippi Valley Historical Review 49
(September 1962): 269-290.

3400. Huber, John P. "General Josiah
Harmar's Command: Military Policy in the
Old Northwest, 1784-1791." Ph.D. disser-
tation, University of Michigan, 1968.

3401. Hunt, Samuel F. "General Anthony
Wayne and the Battle of 'Fallen Timbers.'"
Ohio Archaeological and Historical Quar-
terly 9 (October 1900): 214-237.

3402. Jackson, James. "The Letter Book of
General James Jackson, 1788-1796."
Georgia Historical Quarterly 37 (September
1953): 220-249; (December 1953): 299-329.

3403. Jacobs, James Ripley. The Beginning

of the U.S. Army, 1783-1812. Princeton: Princeton University Press, 1947.

3404. Knopf, Richard C. "Crime and Punishment in the Legion, 1792-1793." Bulletin of the Historical and Philosophical Society of Ohio 14 (July 1956): 232-238.

3405. Knopf, Richard C., ed. Anthony Wayne, a Name in Arms: The Wayne-Knox-Pickering-McHenry Correspondence. Pittsburgh: University of Pittsburgh Press, 1960.

3406. _____. "A Precise Journal of General Wayne's Last Campaign." Proceedings of the American Antiquarian Society 64 (October 20, 1954): 273-302.

3407. _____. "Two Journals of the Kentucky Volunteers, 1793 and 1794." Filson Club History Quarterly 27 (July 1953): 247-281.

3408. _____. "Wayne's Western Campaign: The Wayne-Knox Correspondence." Pennsylvania Magazine of History and Biography 78 (July 1954): 298-341; (October 1954): 424-455.

3409. Kohn, Richard H. "General Wilkinson's Vendetta with General Wayne: Politics and Command in the American Army, 1791-1796." Filson Club History Quarterly 45 (October 1971): 361-372.

3410. McGrane, R. C., ed. "William Clark's Journal of General Wayne's Campaign." Mississippi Valley Historical Review 1 (December 1914): 418-444.

3411. Meek, Basil. "General Harmar's Expedition." Ohio Archaeological and Historical Quarterly 20 (January 1911): 74-108.

3412. Peckham, Howard H. "Josiah Harmar and His Indian Expedition." Ohio State Archaeological and Historical Quarterly 55 (July-September 1946): 227-241.

3413. Pirtle, Alfred. The Battle of Tippecanoe. Filson Club Publications, no. 15. Louisville: John P. Morton and Company, 1900.

3414. Priddy, O. W. "Wayne's Strategic Advance from Fort Greenville to Grand Glaize." Ohio Archaeological and Historical Quarterly 39 (January 1930): 42-76.

3415. Quaife, Milo M., ed. "Fort Knox Orderly Book, 1793-97." Indiana Magazine of History 32 (June 1936): 137-169.

3416. _____. "General James Wilkinson's Narrative of the Fallen Timbers Campaign." Mississippi Valley Historical Review 16 (June 1929): 81-90.

3417. _____. "A Picture of the First United States Army: The Journal of Captain Samuel Newman." Wisconsin Magazine of History 2 (September 1918): 40-73.

3418. Robertson, James. "The Correspondence of General James Robertson." American Historical Magazine 2-5 (1897-1900): passim.

3419. St. Clair, Arthur. A Narrative of the Manner in Which the Campaign against the Indians, in the Year One Thousand Seven Hundred and Ninety-one, Was Conducted, under the Command of Major General St. Clair. Philadelphia: Jane Aitken, 1812.

3420. Sargent, Winthrop. Diary of Col. Winthrop Sargent, Adjutant General of the United States' Army, during the Campaign of MDCCXCI. Wormsloe, Georgia, 1851. Reprinted as "Winthrop Sargent's Diary While with General Arthur St. Clair's Expedition against the Indians." Ohio Archaeological and Historical Quarterly 33 (July 1924): 237-273.

3421. Smith, Dwight L. "The Contest with the Indians." American Heritage 4 (Spring 1953): 32-37, 69-70.

3422. _____. "Provocation and Occurrence of Indian-White Warfare in the Early American Period in the Old Northwest." Northwest Ohio Quarterly 33 (Summer 1961): 132-147.

3423. _____. "Wayne and the Treaty of Greene Ville." Ohio State Archaeological and Historical Quarterly 63 (January 1954): 1-7.

3424. _____. "Wayne's Peace with the Indians of the Old Northwest, 1795." Ohio State Archaeological and Historical Quarterly 59 (July 1950): 239-255.

3425. Smith, Dwight L., ed. "From Greene Ville to Fallen Timbers: A Journal of the Wayne Campaign, July 28-September 14, 1794." Indiana Historical Society Publications 16 (1952): 239-333.

3426. Smith, James. A Treatise, on the Mode and Manner of Indian War . . . Also--a Brief Account of Twenty-Three Campaigns, Carried on against the Indians with the Events, since the Year 1755, Gov. Harrison's Included. Paris, Kentucky: Joel R. Lyle, 1812. Facsimile reprint, Chicago: Barnard and Miller, 1948.

3427. Symmes, John Cleves. "John Cleves Symmes to Elias Boudinot." Quarterly Publication of the Historical and Philosophical Society of Ohio 5 (July-September 1910): 93-101.

3428. Thornbrough, Gayle. "Tippecanoe." American Heritage 2 (Autumn 1950): 16-19.

3429. Thornbrough, Gayle, ed. Outpost on the Wabash, 1787-1791. Indianapolis:

Indiana Historical Society, 1957. Letters of Josiah Harmar and John Francis Hamtramck and other documents from the Harmar Papers.

3430. Twiggs, John. "The Creek Troubles of 1793," edited by E. Merton Coulter. Georgia Historical Quarterly 11 (September 1927): 274-280.

3431. Underwood, Thomas Taylor. Journal, Thomas Taylor Underwood, March 26, 1792 to March 18, 1800: An Old Soldier in Wayne's Army. Edited by Lee Shepard. Cincinnati: Society of Colonial Wars in the State of Ohio, 1945.

3432. Van Cleve, Benjamin. "Memoirs of Benjamin Van Cleve," edited by Beverly W. Bond, Jr. Quarterly Publication of the Historical and Philosophical Society of Ohio 17 (January-June 1922): 1-71.

3433. Van Every, Dale. "President Washington's Calculated Risk." American Heritage 9 (June 1958): 56-61, 109-111.

3434. Wilson, Frazer Ells. The Peace of Mad Anthony: An Account of the Subjugation of the North-Western Indian Tribes and the Treaty of Greenville by Which the Territory Beyond the Ohio Was Opened for Anglo-Saxon Settlement. Greenville, Ohio: C. R. Kemble, 1909.

3435. _____. "St. Clair's Defeat." Ohio Archaeological and Historical Quarterly 11 (July 1902): 30-43.

3436. Winger, Otho. "The Indians Who Opposed Harmar." Ohio State Archaeological and Historical Quarterly 50 (January-March 1941): 55-59.

Indians in the War of 1812

Indian-white conflicts on the frontier merged into the War of 1812. Both in the north and in the south, Indians fought against American regular and volunteer troops. General histories of the War of 1812, most of which contain considerable material on Indian affairs, are not listed. The items given here are studies or documents that pertain particularly to Indians in the war.

3437. Brannon, Peter A., ed. "Journal of James A. Tait for the Year 1813." Georgia Historical Quarterly 8 (September 1924): 229-239.

3438. Cruikshank, Ernest Alexander. "The Employment of Indians in the War of 1812." Annual Report of the American Historical Association for the Year 1895, pp. 319-335.

3439. DeWitt, John H., ed. "Letters of General John Coffee to His Wife, 1813-1815." Tennessee Historical Magazine 2 (December 1916): 264-295."

3440. Doster, James F., ed. "Letters Relating to the Tragedy at Fort Mims: August-September 1813." Alabama Review 14 (October 1961): 269-285.

3441. Edmunds, R. David. "The Illinois River Potawatomi in the War of 1812." Journal of the Illinois State Historical Society 62 (Winter 1969): 341-362.

3442. Eggleston, George Cary. Red Eagle and the War with the Creek Indians of Alabama. New York: Dodd, Mead and Company, 1878.

3443. Faust, Richard H. "Another Look at General Jackson and the Indians of the Mississippi Territory." Alabama Review 28 (July 1975): 202-217.

3444. Halbert, Henry Sale. "Creek War Incidents." Transactions of the Alabama Historical Society, 1897-1898 2 (1898): 95-119.

3445. Halbert, Henry Sale, and T. H. Ball. The Creek War of 1813 and 1814. Chicago: Donohue and Henneberry, 1895.

3446. Hall, Arthur H. "The Red Stick War: Creek Indian Affairs during the War of 1812." Chronicles of Oklahoma 12 (September 1934): 264-293.

3447. Heath, Herschel. "The Indians as a Factor in the War of 1812." Ph.D. dissertation, Clark University, 1933.

3448. Holland, James W. Andrew Jackson and the Creek War: Victory at Horseshoe. University, Alabama: University of Alabama Press, 1969.

3449. _____. "Andrew Jackson and the Creek War: Victory at the Horseshoe." Alabama Review 21 (October 1968): 243-275.

3450. Horsman, Reginald. "The Role of the Indian in the War." In After Tippecanoe: Some Aspects of the War of 1812, edited by Philip P. Mason, pp. 60-77. East Lansing: Michigan State University Press, 1963.

3451. _____. "Wisconsin and the War of 1812." Wisconsin Magazine of History 46 (Autumn 1962): 3-15.

3452. Kellogg, Louise Phelps. "The Capture of Mackinac in 1812." Proceedings of the State Historical Society of Wisconsin, 1912, pp. 124-145.

3453. Kinzie, Juliette Augusta. Narrative of the Massacre at Chicago, August 15, 1812, and of Some Preceding Events. Chicago: Fergus Printing Company, 1914. Originally published in 1844.

3454. Mahon, John K. "British Strategy and Southern Indians: War of 1812." Florida Historical Quarterly 44 (April 1966): 285-302.

3455. Martin, Thomas W. The Story of Horseshoe Bend National Military Park. New York: Newcomen Society in North America, 1960.

3456. Nunez, Theron A. "Creek Nativism and the Creek War of 1813-1814." Ethnohistory 5 (Winter 1958): 1-47; (Spring 1958): 131-175; (Summer 1958): 292-301.

3457. Orr, William Gates. "Surrender of Weatherford." Transactions of the Alabama Historical Society, 1897-1898 2 (1898): 57-78.

3458. Owsley, Frank L., Jr. "British and Indian Activities in Spanish West Florida during the War of 1812." Florida Historical Quarterly 46 (October 1967): 111-123.

3459. _____. "The Fort Mims Massacre." Alabama Review 24 (July 1971): 192-204.

3460. Parker, Arthur C. "The Senecas in the War of 1812." Proceedings of the New York State Historical Association 15 (1916): 78-90.

3461. Pokagon, Simon. "The Pottawatomies in the War of 1812." Arena 26 (July 1901): 48-55.

3462. Pratt, Julius W. "Fur Trade Strategy and the American Left Flank in the War of 1812." American Historical Review 40 (January 1935): 246-273.

3463. Quaife, Milo M., ed. "The Fort Dearborn Massacre." Mississippi Valley Historical Review 1 (March 1915): 561-573.

3464. Smelser, Marshall. "Tecumseh, Harrison, and the War of 1812." Indiana Magazine of History 65 (March 1969): 25-44.

3465. Stanley, George F. G. "The Indians in the War of 1812." Canadian Historical Review 31 (June 1950): 145-165.

3466. _____. "The Significance of the Six Nations' Participation in the War of 1812." Ontario History 55 (December 1963): 215-231.

3467. West, Elizabeth H. "A Prelude to the Creek War of 1813-1814." Florida Historical Quarterly 18 (April 1940): 249-260.

3468. Wickliffe, Charles A. "Tecumseh and the Battle of the Thames," edited by G. Glenn Clift. Register of the Kentucky Historical Society 60 (January 1962): 45-49.

3469. Williams, Mentor L. "John Kinzie's Narrative of the Fort Dearborn Massacre." Journal of the Illinois State Historical Society 46 (Winter 1953): 343-362.

3470. Wright, Marcus J. "The Battle of Tohopeka, or Horse-Shoe: General Andrew Jackson's Original Report." Magazine of American History 19 (January 1888): 45-49.

First Seminole War

In 1817-1818 the United States used military force on the Florida border to chastise Indians who harbored Negro and white fugitives. There are few specific studies on this so-called First Seminole War, which has to be studied in biographies of Andrew Jackson and other general works.

3471. Coulter, E. Merton. "The Chehaw Affair." Georgia Historical Quarterly 49 (December 1965): 369-395.

3472. Porter, Kenneth W. "Negroes and the Seminole War, 1817-1818." Journal of Negro History 36 (July 1951): 249-280.

3473. Wright, J. Leitch, Jr. "A Note on the First Seminole War As Seen by the Indians, Negroes, and Their British Advisers." Journal of Southern History 34 (November 1968): 565-575.

Protection of the Santa Fe Trail

When trade between the Mississippi Valley and Santa Fe opened up in the 1820s, military protection against the Indians was provided by United States troops. The military escorts were withdrawn when the caravans were able to protect themselves.

3474. Beers, Henry Putney. "Military Protection on the Santa Fe Trail to 1843." New Mexico Historical Review 12 (April 1937): 113-133.

3475. Connelley, William E., ed. "A Journal of the Santa Fe Trail." Mississippi Valley Historical Review 12 (June 1925): 72-98; (September 1925): 227-255.

3476. Goldman, Henry H. "A Survey of Federal Escorts of the Santa Fe Trade, 1829-1843." Journal of the West 5 (October 1966): 504-516.

3477. Koester, Susan. "The Indian Threat along the Santa Fe Trail." Pacific Historian 17 (Winter 1973): 13-28.

3478. Oliva, Leo E. Soldiers on the Santa Fe Trail. Norman: University of Oklahoma Press, 1967.

3479. Perrine, Fred S., ed. "Military Escorts on the Santa Fe Trail." New Mexico Historical Review 2 (April 1927): 175-193; (July 1927): 269-304; 3 (July 1928): 265-300. Report and Journal of

Major Bennet Riley.

3480. Young, Otis E. "Dragoons on the Santa Fe Trail in the Autumn of 1843." Chronicles of Oklahoma 32 (Spring 1954): 42-51.

3481. _____. The First Military Escort on the Santa Fe Trail, 1829: From the Journal and Reports of Major Bennet Riley and Lieutenant Philip St. George Cooke. Glendale, California: Arthur H. Clark Company, 1952.

3482. _____. "Military Protection of the Santa Fe Trail and Trade." Missouri Historical Review 49 (October 1954): 19-32.

Black Hawk War

When the Sac chief, Black Hawk, and his British Band insisted on returning to ancestral lands east of the Mississippi, the frontier settlers of Illinois called for military force to remove them. The resulting conflict developed into the Black Hawk War of 1832, the last display of Indian resistance in the Old Northwest.

3483. Anderson, Robert. "Reminiscences of the Black Hawk War." Report and Collections of the State Historical Society of Wisconsin 10 (1888): 167-176.

3484. Armstrong, Perry A. The Sauks and the Black Hawk War, with Biographical Sketches, Etc. Springfield, Illinois: H. W. Rokker, 1887.

3485. Bracken, Charles. "Further Strictures on Governor Ford's History of the Black Hawk War." Annual Report and Collections of the State Historical Society of Wisconsin 2 (1856): 402-414.

3486. Burford, C. C. "Abraham Lincoln and the American Indian in the Central West." Journal of the Illinois State Archaeological Society 6 (January 1949). 15-21.

3487. Eby, Cecil. "That Disgraceful Affair": The Black Hawk War. New York: W. W. Norton and Company, 1973.

3488. Elliott, Charles Winslow. "Winfield Scott and the Black Hawk War." Infantry Journal 41 (September-October 1934): 333-337.

3489. Hagan, William T. Black Hawk's Route through Wisconsin: Report of an Investigation Made by Authority of the Legislature of Wisconsin. Madison: State Historical Society of Wisconsin, 1949.

3490. _____. "The Dodge-Henry Controversy." Journal of the Illinois State Historical Society 50 (Winter 1957): 377-384.

3491. _____. "General Henry Atkinson and the Militia." Military Affairs 23 (Winter 1959-1960): 194-197.

3492. Hamilton, Holman, ed. "Zachary Taylor and the Black Hawk War." Wisconsin Magazine of History 24 (March 1941): 305-315.

3493. Hauberg, John H. "The Black Hawk War, 1831-1832." Illinois State Historical Society Transactions for the Year 1932, pp. 91-134.

3494. Jackson, Alfred A. "Abraham Lincoln in the Black Hawk War." Collections of the State Historical Society of Wisconsin 14 (1898): 118-136.

3495. Jackson, Donald. "Black Hawk--the Last Campaign." Palimpsest 43 (February 1962): 80-94.

3496. Lambert, Joseph I. "The Black Hawk War: A Military Analysis." Journal of the Illinois State Historical Society 32 (December 1939): 442-473.

3497. Lonn, Ella. "Ripples of the Black Hawk War in Northern Indiana." Indiana Magazine of History 20 (September 1924): 288-307.

3498. Nichols, Roger L., ed. "The Battle of Bad Axe: General Atkinson's Report." Wisconsin Magazine of History 50 (Autumn 1966): 54-58.

3499. _____. "The Black Hawk War: Another View." Annals of Iowa 36 (Winter 1963): 525-533.

3500. Parkinson, Peter. "Strictures upon Gov. Ford's History of the Black Hawk War." Annual Report and Collections of the State Historical Society of Wisconsin 2 (1856): 393-401.

3501. Petersen, William J. "The Terms of Peace." Palimpsest 43 (February 1962): 95-111.

3502. Pratt, Harry E. "Abraham Lincoln in the Black Hawk War." In The John H. Hauberg Historical Essays, edited by O. Fritiof Ander, pp. 18-28. Rock Island, Illinois: Augustana College Library, 1954.

3503. Rooney, Elizabeth B. "The Story of the Black Hawk War." Wisconsin Magazine of History 40 (Summer 1957): 274-283.

3504. Smith, Henry. "Indian Campaign of 1832." Report and Collections of the State Historical Society of Wisconsin 10 (1909): 150-166.

3505. Stevens, Frank E. The Black Hawk War, Including a Review of Black Hawk's Life. Chicago: Frank E. Stevens, 1903.

3506. _____. "A Forgotten Hero: General

James Dougherty Henry." Illinois State Historical Society Transactions for the Year 1934, pp. 77-120.

3507. Temple, Wayne C. "Lincoln's Arms and Dress in the Black Hawk War." Lincoln Herald 71 (Winter 1969): 145-149.

3508. Thwaites, Reuben Gold. "The Story of the Black Hawk War." Collections of the State Historical Society of Wisconsin 12 (1892): 217-265.

3509. Van der Zee, Jacob. The Black Hawk War. Iowa City: State Historical Society of Iowa, 1918.

3510. _____. "The Black Hawk War and the Treaty of 1832." Iowa Journal of History and Politics 13 (July 1915): 416-428.

3511. Wakefield, John A. History of the War between the United States and the Sac and Fox Nations of Indians, and Parts of Other Disaffected Tribes of Indians, in the Years Eighteen Hundred and Twenty-Seven, Thirty-One, and Thirty-Two. Jacksonville, Illinois: Calvin Goudy, 1834. Reprinted as Wakefield's History of the Black Hawk War. Edited by Frank E. Stevens. Chicago: Caxton Club, 1908.

3512. Wallace, Anthony F. C. Prelude to Disaster: The Course of Indian-White Relations Which Led to the Black Hawk War of 1832. Springfield: Illinois State Historical Library, 1970. Reprinted from Ellen M. Whitney, ed. The Black Hawk War, 1831-1832.

3513. Whitney, Ellen M., ed. The Black Hawk War, 1831-1832. 3 volumes. Collections of the Illinois State Historical Library, volumes 35-37. Springfield: Illinois State Historical Library, 1970-1975.

Second Seminole War

When the Seminole Indians of Florida refused to move to the West, the United States army was sent to remove them by force. The "Florida War" that resulted lasted from 1835 to 1842. It has been the subject of many studies.

3514. Adams, George R. "The Caloosahatchee Massacre: Its Significance in the Second Seminole War." Florida Historical Quarterly 48 (April 1970): 368-380.

3515. Backus, Electus. "Diary of a Campaign in Florida, in 1837-1838." Historical Magazine 10 (September 1866): 279-285.

3516. Barr, James. A Correct and Authentic Narrative of the Indian War in Florida, with a Description of Maj. Dade's Massacre, and an Account of the Extreme Suf-

fering, for Want of Provisions, of the Army--Having Been Obliged to Eat Horses' and Dogs' Flesh, &c. &c. New York: James Narine, 1836.

3517. Bemrose, John. Reminiscences of the Second Seminole War. Edited by John K. Mahon. Gainesville: University of Florida Press, 1966.

3518. Bittle, George C. "First Campaign of the Second Seminole War." Florida Historical Quarterly 46 (July 1967): 39-45.

3519. _____. "The Florida Militia's Role in the Battle of Withlacoochee." Florida Historical Quarterly 44 (April 1966): 303-311.

3520. Boyd, Mark F. "The Seminole War: Its Background and Onset." Florida Historical Quarterly 30 (July 1951): 3-115.

3521. Brown, Tom O. "Locating Seminole Indian War Forts." Florida Historical Quarterly 40 (January 1962): 310-313.

3522. Buker, George E. "Lieutenant Levin M. Powell, U.S.N., Pioneer of Riverine Warfare." Florida Historical Quarterly 47 (January 1969): 253-275.

3523. _____. "Riverine Warfare: Naval Combat in the Second Seminole War, 1835-1842." Ph.D. dissertation, University of Florida, 1969.

3524. "The Case of Osceola." Magazine of American History 5 (December 1880): 447-450. Statements by R. M. Potter and Thomas S. Jesup.

3525. Chandler, William. "Original Narratives of Indian Attacks in Florida: A Tallahassee Alarm of 1836." Florida Historical Society Quarterly 8 (April 1930): 197-199.

3526. Cobb, Samuel E. "The Florida Militia and the Affair at Withlacoochee." Florida Historical Quarterly 19 (October 1940): 128-139.

3527. Coe, Charles H. Red Patriots: The Story of the Seminoles. Cincinnati: Editor Publishing Company, 1898.

3528. Cohen, M. M. Notices of Florida and the Campaigns. Charleston, South Carolina: Burges and Honour, 1836. Facsimile edition, Gainesville: University of Florida Press, 1964.

3529. Covington, James W. "Cuban Bloodhounds and the Seminoles." Florida Historical Quarterly 33 (October 1954): 111-119.

3530. Covington, James W., ed. "Exploring the Ten Thousand Islands in 1838." Tequesta 18 (1958): 7-13. Report of Thomas Lawson.

3531. Davis, T. Frederick. "The Seminole Council, October 23-25, 1834." Florida Historical Society Quarterly 7 (April 1929): 330-350.

3532. Doherty, Herbert J., Jr. "Richard K. Call vs. the Federal Government on the Seminole War." Florida Historical Quarterly 31 (January 1953): 163-180.

3533. Foreman, Carolyn Thomas. "The Brave Major Moniac and the Creek Volunteers." Chronicles of Oklahoma 23 (Summer 1945): 96-106.

3534. Foreman, Grant, ed. "Report of the Cherokee Deputation into Florida." Chronicles of Oklahoma 9 (December 1931): 423-438.

3535. Forry, Samuel. "Letters of Samuel Forry, Surgeon U.S. Army, 1837-1838." Florida Historical Society Quarterly 6 (January 1928): 133-148; (April 1928): 206-219; 7 (July 1928): 88-105.

3536. Gadsden, James. "Letter of Colonel James Gadsden on the Seminole Council (The News, St. Augustine, July 13, 1839)." Florida Historical Society Quarterly 7 (April 1929): 350-356.

3537. Giddings, Joshua R. The Exiles of Florida; or, The Crimes Committed by Our Government against the Maroons, Who Fled from South Carolina and Other Slave States, Seeking Protection under Spanish Laws. Columbus, Ohio: Follett, Foster and Company, 1858. Facsimile edition, Gainesville: University of Florida Press, 1964.

3538. Hammond, E. A., ed. "Bemrose's Medical Case Notes from the Second Seminole War." Florida Historical Quarterly 47 (April 1969): 401-413.

3539. _____. "Dr. Strobel Reports on Southeast Florida, 1836." Tequesta 21 (1961): 65-75.

3540. Horn, Stanley F., ed. "Notes and Documents: Tennessee Volunteers in the Seminole Campaign of 1836: The Diary of Henry Hollingsworth." Tennessee Historical Quarterly 1 (September 1942): 269-274; (December 1942): 344-366; 2 (March 1943): 61-73; (June 1943): 163-178; (September 1943): 236-256.

3541. Hoyt, William D. "A Soldier's View of the Seminole War, 1838-39." Florida Historical Quarterly 25 (April 1947): 356-362.

3542. "Jacksonville and the Seminole War, 1835-1836." Florida Historical Society Quarterly 3 (January 1925): 10-14; (April 1925): 15-21; 4 (July 1925): 22-30.

3543. Jarvis, Nathan S. "An Army Surgeon's Notes of Frontier Service, 1833-1848." Journal of the Military Service Institution of the United States 39 (July-August 1906): 130-135; (September-October 1906): 275-286; (November-December 1906): 451-460.

3544. Jesup, Thomas Sydney. Seminole Saga: The Jesup Report. Fort Myers Beach, Florida: Island Press, 1973. Reprint of Senate Document no. 507, 25th Congress, 2d session.

3545. Laumer, Frank. "Encounter by the River." Florida Historical Quarterly 46 (April 1968): 322-339.

3546. _____. Massacre! Gainesville: University of Florida Press, 1968. Dade Massacre.

3547. _____. "This Was Fort Dade." Florida Historical Quarterly 45 (July 1966): 1-11.

3548. Mahon, John K. History of the Second Seminole War, 1835-1842. Gainesville: University of Florida Press, 1967.

3549. _____. "Postscript to John Bemrose's Reminiscences." Florida Historical Quarterly 47 (July 1968): 59-62.

3550. Mahon, John K., ed. "The Journal of A. B. Meek and the Second Seminole War, 1836." Florida Historical Quarterly 38 (April 1960): 302-318.

3551. _____. "Letters from the Second Seminole War." Florida Historical Quarterly 36 (April 1958): 331-352. Letters of Joseph R. Smith.

3552. Motte, Jacob Rhett. Journey into Wilderness: An Army Surgeon's Account of Life in Camp and Field during the Creek and Seminole Wars, 1836-1838. Edited by James F. Sunderman. Gainesville: University of Florida Press, 1953.

3553. Moulton, Gary E. "Cherokees and the Second Seminole War." Florida Historical Quarterly 53 (January 1975): 296-305.

3554. "Original Narratives of Indian Attacks in Florida: Indian Murders." Florida Historical Society Quarterly 8 (April 1930): 200-203.

3555. Parker, H. H. "The Battle of Okee-Chobee." American Philatelist 61 (July 1948): 808-810.

3556. Phelps, John W. "Letters of Lieutenant John W. Phelps, U.S.A., 1837-1838." Florida Historical Society Quarterly 6 (October 1927): 67-84.

3557. Pierce, Philip N., and Lewis Meyers.

"The Seven Years War." Marine Corps Gazette 32 (September 1948): 32-38.

3558. Porter, Kenneth Wiggins. "Florida Slaves and Free Negroes in the Seminole War, 1835-1842." Journal of Negro History 28 (October 1943): 390-421.

3559. _____. "Negroes and the Seminole War, 1835-1842." Journal of Southern History 30 (November 1964): 427-450.

3560. _____. "Negro Guides and Interpreters in the Early Stages of the Seminole War, Dec. 28, 1835-Mar. 6, 1837." Journal of Negro History 35 (April 1950): 174-182.

3561. _____. "Seminole Flight from Fort Marion." Florida Historical Quarterly 22 (January 1944): 113-133.

3562. Potter, Woodburne. The War in Florida: Being an Exposition of Its Causes, and an Accurate History of the Campaigns of Generals Clinch, Gaines and Scott. Baltimore: Lewis and Coleman, 1836.

3563. Preble, George Henry. "A Canoe Expedition into the Everglades in 1842." Tequesta 5 (January 1945): 30-51.

3564. Roberts, Albert Hubbard. "The Dade Massacre." Florida Historical Society Quarterly 5 (January 1927): 123-138.

3565. Sheldon, Jane Murray. "Original Narratives of Indian Attacks in Florida: Seminole Attacks near New Smyrna: 1835-1856." Florida Historical Society Quarterly 8 (April 1930): 188-196.

3566. Smith, W. W. Sketch of the Seminole War, and Sketches during a Campaign. Charleston, South Carolina: Dan J. Dowling, 1836.

3567. Sprague, John T. The Origin, Progress, and Conclusion of the Florida War. New York: D. Appleton and Company, 1848. Facsimile edition, Gainesville: University of Florida Press, 1964.

3568. Stafford, Robert Charles. "The Bemrose Manuscript on the Seminole War." Florida Historical Quarterly 18 (April 1940): 285-292.

3569. Sunderman, James F., ed. "Army Surgeon Reports on Lower East Coast, 1838." Tequesta 10 (1950): 25-33. Report of Jacob Rhett Motte.

3570. Van Ness, W. P. "An Incident of the Seminole War." Journal of the Military Service Institution of the United States 50 (March-April 1912): 267-271.

3571. Walker, Hester Perrine. "Massacre at Indian Key, August 7, 1840, and the Death of Doctor Henry Perrine (Narrative of

Hester Perrine Walker, a Survivor)." Florida Historical Society Quarterly 5 (July 1926): 18-42.

3572. White, Frank F., Jr., ed. "A Journal of Lt. Robert C. Buchanan during the Seminole War." Florida Historical Quarterly 29 (October 1950): 132-151.

3573. _____. "Macomb's Mission to the Seminoles: John T. Sprague's Journal Kept during April and May, 1839." Florida Historical Quarterly 35 (October 1956): 130-193.

3574. _____. "A Scouting Expedition along Lake Panasoffkee." Florida Historical Quarterly 31 (April 1953): 282-289. Report of Robert C. Buchanan.

3575. "The White Flag." Florida Historical Quarterly 33 (January-April 1955): 218-234. The surrender of Osceola.

3576. Wik, Reynold M. "Captain Nathaniel Wyche Hunter and the Florida Indian Campaigns, 1837-1844." Florida Historical Quarterly 39 (July 1960): 62-75.

3577. Woodward, A. L. "Indian Massacre in Gadsden County." Florida Historical Society Quarterly 1 (April 1908): 17-25.

3578. Young, Rogers W. "Fort Marion during the Seminole War, 1835-1842." Florida Historical Society Quarterly 13 (April 1935): 193-223.

See also studies on the Seminole Indians and biographies of Osceola.

Mississippi Valley and the Plains

The authorization for mounted troops in the West in 1832 increased military action, as the dragoons crossed the prairies and the plains in summer campaigns intended to overawe the Indians. Included here are reports of these expeditions and other studies dealing with the defense of the plains before the Civil War.

3579. Agnew, Brad. "The 1858 War against the Comanches." Chronicles of Oklahoma 49 (Summer 1971): 211-229.

3580. Ballenger, T. L. "Colonel Albert Sidney Johnston's March through Indian Territory in 1855." Chronicles of Oklahoma 47 (Summer 1969): 132-137.

3581. Barry, Louise. "The Fort Leavenworth-Fort Gibson Military Road and the Founding of Fort Scott." Kansas Historical Quarterly 11 (May 1942): 115-129.

3582. Barry, Louise, ed. "With the First U.S. Cavalry in Indian Country, 1859-1861: Letters to The Daily Times, Leavenworth." Kansas Historical Quarterly 24 (Autumn

1958): 257-284; (Winter 1958): 399-425.

3583. Beers, Henry P. "The Army and the Oregon Trail to 1846." Pacific Northwest Quarterly 28 (October 1937): 339-362.

3584. Benedict, J. W. "Diary of a Campaign against the Comanches." Southwestern Historical Quarterly 32 (April 1929): 300-310.

3585. Birch, James H. "The Battle of Coon Creek." Transactions of the Kansas State Historical Society 10 (1907-1908): 409-413.

3586. Briggs, John Ely, ed. "The Expedition of 1835." Palimpsest 16 (April 1935): 105-136.

3587. Caldwell, Dorothy J. "The Big Neck Affair: Tragedy and Farce on the Missouri Frontier." Missouri Historical Review 64 (July 1970): 391-412.

3588. Call, Ambrose A. "Indians Repelled in Kossuth." Annals of Iowa, 3d series 31 (October 1951): 81-90.

3589. Carleton, James Henry. The Prairie Logbooks: Dragoon Campaigns to the Pawnee Villages in 1844, and to the Rocky Mountains in 1845. Edited by Louis Pelzer. Chicago: Caxton Club, 1943.

3590. Clark, Dan Elbert. "Frontier Defense in Iowa, 1850-1865." Iowa Journal of History and Politics 16 (July 1918): 315-386.

3591. Crimmins, M. L. "First Sergeant John W. Spangler, Company H, Second United States Cavalry." West Texas Historical Association Year Book 26 (October 1950): 68-75. Service in the Indian wars, 1857-1861.

3592. Davis, Carl L., and LeRoy H. Fischer. "Dragoon Life in Indian Territory, 1833-1846." Chronicles of Oklahoma 48 (Spring 1970): 2-24.

3593. Drum, Richard C. "Reminiscences of the Indian Fight at Ash Hollow, 1855." Collections of the Nebraska State Historical Society 16 (1911): 143-150.

3594. Fessler, W. Julian, ed. "Captain Nathan Boone's Journal." Chronicles of Oklahoma 7 (March 1929): 58-105.

3595. Foreman, Carolyn Thomas, ed. "The Cherokee War Path." Chronicles of Oklahoma 9 (September 1931): 233-263.

3596. Foreman, Grant, ed. "A Journal Kept by Douglas Cooper of an Expedition by a Company of Chickasaw in Quest of Comanche Indians." Chronicles of Oklahoma 5 (December 1927): 381-390.

3597. "Frontier Fear of the Indians."

Annals of Iowa, 3d series 29 (April 1948): 315-322.

3598. Gardner, Hamilton. "Captain Philip St. George Cooke and the March of the 1st Dragoons to the Rocky Mountains in 1845." Colorado Magazine 30 (October 1953): 246-269.

3599. _____. "The March of the First Dragoons from Jefferson Barracks to Fort Gibson in 1833-1834." Chronicles of Oklahoma 31 (Spring 1953): 22-36.

3600. Glenn, Robert A. "The Osage War." Missouri Historical Review 14 (January 1920): 201-210.

3601. Godsey, Roy. "The Osage War, 1837." Missouri Historical Review 20 (October 1925): 96-100.

3602. Grimes, J. W. "Apprehended Indian Troubles." Annals of Iowa, 3d series 2 (January 1897): 627-630.

3603. Hafen, LeRoy R., and Ann W. Hafen, eds. Relations with the Indians of the Plains, 1857-1861: A Documentary Account of the Military Campaigns, and Negotiations of Indian Agents--with Reports and Journals of P. G. Lowe, R. M. Peck, J. E. B. Stuart, S. D. Sturgis, and Other Official Papers. Glendale, California: Arthur H. Clark Company, 1959.

3604. Hayden, Willard C. "The Battle of Pierre's Hole." Idaho Yesterdays 16 (Summer 1972): 2-11.

3605. Hildreth, James. Dragoon Campaigns to the Rocky Mountains: Being a History of the Enlistment, Organization, and First Campaigns of the Regiment of United States Dragoons, Together with the Incidents of a Soldier's Life, and Sketches of Scenery and Indian Character. New York: Wiley and Long, 1836.

3606. Hughes, W. J. "'Rip' Ford's Indian Fight on the Canadian." Panhandle-Plains Historical Review 30 (1957): 1-26.

3607. Hughes, Willis B. "The Army and Stephen Watts Kearny in the West, 1819-1846." Ph.D. dissertation, University of Minnesota, 1955.

3608. _____. "The First Dragoons on the Western Frontier, 1834-1846." Arizona and the West 12 (Summer 1970): 115-138.

3609. Hughes, Willis B., ed. "The Heatherly Incident of 1836." Bulletin of the Missouri Historical Society 13 (January 1957): 161-180.

3610. Ingham, Harvey. "Sioux Indians Harassed the Early Iowa Settlers." Annals of Iowa, 3d series 34 (October 1957): 137-141.

3611. "Investigations as to Causes of Indian Hostilities West of the Missouri River, 1824." Annals of Wyoming 15 (July 1943): 198-220. Reports of R. Graham and Joshua Pilcher.

3612. McCann, Lloyd E. "The Grattan Massacre." Nebraska History 37 (March 1956): 1-25.

3613. McKenney, Thomas L. "The Winnebago War of 1827." Collections of the State Historical Society of Wisconsin 5 (1868): 179-187.

3614. Mattison, Ray H., ed. "The Harney Expedition against the Sioux: The Journal of Capt. John B. S. Todd." Nebraska History 43 (June 1962): 89-130.

3615. Morrison, James D. "Travis G. Wright and the Leavenworth Expedition in Oklahoma." Chronicles of Oklahoma 25 (Spring 1947): 7-14.

3616. Munkres, Robert L. "The Plains Indian Threat on the Oregon Trail before 1860." Annals of Wyoming 40 (October 1968): 193-221.

3617. Nasatir, Abraham P. "The International Significance of the Jones and Immell Massacre and of the Aricara Outbreak of 1823." Pacific Northwest Quarterly 30 (January 1939): 77-108.

3618. Nichols, Roger L., ed. "General Henry Atkinson's Report of the Yellowstone Expedition of 1825." Nebraska History 49 (June 1963): 65-82.

3619. Patterson, Bradley H., Jr. "The Pierre's Hole Fight." In Great Western Indian Fights, pp. 30-38. Garden City, New York: Doubleday and Company, 1960.

3620. Pelzer, Louis. Marches of the Dragoons in the Mississippi Valley: An Account of Marches and Activities of the First Regiment of United States Dragoons in the Mississippi Valley between the Years 1833 and 1850. Iowa City: State Historical Society of Iowa, 1917.

3621. Pelzer, Louis, ed. "Captain Ford's Journal of an Expedition to the Rocky Mountains, 29 May to 16 September, 1835." Mississippi Valley Historical Review 12 (March 1926): 550-579. Journal of Lemuel Ford.

3622. _____. "A Journal of Marches by the First United States Dragoons 1834-1835." Iowa Journal of History and Politics 7 (July 1909): 331-378.

3623. Perrine, Fred S., ed. "Hugh Evans' Journal of Colonel Henry Dodge's Expedition to the Rocky Mountains in 1835." Mississippi Valley Historical Review 14 (September 1927): 192-214.

3624. Perrine, Fred S., and Grant Foreman, eds. "The Journal of Hugh Evans, Covering the First and Second Campaigns of the United States Dragoon Regiment in 1834 and 1835: Campaign of 1834." Chronicles of Oklahoma 3 (September 1925): 175-215.

3625. Reese, Calvin Lee. "The United States Army and the Indian: Low Plains Area, 1815-1854." Ph.D. dissertation, University of Southern California, 1963.

3626. Reid, Russell, and Clell G. Gannon, eds. "Journal of the Atkinson-O'Fallon Expedition." North Dakota Historical Quarterly 4 (October 1929): 5-56.

3627. Richards, Charles B. "Organization and Service of the Frontier Guards." Annals of Iowa 11 (April 1913): 1-15.

3628. Robinson, Doane, ed. "Official Correspondence Pertaining to the Leavenworth Expedition of 1823 into South Dakota for the Conquest of the Ree Indians." South Dakota Historical Collections 1 (1902): 181-256.

3629. Robinson, W. Stitt, ed. "The Kiowa and Comanche Campaign of 1860 As Recorded in the Personal Diary of Lt. J. E. B. Stuart." Kansas Historical Quarterly 23 (Winter 1957): 382-400.

3630. Rutland, Robert, ed. "The Dragoons in the Iowa Territory, 1845." Iowa Journal of History 51 (April 1953): 156-182.

3631. _____. "A Journal of the First Dragoons in the Iowa Territory, 1844." Iowa Journal of History 51 (January 1953): 57-78.

3632. Salter, William. "Henry Dodge: Part IV, Colonel U.S. Dragoons, 1833-6." Iowa Historical Record 7 (April 1891): 101-119; 8 (April 1892): 251-267.

3633. Seabrook, S. L. "Expedition of Col. E. V. Sumner against the Cheyenne Indians, 1857." Collections of the Kansas State Historical Society 16 (1923-1925): 306-315.

3634. Shirk, George H. "Peace on the Plains." Chronicles of Oklahoma 28 (Spring 1950): 2-41. Includes "Journal of Colonel Dodge's Expedition from Fort Gibson to the Pawnee Pict Village," by T. B. Wheelock, 1834.

3635. Taylor, Morris F. "The Mail Station and the Military at Camp on Pawnee Fork, 1859-1860." Kansas Historical Quarterly 36 (Spring 1970): 27-39.

3636. Thoburn, Joseph B. "The Dragoon Campaigns to the Rocky Mountains." Chronicles of Oklahoma 7 (March 1930): 35-41.

3637. Van der Zee, Jacob, ed. "Captain Edwin V. Sumner's Dragoon Expedition in the Territory of Iowa in the Summer of 1845." Iowa Journal of History and Politics 11 (April 1913): 258-267.

3638. _____. "Captain James Allen's Dragoon Expedition from Fort Des Moines, Territory of Iowa, in 1844." Iowa Journal of History and Politics 11 (January 1913): 68-108.

3639. Warner, Mildred. "Indians Challenge the Nebraska Territorial Government." Great Plains Journal 9 (Spring 1970): 53-58.

3640. Woolworth, Nancy L. "Captain Edwin V. Sumner's Expedition to Devil's Lake in the Summer of 1845." North Dakota History 28 (April-July 1961): 79-98.

3641. Young, Otis E. "The United States Mounted Ranger Battalion, 1832-1833." Mississippi Valley Historical Review 41 (December 1954): 453-470.

Texas before the Civil War

The Republic of Texas had frontier Indian troubles that continued after Texas became a state. Listed here are accounts of military action relating to Indians in Texas before the Civil War.

3642. Crimmins, M. L., ed. "Colonel Robert E. Lee's Report on Indian Combats in Texas." Southwestern Historical Quarterly 39 (July 1935): 21-32.

3643. Daniell, Forrest. "Texas Pioneer Surveyors and Indians." Southwestern Historical Quarterly 60 (April 1957): 501-506.

3644. Dragoo, Benjamin Crawford, as told to J. Marvin Hunter. "Trailing and Fighting Indians in 1855." Frontier Times 30 (April-June 1953): 180-185.

3645. Fisher, O. Clark. "Battle of Bandera Pass." In Great Western Indian Fights, pp. 41-45. Garden City, New York: Doubleday and Company, 1960.

3646. Hayes, E. M. "Indian Campaigns in Texas: The Battle of Jungle Hollow--Indian Territory, May, 1859." Army and Navy Life 12 (March 1908): 317-320.

3647. Henderson, Harry McCorry. "The Surveyors Fight." Southwestern Historical Quarterly 56 (July 1952): 25-35. Kickapoo Indians, Texas, 1838.

3648. Oates, Stephen B. "They Did Right Because It Was Right." Southwest Review 48 (Autumn 1963): 387-395. Texas Rangers in United States service, 1849-1851.

3649. Richardson, Rupert N., ed. "Documents Relating to West Texas and Her Indian Tribes." West Texas Historical Association Year Book 1 (June 1925): 30-83.

3650. Ritchie, E. B., ed. "Copy of Report of Colonel Samuel Cooper, Assistant Adjutant General of the United States, of Inspection Trip from Fort Graham to the Indian Villages on the Upper Brazos Made in June, 1851." Southwestern Historical Quarterly 42 (April 1939): 327-333.

3651. Shearer, Ernest Charles. "The Callahan Expedition, 1855." Southwest Historical Quarterly 54 (April 1951): 430-451.

3652. Tate, Michael L. "Frontier Defense on the Comanche Ranges of Northwest Texas, 1846-1860." Great Plains Journal 2 (Fall 1971): 41-56.

3653. _____. "Military Relations between the Republic of Texas and the Comanche Indians." Journal of the West 13 (January 1974): 67-77.

3654. Vigness, David M. "Indian Raids on the Lower Rio Grande, 1836-1837." Southwestern Historical Quarterly 59 (July 1955): 14-23.

Military Action in the Southwest

When the United States gained control of the Southwest at the time of the Mexican War, military defense against the Indians was extended to that region.

3655. Anderson, Hattie M., ed. "Mining and Indian Fighting in Arizona and New Mexico, 1858-1861: Memoirs of Hank M. Smith." Panhandle-Plains Historical Review 1 (1928): 67-115.

3656. Bender, Averam B. "Frontier Defense in the Territory of New Mexico, 1846-1853." New Mexico Historical Review 9 (July 1934): 249-272.

3657. _____. "Frontier Defense in the Territory of New Mexico, 1853-1861." New Mexico Historical Review 9 (October 1934): 345-373.

3658. _____. The March of Empire: Frontier Defense in the Southwest, 1848-1860. Lawrence: University of Kansas Press, 1952.

3659. Benson, William Ralganal. "The Stone and Kelsey 'Massacre' on the Shores of Clear Lake in 1849--the Indian Viewpoint." Quarterly of the California Historical Society 11 (September 1932): 266-273.

3660. Chacon, Rafael. "Campaign against

Utes and Apaches in Southern Colorado, 1855." Colorado Magazine 11 (May 1934): 108-112.

3661. Chaput, Donald. "Babes in Arms." Journal of Arizona History 13 (Autumn 1972): 197-204. Warfare in the Southwest, 1853.

3662. DuBois, John Van Deusen. Campaigns in the West, 1856-1861: The Journal and Letters of Colonel John Van Deusen DuBois. Edited by George P. Hammond. Tucson: Arizona Pioneers Historical Society, 1949.

3663. Eccleston, Robert. The Mariposa Indian War, 1850-1851: Diaries of Robert Eccleston: The California Gold Rush, Yosemite, and the High Sierra. Edited by C. Gregory Crampton. Salt Lake City: University of Utah Press, 1957. War against the California Indians.

3664. Evans, William Edward. "The Garra Uprising: Conflict between San Diego Indians and Settlers in 1851." California Historical Society Quarterly 45 (December 1966): 339-349.

3665. Gardner, Hamilton, ed. "Philip St. George Cooke and the Apache, 1854." New Mexico Historical Review 28 (April 1953): 115-132.

3666. Hafen, LeRoy R. "The Fort Pueblo Massacre and the Punitive Expedition against the Utes." Colorado Magazine 4 (March 1927): 49-58.

3667. Johannsen, Robert W., ed. "Edward O. C. Ord on Frontier Defense." California Historical Society Quarterly 35 (March 1956): 23-27.

3668. Lecompte, Janet. "The Manco Burro Pass Massacre." New Mexico Historical Review 41 (October 1966): 305-318.

3669. McClure, Charles R. "Neither Effective nor Financed: The Difficulties of Indian Defense in New Mexico, 1837-1846." Military History of Texas and the Southwest 10 (1972): 73-92.

3670. McNitt, Frank. "Navajo Campaigns and the Occupation of New Mexico, 1847-1848." New Mexico Historical Review 43 (July 1968): 173-194.

3671. Marino, C. C. "The Seboyetanos and the Navahos." New Mexico Historical Review 29 (January 1954): 8-27.

3672. Murphy, Lawrence R. "The United States Army in Taos, 1847-1852." New Mexico Historical Review 47 (January 1972): 33-48.

3673. Myers, Lee. "Illinois Volunteers in New Mexico, 1847-1848." New Mexico Historical Review 47 (January 1972): 5-31.

3674. Smith, Ralph A. "Apache Plunder Trails Southward, 1831-1840." New Mexico Historical Review 37 (January 1962): 20-42.

3675. _____. "Apache 'Ranching' below the Gila, 1841-1845." Arizoniana 3 (Winter 1962): 1-17.

3676. _____. "The Scalp Hunter in the Borderlands 1835-1850." Arizona and the West 6 (Spring 1964): 5-22.

3677. _____. "The Scalp Hunt in Chihuahua-1849." New Mexico Historical Review 40 (April 1965): 117-140.

3678. Taylor, Morris F. "Action at Fort Massachusetts: The Indian Campaign of 1855." Colorado Magazine 42 (Fall 1965): 292-310.

3679. _____. "Campaigns against the Jicarilla Apache, 1854." New Mexico Historical Review 44 (October 1969): 269-291.

3680. _____. "Campaigns against the Jicarilla Apache, 1855." New Mexico Historical Review 45 (April 1970): 119-136.

3681. Utley, Robert M. "Captain John Pope's Plan of 1853 for the Frontier Defense of New Mexico." Arizona and the West 5 (Summer 1963): 149-163.

Other studies, dealing particularly with the Navajo Indians in this period, are listed under Navajo campaigns (3815 to 3830).

Wars in the Pacific Northwest

The flood of population into the Pacific Northwest brought Indian-white conflicts, in part because the administration of Indian affairs lagged behind the influx of settlers. A general outbreak in 1855, known as the Yakima War, did not finally subside until 1858.

3682. Abbot, Henry L. "Reminiscences of the Oregon War of 1855." Journal of the Military Service Institution of the United States 45 (November-December 1909): 436-442.

3683. Andrews, Clarence L. "Warfield's Story of Peo-Peo-Mox-Mox." Washington Historical Quarterly 25 (July 1934): 182-184.

3684. Bagley, Clarence B. "Attitude of the Hudson's Bay Company during the Indian War of 1855-1856." Washington Historical Quarterly 8 (October 1917): 291-307.

3685. _____. "Our First Indian War." Washington Historical Quarterly 1 (October 1906): 34-49.

3686. Baydo, Gerald. "Citizen Soldier in the Indian War of 1855-56." Idaho Yesterdays 15 (Winter 1972): 27-33. Based on diary of Winfield Ebey.

3687. Bischoff, William N. "The Yakima Indian War, 1855-1856: A Problem in Research." Pacific Northwest Quarterly 41 (April 1950): 162-169.

3688. _____. "The Yakima Indian War: 1855-1856." Ph.D. dissertation, Loyola University of Chicago, 1950.

3689. Bischoff, William N., ed. "The Yakima Campaign of 1856." Mid-America 31 (July 1949): 163-208. Reports of Colonel George Wright.

3690. Bledsoe, A. J. The Indian Wars of the Northwest: A California Sketch. San Francisco: Bacon and Company, 1885.

3691. Bonney, W. P. "Monument to Captain Hembree." Washington Historical Quarterly 11 (July 1920): 178-182.

3692. Brandt, John H. "The Navy as an Indian Fighter." United States Naval Institute Proceedings 56 (August 1930): 691. Protection of Seattle, 1855.

3693. Brown, William Compton. The Indian Side of the Story: Being a Concourse of Presentations Historical and Biographical in Character Relating to the Indian Wars, and to Treatment Accorded the Indians, in Washington Territory East of the Cascade Mountains during the Period from 1853 to 1889. Spokane: C. W. Hill Printing Company, 1961.

3694. Burns, Robert Ignatius. "A Bancroft Library Manuscript on the 1858 War." Oregon Historical Quarterly 52 (March 1951): 54-57.

3695. _____. "A Jesuit in the War against the Northern Indians." Records of the American Catholic Historical Society 61 (March 1950): 9-54.

3696. _____. The Jesuits and the Indian Wars of the Northwest. New Haven: Yale University Press, 1966.

3697. Burns, Robert Ignatius, ed. "Pere Joset's Account of the Indian War of 1858." Pacific Northwest Quarterly 38 (October 1947): 285-314.

3698. Chadwick, S. J. "Colonel Steptoe's Battle." Washington Historical Quarterly 2 (July 1908): 333-343.

3699. Clark, Robert Carlton. "Military History of Oregon, 1849-59." Oregon Historical Quarterly 36 (March 1935): 14-59.

3700. Colvig, William M. "Indian Wars of Southern Oregon." Oregon Historical Society Quarterly 4 (September 1903): 227-240.

3701. Cresap, Bernarr. "Captain Edward O. C. Ord in the Rogue River Indian War." Oregon Historical Quarterly 54 (June 1953): 83-90.

3702. "Defending Puget Sound against the Northern Indians." Pacific Northwest Quarterly 36 (January 1945): 69-78.

3703. Dodd, Jack. "The Indians Have an Inning: To-Hoto-Nim-Me." In Great Western Indian Fights, pp. 50-60. Garden City, New York: Doubleday and Company, 1960.

3704. _____. "The Soldiers Have Theirs: Four Lakes and Spokane Plains." In Great Western Indian Fights, pp. 61-72. Garden City, New York: Doubleday and Company, 1960.

3705. Dozier, Jack. "The Coeur D'Alene Indians in the War of 1858." Idaho Yesterdays 5 (Fall 1961): 22-32.

3706. Elliott, T. C. "Steptoe Butte and Steptoe Battle-field." Washington Historical Quarterly 18 (October 1927): 243-253.

3707. Ermatinger, Frank. "Earliest Expedition against Puget Sound Indians," edited by Eva Emery Dye. Washington Historical Quarterly 1 (January 1907): 16-29.

3708. Garth, Thomas R., Jr. "Waiilatpu after the Massacre." Pacific Northwest Quarterly 38 (October 1947): 315-318.

3709. Gates, Charles, M., ed. "Seattle's First Taste of Battle, 1856." Pacific Northwest Quarterly 47 (January 1956): 1-8.

3710. Gosnell, W. B. "Indian War in Washington Territory." Washington Historical Quarterly 17 (October 1926): 289-299.

3711. Graham, Joel. "A Massacre on the Frontier." Washington Historical Quarterly 2 (April 1908): 233-236.

3712. Hacker, Nancy A., and Francis S. Landrum, eds. "Alexander Piper's Reports and Journal." Oregon Historical Quarterly 69 (September 1968): 223-268.

3713. Hembree, Waman C. "Yakima Indian War Diary," edited by Edmond S. Meany. Washington Historical Quarterly 16 (October 1925): 273-283.

3714. Howard, Helen Addison. "The Steptoe

Affair." Montana, the Magazine of Western History 19 (April 1969): 28-36.

3715. Hussey, John Adam, and George Walcott Amers, Jr. "California Preparations to Meet the Walla Walla Invasion, 1846." California Historical Society Quarterly 21 (March 1942): 9-21.

3716. Kelley, John F. "The Steptoe Disaster." Pacific Northwesterner 1 (Winter 1956-1957): 9-16.

3717. Kip, Lawrence. Army Life on the Pacific: A Journal of the Expedition against the Northern Indians, the Tribes of the Coeur d'Alenes, Spokans, and Pelouzes, in the Summer of 1858. New York: Redfield, 1859.

3718. Knuth, Priscilla, ed. "Cavalry in the Indian Country, 1864." Oregon Historical Quarterly 65 (March 1964): 5-118. Journal of John M. Drake.

3719. Manring, B. F. The Conquest of the Coeur d'Alenes, Spokanes and Palouses: The Expeditions of Colonels E. J. Steptoe and George Wright against the "Northern Indians" in 1858. Spokane: Inland Printing Company, 1912.

3720. Merriam, L. C., Jr., ed. "The First Oregon Cavalry and the Oregon Central Military Road Survey of 1865." Oregon Historical Quarterly 60 (March 1959): 89-124. Journal of John Marshall McCall.

3721. Metschan, Phil. "Canyon City 'Fort-Up' 1878." Oregon Historical Quarterly 70 (March 1969): 56-59.

3722. Morris, T. "Army Officer's Report on Indian War and Treaties." Washington Historical Quarterly 19 (April 1928): 134-141.

3723. Nalty, Bernard C., and Truman R. Strobridge. "The Defense of Seattle, 1856: 'And Down Came the Indians.'" Pacific Northwest Quarterly 55 (July 1964): 105-110.

3724. Oliphant, J. Orin, ed. "Journals of the Indian War of 1855-56." Washington Historical Quarterly 15 (January 1924): 11-31. Journals of Robert Moore Painter and William Charles Painter.

3725. Onstad, Preston E. "Camp Henderson, 1864." Oregon Historical Quarterly 65 (September 1964): 297-302.

3726. Prosch, Thomas W. "The Indian War in Washington Territory." Quarterly of the Oregon Historical Society 16 (March 1915): 1-23.

3727. Prosch, Thomas W., ed. "The Indian War of 1858." Washington Historical

Quarterly 2 (April 1908): 237-240. Narrative of Winfield Scott.

3728. Reese, J. W. "OMV's Fort Henrietta: On Winter Duty, 1855-56." Oregon Historical Quarterly 66 (June 1965): 133-160. Oregon Mounted Volunteers in the Yakima Indian War.

3729. Richards, Kent. "Isaac I. Stevens and Federal Military Power in Washington Territory." Pacific Northwest Quarterly 63 (July 1972): 81-86.

3730. Rinehart, William Vance. "War in the Great Northwest." Washington Historical Quarterly 22 (April 1931): 83-98.

3731. Robbins, Harvey. "Journal of Rogue River War, 1855." Oregon Historical Quarterly 34 (December 1933): 345-358.

3732. Santee, J. F. "The Slaying of Pio-Pio-Mox-Mox." Washington Historical Quarterly 25 (April 1934): 128-132.

3733. Sebring, F. M. "The Indian Raid on the Cascades in March, 1856." Washington Historical Quarterly 19 (April 1928): 99-107.

3734. "The Steptoe-Wright Campaign against the Northern Indians in 1858." Journal of the Military Service Institution of the United States 42 (May-June 1908): 475-502. A symposium, with articles by Lawrence Kip, August Wolf, and M. R. Morgan.

3735. Trimble, I. Ridgeway, ed. "Captain C. S. Winder's Account of a Battle with the Indians." Maryland Historical Magazine 35 (March 1940): 56-59.

3736. Victor, Frances Fuller. The Early Indian Wars of Oregon: Compiled from the Oregon Archives and Other Original Sources. Salem, Oregon: F. C. Baker, 1894.

3737. Walsh, Frank K. Indian Battles along the Rogue River, 1855-56: One of America's Wild and Scenic Rivers. Grants Pass, Oregon: Te-cum-tom Publications, 1972.

Third Seminole War

Minor actions against the Florida Indians that occurred in the 1850s are sometimes called the Third Seminole War.

3738. Bittle, George C. "Florida Frontier Incidents during the 1850s." Florida Historical Quarterly 49 (October 1970): 153-160.

3739. Covington, James W. "An Episode in the Third Seminole War." Florida Historical Quarterly 45 (July 1966): 45-49.

3740. Tillis, James Dallas. "Original Narratives of Indian Attacks in Florida:

An Indian Attack of 1856 on the Home of Willoughby Tillis." Florida Historical Quarterly 8 (April 1930): 179-187.

3741. Webb, Alex S. "Campaigning in Florida in 1855." Journal of the Military Service Institution 45 (November-December 1909): 397-429.

Spirit Lake Massacre

An erratic outbreak led by Inkpaduta in northern Iowa and southern Minnesota is known as the Spirit Lake Massacre.

3742. Baker, Miriam Hawthorn. "Inkpaduta's Camp at Smithland." Annals of Iowa 39 (Fall 1967): 81-104.

3743. Flandrau, Charles E. "The Ink-pa-du-ta Massacre of 1857." Collections of the Minnesota Historical Society 3 (1880): 386-407.

3744. Herriott, F. I. "The Aftermath of the Spirit Lake Massacre, March 8-15, 1857." Annals of Iowa 18 (October 1932): 434-470; (January 1933): 482-517; (April 1933): 597-631.

3745. Howe, Orlando C. "The Discovery of the Spirit Lake Massacre." Annals of Iowa 11 (July 1914): 408-424.

3746. Hughes, Thomas. "Causes and Results of the Inkpaduta Massacre." Collections of the Minnesota Historical Society 12 (1908): 263-282.

3747. Laut, Agnes C. "Pioneer Women of the West: Heroines of Spirit Lake, Iowa." Outing 51 (March 1908): 686-698.

3748. Lee, Lorenzo Porter. History of the Spirit Lake Massacre! New Britain, Connecticut: L. P. Lee, 1857. Reprinted, Iowa City: State Historical Society of Iowa, 1971.

3749. Petersen, William J. "The Spirit Lake Massacre." Palimpsest 38 (June 1957): 209-272.

3750. Smith, R. A. "A Risk That Cost Two Lives." Annals of Iowa 11 (July 1914): 424-428.

3751. Teakle, Thomas. The Spirit Lake Massacre. Iowa City: State Historical Society of Iowa, 1918.

INDIAN WARS DURING THE CIVIL WAR AND AFTER

Sioux Uprising of 1862 and Its Aftermath

The Santee Sioux, confined to narrow reservations along the Minnesota River and suffering because of lack of rations, rose up against the unprotected settlers in August 1862. The hostilities then spread to the west, as refugee Sioux moved into Dakota. The United States sent troops up the Missouri River in the mid-1860s to subdue the hostiles.

3752. Adams, Moses N. "The Sioux Outbreak in the Year 1862, with Notes of Missionary Work among the Sioux." Collections of the Minnesota Historical Society 9 (1898-1900): 431-452.

3753. Andrist, Ralph K. "Massacre!" American Heritage 13 (April 1962): 8-17, 108-111.

3754. Athearn, Robert G. "The Fort Buford 'Massacre.'" Mississippi Valley Historical Review 41 (March 1955): 675-684.

3755. Babcock, Willoughby M. "Minnesota's Frontier: A Neglected Sector of the Civil War." Minnesota History 38 (June 1963): 274-286.

3756. _____. "Minnesota's Indian War." Minnesota History 38 (September 1962): 93-98.

3757. Barsness, John, and William Dickinson. "The Sully Expedition of 1864." Montana, the Magazine of Western History 16 (July 1966): 23-29.

3758. Bean, Geraldine. "General Alfred Sully and the Northwest Indian Expedition." North Dakota History 33 (Summer 1966): 240-259.

3759. Bishop, Harriet E. Dakota War Whoop; or, Indian Massacres and War in Minnesota, of 1862-'3. Revised edition. St. Paul, 1864. Reprinted, Chicago: Lakeside Press, 1965.

3760. Brown, Samuel J. In Captivity. Mankato, Minnesota: Mankato Daily Review, 1896. Also published as Senate Document no. 23, 56th Congress, 2d session, serial 4029.

3761. Bryant, Charles S., and Abel B. Murch. A History of the Great Massacre by the Sioux Indians, in Minnesota, Including the Personal Narratives of Many Who Escaped. Cincinnati: Rickey and Carroll, 1864.

3762. Buck, Daniel. Indian Outbreaks. Mankato, Minnesota, 1904. Reprinted, Minneapolis: Ross and Haines, 1965.

3763. Buell, Salmon A. "Judge Flandrau in the Defense of New Ulm during the Sioux Outbreak of 1862." Collections of the Minnesota Historical Society 10, part 2 (1900-1904): 783-818.

3764. Carley, Kenneth. The Sioux Uprising of 1862. St Paul: Minnesota Historical

Society, 1961.

3765. Carley, Kenneth, ed. "As Red Men Viewed It: Three Indian Accounts of the Uprising." Minnesota History 38 (September 1962): 126-149.

3766. _____. "The Sioux Campaign of 1862: Sibley's Letters to His Wife." Minnesota History 38 (September 1962): 99-114.

3767. Connolly, A. P. A Thrilling Narrative of the Minnesota Massacre and the Sioux War of 1862-63. Chicago: A. P. Connolly, 1896.

3768. Connors, Joseph. "The Elusive Hero of Redwood Ferry." Minnesota History 34 (Summer 1955): 233-238.

3769. Daniels, Asa W. "Reminiscences of Little Crow." Collections of the Minnesota Historical Society 12 (1905-1908): 513-530.

3770. _____. "Reminiscences of the Little Crow Uprising." Collections of the Minnesota Historical Society 15 (1909-1914): 323-336.

3771. Davis, Jane S. "Two Sioux War Orders: A Mystery Unraveled." Minnesota History 41 (Fall 1968): 117-125.

3772. Ebell, Adrian J. "The Indian Massacres and War of 1862." Harper's New Monthly Magazine 27 (June 1863): 1-24.

3773. Ferril, Will C. "The Sixteenth Kansas Cavalry in the Black Hills in 1865." Collections of the Kansas State Historical Society 17 (1926-1928): 855-858.

3774. Gluek, Alvin C., Jr. "The Sioux Uprising: A Problem in International Relations." Minnesota History 34 (Winter 1955): 317-324.

3775. Goodwin, Carol G. "The Letters of Private Milton Spencer, 1862-1865: A Soldier's View of Military Life on the Northern Plains." North Dakota History 37 (Fall 1970): 233-269.

3776. Gray, John S. "The Santee Sioux and the Settlers at Lake Shetek." Montana, the Magazine of Western History 25 (January 1975): 42-54.

3777. Heard, Isaac V. D. History of the Sioux War and Massacres of 1862 and 1863. New York: Harper and Brothers, 1863.

3778. Holcombe, Return I., ed. "A Sioux Story of the War: Chief Big Eagle's Story of the Sioux Outbreak of 1862." Collections of the Minnesota Historical Society 6 (1887-1894): 382-400.

3779. Johnson, Roy P. "The Siege at Fort Abercrombie." North Dakota History 24 (January 1957): 5-79.

3780. Jones, Robert H. The Civil War in the Northwest: Nebraska, Wisconsin, Iowa, Minnesota, and the Dakotas. Norman: University of Oklahoma Press, 1960.

3781. _____. "The Northwestern Frontier and the Impact of the Sioux War, 1862." Mid-America 41 (July 1959): 131-153.

3782. Kellogg, Louise Phelps. "Sioux War of 1862 at Superior." Wisconsin Magazine of History 3 (June 1920): 473-477.

3783. King, James T., ed. "The Civil War of Private Morton." North Dakota History 35 (Winter 1968): 8-19. Letters of Thomas F. Morton.

3784. Laut, Agnes C. "Pioneer Women of the West: Heroines of Lake Shetek, Minnesota." Outing 52 (June 1908): 271-286.

3785. "Lincoln's Sioux War Order." Minnesota History 33 (Summer 1952): 77-79.

3786. Lingk, Ray W. "The Northwestern Indian Expedition: The Sully Trail (1864) from the Little Missouri River to the Yellowstone River." North Dakota History 24 (October 1957): 181-200.

3787. Loomis, Noel M. "The Battle of Wood Lake." In Great Western Indian Fights, pp. 86-93. Garden City, New York: Doubleday and Company, 1960.

3788. Minnesota in the Civil and Indian Wars, 1861-1865. 2 volumes. St. Paul: Board of Commissioners on Publication of History of Minnesota in Civil and Indian Wars, 1890-1893.

3789. Moore, S. A. "Hostile Raid into Davis County, Iowa," edited by Edgar R. Harlan. Annals of Iowa 13 (July 1922): 362-374.

3790. "Narrative of Paul Mazakootemane," translated by Stephen R. Riggs. Collections of the Minnesota Historical Society 3 (1870-1880): 82-90.

3791. Oehler, C. M. The Great Sioux Uprising. New York: Oxford University Press, 1959.

3792. "Official Correspondence Pertaining to the War of the Outbreak, 1862-1865." South Dakota Historical Collections 8 (1916): 100-588.

3793. Pattee, John. "Reminiscences of John Pattee." South Dakota Historical Collections 5 (1910): 273-350.

3794. Pfaller, Louis. "The Peace Mission of 1863-1864." North Dakota History 37 (Fall 1970): 293-313.

3795. _____. "Sully's Expedition of

1864: Featuring the Killdeer Mountain and Badlands Battles." North Dakota History 31 (January 1964): 25-77.

3796. Pritchett, John Perry. "Sidelights on the Sibley Expedition from the Diary of a Private." Minnesota History 7 (December 1926): 326-335. Diary of Henry J. Hagadorn.

3797. Pritchett, John Perry, ed. "On the March with Sibley in 1863: The Diary of Private Henry J. Hagadorn." North Dakota Historical Quarterly 5 (January 1931): 103-129.

3798. Quaife, Milo M. "The Panic of 1862 in Wisconsin." Wisconsin Magazine of History 4 (December 1920): 166-195.

3799. Renville, Gabriel. "A Sioux Narrative of the Outbreak in 1862, and of Sibley's Expedition in 1863." Collections of the Minnesota Historical Society 10, part 2 (1900-1904): 595-618.

3800. Roddis, Louis Harry. The Indian Wars of Minnesota. Cedar Rapids, Iowa: Torch Press, 1956.

3801. Ronnenberg, Harold A. "America's Greatest Mass Execution." American Mercury 67 (November 1948): 565-571.

3802. Rothfuss, Hermann E. "German Witnesses of the Sioux Campaigns." North Dakota History 25 (October 1958): 123-133.

3803. Rowen, Richard D., ed. "The Second Nebraska's Campaign against the Sioux." Nebraska History 44 (March 1963): 3-53.

3804. Satterlee, Marion P. A Detailed Account of the Massacre by the Dakota Indians of Minnesota in 1862. Minneapolis: M. P. Satterlee, 1923.

3805. _____. "Narratives of the Sioux War." Collections of the Minnesota Historical Society 15 (1909-1914): 349-370.

3806. Searle, January. "Causes of the Minnesota Massacre." Continental Monthly 6 (August 1864): 174-189.

3807. Snana. "Narration of a Friendly Sioux." Collections of the Minnesota Historical Society 9 (1898-1900): 427-430. With note by Return I. Holcombe.

3808. Sweet, George W. "Incidents of the Threatened Outbreak of Hole-in-the-Day and Other Ojibways at Time of Sioux Massacre of 1862." Collections of the Minnesota Historical Society 6 (1887-1894): 401-408.

3809. Sweet, J. E. De C. "Mrs. J. E. De Camp Sweet's Narrative of Her Captivity in the Sioux Outbreak of 1862." Collec-

tions of the Minnesota Historical Society 6 (1887-1894): 354-380.

3810. Trenerry, Walter N. "The Shooting of Little Crow: Heroism or Murder?" Minnesota History 38 (September 1962): 150-153.

3811. Throne, Mildred. "Iowa Troops in Dakota Territory, 1861-64, Based on the Diaries and Letters of Henry J. Wieneke." Iowa Journal of History 57 (April 1959): 97-190.

3812. Wall, Oscar Garrett. Recollections of the Sioux Massacre. Lake City, Minnesota: M. C. Russell, 1909.

3813. White, Mrs. N. D. "Captivity among the Sioux, August 18 to September 26, 1862." Collections of the Minnesota Historical Society 9 (1898-1900): 395-426.

3814. Wieneke, Henry J., and others. "Iowa Troops in the Sully Campaigns." Iowa Journal of History and Politics 20 (July 1922): 364-443.

Navajo Wars

Military activity in the Southwest during the Civil War involved the Apaches and the Navajos, although it was the latter who received the most attention. Defeated by troops under Kit Carson, the Navajo Indians were moved to the Bosque Redondo in eastern New Mexico.

3815. Anderson, Clinton P. "Canyon de Chelly." In Great Western Indian Fights, pp. 94-101. Garden City, New York: Doubleday and Company, 1960.

3816. Bailey, L. R. The Long Walk: A History of the Navajo Wars, 1846-68. Los Angeles: Westernlore Press, 1964.

3817. Bailey, Paul D. "The Navajo Wars." Arizoniana 2 (Summer 1961): 3-12.

3818. Buell, Crawford R. "The Navajo 'Long Walk': Recollections by Navajos." In The Changing Ways of Southwestern Indians: A Historic Perspective, edited by Albert H. Schroeder, pp. 171-187. Glorieta, New Mexico: Rio Grande Press, 1973.

3819. Burton, Estelle Bennett. "Volunteer Soldiers of New Mexico and Their Conflicts with the Indians in 1862 and 1863." Old Santa Fe 1 (April 1914): 386-419.

3820. Correll, J. Lee. "Navajo Frontiers in Utah and Troublous Times in Monument Valley." Utah Historical Quarterly 39 (Spring 1971): 145-161.

3821. Goldman, Henry H. "General James H.

Carleton and the New Mexico Indian Campaigns, 1862-1866." Journal of the West 2 (April 1963): 156-165.

3822. Heyman, Max L., Jr. "On the Navaho Trail: The Campaign of 1860-61." New Mexico Historical Review 26 (January 1951): 44-63.

3823. Hopkins, Richard C. "Kit Carson and the Navajo Expedition." Montana, the Magazine of Western History 18 (April 1968): 52-61.

3824. Jett, Stephen C., ed. "The Destruction of Navajo Orchards in 1864: Captain John Thompson's Report." Arizona and the West 16 (Winter 1974): 365-378.

3825. Kelly, Lawrence C. Navajo Roundup: Selected Correspondence of Kit Carson's Expedition against the Navajo, 1863-1865. Boulder, Colorado: Pruett Publishing Company, 1970.

3826. Lindgren, Raymond E., ed. "A Diary of Kit Carson's Navaho Campaign, 1863-1864." New Mexico Historical Review 21 (July 1946): 226-246.

3827. McNitt, Frank. "The Long March: 1863-67." In The Changing Ways of Southwestern Indians: A Historic Perspective, edited by Albert H. Schroeder, pp. 145-169. Glorieta, New Mexico: Rio Grande Press, 1973.

3828. _____. Navajo Wars: Military Campaigns, Slave Raids, and Reprisals. Albuquerque: University of New Mexico Press, 1972.

3829. Simpson, James Hervey. Navaho Expedition: Journal of a Military Reconnaissance from Santa Fe, New Mexico, to the Navaho Country Made in 1849. Edited by Frank McNitt. Norman: University of Oklahoma Press, 1964. First published in Philadelphia, 1852.

3830. Walker, J. G., and O. L. Shepherd. The Navajo Reconnaissance: A Military Exploration of the Navajo Country in 1859. Edited by L. R. Bailey. Los Angeles: Westernlore Press, 1964.

Sand Creek Massacre

The massacre of Cheyenne and Arapaho Indians on Sand Creek in November 1864 by Colorado volunteers under Colonel John M. Chivington touched off a tremendous outcry. The following studies tell the story, but one should also see the voluminous reports of official investigations of the event.

3831. Carey, Raymond G. "Colonel Chivington, Brigadier General Connor, and Sand Creek." Westerners Brand Book (Denver)

16 (1960): 103-136.

3832. _____. "The Puzzle of Sand Creek." Colorado Magazine 41 (Fall 1964): 279-298.

3833. Hoig, Stanley. The Sand Creek Massacre. Norman: University of Oklahoma Press, 1961.

3834. Kelsey, Harry. "Background to Sand Creek." Colorado Magazine 45 (Fall 1968): 279-300.

3835. Lecompte, Janet. "Sand Creek." Colorado Magazine 41 (Fall 1964): 315-335.

3836. Mellor, William J. "The Military Investigation of Colonel John M. Chivington Following the Sand Creek Massacre." Chronicles of Oklahoma 16 (December 1938): 444-464.

3837. Mumey, Nolie. "John Milton Chivington: The Misunderstood Man." Brand Book of the Denver Westerners, 1956, pp. 125-148.

3838. Perrigo, Lynn I. "Major Hal Sayr's Diary of the Sand Creek Campaign." Colorado Magazine 15 (March 1938): 41-57.

3839. Sievers, Michael A. "Sands of Sand Creek Historiography." Colorado Magazine 49 (Spring 1972): 116-142.

3840. White, Lonnie J. "From Bloodless to Bloody: The Third Colorado Cavalry and the Sand Creek Massacre." Journal of the West 6 (October 1967): 535-581.

War on the Plains, 1860s

The Sand Creek Massacre was but one episode in a continuing series of conflicts between the army and the Indians of the plains in the 1860s. The central and southern plains were aflame with hostilities, including Custer's Battle of Washita on November 27, 1868.

3841. Anderson, Harry H., ed. "Stand at the Arikaree." Colorado Magazine 41 (Fall 1964): 337-342. Account of Major James S. Brisbin.

3842. Athearn, Robert G. "Colorado and the Indian War of 1868." Colorado Magazine 33 (January 1956): 42-51.

3843. "Battle of the Arickaree (or Beecher Island), September 17-25, 1868." Kansas Historical Quarterly 34 (Spring 1968): frontispiece.

3844. Brill, Charles J. Conquest of the Southern Plains: Uncensored Narratives of the Battle of the Washita and Custer's Southern Campaign. Oklahoma City: Golden Saga Publishers, 1938.

3845. Brininstool, E. A. "The Rescue of Forsyth's Scouts." Collections of the Kansas State Historical Society 17 (1926-1928): 845-851.

3846. Brown, D. Alexander. The Galvanized Yankees. Urbana: University of Illinois Press, 1963.

3847. Chapman, Arthur. "The Indian Fighters of the Arickaree." Harper's Weekly 57 (July 26, 1913): 9, 25-26.

3848. Coad, Mark M. "Story of Indian Fighting in 1864." Nebraska History 6 (January-March 1923): 102-108.

3849. Compton, Lawrence V. "The First Battle of Adobe Walls." In Great Western Indian Fights, pp. 102-107. Garden City, New York: Doubleday and Company, 1960.

3850. Danker, Donald F., ed. "The Journal of an Indian Fighter: The 1869 Diary of Major Frank J. North." Nebraska History 39 (June 1958): 87-177.

3851. Davis, Theodore R. "A Summer on the Plains." Harper's New Monthly Magazine 36 (February 1868): 292-307.

3852. Delahunty, Michael. "The Plum Creek Railroad Attack--1867." Nebraska History 7 (January-March 1924): 38-39.

3853. Dillon, Lee A. "The Indian Massacre of 1866." Proceedings and Collections of the Nebraska State Historical Society 5 (1902): 223-225.

3854. Dixon, James W. "The Hancock Expedition: A Campaign against Hostile Indians in 1867." Army and Navy Life 10 (March 1907): 322-328.

3855. Doster, Frank. "Eleventh Indiana Cavalry in Kansas in 1865." Collections of the Kansas State Historical Society 15 (1919-1922): 524-529.

3856. Ediger, Theodore A., and Vinnie Hoffman. "Some Reminiscences of the Battle of the Washita: Moving Behind's Story of the Battle of the Washita." Chronicles of Oklahoma 33 (Summer 1955): 137-141.

3857. Ellis, John M., and Robert E. Stowers, eds. "The Nevada Indian Uprising of 1860 as Seen by Private Charles A. Scott." Arizona and the West 3 (Winter 1961): 355-376.

3858. Ellis, Richard N. "Volunteer Soldiers in the West, 1865." Military Affairs 34 (April 1970): 53-56.

3859. Emerson, Arthur W. "The Battle of Pyramid Lake." In Great Western Indian Fights, pp. 73-81. Garden City, New York: Doubleday and Company, 1960.

3860. Enochs, James C. "A Clash of Ambition: The Tappan-Chivington Feud." Montana, the Magazine of Western History 15 (July 1965): 58-67.

3861. Filipiak, Jack D. "The Battle of Summit Springs." Colorado Magazine 41 (Fall 1964): 343-354.

3862. Fisher, John R. "The Royal and Duncan Pursuits: Aftermath of the Battle of Summit Springs, 1869." Nebraska History 50 (Fall 1969): 293-308.

3863. Forsyth, G. A. "A Frontier Fight." Harper's New Monthly Magazine 91 (June 1895): 42-62.

3864. Freeman, Winfield. "The Battle of Arickaree." Transactions of the Kansas State Historical Society 6 (1897-1900): 346-357.

3865. Frost, Lawrence. "Battle of the Washita." In Great Western Indian Fights, pp. 175-181. Garden City, New York: Doubleday and Company, 1960.

3866. Garfield, Marvin H. "Defense of the Kansas Frontier, 1864-65." Kansas Historical Quarterly 1 (February 1932): 140-152.

3867. _____. "Defense of the Kansas Frontier, 1866-1867." Kansas Historical Quarterly 1 (August 1932): 326-344.

3868. _____. "Defense of the Kansas Frontier, 1868-1869." Kansas Historical Quarterly 1 (November 1932): 451-473.

3869. Gilles, Albert S., Sr. "Who Killed Jane Riggs?" Southwest Review 57 (Autumn 1972): 318-326.

3870. Griffis, Joseph K. "The Battle of the Washita." Chronicles of Oklahoma 8 (September 1930): 272-281.

3871. Hagerty, Leroy W. "Indian Raids along the Platte and Little Blue Rivers, 1864-1865." Nebraska History 28 (July-September 1947): 176-186; (October-December 1947): 239-260.

3872. Heinzman, George M. "'Don't Let Them Ride over Us.'" American Heritage 18 (February 1967): 44-47, 86-89. Battle of Beecher's Island.

3873. Holden, W. C. "Frontier Defense in Texas during the Civil War." West Texas Historical Association Year Book 4 (June 1928): 16-31.

3874. Howell, Edgar M. "A Special Artist in the Indian Wars: Theodore R. Davis and the Hancock Campaign of 1867." Montana, the Magazine of Western History 15 (April 1965): 2-23.

3875. Hurst, John, and Sigmund Schlesinger. "Battle of the Arikaree." Collections of the Kansas State Historical Society 15 (1921-1922): 530-547.

3876. Hutchins, James S. "The Fight at Beecher Island." In Great Western Indian Fights, pp. 165-174. Garden City, New York: Doubleday and Company, 1960.

3877. Jenness, George B. "The Battle on Beaver Creek." Collections of the Kansas State Historical Society 9 (1905-1906): 443-452.

3878. Keim, De B. Randolph. Sheridan's Troopers on the Borders: A Winter Campaign on the Plains. Philadelphia: David McKay, 1885.

3879. King, James T. "The Republican River Expedition, June-July, 1869: I, On the March." Nebraska History 41 (September 1960): 165-199.

3880. _____. "The Republican River Expedition, June-July, 1869: II, The Battle of Summit Springs." Nebraska History 41 (December 1960): 281-297.

3881. McBee, John, as told to William E. Connelley. "John McBee's Account of the Expedition of the Nineteenth Kansas." Collections of the Kansas State Historical Society 17 (1926-1928): 361-374.

3882. McClure, C. B., ed. "The Battle of Adobe Walls, 1864." Panhandle-Plains Historical Review 21 (1948): 18-65.

3883. Moore, Horace L. "The Nineteenth Kansas Cavalry in the Washita Campaign." Chronicles of Oklahoma 2 (December 1924): 350-365.

3884. Murphy, John. "Reminiscences of the Washita Campaign and of the Darlington Indian Agency." Chronicles of Oklahoma 1 (June 1923): 259-278.

3885. Nesbitt, Paul. "Battle of the Washita." Chronicles of Oklahoma 3 (April 1925): 3-32.

3886. Russell, Don. "Jeb Stuart's Other Indian Fight." Civil War Times Illustrated 12 (January 1974): 10-17.

3887. Shirk, George H. "Campaigning with Sheridan: A Farrier's Diary." Chronicles of Oklahoma 37 (Spring 1959): 68-105. Diary of Private Winfield S. Harvey.

3888. _____. "The Case of the Plagiarized Journal." Chronicles of Oklahoma 36 (Winter 1958-1959): 371-410.

3889. Spotts, David L. Campaigning with Custer and the Nineteenth Kansas Volunteer Cavalry in the Washita Campaign, 1868-'69. Edited by E. A. Brininstool. Los Angeles: Wetzel Publishing Company, 1928.

3890. "Survivors Tell of Forsyth Fight." Westerners Brand Book (Chicago) 29 (June 1972): 25-27, 30-32.

3891. Taylor, Morris F. "The Carr-Penrose Expedition: General Sheridan's Winter Campaign, 1868-1869." Chronicles of Oklahoma 51 (Summer 1973): 159-176.

3892. Unrau, William E. "A Prelude to War." Colorado Magazine 41 (Fall 1964): 299-313.

3893. Utley, Robert M. "General Crook and the Paiutes." American History Illustrated 8 (July 1973): 38-42.

3894. _____. "Kit Carson and the Adobe Walls Campaign." American West 2 (Winter 1965): 4-11, 73-75.

3895. Ware, Eugene F. The Indian War of 1864: Being a Fragment of the Early History of Kansas, Nebraska, Colorado, and Wyoming. Topeka, Kansas: Crane and Company, 1911. Reprinted, New York: St. Martin's Press, 1960.

3896. White, Lonnie J. "The Battle of Beecher Island: The Scouts Hold Fast on the Arickaree." Journal of the West 5 (January 1966): 1-24.

3897. _____. "The Cheyenne Barrier on the Kansas Frontier, 1868-1869." Arizona and the West 4 (Spring 1962): 51-64.

3898. _____. "General Sully's Expedition to the North Canadian, 1868." Journal of the West 11 (January 1972): 75-98.

3899. _____. "The Hancock and Custer Expeditions of 1867." Journal of the West 5 (July 1966): 355-378.

3900. _____. "Indian Raids on the Kansas Frontier, 1869." Kansas Historical Quarterly 38 (Winter 1972): 369-388.

3901. _____. "The Santa Fe Trail in '65: The Military Defense of the Road." Military History of Texas and the Southwest 9 (1971): 107-128.

3902. _____. "Warpaths on the Southern Plains: The Battles of the Saline River and Prairie Dog Creek." Journal of the West 4 (October 1965): 485-503.

3903. _____. "Winter Campaigning with Sheridan and Custer: The Expedition of the Nineteenth Kansas Volunteer Cavalry." Journal of the West 6 (January 1967): 68-98.

3904. Willard, James F. "The Tyler Rangers: The Black Hawk Company and the Indian Uprising of 1864." Colorado Magazine 7 (July 1930): 147-152.

3905. Woodward, R. O. "With the Troops in

Colorado, 1865." Colorado Magazine 3
(May 1926): 53-54.

Bozeman Trail

Miners seeking a short supply route to
the Montana mines established a road running north from the Platte River through
the Powder River hunting grounds of the
Sioux and Cheyenne Indians. This Bozeman
Trail, protected by a string of military
posts, was continually under attack. The
troops were withdrawn in 1868--a victory
for the Indians.

3906. Appleman, Roy E. "The Fetterman
Fight." In Great Western Indian Fights,
pp. 117-131. Garden City, New York:
Doubleday and Company, 1960.

3907. _____. "The Hayfield Fight." In
Great Western Indian Fights, pp. 132-
147. Garden City, New York: Doubleday
and Company, 1960.

3908. _____. "The Wagon Box Fight."
In Great Western Indian Fights, pp. 148-
162. Garden City, New York: Doubleday
and Company, 1960.

3909. Barrett, Francis A. "The Greatest
Ride in Wyoming History." Annals of
Wyoming 38 (October 1966): 223-228.

3910. Bate, Walter N. "Eyewitness Reports
of the Wagon Box Fight." Annals of
Wyoming 41 (October 1969): 193-202.

3911. Carrington, Frances C. My Army Life
and the Fort Phil. Kearny Massacre.
Philadelphia: J. B. Lippincott Company,
1910.

3912. Greene, Jerome A. "The Hayfield
Fight: A Reappraisal of a Neglected Ac-
tion." Montana, the Magazine of Western
History 22 (October 1972): 30-43.

3913. Guthrie, John. "The Fetterman Massacre." Annals of Wyoming 9 (October
1932): 714-718.

3914. Hafen, LeRoy R., and Ann W. Hafen,
eds. Powder River Campaigns and Sawyer's
Expedition of 1865: A Documentary Account
Comprising Official Reports, Diaries,
Contemporary Newspaper Accounts, and Per-
sonal Narratives. Glendale, California:
Arthur H. Clark Company, 1961.

3915. Hampton, H. D. "The Powder River
Indian Expedition of 1865." Montana, the
Magazine of Western History 14 (Autumn
1964): 2-15.

3916. Hebard, Grace Raymond, and E. A.
Brininstool. The Bozeman Trail: Historical Accounts of the Blazing of the Overland Routes into the Northwest, and the
Fights with Red Cloud's Warriors. 2

volumes. Cleveland: Arthur H. Clark
Company, 1922.

3917. Hull, Myra E., ed. "Soldiering on
the High Plains: The Diary of Lewis Byram
Hull, 1864-1866." Kansas Historical Quarterly 7 (February 1938): 3-53.

3918. Johnson, Dorothy M. The Bloody
Bozeman: The Perilous Trail to Montana's
Gold. New York: McGraw Hill Book Com-
pany, 1971.

3919. Jones, Brian. "John Richard, Jr.,
and the Killing at Fetterman." Annals
of Wyoming 43 (Fall 1971): 237-257.

3920. Keenan, Jerry. "Max Littmann: Immigrant Soldier in the Wagon Box Fight."
Western States Jewish Historical Quarterly 6 (January 1974): 111-119.

3921. _____. "The Wagon Box Fight."
Journal of the West 11 (January 1972):
51-74.

3922. Marshall, Anthony D. "The Phil
Kearney Fort Massacre, December 1866."
Overland Magazine 61 (March 1913):
228-230.

3923. Murray, Robert A. "The Wagon Box
Fight: A Centennial Appraisal." Annals
of Wyoming 39 (April 1967): 104-107.

3924. Olson, James C. "The 'Lasting Peace'
of Fort Laramie: Prelude to Massacre."
American West 2 (Winter 1965): 46-53.

3925. Parsons, John E., ed. "The Cheyenne
at Fort Fetterman." Montana, the
Magazine of Western History 9 (April
1959): 16-27. Report of Colonel George
A. Woodward.

3926. Pfaller, Louis L., ed. "The Galpin
Journal: Dramatic Record of an Odyssey
of Peace." Montana, the Magazine of
Western History 18 (April 1968): 2-23.

3927. Richardson, Ernest M. "The Forgotten
Haycutters at Fort C. F. Smith." Montana,
the Magazine of Western History 9 (Summer
1959): 22-33.

3928. Sinclair, F. H. "White Man's
Medicine Fight: An Account of the Fort
Phil Kearny 'Wagon Box Battle.'" Mon-
tana, the Magazine of Western History 6
(July 1956): 1-10.

3929. Sterling, Edward M. "The Winter Ride
of Portugee Phillips." Montana, the
Magazine of Western History 15 (Winter
1965): 2-11.

3930. "A Survivor's Story of Wagon Box
Fight." Westerners Brand Book (Chicago)
29 (July 1972): 33-35, 37-40.

3931. Thane, James L., Jr. "The Montana
'Indian War' of 1867." Arizona and

the West 10 (Summer 1968): 153-170.

3932. Vaughn, J. W. The Battle of Platte Bridge. Norman: University of Oklahoma Press, 1963.

Modoc War

A serious test of the "peace policy" came in 1872-1873, in a war with the Modoc Indians in northeastern California. General Canby was murdered by the Modoc leader, Captain Jack, when the whites met in a peace conference with the Indians on Good Friday, 1873.

3933. Boyle, William Henry. Personal Observations on the Conduct of the Modoc War. Edited by Richard H. Dillon. Los Angeles: Dawson's Book Shop, 1959.

3934. Brown, J. Henry. "The Biggest Little War in American History." Oregon Historical Quarterly 43 (March 1942): 37-39.

3935. Brown, William Samuel. California Northeast, the Bloody Ground. Oakland, California: Biobooks, 1951.

3936. Dillon, Richard H. Burnt-Out Fires: California's Modoc Indian War. Englewood Cliffs, New Jersey: Prentice-Hall, 1973.

3937. _____. "Costs of the Modoc War." California Historical Society Quarterly 28 (June 1949): 161-164.

3938. _____. "Fort Klamath and the Modoc War." Westerners Brand Book (New York) 18, no. 3 (1971): 56-57, 66-68.

3939. _____. "Lost River Raid." In Troopers West: Military and Indian Affairs on the American Frontier, edited by Ray Brandes, pp. 77-91. San Diego: Frontier Heritage Press, 1970.

3940. FitzGerald, Maurice. "The Modoc War: Reminiscences of the Campaign against the Indian Uprising in the Lava Beds of Northern California and Southern Oregon in 1872-'73." Americana 21 (October 1927): 498-521.

3941. Jones, Joseph Roy. Saddlebags in Siskiyou. Yreka, California: News-Journal Print Shop, 1953.

3942. Kerr, James T. "The Modoc War of 1873." Proceedings of the Annual Meeting and Dinner of the Order of Indian Wars of the United States, January 24, 1931, pp. 24-52.

3943. Lockley, Fred. "How the Modoc Indian War Started." Overland Monthly and Out West Magazine 81 (November 1923): 12-14, 43.

3944. Meacham, Alfred B. "The Tragedy of the Lava-Beds: A Lecture Delivered by Alfred B. Meacham, in Park Street Church, Boston, Massachusetts, May 24, 1874." Printed with T. A. Bland. Life of Alfred B. Meacham. Washington: T. A. and M. C. Bland, 1883.

3945. _____. Wigwam and War-path; or, The Royal Chief in Chains. 2d edition revised. Boston: John P. Dale and Company, 1875.

3946. _____. Wi-ne-ma (the Woman-Chief) and Her People. Hartford: American Publishing Company, 1876.

3947. Murray, Keith A. The Modocs and Their War. Norman: University of Oklahoma Press, 1959.

3948. Payne, Doris Palmer. Captain Jack, Modoc Renegade. Portland: Binford and Mort, 1938.

3949. Renner, F. G. "Blood on the Lava." In Great Western Indian Fights, pp. 192-199. Garden City, New York: Doubleday and Company, 1960.

3950. Riddle, Jeff C. The Indian History of the Modoc War and the Causes That Led to It. San Francisco, 1914. Facsimile reprint, Medrod, Oregon: Pine Cone Publishers, 1973.

3951. Santee, J. F. "Edward R. S. Canby, Modoc War, 1873." Oregon Historical Quarterly 33 (March 1932): 70-78.

3952. Smith, Harlan I. "Modoc Veterans to Return Home." Southern Workman 38 (August 1909): 450-452.

3953. Thompson, Erwin N. Modoc War: Its Military History and Topography. Sacramento: Argus Books, 1971.

War on the Southern Plains, 1870s

Southern plains tribes refused to be restricted to the reservations established for them in western Indian Territory. When they went out to raid, they came in conflict with the troops who were directed to keep them on the reservations. Of particular importance was the Red River War of 1874-1875, which brought defeat to the Indians.

3954. Archambeau, Ernest R., ed. "The Battle of Lyman's Wagon Train." Panhandle-Plains Historical Review 36 (1963): 89-101.

3955. Capps, Benjamin. The Warren Wagon-train Raid: The First Complete Account of an Historic Indian Attack and Its Aftermath. New York: Dial Press, 1974.

3956. Carriker, Robert C. "Mercenary Heroes: The Scouting Detachment of the

Indian Territory Expedition, 1874-1875."
Chronicles of Oklahoma 51 (Fall 1973):
309-324.

3957. Carriker, Robert C., ed. "Thompson
McFadden's Diary of an Indian Campaign,
1874." Southwestern Historical Quarterly
75 (October 1971): 198-232.

3958. Crane, R. C. "The Settlement in
1874-5 of Indian Troubles in West Texas."
West Texas Historical Association Year-
Book 1 (June 1925): 3-14.

3959. Crimmins, M. L. "General Randolph B.
Marcy's Last Tour of Texas." West Texas
Historical Association Year Book 25
(October 1949): 74-86.

3960. Dykes, J. C. "The Battle of Palo
Duro Canyon." In Great Western Indian
Fights, pp. 214-220. Garden City, New
York: Doubleday and Company, 1960.

3961. _____. "The Second Battle of
Adobe Walls." In Great Western Indian
Fights, pp. 203-213. Garden City, New
York: Doubleday and Company, 1960.

3962. Fleming, Elvis Eugene. "Captain
Nicholas Nolan: Lost on the Staked
Plains." Texana 4 (Spring 1966): 1-13.

3963. Harrison, Lowell H. "Damage Suits
for Indian Depredations in the Adobe
Walls Area, 1874." Panhandle-Plains
Historical Review 36 (1963): 37-60.

3964. _____. "Indians vs. Buffalo
Hunters at Adobe Walls." American History Illustrated 2 (April 1967): 18-27.

3965. Leckie, William H. The Military
Conquest of the Southern Plains. Norman:
University of Oklahoma Press, 1963.

3966. _____. "The Red River War: 1874-
1875." Panhandle-Plains Historical Review 29 (1956): 78-100.

3967. Marshall, J. T. The Miles Expedition
of 1874-1875: An Eyewitness Account of
the Red River War. Edited by Lonnie J.
White. Austin, Texas: Encino Press,
1971.

3968. "The Mexican and Indian Raid of '78."
Quarterly of the Texas State Historical
Association 5 (January 1902): 212-251.

3969. Nye, Wilbur Sturtevant. Plains Indian Raiders: The Final Phases of Warfare from the Arkansas to the Red River.
Norman: University of Oklahoma Press,
1968.

3970. Peery, Dan W. "The Kiowa's Defiance."
Chronicles of Oklahoma 13 (March 1935):
30-36.

3971. Rickey, Don, Jr. "Battle of Wolf
Mountain." Montana, the Magazine of

Western History 13 (April 1963): 44-54.

3972. Rister, C. C. "The Significance of
the Jacksboro Indian Affair of 1871."
Southwestern Historical Quarterly 29
(January 1926): 181-200.

3973. _____. The Southwestern Frontier--
1865-1881. Cleveland: Arthur H. Clark
Company, 1928.

3974. Schmitt, Karl. "Wichita-Kiowa
Relations and the 1874 Outbreak." Chronicles of Oklahoma 28 (Summer 1950): 154-
160.

3975. Taylor, Joe F., ed. "The Indian
Campaign on the Staked Plains, 1874-1875:
Military Correspondence from War Department Adjutant General's Office, File
2815-1874." Panhandle-Plains Historical
Review 34 (1961): 1-216; 35 (1962):
215-362.

3976. Taylor, Morris F. "Plains Indians
on the New Mexico-Colorado Border: The
Last Phase, 1870-1876." New Mexico Historical Review 46 (October 1971): 315-
336.

3977. Wallace, Edward Seccomb. "The Mackenzie Raid." Westerners New York Posse
Brand Book 4 (1958): 73, 75-76, 87, 89-
90.

3978. Wallace, Ernest, and Adrian S.
Anderson. "R. S. Mackenzie and the Kickapoos: The Raid into Mexico in 1873."
Arizona and the West 7 (Summer 1965):
105-126.

3979. West, G. Derek. "The Battle of
Adobe Walls (1874)." Panhandle-Plains
Historical Review 36 (1963): 1-36.

3980. _____. "The Battle of Sappa
Creek (1875)." Kansas Historical Quarterly 34 (Summer 1968): 150-178.

3981. White, Lonnie J. "Indian Battles in
the Texas Panhandle, 1874." Journal of
the West 6 (April 1967): 278-309.

3982. White, Lonnie J., ed. "Kansas
Newspaper Items Relating to the Red River
War of 1874-1875." Panhandle-Plains His-
torical Review 36 (1963): 71-88.

Black Hills Expedition, 1874

A prelude to the Sioux War of 1876 was
Custer's expedition to explore the Black
Hills in 1874. Reports of gold in the
region increased white demands for the Indian lands.

3983. Gerber, Max E. "The Custer Expedition of 1874: A New Look." North Dakota
History 40 (Winter 1973): 5-23.

3984. Jackson, Donald. Custer's Gold:

The United States Cavalry Expedition of 1874. New Haven: Yale University Press, 1966.

3985. Keenan, Jerry. "Exploring the Black Hills: An Account of the Custer Expedition." Journal of the West 6 (April 1967): 248-261.

3986. Krause, Herbert, and Gary D. Olson. Prelude to Glory: A Newspaper Accounting of Custer's 1874 Expedition to the Black Hills. Sioux Falls: Brevet Press, 1974.

3987. McAndrews, Eugene V., ed. "An Army Engineer's Journal of Custer's Black Hills Expedition, July 2, 1874--August 23, 1874." Journal of the West 13 (January 1974): 78-85. Journal of William Ludlow.

3988. Moyne, Ernest J., ed. "Fred Snow's Account of the Custer Expedition of 1874." North Dakota History 27 (Summer-Fall 1960): 143-151.

3989. O'Harra, Cleophas C. "Custer's Black Hills Expedition of 1874." Black Hills Engineer 17 (November 1929): 221-286.

3990. Radabaugh, J. S. "Custer Explores the Black Hills 1874." Military Affairs 26 (Winter 1962-1963): 162-170.

3991. Wemett, W. M. "Custer's Expedition to the Black Hills in 1874." North Dakota Historical Quarterly 6 (April 1932): 292-301.

Little Big Horn

No other military encounter with the Indians has generated as much writing as Custer's defeat at the Little Big Horn in June 1876. The battle has attracted much attention from amateur as well as professional historians. A bibliography, which indicates the extent and range of the Little Big Horn literature, is the following.

3992. Dustin, Fred. "Bibliography of the Battle of the Little Big Horn." In The Custer Myth: A Source Book of Custeriana, edited by W. A. Graham, pp. 382-405. Harrisburg, Pennsylvania: Stackpole Company, 1953.

A selected list of books and articles, including a few accounts by contemporaries, is given here.

3993. Abstract of the Official Record of Proceedings of the Reno Court of Inquiry. Harrisburg, Pennsylvania: Stackpole Company, 1954.

3994. Anderson, Harry H. "Cheyennes at the Little Big Horn." North Dakota History 27 (Spring 1960): 81-94.

3995. Bellah, James Warner. "Thirty-Nine Days to Glory." Holiday 26 (September 1959): 68-69, 124-128.

3996. Brackett, William S. "Custer's Last Battle on the Little Big Horn in Montana, June 25, 1876." Historical Society of Montana Contributions 4 (1903): 259-276.

3997. Brininstool, E. A. "The Custer Battle Continues." Montana Magazine of History 4 (Fall 1954): 62-63.

3998. _____. The Custer Fight: Captain Benteen's Story of the Battle of the Little Big Horn, June 25-26, 1876. Hollywood, California, 1933.

3999. _____. Troopers with Custer: Historic Incidents of the Battle of the Little Big Horn. Harrisburg, Pennsylvania: Stackpole Company, 1952. Revised and expanded edition of A Trooper with Custer.

4000. _____. A Trooper with Custer and Other Historic Incidents of the Battle of the Little Big Horn. Columbus, Ohio: Hunter-Trapper Company, 1925.

4001. Britt, Albert. "Custer's Last Fight." Pacific Historical Review 13 (March 1944): 12-20.

4002. Bronson, D. W. "The Story of the Little Big Horn." Overland Monthly, 2d series 49 (January 1907): 49-56.

4003. Brown, Dee. Showdown at Little Big Horn. New York: Berkeley Publishing Corporation, 1971.

4004. Bruce, Robert, comp. Custer's Last Battle. New York: National Highways Association, 1927.

4005. Carroll, John M., ed. The Benteen-Goldin Letters on Custer and His Last Battle. New York: Liveright, 1974.

4006. _____. The Two Battles of the Little Big Horn. New York: Liveright, 1974.

4007. Coburn, Wallace David. "The Battle of the Little Big Horn." Montana, the Magazine of Western History 6 (July 1956): 28-41. Based on account of Major Will A. Logan.

4008. Coughlan, T. M. "The Battle of the Little Big Horn: A Tactical Study." Cavalry Journal 43 (January-February 1934): 13-21.

4009. Cullens, J. "Custer's Last Stand." Army Quarterly and Defence Journal 90 (April 1965): 104-109.

4010. De Rudio, Charles. "An Incident in the Little Big Horn Fight." Harper's

Weekly 41 (September 25, 1897): 949-950.

4011. Dippie, Brian W. "Bards of the Little Big Horn." *Western American Literature* 1 (Fall 1966): 175-195.

4012. _____. "Brush, Palette and the Custer Battle: A Second Look." *Montana, the Magazine of Western History* 24 (January 1974): 55-67.

4013. _____. "The Southern Response to Custer's Last Stand." *Montana, the Magazine of Western History* 21 (April 1971): 18-31.

4014. _____. "What Will Congress Do about It? The Congressional Reaction to the Little Big Horn Disaster." *North Dakota History* 37 (Summer 1970): 161-189.

4015. duMont, John S., ed. "A Debate of Authors on the Custer Fight." *Westerners Brand Book* (Chicago) 30 (July 1973): 33-35, 37-40; (August 1973): 41-48.

4016. Dustin, Fred. *The Custer Tragedy: Events Leading Up to and Following the Little Big Horn Campaign of 1876.* Ann Arbor: Edwards Brothers, 1939.

4017. Eastman, Charles A. "The Story of the Little Big Horn." *Chautauquan* 31 (July 1900): 353-358.

4018. Ege, Robert J. "Isaiah Dorman: Negro Casualty with Reno." *Montana, the Magazine of Western History* 16 (Winter 1966): 35-40.

4019. _____. "Legend Was a Man Named Keogh." *Montana, the Magazine of Western History* 16 (Spring 1966): 27-39.

4020. Fife, Austin, and Alta Fife. "Ballads of the Little Big Horn." *American West* 4 (February 1967): 46-49, 86-89.

4021. Fry, James B. "Comments by General Fry on the Custer Battle." *Century Illustrated Monthly Magazine* 43 (January 1892): 385-387.

4022. Godfrey, Edward S. "Custer's Last Battle." *Historical Society of Montana Contributions* 9 (1922-1923): 144-212. Reprinted from *Century* 43 (January 1892): 358-384.

4023. _____. *The Field Diary of Lt. Edward Settle Godfrey, Commanding Co. K, 7th Cavalry Regiment under Lt. Colonel George Armstrong Custer in the Sioux Encounter at the Battle of the Little Big Horn.* Edited with an Introduction and Notes by Edgar I. Stewart and Jane R. Stewart Together with a Note on the Kicking Bear Pictograph by Carl S. Dentzel. Portland, Oregon: Campoeg Press, 1957.

4024. Graham, W. A. "The Custer Myth." *American Heritage* 5 (Summer 1954): 30-35.

4025. _____. *The Story of the Little Big Horn, Custer's Last Fight.* New York: Century Company, 1926.

4026. Graham, W. A., ed. *The Custer Myth: A Source Book of Custeriana.* Harrisburg, Pennsylvania: Stackpole Company, 1953.

4027. _____. *The Official Record of a Court of Inquiry Convened at Chicago, Illinois, January 13, 1879, by the President of the United States upon the Request of Major Marcus A. Reno, 7th U.S. Cavalry, to Investigate His Conduct at the Battle of the Little Big Horn, June 25-26, 1876.* Pacific Palisades, California, 1951.

4028. Gray, John S. "Arikara Scouts with Custer." *North Dakota History* 35 (Spring 1968): 442-478.

4029. Hanson, Joseph Mills. *The Conquest of the Missouri: Being the Story of the Life and Exploits of Captain Grant Marsh.* Chicago: A. C. McClurg and Company, 1909. Marsh was captain of the steamboat that took part in the campaign.

4030. Hunt, Frazier, and Robert Hunt. *I Fought with Custer: The Story of Sergeant Charles Windolph, Last Survivor of the Battle of the Little Big Horn.* New York: Charles Scribner's Sons, 1947.

4031. Kanipe, Daniel A. "A New Story of Custer's Last Battle, Told by the Messenger Boy Who Survived." *Historical Society of Montana Contributions* 4 (1903): 277-283.

4032. Kellogg, Mark. "Notes of the Little Big Horn Expedition under General Custer, 1876." *Historical Society of Montana Contributions* 9 (1922-1923): 213-225.

4033. King, Charles. "Custer's Last Battle." *Harper's New Monthly Magazine* 81 (August 1890): 378-387.

4034. Knight, Oliver. "Mark Kellogg Telegraphed for Custer's Rescue." *North Dakota History* 27 (Spring 1960): 95-99.

4035. Koury, Michael J., ed. *Diaries of the Little Big Horn.* Bellevue, Nebraska: Old Army Press, 1968.

4036. Kuhlman, Charles. *General George A. Custer: A Lost Trail and the Gall Saga.* Billings, Montana, 1940.

4037. _____. *Legend into History: The Custer Mystery, an Analytical Study of the Battle of the Little Big Horn.* Harrisburg, Pennsylvania: Stackpole Company, 1951.

4038. Lane, Harrison. "Brush, Palette and the Battle of the Little Big Horn." Montana, the Magazine of Western History 23 (July 1973): 66-80.

4039. _____. "Custer's Massacre: How the News First Reached the Outer World." Montana Magazine of History 3 (Summer 1953): 46-53.

4040. _____. "Gunfire and a June Afternoon." Ph.D. dissertation, University of Minnesota, 1971.

4041. Langley, Harold D., ed. "The Custer Battle and the Critique of an Adventurer." Montana, the Magazine of Western History 22 (Spring 1972): 20-33. Account of Charles F. Henningsen.

4042. Libby, O. G., ed. The Arikara Narrative of the Campaign against the Hostile Dakotas, June, 1876. Bismarck: State Historical Society of North Dakota, 1920.

4043. Lockwood, John C. Custer Fell First: The Adventures of John C. Lockwood. Edited by J. C. Ryan. San Antonio: Naylor Company, 1966.

4044. Luce, Edward S. "Custer Battlefield." American Heritage 5 (Summer 1954): 36-43.

4045. McConnell, Roland C. "Isaiah Dorman and the Custer Expedition." Journal of Negro History 33 (July 1948): 344-352.

4046. Magnussen, Daniel Osar. "An Examination of a Rediscovered Custer Manuscript." Ph.D. dissertation, University of Montana, 1972. Manuscript of Private Peter Thompson.

4047. Marquis, Thomas B. Custer on the Little Big Horn. Edited by Anna Rose Octavia Heil. Lodi, California: Endkian Publishing Company, 1967. Published earlier as separate booklets.

4048. Miller, David Humphreys. Custer's Fall: The Indian Side of the Story. New York: Duell, Sloan, and Pearce, 1957.

4049. _____. "Echoes of the Little Bighorn." American Heritage 22 (June 1971): 28-39; (October 1971): 108.

4050. Noyes, Lee. "Major Marcus A. Reno at the Little Big Horn." North Dakota History 28 (Winter 1961): 5-11.

4051. Nye, E. L. "Cavalry Horse." Montana, the Magazine of Western History 7 (April 1957): 40-45.

4052. Rawling, G. S. "Custer's Last Stand." History Today 12 (January 1962): 57-66.

4053. Rector, William G. "Fields of Fire: The Reno-Benteen Defense Perimeter." Montana, the Magazine of Western History 16 (Spring 1966): 65-72.

4054. Rinehart, Mary Roberts. "To Wyoming." Saturday Evening Post 199 (October 2, 1926): 16-17 +. Custer battle anniversary.

4055. Rosenberg, Bruce A. "How Custer's 'Last Stand' Got Its Name." Georgia Review 26 (Fall 1972): 279-296.

4056. Sandoz, Mari. The Battle of the Little Big Horn. Philadelphia: J. B. Lippincott Company, 1966.

4057. _____. "The Grisly Epilogue." American Heritage 17 (April 1966): 73.

4058. Schoenberger, Dale T. "Custer's Scouts." Montana, the Magazine of Western History 16 (Spring 1966): 40-49.

4059. Schulte, Marie Louise. "Catholic Press Reaction to the Custer Disaster." Mid-America 37 (October 1955): 204-214.

4060. "Sitting Bull's Version of Little Big Horn." American History Illustrated 1 (August 1966): 31.

4061. Stands in Timber, John. "Last Ghastly Moments at the Little Bighorn," edited by Margot Liberty. American Heritage 17 (April 1966): 14-21, 72.

4062. Stewart, Edgar I. "The Custer Battle and Widow's Weeds." Montana, the Magazine of Western History 22 (Winter 1972): 52-59.

4063. _____. Custer's Luck. Norman: University of Oklahoma Press, 1955.

4064. _____. "The Literature of the Custer Fight." Pacific Northwesterner 1 (Winter 1956-1957): 1-8.

4065. _____. "The Little Big Horn: 90 Years Later." Montana, the Magazine of Western History 16 (Spring 1966): 2-13.

4066. _____. "Variations on a Minor Theme: Some Controversial Problems of the Custer Fight." Montana Magazine of History 1 (July 1951): 23-35.

4067. _____. "Which Indian Killed Custer." Montana, the Magazine of Western History 8 (Summer 1958): 26-32.

4068. Stewart, Edgar I., and E. S. Luce. "The Reno Scout." Montana, the Magazine of Western History 10 (Summer 1960): 22-28.

4069. Terrell, John Upton, and George Walton. Faint the Trumpet Sounds: The Life and Trial of Major Reno. New York: David McKay Company, 1966.

4070. Utley, Robert M. "The Battle of the

Little Bighorn." In Great Western Indian Fights, pp. 235-253. Garden City, New York: Doubleday and Company, 1960.

4071. _____. Custer and the Great Controversy: The Origin and Development of a Legend. Los Angeles: Westernlore Press, 1962.

4072. _____. Custer Battlefield National Monument, Montana. Historical Handbook Series, no. 1. Washington: National Park Service, 1969.

4073. _____. "The Custer Battle in the Contemporary Press." North Dakota History 22 (January-April 1955): 75-88.

4074. Vestal, Stanley. "The Man Who Killed Custer." American Heritage 8 (February 1957): 4-9, 90-91.

4075. Wilcox, E. V. "Selenium versus General Custer." Agricultural History 18 (July 1944): 105-106.

See also the biographical writings on Custer and general accounts of the war on the northern plains in the 1870s.

War on the Northern Plains, 1870s

The defeat on the Little Big Horn was the most dramatic incident in a decade of war on the northern plains, as the policy of placing the Indians on reservations was implemented. Other military activity--both before and after that famous encounter--is treated in the studies listed here.

4076. Anderson, Harry H. "A Challenge to Brown's Indian Wars Thesis." Montana, the Magazine of Western History 12 (January 1961): 40-49.

4077. _____. "Indian Peace-Talkers and the Conclusion of the Sioux War of 1876." Nebraska History 44 (December 1963): 233-254.

4078. _____. "Nelson A. Miles and the Sioux War of 1876-77." Westerners Brand Book (Chicago) 16 (June 1959): 25-27, 32.

4079. Athearn, Robert G., ed. "A Winter Campaign against the Sioux." Mississippi Valley Historical Review 35 (September 1948): 272-285. Account by Major Alfred L. Hough of campaign against the Sioux in 1878.

4080. Braden, Charles. "The Yellowstone Expedition of 1873." Journal of the United States Cavalry Association 16 (October 1905): 218-241.

4081. Bradley, James H. The March of the Montana Column: A Prelude to the Custer Disaster. Edited by Edgar I. Stewart.

Norman: University of Oklahoma Press, 1961.

4082. Bragg, William Frederick. "Feed 'em in the Winter, Fight 'em in the Summer." Westerners Brand Book (Chicago) 13 (June 1956): 25-27, 31-32.

4083. Brown, Lisle G. "The Yellowstone Supply Depot." North Dakota History 40 (Winter 1973): 24-33.

4084. Brown, Mark H. "Muddled Men Have Muddied the Yellowstone's True Colors." Montana, the Magazine of Western History 11 (January 1961): 28-37.

4085. _____. "A New Focus on the Sioux War: Barrier to the Cattlemen." Montana, the Magazine of Western History 11 (Autumn 1961): 76-85.

4086. Capron, Cynthia J. "The Indian Border War of 1876." Journal of the Illinois State Historical Society 13 (January 1921): 476-503.

4087. Cox, John E. "Soldiering in Dakota Territory in the Seventies: A Communication." North Dakota Historical Quarterly 6 (October 1931): 63-81.

4088. Daniel, Forrest W. "Dismounting the Sioux." North Dakota History 41 (Summer 1974): 9-13.

4089. Dempsey, Hugh A. "Sweetgrass Hills Massacre." Montana, the Magazine of Western History 7 (April 1957): 12-18.

4090. Dobak, William A. "Yellow-Leg Journalists: Enlisted Men as Newspaper Reporters in the Sioux Campaign, 1876." Journal of the West 13 (January 1974): 86-112.

4091. Ege, Robert J. "Tell Baker to Strike Them Hard!" Incident on the Marias, 23 January 1870. Bellevue, Nebraska: Old Army Press, 1970. Baker massacre of Piegans.

4092. Finerty, John Frederick. War-Path and Bivouac; or, The Conquest of the Sioux, a Narrative of Stirring Personal Experiences and Adventures in the Big Horn and Yellowstone Expedition of 1876 and in the Campaign on the British Border in 1879. Chicago, 1890. Reprinted, Norman: University of Oklahoma Press, 1961.

4093. Gibbon, John. "Hunting Sitting Bull." American Catholic Quarterly Review 2 (October 1877): 665-694.

4094. _____. "Last Summer's Expedition against the Sioux and Its Great Catastrophe." American Catholic Quarterly Review 2 (April 1877): 271-304.

4095. Gray, John S. "The Lame Deer Fight Ends the Sioux War." Westerners Brand Book (Chicago) 31 (May 1974): 17-19, 23-24.

4096. _____. "Sitting Bull Strikes the Glendive Supply Trains." Westerners Brand Book (Chicago) 28 (June 1971): 25-27, 31-32.

4097. Gray, John S., ed. "Captain Clifford's Newspaper Dispatches." Westerners Brand Book (Chicago) 27 (January 1971): 81-83, 88. Walter Clifford.

4098. _____. "Captain Clifford's Story of the Sioux War of 1876." Westerners Brand Book (Chicago) 26 (December 1969): 73-78; (January 1970): 81-83, 86-88; 29 (August 1972): 41-43, 48. Walter Clifford.

4099. Gregg, Thomas B. "Four Indian Horsemen Who Set the Pace for Custer." Outlook 138 (December 31, 1924): 727-728.

4100. Haines, Francis, ed. "Letters of an Army Captain on the Sioux Campaign of 1879-1880." Pacific Northwest Quarterly 39 (January 1948): 39-64. Letters of Eli Huggins.

4101. Hardin, Edward E. "An Army Lieutenant in Montana, 1874-76," edited by Ralph W. Donnelly. Military Affairs 23 (1959): 85-91.

4102. Howe, George Frederick, ed. "Expedition to the Yellowstone River in 1873: Letters of a Young Cavalry Officer." Mississippi Valley Historical Review 39 (December 1952): 519-534. Letters of Charles W. Larned.

4103. Hughes, Robert P. "The Campaign against the Sioux in 1876." Journal of the Military Service Institution of the United States 18 (January 1896): 1-44.

4104. Hutchins, James S. "Poison in the Pemmican: The Yellowstone Wagon-Road Prospecting Expedition of 1874." Montana, the Magazine of Western History 8 (July 1958): 8-25.

4105. Johnson, Barry C. "Reno as Escort Commander." Westerners Brand Book (Chicago) 29 (September 1972): 49-56.

4106. Jordan, Weymouth T., Jr., ed. "Lieutenant C. D. Cowles at North Platte Station, 1876." Nebraska History 52 (Spring 1971): 89-91.

4107. Keirnes, Helen R. "Final Days of the Indian Campaign of 1876-1877: Aftermath of the Little Big Horn." South Dakota Department of History Report and Historical Collections 36 (1972): 445-523.

4108. King, James T. "General Crook at Camp Cloud Peak: 'I Am at a Loss What to Do.'" Journal of the West 11 (January 1972): 114-127.

4109. Knight, Oliver. "War or Peace: The Anxious Wait for Crazy Horse." Nebraska History 54 (Winter 1973): 521-544.

4110. Leermakers, J. A. "The Battle of the Rosebud." In Great Western Indian Fights, pp. 225-234. Garden City, New York: Doubleday and Company, 1960.

4111. Luce, Edward S., ed. "The Diary and Letters of Dr. James M. DeWolf, Acting Assistant Surgeon, U.S. Army: His Record of the Sioux Expedition of 1876 As Kept until His Death." North Dakota History 25 (April-July 1958): 33-81.

4112. Mears, David T. "Campaigning against Crazy Horse." Proceedings and Collections of the Nebraska State Historical Society, 2d series 10 (1907): 68-77.

4113. McBlain, John F. "The Last Fight of the Sioux War of 1876-77." Journal of the United States Cavalry Association 10 (June 1897): 122-127.

4114. Miles, Nelson A. "My First Fights on the Plains." Cosmopolitan Magazine 50 (May 1911): 792-802.

4115. _____. "Rounding Up the Red Men." Cosmopolitan Magazine 51 (June 1911): 105-114.

4116. Nohl, Lessing H., Jr. "Mackenzie against Dull Knife: Breaking the Northern Cheyennes in 1876." In Probing the American West: Papers from the Santa Fe Conference, edited by K. Ross Toole and others, pp. 86-92. Santa Fe: Museum of New Mexico Press, 1962.

4117. Nottage, James H., ed. "The Big Horn and Yellowstone Expedition of 1876: As Seen through the Letters of Captain Gerhard Luke Luhn." Annals of Wyoming 45 (Spring 1973): 27-46.

4118. Parsons, John E. "Sioux Resistance on the Yellowstone, 1872." Westerners New York Posse Brand Book 3 (1956): 1, 3-4, 6.

4119. Powell, Peter J. "High Bull's Victory Roster." Montana, the Magazine of Western History 25 (January 1975): 14-21.

4120. "Report of E. P. Goodwin, J. A. Campbell, and S. R. Hosmer, Special Commissioners to Investigate Facts Connected with the 'Rawlings Spring Massacre,' in Wyoming Territory, in June 1873." Annals of Wyoming 17 (July 1945): 161-169.

4121. Robinson, Frank U. "The Battle of Snake Mountain." Military Affairs 14

(Summer 1950): 92-98.

4122. Rolston, Alan. "The Yellowstone Expedition of 1873." Montana, the Magazine of Western History 20 (Spring 1970): 20-29.

4123. Russell, Don. "The Duel on the War Bonnet." Journal of the American Military History Foundation 1 (Summer 1937): 55-69.

4124. Self, Zenobia. "Court-Martial of J. J. Reynolds." Military Affairs 37 (April 1973): 52-56.

4125. Smith, Cornelius C., Jr. "Crook and Crazy Horse." Montana, the Magazine of Western History 16 (Spring 1966): 14-26.

4126. Smith, John E. "Indian Troubles (Communications on Indian Troubles of 1872-1874)." Annals of Wyoming 9 (January 1933): 755-760.

4127. Stewart, Edgar I. "Major Brisbin's Relief of Fort Pease: A Prelude to the Bloody Little Big Horn Massacre." Montana, the Magazine of Western History 6 (July 1956): 23-27.

4128. Utley, Robert M. "The Sioux War of 1876." Corral Dust (Potomac Westerners) 2 (March 1957): 3-4.

4129. Vaughn, J. W. The Reynolds Campaign on Powder River. Norman: University of Oklahoma Press, 1961.

4130. _____. With Crook at the Rosebud. Harrisburg, Pennsylvania: Stackpole Company, 1956.

4131. Wilson, Wesley C. "The U.S. Army and the Piegans: The Baker Massacre on the Marias, 1870." North Dakota History 32 (January 1965): 40-58.

Nez Perce War

Nez Perce Indians, who refused to leave their homes in eastern Oregon, came into open conflict with white settlers in 1877. The Indians, led by Chief Joseph, decided upon flight and intended to seek refuge in Canada. The Nez Perce evaded and fought off the pursuing troops, but they were stopped in northern Montana before they reached their goal.

4132. Alcorn, Rowena L., and Gordon D. Alcorn. "Aged Nez Perce Recalls the 1877 Tragedy." Montana, the Magazine of Western History 15 (October 1965): 54-67.

4133. _____. "Old Nez Perce Recalls Tragic Retreat of 1877." Montana, the Magazine of Western History 13 (January 1963): 66-74.

4134. Baird, G. W. "The Capture of Chief Joseph and the Nez-Perces." International Review 7 (August 1879): 209-215.

4135. Beal, Merrill D. "I Will Fight No More Forever": Chief Joseph and the Nez Perce War. Seattle: University of Washington Press, 1963.

4136. Brown, Mark H. "The Chessmen of War." Idaho Yesterdays 10 (Winter 1966-1967): 22-29.

4137. _____. The Flight of the Nez Perce. New York: G. P. Putnam's Sons, 1967.

4138. Buck, Amos. "Review of the Battle of the Big Hole." Contributions to the Historical Society of Montana 7 (1910): 117-130.

4139. Burns, Robert Ignatius. "Coeur d'Alene Diplomacy in the Nez Perce War of 1877." Records of the American Catholic Historical Society of Philadelphia 63 (March 1952): 37-60.

4140. _____. "The Jesuits, the Northern Indians, and the Nez Perce War of 1877." Pacific Northwest Quarterly 42 (January 1951): 40-76.

4141. Carpenter, John A. "General Howard and the Nez Perce War of 1877." Pacific Northwest Quarterly 49 (October 1958): 129-145.

4142. Cave, Will. Nez Perce Indian War of 1877, and Battle of the Big Hole. Missoula, Montana, n.d.

4143. Chalmers, Harvey. The Last Stand of the Nez Perce: Destruction of a People. New York: Twayne Publishers, 1962.

4144. Gibbon, John. "The Battle of the Big Hole." Harper's Weekly 39 (December 21, 1895): 1215-1216; (December 28, 1895): 1235-1236.

4145. _____. "The Pursuit of 'Joseph.'" American Catholic Quarterly Review 4 (April 1879): 317-344.

4146. Goodenough, Daniel, Jr. "Lost on Cold Creek: Modern Explorers Track the Nez Perce." Montana, the Magazine of Western History 24 (October 1974): 16-29.

4147. Haines, Francis. "Chief Joseph and the Nez Perce Warriors." Pacific Northwest Quarterly 45 (January 1954): 1-7.

4148. Haines, Francis, ed. "The Skirmish at Cottonwood." Idaho Yesterdays 2 (Spring 1958): 2-7. Account of George M. Shearer.

4149. Horner, J. H., and Grace Butterfield. "The Nez Perce-Findley Affair." Oregon

Historical Quarterly 40 (March 1939): 40-51.

4150. Howard, O. O. "The True Story of the Wallowa Campaign." North American Review 129 (July 1879): 53-64.

4151. Josephy, Alvin M., Jr. "The Last Stand of Chief Joseph." American Heritage 9 (February 1958): 36-43, 78-81.

4152. Mueller, Oscar O. "The Nez Perce at Cow Island." Montana, the Magazine of Western History 14 (April 1964): 50-53.

4153. Phillips, Paul C., ed. "The Battle of the Big Hole." Frontier: A Magazine of the Northwest 10 (November 1929): 63-80.

4154. Redfield, Francis M. "Reminiscences of Francis M. Redfield: Chief Joseph's War," edited by Floy Laird. Pacific Northwest Quarterly 27 (January 1936): 66-77.

4155. Rhodes, Charles D. "Chief Joseph and the Nez Perce Campaign of 1877." Proceedings of the Annual Meeting of the Order of Indian Wars of the United States, February 18, 1938, pp. 19-48.

4156. Romeyn, Henry. "The Capture of Chief Joseph and the Nez Perce Indians." Contributions to the Historical Society of Montana 2 (1896): 283-291.

4157. Sutherland, Thomas A. Howard's Campaign against the Nez Perce Indians. Portland: A. G. Walling, 1878.

4158. Titus, Nelson C. "The Last Stand of the Nez Perces." Washington Historical Quarterly 6 (July 1915): 145-153.

4159. Wells, Merle W. "The Nez Perce and Their War." Pacific Northwest Quarterly 55 (January 1964): 35-37.

See also general studies on the Nez Perce Indians and biographies of Chief Joseph.

Flight of the Northern Cheyennes

Northern Cheyennes, led by Dull Knife and Little Wolf, fled from the Indian Territory in 1878 to return to their northern homelands. United States troops pursued them and imprisoned Dull Knife's band at Fort Robinson. Many of the band were killed when they attempted to escape in early 1879.

4160. Allred, B. W. "The Massacre of the Dull Knife Band." In Great Western Indian Fights, pp. 295-302. Garden City, New York: Doubleday and Company, 1960.

4161. Bronson, Edgar Beecher. "A Finish Fight for a Birthright." Pearson's Magazine 21 (January 1909): 103-109; (February 1909): 205-213; (March 1909): 257-262.

4162. Brown, George W. "Kansas Indian Wars." Kansas Historical Collections 17 (1926-1928): 134-139.

4163. Collins, Dennis. The Indians' Last Fight; or, The Dull Knife Raid. Girard, Kansas: Press of the Appeal to Reason, 1915.

4164. Covington, James Warren. "Causes of the Dull Knife Raid, 1878." Chronicles of Oklahoma 26 (Spring 1948): 13-22.

4165. Grange, Roger T. "Treating the Wounded at Fort Robinson." Nebraska History 45 (September 1964): 273-294.

4166. Keith, A. N. "Dull Knife's Cheyenne Raid of 1878." Nebraska History 7 (October 1924): 116-119.

4167. Powers, Ramon. "The Northern Cheyenne Trek through Western Kansas in 1878: Frontiersmen, Indians and Cultural Conflict." Trail Guide 16 (September-December 1972): 2-35.

4168. Wright, Peter M. "The Pursuit of Dull Knife from Fort Reno in 1878-1879." Chronicles of Oklahoma 46 (Summer 1968): 141-154.

See also general studies on the Cheyenne Indians and biographies of the leaders.

Bannocks, Paiutes, Sheepeaters

Indians in Idaho came into conflict with the army in 1878 and 1879. Studies listed here concern the Bannock, Paiute, and Sheepeater Indian troubles and other related events.

4169. Adams, J. "In the Stronghold of the Piutes." Overland Monthly, 2d series 22 (December 1893): 583-593.

4170. Brimlow, George F. The Bannock Indian War of 1878. Caldwell, Idaho: Caxton Printers, 1938.

4171. Brimlow, George F., ed. "Two Cavalrymen's Diaries of the Bannock War, 1878." Oregon Historical Quarterly 68 (September 1967): 221-258; (December 1967): 293-316. Diaries of Lieutenant William C. Brown and Private Frederick W. Mayer.

4172. Brown, W. C. "The Sheepeater Campaign, Idaho--1879." Tenth Biennial Report of the State Historical Society of Idaho 10 (1925-1926): 27-51. Reprinted, Boise, Idaho: Syms-York Company, 1926.

4173. Davison, Stanley R., ed. "The Bannock-Piute War of 1878: Letters of Major Edwin C. Mason." Journal of the West 11 (January 1972): 128-142.

4174. Egan, Ferol. Sand in a Whirlwind: The Paiute Indian War of 1860. Garden City, New York: Doubleday and Company, 1972.

4175. Faulkner, Mont E. "Emigrant-Indian Confrontation in Southeastern Idaho, 1841-1863." Rendezvous 2 (Winter 1967): 43-58.

4176. Hardin, C. B. "The Sheepeater Campaign." Journal of the Military Service Institution of the United States 47 (July-August 1910): 25-40.

4177. Hines, Clarence, ed. "Indian Agent's Letter-Book: I, The Piute Bannock Raid of July, 1878." Oregon Historical Quarterly 39 (March 1938): 8-15. Letterbook of N. A. Cornoyer.

4178. Howard, Oliver O. "Indian War Papers--Causes of the Piute and Bannock War." Overland Monthly 9 (May 1887): 492-498.

4179. _____. "Outbreak of the Piute and Bannock War." Overland Monthly 9 (June 1887): 587-592.

4180. Madsen, Brigham D. "Shoshoni-Bannock Marauders on the Oregon Trail, 1859-1863." Utah Historical Quarterly 35 (Winter 1967): 3-30.

4181. Mark, Frederick A. "The Bannack Indian War of 1878." In Great Western Indian Fights, pp. 270-280. Garden City, New York: Doubleday and Company, 1960.

4182. Miller, William C., ed. "The Pyramid Lake Indian War of 1860." Nevada Historical Society Quarterly 1 (November 1957): 98-113.

4183. Shearer, George M. "The Battle of Vinegar Hill." Idaho Yesterdays 12 (Spring 1968): 16-21.

4184. Watson, Chandler B. "Recollections of the Bannock War." Oregon Historical Quarterly 68 (December 1967): 317-329.

4185. Yeckel, Carl. "The Sheepeater Campaign." Idaho Yesterdays 15 (Summer 1971): 2-9.

Ute Conflicts

The growth of white population in Colorado and the spread of mining activity forced the Ute Indians onto reservations, and Indain-white tension increased. A new agent at the White River Agency, the agricultural reformer Nathan C. Meeker, further irritated the Utes. When he called for military aid, the Indians killed him and

other agency personnel in 1879. Listed here are accounts of that event and other studies of Colorado Indian-white conflicts.

4186. Athearn, Robert G., ed. "Major Hough's March into Southern Ute Country, 1879." Colorado Magazine 25 (May 1948): 97-109.

4187. Burkey, Elmer R. "The Thornburgh Battle with the Utes on Milk Creek." Colorado Magazine 13 (May 1936): 90-110.

4188. Covington, James W., ed. "Ute Scalp Dance in Denver." Colorado Magazine 30 (April 1953): 119-124.

4189. Cox, Mrs. C. N. "Late Indian Troubles in the San Juan Country." Colorado Magazine 16 (January 1939): 30-34.

4190. Culmsee, Carlton. Utah's Black Hawk War: Lore and Reminiscences of Participants. Logan: Utah State University Press, 1973.

4191. Dawson, Thomas F., and F. J. V. Skiff. The Ute War: A History of the White River Massacre and the Privations and Hardships of the Captive White Women among the Hostiles on Grand River. Denver: Tribune Publishing House, 1879. Facsimile edition, Boulder, Colorado: Johnson Publishing Company, 1964. Contemporary newspaper accounts.

4192. Edwards, W. W. "The Campaign against the Utes." Army and Navy Life 11 (October 1907): 400-407.

4193. Emmitt, Robert. The Last War Trail: The Utes and the Settlement of Colorado. Norman: University of Oklahoma Press, 1954.

4194. Johnson, Jerome W. "Murder on the Uncompahgre." Colorado Magazine 43 (Summer 1966): 209-224.

4195. McMechen, Edgar C., ed. "Jordan Bean's Story and the Castle Valley Indian Fight." Colorado Magazine 20 (January 1943): 17-25.

4196. Moody, Marshall D. "The Meeker Massacre." Colorado Magazine 30 (April 1953): 91-104.

4197. Nankivell, John H. "Colorado's Last Indian 'War.'" Colorado Magazine 10 (November 1933): 222-234.

4198. Opler, Marvin K. "The Ute Indian War of 1879." El Palacio 46 (November 1939): 255-262.

4199. Rankin, M. Wilson. "The Meeker Massacre: From Reminiscences of Frontier Days." Annals of Wyoming 16 (July 1944): 87-145.

4200. Riddle, Jack P. "Besieged on Milk

Creek." In Great Western Indian Fights, pp. 281-291. Garden City, New York: Doubleday and Company, 1960. Meeker massacre.

4201. Ross, A. R. "Indian Raids in Colorado, 1875." Colorado Magazine 24 (November 1947): 258-263.

4202. Spooner, H. W. "The Outbreak of September, 1879." Journal of the United States Cavalry Association 20 (May 1910): 1124-1128.

4203. Sprague, Marshall. "The Bloody End of Meeker's Utopia." American Heritage 8 (October 1957): 36-39, 90-94.

4204. _____. Massacre: The Tragedy of White River. Boston: Little Brown and Company, 1957.

4205. Sumner, E. V. "Besieged by the Utes: The Massacre of 1879." Century Illustrated Monthly Magazine 42 (October 1891): 837-847.

4206. Walker, Don D., ed. "Cowboys, Indians and Cavalry: A Cattleman's Account of the Fights of 1884." Utah Historical Quarterly 34 (Summer 1966): 255-262.

Apache Wars

The Southwest was the scene of much military activity in the two decades following the Civil War, culminating with the surrender of Geronimo in 1886. Listed here are accounts of the Geronimo campaign, of earlier conflicts with the Apaches, and of humanitarian concern for the Apache prisoners after the war.

4207. "Apache Prisoners in Fort Marion." Lend a Hand 2 (June 1887): 324-327.

4208. Ball, Eve. "Cibicu, an Apache Interpretation." In Troopers West: Military and Indian Affairs on the American Frontier, edited by Ray Brandes, pp. 121-133. San Diego: Frontier Heritage Press, 1970. Based on interviews with Ace Daklugie.

4209. Barnes, Will C. "The Apaches' Last Stand in Arizona: The Battle of the Big Dry Wash." Arizona Historical Review 3 (January 1931): 36-59.

4210. Barney, James M. Tales of Apache Warfare: True Stories of Massacres, Fights and Raids in Arizona and New Mexico. Phoenix, Arizona, 1933.

4211. Basso, Keith H., ed. Western Apache Raiding and Warfare: From the Notes of Grenville Goodwin. Tucson: University of Arizona Press, 1971.

4212. Benson, H. C. "The Geronimo Cam-

paign." Army and Navy Journal 46 (July 3, 1909): 1240-1241.

4213. Betzinez, Jason. I Fought with Geronimo. Edited by Wilbur Sturtevant Nye. Harrisburg, Pennsylvania: Stackpole Company, 1959.

4214. Bigelow, John, Jr. On the Bloody Trail of Geronimo. Edited by Arthur Woodward. Los Angeles: Westernlore Press, 1958. Reprinted from Outing, 1886-1887.

4215. Blankenburg, William B. "The Role of the Press in an Indian Massacre, 1871." Journalism Quarterly 45 (Spring 1968): 61-70. Camp Grant Massacre.

4216. Bourke, John G. An Apache Campaign in the Sierra Madre: An Account of the Expedition in Pursuit of Hostile Chiricahua Apache in the Spring of 1883. New York: C. Scribner's Sons, 1886.

4217. _____. "General Crook in the Indian Country." Century Magazine 41 (March 1891): 643-660.

4218. _____. On the Border with Crook. New York: Charles Scribner's Sons, 1891.

4218a. Byars, Charles, ed. "Gatewood Reports to His Wife from Geronimo's Camp." Journal of Arizona History 7 (Summer 1966): 76-81.

4219. Cargill, Andrew Hays. "The Camp Grant Massacre." Arizona Historical Review 7 (July 1936): 73-79.

4220. Carr, Camillo Casatti Cadmus. A Cavalryman in Indian Country. Foreword and annotation by Dan L. Thrapp. Ashland, Oregon: Lewis Osborne, 1974. Originally published as "'The Days of the Empire'--Arizona, 1866-1869." Journal of the United States Cavalry Association 2 (March 1889): 4-22.

4221. Clay, Thomas J. "Some Unwritten Incidents of the Geronimo Campaign." Proceedings of the Annual Meeting and Dinner of the Order of Indian Wars of the United States, January 26, 1929, pp. 62-65.

4222. Clum, John P. "Apache Misrule: A Bungling Agent Sets the Military Arm in Motion." New Mexico Historical Review 5 (April 1930): 138-153; (July 1930): 221-239. Also published in Arizona Historical Review 4 (April 1931): 56-68; (July 1931): 52-64; (October 1931): 64-71.

4223. Crimmins, Martin L. "Colonel Buell's Expedition into Mexico in 1880." New Mexico Historical Review 10 (April 1935): 133-142.

4224. Crook, George. "The Apache Problem."

Journal of the Military Service Institution of the United States 7 (October 1886): 257-269.

4225. _____. Resumé of Operations against Apache Indians, 1882 to 1886. Notes and introduction by Barry C. Johnson. London: Johnson-Taunton Military Press, 1971. First published in 1886.

4226. Cruse, Thomas. Apache Days and After. Edited by Eugene Cunningham. Caldwell, Idaho: Caxton Printers, 1941.

4227. Daly, Henry W. "The Geronimo Campaign." Arizona Historical Review 3 (July 1930): 26-44.

4228. _____. "The Geronimo Campaign." Journal of the United States Cavalry Association 19 (July 1908): 68-103; (October 1908): 247-262.

4229. Davis, Britton. "The Difficulties of Indian Warfare." Army-Navy Journal 23 (October 24, 1885): 243-244.

4230. _____. The Truth about Geronimo. New Haven: Yale University Press, 1929.

4230a. Davis, O. K. "Our 'Prisoners of War.'" North American Review 195 (March 1912): 356-367.

4231. East, Omega G. "Apache Indians in Fort Marion, 1886-1887." El Escribano 6 (January 1969): 11-27; (April 1969): 3-23; (July 1969): 4-23; (October 1969): 20-38.

4232. East, Omega G., and Albert C. Manucy. "Arizona Apaches as 'Guests' in Florida." Florida Historical Quarterly 30 (January 1952): 294-300.

4233. Eaton, George O. "A String for the Bow: An Incident of the Apache Wars," edited by Don Russell. Winners of the West 15 (September 1938): 1, 3.

4234. Elliott, Charles P. "The Geronimo Campaign of 1885-6." Journal of the United States Cavalry Association 21 (September 1910): 211-236.

4235. Faulk, Odie B. The Geronimo Campaign. New York: Oxford University Press, 1969.

4236. Fiebeger, G. J. "General Crook's Campaign in Old Mexico in 1883: Events Leading Up to It and Personal Experiences in the Campaign." Proceedings of the Annual Meeting of the Order of Indian Wars of the United States, February 20, 1936, pp. 22-32.

4237. Forsyth, George A. "An Apache Raid." Harper's Weekly 43 (January 14, 1899): 43-47.

4238. Fountain, Samuel W. "Lieutenant Fountain's Fight with the Apache Indians at Lillie's Ranch Mogollon Mountains, December 9, 1885, and at Dry Creek, December 19, 1885." Proceedings of the Annual Meeting and Dinner of the Order of Indian Wars of the United States, January 19, 1928, pp. 33-41.

4239. Gaines, William H., Jr. "'Boldly and Alone.'" Virginia Cavalcade 5 (Spring 1956): 39-43. On Charles B. Gatewood.

4240. Gates, John Morgan. "General George Crook's First Apache Campaign: The Use of Mobile, Self-Contained Units against the Apache in the Military Department of Arizona, 1871-1873." Journal of the West 6 (April 1967): 310-320.

4241. Gatewood, Charles B. "Lieut. Charles B. Gatewood, 6th U.S. Cavalry, and the Surrender of Geronimo." Arizona Historical Review 4 (April 1931): 29-44.

4242. _____. "Lieutenant Charles B. Gatewood, 6th U.S. Cavalry, and the Surrender of Geronimo," edited by Edward S. Godfrey. Proceedings of the Annual Meeting and Dinner of the Order of Indian Wars of the United States, January 26, 1929, pp. 45-61.

4243. Goodman, David M. "Apaches as Prisoners of War, 1886-1894." Ph.D. dissertation, Texas Christian University, 1969.

4244. Gordon, Dudley, ed. "Lummis as War Correspondent in Arizona." American West 2 (Summer 1965): 4-12.

4245. Greene, Jerome A. "The Crawford Affair: International Implications of the Geronimo Campaign." Journal of the West 11 (January 1972): 143-153.

4246. Gressley, Gene M., ed. "A Soldier with Crook: The Letters of Henry R. Porter." Montana, the Magazine of Western History 8 (Summer 1958): 33-47.

4247. Hagemann, E. R. "Scout out from Camp McDowell." Arizoniana 5 (Fall 1964): 29-47.

4248. Hammond, George P. "The Camp Grant Massacre: A Chapter in Apache History." Proceedings of the Pacific Coast Branch of the American Historical Association, 1929, pp. 200-215.

4249. Hanna, Robert. "With Crawford in Mexico." Arizona Historical Review 6 (April 1935): 56-65.

4250. Hastings, James Rodney. "The Tragedy at Camp Grant in 1871." Arizona and the West 1 (Summer 1959): 146-160.

4251. Irwin, B. J. D. "The Apache Pass

Fight." Infantry Journal 32 (April 1928): 368-375.

4252. Kelly, George H. "How Geronimo Was Finally Overcome and Deported from Arizona." Arizona Historical Review 1 (October 1928): 36-44.

4253. Lane, Jack C., ed. Chasing Geronimo: The Journal of Leonard Wood, May-September, 1886. Albuquerque: University of New Mexico Press, 1970.

4254. Leiby, Austin Nelson. "The Marmon Battalion and the Apache Campaign of 1885." In The Changing Ways of Southwestern Indians: A Historic Perspective, edited by Albert H. Schroeder, pp. 211-229. Glorieta, New Mexico: Rio Grande Press, 1973.

4255. Lummis, Charles F. "The Apache Warrior." Kansas Magazine 6 (September 1886): 225-232.

4256. _____. General Crook and the Apache Wars. Edited by Turbese Lummis Fiske. Flagstaff, Arizona: Northland Press, 1966. Newspaper dispatches of 1886.

4257. McClintock, James H. "Fighting Apaches: Narrative of the Fifth Cavalry's Deadly Conflict in the Superstition Mountains of Arizona." Sunset Magazine 18 (February 1907): 340-343.

4258. Mazzanovitch, Anton. Trailing Geronimo. Edited by E. A. Brininstool. Los Angeles: Gem Publishing Company, 1926. 3d edition, New York, 1931.

4259. Mehren, Lawrence L., ed. "Scouting for Mescaleros: The Price Campaign of 1873." Arizona and the West 10 (Summer 1968): 171-190.

4260. Miles, Nelson A. "On the Trail of Geronimo." Cosmopolitan Magazine 51 (July 1911): 249-262.

4261. Morgan, George H. "The Fight at the Big Dry Wash in the Mogollon Mountains, Arizona, July 17, 1882, with Renegade Apache Scouts from the San Carlos Indian Reservation." Proceedings of the Annual Meeting of the Order of Indian Wars of the United States, February 24, 1940, pp. 21-28.

4262. Opler, Morris E. "A Chiricahua Apache's Account of the Geronimo Campaign of 1886." New Mexico Historical Review 13 (October 1938): 360-386.

4263. Parker, James. "The Geronimo Campaign." Proceedings of the Annual Meeting and Dinner of the Order of Indian Wars of the United States, January 26, 1929, pp. 32-44.

4264. Powers, Nellie Brown. "A Ride from Geronimo, the Apache." New Mexico Historical Review 36 (April 1961): 89-96.

4265. Reeve, Frank D., ed. "Puritan and Apache: A Diary." New Mexico Historical Review 23 (October 1948): 269-301; 24 (January 1949): 12-53.

4266. _____. "War and Peace: Two Arizona Diaries." New Mexico Historical Review 24 (April 1949): 95-129. Diaries of F. A. Cook and Ammon M. Tenney.

4267. Romer, Margaret. "General Howard Made Apache Peace in Pow-Wow." Journal of the West 1 (July 1962): 98-102.

4268. Rothenberg, Gunther Erich. "General George H. Crook and the Apaches, 1872-73." Westerners Brand Book (Chicago) 13 (September 1956): 49-51, 54-56.

4269. Sacks, Benjamin H., ed. "New Evidence on the Bascom Affair." Arizona and the West 4 (Autumn 1962): 261-278.

4270. Schellie, Don. Vast Domain of Blood: The Story of the Camp Grant Massacre. Los Angeles: Westernlore Press, 1968.

4271. Schoenberger, Dale T. "Lieutenant George N. Bascom at Apache Pass, 1861." Chronicles of Oklahoma 51 (Spring 1973): 84-91.

4272. Shipp, W. E. "Captain Crawford's Last Expedition." Journal of the United States Cavalry Association 19 (October 1908): 278-300.

4273. Steelhammer, Charles. "With the Apache Indians during the Revolt of 1879." Military Affairs 18 (Summer 1954): 86-88.

4274. Stout, Joseph A., Jr. Apache Lightning: The Last Great Battles of the Ojo Calientes. New York: Oxford University Press, 1974.

4275. Stout, Joseph A., Jr., ed. "Soldiering and Suffering in the Geronimo Campaign: Reminiscences of Lawrence R. Jerome." Journal of the West 11 (January 1972): 154-169.

4276. Thrapp, Dan L. The Conquest of Apacheria. Norman: University of Oklahoma Press, 1967.

4277. _____. General Crook and the Sierra Madre Adventure. Norman: University of Oklahoma Press, 1972.

4278. _____. "Where Was the Battle of Turret Peak Fought." In Troopers West: Military and Indian Affairs on the American Frontier, edited by Ray Brandes, pp. 105-119. San Diego: Frontier Heritage Press, 1970.

4279. Turcheneske, John A., Jr. "Arizonans and the Apache Prisoners at Mount Vernon Barracks, Alabama: 'They Do Not Die Fast Enough!'" Military History of Texas and the Southwest 11 (1973): 197-226.

4280. _____. "The Arizona Press and Geronimo's Surrender." Journal of Arizona History 14 (Summer 1973): 133-148.

4281. Utley, Robert M. "The Bascom Affair: A Reconstruction." Arizona and the West 3 (Spring 1961): 59-68.

4282. _____. "The Surrender of Geronimo." Arizoniana 4 (Spring 1963): 1-9.

4282a. Valpulic, Marian E., and Harold H. Longfellow, eds. "The Fight at Chiricahua Pass in 1869 As Described by L. L. Dorr, M.D." Arizona and the West 13 (Winter 1971): 369-378.

4283. Wallace, Andrew. "The Mescalero Apaches at Fort Stanton." In The Changing Ways of Southwestern Indians: A Historic Perspective, edited by Albert H. Schroeder, pp. 125-143. Glorieta, New Mexico: Rio Grande Press, 1973.

4284. Webb, Walter Prescott. "Last War Trail of Victorio." True West 4 (March-April 1957): 20-21, 43.

4285. Welsh, Herbert. The Apache Prisoners in Fort Marion, St. Augustine, Florida. Philadelphia: Indian Rights Association, 1887.

4286. Wilson, John P., ed. "Lt. H. B. Cushing: Indian Fighter Extraordinary." El Palacio 76 (Spring 1969): 40-46.

4287. Woodward, Arthur. "Side Lights on Fifty Years of Apache Warfare, 1836-1886." Arizoniana 2 (Fall 1961): 3-14.

4288. Woody, Clara T., ed. "The Woolsey Expeditions of 1864." Arizona and the West 4 (Summer 1962): 157-176.

See also general studies on the Apaches and biographical studies of Geronimo and other Apache leaders. Much of the material listed under Scouts (4696 to 4723) pertains to the Apache campaigns.

Ghost Dance and Wounded Knee

The end of the Indian wars came with the battle at Wounded Knee creek on the Pine Ridge Reservation in December 1890. The Sioux, grasping at the promises of a "Messiah" who preached the ghost dance, were subdued by military force. Included here are accounts of the ghost dance that pertain to the Wounded Knee encounter.

4289. Bell, Joseph N. "The Massacre of Wounded Knee." Coronet 40 (June 1956): 78-80.

4290. Bland, T. A. A Brief History of the Late Military Invasion of the Home of the Sioux. Washington: National Indian Defence Association, 1891.

4291. Bourke, John G. "The Indian Messiah." Nation 51 (December 4, 1890): 439-440.

4292. Boyd, James P. Recent Indian Wars under the Lead of Sitting Bull, and Other Chiefs: With a Full Account of the Messiah Craze, and Ghost Dances. Philadelphia: Publishers Union, 1891.

4293. Brown, D. Alexander. "The Ghost Dance and Battle of Wounded Knee." American History Illustrated 1 (December 1966): 4-16.

4294. Colby, L. W. "The Sioux Indian War of 1890-'91." Transactions and Reports of the Nebraska State Historical Society 3 (1892): 144-190.

4295. Dougherty, W. E. "The Recent Indian Craze." Journal of the Military Service Institution of the United States 12 (May 1891): 576-578.

4296. Eastman, Elaine Goodale. "The Ghost Dance War and Wounded Knee Massacre of 1890-91." Nebraska History 26 (January-March 1945): 26-42.

4297. Gilmore, Melvin R. "The Truth of the Wounded Knee Massacre." American Indian Magazine 5 (October-December 1917): 240-252.

4298. Gresham, John C. "The Story of Wounded Knee." Harper's Weekly 35 (February 7, 1891): 106-107.

4299. Harvey, Philip F. "The Last Stand of the Sioux." Army and Navy Life 12 (February 1908): 225-236.

4300. Hawthorne, H. L. "The Sioux Campaign of 1890-91." Journal of the Military Service Institution of the United States 19 (July 1896): 185-187.

4301. Hilliard, John Northern. "Sitting Bull's Capture and the Messiah Craze." Southern Workman 39 (October 1910): 545-551.

4302. Howard, Oliver O. "The Indian Rising." New Review 4 (February 1891): 161-170.

4303. Johnson, Dorothy M. "Ghost Dance: Last Hope of the Sioux." Montana, the Magazine of Western History 6 (Summer 1956): 42-50.

4304. Kelley, Alexander, and Pierre Bovis, eds. Pine Ridge, 1890: An Eye Witness Account of the Events Surrounding the Fighting at Wounded Knee. San Francisco: Pierre Bovis, 1971. Newspaper articles written by William Fitch Kelley.

4305. Kelley, W. F. "The Indian Troubles and the Battle of Wounded Knee." Transactions and Reports of the Nebraska State Historical Society 4 (1891-1892): 30-50.

4306. Lyons, T. D. "Preparedness-1890." Commonweal 32 (September 20, 1940): 443-445.

4307. McCann, Frank D., Jr. "The Ghost Dance: Last Hope of Western Tribes." Montana, the Magazine of Western History 16 (Winter 1966): 25-34.

4308. McGregor, James H. The Wounded Knee Massacre from Viewpoint of the Sioux. Baltimore: Wirth Brothers, 1940.

4309. Mattes, Merrill J. "The Enigma of Wounded Knee." Plains Anthropologist 5 (May 1960): 1-11.

4310. Maus, Marion P. "The New Indian Messiah." Harper's Weekly 34 (December 6, 1890): 947.

4311. Metcalf, George. "Tragedy at Wounded Knee." In Great Western Indian Fights, pp. 307-317. Garden City, New York: Doubleday and Company, 1960.

4312. Miles, Nelson A. "The War with the 'Messiah.'" Cosmopolitan Magazine 51 (September 1911): 522-533.

4313. Miller, David Humphreys. Ghost Dance. New York: Duell, Sloan and Pearce, 1959.

4314. Mooney, James. "The Indian Ghost Dance." Collections of the Nebraska State Historical Society 16 (1911): 168-182.

4315. _____. The Ghost-Dance Religion and the Sioux Outbreak of 1890. Annual Report of the Bureau of Ethnology, 1892-1893, part 2. Washington: Government Printing Office, 1896. Abridged edition, edited by Anthony F. C. Wallace. Chicago: University of Chicago Press, 1965.

4316. Paige, Harry W. "Wounded Knee: The Tragedy and the Dream." Westerners Brand Book (New York) 18, no. 2 (1971): 25-26, 34.

4317. Pfaller, Louis. "Indian Scare of 1890." North Dakota History 39 (Spring 1972): 4-17, 36.

4318. Remington, Frederic. "The Sioux Outbreak in South Dakota." Harper's Weekly 35 (January 24, 1891): 57, 61-62.

4319. Richardson, W. P. "Some Observations upon the Sioux Campaign of 1890-91." Journal of the Military Service Institution of the United States 18 (May 1896): 512-531.

4320. Rockefeller, Alfred, Jr. "The Sioux Troubles of 1890-1891." Ph.D. dissertation, Northwestern University, 1949.

4321. Scott, E. D. "Wounded Knee: A Look at the Record." Field Artillery Journal 29 (January-February 1939): 5-24.

4322. Seymour, Charles G. "The Sioux Rebellion: The Final Review." Harper's Weekly 35 (February 7, 1891): 106, 108-109.

4323. Seymour, Forrest W. "A Look Back at Wounded Knee." Proceedings of the American Antiquarian Society 84 (April 17, 1974): 33-42.

4324. Sheldon, Addison E. "After Wounded Knee--a Recollection." Nebraska History 22 (January-March 1941): 45.

4325. Spindler, Will H. Tragedy Strikes at Wounded Knee. Gordon, Nebraska: Gordon Journal, 1955. Reprinted Vermillion: University of South Dakota, 1972.

4326. Sword, George. "The Story of the Ghost Dance," translated by Emma Sickels. Folk-Lorist 1 (July 1892): 28-31.

4327. Traub, Peter E. "The First Act of the Last Sioux Campaign." Journal of the United States Cavalry Association 15 (April 1905): 872-879.

4328. Watson, Elmo Scott. "The Last Indian War, 1890-91--a Study of Newspaper Jingoism." Journalism Quarterly 20 (September 1943): 205-219.

4329. _____. "Pine Ridge, 1890-91." Westerners Brand Book (Denver), 1945, pp. 1-11.

4330. Watson, Julia S. "A Sketch of George H. Harries, Reporter of Wounded Knee." Westerners New York Posse Brand Book 3 (1956): 73-76, 90.

4331. Welsh, Herbert. "The Meaning of the Dakota Outbreak." Scribner's Magazine 9 (April 1891): 439-452.

4332. Wilson, George. "The Sioux War." Nation 52 (January 8, 1891): 29-30.

4333. Youngkin, Stephen D. "Prelude to Wounded Knee: The Military Point of View." South Dakota History 4 (Summer 1974): 333-351.

Full accounts of Wounded Knee appear also in a number of works on the Sioux or on the Indian wars. The best account is given by Utley (8489). See also the studies on the ghost dance which do not have special reference to the military clash (9072 to 9083).

Post-1890 Encounters

Although the Indian wars can be said to have ended with the Sioux troubles of 1890-91, occasional later conflicts between Indians and whites have attracted writers.

4334. Browning, D. M. "Indian Disturbances in 'Jackson Hole' Country, Wyoming, 1895." Annals of Wyoming 16 (January 1944): 5-33.

4335. McKibbin, Davidson B. "Revolt of the Navaho, 1913." New Mexico Historical Review 29 (October 1954): 259-289.

4336. Parkhill, Forbes. The Last of the Indian Wars. New York: Collier Books, 1961. Deals with the "Ute War" of 1915.

4337. Perry, Frank Vernon. "The Last Indian Uprising in the United States: Little High Rock Canyon, Nevada, January 19, 1911." Nevada Historical Society Quarterly 15 (Winter 1972): 23-37.

4338. Richardson, Ernest M. "Battle of Lightning Creek." Montana, the Magazine of Western History 10 (July 1960): 42-52.

4339. Roddis, Louis H. "The Last Indian Uprising in the United States." Minnesota History Bulletin 3 (February 1920): 272-290. Chippewa at Leech Lake, Minnesota, 1898.

4340. Underhill, Lonnie E., and Daniel F. Littlefield, Jr. "The Cheyenne 'Outbreak' of 1897." Montana, the Magazine of Western History 24 (October 1974): 30-41.

4341. Underhill, Lonnie E., and Daniel F. Littlefield, Jr., eds. "The Cheyenne 'Outbreak' of 1897 As Reported by Hamlin Garland." Arizona and the West 15 (Autumn 1973): 257-274.

4342. Wharfield, H. B. "A Fight with the Yaquis at Bear Valley, 1918." Arizoniana 4 (Fall 1963): 1-8.

4343. Wold, Pauline. "Some Recollections of the Leech Lake Uprising." Minnesota History 24 (June 1943): 142-148.

UNITED STATES MILITARY POSTS

The United States government established posts along the frontiers in order to assert its authority over new territory and to protect travelers and settlers. The history of these posts is part of the history of military relations with the Indians.

General Studies

A few works provide a comprehensive coverage of the fronteir military establishments.

4344. Grant, Bruce. American Forts, Yesterday and Today. New York: Dutton, 1965.

4345. Frazer, Robert W. Forts of the West: Military Forts and Presidios and Posts Commonly Called Forts West of the Mississippi River to 1898. Norman: University of Oklahoma Press, 1965.

4346. Hart, Herbert M. Old Forts of the Far West. Seattle: Superior Publishing Company, 1965.

4347. _____. Old Forts of the Northwest. Seattle: Superior Publishing Company, 1963.

4348. _____. Old Forts of the Southwest. Seattle: Superior Publishing Company, 1964.

4349. _____. Pioneer Forts of the West. Seattle: Superior Publishing Company, 1968.

4350. Prucha, Francis Paul. A Guide to the Military Posts of the United States, 1789-1895. Madison: State Historical Society of Wisconsin, 1964.

4351. Ruth, Kent. Great Day in the West: Forts, Posts, and Rendezvous beyond the Mississippi. Norman: University of Oklahoma Press, 1963.

The East, the Great Lakes, and the Mississippi Valley

The forts in the East, on the Great Lakes, and in the Ohio and Mississippi valleys formed the first cordons of frontier defense. As American authority advanced westward after the Revolutionary War and the War of 1812, new posts were built and older ones abandoned, although some forts, like Fort Snelling and Jefferson Barracks, became permanent establishments.

4352. Agnew, Daniel. Fort McIntosh: Its Times and Men. Pittsburgh, 1893.

4353. Aleshire, Ruth Cory. "Warsaw and Fort Edwards on the Mississippi." Transactions of the Illinois State Historical Society for the Year 1930, pp. 200-209.

4354. Andrews, Roger. Old Fort Mackinac on the Hill of History. Menominee, Michigan: Herald-Leader Press, 1938.

4355. Bald, F. Clever. "Fort Miami." Historical Society of Northwestern Ohio Quarterly Bulletin 15 (July 1943): 127-138.

4356. Briggs, John Ely. "The Second Fort Des Moines." Palimpsest 24 (May 1943): 161-172.

4357. Caldwell, Norman W. "Cantonment

Wilkinsonville." Mid-America 31 (January 1949): 3-28.

4358. _____. "Fort Massac: The American Frontier Post, 1778-1805." Journal of the Illinois State Historical Society 43 (Winter 1950): 265-281.

4359. _____. "Fort Massac: Since 1805." Journal of the Illinois State Historical Society 44 (Spring 1951): 47-60.

4360. Chase, Lew Allen. "Fort Wilkins, Copper Harbor, Mich." Michigan History Magazine 4 (April-July 1920): 608-611.

4361. Emery, B. Frank. "Fort Saginaw." Michigan History Magazine 30 (July-September 1946): 476-503.

4362. _____. Fort Saginaw, 1822-1823: The Story of a Forgotten Frontier Post. Detroit, 1932.

4363. _____. Fort Wilkins, 1844-46: A Frontier Stockaded Post Built to Protect Michigan's First Copper Mines. Detroit, 1932.

4364. Fisher, James. "Fort Wilkins." Michigan History Magazine 29 (April-June 1945): 155-165.

4365. "Fort Atkinson, Iowa." Annals of Iowa, 3d series 4 (July 1900): 448-453.

4366. "Fort Des Moines (No. 1), Iowa." Annals of Iowa, 3d series 3 (April-July 1898): 351-363.

4367. "Fort Des Moines, No. 2." Annals of Iowa, 3d series 4 (October 1899): 161-178.

4368. "Fort Dodge, Iowa." Annals of Iowa, 3d series 4 (October 1900): 534-538.

4369. Fort Harrison on the Banks of the Wabash, 1812-1912. Terre Haute, Indiana: Fort Harrison Centennial Association, 1912.

4370. "Fort Sanford, Iowa." Annals of Iowa, 3d series 4 (January 1900): 289-293.

4371. Gallaher, Ruth A. Fort Des Moines in Iowa History. Iowa City: State Historical Society of Iowa, 1919.

4372. Graham, A. A. "The Military Posts, Forts and Battlefields within the State of Ohio." Ohio Archaeological and Historical Publications 3 (1891): 300-314.

4373. Graham, Louis E. "Fort McIntosh." Western Pennsylvania Historical Magazine 15 (May 1932): 93-119.

4374. Grant, Joseph H. "Old Fort Snelling." Quartermaster Review 13 (March-April 1934): 21-24, 71-72.

4375. Gregg, Kate L. "Building of the First American Fort West of the Mississippi." Missouri Historical Review 30 (July 1936): 345-364. Fort Belle Fontaine.

4376. Griswold, Bert J., ed. Fort Wayne, Gateway of the West, 1802-1813. Indiana Historical Collections, volume 15. Indianapolis: Historical Bureau of the Indiana Library and Historical Department, 1927.

4377. Hansen, Marcus L. Old Fort Snelling. Iowa City: State Historical Society of Iowa, 1917.

4378. _____. Old Fort Snelling, 1819-1858. Iowa City: State Historical Society of Iowa, 1918.

4379. Holcombe, Return I. "Fort Snelling." American Historical Magazine 1 (March 1906): 110-133.

4380. Holt, John R. Historic Fort Snelling. Fort Snelling, Minnesota, 1938.

4381. Jackson, Donald. "Old Fort Madison, 1808-1813." Palimpsest 39 (January 1958): 1-64.

4382. Jenks, William L. "Fort Gratiot and Its Builder Gen. Charles Gratiot." Michigan History Magazine 4 (January 1920): 141-155.

4383. Johnson, Richard W. "Fort Snelling and Its History." Western Magazine 15 (July 1920): 44-46; (October 1920): 170-173.

4384. _____. "Fort Snelling from Its Foundation to the Present Time." Collections of the Minnesota Historical Society 8 (1898): 427-448.

4385. Jones, Evan. Citadel in the Wilderness: The Story of Fort Snelling and the Old Northwest Frontier. New York: Coward-McCann, 1966.

4386. Jones, Robert Ralston. Fort Washington at Cincinnati, Ohio. Cincinnati: Society of Colonial Wars in the State of Ohio, 1902.

4387. Kellogg, Louise Phelps. "Old Fort Howard." Wisconsin Magazine of History 18 (December 1934): 125-140.

4388. Mahan, Bruce E. "Old Fort Atkinson." Palimpsest 2 (November 1921): 333-350.

4389. _____. "Old Fort Crawford." Palimpsest 42 (October 1961): 449-512.

4390. _____. Old Fort Crawford and the Frontier. Iowa City: State Historical Society of Iowa, 1926.

4391. Miller, W. C. "History of Fort Hamilton." Ohio Archaeological and

Historical Publications 13 (1904): 97-111.

4392. Mueller, Richard E. "Jefferson Barracks: The Early Years." Missouri Historical Review 67 (October 1972): 7-30.

4393. Nichols, Roger L. "The Founding of Fort Atkinson." Annals of Iowa 37 (Spring 1965): 589-597.

4394. Norton, W. T. "Old Fort Belle Fontaine." Journal of the Illinois State Historical Society 4 (October 1911): 334-339.

4395. Peck, Maria. "Fort Armstrong." Annals of Iowa, 3d series 1 (January 1895): 602-613.

4396. Pride, Woodbury Freeman. The History of Fort Riley. Fort Riley, Kansas, 1926.

4397. Prucha, Francis Paul. "Fort Ripley: The Post and the Military Reservation." Minnesota History 28 (September 1947): 205-224.

4398. Pugh, Edwin V. "Fort McIntosh." Pitt 47 (Autumn 1952): 14-17.

4399. Quaife, Milo M. Chicago and the Old Northwest, 1673-1835: A Study of the Evolution of the Northwestern Frontier Together with a History of Fort Dearborn. Chicago: University of Chicago Press, 1913.

4400. Randall, E. O. "Fort St. Clair." Ohio Archaeological and Historical Publications 11 (1902): 161-163.

4401. Scanlan, Peter L. Prairie du Chien: French, British, American. Menasha, Wisconsin, 1937.

4402. Simmons, David. "Anthony Wayne's Forts." Old Fort News, Winter 1973.

4403. Slaughter, Linda W. "Fort Abercrombie." Collections of the State Historical Society of North Dakota 1 (1906): 412-423.

4404. Tanner, George C. "History of Fort Ripley, 1849 to 1859, Based on the Diary of Rev. Solon W. Manney, D.D., Chaplain of This Post from 1851 to 1859." Collections of the Minnesota Historical Society 10, part 1 (February 1905): 179-202.

4405. Turner, Andrew J. "The History of Fort Winnebago." Collections of the State Historical Society of Wisconsin 14 (1898): 65-103.

4406. Van der Zee, Jacob. "Forts in the Iowa Country." Iowa Journal of History and Politics 12 (April 1914): 163-204.

4407. _____. Old Fort Madison. Iowa

City: State Historical Society of Iowa, 1918.

4408. Webb, Henry W. "The Story of Jefferson Barracks." New Mexico Historical Review 21 (July 1946): 185-208.

4409. Wilson, Frazer Ells. Fort Jefferson: The Frontier Post of the Upper Miami Valley. N.p., 1950.

4410. Woehrmann, Paul. At the Headwaters of the Maumee: A History of the Forts of Fort Wayne. Indianapolis: Indiana Historical Society, 1971.

Central and Northern Plains and the Mountains

White expansion westward brought the government into contact with new Indian tribes, and a new series of forts was established--along the Missouri River, across the plains of Kansas and Nebraska, and in the Rocky Mountains. Much of the history of the wars with the plains Indians appears in the story of these posts.

4411. Anderson, James. "Fort Osage: An Incident of Territorial Missouri." Bulletin of the Missouri Historical Society 4 (April 1948): 174-176.

4412. Athearn, Robert G. Forts of the Upper Missouri. Englewood Cliffs, New Jersey: Prentice-Hall, 1967.

4413. Baird, W. David. "Fort Smith and the Red Man." Arkansas Historical Quarterly 30 (Winter 1971): 337-348.

4414. Barry, Louise. "Fort Aubrey." Kansas Historical Quarterly 39 (Summer 1973): 188-198.

4415. Beach, James H. "Old Fort Hays." Collections of the Kansas Historical Society 11 (1910): 571-581.

4416. Bearss, Edwin C. "In Quest of Peace on the Indian Border: The Establishment of Fort Smith." Arkansas Historical Quarterly 23 (Summer 1964): 123-153.

4417. Bearss, Edwin C., and Arrell M. Gibson. Fort Smith: Little Gibraltar on the Arkansas. Norman: University of Oklahoma Press, 1969.

4418. Blades, Thomas E., and John W. Wike. "Fort Missoula." Military Affairs 13 (Spring 1949): 29-36.

4419. Brown, Dee. Fort Phil Kearny: An American Saga. New York: Putnam, 1962.

4420. Campbell, Hortense Balderston. "Camp Beecher." Kansas Historical Quarterly 3 (May 1934): 172-185.

4421. Chambers, Alexander. "Fort Bridger." Annals of Wyoming 5 (October 1927- January 1928): 91-95.

4422. Chappell, Gordon Stelling. "Surgeon at Fort Sidney: Captain Walter Reed's Experiences at a Nebraska Military Post, 1883-1884." Nebraska History 54 (Fall 1973): 419-443.

4423. Corbusier, William T. "Camp Sheridan, Nebraska." Nebraska History 42 (March 1961): 29-53.

4424. "Dakota Military Posts." South Dakota Historical Collections 7 (1916): 77-99.

4425. Day, Daniel S. "Fort Sedgwick." Colorado Magazine 42 (Winter 1965): 17-35.

4426. De Noyer, Charles. "The History of Fort Totten." Collections of the State Historical Society of North Dakota 3 (1910): 178-236.

4427. Dunn, Adrian R. "A History of Old Fort Berthold." North Dakota History 30 (October 1963): 157-240.

4428. _____. A History of Old Fort Berthold. Bismarck: North Dakota State Historical Society, 1964.

4429. "Early Military Posts, Missions and Camps." Transactions of the Kansas State Historical Society 1-2 (1881): 263-270.

4430. Edwards, Paul M. "Fort Wadsworth and the Friendly Santee Sioux, 1864-1892." South Dakota Department of History, Report and Historical Collections 31 (1962): 74-156.

4431. Ellison, Robert S. Fort Bridger, Wyoming: A Brief History. Casper, Wyoming: Historical Landmark Commission of Wyoming, 1931.

4432. "Fort Abercrombie, 1857-1877." Collections of the State Historical Society of North Dakota 2, part 2 (1908): 7-34.

4433. Garfield, Marvin H. "The Military Post as a Factor in the Frontier Defense of Kansas, 1865-1869." Kansas Historical Quarterly 1 (November 1931): 50-62.

4434. Goplen, Arnold O. "Fort Abraham Lincoln: A Typical Frontier Military Post." North Dakota History 13 (October 1946): 176-221.

4435. Grange, Roger T., Jr. "Fort Robinson, Outpost on the Plains." Nebraska History 39 (September 1958): 191-240.

4436. Gregg, Kate L. "The History of Fort Osage." Missouri Historical Review 34 (July 1940): 439-488.

4437. Hafen, LeRoy R., and Francis Marion Young. Fort Laramie and the Pageant of the West, 1834-1890. Glendale, California: Arthur H. Clark Company, 1938.

4438. Hagen, Olaf T. "Platte Bridge Station and Fort Caspar." Annals of Wyoming 27 (April 1955): 3-17.

4439. Haskett, James N. "The Final Chapter in the Story of the First Fort Smith." Arkansas Historical Quarterly 25 (Autumn 1966): 214-228.

4440. Hieb, David L. Fort Laramie National Monument, Wyoming. National Park Service Historical Handbook Series, no. 20. Washington: Government Printing Office, 1954.

4441. Hoekman, Steven. "The History of Fort Sully." South Dakota Historical Collections and Report 26 (1952): 222-277.

4442. Holtz, Milton E. "Old Fort Kearny, 1846-1848: Symbol of a Changing Frontier." Montana, the Magazine of Western History 22 (October 1972): 44-55.

4443. Hummel, Edward A. "The Story of Fort Sisseton." South Dakota Historical Review 2 (1937): 126-144.

4444. Hunt, Elvid. History of Fort Leavenworth, 1827-1927. Fort Leavenworth, Kansas: General Service Schools Press, 1926. 2d edition, 1937.

4445. Hurt, R. Douglas. "Fort Wallace, Kansas, 1865-1882: A Frontier Post during the Indian Wars." Red River Valley Historical Review 1 (Spring 1974): 132-145.

4446. Johnson, Sally A. "Cantonment Missouri, 1819-1820." Nebraska History 37 (June 1956): 121-133.

4447. _____. "Fort Atkinson at Council Bluffs." Nebraska History 38 (September 1957): 229-236.

4448. _____. "The Sixth's Elysian Fields: Fort Atkinson on the Council Bluffs." Nebraska History 40 (March 1959): 1-38.

4449. Kendall, Jane R. "History of Fort Francis E. Warren." Annals of Wyoming 18 (January 1946): 3-66.

4450. Kirkus, Peggy Dickey. "Fort David A. Russell: A Study of Its History from 1867 to 1890: With a Brief Summary of Events from 1890 to the Present." Annals of Wyoming 40 (October 1968): 161-192; 41 (April 1969): 83-111.

4451. Koury, Michael J. Military Posts of

Montana. Bellevue, Nebraska: Old Army Press, 1970.

4452. Layton, Stanford J. "Fort Rawlins, Utah: A Question of Mission and Means." Utah Historical Quarterly 42 (Winter 1974): 68-83.

4453. Mantor, Lyle E. "Fort Kearny and the Westward Movement." Nebraska History 29 (September 1948): 175-207.

4454. Mattes, Merrill J. "Fort Laramie Centennial: 1849-1949." Westerners Brand Book (Chicago) 6 (April 1949): 9-11, 13-16.

4455. _____. "Fort Laramie, Guardian of the Oregon Trail: A Commemorative Essay." Annals of Wyoming 17 (January 1945): 3-20.

4456. _____. "Fort Mitchell, Scotts Bluff, Nebraska Territory." Nebraska History 33 (March 1952): 1-34.

4457. _____. "A History of Old Fort Mitchell." Nebraska History 24 (April-June 1943): 71-82.

4458. _____. "Revival at Old Fort Randall." Military Engineer 44 (March-April 1952): 88-93.

4459. Mattison, Ray H. "The Army Post on the Northern Plains, 1865-1886." Nebraska History 35 (March 1954): 17-43.

4460. _____. "Fort Rice--North Dakota's First Missouri River Military Post." North Dakota History 20 (April 1953): 87-108.

4461. _____. "Old Fort Stevenson--a Typical Missouri River Military Post." North Dakota History 18 (April-July 1951): 53-91.

4462. Mokler, Alfred James. Fort Caspar (Platte Bridge Station). Casper, Wyoming: Prairie Publishing Company, 1939.

4463. Montgomery, Mrs. Frank C. "Fort Wallace and Its Relation to the Frontier." Collections of the Kansas State Historical Society 17 (1926-1928): 189-283.

4464. Mullin, Cora Phoebe. "The Founding of Fort Hartsuff." Nebraska History Magazine 12 (April-June 1929): 129-140.

4465. Murray, Robert A. "Fort Fred Steele: Desert Outpost on the Union Pacific." Annals of Wyoming 44 (Fall 1972): 139-206.

4466. _____. Military Posts in the Powder River Country of Wyoming, 1865-1894. Lincoln: University of Nebraska Press, 1968.

4467. Nadeau, Remi. Fort Laramie and the Sioux Indians. Englewood Cliffs, New Jersey: Prentice-Hall, 1967.

4468. Nelson, Vance E., ed. "Fort Robinson during the 1880's: An Oklahoma Newspaperman Visits the Post." Nebraska History 55 (Summer 1974): 181-202. Articles by William Edwards Annin.

4469. Oliva, Leo E. "Fort Atkinson in the Santa Fe Trail, 1850-1854." Kansas Historical Quarterly 40 (Summer 1974): 212-233.

4470. _____. "Fortifications on the Plains: Fort Dodge, Kansas, 1864-1882." 1960 Brand Book of the Denver Posse of Westerners 16 (1961): 136-179.

4471. Pedersen, Lyman Clarence, Jr. "History of Fort Douglas, Utah." Ph.D. dissertation, Brigham Young University, 1967.

4472. Reinhardt, George C. "Fort Leavenworth Is Born." Military Review 33 (October 1953): 3-8.

4473. _____. "Fort Leavenworth Grows Up." Military Review 33 (March 1954): 16-33.

4474. Riley, Paul D. "Dr. David Franklin Powell and Fort McPherson." Nebraska History 51 (Summer 1970): 153-170.

4475. Rothermich, Albert E., ed. "Early Days at Fort Missoula." Frontier and Midland 16 (Spring 1936): 225-235.

4476. Ryan, Garry David. "Camp Walbach, Nebraska Territory, 1858-1859: The Military Post at Cheyenne Pass." Annals of Wyoming 35 (April 1963): 5-20.

4477. Sheldon, Addison E. "Old Fort Kearny." Publications of the Nebraska State Historical Society 21 (1930): 269-279.

4478. Slaughter, Linda W. "Fort Randall." Collections of the State Historical Society of North Dakota 1 (1906): 423-429.

4479. Spear, Elsa. Fort Phil Kearny, Dakota Territory, 1866-1868. Sheridan, Wyoming: Quick Printing Company, 1939.

4480. Spring, Agnes Wright. "The Founding of Fort Collins, United States Military Post." Colorado Magazine 10 (March 1933): 47-55.

4481. Strate, David Kay. Sentinel to the Cimarron: The Frontier Experience of Fort Dodge, Kansas. Dodge City, Kansas: Cultural Heritage and Arts Center, 1970.

4482. Sweet, J. H. "Old Fort Kearny."

Nebraska History 27 (October-December 1946): 233-243.

4483. Taylor, Morris F. "Fort Stevens, Fort Reynolds, and the Defense of Southern Colorado." *Colorado Magazine* 49 (Spring 1972): 143-162.

4484. _____. "Fort Wise." *Colorado Magazine* 46 (Spring 1969): 93-119.

4485. Unrau, William E. "The Story of Fort Larned." *Kansas Historical Quarterly* 23 (Autumn 1957): 257-280.

4486. Upton, Richard, ed. *Fort Custer on the Big Horn, 1877-1898: Its History and Personalities As Told and Pictured by Its Contemporaries.* Glendale, California: Arthur H. Clark Company, 1973.

4487. Walton, George H. *Sentinel of the Plains: Fort Leavenworth and the American West.* Englewood Cliffs, New Jersey: Prentice-Hall, 1973.

4488. Watkins, Albert. "History of Fort Kearny." *Collections of the Nebraska State Historical Society* 16 (1911): 227-267.

4489. Welty, Raymond L. "The Army Fort of the Frontier, 1860-1870." *North Dakota Historical Quarterly* 2 (April 1928): 155-167.

4490. Wertenberger, Mildred. "Fort Totten, Dakota Territory, 1867." *North Dakota History* 34 (Spring 1967): 125-146.

4491. Wesley, Edgar Bruce. "Life at a Frontier Post: Fort Atkinson, 1823-1826." *Journal of the American Military Institute* 3 (Winter 1939): 203-209.

4492. _____. "Life at Fort Atkinson." *Nebraska History* 30 (December 1949): 348-358.

4493. Willman, Lillian M. "The History of Fort Kearny." *Publications of the Nebraska State Historical Society* 21 (1930): 211-249.

Oklahoma and Texas

Indian hostilities on the southern plains called for numerous military establishments.

4494. Barrett, Arrie. "Western Frontier Forts of Texas, 1845-1861." *West Texas Historical Association Year Book* 7 (1931): 115-139.

4495. Braly, Earl Burk. "Fort Belknap of the Texas Frontier." *West Texas Historical Association Year Book* 30 (October 1954): 83-114.

4496. "A Brief History of Fort Sill and the Field Artillery School." *Field Artillery Journal* 23 (November-December 1933): 528-541.

4497. Brown, Marion T. *Letters from Fort Sill, 1886-1887.* Edited by C. Richard King. Austin: Encino Press, 1970.

4498. Carriker, Robert C. *Fort Supply, Indian Territory: Frontier Outpost on the Plains.* Norman: University of Oklahoma Press, 1970.

4499. Chapman, John. "Fort Concho." *Southwest Review* 25 (April 1940): 258-286.

4500. _____. "Fort Griffin." *Southwest Review* 27 (Summer 1942): 426-455.

4501. _____. "Old Fort Richardson." *Southwest Review* 38 (Winter 1953): 62-69.

4502. Crimmins, M. L. "Camp Cooper and Fort Griffin, Texas." *West Texas Historical Association Year Book* 17 (October 1941): 32-43.

4503. _____. "The First Line of Army Posts Established in West Texas in 1849." *West Texas Historical Association Year Book* 19 (1943): 121-127.

4504. _____. "Fort Elliott, Texas." *West Texas Historical Association Year Book* 23 (October 1947): 3-12.

4505. _____. "Fort McKavett, Texas." *Southwestern Historical Quarterly* 38 (July 1934): 28-39.

4506. _____. "General Mackenzie and Fort Concho." *West Texas Historical Association Year Book* 10 (October 1934): 16-31.

4507. _____. "History of Camp Colorado, Texas." *Frontier Times* 13 (May 1936): 402-408.

4508. _____. "The Military History of Camp Colorado." *West Texas Historical Association Year Book* 28 (October 1952): 71-80.

4509. _____. "Old Fort Duncan: A Frontier Post." *Frontier Times* 15 (June 1938): 379-385.

4510. _____. "Old Fort Richardson." *Frontier Times* 17 (July 1940): 421-424.

4511. Crook, Cornelia, and Garland Crook. "Fort Lincoln, Texas." *Texas Military History* 4 (Fall 1964): 145-161.

4512. Fletcher, Henry T. "Old Fort Lancaster." *West Texas Historical and Scientific Society Publications* 4 (1932): 33-44.

4513. Foreman, Grant. "The Centennial of Fort Gibson." *Chronicles of Oklahoma* 2 (June 1924): 119-128.

4514. _____. Fort Gibson: A Brief History. 2d edition. Norman: University of Oklahoma Press, 1943.

4515. Griswold, Gillett. "Old Fort Sill: The First Seven Years." Chronicles of Oklahoma 36 (Spring 1958): 2-14.

4516. Haley, James Evetts. Fort Concho and the Texas Frontier. San Angelo, Texas: San Angelo Standard-Times, 1952.

4517. Hatcher, John H. "Fort Phantom Hill." Texas Military History 3 (Fall 1963): 154-164.

4518. Hopper, W. L. "The Birth and Death of an Army Fort." Military History of Texas and the Southwest 10 (1972): 273-277. Fort Stockton.

4519. Kalisch, Philip A., and Beatrice J. Kalisch. "Indian Territory Forts: Charnel Houses of the Frontier, 1839-1865." Chronicles of Oklahoma 50 (Spring 1972): 65-81.

4520. Knight, Oliver. Fort Worth, Outpost on the Trinity. Norman: University of Oklahoma Press, 1953.

4521. Lackey, Vinson. The Forts of Oklahoma. Edited by Muriel O. Lackey. Tulsa, Oklahoma, 1963.

4522. Morrison, William Brown. "Fort Arbuckle." Chronicles of Oklahoma 6 (March 1928): 26-34.

4523. _____. "Fort Towson." Chronicles of Oklahoma 8 (June 1930): 226-232.

4524. _____. "Fort Washita." Chronicles of Oklahoma 5 (June 1927): 251-258.

4525. _____. Military Posts and Camps in Oklahoma. Oklahoma City: Harlow Publishing Corporation, 1936.

4526. Mueller, Esther. "Old Fort Martin Scott, at Fredericksburg." Frontier Times 14 (August 1937): 463-468.

4527. Nye, Wilbur Sturtevant. Carbine and Lance: The Story of Old Fort Sill. Norman: University of Oklahoma Press, 1937. 3d edition, revised, 1969.

4528. Oneal, Ben G. "The Beginnings of Fort Belknap." Southwestern Historical Quarterly 61 (April 1958): 508-521.

4529. Oswald, James M. "History of Fort Elliott." Panhandle-Plains Historical Review 32 (1959): 1-59.

4530. Rister, Carl Coke. "The Border Post of Phantom Hill." West Texas Historical Association Year Book 14 (October 1938): 3-13.

4531. _____. "Fort Griffin." West Texas Historical Association Year Book 1 (June 1925): 15-24.

4532. _____. Fort Griffin on the Texas Frontier. Norman: University of Oklahoma Press, 1956.

4533. Sanger, Donald Bridgman. The Story of Old Fort Bliss. El Paso: Hughes-Buie Company, 1933.

4534. Scobee, Barry. Old Fort Davis. San Antonio, Texas: Naylor Company, 1947.

4535. Sides, Joseph C. Fort Brown Historical: History of Fort Brown, Texas, Border Post on the Rio Grande. San Antonio, Texas: Naylor Company, 1942.

4536. Swett, Morris. Fort Sill: A History. Fort Sill, Oklahoma, 1921.

4537. Whisenhunt, Donald W. "Fort Richardson: Outpost on the Texas Frontier." Southwestern Studies 5, no. 4 (1968): 3-46.

4538. Wright, Muriel H. "A History of Fort Cobb." Chronicles of Oklahoma 34 (Spring 1956): 53-71.

The Southwest

American occupation of the Southwest after the Mexican War brought frequent conflict with the Indians of the region. Numerous military posts were built in New Mexico and Arizona to protect the white miners and settlers.

4539. Avillo, Philip J., Jr. "Fort Mojave: Outpost on the Upper Colorado." Journal of Arizona History 11 (Summer 1970): 77-100.

4540. Ayres, Mary C. "History of Fort Lewis, Colorado." Colorado Magazine 8 (May 1931): 81-92.

4541. Bender, Averam B. "Military Posts in the Southwest, 1848-1860." New Mexico Historical Review 16 (April 1941): 125-147.

4542. Brandes, Ray. Frontier Military Posts of Arizona. Globe, Arizona: D. S. King, 1960.

4543. _____. "A Guide to the History of the U.S. Army Installations in Arizona, 1849-1886." Arizona and the West 1 (Spring 1959): 42-65.

4544. Chapel, William L. "Camp Rucker: Outpost in Apacheria." Journal of Arizona History 14 (Summer 1973): 95-112.

4545. Cohrs, Timothy. "Fort Selden, New Mexico." El Palacio 79 (March 1974): 13-39.

4546. Crimmins, M. L. "Fort Fillmore."

New Mexico Historical Review 6 (October 1931): 327-333.

4547. _____. "Fort Massachusetts, First United States Military Post in Colorado." Colorado Magazine 14 (July 1937): 128-135.

4548. Crocchiola, Stanley Francis Louis [F. Stanley]. Fort Bascom, Commanche-Kiowa Barrier. Pampa, Texas: Pampa Print Shop, 1961.

4549. _____. The Fort Conrad, New Mexico, Story. Dumas, Texas, 1961.

4550. _____. Fort Craig. Pampa, Texas: Pampa Print Shop, 1963.

4551. _____. The Fort Fillmore, New Mexico, Story. Pantex, Texas, 1961.

4552. _____. Fort Stanton. Pampa, Texas: Pampa Print Shop, 1964.

4553. _____. The Fort Thorn, New Mexico, Story. Pep, Texas, 1965.

4554. _____. The Fort Tulerosa, New Mexico, Story. Pep, Texas, 1968.

4555. _____. Fort Union (New Mexico). Rotan, Texas, 1953.

4556. Egan, Ferol. "The Building of Fort Churchill: Blueprint for a Military Fiasco, 1860." American West 9 (March 1972): 4-9.

4557. Emmett, Chris. Fort Union and the Winning of the Southwest. Norman: University of Oklahoma Press, 1965.

4558. Foster, James Monroe, Jr. "Fort Bascom, New Mexico." New Mexico Historical Review 35 (January 1960): 30-62.

4559. Kayser, David. "Fort Tulerosa: 1872-1874." El Palacio 79 (September 1973): 24-27.

4560. Kelly, Lawrence C. "Where Was Fort Canby?" New Mexico Historical Review 42 (January 1967): 49-62.

4561. Lockwood, Frank C. "Early Military Posts in Arizona." Arizona Historical Review 2 (January 1930): 91-97.

4562. McNitt, Frank. "Fort Sumner: A Study in Origins." New Mexico Historical Review 45 (April 1970): 101-117.

4563. _____. "Old Fort Wingate: The Inspection Reports." El Palacio 78 (June 1972): 30-36.

4564. Murphy, Lawrence R. "Cantonment Burgwin, New Mexico, 1852-1860." Arizona and the West 15 (Spring 1973): 5-26.

4565. Myers, Lee. "Fort Webster on the Mimbres River." New Mexico Historical

Review 41 (January 1966): 47-57.

4566. Nankivell, John H. "Fort Crawford, Colorado, 1880-1890." Colorado Magazine 11 (January 1934): 54-64.

4567. _____. "Fort Garland, Colorado." Colorado Magazine 16 (January 1939): 13-28.

4568. Pierson, Lloyd. "A Short History of Camp Verde, Arizona, to 1890." El Palacio 64 (November-December 1957): 323-339.

4569. Sacks, B. "The Origins of Fort Buchanan: Myth and Fact." Arizona and the West 7 (Autumn 1965): 207-226.

4570. Schilling, Frank A. "Military Posts of the Old Frontier: Arizona--New Mexico." Historical Society of Southern California Quarterly 42 (June 1960): 133-149.

4571. Sleight, Eleanor Friend. "Fort Defiance." El Palacio 60 (January 1953): 3-11.

4572. Stewart, Ronald L. "Fort Sumner: An Adobe Post on the Pecos." El Palacio 77 (Fall 1971): 12-16.

4573. Utley, Robert M. "Fort Union and the Santa Fe Trail." New Mexico Historical Review 36 (January 1961): 36-48.

4574. _____. Fort Union National Monument, New Mexico. National Park Service Historical Handbook Series, no. 35. Washington: National Park Service, 1962.

4575. _____. "The Past and Future of Old Fort Bowie." Arizoniana 5 (Winter 1964): 55-60.

4576. Vandenbusche, Duane. "Life at a Frontier Post: Fort Garland." Colorado Magazine 43 (Spring 1966): 132-148.

4577. Wood, Henry. "Fort Union: End of the Santa Fe Trail." Westerners Brand Book (Denver) 3 (1947): 205-256.

California and the Pacific Northwest

Movement of Americans into the Pacific Northwest and into California in the 1840s and 1850s expanded defense lines, and forts were built on the new Indian frontiers.

4578. Beckham, Stephen Dow. "Lonely Outpost: The Army's Fort Umpqua." Oregon Historical Quarterly 70 (September 1969): 233-257.

4579. Cowell, Ray Theodore. "History of Fort Townsend." Washington Historical Quarterly 16 (October 1925): 284-289.

4580. Culverwell, Albert. "Stronghold in the Yakima Country: Fort Simcoe and the Indian War, 1856-59." Pacific Northwest Quarterly 46 (April 1955): 46-51.

4581. _____. Stronghold in the Yakima Country: The Story of Fort Simcoe, 1856-1859. Olympia, Washington: Washington State Parks and Recreation Commission, 1956.

4582. Giffen, Helen S. "Camp Independence--an Owens Valley Outpost." Historical Society of Southern California Quarterly 24 (December 1942): 129-142.

4583. _____. "Fort Miller--a Memory of the San Joaquin." Journal of the West 2 (April 1963): 205-212.

4584. _____. "Fort Miller and Millerton: Memories of the Southern Mines." Historical Society of Southern California Quarterly 21 (March 1939): 5-16.

4585. Guie, H. Dean. Bugles in the Valley: Garnett's Fort Simcoe. Yakima, Washington, 1956.

4586. Hoop, Oscar Winslow. "History of Fort Hoskins, 1856-65." Oregon Historical Quarterly 30 (December 1929): 346-361.

4587. Kenny, Judith Keyes. "The Founding of Camp Watson." Oregon Historical Quarterly 58 (March 1957): 5-16.

4588. Knuth, Priscilla. "Picturesque Frontier: The Army's Fort Dalles." Oregon Historical Quarterly 68 (March 1967): 5-52.

4589. Oliphant, J. Orin. "Old Fort Colville." Washington Historical Quarterly 16 (January 1925): 29-48.

4590. Onstad, Preston E. "The Fort on the Luckiamute: A Resurvey of Fort Hoskins." Oregon Historical Quarterly 65 (June 1964): 173-196.

4591. Rogers, Fred B. "Early Military Posts of Del Norte County." California Historical Society Quarterly 26 (March 1947): 1-11.

4592. _____. "Early Military Posts of Mendocino County, California." California Historical Society Quarterly 27 (September 1948): 215-228.

4593. Waitman, Leonard. "The History of Camp Cady." Historical Society of Southern California Quarterly 36 (March 1954): 49-91.

4594. Whiting, J. S. Forts of the State of Washington: A Record of Military and Semi-Military Establishments Designated as Forts from May 29, 1792, to November 15, 1951. Seattle, 1951.

4595. Whiting, J. S., and Richard J. Whiting. Forts of the State of California. Seattle, 1960.

4596. Winans, W. P. "Fort Colville 1859 to 1869." Washington Historical Quarterly 3 (October 1908): 78-82.

4597. Woodward, Arthur. "Fort Tejon--a Nursery of the Army." In Helen S. Giffen and Arthur Woodward, The Story of El Tejon, pp. 57-137. Los Angeles: Dawson's Book Shop, 1942.

MILITARY PERSONNEL

Army Officers

Many military men had great interest in Indian affairs and had influence in both military relations with the Indians and in the formulation of Indian policy. Biographical writings by and about some important officers, with a few related accounts, are listed here. No attempt has been made to list the numerous reminiscences published by soldiers in the Indian wars, although some of them are entered under the appropriate military engagement. Material on Custer is entered separately below.

4598. Athearn, Robert G. William Tecumseh Sherman and the Settlement of the West. Norman: University of Oklahoma Press, 1956.

4599. Bailey, John W. "General Terry and the Decline of the Sioux, 1866-1890." Ph.D. dissertation, Marquette University, 1974.

4600. Bourke, John G. "Bourke on the Southwest," edited by Lansing B. Bloom. New Mexico Historical Review 8 (January 1933): 1-30; 9 (January 1934): 33-77; (April 1934): 159-183; (July 1934): 273-289; (October 1934): 375-435; 10 (January 1935): 1-35; (October 1935): 271-322; 11 (January 1936): 77-122; (April 1936): 188-207; (July 1936): 217-282; 12 (January 1937): 41-77; (October 1937): 337-379; 13 (April 1938): 192-238.

4601. Carlson, Paul Howard. "William R. Shafter: Military Commander in the American West." Ph.D. dissertation, Texas Tech University, 1973.

4602. Carpenter, John A. Sword and Olive Branch: Oliver Otis Howard. Pittsburgh: University of Pittsburgh Press, 1964.

4603. Carter, Harvey Lewis. 'Dear Old Kit': The Historical Christopher Carson, with a New Edition of the Carson Memoirs. Norman: University of Oklahoma Press, 1968.

4604. Clarke, Dwight L. Stephen Watts

Kearny: Soldier of the West. Norman: University of Oklahoma Press, 1961.

4605. Cooke, Philip St. George. Scenes and Adventures in the Army; or, Romance of Military Life. Philadelphia: Lindsay and Blakiston, 1857.

4606. Crook, George. General George Crook, His Autobiography. Edited and annotated by Martin F. Schmitt. Norman: University of Oklahoma Press, 1946.

4607. Davidson, Homer K. Black Jack Davidson, a Cavalry Commander on the Western Frontier: The Life of General John W. Davidson. Glendale, California: Arthur H. Clark Company, 1974.

4608. Elliott, Charles W. Winfield Scott: The Soldier and the Man. New York: Macmillan Company, 1937.

4609. Ellis, Richard N. "After Bull Run: The Later Career of Gen. John Pope." Montana, the Magazine of Western History 19 (Autumn 1969): 46-57.

4610. _____. "General John Pope and the Southern Plains Indians, 1875-1883." Southwestern Historical Quarterly 72 (October 1968): 152-169.

4611. _____. General Pope and U.S. Indian Policy. Albuquerque: University of New Mexico Press, 1970.

4612. _____. "The Humanitarian Generals." Western Historical Quarterly 3 (April 1972): 169-178.

4613. _____. "The Humanitarian Soldiers." Journal of Arizona History 10 (Summer 1969): 53-66.

4614. Foreman, Carolyn Thomas. "General Philip St. George Cooke." Chronicles of Oklahoma 32 (Summer 1954): 195-213.

4615. Forsyth, George A. Thrilling Days in Army Life. New York: Harper and Brothers, 1900.

4616. Griswold, Oliver. "William Selby Harney: Indian Fighter." Tequesta 9 (1949): 73-80.

4617. Hagemann, E. R., ed. Fighting Rebels and Redskins: Experiences in Army Life of Colonel George B. Sanford, 1861-1892. Norman: University of Oklahoma Press, 1969.

4618. Hamilton, Holman. Zachary Taylor: Soldier of the Republic. Indianapolis: Bobbs-Merrill Company, 1941.

4619. Hay, Thomas Robson, and M. R. Werner. The Admirable Trumpeter: A Biography of General James Wilkinson. Garden City, New York: Doubleday, Doran and Company, 1941.

4620. Heyman, Max L., Jr. Prudent Soldier: A Biography of Major General E. R. S. Canby, 1817-1873. Glendale, California: Arthur H. Clark Company, 1959.

4621. Hinton, Harwood P. "The Military Career of John Ellis Wool, 1812-1863." Ph.D. dissertation, University of Wisconsin, 1960.

4622. Hitchcock, Ethan Allen. Fifty Years in Camp and Field: Diary of Major-General Ethan Allen Hitchcock, U.S.A., edited by W. A. Croffut. New York: G. P. Putnam's Sons, 1909.

4623. Howard, Oliver O. My Life and Experiences among Our Hostile Indians. Hartford, Connecticut: A. D. Worthington and Company, 1907.

4624. Hunt, Aurora. Major General James Henry Carleton, 1814-1873: Western Frontier Dragoon. Glendale, California: Arthur H. Clark Company, 1958.

4625. Jacobs, James Ripley. Tarnished Warrior, Major-General James Wilkinson. New York: Macmillan Company, 1938.

4626. Johnson, Virginia Weisel. The Unregimented General: A Biography of Nelson A. Miles. Boston: Houghton Mifflin, 1962.

4627. Keyes, E. D. Fifty Years' Observations of Men and Events, Civil and Military. New York: Charles Scribner's Sons, 1885.

4628. King, James T. "George Crook: Indian Fighter and Humanitarian." Arizona and the West 9 (Winter 1967): 333-348.

4629. _____. "Needed: A Re-evaluation of General George Crook." Nebraska History 45 (September 1964): 223-236.

4630. _____. War Eagle: A Life of General Eugene A. Carr. Lincoln: University of Nebraska Press, 1963.

4631. Kroeker, Marvin. "Colonel W. B. Hazen in the Indian Territory, 1868-1869." Chronicles of Oklahoma 42 (Spring 1964): 53-73.

4632. _____. "William B. Hazen: A Military Career in the Frontier West, 1855-1880." Ph.D. dissertation, University of Oklahoma, 1967.

4633. Long, William Wallace. "A Biography of Major General Edwin Vose Sumner, U.S.A., 1797-1863." Ph.D. dissertation, University of New Mexico, 1971.

4634. McCall, George A. Letters from the Frontiers, Written during a Period of Thirty Years' Service in the Army of the United States. Philadelphia: J. B.

Lippincott and Company, 1868.

4635. Marcy, Randolph B. Thirty Years
of Army Life on the Border. New York:
Harper and Brothers, 1866.

4636. Mattes, Merrill J. Indians, Infants,
and Infantry: Andrew and Elizabeth Burt
on the Frontier. Denver: Old West Publishing Company, 1960.

4637. Miles, Nelson A. Personal Recollections and Observations. Chicago: Werner
Company, 1896.

4638. _____. Serving the Republic:
Memoirs of the Civil and Military Life
of Nelson A. Miles. New York: Harper
and Brothers, 1911.

4639. Mills, Anson. My Story. Edited by
C. H. Claudy. Washington, 1918.

4640. Nalty, Bernard C., and Truman R.
Strobridge. "Captain Emmet Crawford:
Commander of Apache Scouts 1882-1886."
Arizona and the West 6 (Spring 1964):
30-40.

4641. _____. "Emmet Crawford, Pennsylvania Volunteer Turned Indian Fighter."
Pennsylvania History 33 (April 1966):
204-214.

4642. Nichols, Roger L. General Henry
Atkinson: A Western Military Career.
Norman: University of Oklahoma Press,
1965.

4643. Nohl, Lessing H., Jr. "Bad Hand:
The Military Career of Ranald Slidell
Mackenzie, 1871-1889." Ph.D. disserta-
tion, University of New Mexico, 1962.

4644. Peterson, Clell T. "Charles King:
Soldier and Novelist." American Book
Collector 16 (December 1965): 8-12.

4645. Reed, William. "William Babcock
Hazen: Curmudgeon or Crusader?" In
Troopers West: Military and Indian Af-
fairs on the American Frontier, edited
by Ray Brandes, pp. 135-147. San Diego:
Frontier Heritage Press, 1970.

4646. Rister, Carl Coke. Border Command:
General Phil Sheridan in the West.
Norman: University of Oklahoma Press,
1944.

4647. Russell, Don. "Captain Charles King,
Chronicler of the Frontier." Westerners
Brand Book (Chicago) 9 (March 1952): 1-3,
7-8.

4648. _____. One Hundred and Three
Fights and Scrimmages: The Story of
General Reuben F. Bernard. Washington:
United States Cavalry Association, 1936.

4649. Scott, Winfield. Memoirs of Lieut.-
General Scott, LL.D., Written by Him-

self. 2 volumes. New York: Sheldon and
Company, 1864.

4650. Sheridan, Philip H. Personal Memoirs
of P. H. Sheridan, General, United
States Army. 2 volumes. New York: C. L.
Webster and Company, 1888.

4651. Silver, James W. "Edmund Pendleton
Gaines and Frontier Problems, 1801-1849."
Journal of Southern History 1 (August
1935): 320-344.

4652. _____. Edmund Pendleton Gaines,
Frontier General. Baton Rouge: Louisiana State University Press, 1949.

4653. Spring, Agnes Wright. Caspar Collins: The Life and Exploits of an Indian Fighter of the Sixties. New York:
Columbia University Press, 1927.

4654. Trobriand, Philippe Regis de. Military Life in Dakota: The Journal of
Philippe Regis de Trobriand, translated and edited by Lucile M. Kane. St.
Paul: Alvord Memorial Commission, 1951.

4655. Walker, Henry P. "George Crook,
'The Gray Fox': Prudent, Compassionate
Indian Fighter." Montana, the Magazine
of Western History 17 (April 1967): 2-13.

4656. Wallace, Andrew. "General August
V. Kautz in Arizona, 1874-1878."
Arizoniana 4 (Winter 1963): 54-65.

4657. _____. "Soldier in the Southwest: The Career of General A. V. Kautz,
1869-1886." Ph.D. dissertation, University of Arizona, 1968.

4658. Wallace, Edward S. "Border Warrior."
American Heritage 9 (June 1958): 22-25,
101-105. Ranald Slidell Mackenzie.

4659. Wallace, Ernest. "Prompt in the
Saddle: The Military Career of Ranald S.
Mackenzie." Military History of Texas
and the Southwest 9 (1971): 161-189.

4660. _____. Ranald S. Mackenzie on
the Texas Frontier. Lubbock, Texas:
West Texas Museum Association, 1964.

4661. Young, Otis E. The West of Philip
St. George Cooke, 1809-1895. Glendale,
California: Arthur H. Clark Company,
1955.

4662. Zimmerman, Jean L. "Colonel Ranald
S. Mackenzie at Fort Sill." Chronicles
of Oklahoma 44 (Spring 1966): 12-21.

George Armstrong Custer

In addition to the large number of writings about particular military exploits
of Custer, especially the Battle of the
Little Big Horn, there are biographical
works on the general.

4663. Bell, Gordon L., and Beth L. Bell. "General Custer in North Dakota." North Dakota History 31 (April 1964): 101-113.

4664. Brigham, Earl K. "Custer's Meeting with Secretary of War Belknap at Fort Abraham Lincoln." North Dakota History 19 (April 1952): 129-131.

4665. Byrne, P. E. "The Custer Myth." North Dakota Historical Quarterly 6 (April 1932): 187-200.

4666. Custer, Elizabeth B. "Boots and Saddles"; or, Life in Dakota with General Custer. New York: Harper and Brothers, 1885.

4667. _____. Following the Guidon. New York: Harper and Brothers, 1890.

4668. _____. Tenting on the Plains; or, General Custer in Kansas and Texas. New York: C. L. Webster and Company, 1887.

4669. Custer, George Armstrong. My Life on the Plains; or, Personal Experiences with Indians. New York: Sheldon and Company, 1874.

4670. _____. Wild Life on the Plains and Horrors of Indian Warfare. St. Louis: Royal Publishing Company, 1891. Pirated edition of My Life on the Plains with much added material.

4671. Dellenbaugh, Frederick S. George Armstrong Custer. New York: Macmillan Company, 1917.

4672. Ege, Robert J. Curse Not His Curls. Fort Collins, Colorado: Old Army Press, 1974.

4673. Fougera, Katherine Gibson. With Custer's Cavalry. Caldwell, Idaho: Caxton Printers, 1940.

4674. Frost, Lawrence A. The Court-Martial of General George Armstrong Custer. Norman: University of Oklahoma Press, 1968.

4675. _____. "Let's Have a Fair Fight!" Westerner's Brand Book (Chicago) 14 (June 1957): 25-27, 29-32.

4676. Gray, John S. "Custer Throws a Boomerang." Montana, the Magazine of Western History 11 (April 1961): 2-12.

4677. Hofling, Charles K. "General Custer and the Battle of the Little Big Horn." Psychoanalytic Review 54 (Summer 1967): 303-328. Reprinted under the title, "George Armstrong Custer: A Psychoanalytic Approach." Montana, the Magazine of Western History 21 (Spring 1971): 32-43.

4678. Johnson, Dorothy M. "Custer Rides Again." Montana, the Magazine of Western History 17 (Spring 1967): 53-63.

4679. Josephy, Alvin M., Jr. "The Custer Myth." Life 71 (July 2, 1971): 48-52, 55-59.

4680. Kinsley, D. A. Favor the Bold: Custer the Indian Fighter. 2 volumes. New York: Holt, Rinehart and Winston, 1967-1968.

4681. Merington, Marguerite, ed. The Custer Story: The Life and Intimate Letters of General George A. Custer and His Wife Elizabeth. New York: Devin-Adair, 1950.

4682. Millbrook, Minnie Dubbs. "The Boy General and How He Grew: George Custer after Appomattox." Montana, the Magazine of Western History 23 (April 1973): 34-43.

4683. _____. "Custer's First Scout in the West." Kansas Historical Quarterly 39 (Spring 1973): 75-95.

4684. _____. "A Monument to Custer." Montana, the Magazine of Western History 24 (April 1974): 18-33.

4685. _____. "The West Breaks in General Custer." Kansas Historical Quarterly 36 (Summer 1970): 113-148.

4686. Monaghan, Jay. Custer: The Life of General George Armstrong Custer. Boston: Little, Brown and Company, 1959.

4687. Murray, Robert A. "The Custer Court-Martial." Annals of Wyoming 36 (October 1964): 174-184.

4688. Ronsheim, Milton. The Life of General Custer. Cadiz, Ohio, 1929.

4689. Rosenberg, Bruce A. Custer and the Epic of Defeat. University Park: Pennsylvania State University Press, 1974.

4690. Steckmesser, Kent L. "Custer in Fiction: George A. Custer, Hero or Villain?" American West 1 (Fall 1964): 47-52, 63-64.

4691. Stewart, Edgar I. "A Psychoanalytic Approach to Custer: Some Reflections." Montana, the Magazine of Western History 21 (July 1971): 74-77.

4692. Stewart, Edgar I., ed. "I Rode with Custer." Montana Magazine of History 4 (Summer 1954): 17-29. Account of Edwin Pickard.

4693. Utley, Robert M. "Custer: Hero or Butcher?" American History Illustrated 5 (February 1971): 4-9, 43-48.

4694. Van de Water, Frederick F. Glory Hunter: A Life of General Custer. Indianapolis: Bobbs-Merrill Company, 1934.

4695. Whittaker, Frederick. A Complete Life of General George A. Custer. New York: Sheldon and Company, 1876.

Indian Scouts

In many of the Indian wars the United States army was aided by Indians who acted as scouts. Listed here are studies of those men and of white scouts in the Indian wars.

4696. Ball, Eve. "The Apache Scouts: A Chiricahua Appraisal." Arizona and the West 7 (Winter 1965): 315-328.

4697. Cook, James H. Fifty Years on the Old Frontier, as Cowboy, Hunter, Guide, Scout, and Ranchman. New Haven: Yale University Press, 1923.

4698. Cullinane, Daniel B. "The Last Indian Scouts." Password 5 (July 1960): 101-104.

4699. Danker, Donald F. "The North Brothers and the Pawnee Scouts." Nebraska History 42 (September 1961): 161-179.

4700. Doerner, Rita. "Sinew Riley, Apache Scout." Journal of Arizona History 14 (Winter 1973): 271-280.

4701. Downey, Fairfax, and Jacques Noel Jacobsen, Jr. The Red/Bluecoats: The Indian Scouts, U.S. Army. Fort Collins, Colorado: Old Army Press, 1973.

4702. Ellis, Richard N. "Copper-Skinned Soldiers: The Apache Scouts." Great Plains Journal 5 (Spring 1966): 51-67.

4703. Goodwin, Grenville, ed. "Experiences of an Indian Scout: Excerpts from the Life of John Rope, an 'Old Timer' of the White Mountain Apaches." Arizona Historical Review 7 (January 1936): 31-68; (April 1936): 31-73.

4704. Gray, John S. "What Made Johnnie Bruguier Run?" Montana, the Magazine of Western History 14 (April 1964): 34-39.

4705. _____. "Will Comstock, Scout: The Natty Bumpo of Kansas." Montana, the Magazine of Western History 20 (July 1970): 2-15.

4706. Grinnell, George Bird. Two Great Scouts and Their Pawnee Battalion: The Experiences of Frank J. North and Luther H. North, Pioneers in the Great West, 1856-1882, and Their Defence of the Building of the Union Pacific Railroad. Cleveland: Arthur H. Clark Company, 1928.

4707. Innis, Ben. Bloody Knife! Custer's Favorite Scout. Fort Collins, Colorado: Old Army Press, 1973.

4708. Kelly, Luther S. "Yellowstone Kelly":

The Memoirs of Luther S. Kelly. Edited by Milo M. Quaife. New Haven: Yale University Press, 1926.

4709. Kinsley, H. B. "Frank Grouard--Government Scout in the Days of Sitting Bull." Overland Monthly 81 (August 1923): 18-19, 38-39, 47.

4710. Lyon, Kuana Fraser. "Archie McIntosh, the Scottish Indian Scout." Journal of Arizona History 7 (Autumn 1966): 103-122.

4711. Mason, Joyce Evelyn. "The Use of Indian Scouts in the Apache Wars, 1870-1886." Ph.D. dissertation, Indiana University, 1970.

4712. Porter, Kenneth Wiggins. "The Seminole Negro-Indian Scouts, 1870-1881." Southwestern Historical Quarterly 55 (January 1952): 358-377.

4713. Simms, D. Harper. "The Apache Scouts Who Won a War." In Great Western Indian Fights, pp. 257-265. Garden City, New York: Doubleday and Company, 1960.

4714. _____. "The Incredible Story of the Chiricahua Scouts." Westerners Brand Book (Chicago) 13 (August 1956): 41-43, 46-48.

4715. Swett, Morris. "Sergeant I-See-O, Kiowa Indian Scout." Chronicles of Oklahoma 13 (September 1935): 341-354.

4716. Thrapp, Dan L. Al Sieber: Chief of Scouts. Norman: University of Oklahoma Press, 1964.

4717. _____. "Dan O'Leary, Arizona Scout: A Vignette." Arizona and the West 7 (Winter 1965): 287-298.

4718. Wellman, Paul I. "Some Famous Kansas Frontier Scouts." Kansas Historical Quarterly 1 (August 1932): 345-359.

4719. Wharfield, H. B. Apache Indian Scouts. El Cajon, California, 1964.

4720. _____. "Apache Kid and the Record." Journal of Arizona History 6 (Spring 1965): 37-46.

4721. _____. With Scouts and Cavalry at Fort Apache. Edited by John Alexander Carroll. Tucson: Arizona Pioneer's Historical Society, 1965.

4722. Williamson, Dan R. "Al Sieber, Famous Scout of the Southwest." Arizona Historical Review 3 (January 1931): 60-76.

4723. _____. "Story of Oskay De No Tah, the Flying Fighter." Arizona Historical Review 3 (October 1930): 78-83.

GOVERNMENT EXPLORATIONS

The federal government sponsored explorations of the West, which brought whites into relations with Indians, often for the first time. Many of the expeditions were conducted by army officers or had army escorts.

The following bibliography is a useful guide to official reports of government explorations.

4724. Hasse, Adelaide R., comp. Reports of Explorations Printed in the Documents of the U.S. Government (a Contribution towards a Bibliography). Washington: Government Printing Office, 1899. Reprint, New York: Burt Franklin, 1969.

Listed here are reports of a number of significant explorations and some accounts of them by historians.

4725. Bakeless, John. Lewis and Clark, Partners in Discovery. New York: W. Morrow, 1947.

4726. Bartlett, Richard A. Great Surveys of the American West. Norman: University of Oklahoma Press, 1962.

4727. Bell, John R. The Journal of Captain John R. Bell, Official Journalist for the Stephen H. Long Expedition to the Rocky Mountains, 1820. Edited by Harlin M. Fuller and LeRoy R. Hafen. The Far West and the Rockies Historical Series, 1820-1875, volume 6. Glendale, California: Arthur H. Clark Company, 1957.

4728. Bender, Averam B. "The Texas Frontier, 1848-1861: II, Government Explorations in Texas, 1851-1860." Southwestern Historical Quarterly 38 (October 1934): 135-148.

4729. Clark, William. The Field Notes of Captain William Clark, 1803-1805. Edited by Ernest Staples Osgood. New Haven: Yale University Press, 1964.

4730. Coues, Elliott, ed. The Expeditions of Zebulon Montgomery Pike, to Headwaters of the Mississippi, through Louisiana Territory, and in New Spain, during the Years 1805-6-7. 3 volumes. New York: F. P. Harper, 1895.

4731. _____. History of the Expedition under the Command of Lewis and Clark, to the Sources of the Missouri River, Thence across the Rocky Mountains and down the Columbia River to the Pacific Ocean, Performed during the Years 1804-5-6, by Order of the Government of the United States. 4 volumes. New York: F. P. Harper, 1893.

4732. Cutright, Paul Russell. "Lewis on the Marias, 1806." Montana, the Magazine of Western History 18 (July 1968): 30-43.

4733. Doty, James Duane. "Official Journal, 1820, Expedition with Cass and Schoolcraft." Collections of the State Historical Society of Wisconsin 13 (1895): 163-219.

4734. Fremont, John Charles. Report of the Exploring Expedition to the Rocky Mountains in the Year 1842, and to Oregon and North California in the Years 1843-'44. Washington: Gales and Seaton, 1845.

4735. Goetzmann, William H. Army Exploration in the American West, 1803-1863. New Haven: Yale University Press, 1959.

4736. _____. Exploration and Empire: The Explorer and the Scientist in the Winning of the American West. New York: Alfred A. Knopf, 1966.

4737. Goodwin, Cardinal L. "A Larger View of the Yellowstone Expedition, 1819-1820." Mississippi Valley Historical Review 4 (December 1917): 299-313.

4738. Guinness, Ralph B. "The Purpose of the Lewis and Clark Expedition." Mississippi Valley Historical Review 20 (June 1933): 90-100.

4739. Hollon, W. Eugene. Beyond the Cross Timbers: The Travels of Randolph B. Marcy, 1812-1887. Norman: University of Oklahoma Press, 1955.

4740. _____. Lost Pathfinder: Zebulon Montgomery Pike. Norman: University of Oklahoma Press, 1949.

4741. Jackson, Donald. "Lewis and Clark among the Oto." Nebraska History 41 (December 1960): 237-248.

4742. _____. "Zebulon Pike and Nebraska." Nebraska History 47 (December 1966): 355-369.

4743. Jackson, Donald, ed. The Journals of Zebulon Montgomery Pike with Letters and Related Documents. 2 volumes. Norman: University of Oklahoma Press, 1966.

4744. _____. Letters of the Lewis and Clark Expedition with Related Documents, 1783-1854. Urbana: University of Illinois Press, 1962.

4745. Jackson, Donald, and Mary Lee Spence, eds. The Expeditions of John Charles Fremont. Volume 1, Travels from 1838 to 1844. Urbana: University of Illinois Press, 1970.

4746. James, Edwin. An Account of an Expedition from Pittsburgh to the Rocky Mountains, Performed in the Years 1819, 1820. 2 volumes and atlas. Philadelphia: H. C. Carey and I. Lea, 1822-1823. 3 volumes. London: Longman, Hurst, Rees, Orme, and Brown, 1823. An account of the Stephen H. Long expediton.

4747. Kearny, Stephen Watts. "Journal of Stephen Watts Kearny: Part I, the Council Bluffs--St. Peter's Exploration (1820)," edited by Valentine Mott Porter. Missouri Historical Society Collections 3 (January 1908): 8-29; (April 1908): 99-131.

4748. Keating, William H. Narrative of an Expedition to the Source of St. Peter's River, Lake Winnepeek, Lake of the Woods, &c. &c. Performed in the Year 1823, by Order of the Hon. J. C. Calhoun, Secretary of War, under the Command of Stephen H. Long, Major U.S.T.E. 2 volumes. Philadelphia: H. C. Carey and I. Lea, 1824.

4749. Quaife, Milo M., ed. The Journals of Captain Meriwether Lewis and Sergeant John Ordway Kept on the Expedition of Western Exploration, 1803-1806. Madison: State Historical Society of Wisconsin, 1916.

4750. Ray, Verne F. Lewis and Clark and the Nez Perce Indians. Washington: Potomac Corral of the Westerners, 1971.

4751. Schoolcraft, Henry R. Narrative

Journal of Travels through the Northwestern Region of the United States Extending from Detroit through the Great Chain of American Lakes to the Sources of the Mississippi River, in the Year 1820. Edited by Mentor L. Williams. East Lansing: Michigan State College Press, 1953.

4752. Stegner, Wallace. Beyond the Hundredth Meridian: John Wesley Powell and the Second Opening of the West. Boston: Houghton Mifflin Company, 1954.

4753. Thwaites, Reuben Gold, ed. Original Journals of the Lewis and Clark Expedition, 1804-1806. 8 volumes. New York: Dodd, Mead, and Company, 1904-1905.

4754. Trowbridge, Charles C. "With Cass in the Northwest in 1820," edited by Ralph H. Brown. Minnesota History 23 (June 1942): 126-148; (September 1942): 233-252; (December 1942): 320-348.

4755. Wallace, Edward S. The Great Reconnaissance: Soldiers, Artists and Scientists on the Frontier 1848-1861. Boston: Little, Brown and Company, 1955.

4756. Wesley, Edgar B. "A Still Larger View of the So-Called Yellowstone Expedition." North Dakota Historical Quarterly 5 (July 1931): 219-238.

See also bibliographies and collections of western travels.

10
Trade and Traders

The first contacts between Indians and whites were often those of trade, and the regulation of the fur trade became an important element in government Indian policy.

GENERAL STUDIES ON INDIAN TRADE

The following bibliographies, although outdated, list numerous works on the fur trade.

4757. Cuthbertson, Stuart, and John C. Ewers. A Preliminary Bibliography on the American Fur Trade. St. Louis: Department of the Interior, National Park Service, 1939.

4758. Phillips, Paul Chrisler. "Bibliography." In The Fur Trade, 2: 577-656. 2 volumes. Norman: University of Oklahoma Press, 1961.

A number of studies deal with Indian trade comprehensively. Others discuss some particular aspect of the trade.

4759. Bolus, Malvina, ed. People and Pelts (Selected Papers: Second North American Fur Trade Conference). Winnipeg: Peguis Publishers, 1972.

4760. Clayton, James L. "The Growth and Economic Significance of the Fur Trade, 1790-1890." Minnesota History 40 (Winter 1966): 210-220.

4761. _____. "The Impact of Traders' Claims on the American Fur Trade." In The Frontier in American Development: Essays in Honor of Paul Wallace Gates, edited by David M. Ellis, pp. 299-322. Ithaca, New York: Cornell University Press, 1969.

4762. Courville, Cyril B. "Trade Tomahawks." Masterkey 37 (October-December 1963): 124-136.

4763. Finney, Frank F. "Troubles of Indian Traders Brings Senate Investigation." Chronicles of Oklahoma 36 (Spring 1958): 15-20.

4764. Goodwin, Cardinal. "The Fur Trade and the Northwest Boundary, 1783-1814." Annual Report of the American Historical Association for the Year 1921, pp. 200-204.

4765. Greenbie, Sydney. Frontiers and the Fur Trade. New York: John Day Company, 1929.

4766. Hickerson, Harold. "Fur Trade Colonialism and the North American Indians." Journal of Ethnic Studies 1 (Summer 1973): 15-44.

4767. Innis, Harold A. "Interrelations between the Fur Trade of Canada and the United States." Mississippi Valley Historical Review 20 (December 1933): 321-332.

4768. Kidd, Kenneth E. "Trade Goods Research Techniques." American Antiquity 20 (July 1954): 1-8.

4769. King, James C. "The Frontier Gunsmith and Indian Relations." Western Pennsylvania Historical Magazine 50 (January 1967): 23-32.

4770. Laut, Agnes C. The Fur Trade of America. New York: Macmillan Company, 1921.

4771. McManus, John C. "An Economic Analysis of Indian Behavior in the North American Fur Trade." Journal of Economic History 32 (March 1972): 36-53.

4772. Morgan, Dale L. "The Fur Trade and Its Historians." Minnesota History 40 (Winter 1966): 151-156.

4773. North American Fur Trade Conference. Aspects of the Fur Trade: Selected Papers. St. Paul: Minnesota Historical Society, 1967.

4774. Phillips, Paul Chrisler. The Fur Trade. 2 volumes. Norman: University of Oklahoma Press, 1961.

4775. Porter, Kenneth W. "Negroes and the Fur Trade." Minnesota History 15 (December 1934): 421-433.

4776. Quimby, George Irving. Indian Culture

and European Trade Goods: The Archaeology of the Historic Period in the Western Great Lakes Region. Madison: University of Wisconsin Press, 1966.

4777. Smith, Wallis. "The Fur Trade and the Frontier: A Study of an Inter-Cultural Alliance." Anthropologica 15 (1973): 21-35.

4778. Trennert, Robert A., Jr. "The Fur Trader as Indian Administrator: Conflict of Interest or Wise Policy?" South Dakota History 5 (Winter 1974): 1-19.

4779. _____. "William Medill's War with the Indian Traders, 1847." Ohio History 82 (Winter-Spring 1973): 46-62.

4780. Vandiveer, Clarence A. The Fur Trade and Early Western Explorations. Cleveland: Arthur H. Clark Company, 1929.

4781. Washburn, Wilcomb E. "Symbol, Utility, and Aesthetics in the Indian Fur Trade." Minnesota History 40 (Winter 1966-1967): 198-202.

COLONIAL INDIAN TRADE

The following is a preliminary bibliography on the colonial fur trade.

4782. Donnelly, Joseph P. A Tentative Bibliography for the Colonial Fur Trade in the American Colonies: 1608-1800. Saint Louis University Studies, Monograph Series, Social Science, no. 2. St. Louis: Saint Louis University Press, 1947.

The colonial fur trade was a chief point of contact between the colonists and the Indians, and traders became important diplomatic as well as economic figures.

4783. Anderson, Niles, and Edward G. Williams. "The Venango Path As Thomas Hutchins Knew It." Western Pennsylvania Historical Magazine 49 (January 1966): 1-18; (April 1966): 141-154.

4784. Andrews, Charles M. "Anglo-French Commercial Rivalry, 1700-1754: The Western Phase." American Historical Review 20 (April 1915): 539-556; (July 1915): 761-780.

4785. Armour, David A. "The Merchants of Albany, New York, 1686-1760." Ph.D. dissertation, Northwestern University, 1965.

4786. "Articles, Settlement and Offices of the Free Society of Traders in Pennsylvania." Pennsylvania Magazine of History and Biography 5 (1881): 37-50.

4787. Babcock, H. L. "The Beaver as a Factor in the Development of New England." Americana 11 (April 1916): 181-196.

4788. Bauman, Robert F. "The Ottawas of the Lakes, 1615-1766." Ohio Northwest Quarterly 31 (Autumn 1958): 186-210; (Winter 1958-1959): 38-64; 32 (Summer 1960): 86-101; (Autumn 1960): 138-172; 33 (Winter 1960-1961): 7-40; 35 (Spring 1963): 70-97; 36 (Winter 1964): 60-78; (Summer 1964): 146-167. A series of articles, under various titles, dealing chiefly with trade relations.

4789. Beauchamp, William M. The Life of Conrad Weiser As It Relates to His Services as Official Interpreter between New York and Pennsylvania, and as Envoy between Philadelphia and the Onondaga Councils. Syracuse: Onondaga Historical Association, 1925.

4790. Bolton, Herbert E. "Spanish Resistance to the Carolina Traders in Western Georgia (1680-1704)." Georgia Historical Quarterly 9 (June 1925): 115-130.

4791. Broshar, Helen. "The First Push Westward of the Albany Traders." Mississippi Valley Historical Review 7 (December 1920): 228-241.

4792. Buffinton, Arthur H. "New England and the Western Fur Trade, 1629-1675." Publications of the Colonial Society of Massachusetts, Transactions 18 (1915-1916): 160-192.

4793. _____. "The Policy of Albany and English Westward Expansion." Mississippi Valley Historical Review 8 (March 1922): 327-366.

4794. Crane, Verner W. "The Tennessee River as the Road to Carolina: The Beginnings of Exploration and Trade." Mississippi Valley Historical Review 3 (June 1916): 3-18.

4795. Croghan, George. "Letters of Colonel George Croghan." Pennsylvania Magazine of History and Biography 15 (1891): 429-439.

4796. Darlington, William M., ed. Christopher Gist's Journals with Historical, Geographical and Ethnological Notes and Biographies of His Contemporaries. Pittsburgh: J. R. Weldin and Company, 1893.

4797. Diffenderffer, F. R. "Indian Trader Troubles." Historical Papers and Addresses of the Lancaster County Historical Society 9 (1905): 305-326.

4798. Downes, Randolph C. "Problems of Trade in Early Western Pennsylvania." Western Pennsylvania Historical Magazine 13 (October 1930): 261-271.

4799. Fant, H. B. "The Indian Trade Policy of the Trustees for Establishing the

Colony of Georgia in America." Georgia Historical Society Quarterly 15 (September 1931): 207-222.

4800. Franklin, W. Neil. "Pennsylvania-Virginia Rivalry for the Indian Trade of the Ohio Valley." Mississippi Valley Historical Review 20 (March 1934): 463-480.

4801. _____. "Virginia and the Cherokee Indian Trade, 1673-1752." East Tennessee Historical Society's Publications, no. 4 (January 1932): 3-21.

4802. _____. "Virginia and the Cherokee Indian Trade, 1753-1775." East Tennessee Historical Society's Publications, no. 5 (January 1933): 22-38.

4803. Franklin, W. Neil, ed. "Act for the Better Regulation of the Indian Trade, Virginia, 1714." Virginia Magazine of History and Biography 72 (April 1964): 141-151.

4804. Goff, John H. "The Path to Oakfuskee: Upper Trading Route in Alabama to the Creek Indians." Georgia Historical Quarterly 39 (June 1955): 152-171.

4805. _____. "The Path to Oakfuskee: Upper Trading Route in Georgia to the Creek Indians." Georgia Historical Quarterly 39 (March 1955): 1-36.

4806. Goggin, John M. "A Florida Indian Trading Post, circa 1763-1784." Southern Indian Studies 1 (October 1949): 35-38.

4807. Graeff, Arthur D. Conrad Weiser, Pennsylvania Peacemaker. Allentown, Pennsylvania: Schlecter's, 1945.

4808. Grant, Ludovick. "Historical Relation of Facts Delivered by Ludovick Grant, Indian Trader, to His Excellency the Governor of South Carolina." South Carolina Historical and Geneological Magazine 10 (January 1909): 54-68.

4809. Hanna, Charles A. The Wilderness Trail; or, The Ventures and Adventures of the Pennsylvania Traders on the Allegheny Path. 2 volumes. New York: G. P. Putnam's Sons, 1911.

4810. Hunter, William A. "Traders on the Ohio: 1730." Western Pennsylvania Historical Magazine 35 (June 1952): 85-92.

4811. Jacobs, Wilbur R. "Unsavory Sidelights on the Colonial Fur Trade." New York History 34 (April 1953): 135-148.

4812. Jennings, Francis. "The Indian Trade of the Susquehanna Valley." Proceedings of the American Philosophical Society 110 (1966): 406-424.

4813. Judd, Sylvester. "The Fur Trade on Connecticut River in the Seventeenth Century." New-England Historical and Genealogical Register 11 (July 1857): 217-219.

4814. King, James C. "Indian Credit as a Source of Friction in the Colonial Fur Trade." Western Pennsylvania Historical Magazine 49 (January 1966): 57-65.

4815. Lawson, Murray G. Fur: A Study in English Mercantilism, 1700-1775. Toronto: University of Toronto Press, 1943.

4816. Lunn, Jean. "The Illegal Fur Trade Out of New France, 1713-60." Canadian Historical Association Report, 1939, pp. 61-76.

4817. MacFarlane, Ronald Oliver. "The Massachusetts Bay Truck-Houses in Diplomacy with the Indians." New England Quarterly 11 (March 1938): 48-65.

4818. Moloney, Francis X. The Fur Trade in New England, 1620-1676. Cambridge: Harvard University Press, 1931.

4819. Montgomery, Thomas Lynch, ed. "Indian Traders, 1743-1775." Pennsylvania Archives, 5th series 1 (1906): 369-379.

4820. Morrison, A. J. "The Virginia Indian Trade to 1673." William and Mary College Quarterly Historical Magazine, 2d series 1 (October 1921): 217-236.

4821. Murray, Jean E. "The Early Fur Trade in New France and New Netherland." Canadian Historical Review 19 (December 1938): 365-377.

4822. Nash, Gary B. "The Quest for the Susquehanna Valley: New York, Pennsylvania, and the Seventeenth-Century Fur Trade." New York History 48 (January 1967): 3-27.

4823. Norton, Thomas Elliot. The Fur Trade in Colonial New York, 1686-1776. Madison: University of Wisconsin Press, 1974.

4824. LeFave, Don. "Time of the Whitetail: The Charles Town Indian Trade 1690-1715." Studies in History and Society 5 (Fall 1973): 5-15.

4825. Reid, Marjorie. "The Quebec Fur Traders and Western Policy 1763-1774." Canadian Historical Review 6 (March 1925): 15-32.

4826. Roberts, William I. "The Fur Trade of New England in the Seventeenth Century." Ph.D. dissertation, University of Pennsylvania, 1958.

4827. Rothrock, Mary U. "Carolina Traders among the Overhill Cherokees, 1690-1760." East Tennessee Historical Society's Publications, no. 1 (1929): 3-18.

4828. Stevens, Wayne E. "The Organization of the British Fur Trade, 1760-1800." Mississippi Valley Historical Review 3 (September 1916): 172-202.

4829. Trelease, Allen W. "The Iroquois and the Western Fur Trade: A Problem in Interpretation." Mississippi Valley Historical Review 49 (June 1962): 32-51.

4830. Trigger, Bruce G. "The Jesuits and the Fur Trade." Ethnohistory 12 (Winter 1965): 30-53.

4831. Volwiler, Albert T. George Croghan and the Westward Movement, 1741-1782. Cleveland: Arthur H. Clark Company, 1926.

4832. Wainwright, Nicholas B. George Croghan, Wilderness Diplomat. Chapel Hill: University of North Carolina Press, 1959.

4833. _____. "An Indian Trade Failure: The Story of the Hockley, Trent and Croghan Company, 1748-1752." Pennsylvania Magazine of History and Biography 72 (October 1948): 343-375.

4834. Wainwright, Nicholas B., ed. "The Opinions of George Croghan on the American Indians." Pennsylvania Magazine of History and Biography 71 (April 1947): 152-159.

4835. Wallace, Paul A. W. Conrad Weiser, 1696-1760, Friend of Colonist and Mohawk. Philadelphia: University of Pennsylvania Press, 1945.

4836. Williams, Meade C. "The Early Fur Trade in North America." Collections and Researches Made by the Michigan Pioneer and Historical Society 35 (1905-1906): 58-73.

4837. Witthoft, John. "Archaeology as a Key to the Colonial Fur Trade." Minnesota History 40 (Winter 1966): 203-209.

4838. Zimmerman, Albright G. "European Trade Relations in the 17th and 18th Centuries." In A Delaware Indian Symposium, edited by Herbert C. Kraft, pp. 57-70. Harrisburg: Pennsylvania Historical and Museum Commission, 1974.

4739. _____. "The Indian Trade of Colonial Pennsylvania." Ph.D. dissertation, University of Delaware, 1966.

THE EAST AND THE MISSISSIPPI VALLEY

The Trans-Appalachian West and the Great Lakes region were invaded by fur traders at an early date, and traders on the Upper Mississippi, too, were often the first contact between white and Indian cultures. The works listed here deal chiefly with the fur trade and traders of these regions.

4840. Adams, John Arthur. "The Indian Trader of the Upper Ohio Valley." Western Pennsylvania Historical Magazine 17 (September 1934): 163-174.

4841. Anson, Bert. "The Fur Traders in Northern Indiana, 1796-1850." Ph.D. dissertation, Indiana University, 1953.

4842. Barnes, Frederick W. "The Fur Traders of Early Oswego." Proceedings of the New York State Historical Association 13 (1914): 128-137.

4843. Barnhart, Warren Lynn. "The Letter Books of Charles Gratiot, Fur Trader: The Nomadic Years, 1769-1797." Ph.D. dissertation, Saint Louis University, 1972.

4844. Brady, Francis X. "W. G. and G. W. Ewing, Pioneer Mercantile Capitalists." Ed.D. dissertation, Ball State University, 1965.

4845. Brannon, Peter A. "The Pensacola Indian Trade." Florida Historical Quarterly 31 (July 1952): 1-15.

4846. _____. The Southern Indian Trade, Being Particularly a Study of Material from the Tallapoosa River Valley of Alabama. Montgomery, Alabama: Paragon Press, 1935.

4847. Bridgewater, William R. "The American Fur Company." Ph.D. dissertation, Yale University, 1938.

4848. Brown, J. A. "Panton, Leslie and Company: Indian Traders of Pensacola and St. Augustine." Florida Historical Quarterly 37 (January-April 1959): 328-336.

4849. Clayton, James L. "The American Fur Company: The Final Years." Ph.D. dissertation, Cornell University, 1964.

4850. Craig, Alan, and David McJunkin. "Stranahan's: Last of the Seminole Trading Posts." Florida Anthropologist 24 (June 1971): 45-50.

4851. Cruikshank, Ernest Alexander. "Robert Dickson, the Indian Trader." Collections of the State Historical Society of Wisconsin 12 (1892): 133-153.

4852. Davidson, Gordon C. "The North West Company." Ph.D. dissertation, University of California, 1916.

4853. Dunham, Douglas. "The French Element in the American Fur Trade, 1760-1816." Ph.D. dissertation, University of Michigan, 1950.

4854. Gates, Charles M., ed. Five Fur Traders of the Northwest. Minneapolis:

University of Minnesota Press, 1933.

4855. Gilman, Rhoda R. "The Fur Trade in the Upper Mississippi Valley, 1630-1850." Wisconsin Magazine of History 58 (Autumn 1974): 3-18.

4856. "The Indian Trade of Rock River Valley." Wisconsin Magazine of History 2 (September 1918): 98-100.

4857. Irwin, Matthew. "The Fur Trade and Factory System at Green Bay, 1816-21," edited by Lyman C. Draper. Report and Collections of the State Historical Society of Wisconsin 7 (1873-1876): 269-288.

4858. Jackson, Marjorie Gordon. "The Beginning of British Trade at Michilimackinac." Minnesota History 11 (September 1930): 231-270.

4859. Johnson, Ida Amanda. The Michigan Fur Trade. Lansing: Michigan Historical Commission, 1919.

4860. Kellogg, Louise Phelps. "The First Traders in Wisconsin." Wisconsin Magazine of History 5 (June 1922): 348-359.

4861. _____. "The Fur Trade in Wisconsin." Wisconsin Archeologist 17 (September 1918): 55-60.

4862. Kelton, Dwight H. "The American Fur Company." Report of the Pioneer Society of the State of Michigan 6 (1883): 343-347.

4863. Kersey, Harry A., Jr. "Pelts, Plumes, and Hides: White Traders among the Seminole Indians, 1890-1930." Florida Historical Quarterly 51 (January 1973): 250-266.

4864. Kinnaird, Lawrence. "The Significance of William August Bowles' Seizure of Panton's Apalachee Store in 1792." Florida Historical Society Quarterly 9 (January 1931): 156-192.

4865. Lasselle, Charles B. "The Old Indian Traders of Indiana." Indiana Quarterly Magazine of History 2 (March 1906): 1-13.

4866. Lavender, David. The Fist in the Wilderness. Garden City, New York: Doubleday and Company, 1964. American Fur Company.

4867. _____. "Some American Characteristics of the American Fur Company." Minnesota History 40 (Winter 1966): 178-187.

4868. Lippincott, Isaac. "A Century and a Half of Fur Trade at St. Louis." Washington University Studies 3 (April 1916): 205-242.

4869. Martin, Deborah Beaumont. "The Fox River in the Days of the Fur Trade." Proceedings of the State Historical Society of Wisconsin, 1899, pp. 117-127.

4870. Massie, Dennis. "Jacob Smith in the Saginaw Valley." Michigan History 51 (Summer 1967): 117-129.

4871. Neill, Edward D. "Indian Trade: A Sketch of the Early Trade and Traders of Minnesota." Annals of the Minnesota Historical Society, 1852, pp. 29-47.

4872. Nute, Grace Lee. "Posts in the Minnesota Fur-Trading Area, 1660-1855." Minnesota History 11 (December 1930): 353-385.

4873. Overton, George. "Trade Goods: Grignon-Porlier Post." Wisconsin Archeologist, new series 21 (December 1940): 71-73.

4874. Phillips, Paul Chrisler. "The Fur Trade in the Maumee-Wabash Country." In Studies in American History Inscribed to James Albert Woodburn, pp. 91-118. Bloomington: Indiana University Press, 1926.

4875. Porter, Kenneth Wiggins. John Jacob Astor, Business Man. 2 volumes. Cambridge: Harvard University Press, 1931. American Fur Company.

4876. Richmond, Rebecca L. "The Fur Traders of the Grand River Valley." Publications of the Historical Society of Grand Rapids 1 (1907): 35-47.

4877. Robeson, George F. "Fur Trade in Early Iowa." Palimpsest 6 (January 1925): 14-29.

4878. _____. "Life among the Fur Traders." Palimpsest 6 (January 1925): 30-41.

4879. Robinson, Mary F. "Rix Robinson, Fur Trader." Michigan History Magazine 6 (1922): 277-287.

4880. Ruckman, J. Ward. "Ramsay Crooks and the Fur Trade of the Northwest." Minnesota History 7 (March 1926): 18-31.

4881. Stevens, Wayne E. "The Fur Trade in Minnesota during the British Regime." Minnesota History Bulletin 5 (February 1923): 3-13.

4882. _____. "Fur-Trading Companies in the Northwest, 1760-1816." Proceedings of the Mississippi Valley Historical Association 9, part 2 (1916-1917): 283-291.

4883. _____. The Northwest Fur Trade, 1763-1800. University of Illinois Studies in the Social Sciences, volume 14, no. 3.

Urbana: University of Illinois, 1926.

4884. Thwaites, Reuben Gold, ed. "The Fur-Trade in Wisconsin, 1815-1817." Collections of the State Historical Society of Wisconsin 19 (1910): 375-488.

4885. _____. "The Fur-Trade in Wisconsin, 1812-1825." Collections of the State Historical Society of Wisconsin 20 (1911): 1-395.

4886. _____. "Fur Trade on the Upper Lakes, 1778-1815." Collections of the State Historical Society of Wisconsin 19 (1910): 234-374.

4887. Tohill, Louis Arthur. "Robert Dickson, British Fur Trader on the Upper Mississippi." North Dakota Historical Quarterly 3 (October 1928): 5-49; (January 1929): 83-128; (April 1929): 182-203.

4888. _____. "Robert Dickson, the Fur Trade, and the Minnesota Boundary." Minnesota History 6 (December 1925): 330-342.

4889. Truett, Randle Bond. Trade and Travel around the Southern Appalachians before 1830. Chapel Hill: University of North Carolina Press, 1935.

4890. Turner, Frederick Jackson. "The Character and Influence of the Fur Trade in Wisconsin." Proceedings of the State Historical Society of Wisconsin, 1889, pp. 52-98.

4891. _____. The Character and Influence of the Indian Trade in Wisconsin: A Study of the Trading Post as an Institution. Johns Hopkins University Studies in Historical and Political Science, 9th series 11-12. Baltimore: Johns Hopkins Press, 1891.

4892. Upham, Warren. "Founders of the Fur Trade in Northern Minnesota." Magazine of History with Notes and Queries 4 (October 1906): 187-197.

4893. Utley, Henry M. "The Fur Trade in the Early Development of the Northwest." American Historical Magazine 1 (January 1906): 45-51.

4894. Van der Zee, Jacob. "Fur Trade Operations in the Eastern Iowa Country from 1800 to 1833." Iowa Journal of History and Politics 12 (October 1914): 479-567.

4895. Weissert, Charles A. "The Indians and the Trading Posts in the Northwest of Barry County, Michigan." Collections and Researches Made by the Michigan Pioneer and Historical Society 38 (1912): 654-672.

4896. Wesley, Edgar B. "Some Official

Aspects of the Fur Trade in the Northwest, 1815-1825." North Dakota Historical Quarterly 6 (April 1932): 201-209.

4897. White, David H. "The John Forbes Company: Heir to the Florida Indian Trade: 1801-1819." Ph.D. dissertation, University of Alabama, 1973.

4898. Williams, Samuel C. "The Father of Sequoyah: Nathaniel Gist." Chronicles of Oklahoma 15 (March 1937): 3-20.

4899. _____. "Nathaniel Gist, Father of Sequoyah." East Tennessee Historical Society's Publications no. 5 (1933): 39-54.

THE TRANS-MISSISSIPPI WEST

The fur trade moved quickly to the regions west of the Mississippi, into the headwaters of the Missouri, the Platte, and other rivers, into the Rocky Mountains, the Pacific Northwest, and the Southwest--wherever the lure of furs drew the adventurous traders. The trade and its effects on whites and Indians are studied in the works listed here, as well as the activities of Indian traders in the West in more recent times.

4900. Adams, William Y. Shonto: A Study of the Role of the Trader in a Modern Navajo Community. Bureau of American Ethnology, Bulletin 188. Washington: U.S. Government Printing Office, 1963.

4901. Albrecht, Dorothy E. "John Lorenzo Hubbell, Navajo Indian Trader." Arizoniana 4 (Fall 1963): 33-40.

4902. Alter, J. Cecil. James Bridger, Trapper, Frontiersman, Scout and Guide: A Historical Narrative. Salt Lake City: Shepard Book Company, 1925.

4903. Barker, Eugene C. "A Glimpse of the Texas Fur Trade in 1832." Southwestern Historical Quarterly 19 (January 1916): 279-282.

4904. Beidleman, Richard G. "Nathaniel Wyeth's Fort Hall." Oregon Historical Quarterly 58 (September 1957): 197-250.

4905. Boller, Henry A. Among the Indians, Eight Years in the Far West, 1858-1866: Embracing Sketches of Montana and Salt Lake. Philadelphia: T. Ellwood Zell, 1868.

4906. Bradley, James H. "Sketch of the Fur Trade of the Upper Missouri River." Contributions to the Historical Society of Montana 8 (1917): 177-196; 9 (1923): 317-335.

4907. Brandon, William. "The Wild Freedom

of the Mountain Men." American Heritage 6 (August 1955): 4-9.

4908. Brooks, George R., ed. "The Private Journal of Robert Campbell." Bulletin of the Missouri Historical Society 20 (October 1963): 3-24; (January 1964): 107-118.

4909. Brown, Jennie Broughton. Fort Hall on the Oregon Trail: A Historical Study. Caldwell, Idaho: Caxton Printers, 1932.

4910. Burns, Peter J. "The Short, Incredible Life of Jedediah Strong Smith." Montana, the Magazine of Western History 17 (January 1967): 44-55.

4911. Chittenden, Hiram Martin. The American Fur Trade of the Far West. 3 volumes. New York: Francis P. Harper, 1902.

4912. Cleland, Robert Glass. This Reckless Breed of Men: The Trappers and Fur Traders of the Southwest. New York: Alfred A. Knopf, 1950.

4913. Clokey, Richard M. "The Life of William H. Ashley." Ph.D. dissertation, University of Wisconsin, 1969.

4914. Dale, Harrison Clifford, ed. The Ashley-Smith Explorations and the Discovery of a Central Route to the Pacific, 1822-1829. Cleveland: Arthur H. Clark Company, 1918.

4915. De Voto, Bernard. Across the Wide Missouri. Boston: Houghton Mifflin Company, 1947.

4916. Dougherty, Dolorita Marie. "A History of Fort Union (North Dakota) 1829-1867." Ph.D. dissertation, Saint Louis University, 1957.

4917. Dunwiddie, Peter W. "The Nature of the Relationship between the Blackfeet Indians and the Men of the Fur Trade." Annals of Wyoming 46 (Spring 1974): 123-133.

4918. Ewers, John C. "The Indian Trade on the Upper Missouri before Lewis and Clark: An Interpretation." Bulletin of the Missouri Historical Society 10 (July 1954): 429-446.

4919. Elliott, T. C. "The Fur Trade in the Columbia River Basin Prior to 1811." Washington Historical Quarterly 6 (January 1915): 3-10.

4920. Finney, Frank F. "John N. Florer: Pioneer Osage Trader." Chronicles of Oklahoma 33 (Summer 1955): 142-144.

4921. Finney, James Edwin, as told to Joseph B. Thoburn. "Reminiscences of a Trader in the Osage Country." Chronicles

of Oklahoma 33 (Summer 1955): 145-158.

4922. Frost, Donald McKay. "Notes on General Ashley, the Overland Trail, and South Pass." Proceedings of the American Antiquarian Society 54 (October 18, 1944): 161-312.

4923. Fynn, Arthur J. "Furs and Forts of the Rocky Mountain West." Colorado Magazine 8 (November 1931): 209-222; 9 (March 1932): 45-57.

4924. Gale, Frederick C. "Jedediah Smith Meets Indians and Vice Versa." Pacific Historian 10 (Spring 1966): 34-38.

4925. Gerber, Max E. "The Steamboat and Indians of the Upper Missouri." South Dakota History 4 (Spring 1974): 139-160.

4926. Gillmor, Frances, and Louisa Wade Wetherill. Traders to the Navajos: The Story of the Wetherills of Kayenta. Boston: Houghton Mifflin, 1934.

4927. Gilman, Rhoda R. "Last Days of the Upper Missouri Fur Trade." Minnesota History 42 (Winter 1970): 122-140.

4928. Goodwin, Cardinal. "Manuel Lisa." Overland Monthly 69 (February 1917): 151-155.

4929. Gowans, Frederick Ross. "A History of Fort Bridger from 1841-1858." Ph.D. dissertation, Brigham Young University, 1972.

4930. Grinnell, George Bird. "Bent's Old Fort and Its Builders." Collections of the Kansas State Historical Society 15 (1919-1922): 28-91.

4931. Hafen, LeRoy R. "The Early Fur Trade Posts on the South Platte." Mississippi Valley Historical Review 12 (December 1925): 334-341.

4932. _____. "Fort Jackson and the Early Fur Trade on the South Platte." Colorado Magazine 5 (February 1928): 9-17.

4933. _____. "Fort Vasquez." Colorado Magazine 41 (Summer 1964): 199-212.

4934. Hafen, LeRoy R., ed. The Mountain Men and the Fur Trade of the Far West: Biographical Sketches of the Participants by Scholars of the Subject. 10 volumes. Glendale, California: Arthur H. Clark Company, 1965-1972.

4935. Haley, J. Evetts. "The Comanchero Trade." Southwestern Historical Quarterly 38 (January 1935): 157-176.

4936. Halliburton, R., Jr. "John Colter's Bare Escape." American History Illustrated 9 (November 1974): 12-17.

197

4937. _____. "John Colter's Run for Life." Great Plains Journal 3 (Fall 1963): 32-34.

4938. Hamilton, William T. "A Trading Expedition among the Indians in 1858, from Fort Walla Walla to the Blackfoot Country and Return." Contributions to the Historical Society of Montana 3 (1900): 33-123.

4939. Harper, Elizabeth Ann. "The Taovayas Indians in Frontier Trade and Diplomacy, 1719-1768." Chronicles of Oklahoma 31 (Autumn 1953): 268-289.

4940. _____. "The Taovayas Indians in Frontier Trade and Diplomacy, 1769-1779." Southwestern Historical Quarterly 57 (October 1953): 181-201.

4941. _____. "The Taovayas Indians in Frontier Trade and Diplomacy, 1779-1835." Panhandle-Plains Historical Review 26 (1953): 41-72.

4942. Harris, Henry, Jr. "The Indians and the Fur Men." Utah Historical Quarterly 39 (Spring 1971): 128.

4943. Harrison, Lowell H., ed. "Three Comancheros and a Trader." Panhandle-Plains Historical Review 38 (1965): 73-93.

4944. Harvey, James Rose. "A Trader with the Utes, and the Murder of Chief Shavano." Colorado Magazine 20 (May 1943): 99-108. Story of Arthur C. Moulton.

4945. Hegemann, Elizabeth Compton. Navaho Trading Days. Albuquerque: University of New Mexico Press, 1963.

4946. Hill, Joseph J. "Antoine Robidoux, Kingpin in the Colorado River Fur Trade, 1824-1844." Colorado Magazine 6 (July 1930): 125-132.

4947. _____. "Ewing Young in the Fur Trade of the Far Southwest, 1822-1834." Oregon Historical Quarterly 24 (March 1923): 1-35.

4948. _____. "New Light on Pattie and the Southwestern Fur Trade." Southwestern Historical Quarterly 26 (January 1922): 243-254.

4949. Holmes, Kenneth L. "Ewing Young, Enterprising Trapper." Ph.D. dissertation, University of Oregon, 1963.

4950. Irving, Washington. Astoria; or, Anecdotes of an Enterprise beyond the Rocky Mountains. Revised edition. New York: G. P. Putnam, 1849. First published in Philadelphia, 1836.

4951. Jablow, Joseph. The Cheyenne in Plains Indian Trade Relations, 1795-1840.

Monographs of the American Ethnological Society, no. 19. New York: J. J. Augustin, 1951.

4952. Johnson, Roy P. "Fur Trader Chaboillez at Pembina." North Dakota History 32 (April 1965): 83-99.

4953. Kardas, Susan. "'The People Bought This and the Clatsop Became Rich': A View of Nineteenth Century Fur Trade Relationships on the Lower Colombia between Chinookan Speakers, Whites, and Kanakas." Ph.D. dissertation, Bryn Mawr College, 1971.

4954. Keeling, Henry C. "My Experience with the Cheyenne Indians," edited by Joseph B. Thoburn. Chronicles of Oklahoma 3 (April 1925): 59-73.

4955. Kime, Wayne R. "Alfred Seton's Journal: A Source for Irving's Tonquin Disaster Account." Oregon Historical Quarterly 71 (December 1970): 309-324.

4956. Knight, Oliver. "An Oklahoma Indian Trader as a Frontiersman of Commerce." Journal of Southern History 23 (May 1957): 203-219.

4957. Koch, Peter. "A Trading Expedition among the Crow Indians, 1873-1874," edited by Carl B. Cone. Mississippi Valley Historical Review 31 (December 1944): 407-430.

4958. Larpenteur, Charles. Forty Years a Fur Trader on the Upper Missouri: The Personal Narrative of Charles Larpenteur, 1833-1872. Edited by Elliott Coues. 2 volumes. New York: Francis P. Harper, 1898.

4959. Lecompte, Janet. "Bent, St. Vrain and Company among the Comanche and Kiowa." Colorado Magazine 49 (Fall 1972): 273-293.

4960. _____. "Gantt's Fort and Bent's Picket Post." Colorado Magazine 41 (Spring 1964): 111-125.

4961. Lewis, Anna. "Trading Post at the Crossing of the Chickasaw Trails." Chronicles of Oklahoma 12 (December 1934): 447-453.

4962. Lewis, Oscar. The Effects of White Contact upon Blackfoot Culture, with Special Reference to the Role of the Fur Trade. Monographs of the American Ethnological Society, no. 6. New York: J. J. Augustin, 1942.

4963. Lewis, William S. "Francis Heron, Fur Trader: Other Herons." Washington Historical Quarterly 11 (January 1920): 29-34.

4964. Lubers, H. L. "William Bent's Family and the Indians of the Plains."

Colorado Magazine 13 (January 1936): 19-22.

4965. Luttig, John C. *Journal of a Fur Trading Expedition to the Upper Missouri, 1812-1813.* Edited by Stella M. Drumm. St. Louis: Missouri Historical Society, 1920.

4966. McFadden, Marguerite. "Intruders or Injustice?" *Chronicles of Oklahoma* 48 (Winter 1970-1971): 431-449.

4967. McNitt, Frank. *The Indian Traders.* Norman: University of Oklahoma Press, 1962.

4968. Mattison, Ray H. "Fort Union: Its Role in the Upper Missouri Fur Trade." *North Dakota History* 29 (January-April 1962): 181-208.

4969. _____. "The Upper Missouri Fur Trade: Its Methods of Operation." *Nebraska History* 42 (March 1961): 1-28.

4970. Mattison, Ray H., ed. "Henry A. Boller: Upper Missouri River Fur Trader." *North Dakota History* 33 (Spring 1966): 106-219.

4971. _____. "Journal of a Trip to, and Residence in, the Indian Country, Commenced Saturday, May 22d, 1858." *North Dakota History* 33 (Summer 1966): 260-315. Journal of Henry A. Boller.

4972. Miller, David E. "Peter Skene Ogden Discovered Indians." In *Essays on the American West, 1972-1973,* edited by Thomas G. Alexander, pp. 137-166. Charles Redd Monographs in Western History, no. 3. Provo, Utah: Brigham Young University Press, 1974.

4973. Mitchell, Annie R. "Major James D. Savage and the Tularenos." *California Historical Society Quarterly* 28 (December 1949): 323-341.

4974. Mitchell, Daniel Holmes. "An Indian Trader's Plea for Justice, 1906," edited by Clifford E. Trafzer. *New Mexico Historical Review* 47 (July 1972): 239-256.

4975. Monahan, Forrest D., Jr. "Trade Goods on the Prairie: The Kiowa Tribe and White Trade Goods, 1794-1875." Ph.D. dissertation, University of Oklahoma, 1965.

4976. Morgan, Dale L. *Jedediah Smith and the Opening of the West.* Indianapolis: Bobbs-Merrill Company, 1953.

4977. Morgan, Dale L., ed. *The West of William H. Ashley.* Denver: Old West Publishing Company, 1964.

4978. Morris, Wayne. "Auguste Pierre Chouteau, Merchant Prince at the Three Forks of the Arkansas." *Chronicles of Oklahoma* 48 (Summer 1970): 155-163.

4979. _____. "The Wichita Exchange: Trade on Oklahoma's Fur Frontier, 1719-1812." *Great Plains Journal* 9 (Spring 1970): 79-84.

4980. Mumey, Nolie. *The Life of Jim Baker, 1818-1898: Trapper, Scout, Guide and Indian Fighter.* Denver: World Press, 1931.

4981. Nasatir, A. P., ed. *Before Lewis and Clark: Documents Illustrating the History of the Missouri, 1785-1804.* 2 volumes. St. Louis: St. Louis Historical Documents Foundation, 1952.

4982. Neihardt, John G. *The Splendid Wayfaring: The Story of the Exploits of Jedediah Smith and His Comrades, the Ashley-Henry Men, Discoverers and Explorers of the Great Central Route from the Missouri River to the Pacific Ocean, 1822-1831.* New York: Macmillan Company, 1920.

4983. Nunis, Doyce B., Jr. "The Fur Men: Key to Westward Expansion, 1822-1830." *Historian* 23 (February 1961): 167-190.

4984. Oglesby, Richard E. *Manuel Lisa and the Opening of the Missouri Fur Trade.* Norman: University of Oklahoma Press, 1963.

4985. O'Meara, Walter. *Daughters of the Country: The Women of the Fur Traders and Mountain Men.* New York: Harcourt, Brace and World, 1968.

4986. Pearsall, Marion. "Contributions of Early Explorers and Traders to the Ethnography of the Northwest." *Pacific Northwest Quarterly* 40 (October 1949): 316-326.

4987. Phillips, George H. "The Indian Ring in Dakota Territory, 1870-1890." *South Dakota History* 2 (Fall 1972): 345-376.

4988. Pope, Polly. "Trade in the Plains: Affluence and Its Effects." *Kroeber Anthropological Society Papers* 34 (Spring 1966): 53-61.

4989. Raemsch, Bruce E. "The Indianization of the Mountain Men." Ph.D. dissertation, University of Pennsylvania, 1966.

4990. Rister, Carl Coke. "Harmful Practices of Indian Traders of the Southwest, 1865-1876." *New Mexico Historical Review* 6 (July 1931): 231-248.

4991. Robertson, Frank C. *Fort Hall: Gateway to the Oregon Country.* New York: Hastings House, 1963.

4992. Rowe, David C. "Government Relations with the Fur Trappers of the Upper Missouri: 1820-1840." North Dakota History 35 (Spring 1968): 481-505.

4993. Sears, Paul M. "Gallup Merchants Like It--When Indians Come to Town." New Mexico Business 7 (November 1954): 2-8.

4994. Smith, Alson J. Men against the Mountains: Jedediah Smith and the South West Expedition of 1826-1829. New York: John Day Company, 1965.

4995. Smith, Jedediah. The Travels of Jedediah Smith: A Documentary Outline Including the Journal of the Great American Pathfinder. Edited by Maurice S. Sullivan. Santa Ana, California: Fine Arts Press, 1934.

4996. Sneed, R. A. "The Reminiscences of an Indian Trader." Chronicles of Oklahoma 14 (June 1936): 135-155. At Fort Sill and Anadarko, 1885-1890.

4997. Socwell, Clarence P. "Peter Skene Ogden: Fur Trader Extraordinaire." American West 10 (May 1973): 42-47, 61.

4998. Sperlin, O. B. "Washington Forts of the Fur Trade Regime." Washington Historical Quarterly 8 (April 1917): 102-113.

4999. Stevens, Harry R. "A Company of Hands and Traders: Origins of the Glenn-Fowler Expedition of 1821-1822." New Mexico Historical Review 46 (July 1971): 181-221.

5000. Sturgis, William. "The Northwest Fur Trade." Merchants' Magazine and Commercial Review 14 (June 1846): 532-539. Report by Elliot C. Cowdin of a lecture given by Sturgis.

5001. _____. The Northwest Fur Trade and the Indians of the Oregon Country, 1788-1830. Old South Leaflets, no. 219. Boston: Old South Association, n.d.

5002. Sullivan, Maurice S. Jedediah Smith, Trader and Trail Breaker. New York: Press of the Pioneers, 1936.

5003. Sunder, John E. The Fur Trade on the Upper Missouri, 1840-1865. Norman: University of Oklahoma Press, 1965.

5004. _____. Joshua Pilcher: Fur Trader and Indian Agent. Norman: University of Oklahoma Press, 1968.

5005. Unrau, William E. "The Council Grove Merchants and Kansas Indians, 1855-1870." Kansas Historical Quarterly 34 (Autumn 1968): 266-281.

5006. Weber, David J. The Taos Trappers: The Fur Trade in the Far Southwest, 1540-1846. Norman: University of Oklahoma Press, 1971.

5007. Wike, Joyce. "Problems in Fur Trade Analysis: The Northwest Coast." American Anthropologist 60 (December 1958): 1086-1101.

LIQUOR AND THE LIQUOR TRADE

Tremendous evil came from the use of liquor by the Indians, yet many traders continued to ply the Indians with alcohol, and government prohibitions seemed almost useless.

5008. Bearss, Edwin C. "The Arkansas Whiskey War: A Fort Smith Case Study." Journal of the West 7 (April 1968): 143-172.

5009. Bourke, John G. "Distillation by Early American Indians." American Anthropologist 7 (July 1894): 297-299.

5010. Covington, James W., ed. "The Indian Liquor Trade at Peoria 1864." Journal of the Illinois State Historical Society 46 (Summer 1953): 142-150.

5011. Dempsey, Hugh A. "Howell Harris and the Whiskey Trade." Montana Magazine of History 3 (Spring 1953): 1-8.

5012. Donnelly, Joseph Peter. "The Liquor Traffic among the Aborigines of the New Northwest, 1800-1860." Ph.D. dissertation, St. Louis University, 1940.

5013. Finney, Frank F. "The Osage Indians and the Liquor Problem before Oklahoma Statehood." Chronicles of Oklahoma 34 (Winter 1956-1957): 456-464.

5014. Foreman, Grant. "A Century of Prohibition." Chronicles of Oklahoma 12 (June 1934): 133-141.

5015. Franklin, J. L. "The Fight for Prohibition in Oklahoma Territory." Social Science Quarterly 49 (March 1969): 876-885.

5016. Frederikson, Otto F. The Liquor Question among the Indian Tribes in Kansas, 1804-1881. Bulletin of the University of Kansas, Humanistic Studies, volume 4, no. 4. Lawrence, Kansas, 1932.

5017. Heaston, Michael D. "Whiskey Regulation and Indian Land Titles in New Mexico Territory, 1851-1861." Journal of the West 10 (July 1971): 474-483.

5018. Hudson, Peter J. "Temperance Meetings among the Choctaws." Chronicles of Oklahoma 12 (June 1934): 130-132.

5019. Johnson, William E. The Federal Government and the Liquor Traffic. Westerville, Ohio: American Issue Publishing Company, 1917.

5020. Parish, John C. "Liquor and the Indians." Palimpsest 3 (July 1922): 201-213.

5021. Stein, Gary C. "A Fearful Drunkenness: The Liquor Trade to the Western Indians As Seen by European Travellers in America, 1800-1860." Red River Valley Historical Review 1 (Summer 1974): 109-121.

5022. Winkler, Allen M. "Drinking on the American Frontier." Quarterly Journal of Studies on Alcohol 29 (June 1968): 413-445.

For recent studies on alcohol problems among the Indians, see the section on Alcoholism (7159 to 7201).

11
Missions and Missionaries

Missionary zeal to convert the Indians to Christianity accounted for much of the contact between Indians and whites in the United States. Both Catholics and Protestants established and staffed missions and schools among the tribes, from earliest colonial days up to the present time. The studies listed in this section include those on the educational work of the various denominations as well as those that deal with strictly religious work, and biographical studies on missionaries as well as accounts of the missionary enterprises. The materials are classified by religious denomination, except for general works and studies of colonial missionary activity.

GENERAL STUDIES

Listed here are works that treat theoretically or analytically of missionary activity and studies that cover more than one denomination. Also included are a few items that do not fit under the specific denominational headings used below.

5023. Ames, Michael. "Missionaries' Toil for Souls and Survival: Introducing Christianity to the Pacific Northwest." American West 10 (January 1973): 28-33, 63.

5024. Ashenhurst, James O. "Difficulties in Missions to American Indians." Missionary Review of the World 31 (July 1908): 516-519.

5025. Bass, Althea. "With Benefit of Grammar." Colophon 2 (Autumn 1937): 517-536. Efforts of John Eliot and Ann Eliza Worcester Robertson to translate the Bible into Indian languages.

5026. Beaver, R. Pierce. "American Missionary Efforts to Influence Government Indian Policy." Journal of Church and State 5 (May 1963): 77-94.

5027. _____. Church, State, and the American Indians: Two and a Half Centuries of Partnership in Missions Between Protestant Churches and Government. St.

Louis: Concordia Publishing House, 1966.

5028. _____. "Church, State, and the Indians: Indian Missions in the New Nation." Journal of Church and State 4 (May 1962): 11-30.

5029. Berkhofer, Robert F., Jr. "Model Zions for the American Indian." American Quarterly 15 (Summer 1963): 176-190.

5030. _____. "Protestants, Pagans, and Sequences among the North American Indians, 1760-1860." Ethnohistory 10 (Summer 1963): 201-232.

5031. _____. Salvation and the Savage: An Analysis of Protestant Missions and American Indian Response, 1787-1862. Lexington: University of Kentucky Press, 1965. Paperback edition with new introduction, New York: Atheneum, 1972.

5032. Brickman, Helen. "New Trails for the American Indian." International Journal of Religious Education 7 (October 1930): 22-23, 48.

5033. Bryant, Keith L., Jr. "The Choctaw Nation in 1843: A Missionary's View." Chronicles of Oklahoma 44 (Autumn 1966): 319-321. Letter of Jared Olmstead.

5034. Chase, Don M. "Was It Jedediah Smith?" Pacific Historian 15 (Fall 1971): 3-10. On Nez Perce mission to St. Louis, 1831.

5035. Clark, David W. "A Note on the Functioning of Christianity among Indians." In The Changing Indian, edited by Oliver La Farge, pp. 163-165. Norman: University of Oklahoma Press, 1942.

5036. Clark, John W. "American Indians and the Gospel." Missionary Review of the World 36 (November 1913): 830-836.

5037. Cloud, Henry Roe. "Are Missions to Indians Effective?" Missionary Review of the World 55 (July 1932): 401-404.

5038. Collins, Linton McGee. "Activities of the Missionaries among the Cherokees." Georgia Historical Quarterly 6

(December 1922): 285-322.

5039. Cornelison, J. M. "American Indians as Christians." Missionary Review of the World 38 (July 1915): 529-530.

5040. Corwin, Hugh D. "Protestant Missionary Work among the Comanches and Kiowas." Chronicles of Oklahoma 46 (Spring 1968): 41-57.

5041. De Korne, John Cornelius. Navaho and Zuni for Christ: Fifty Years of Indian Missions. Grand Rapids, Michigan: Christian Reformed Board of Missions, 1947.

5042. DeRosier, Arthur H., Jr. "Pioneers with Conflicting Ideals: Christianity and Slavery in the Choctaw Nation." Journal of Mississippi History 21 (July 1959): 174-189.

5043. Drury, Clifford M. "Another Myth Answered." Pacific Historian 17 (Spring 1973): 43-48. Rejoinder by Don Chase, pp. 49-52. Nez Perce mission to St. Louis, 1831.

5044. _____. "Christian Beginnings in California and Indian Mission Beginnings in Old Oregon." Far-Westerner 13 (October 1972): 1-6.

5045. _____. "The Nez Perce 'Delegation' of 1831." Oregon Historical Quarterly 40 (September 1939): 283-287.

5046. _____. "Oregon Indians in the Red River School." Pacific Historical Review 7 (March 1938): 50-60.

5047. _____. "Protestant Missionaries in Oregon: A Bibliographic Survey." Oregon Historical Quarterly 50 (September 1949): 209-221.

5048. Dryden, Cecil P. Give All to Oregon! Missionary Pioneers of the Far West. New York: Hastings House, 1968.

5049. Dusenberry, Verne. "Montana Indians and the Pentecostals." Christian Century 75 (July 23, 1958): 850-851.

5050. Eastman, Elaine Goodale. "The American Indian and His Religion." Missionary Review of the World 60 (March 1937): 128-130.

5051. Edwards, Martha Letitia. "Government Patronage of Indian Missions." Ph.D. dissertation, University of Wisconsin, 1916.

5052. _____. "A Problem of Church and State in the 1870's." Mississippi Valley Historical Review 11 (June 1924): 37-53.

5053. Eells, Myron. History of Indian

Missions on the Pacific Coast, Oregon, Washington and Idaho. Philadelphia: American Sunday-School Union, 1882.

5054. Elliott, R. C. "Religion among the Flatheads." Oregon Historical Quarterly 37 (March 1936): 1-8.

5055. Elsbree, Oliver Wendell. The Rise of the Missionary Spirit in America, 1790-1815. Williamsport, Pennsylvania: Williamsport Printing and Binding Company, 1928.

5056. Facing the Future in Indian Missions. New York: Council of Women for Home Missions and Missionary Education Movement, 1932. Includes "A Social Outlook on Indian Missions," by Lewis Meriam, pp. 3-141, and "The Church and the Indian," by George W. Hinman, pp. 145-208.

5057. Farr, Eugene Ijams. "Religious Assimilation: A Case Study--the Adoption of Christianity by the Choctaw Indians of Mississippi." Th.D. dissertation, New Orleans Baptist Theological Seminary, 1948.

5058. Fey, Harold E. "Confer on Indian Missions: National Fellowship of Indian Workers." Christian Century 72 (July 27, 1955): 861-863.

5059. Freeman, John F. "The Indian Convert: Theme and Variation." Ethnohistory 12 (Spring 1965): 113-128.

5060. Graves, Mrs. W. W. "In the Land of the Osages--Harmony Mission." Missouri Historical Review 19 (April 1925): 409-418.

5061. Haines, Francis. "The Nez Perce Delegation to St. Louis in 1831." Pacific Historical Review 6 (March 1937): 71-78.

5062. Halkett, John. Historical Notes Respecting the Indians of North America: With Remarks on the Attempts Made to Convert and Civilize Them. London: Archibald Constable and Company, 1825.

5063. Hall, C. L. "The Advance of an Indian Community in a Quarter of a Century." American Missionary 56 (April 1902): 184-187.

5064. Harper, Richard H. "American Indians --Pagan and Christian." Missionary Review of the World 55 (July-August 1932): 395-398.

5065. _____. "The Missionary Work of the Reformed (Dutch) Church in America in Oklahoma." Chronicles of Oklahoma 18 (September 1940): 252-265; (December 1940): 328-347; 19 (June 1941): 170-179.

5066. Harrod, Howard L. "The Blackfeet and the Divine 'Establishment.'" Montana, the Magazine of Western History 22 (Winter 1972): 42-51.

5067. _____. "Early Protestant Missions among the Blackfeet Indians, 1850-1900." Methodist History 5 (July 1967): 15-24.

5068. _____. Mission among the Blackfeet. Norman: University of Oklahoma Press, 1971.

5069. Harvey, R. E. "Faith and Works in the Black Hawk Purchase." Annals of Iowa, 3d series 21 (April 1938): 241-282.

5070. Hinds, Roland. "Early Creek Missions." Chronicles of Oklahoma 17 (March 1939): 48-61.

5071. Hinman, George W. The American Indian and Christian Missions. New York: Fleming H. Revell Company, 1933.

5072. _____. Christian Activities among American Indians. Boston: Society for Propagating the Gospel among the Indians and Others in North America, 1933.

5073. Holway, Hope. "Union Mission, 1826-1837." Chronicles of Oklahoma 40 (Winter 1962-1963): 355-378.

5074. Howard, Harold Charles. "The Protestant Missionary and the Government Indian Policy, 1775-1850." Ph.D. dissertation, Loyola University of Chicago, 1965.

5075. Huffman, James. "Indian Reservations about the Church." Christianity Today 13 (September 12, 1969): 54-55.

5076. Hume, C. Ross. "Notes of Missions and Missionaries of Kiowa, Comanche and Wichita Indian Reservations." Chronicles of Oklahoma 29 (Spring 1951): 113-116.

5077. Humphreys, Mary Gay, ed. Missionary Explorers among the American Indians. New York: Charles Scribner's Sons, 1913.

5078. Jackson, Joe C. "Church School Education in the Creek Nation, 1898-1907." Chronicles of Oklahoma 46 (Autumn 1968): 312-330.

5079. Jessett, Thomas E. "Christian Missions and the Dichotomy in Western Civilization." Anglican Theological Review 40 (April 1958): 119-130.

5080. _____. "Christian Missions to the Indians of Oregon." Church History 28 (June 1959): 147-156.

5081. Lambert, Bernard. "Mission Priorities: Indians or Miners?" Michigan History 51 (Winter 1967): 323-334.

5082. Lewitt, Robert T. "Indian Missions and Antislavery Sentiment: A Conflict of Evangelical and Humanitarian Ideals." Mississippi Valley Historical Review 50 (June 1963): 39-55.

5083. Lindquist, G. E. E. "Christian Work among Indians, Including Problems of Religious Life." Journal of Religious Thought 7 (Spring-Summer 1950): 128-135.

5084. _____. "Early Work among the Indians." Missionary Review of the World 60 (November 1937): 533-538.

5085. _____. Indians in Transition: A Study of Protestant Missions to Indians in the United States. New York: Division of Home Missions, National Council of Churches of Christ in the U.S.A., 1951.

5086. _____. The Red Man in the United States: An Intimate Study of the Social, Economic and Religious Life of the American Indian. New York: George H. Doran Company, 1923.

5087. McLoughlin, William G. "Civil Disobedience and Evangelism among the Missionaries to the Cherokees, 1829-1839." Journal of Presbyterian History 51 (Summer 1973): 116-139.

5088. _____. "Red, White, and Black in the Antebellum South." Baptist History and Heritage 7 (April 1972): 69-75.

5089. Malone, Henry Thompson. "The Early Nineteenth Century Missionaries in the Cherokee Country." Tennessee Historical Quarterly 10 (June 1951): 127-139.

5090. Mattison, Ray H. "Indian Missions and Missionaries on the Upper Missouri to 1900." Nebraska History 38 (June 1957): 127-154.

5091. "Missionaries vs. Native Americans in the Northwest: A Bibliography for Re-evaluation." Indian Historian 5 (Summer 1972): 46-48.

5092. Moffett, Thomas C. The American Indian on the New Trail: The Red Man of the United States and the Christian Gospel. New York: Presbyterian Department of Missionary Education, 1914.

5093. _____. "The First Americans-- the Indians." Missionary Review of the World 42 (November 1919): 856-859.

5094. _____. "Red Men and the Gospel." Missionary Review of the World 38 (October 1915): 745-754.

5095. Muntz, E. E. "Christianity and the American Indian." Nineteenth Century and After 101 (January 1927): 58-72.

5096. Nute, Grace Lee. "Early Day Missionaries to the Indians, Missionaries among the Sioux and Chippewa in Minnesota: A Brief Sketch Based on Diaries and Letters in Manuscript Division of Minnesota Historical Society." Western Magazine 24 (October 1924): 110-112.

5097. Oliphant, J. Orin. "Francis Haines and William Walker: A Critique." Pacific Historical Review 14 (June 1945): 211-216. On Indian delegation to St. Louis in 1831.

5098. _____. "George Simpson and Oregon Missions." Pacific Historical Review 6 (September 1937): 213-248.

5099. _____. "A Project for a Christian Mission on the Northwest Coast of America, 1798." Pacific Northwest Quarterly 36 (April 1945): 99-114.

5100. Rapoport, Robert Norman. Changing Navaho Religious Values: A Study of the Christian Missions to the Rimrock Navahos. Papers of the Peabody Museum of American Archaeology and Ethnology, Harvard University, volume 41, no. 2. Cambridge, Massachusetts: Peabody Museum, 1954.

5101. Rhodes, Willard. "The Christian Hymnology of the North American Indians." In Men and Cultures: Selected Papers of the Fifth International Congress of Anthropological and Ethnological Sciences, Philadelphia, September 1-9, 1956, edited by Anthony F. C. Wallace, pp. 324-331. Philadelphia: University of Pennsylvania Press, 1960.

5102. Riggs, Stephen R. "Protestant Missions in the Northwest." Collections of the Minnesota Historical Society 6 (1887-1894): 117-188.

5103. Rothensteiner, John. "The Flat-Head and Nez Perce Delegation to St. Louis, 1831-1839." St. Louis Catholic Historical Review 2 (October 1920): 183-197.

5104. Rushdoony, Rousas John. "Christian Missions and Indian Culture." Westminster Theological Journal 12 (November 1949): 1-12.

5105. Sanders, Helen FitzGerald. "Some Indian Missions of the Northwest." Overland Monthly 55 (June 1910): 561-573.

5106. Schaeffer, Claude E. "Early Christian Mission of the Kutenai Indians." Oregon Historical Quarterly 71 (December 1970): 325-348.

5107. Schusky, Ernest L. "Mission and Government Policy in Dakota Indian Communities." Practical Anthropology 10 (May-June 1963): 109-114.

5108. Simmons, Benjamin F. "The Beginning

of Church of the Brethren Work among Indian Americans." Brethren Life and Thought 14 (Summer 1969): 183-186.

5109. Spalding, Arminta Scott. "From the Natchez Trace to Oklahoma: Development of Christian Civilization among the Choctaws, 1800-1860." Chronicles of Oklahoma 45 (Spring 1967): 2-24.

5110. Stevens, Michael E. "Catholic and Protestant Missionaries among Wisconsin Indians: The Territorial Period." Wisconsin Magazine of History 58 (Winter 1974-1975): 140-148.

5111. Stock, Harry Thomas. "A Resume of Christian Missions among the American Indians." American Journal of Theology 24 (July 1920): 368-385.

5112. Thomas, Robert K. "The Role of the Church in Indian Adjustment." Kansas Journal of Sociology 3 (Winter 1967): 20-28.

5113. Wardell, Morris L. "Protestant Missions among the Osages, 1820 to 1838." Chronicles of Oklahoma 2 (September 1924): 285-297.

5114. Warner, Michael J. "The Fertile Ground: The Beginnings of Protestant Missionary Work with the Navajos, 1852-1890." In The Changing Ways of Southwestern Indians: A Historic Perspective, edited by Albert H. Schroeder, pp. 189-203. Glorieta, New Mexico: Rio Grande Press, 1973.

5115. _____. "Protestant Missionary Activity among the Navajo, 1890-1912." New Mexico Historical Review 45 (July 1970): 209-232.

5116. Webb, Murl L. "Religious and Educational Efforts among Texas Indians in the 1850's." Southwestern Historical Quarterly 69 (July 1965): 22-37.

5117. Williams, Samuel C. "Christian Missions to the Overhill Cherokees." Chronicles of Oklahoma 12 (March 1934): 66-73.

5118. Wyeth, Walter N. Poor Lo! Early Indian Missions: A Memorial. Philadelphia: W. N. Wyeth, 1896.

A good deal of information about Indian missions can be gleaned from periodicals published by religious groups. Most of the denominations prominent in Indian missionary work issued mission magazines, which frequently carried reports from the Indian missionaries in the field and other Indian news. See such journals as the Baptist Home Mission Monthly, Missionary Herald, Missionary Review of the World, and Woodstock Letters.

COLONIAL MISSIONS

In all parts of the colonies efforts were made to convert the Indians. In New England, especially, there was much activity in the early years, sparked by John Eliot and his associates.

5119. Beaver, R. Pierce. "Methods in American Missions to the Indians in the Seventeenth and Eighteenth Centuries: Calvinist Models for Protestant Foreign Missions." Journal of Presbyterian History 47 (June 1969): 124-148.

5120. Brain, Belle M. "Samson Occom, the Famous Indian Preacher of New England." Missionary Review of the World 33 (December 1910): 913-919.

5121. Busk, Henry William. A Sketch of the Origin and the Recent History of the New England Company by the Senior Member of the Company. London: Spottiswoode and Company, 1884.

5122. Chesterman, A. de M. "The Journals of David Brainerd and of William Carey." Baptist Quarterly, new series 19 (October 1961): 147-156.

5123. Corwin, Charles E. "Efforts of the Dutch-American Colonial Pastors for the Conversion of the Indians." Journal of the Presbyterian Historical Society 12 (October 1925): 225-246.

5124. "Documents of the Society for Promoting and Propagating the Gospel in New England." New-England Historical and Genealogical Register 36 (October 1882): 371-376.

5125. Eames, Wilberforce. Bibliographic Notes on Eliot's Indian Bible and on His Other Translations and Works in the Indian Language of Massachusetts. Washington: Government Printing Office, 1890.

5126. Edwards, Jonathan. Memoirs of the Rev. David Brainerd, Missionary to the Indians on the Borders of New-York, New-Jersey, and Pennsylvania: Chiefly Taken from His Own Diary. Edited by Sereno Edwards Dwight. New Haven: S. Converse, 1822. Enlarged edition of a work published in Boston, 1749.

5127. Francis, Convers. Life of John Eliot, the Apostle to the Indians. Boston: Hilliard, Gray and Company, 1836.

5128. Hare, Lloyd C. M. Thomas Mayhew: Patriarch to the Indians (1593-1682). New York: D. Appleton and Company, 1932.

5129. Harling, Frederick Farnham. "A Biography of John Eliot, 1604-1690." Ph.D. dissertation, Boston University, 1965.

5130. Hawkins, Ernest. Historical Notices of the Missions of the Church of England in the North American Colonies, Previous to the Independence of the United States. London: B. Fellowes, 1845.

5131. Jennings, Francis. "Goals and Functions of Puritan Missions to the Indians." Ethnohistory 18 (Summer 1971): 197-212.

5132. Johnson, Edward Payson. "Christian Work among the North American Indians during the Eighteenth Century." Papers of the American Society of Church History, 2d series 6 (1921): 3-41.

5133. Johnson, Margery R. "The Mayhew Mission to the Indians, 1643-1806." Ph.D. dissertation, Clark University, 1966.

5134. Jones, Jerome W. "The Established Virginia Church and the Conversion of Negroes and Indians, 1620-1760." Journal of Negro History 46 (January 1961): 12-23.

5135. Kellaway, William. The New England Company, 1649-1776: Missionary Society to the American Indians. New York: Barnes and Noble, 1962.

5136. Kemp, William Webb. "The Support of Schools in Colonial New York by the Society for the Propagation of the Gospel in Foreign Parts." Ph.D. dissertation, Columbia University, 1914.

5137. Klingberg, Frank J. Anglican Humanitarianism in Colonial New York. Philadelphia: Church Historical Society, 1940.

5138. _____. "The Anglican Minority in Colonial Pennsylvania, with Particular Reference to the Indian." Pennsylvania Magazine of History and Biography 65 (July 1941): 276-299.

5139. _____. "The Indian Frontier in South Carolina As Seen by the S. P. G. Missionary." Journal of Southern History 5 (November 1939): 479-500.

5140. _____. "The Noble Savage As Seen by the Missionary of the Society for the Propagation of the Gospel in Colonial New York, 1702-1750." Historical Magazine of the Protestant Episcopal Church 8 (March 1939): 128-165.

5141. Lennox, Herbert J. "Samuel Kirkland's Mission to the Iroquois." Ph.D. dissertation, University of Chicago, 1932.

5142. Lewis, Norman. "English Missionary Interest in the Indians of North America, 1578-1700." Ph.D. dissertation, University of Washington, 1968.

5143. Lothrop, Samuel K. Life of Samuel Kirkland. Boston: Charles C. Little and James Brown, 1847.

5144. Love, W. DeLoss. Samson Occom and the Christian Indians of New England. Boston: Pilgrim Press, 1899.

5145. Lydekker, John Wolfe. The Faithful Mohawks. New York: Macmillan Company, 1938.

5146. McCallum, James Dow. Eleazar Wheelock, Founder of Dartmouth College. Hanover, New Hampshire: Dartmouth College Publications, 1939.

5147. Moore, Martin. Memoirs of the Life and Character of Rev. John Eliot, Apostle of the N. A. Indians. Boston: T. Bedlington, 1822. Revised and corrected edition, Memoir of Eliot of the North American Indians. Boston: Seth Goldsmith and Crocker and Brewster, 1842.

5148. Morison, Samuel Eliot. "John Eliot, Apostle to the Indians." In Builders of the Bay Colony, pp. 289-319. Boston: Houghton Mifflin Company, 1930.

5149. Pierson, Arthur T. "John Eliot, Apostle to the Red Indians." Missionary Review of the World 24 (September 1901): 641-645.

5150. Richardson, Leon Burr, ed. An Indian Preacher in England: Being Letters and Diaries Relating to the Mission of the Reverend Samson Occom and the Reverend Nathaniel Whitaker to Collect Funds in England for the Benefit of Eleazar Wheelock's Indian Charity School, from Which Grew Dartmouth College. Hanover, New Hampshire: Dartmouth College Publications, 1933.

5151. Robinson, W. Stitt, Jr. "Indian Education and Missions in Colonial Virginia." Journal of Southern History 18 (May 1952): 152-168.

5152. Russell, Francis. "Apostle to the Indians." American Heritage 9 (December 1957): 4-9, 117-119. John Eliot.

5153. Salisbury, Neal. "Red Puritans: The 'Praying Indians' of Massachusetts Bay and John Eliot." William and Mary Quarterly 31 (January 1974): 27-54.

5154. Stryker, Melancthon Woolsey. "Samuel Kirkland and the Oneida Indians." Proceedings of the New York State Historical Association 14 (1915): 101-107.

5155. Taylor, Maxwell Ford, Jr. "The Influence of Religion on White Attitudes toward Indians in the Early Settlement of Virginia." Ph.D. dissertation, Emory University, 1970.

5156. Thayer, Theodore. "The Friendly Association." Pennsylvania Magazine of

History 67 (October 1943): 356-376.

5157. Thorp, Willard. "Samuel Kirkland, Missionary for the Six Nations: Founder of Hamilton College." In Lives of Eighteen from Princeton, edited by Willard Thorp, pp. 24-50. Princeton: Princeton University Press, 1946.

5158. Trumbull, J. Hammond. Origin and Early Progress of Indian Missions in New England, with a List of Books in the Indian Language Printed at Cambridge and Boston, 1653-1721. Worcester, Massachusetts, 1874.

5159. Weis, Frederick L. "The New England Company of 1649 and Its Missionary Enterprises." Publications of the Colonial Society of Massachusetts, Transactions 38 (1947-1951): 134-218.

5160. Williams, Samuel C. "An Account of the Presbyterian Mission to the Cherokees, 1757-1759." Tennessee Historical Magazine, 2d series 1 (January 1931): 125-138.

5161. Winship, George Parker. "The Eliot Indian Tracts." In Bibliographical Essays: A Tribute to Wilberforce Eames, pp. 179-192. N.p., 1924.

5162. _____. "Samuel Sewall and the New England Company." Proceedings of the Massachusetts Historical Society 67 (1941-1944): 55-110.

5163. Winship, George Parker, ed. The New England Company of 1649 and John Eliot. Publications of the Prince Society, 36. Boston: Prince Society, 1920.

5164. Winslow, Ola E. John Eliot: "Apostle to the Indians." Boston: Houghton Mifflin Company, 1968.

For numerous eighteenth century publications of John Eliot and other missionaries, see the listings in Vail's Voice of the Old Frontier (276). Studies of colonial missionary work are also found under particular denominations below.

BAPTIST MISSIONS

The Baptists, although less active in Indian work than the Methodists and Presbyterians, had some important missions. One of their missionaries, Isaac McCoy, played a significant role in the movement of eastern Indians to the West.

5165. Adams, Franklin G. "Reverend Isaac McCoy." Kansas Historical Collections 2 (1881): 271-275.

5166. Balyeat, Frank A. "Joseph Samuel Murrow, Apostle to the Indians." Chronicles of Oklahoma 35 (Autumn 1957): 297-313.

5167. Belt, Loren James. "Baptist Missions to the Indians of the Five Civilized Tribes of Oklahoma." Th.D. dissertation, Central Baptist Theological Seminary, 1955.

5168. Bolt, Robert. "Reverend Leonard Slater in the Grand River Valley." Michigan History 51 (Fall 1967): 241-251.

5169. Cady, John F. "Isaac McCoy's Mission to the Indians of Indiana and Michigan." Indiana History Bulletin 16 (February 1939): 100-113.

5170. Carleton, William A. "Not Yours but You." Quarterly Review: A Survey of Southern Baptist Progress 16 (April-June 1956): 60-65, 96. On the work of Joseph Samuel Murrow.

5171. Corwin, Hugh D. "Saddle Mountain Mission and Church." Chronicles of Oklahoma 36 (Summer 1958): 118-130.

5172. Crawford, Isabel. Kiowa: The History of a Blanket Indian Mission. New York: Fleming H. Revell Company, 1915.

5173. Cumming, John. "A Puritan among the Chippewas." Michigan History 51 (Fall 1967): 213-225. Abel Bingham, 1827-1855.

5174. Dane, John Preston. "A History of Baptist Missions among the Plains Indians of Oklahoma." Th.D. dissertation, Central Baptist Theological Seminary, 1955.

5175. Fauth, Albert H. "A History of the American Indian Mission Association and Its Contribution to Baptist Indian Missions." Th.D. dissertation, Central Baptist Theological Seminary, 1953.

5176. Fife, Sharon A. "Baptist Indian Church: Thlewarle Mekko Sapkv Coko." Chronicles of Oklahoma 48 (Winter 1970-1971): 450-466.

5177. Fleming, Robert. Sketch of the Life of Elder Humphrey Posey, First Baptist Missionary to the Cherokee Indians and Founder of Valley Town School, North Carolina. Philadelphia: King and Baird, 1852.

5178. Foreman, Carolyn Thomas. "North Fork Town." Chronicles of Oklahoma 29 (Spring 1951): 79-111.

5179. Gammell, William. A History of American Baptist Missions in Asia, Africa, Europe and North America. Boston: Gould, Kendall and Lincoln, 1849.

5180. Hamilton, Robert. The Gospel among the Red Man: The History of the Southern Baptist Indian Missions. Nashville: Baptist Sunday School Board, 1930.

5181. Hill, Esther Clark. "Some Backgrounds of Early Baptist Missions in Kansas Based on Letters in the Pratt Collection of Manuscripts and Documents." Kansas Historical Quarterly 1 (February 1932): 89-103.

5182. House, R. Morton. "'The Only Way' Church and the Sac and Fox Indians." Chronicles of Oklahoma 43 (Winter 1965-1966): 443-466.

5183. Hutcherson, Curtis A. "The Contributions of Dr. Johnston Lykins and Robert Simerwell to the Preservation, Advancement and Evangelization of the American Indians." Th.D. dissertation, Central Baptist Theological Seminary, 1952.

5184. Lempenau, Mary Carswell. "Baptist Mission for Indians." Daughters of the American Revolution Magazine 86 (August 1952): 873-874, 888.

5185. McCormick, Calvin. The Memoir of Miss Eliza McCoy. Dallas, Texas, 1892.

5186. McCoy, Isaac. History of Baptist Indian Missions: Embracing Remarks on the Former and Present Condition of the Aboriginal Tribes, Their Settlement within the Indian Territory, and Their Future Prospects. Washington: William M. Morrison; New York: H. and S. Raynor, 1840. Reprint, with a new introduction by Robert F. Berkhofer, Jr., New York: Johnson Reprint Corporation, 1970.

5187. McDonald, Joseph R. "A History of the Western Oklahoma Indian Baptist Association." Th.D. dissertation, Central Baptist Theological Seminary, 1957.

5188. Mason, Zane Allen. Frontiersmen of the Faith: A History of Baptist Pioneer Work in Texas, 1865-1885. San Antonio: Naylor Company, 1970.

5189. Moffitt, James W. "Early Baptist Missionary Work among the Cherokees." East Tennessee Historical Society's Publications no. 12 (1940): 16-27.

5190. _____. "A History of Early Baptist Missions among the Five Civilized Tribes." Ph.D. dissertation, University of Oklahoma, 1946.

5191. _____. "Some Results of Early Baptist Indian Missions, 1801-1861." Review and Expositor: A Baptist Theological Quarterly 45 (April 1948): 209-216.

5192. Olsen, Olaf Severn. "A History of the Baptists of the Rocky Mountain Region,

1849-1890." Ph.D. dissertation, University of Colorado, 1953.

5193. Peck, Solomon. "History of the Missions of the Baptist General Convention." In History of American Missions to the Heathen, from Their Commencement to the Present Time, edited by Joseph Tracy, pp. 353-620. Worcester, Massachusetts: Spooner and Howland, 1840.

5194. Rister, Carl Coke. Baptist Missions among the American Indians. Atlanta, Georgia: Home Mission Board Southern Baptist Convention, 1944.

5195. Roustio, Edward. "A History of the Life of Isaac McCoy in Relationship to Early Indian Migrations and Missions As Revealed in His Unpublished Manuscripts." Th.D. dissertation, Central Baptist Theological Seminary, 1954.

5196. Routh, E. C. "Early Missionaries to the Cherokees." Chronicles of Oklahoma 15 (December 1937): 449-465.

5197. Schultz, George A. An Indian Canaan: Isaac McCoy and the Vision of an Indian State. Norman: University of Oklahoma Press, 1972.

5198. Torbet, Robert G. Venture of Faith: The Story of the American Baptist Foreign Mission Society and the Woman's American Baptist Foreign Mission Society, 1814-1954. Philadelphia: Judson Press, 1955.

5199. "Two Minute Books of Kansas Missions in the Forties." Kansas Historical Quarterly 2 (August 1933): 227-250.

5200. West, Sam. "Brief Statement of Facts Concerning Old Baptist Mission Church, Cherokee Nation." Chronicles of Oklahoma 24 (Spring 1946): 106-107.

5201. Wyeth, Walter N. Isaac McCoy: A Memorial. Philadelphia: W. N. Wyeth, 1895.

5202. Yeager, Randolph O. "Indian Enterprises of Isaac McCoy, 1817-1846." Ph.D. dissertation, University of Oklahoma, 1954.

CATHOLIC MISSIONS

Roman Catholics devoted much energy and money to evangelizing the Indians; many of the missionaries were members of religious orders like the Jesuits or Franciscans or the numerous congregations of nuns. A good deal of the missionary activity was concerned with education.

Studies on Catholic missions in the Southwest before the advent of the Anglo-Americans are not included in the listing here.

5203. Adney, John R. "Who Was Father Mazzuchelli?" Annals of Iowa, 3d series 39 (Winter 1969): 552-560.

5204. Agatha, Mother M. "Catholic Education and the Indian." In Essays on Catholic Education in the United States, edited by Roy Joseph Deferrari, pp. 523-553. Washington: Catholic University of America Press, 1942.

5205. Aldrich, Vernice M., ed. "Father George Antoine Belcourt, Red River Missionary." North Dakota Historical Quarterly 2 (October 1927): 30-52.

5206. Antrei, Albert. "Father Pierre De Smet." Montana, the Magazine of Western History 13 (April 1963): 24-43.

5207. Bagley, Clarence B., ed. Early Catholic Missions in Old Oregon. 2 volumes. Seattle: Lowman and Hanford Company, 1932.

5208. Betschart, Ildefons. "Bishop Martin Marty, O.S.B.--1834-1896: 'The Apostle to the Sioux Indians.'" Records of the American Catholic Historical Society of Philadelphia 49 (June 1938): 97-134; (September 1938): 214-248; 50 (March 1939): 33-64.

5209. Bischoff, William N. The Jesuits in Old Oregon: A Sketch of Jesuit Activities in the Pacific Northwest. Caldwell, Idaho: Caxton Printers, 1945.

5210. "Bright Vignettes of a Lost World." Life 63 (December 1, 1967): 52-59. Journals and paintings of Nicolas Point.

5211. Brouillet, J. B. A. The Bureau of Catholic Indian Missions--the Work of the Decade Ending December 31, 1883. Washington, 1883.

5212. _____. Work of the Catholic Indian Missions of the United States of America. Washington, 1879.

5213. Buetow, Harold A. "The Underprivileged and Roman Catholic Education." Journal of Negro Education 40 (Fall 1971): 373-389.

5214. Bureau of Catholic Indian Missions. Status of the Catholic Indian Missions in the United States, 1876. Baltimore, 1876.

5215. Cameron, Jean. "Ka-ou-shin, the Blackrobe." Catholic World 121 (August 1925): 677-681. Father Joseph Cataldo.

5216. Cassal, Hilary. "Missionary Tour in the Chickasaw Nation and Western Indian Territory." Chronicles of Oklahoma 34 (Winter 1956-1957): 397-416.

5217. Chapman, Berlin B. "Valuable Manuscripts on Oklahoma Indian History in the Bureau of Catholic Indian Missions, Washington, D.C." Chronicles of Oklahoma 26 (Summer 1948): 247.

5218. Clark, Ella E. "Mission in the Wilderness." Montana Magazine of History 5 (Winter 1955): 51-57. St. Ignatius Mission, Montana.

5219. _____. "The Old Mission." Idaho Yesterdays 15 (Fall 1971): 18-27. Coeur d'Alene Mission.

5220. Cody, Edmund R. History of the Coeur d'Alene Mission of the Sacred Heart. Caldwell, Idaho: Caxton Printers, 1930.

5221. Collins, Dabney Otis. "A Happening at Oglala." American West 6 (March 1969): 15-19.

5222. Connolly, James B. "Father De Smet in North Dakota." North Dakota History 27 (January 1960): 5-24.

5223. Corrigan, Joseph M. "Father Peter De Smet--Mighty Sower, 1801-1873." Records of the American Catholic Historical Society of Philadelphia 27 (June 1916): 95-112; (September 1916): 259-274.

5224. Davis, William L. A History of St. Ignatius Mission. Spokane, Washington, 1954.

5225. _____. "Mission St. Anne of the Cayuse Indians, 1847-1848." Ph.D. dissertation, University of California, 1943.

5226. _____. "Peter John De Smet: The Journey of 1840." Pacific Northwest Quarterly 35 (January 1944): 29-43; (April 1944): 121-142.

5227. _____. "Peter John De Smet: Missionary to the Potawatomi, 1837-1840." Pacific Northwest Quarterly 33 (April 1942): 123-152.

5228. _____. "Peter John De Smet: The Years of Preparation, 1801-1837." Pacific Northwest Quarterly 32 (April 1941): 167-196.

5229. De Smet, Pierre Jean. Letters and Sketches, with a Narrative of a Year's Residence among the Indian Tribes of the Rocky Mountains. Philadelphia: M. Fithian, 1843.

5230. _____. Life, Letters, and Travels of Father Pierre-Jean De Smet, S.J., 1801-1873, Missionary Labors and Adventures among the Wild Tribes of the North American Indians, Embracing Minute Descriptions of Their Manners, Customs, Games, Modes of Warfare and Torture, Legends, Traditions, etc. Edited by H. M. Chittenden and A. T. Richardson. 4 volumes. New York: Francis P. Harper, 1905.

5231. _____. New Indian Sketches. New York: D. and J. Sadlier and Company, 1863.

5232. _____. Oregon Missions and Travels over the Rocky Mountains in 1845-46. New York: Edward Dunigan, 1847.

5233. _____. Western Missions and Missionaries: A Series of Letters. New York: P. J. Kenedy, 1859.

5234. Donnelly, Joseph P. "Father Jacques Marquette and the Indians of Upper Michigan." Records of the American Catholic Historical Society of Philadelphia 80 (March 1969): 39-52.

5235. _____. Jacques Marquette, S.J., 1637-1675. Chicago: Loyola University Press, 1968.

5236. _____. Thwaites' Jesuit Relations: Errata and Addenda. Chicago: Loyola University Press, 1967. See the "Bibliography, 1906-66," pp. 211-269.

5237. Donnelly, Joseph P., ed. Wilderness Kingdom: Indian Life in the Rocky Mountains 1840-1847, the Journals and Paintings of Nicolas Point. New York: Holt, Rinehart and Winston, 1967.

5238. Donnelly, William Patrick. "Father Pierre-Jean De Smet: United States Ambassador to the Indians." Historical Records and Studies 24 (1934): 7-142.

5239. _____. "Nineteenth Century Jesuit Reductions in the United States." Mid-America 17 (April 1935): 69-83.

5240. Donohue, Arthur Thomas. "A History of the Early Jesuit Missions in Kansas." Ph.D. dissertation, University of Kansas, 1931.

5241. Duignan, Peter. "Early Jesuit Missionaries: A Suggestion for Further Study." American Anthropologist 60 (August 1958): 725-732.

5242. Duratschek, Mary Claudia. Crusading Along Sioux Trails: A History of the Catholic Missions in South Dakota. St. Meinrad, Indiana, 1947.

5243. _____. Under the Shadow of His Wings: History of Sacred Heart Convent of Benedictine Sisters, Yankton, South Dakota, 1880-1970. Aberdeen, South Dakota: North Plains Press, 1971.

5244. Eberschweiler, Frederic. "An Indian Clergy Impossible." Catholic World 65 (September 1897): 815-824.

5245. Eckert, Robert P., Jr. "A Missionary in the Wilderness." Catholic World 144 (February 1937): 590-595. Father Samuel Mazzuchelli.

5246. Elliott, Richard R. "The Apostolate of Father Baraga among the Chippewas and Whites of Lake Superior." American Catholic Quarterly Review 21 (July 1896): 596-617.

5247. Emerson, Dorothy. Among the Mescalero Apaches: The Story of Father Albert Braun, O.F.M. Tucson: University of Arizona Press, 1973.

5248. Fightmaster, Maxine. "Sacred Heart Mission among the Potawatomi Indians." Chronicles of Oklahoma 50 (Summer 1972): 156-176.

5249. Fitzgerald, Mary Clement. "Bishop Marty and His Sioux Missions, 1876-1896." South Dakota Historical Collections 20 (1940): 523-558.

5250. Fitzgerald, Mary Paul. "John Baptist Miege, S.J., 1815-1884, First Vicar Apostolic of the Indian Territory: A Study in Frontier History." Historical Records and Studies 24 (1934): 284-362.

5251. _____. Beacon on the Plains. Leavenworth, Kansas: Saint Mary College, 1939.

5252. _____. "Osage Mission, a Factor in the Making of Kansas." Mid-America 19 (July 1937): 182-196.

5253. Flick, Lawrence F. "The Papago Indians and Their Church." Records of the American Catholic Historical Society of Philadelphia 5 (December 1894): 385-416.

5254. Flynn, William J. "Glorious Work to Be Abandoned? Catholic Indian Missions." Commonweal 20 (June 8, 1934): 163.

5255. Forbis, Richard. "The Flathead Apostasy, an Interpretation." Montana Magazine of History 1 (October 1951): 35-40.

5256. Foreman, Carolyn Thomas. "St. Agnes Academy for the Choctaws." Chronicles of Oklahoma 48 (Autumn 1970): 323-330.

5257. Gachet, Anthony Maria. "Five Years in America (Cinq Ans en Amerique): Journal of a Missionary among the Redskins --Journal, 1859," translated by Joseph Schafer. Wisconsin Magazine of History 18 (September 1934): 66-76; (December 1934): 191-204; (March 1935): 345-359.

5258. Gailland, Maurice. "Early Years at St. Mary's Pottowatomie Mission: From the Diary of Father Maurice Gailland, S.J.," edited by James M. Burke. Kansas Historical Quarterly 20 (August 1953): 501-529.

5259. Garraghan, Gilbert J. Chapters in Frontier History: Research Studies in the Making of the West. Milwaukee: Bruce Publishing Company, 1934.

5260. _____. Jesuits of the Middle United States. 3 volumes. New York: America Press, 1938.

5261. _____. "The Kickapoo Mission." St. Louis Catholic Historical Review 4 (January-April 1922): 25-50.

5262. _____. "Nicolas Point, Jesuit Missionary in Montana of the Forties." In The Trans-Mississippi West: Papers Read at a Conference Held at the University of Colorado, June 18-June 21, 1929, edited by James F. Willard and Colin B. Goodykoontz, pp. 43-63. Boulder: University of Colorado Press, 1930.

5263. _____. "The Potawatomi Mission of Council Bluffs." St. Louis Catholic Historical Review 3 (July 1921): 155-173.

5264. _____. "St. Regis Seminary--First Catholic Indian School (1823-1831)." Catholic Historical Review 4 (January 1919): 452-478.

5265. Garraghan, Gilbert J., ed. "An Early Missouri River Journal." Mid-America 13 (January 1931): 236-254. Journal of Nicolas Point.

5266. _____. "Father De Smet's Sioux Peace Mission of 1868 and the Journal of Charles Galpin." Mid-America 13 (October 1930): 141-163.

5267. Gerlach, Dominic B. "St. Joseph's Indian Normal School, 1888-1896." Indiana Magazine of History 69 (March 1973): 1-42.

5268. Graham, Hugh. "Catholic Missionary Schools among the Indians of Minnesota." Mid-America 13 (January 1931): 199-206.

5269. Graves, W. W. Life and Letters of Fathers Ponziglione, Schoenmakers, and Other Early Jesuits at Osage Mission. St. Paul, Kansas: W. W. Graves, 1916.

5270. Hamilton, Raphael N. "Jesuit Mission at Sault Ste. Marie." Michigan History 52 (Summer 1968): 123-132.

5271. _____. Marquette's Explorations: The Narratives Reexamined. Madison: University of Wisconsin Press, 1970.

5272. Hoecken, Christian. "Letters of Father Christian Hoecken." United States Catholic Magazine and Monthly Review 6 (February 1847): 89-92; (March 1847): 149-151; (April 1847): 214-216.

5273. Hoffman, Matthias M. "The Winnebago Mission: A Cause Celebre." Mid-America 13 (July 1930): 26-52.

5274. Jacobs, Hubert, ed. "The Potawatomi Mission 1854." Mid-America 36 (October 1954): 220-248. Letter of Maurice Gailland.

5275. "Journal of Father Vitry of the Society of Jesus, Army Chaplain during the War against the Chickasaw from 1738 to the Beginning of 1740." Mid-America 28 (January 1946): 30-59.

5276. Karol, Joseph. "What Happened to the Potawatomi?" American Ecclesiastical Review 129 (December 1953): 361-367.

5277. Kehoe, Mary Urban. "The Educational Activities of Distinguished Catholic Missionaries among the Five Civilized Tribes." Chronicles of Oklahoma 24 (Summer 1946): 166-182.

5278. Kellogg, Louise Phelps. "The First Missionary in Wisconsin." Wisconsin Magazine of History 4 (June 1921): 417-425. Father Rene Menard.

5279. Kenton, Edna, ed. The Jesuit Relations and Allied Documents: Travels and Explorations of the Jesuit Missionaries in North America (1610-1791). New York: Albert and Charles Boni, 1925. Reprinted New York: Vanguard Press, 1954.

5280. Kinlicheeny, Jeanette. "Viewpoints: Indian." Momentum 3 (December 1972): 44-46.

5281. Laracy, John. "Sacred Heart Mission and Abbey." Chronicles of Oklahoma 5 (1927): 234-250. Includes "Diary of a Young French Immigrant," Joseph Lanchet.

5282. Laveille, E. The Life of Father De Smet, S.J. (1801-1873). Translated by Marian Lindsay. New York: P. J. Kenedy and Sons, 1915.

5283. Leger, Mary Celeste. "Catholic Indian Missions in Maine (1611-1820)." Ph.D. dissertation, Catholic University of America, 1929.

5284. Lothrop, Gloria Ricci. "Father Gregory Mengarini, an Italian Jesuit Missionary in the Transmontane West: His Life and Memoirs." Ph.D. dissertation, University of Southern California, 1970.

5285. McCoy, James C. Jesuit Relations of Canada, 1632-1673: A Bibliography. Paris: Arthur Rau, 1937.

5286. McDermott, John Francis. "De Smet's Illustrator: Father Nicolas Point." Nebraska History 33 (March 1952): 35-40.

5287. McDonald, Grace. "Father Francis

Pierz, Missionary." Minnesota History 10 (June 1929): 107-125.

5288. Magaret, Helene. Father De Smet, Pioneer Priest of the Rockies. New York: Farrar and Rinehart, 1940.

5289. _____. "Marty." Catholic World 160 (December 1944): 220-225. St. Paul's Indian Mission, South Dakota.

5290. Mallett, Edmond. "The Origin of the Flathead Mission of the Rocky Mountains." Records of the American Catholic Historical Society of Philadelphia 2 (1886-1888): 174-205.

5291. "Marquette League Jubilee." America 91 (September 18, 1954): 579-580.

5292. Mazzuchelli, Samuel. Memoirs, Historical and Edifying, of a Missionary Apostolic of the Order of Saint Dominic among Various Indian Tribes and among the Catholics and Protestants in the United States of America. Translated by Mary Benedicta Kennedy. Chicago: W. F. Hall Printing Company, 1915.

5293. Michalicka, John. "First Catholic Church in Indian Territory--1872: St. Patrick's Church at Atoka." Chronicles of Oklahoma 50 (Winter 1972): 479-485.

5294. Mullin, Frank Anthony. "Father De Smet and the Pottawattamie Indian Mission." Iowa Journal of History and Politics 23 (April 1925): 192-216.

5295. Mulvey, Mary Doris. French Catholic Missionaries in the Present United States (1604-1791). Washington: Catholic University of America, 1936.

5296. Nieberding, Velma. "Catholic Education among the Osage." Chronicles of Oklahoma 32 (Autumn 1954): 290-307.

5297. _____. "Chief Splitlog and the Cayuga Mission Church." Chronicles of Oklahoma 32 (Spring 1954): 18-28.

5298. _____. "St. Agnes School of the Choctaws." Chronicles of Oklahoma 33 (Summer 1955): 183-192.

5299. _____. "St. Mary's of the Quapaws, 1894-1927." Chronicles of Oklahoma 31 (Spring 1953): 2-14.

5300. _____. "The Very Reverend Urban DeHasque, S.T.D., L.L.D., Pioneer Priest of Indian Territory." Chronicles of Oklahoma 38 (Spring 1960): 35-42.

5301. Nieberding, Velma, ed. "A Trip to Quapaw in 1903." Chronicles of Oklahoma 31 (Summer 1953): 142-167. Report of Sister M. Laurence.

5302. Nolan, Charles E. "Recollections of Tulsa, Indian Territory, from Sister Mary

Agnes New Church, O.Carm." Chronicles of Oklahoma 49 (Spring 1971): 92-99.

5303. Norton, Mary Aquinas. Catholic Missionary Activities in the Northwest, 1818-1864. Washington: Catholic University of America Press, 1930.

5304. _____. "Catholic Missions and Missionaries among the Indians of Dakota." North Dakota Historical Quarterly 5 (April 1931): 149-165.

5305. O'Brien, F. A. "Father Frank Piertz." Michigan Historical Collections 39 (1915): 225-232.

5306. _____. "Lady Antoinette Von Hoeffern." Michigan Historical Collections 39 (1915): 221-224.

5307. O'Connor, Thomas F. "Pierre De Smet: Frontier Missionary." Mid-America 17 (July 1935): 191-196.

5308. O'Conor, J. F. X. "The Jesuit Indian Missions in the United States, 1565 to 1916." Proceedings of the Nineteenth International Congress of Americanists, 1915, pp. 487-502.

5309. O'Dwyer, George F. "Catholic Indians of Maine." Catholic World 135 (April 1932): 81-84.

5310. O'Hara, Edwin V. "Catholic Pioneers of the Oregon Country." Catholic Historical Review 3 (July 1917): 187-201.

5311. _____. "De Smet in the Oregon Country." Quarterly of the Oregon Historical Society 10 (September 1909): 239-262.

5313. Ondracek, Elaine. "In Search of Ethete." Delta Kappa Gamma Bulletin 36 (Summer 1970): 42-46. St. Stephen's Indian Mission School, Wyoming.

5314. Owens, M. Lillianna. "The Guiding Light of the Osages." Catholic Educational Review 39 (September 1941): 414-420.

5315. Palladino, L. B. Anthony Ravalli, S.J., Forty Years a Missionary in the Rocky Mountains. Helena, Montana: G. E. Boos and Company, 1884.

5316. _____. Indian and White in the Northwest: A History of Catholicity in Montana, 1831-1891. 2d edition, revised and enlarged. Lancaster, Pennsylvania: Wickersham Publishing Company, 1922. Original edition, 1894.

5317. Palm, Mary Borgias. The Jesuit Missions of the Illinois Country, 1673-1763. Cleveland, 1933.

5318. Pare, George. "The St. Joseph Mission." Mississippi Valley Historical Review 17 (June 1930): 24-54.

5319. Partoll, Albert J., ed. "Father Mengarini's Narrative of the Rockies." Frontier and Midland: A Magazine of the West 18 (Spring 1938): 192-202; (Summer 1938): 258-266.

5320. Petersen, William J. "The Joliet-Marquette Expedition." Palimpsest 49 (October 1968): 416-446.

5321. Phillips, Paul C. "Jesuit Missionaries as Doctors." In Medicine in the Making of Montana, pp. 34-40. Missoula: Montana Medical Association, 1962.

5322. Point, Nicolas. "Religion and Superstition: Vignettes of a Wilderness Mission." American West 4 (November 1967): 34-43, 70-73.

5323. Raufer, Maria Ilma. Black Robes and Indians on the Last Frontier: A Story of Heroism. Milwaukee: Bruce Publishing Company, 1966. St. Mary's Mission, Omak, Washington.

5324. Reilly, Louis W. "Father Ravalli, Pioneer Indian Missionary." Catholic World 125 (April 1927): 67-73.

5325. Reyes, Paul. "An Indian 'Uprising' Five Years Later." Christian Century 88 (January 20, 1971): 80-84.

5326. Riggs, Francis Mary. Attitudes of Missionary Sisters toward American Indian Acculturation. Studies in Sociology, no. 72. Washington: Catholic University of America, 1967.

5327. Ronda, James P. "The European Indian: Jesuit Civilization Planning in New France." Church History 41 (September 1972): 385-395.

5328. Rothensteiner, John. "Early Missionary Efforts among the Indians in the Diocese of St. Louis." St. Louis Catholic Historical Review 2 (April-July 1920): 57-96.

5329. St. Hilaire, Theodore J. "Pedagogy in the Wilderness." Oregon Historical Quarterly 63 (1962): 55-60.

5330. St. Luke, Mary. "Montana Missions." Records of the American Catholic Historical Society of Philadelphia 34 (March 1923): 32-49.

5331. Schaeffer, Claude. "The First Jesuit Mission to the Flathead, 1840-1850: A Study in Culture Conflicts." Pacific Northwest Quarterly 28 (July 1937): 227-250.

5332. Schimberg, Albert P. "Father Van

den Broek." Catholic World 113 (June 1921): 328-333.

5333. Schoenberg, Wilfred P. "Historic St. Peter's Mission: Landmark of the Jesuits and the Ursulines among the Blackfeet." Montana, the Magazine of Western History 11 (Winter 1961): 68-85.

5334. _____. Jesuit Mission Presses in the Pacific Northwest: A History and Bibliography of Imprints, 1876-1899. Portland, Oregon: Champoeg Press, 1957.

5335. _____. Jesuits in Montana, 1840-1960. Portland, Oregon, 1960.

5336. _____. Jesuits in Oregon, 1844-1959. Portland, Oregon: Oregon-Jesuit, 1959.

5337. Shea, John Gilmary. History of the Catholic Missions among the Indian Tribes of the United States 1529-1854. New York: Edward Dunigan and Brother, 1855.

5338. Stephan, J. A. The Bureau of Catholic Indian Missions, 1874 to 1895. Washington: Church News Publishing Company, 1895.

5339. _____. Report of Rev. J. A. Stephan, Director, to Rt. Rev. Bishop M. Marty, President of the Bureau of Catholic Indian Missions for the Year 1891-'92. Washington: Gedney and Roberts Company, 1892.

5340. Terrell, John U. Black Robe, the Life of Pierre-Jean de Smet, Missionary, Explorer, Pioneer. Garden City, New York: Doubleday and Company, 1964.

5341. Thomas, Mary Ursula. "The Catholic Church on the Oklahoma Frontier, 1824-1907." Ph.D. dissertation, Saint Louis University, 1938.

5342. Thompson, Erwin N. "Joseph M. Cataldo and Saint Joseph's Mission." Idaho Yesterdays 18 (Summer 1974): 19-29.

5343. Thwaites, Reuben Gold, ed. "Documents Relating to the Catholic Church in Green Bay, and the Mission at Little Chute, 1825-40." Collections of the State Historical Society of Wisconsin 14 (1898): 162-205.

5344. _____. The Jesuit Relations and Allied Documents, 1610-1791. 73 volumes. Cleveland: Burrows Brothers, 1896-1901.

5345. Trecy, Jeremiah F. "The First Catholic Missions in Nebraska." Mid-America 14 (January 1932): 269-275.

5346. Treutlein, Theodore H. "The Jesuit Missionary in the Role of Physician." Mid-America 22 (April 1940): 120-141.

5347. Van der Heyden, J. "Monsignor Adrian J. Croquet, Indian Missionary, (1818-1902) and Some of His Letters." Records of the American Catholic Historical Society of Philadelphia 16 (June 1905): 121-161; (September 1905): 268-295; (December 1905): 456-462; 17 (March 1906): 86-96; (June 1906): 220-242; (September 1906): 267-288.

5348. Verwyst, Chrysostom. Life and Letters of Rt. Rev. Frederic Baraga. Milwaukee: M. H. Wiltzius and Company, 1900.

5349. _____. Missionary Labors of Fathers Marquette, Menard, and Allouez in the Lake Superior Region. Chicago: Hoffman Brothers, 1886.

5350. Vollmar, E. R., ed. "Missionary Life in Colorado, 1874." Mid-America 35 (July 1953): 175-180.

5351. Weber, Francis J. "A Missionary's Plea for Governmental Assistance." Records of the American Catholic Historical Society of Philadelphia 77 (December 1966): 242-249.

5352. White, Mary Afra. "Catholic Indian Missionary Influence in the Development of Catholic Education in Montana, 1840-1903." Ph.D. dissertation, Saint Louis University, 1940.

5353. Wilken, Robert L. Anselm Weber, O.F.M., Missionary to the Navaho, 1898-1921. Milwaukee: Bruce Publishing Company, 1955.

5354. Woolworth, Nancy L. "The Grand Portage Mission, 1731-1965." Minnesota History 39 (Winter 1965): 301-310.

5355. Wooten, Dudley G. "Noble Ursuline." Catholic World 111 (August 1920): 588-602. Sister Mary A. Madeus (Sarah Theresa Dunne).

5356. Zens, M. Serena. "The Educational Work of the Catholic Church among the Indians of South Dakota from the Beginning to 1935." South Dakota Historical Collections 20 (1940): 299-356.

5357. Zerwekh, Edward Mary. "John Baptist Salpointe, 1825-1894." New Mexico Historical Review 37 (January 1962): 1-19; (April 1962): 132-154; (July 1962): 214-229.

See also the items listed under Church-State Conflict in Indian Education (6108 to 6137).

EPISCOPAL CHURCH MISSIONS

Episcopalian missionaries were active, especially among the Sioux, and notable church leaders like bishops Henry B. Whipple and William H. Hare worked zealously among the Indians.

5358. Aldrich, Vernice M. "Biographical Sketch of Joseph A. Gilfillan, Indian Missionary--1838-1913." North Dakota Historical Quarterly 1 (July 1927): 41-45.

5359. Barnds, William Joseph. "The Ministry of the Reverend Samuel Dutton Hinman, among the Sioux." Historical Magazine of the Protestant Episcopal Church 38 (December 1969): 393-401.

5360. Bloomfield, J. K. The Oneidas. New York: Alden Brothers, 1907.

5361. Botkin, Sam L. "Indian Missions of the Episcopal Church in Oklahoma." Chronicles of Oklahoma 36 (Spring 1958): 40-47.

5362. Breck, Charles. The Life of the Reverend James Lloyd Breck, D. D., Chiefly from Letters Written by Himself. New York: E. and J. B. Young and Company, 1883.

5363. Daniels, Roger. "The Fierce-Fighting Sioux Turned Christian." Mentor 12 (March 1924): 43-45.

5364. Doig, Ivan. "The Tribe That Learned the Gospel of Capitalism." American West 11 (March 1974): 42-47. William Duncan and the Tsimshean Indians.

5365. Emery, Julia C. A Century of Endeavor, 1821-1921: A Record of the First Hundred Years of the Domestic and Foreign Missionary Society of the Protestant Episcopal Church in the United States of America. New York: Department of Missions, 1921.

5366. Foreman, Carolyn Thomas, ed. "Journal of a Tour in the Indian Territory." Chronicles of Oklahoma 10 (June 1932): 219-256. N. Sayre Harris, Secretary and General Agent of the Protestant Episcopal Church, 1844.

5367. Goodwin, Gerald J. "Christianity, Civilization and the Savage: The Anglican Mission to the American Indian." Historical Magazine of the Protestant Episcopal Church 42 (June 1973): 93-110.

5368. Greene, Howard. The Reverend Richard Fish Cadle, a Missionary of the Protestant Episcopal Church in the Territories of Michigan and Wisconsin in the Early Nineteenth Century. Waukesha, Wisconsin: Davis-Greene Corporation, 1936.

5369. Hare, William Hobart. Glimpses into the Life of the Indian Schools in South Dakota. New York: L. F. Eggers, 1908.

5370. Hinman, Samuel Dutton. Journal of the Reverend S. D. Hinman, Missionary to the Santee Sioux Indians. Compiled by William Welsh. Philadelphia: McCalla and Stavey, 1869.

5371. Hock, Alvin Scollay. "The Church in Indian Territory." Protestant Episcopal Church Historical Magazine 8 (December 1939): 372-387.

5372. Holcombe, Theodore I. An Apostle of the Wilderness: James Lloyd Breck, D.D., His Missions and His Schools. New York: Thomas Whittaker, 1903.

5373. Howe, M. A. DeWolfe. "An Apostle to the Sioux: Bishop Hare of South Dakota." Atlantic Monthly 108 (September 1911): 359-370.

5374. _____. The Life and Labors of Bishop Hare, Apostle to the Sioux. New York: Sturgis and Walton Company, 1912.

5375. Jessett, Thomas E. "Anglicanism among the Indians of Washington Territory." Pacific Northwest Quarterly 42 (July 1951): 224-241.

5376. _____. "Origins of the Episcopal Church in the Pacific Northwest." Oregon Historical Quarterly 48 (September 1947): 225-244; (December 1947): 287-308.

5377. _____. "The Origins of the Episcopal Church in Western Washington." Pacific Northwest Quarterly 37 (October 1946): 303-312.

5378. Kent, Herbert Richard. "Four Decades of Missionary Enterprise: An Institutional History of the Episcopal Church in the Pacific Northwest, 1851-1889." Ph.D. dissertation, University of Texas, 1967.

5379. Kersey, Harry A., and Donald E. Pullease. "Bishop William Crane Gray's Mission to the Seminole Indians in Florida, 1893-1914." Historical Magazine of the Protestant Episcopal Church 42 (September 1973): 257-273.

5380. Pipes, Nellie B., ed. "Indian Conditions in 1836-1838." Oregon Historical Quarterly 32 (December 1931): 332-342. Report of the Reverend Herbert Beaver.

5381. Prosch, Mrs. Thomas W. "The Protestant Episcopal as a Missionary and Pioneer Church." Washington Historical Quarterly 1 (April 1907): 125-130.

5382. Smith, Franklin C. "Pioneer Beginnings at Emmanuel, Shawnee." Chronicles of Oklahoma 24 (Spring 1946): 2-14.

5383. Stinson, Richard L. "The Development of Indian Mission Policy and Practice in the National Period." Historical Magazine of the Protestant Episcopal Church 37 (March 1968): 51-65.

5384. Thwaites, Reuben Gold, ed. "Documents Relating to the Episcopal Church and Mission in Green Bay, 1825-1841." Collections of the State Historical Society of Wisconsin 14 (1898): 450-515.

5385. Whipple, Henry Benjamin. "Civilization and Christianization of the Ojibways of Minnesota." Collections of the Minnesota Historical Society 9 (1898-1900): 129-142.

5386. _____. Lights and Shadows of a Long Episcopate. New York: Macmillan Company, 1899.

5387. Wicks, J. B. "A Chapter from the Indian Territory: Story of the Indian Territory Mission." Protestant Episcopal Church Historical Magazine 3 (December 1934): 262-269.

5388. Woodruff, K. Brent. "The Episcopal Mission to the Dakotas, 1860-1898." South Dakota Historical Collections 17 (1934): 553-603.

LUTHERAN MISSIONS

The Lutherans were involved in mission work among the Indians to a very limited extent. That fact is reflected in the paucity of historical studies on Lutheran Indian missions.

5389. Greenholt, Homer Reginald. "A Study of Wilhelm Loehe, His Colonies and the Lutheran Indian Missions in the Saginaw Valley of Michigan." Ph.D. dissertation, University of Chicago, 1937.

5390. Hill, Burton S. "Frontier Powder River Mission." Annals of Wyoming 38 (October 1966): 215-222.

5391. Keiser, Albert. Lutheran Mission Work among the American Indians. Minneapolis: Augsburg Publishing House, 1922.

5392. Kjaer, Jens Christian. "The Lutheran Mission at Oaks, Oklahoma." Chronicles of Oklahoma 28 (Spring 1950): 42-51.

5393. Luckhard, Charles F. Faith in the Forest: A True Story of Pioneer Lutheran Missionaries, Laboring among the Chippewa Indians in Michigan, 1833-1868. Sebewaing, Michigan, 1952.

5394. Morstad, Alexander E. The Reverend Erik Olsen Morstad: His Missionary Work among the Wisconsin Pottawatomie Indians. Clearwater, Florida: Eldnar Press, 1971.

5395. Schoenfuhs, Walter P. "'O Tebeningeion'--'O Dearest Jesus.'" Concordia

Historical Institute Quarterly 37 (October 1964): 95-114.

5396. Suelflow, Roy A. "Lutheran Missions in the Saginaw Valley." Michigan History 51 (Fall 1967): 226-240.

5397. Trexler, Edgar R. "Lutherans and American Indians: A Confrontation." Christian Century 87 (September 16, 1970): 1103-1105.

5398. Wagner, Oswald F. "Lutheran Zealots among the Crows." Montana, the Magazine of Western History 22 (Spring 1972): 2-19.

MENNONITE MISSIONS

The Mennonites conducted some missions, chiefly with the Cheyenne Indians in Oklahoma and in Montana.

5399. Among the Cheyenne and Arapaho Indians in Oklahoma: Seventy-five Years of General Conference Mission Work. Newton, Kansas: Board of Missions, General Conference, Mennonite Church, 1955.

5400. Habegger, Lois R. Cheyenne Trails: A History of Mennonites and Cheyennes in Montana. Newton, Kansas: Mennonite Publication Office, 1959.

5401. Kaufman, Edmund G. "Mennonite Missions among the Oklahoma Indians." Chronicles of Oklahoma 40 (Spring 1962): 41-54.

5402. Linscheid, Ruth C. Red Moon. Newton, Kansas, 1973. Story of Henry J. Kliewer, Mennonite missionary to the Cheyennes.

5403. Petter, Rodolphe C. Reminiscences of Past Years in Mission Service among the Cheyenne. Newton, Kansas: Herald Publishing Company, 1936.

METHODIST MISSIONS

The Methodists had an early Wyandot mission in Ohio, a famous manual labor school for the Shawnee Indians in Kansas, missions in Indian Territory, and numerous missionary enterprises in the Pacific Northwest.

5404. Anderson, James. "The Methodist Shawnee Mission in Johnson County, Kansas, 1830-1862." Trail Guide 1 (January 1956): 7-20.

5405. Babcock, Sidney H. "John Jasper Methvin, 1846-1941." Chronicles of Oklahoma 19 (June 1941): 113-118.

5406. Babcock, Sidney Henry, and John Y. Bryce. History of Methodism in Oklahoma:

Story of the Indian Mission Annual Conference of the Methodist Episcopal Church,
South. Oklahoma City: Times Journal Publishing Company, 1937.

5407. Ballenger, T. L. "Joseph Franklin
Thompson: An Early Cherokee Leader."
Chronicles of Oklahoma 30 (Autumn 1952):
285-291.

5408. Barclay, Wade Crawford. History of
Methodist Missions: Part One, Early
American Methodism, 1769-1844. 2 volumes.
New York: Board of Missions and Church
Extension of the Methodist Church, 1949-
1950.

5409. _____. History of Methodist Missions: Part Two, The Methodist Church,
1845-1939. New York: Board of Missions
and Church Extension of the Methodist
Church, 1957.

5410. Barnes, Lela, ed. "Letters of Allen
T. Ward, 1842-1851, from the Shawnee
and Kaw (Methodist) Missions." Kansas
Historical Quarterly 33 (Autumn 1967):
321-377.

5411. Benson, Henry C. Life among the
Choctaws, and Sketches of the South-
West. Cincinnati: L. Swornstedt and A.
Poe, for the Methodist Episcopal Church,
1860. Account by a Methodist missionary.

5412. Brewer, Phil D. "Rev. Willis F.
Folsom." Chronicles of Oklahoma 4 (March
1926): 55-60.

5413. Brosnan, Cornelius J. Jason Lee:
Prophet of the New Oregon. New York:
Macmillan Company, 1932.

5414. Brunson, Alfred. A Western Pioneer;
or, Incidents of the Life and Times of
Rev. Alfred Brunson, A.M., D.D., Embracing a Period of Over Seventy Years.
2 volumes. Cincinnati: Hitchcock and
Walden, 1872-1879.

5415. Bryce, J. Y. "Beginning of Methodism
in Indian Territory." Chronicles of
Oklahoma 7 (December 1929): 475-486.

5416. Caldwell, Martha B., ed. Annals of
Shawnee Methodist Mission and Indian
Manual Labor School. Topeka: Kansas
State Historical Society, 1939.

5417. Canse, John Martin. "Jason Lee: New
Evidence on the Missionary and Colonizer."
Washington Historical Quarterly 6 (October
1915): 251-263.

5418. _____. "The Oregon Mission--Its
Transition." Washington Historical Quarterly 25 (July 1934): 203-209.

5419. _____. Pilgrim and Pioneer: Dawn
in the Northwest. New York: Abingdon
Press, 1930. On Jason Lee.

5420. Canse, John M., ed. "The Diary of
Henry Bridgeman Brewer, Being a Log
of the Lausanne and the Time-Book of the
Dalles Mission." Oregon Historical
Quarterly 29 (June 1928): 189-208;
(September 1928): 288-309; (December
1928): 347-362; 30 (March 1929): 53-62;
(June 1929): 111-119.

5421. Carey, Charles Henry, ed. "Diary of
Reverend George Gary." Quarterly of the
Oregon Historical Society 24 (March 1923):
68-105; (June 1923): 152-185; (September
1923): 269-333; (December 1923): 386-433.

5422. _____. "Methodist Annual Reports
Relative to the Willamette Mission (1834-
1848)." Quarterly of the Oregon Historical Society 23 (December 1922): 303-364.

5423. _____. "The Mission Record Book
of the Methodist Episcopal Church, Willamette Station, Oregon Territory, North
America, Commenced 1834." Quarterly of
the Oregon Historical Society 23 (September 1922): 230-266.

5424. Chisholm, Johnnie Bishop. "Harley
Institute." Chronicles of Oklahoma 4
(June 1926): 116-128.

5425. Copway, George. The Life, History,
and Travels of Kah-ge-ga-gah-bowh,
(George Copway), a Young Indian Chief
of the Ojebwa Nation, a Convert to the
Christian Faith, and a Missionary to His
People for Twelve Years. Albany: Weed
and Parsons, 1847.

5426. _____. The Life, Letters and
Speeches of Kah-ge-ga-gah-bowh, or G.
Copway, Chief Ojibway Nation. New York:
S. W. Benedict, 1850.

5427. Corwin, Hugh D. "The Folsom Training
School." Chronicles of Oklahoma 42
(Spring 1964): 46-52.

5428. Decker, Robert James. "Jason Lee,
Missionary to Oregon: A Re-evaluation."
Ph.D. dissertation, Indiana University,
1961.

5429. Drury, Clifford M. "The Oregonian
and Indian's Advocate." Pacific Northwest Quarterly 56 (October 1965): 159-167.

5430. Dunkle, W. F. "A Choctaw Indian's
Diary." Chronicles of Oklahoma 4 (March
1926): 61-69. Diary of Willis F. Folsom.

5431. Eichenberger, Flora Paine. "A
Reminiscence of a Methodist Minister's
Daughter." Chronicles of Oklahoma 7
(September 1929): 260-265.

5432. Fenton, William D. "Father Wilbur and
His Work." Quarterly of the Oregon Historical Society 10 (June 1909): 16-30.

5433. Finley, James B. History of the

Wyandott Mission at Upper Sandusky, Ohio, under the Direction of the Methodist Episcopal Church. Cincinnati: J. F. Wright and L. Swormstedt, 1840.

5434. _____. Life among the Indians; or, Personal Reminiscences and Historical Incidents Illustrative of Indian Life and Character. Edited by D. W. Clark. Cincinnati: Methodist Book Concern, 1857.

5435. _____. Selected Chapters from the History of the Wyandott Mission at Upper Sandusky, Ohio, under the Direction of the Methodist Episcopal Church. Edited by R. T. Stevenson. Cincinnati: Methodist Book Concern, 1916. Original work published in 1840.

5436. Gatke, Robert Moulton. "The First Indian School of the Pacific Northwest." Oregon Historical Society Quarterly 23 (March 1922): 70-83.

5437. Gatke, Robert Moulton, ed. "Documents of Mission History, 1833-43." Oregon Historical Quarterly 36 (March 1935): 71-94; (June 1935): 163-181.

5438. _____. "The Letters of the Rev. William M. Roberts, Third Superintendent of the Oregon Mission." Quarterly of the Oregon Historical Society 21 (March 1920): 33-48; 22 (September 1921): 225-251; 23 (June 1922): 163-191.

5439. Goode, William H. Outposts of Zion, with Limnings of Mission Life. Cincinnati: Poe and Hitchcock, 1863.

5440. Green, Frank L. "H. K. W. Perkins, Missionary to the Dalles." Methodist History 9 (April 1971): 34-44.

5441. Hall, B. M. The Life of Rev. John Clark. New York: Carlton and Porter, 1856.

5442. Hillgen, Marcella M. "The Wascopan Mission." Oregon Historical Quarterly 39 (September 1938): 222-234.

5443. Hoon, John. "The Wyandotte Indian Mission (the First Missionary Project in the World under the Auspices of the Methodist Episcopal Church of America)." Wesleyan Quarterly Review 3 (February 1966): 36-52.

5444. Howell, Erle. "James Harvey Wilbur: Indian Missionary--Founder of Methodism in the Inland Empire." Methodist History 7 (January 1969): 17-27.

5445. "Jason Lee Memorial Addresses." Quarterly of the Oregon Historical Society 7 (September 1906): 225-287.

5446. Johnson, William, and others. "Letters from the Indian Missions in Kansas." Kansas Historical Society Collections

16 (1925): 227-271.

5447. Kilpatrick, Jack Frederick. "Documents from Echota Methodist Mission." Southern Indian Studies 14 (October 1962): 29-31.

5448. Lee, Daniel, and J. H. Frost. Ten Years in Oregon. New York: J. Collord, 1844.

5449. Lutz, J. J. "The Methodist Missions among the Indian Tribes in Kansas." Transactions of the Kansas State Historical Society 9 (1905-1906): 160-235.

5450. Meany, Edmond S. "Last Survivor of the Oregon Mission of 1840." Washington Historical Quarterly 2 (October 1907): 12-23.

5451. Methvin, J. J. "Reminiscences of Life among the Indians." Chronicles of Oklahoma 5 (June 1927): 166-179.

5452. Mitchell, Joseph. The Missionary Pioneer; or, A Brief Memoir of the Life, Labours, and Death of John Stewart, (Man of Colour), Founder, under God, of the Mission among the Wyandotts at Upper Sandusky, Ohio. New York, 1827.

5453. Moore, F. M. A Brief History of the Missionary Work in the Indian Territory, of the Indian Mission Conference, Methodist Episcopal Church, South, and an Appendix Containing Personal Sketches of Many of the Early Workers in This Field. Muskogee: Phoenix Printing Company, 1899.

5454. Norwood, Frederick A. "The Invisible American--Methodism and the Indian." Methodist History 8 (January 1970): 3-24.

5455. Oliphant, J. Orin, ed. "Lee-Greene Correspondence, 1839." Oregon Historical Quarterly 35 (September 1934): 263-268.

5456. Patton, William. "Journal of a Visit to Indian Missions, Missouri Conference." Bulletin of the Missouri Historical Society 10 (January 1954): 167-180.

5457. Peacock, Mary Thomas. "Methodist Mission Work among the Cherokee Indians before the Removal." Methodist History 3 (April 1965): 20-39.

5458. Pipes, Nellie B., ed. "Journal of J. H. Frost, 1840-43." Oregon Historical Quarterly 35 (March 1934): 50-73; (June 1934): 139-167; (September 1934): 235-262; (December 1934): 348-375.

5459. Pitezel, John H. Lights and Shades of Missionary Life: Containing Travels, Sketches, Incidents, and Missionary Efforts, during Nine Years Spent in the Region of Lake Superior. Cincinnati: Western Book Concern, 1860. First published in 1857.

5460. Randolph, J. Ralph. "John Wesley and the American Indian: A Study in Disillusionment." Methodist History 10 (April 1972): 3-11.

5461. Riggin, F. A. "Piegan Indian Mission: An Example of What Is Being Done." In Methodism and the Republic, edited by Ward Platt, pp. 299-308. Philadelphia: Board of Home Missions and Church Extension of the Methodist Episcopal Church, n.d.

5462. Riley, Ruth E. "The Story of Shawnee Indian Mission." National Historical Magazine 73 (March 1939): 32-34.

5463. Ross, Edith Connelley. "The Old Shawnee Mission." Kansas State Historical Society Collections 17 (1928): 417-435.

5464. Schaeffer, Claude E. "William Brooks, Chinook Publicist." Oregon Historical Quarterly 64 (March 1963): 41-54.

5465. Schlup, Emil. "The Wyandot Mission." Ohio Archaeological and Historical Society Quarterly 15 (April 1906): 163-181.

5466. Schomburg, Arthur A. "Two Negro Missionaries to the American Indians, John Marrant and John Stewart." Journal of Negro History 21 (October 1936): 394-405.

5467. Seiber, Richard A. "David E. Blain: The Methodist Church in Washington, 1853-1861." Methodist History 1 (April 1963): 1-17.

5468. Stewart, Martha. "The Indian Mission Conference of Oklahoma." Chronicles of Oklahoma 40 (Winter 1962-1963): 330-336.

5469. Thacker, Joseph Allen, Jr. "James B. Finley: A Biography." Ph.D. dissertation, University of Kentucky, 1967.

5470. Vernon, Walter N. "Early Echoes from Bloomfield Academy." Chronicles of Oklahoma 52 (Summer 1974): 237-243.

MORAVIAN MISSIONS

The Moravians were among the most zealous of Protestant groups in missionary activity among the Indians and produced outstanding leaders in the work like David Zeisberger and John Heckewelder.

5471. Brady, Arthur W. "The Moravian Mission in Indiana." Mississippi Valley Historical Review, extra no. (November 1921): 286-298.

5472. Brain, Belle M. "David Zeisberger, the Apostle to the Delawares." Missionary Review of the World 32 (November 1909): 821-831.

5473. Dahlinger, Charles W. "The Moravians and Their Missions among the Indians of the Ohio Valley." Western Pennsylvania Historical Magazine 3 (April 1920): 45-67.

5474. De Baillou, Clemens. "The Diaries of the Moravian Brotherhood at the Cherokee Mission in Spring Place, Georgia for the Years 1800-1804," translated by William L. Boletta. Georgia Historical Quarterly 54 (Winter 1970): 571-576.

5475. De Schweinitz, Edmund. The Life and Times of David Zeisberger, the Western Pioneer and Apostle of the Indians. Philadelphia: J. B. Lippincott, 1871.

5476. Dunn, Jacob P. "The Moravian Mission near Anderson." Indiana Quarterly Magazine of History 9 (June 1913): 73-83.

5477. Gipson, Lawrence H., ed. The Moravian Indian Mission on White River: Diaries and Letters, May 5, 1799, to November 12, 1806. Indiana Historical Collections, 23. Indianapolis: Indiana Historical Bureau, 1938.

5478. Gray, Elma E., and Leslie Robb Gray. Wilderness Christians: The Moravian Mission to the Delaware Indians. Ithaca: Cornell University Press, 1956.

5479. Hamilton, J. Taylor. "The Contacts of the Moravian Church with the Iroquois League." Transactions of the Moravian Historical Society 11 (1931): 28-55.

5480. Hamilton, Kenneth G. "Cultural Contributions of Moravian Missions among the Indians." Pennsylvania History 18 (January 1951): 1-15.

5481. Heckewelder, John. A Narrative of the Mission of the United Brethren among the Delaware and Mohegan Indians, from Its Commencement, in the Year 1740, to the Close of the Year 1808. Philadelphia: McCarty and Davis, 1820.

5482. Hutton, J. E. A History of Moravian Missions. London: Moravian Publication Office, 1923.

5483. Jordan, Albert F. "The Moravians and the Indians during the French and Indian War." Transactions of the Moravian Historical Society 22, part 1 (1969): 1-14.

5484. Kohnova, Marie J. "The Moravians and Their Missionaries: A Problem in Americanization." Mississippi Valley Historical Review 19 (December 1932): 348-361.

5485. Lackey, Vinson. "New Springplace."

Chronicles of Oklahoma 17 (June 1939): 178-183.

5486. Loskiel, George Henry. History of the Mission of the United Brethren among the Indians in North America. Translated by Christian I. LaTrobe. London: Brethren's Society for the Furtherance of the Gospel, 1794.

5487. _____. The History of the Moravian Mission among the Indians in North America from Its Commencement to the Present Time. London: T. Allman, 1838.

5488. Luckenbach, Abraham. "The Autobiography of Abraham Luckenbach," translated by Harry Emilius Stocker. Transactions of the Moravian Historical Society 10 (1917): 359-408.

5489. McHugh, Thomas F. "The Moravian Mission to the American Indians: Early American Peace Corps." Pennsylvania History 33 (October 1966): 412-431.

5490. Mauelshagen, Carl, and Gerald H. Davis. "The Moravians' Plan for a Mission among the Creek Indians, 1803-1804." Georgia Historical Quarterly 51 (September 1967): 358-364.

5491. "Moravians among the Indians." American Historical Record 1 (January 1872): 11-12.

5492. Muller, Paul Eugene. "David Zeisberger's Official Diary, Fairfield, 1791-1795." Transactions of the Moravian Historical Society 19, part 1 (1963): 5-229.

5493. Reichel, Levin T. "Our Indian Mission, 1740-1850." Moravian Church Miscellany 5 (November 1854): 338-348; (December 1854): 366-369.

5494. Schwarze, Edmund. History of the Moravian Missions among Southern Indian Tribes of the United States. Bethlehem, Pennsylvania: Times Publishing Company, 1923.

5495. Scott, Nancy E. "Lights and Shadows of the Moravian Mission." Michigan History Magazine 23 (Autumn 1939): 367-376.

5496. Stocker, Harvey Emilius. "A History of the Moravian Missions among the Indians on the White River in Indiana." Transactions of the Moravian Historical Society 10 (1917): 235-357.

5497. Thompson, Robert Ellis. "Zeisberger's Mission to the Indians." Penn Monthly 2 (February 1871): 97-106; (April 1871): 188-197.

5498. Wallace, Paul A. W. "The Moravian Records." Indiana Magazine of

History 48 (June 1952): 141-160.

5499. _____. "They Knew the Indians: The Men Who Wrote the Moravian Records." Proceedings of the American Philosophical Society 95 (June 1951): 290-295.

5500. Wallace, Paul A. W., ed. Thirty Thousand Miles with John Heckewelder. Pittsburgh: University of Pittsburgh Press, 1958. The journals of the missionary.

5501. Weinland, Joseph E. "Pioneer Mission in Ohio." Missionary Review of the World 53 (December 1930): 953.

5502. Weller, Arthur. "Missionaries in Ohio." National Republic 20 (September 1932): 20-21, 31.

5503. Wright, Muriel H. Springplace: Moravian Mission and the Ward Family of the Cherokee Nation. Guthrie, Oklahoma: Co-operative Publishing Company, 1940.

5504. Zeisberger, David. Diary of David Zeisberger, a Moravian Missionary among the Indians of Ohio. 2 volumes. Edited by Eugene F. Bliss. Cincinnati: Robert Clarke and Company, 1885.

MORMON MISSIONS

The Mormons had special missions to the Indians, and studies of those missions are listed here. Included also are some accounts of more general Mormon-Indian relations.

5505. Alter, J. Cecil, ed. "The Mormons and the Indians: News Items and Editorials from the Mormon Press." Utah Historical Quarterly 12 (January-April 1944): 49-68.

5506. Brooks, Juanita. "Indian Relations on the Mormon Frontier." Utah Historical Quarterly 12 (January-April 1944): 1-48.

5507. _____. "Indian Sketches from the Journals of T. D. Brown and Jacob Hamblin." Utah Historical Quarterly 29 (October 1961): 347-360.

5508. Brooks, Juanita, ed. Journal of the Southern Indian Mission: Diary of Thomas D. Brown. Logan: Utah State University Press, 1972.

5509. Coates, Lawrence G. "Mormons and Social Change among the Shoshoni, 1853-1900." Idaho Yesterdays 15 (Winter 1972): 3-11.

5510. Foreman, Grant, ed. "Missionaries of the Latter Day Saints Church in Indian Territory." Chronicles of Oklahoma 13

(June 1935): 196-213.

5511. Green, Doyle L. "The Southwest Indian Mission." Improvement Era 58 (April 1955): 233-235, 262-265.

5512. Jennings, Warren A. "The First Mormon Mission to the Indians." Kansas Historical Quarterly 37 (Autumn 1971): 288-299.

5513. Jenson, Andrew. "The Elk Mountain Mission." Utah Genealogical and Historical Magazine 4 (October 1913): 188-200.

5514. Kimball, Spencer W. "The Lamanite." Improvement Era 58 (April 1955): 226-228 +.

5515. Nash, John D. "The Salmon River Mission of 1855." Idaho Yesterdays 11 (Spring 1967): 22-31.

5516. Parry, Keith William John. "To Raise These People Up: An Examination of a Mormon Mission to an Indian Community as an Agent of Social Change." Ph.D. dissertation, University of Rochester, 1972.

5517. Peterson, Charles S. "The Hopis and the Mormons 1858-1873." Utah Historical Quarterly 39 (Spring 1971): 179-194.

5518. Smiley, Winn Whiting, "Ammon M. Tenney: Mormon Missionary to the Indians." Journal of Arizona History 13 (Summer 1972): 82-108.

5519. Stowell, Addie. The Red Man's Hope. Dallas: Royal Publishing Company, 1963. Elder Hubert Case and his ministry among the Indians.

5520. Tarcay, Eileen. "Among the Lamanites: The Indians and the Mormons." Western Folklore 28 (April 1959): 131-134.

5521. Zobell, Albert L., Jr. "Missionary Work among the Indians." Improvement Era 58 (April 1955): 242-243, 270-274.

PRESBYTERIAN, CONGREGATIONAL, AND ABCFM MISSIONS

Presbyterians, Congregationalists, and the American Board of Commissioners for Foreign Missions, an organization made up largely of members of those denominations, had numerous missions among the Indians. Notable are the early work of the ABCFM among the southern Indians and its later activities in the Pacific Northwest.

5522. Alden, Timothy. An Account of Sundry Missions Performed among the Senecas and Munsees: In a Series of Letters. New York: J. Seymour, 1827.

5523. Allen, Penelope Johnson. "Brainerd Mission." Daughters of the American Revolution Magazine 68 (June 1934): 347-349.

5524. Allis, Samuel. "Forty Years among the Indians and on the Eastern Border of Nebraska." Transactions and Reports of the Nebraska State Historical Society 2 (1885-1887): 133-166.

5525. Anderson, Charles A. "Index of American Indian Correspondence." Journal of the Presbyterian Historical Society 31 (March 1953): 63-70. Material in the library of the Presbyterian Historical Society.

5526. Anderson, Charles A., ed. "Diaries of Peter Dougherty." Journal of the Presbyterian Historical Society 30 (June 1952): 95-114; (September 1952): 175-192; (December 1952): 236-253.

5527. _____. "Frontier Mackinac Island, 1823-1834: Letters of William Montague and Amanda White Ferry." Journal of the Presbyterian Historical Society 25 (December 1947): 192-222; 26 (June 1948): 101-127; (September 1948): 182-191.

5528. _____. "Letters of Amanda R. McFarland." Journal of the Presbyterian Historical Society 34 (June 1956): 83-102; (December 1956): 226-244; 35 (March 1957): 33-56.

5529. Anderson, Rufus. Memorial Volume of the First Fifty Years of the American Board of Commissioners for Foreign Missions. Boston: The Board, 1861.

5530. "An Indian Mission in Arizona." Missionary Review of the World 49 (August 1926): 609-616.

5531. Bailey, Alvin Keith. "The Strategy of Sheldon Jackson in Opening the West for National Missions, 1860-1880." Ph.D. dissertation, Yale University, 1948.

5532. Ballou, Howard Malcolm. "The History of the Oregon Mission Press." Quarterly of the Oregon Historical Society 23 (March 1922): 39-52; (June 1922): 95-110.

5533. Bartlett, S. C. Historical Sketch of the Missions of the American Board among the North American Indians. Boston: The Board, 1876.

5534. Barton, Winifred W. John P. Williamson: A Brother to the Sioux. New York: Fleming H. Revell Company, 1919.

5535. Bass, Althea. Cherokee Messenger.

Norman: University of Oklahoma Press, 1936. Samuel Austin Worcester.

5536. _____. "William Schenck Robertson." Chronicles of Oklahoma 37 (Spring 1959): 28-34.

5537. Bass, Dorothy C. "Gideon Blackburn's Mission to the Cherokees: Christianization and Civilization." Journal of Presbyterian History 52 (Fall 1974): 203-226.

5538. Belknap, George P. "Authentic Account of the Murder of Dr. Whitman: The History of a Pamphlet." Papers of the Bibliographical Society of America 55 (Fourth Quarter 1961): 319-346.

5539. Blegen, Theodore C. "The Pond Brothers." Minnesota History 15 (September 1934): 273-281.

5540. Blue, George Verne. "Green's Missionary Report on Oregon, 1829." Oregon Historical Quarterly 30 (September 1929): 259-271.

5541. Bourne, Edward Gaylord. "The Legend of Marcus Whitman." American Historical Review 6 (January 1901): 276-300.

5542. _____. "The Legend of Marcus Whitman." In Essays in Historical Criticism, pp. 3-109. New York: Charles Scribner's Sons, 1901.

5543. Brain, Belle Marvel. The Redemption of the Red Man: An Account of Presbyterian Missions to the North American Indians of the Present Day. New York: Board of Home Missions of the Presbyterian Church in the U.S.A., 1904.

5544. Brown, James Haldane. "Presbyterian Social Influence in Early Ohio." Journal of the Presbyterian Historical Society 30 (December 1952): 209-235.

5545. Bullen, Robert W. "Joseph Bullen: Some Biographical Notes." Journal of Mississippi History 27 (August 1965): 265-267.

5546. Caswell, Harriet S. Our Life among the Iroquois Indians. Boston: Congregational Sunday-School and Publishing Society, 1892.

5547. Craker, Ruth. First Protestant Mission in the Grand Traverse Region. East Jordan, Michigan, 1932.

5548. Crawford, Mary M. "Indian Missionaries to Indians: Nez Perce Indians." Missionary Review of the World 55 (July 1932): 430-431.

5549. Davidson, J. N. Muh-he-ka-ne-ok: A History of the Stockbridge Nation. Milwaukee: Silas Chapman, 1893.

5550. Davison, Stanley. "Worker in God's Wilderness." Montana, the Magazine of Western History 7 (Winter 1957): 8-17. Samuel Parker.

5551. Denison, Natalie Morrison. "Missions and Missionaries of the Presbyterian Church, U.S., among the Choctaws--1866-1907." Chronicles of Oklahoma 24 (Winter 1946-1947): 426-448.

5552. De Rosier, Arthur H., Jr. "Cyrus Kingsbury--Missionary to the Choctaws." Journal of Presbyterian History 50 (Winter 1972): 267-287.

5553. Drury, Clifford Merrill. Elkanah and Mary Walker, Pioneers among the Spokanes. Caldwell, Idaho: Caxton Printers, 1940.

5554. _____. Henry Harmon Spalding: Pioneer of Old Oregon. Caldwell, Idaho: Caxton Printers, 1936.

5555. _____. Marcus and Narcissa Whitman and the Opening of Old Oregon. 2 volumes. Glendale, California: Arthur H. Clark Company, 1973.

5556. _____. Marcus Whitman, M.D., Pioneer and Martyr. Caldwell, Idaho: Caxton Printers, 1937.

5557. Drury, Clifford M., ed. The Diaries and Letters of Henry H. Spalding and Asa Bowen Smith Relating to the Nez Perce Mission, 1838-1842. Glendale, California: Arthur H. Clark Company, 1958.

5558. _____. "Gray's Journal of 1838." Pacific Northwest Quarterly 29 (April 1938): 277-282.

5559. Dunbar, John. "Letters Concerning the Presbyterian Mission in the Pawnee Country, Near Bellevue, Neb. 1831-1849." Collections of the Kansas State Historical Society 14 (1918): 570-784.

5560. _____. "The Presbyterian Mission among the Pawnee Indians in Nebraska, 1834-1836." Collections of the Kansas State Historical Society 11 (1910): 323-332.

5561. Eaches, Owen Philips. "A First-Century Saint in the Eighteenth." Crozer Quarterly 3 (April 1926): 190-195. David Brainerd.

5562. Edwards, John. "An Account of My Escape from the South in 1861," edited by Muriel H. Wright. Chronicles of Oklahoma 43 (Spring 1965): 58-89.

5563. Eells, Myron. Ten Years of Missionary Work among the Indians at Skokomish, Washington Territory, 1874-1884. Boston: Congregational Sunday-School and Publishing Society, 1886.

5564. Faust, Harold S. "The Growth of Presbyterian Missions to the American Indians during the National Period." Journal of the Presbyterian Historical Society 22 (September 1944): 88-123; (December 1944): 137-171.

5565. Fenton, William N. "Toward the Gradual Civilization of the Indian Natives: The Missionary and Linguistic Work of Asher Wright (1803-1875) among the Senecas of Western New York." Proceedings of the American Philosophical Society 100 (December 17, 1956): 567-581.

5566. Foreman, Carolyn Thomas. "Augusta Robertson Moore." Chronicles of Oklahoma 13 (December 1935): 399-420.

5567. _____. "The Cherokee Gospel Tidings of Dwight Mission." Chronicles of Oklahoma 12 (December 1934): 454-469.

5568. _____. "Fairfield Mission." Chronicles of Oklahoma 27 (Winter 1959-1960): 373-388.

5569. _____. "The Foreign Mission School at Cornwall, Connecticut." Chronicles of Oklahoma 7 (September 1929): 242-259.

5570. _____. "Hopefield Mission in Osage Nation, 1823-1837." Chronicles of Oklahoma 28 (Summer 1950): 193-205.

5571. Foreman, Grant, ed. "Dwight Mission." Chronicles of Oklahoma 12 (March 1934): 42-51. Letter of Alfred Finney.

5572. Foreman, Minta Ross. "Reverend Stephen Foreman, Cherokee Missionary." Chronicles of Oklahoma 18 (September 1940): 229-242.

5573. Foster, Frank Hugh. "The Oberlin Ojibway Mission." Papers of the Ohio Church History Society 2 (1892): 1-25.

5574. Garrett, Kathleen. "Worcester, the Pride of the West." Chronicles of Oklahoma 30 (Winter 1952-1953): 386-396. Worcester Academy, Vinita, Cherokee Nation.

5575. Gates, Charles M. "The Lac Qui Parle Indian Mission." Minnesota History 16 (June 1935): 133-151.

5576. Geary, E. R. "Historical Narrative of the Presbytery of Oregon." Journal of the Presbyterian Historical Society 38 (June 1960): 103-109; (September 1960): 166-181.

5577. Graves, William W. The First Protestant Osage Missions, 1820-1837. Oswego, Kansas: Carpenter Press, 1949.

5578. Green, Ashbel. A Historical Sketch or Compendious View of the Domestic and Foreign Missions in the Presbyterian Church of the United States of America. Philadelphia: W. S. Martien, 1838. Reprinted as Presbyterian Missions. Edited by John C. Lowrie. New York: A. D. F. Randolph and Company, 1893.

5579. Green, Norma Kidd. "The Presbyterian Mission to the Omaha Indian Tribe." Nebraska History 48 (Autumn 1967): 267-289.

5580. Hamilton, William. "Letters of William Hamilton, 1811-1891," edited by Charles A. Anderson. Journal of the Presbyterian Historical Society 35 (September 1957): 157-170.

5581. _____. "More Letters of William Hamilton, 1811-1891." Journal of the Presbyterian Historical Society 36 (March 1958): 53-65.

5582. Hickerson, Harold. "Willaim T. Boutwell of the American Board and the Pillager Chippewa: The History of a Failure." Ethnohistory 12 (Winter 1965): 1-29.

5583. Hiemstra, William L. "Early Presbyterian Missions among the Choctaw and Chickasaw Indians in Mississippi." Journal of Mississippi History 10 (January 1948): 8-16.

5584. _____. "Presbyterian Missionaries and Mission Churches among the Choctaw and Chickasaw Indians, 1832-1865." Chronicles of Oklahoma 26 (Winter 1948-1949): 459-467.

5585. _____. "Presbyterian Missions among Choctaw and Chickasaw Indians, 1860." Journal of the Presbyterian Historical Society 37 (March 1959): 51-59.

5586. _____. "Presbyterian Mission Schools among the Choctaws and Chickasaws, 1845-1861." Chronicles of Oklahoma 27 (Spring 1949): 33-40.

5587. Hinckley, Theodore C. "The Alaska Labors of Sheldon Jackson, 1877-1890." Ph.D. dissertation, Indiana University, 1961.

5588. _____. "The Early Alaskan Ministry of S. Hall Young, 1878-1888." Journal of Presbyterian History 46 (September 1968): 175-196.

5589. _____. "Sheldon Jackson as Preserver of Alaska's Native Culture." Pacific Historical Review 33 (November 1964): 411-424.

5590. Holway, Hope. "Ann Eliza Worcester Robertson as a Linguist." Chronicles of Oklahoma 37 (Spring 1959): 35-44.

5591. Hunnewell, James F., ed. The Society for Propagating the Gospel among the Indians and Others in North America, 1787-1887. Boston: University Press, 1887.

5592. Hunt, Elizabeth H., ed. "Two Letters from Pine Ridge Mission." Chronicles of Oklahoma 50 (Summer 1972): 219-225. Letters of Electa May Kingsbury.

5593. Husband, Michael B. "William I. Marshall and the Legend of Marcus Whitman." Pacific Northwest Quarterly 64 (April 1973): 57-69.

5594. Jackson, Sheldon. Alaska, and Missions on the North Pacific Coast. New York: Dodd, Mead and Company, 1880.

5595. Jacobsen, Ethel C. "Life in an Indian Village." North Dakota History 26 (Spring 1959): 45-92. Deals with period 1889-1892.

5596. Jones, Dorsey D. "Cephas Washburn and His Work in Arkansas." Arkansas Historical Quarterly 3 (Summer 1944): 125-136.

5597. Jones, Nard. The Great Command: The Story of Marcus and Narcissa Whitman and the Oregon Country Pioneers. Boston: Little, Brown and Company, 1959.

5598. Klett, Guy S., ed. "Correspondence of the Western Foreign Missionary Society." Journal of the Presbyterian Historical Society 36 (June 1958): 89-113; 37 (March 1959): 31-43.

5599. _____. "Missionary Endeavors of the Presbyterian Church among the Blackfeet Indians in the 1850's." Journal of the Presbyterian Historical Society 19 (December 1941): 327-354.

5600. Lauderdale, Virginia E. "Tullahassee Mission." Chronicles of Oklahoma 26 (Autumn 1948): 285-300.

5601. "Letter of Cyrus Kingsbury to Mission Headquarters." Journal of the Presbyterian Historical Society 37 (March 1959): 50.

5602. Lewis, Anna, ed. "Diary of a Missionary to the Choctaws, 1860-1861." Chronicles of Oklahoma 17 (December 1939): 428-447.

5603. _____. "The Diary of Sue McBeth, a Missionary to the Choctaws, 1860-1861." Chronicles of Oklahoma 21 (June 1943): 186-195.

5604. _____. "Letters Regarding Choctaw Missions and Missionaries." Chronicles of Oklahoma 17 (September 1939): 275-285.

5605. Life and Letters of Miss Mary C. Greenleaf, Missionary to the Chickasaw Indians. Boston: Massachusetts Sabbath School Society, 1858.

5606. Limouze, Arthur H. "The Whitman-Spalding Centennial." Missionary Review of the World 59 (May 1936): 243-245.

5607. Lindsey, Lilah Denton. "Memories of the Indian Territory Mission Field." Chronicles of Oklahoma 36 (Summer 1958): 181-198.

5608. Loomis, Augustus W. "Scenes in the Indian Territory: Kowetah Mission," edited by Muriel H. Wright. Chronicles of Oklahoma 46 (Spring 1968): 64-72.

5609. Love, William A. "The Mayhew Mission to the Choctaws." Publications of the Mississippi Historical Society 11 (1910): 363-402.

5610. McLoughlin, William G. "The Choctaw Slave Burning: A Crisis in Mission Work among the Indians." Journal of the West 13 (January 1974): 113-127.

5611. _____. "Indian Slaveholders and Presbyterian Missionaries, 1837-1861." Church History 42 (December 1973): 535-551.

5612. Miller, Lona Eaton. "Wheelock Mission." Chronicles of Oklahoma 29 (Autumn 1951): 314-323.

5613. "Mission Work among the Omaha Indians." Journal of the Presbyterian Historical Society 38 (September 1960): 182-190. Letter of William Hamilton.

5614. Morrill, Allen C., and Eleanor D. Morrill. "The McBeth Nez Perce Mission Centennial, Utah, 1874-1974." Journal of Presbyterian History 52 (Summer 1974): 123-136.

5615. _____. "'Old Church Made New.'" Idaho Yesterdays 16 (Summer 1972): 16-25. Mission among the Nez Perces.

5616. Morrison, James D. "Note on Abolitionism in the Choctaw Nation." Chronicles of Oklahoma 38 (Spring 1960): 78-84.

5617. Morrison, T. F. "Mission Neosho, the First Kansas Mission." Kansas Historical Quarterly 4 (August 1935): 227-234.

5618. Morrison, William Brown. "The Choctaw Mission of the American Board of Commissioners for Foreign Missions." Chronicles of Oklahoma 4 (June 1926): 166-183.

5619. _____. The Red Man's Trail.

Richmond, Virginia: Presbyterian Committee of Publication, 1932.

5620. Neill, Edward D. "Memoir of William T. Boutwell, the First Christian Minister Resident among the Indians of Minnesota." Macalester College Contributions, 2d series no. 1 (1892): 1-59.

5621. _____. "A Memorial of the Brothers Pond, the First Resident Missionaries among the Dakotahs." Macalester College Contributions, 2d series no. 8 (1892): 159-198.

5622. Nichols, Roger L. "A Missionary Journey to the Sac-Fox Indians, 1834." Annals of Iowa 36 (Spring 1962): 301-315.

5623. Oliphant, J. Orin, ed. "A Letter by Henry H. Spalding from the Rocky Mountains." Oregon Historical Quarterly 51 (June 1950): 127-133.

5624. _____. Through the South and the West with Jeremiah Evarts in 1826. Lewisburg, Pennsylvania: Bucknell University Press, 1956.

5625. Olsen, Louise P. "Mary Clementine Collins: Dacotah Missionary." North Dakota History 19 (January 1952): 59-81.

5626. Parker, Samuel. Journal of an Exploring Tour beyond the Rocky Mountains, under the Direction of the American Board of Commissioners for Foreign Misisons, Performed in the Years 1835, 1836 and 1837. Ithaca, New York, 1838.

5627. Paul, Peter J. "Some Facts in the Early Missionary History of the Northwest: The Legend of Marcus Whitman." Records of the American Catholic Historical Society of Philadelphia 40 (June 1929): 97-122.

5628. Phelps, Dawson A. "The Chickasaw Mission." Journal of Mississippi History 13 (October 1951): 226-235.

5629. _____. "The Choctaw Mission: An Experiment in Civilization." Journal of Mississippi History 14 (January 1952): 35-62.

5630. Phillips, Clifton Jackson. Protestant America and the Pagan World: The First Half Century of the American Board of Commissioners for Foreign Missions, 1810-1860. Cambridge: Harvard University Press, 1969.

5631. Phillips, Paul C., ed. "The Oregon Missions As Shown in the Walker Letters, 1839-1851." Frontier: A Magazine of the Northwest 2 (November 1930): 74-89. Letters of Elkanah Walker.

5632. Pipes, Nellie B. "The Protestant Ladder." Oregon Historical Quarterly 37 (September 1936): 237-240.

5633. Pipes, Nellie B., ed. "Spalding Mission, 1843." Oregon Historical Quarterly 33 (December 1932): 348-354.

5634. Plank, Pryor. "The Iowa Sac and Fox Mission and Its Missionaries, Rev. Samuel M. Irvin and Wife." Transactions of the Kansas State Historical Society 10 (1907-1908): 312-325.

5635. Pond, Samuel W. "Two Missionaries in the Sioux Country," edited by Theodore C. Blegen. Minnesota History 21 (March 1940): 15-32; (June 1940): 158-175; (September 1940): 272-283.

5636. Pond, Samuel W., Jr. Two Volunteer Missionaries among the Dakotas; or, The Story of the Labors of Samuel W. and Gideon H. Pond. Boston: Congregational Sunday-School and Publishing Society, 1893.

5637. Queener, V. M. "Gideon Blackburn." East Tennessee Historical Society's Publications no. 6 (1934): 12-28.

5638. Rainwater, Percy L. "Indian Missions and Missionaries." Journal of Mississippi History 28 (February 1965): 15-39.

5639. Reed, Ora Eddleman. "The Robe Family--Missionaries." Chronicles of Oklahoma 26 (Autumn 1948): 301-312.

5640. Riggs, Stephen R. "The Dakota Mission." Collections of the Minnesota Historical Society 3 (1870-1880): 114-128.

5641. _____. "Journal of a Tour from Lac-Qui-Parle to the Missouri River." South Dakota Historical Collections 13 (1926): 330-344.

5642. _____. Mary and I: Forty Years with the Sioux. Chicago: W. G. Holmes, 1880.

5643. _____. Tah-koo Wah-kan; or, The Gospel among the Dakotas. Boston: Congregational Sabbath-School and Publishing Society, 1869.

5644. Ross, Nancy Wilson. "Murder at the Place of Rye Grass." American Heritage 10 (August 1959): 85-91. The Whitmans.

5645. Scott, Leslie M. "John Fiske's Change of Attitude on the Whitman Legend." Quarterly of the Oregon Historical Society 13 (June 1912): 160-174.

5646. Shirk, George H., ed. "Some Letters from the Reverend Samuel A. Worcester at Park Hill." Chronicles of Oklahoma 26 (Winter 1948-1949): 468-478.

5647. Smoot, Joseph G. "An Account of Alabama Indian Missions and Presbyterian Churches in 1828, from the Travel Diary of William S. Potts." Alabama Review 18 (April 1965): 134-152.

5648. "Soldier Brown and Sheldon Jackson." Alaska Journal 1 (Autumn 1971): 60-62.

5649. Strong, William E. The Story of the American Board: An Account of the First Hundred Years of the American Board of Commissioners for Foreign Missions. Boston: Pilgrim Press, 1910.

5650. Thoburn, Joseph B., ed. "Letters of Cassandra Sawyer Lockwood: Dwight Mission, 1834." Chronicles of Oklahoma 33 (Summer 1955): 202-237.

5651. Thompson, Erwin N. "Narcissa Whitman." Montana, the Magazine of Western History 13 (Winter 1963): 15-27.

5652. Thomson, Louise. "A Cross-Section in the Life of a Missionary Teacher among the Indians." Chronicles of Oklahoma 17 (September 1939): 328-332.

5653. Thwaites, Reuben Gold, ed. "Documents Relating to the Stockbridge Mission, 1825-48." Collections of the State Historical Society of Wisconsin 15 (1900): 39-204.

5654. Torrey, Charles Cutler. "Notes of a Missionary among the Cherokees," edited by Grant Foreman. Chronicles of Oklahoma 16 (June 1938): 171-189.

5655. Tracy, E. C. Memoir of the Life of Jeremiah Evarts, Esq. Boston: Crocker and Brewster, 1845.

5656. Tracy, Joseph. "History of the American Board of Commissioners for Foreign Missions." In History of American Missions to the Heathen, from Their Commencement to the Present Time, edited by Joseph Tracy, pp. 9-346. Worcester, Massachusetts: Spooner and Howland, 1840.

5657. Tuttle, Sarah. Conversations on the Choctaw Mission. Boston: Massachusetts Sabbath School Union, 1830.

5658. _____. Conversations on the Mackinaw and Green-Bay Indian Missions. Boston: Massachusetts Sabbath School Union, 1831.

5659. _____. Conversations on the Mission to the Arkansas Cherokees. Boston: Massachusetts Sabbath School Society, 1833.

5660. _____. History of the American

Mission to the Pawnee Indians. Boston: Massachusetts Sabbath School Society, 1838.

5661. _____. History of the Sioux or Dakota Mission. Boston: Massachusetts Sabbath School Society, 1841.

5662. _____. Hugh Clifford; or, Prospective Missions on the Northwest Coast and at the Washington Islands. Boston: Massachusetts Sabbath School Union, 1832.

5663. _____. Letters and Conversations on the Cherokee Mission. Boston: Massachusetts Sabbath School Union, 1830.

5664. _____. Letters and Conversations on the Indian Missions at Seneca, Tuscarora, Cattaraugus, in the State of New York, and Maumee, in the State of Ohio. Boston: Massachusetts Sabbath School Union, 1831.

5665. _____. Letters on the Chickasaw and Osage Missions. Boston: Massachusetts Sabbath School Union, 1831.

5666. Virtue, Ethel B. "The Pond Papers." Minnesota History Bulletin 3 (May 1919): 82-86. Samuel W. and Gideon H. Pond.

5667. Vogel, Virgil J. "The Missionary as Acculturation Agent: Peter Dougherty and the Indians of Grand Traverse." Michigan History 51 (Fall 1967): 185-201.

5668. Walker, Robert S. Torchlights to the Cherokees: The Brainerd Mission. New York: Macmillan Company, 1931.

5669. Washburn, Cephas. Reminiscences of the Indians. Richmond, Virginia: Presbyterian Committee of Publication, 1869.

5670. White, Pliny H. "A Memorial of Rev. Samuel Austin Worcester." Congregational Quarterly 3 (July 1861): 279-285.

5671. Whitman, Marcus. "Journal and Report by Dr. Marcus Whitman of His Tour of Exploration with Rev. Samuel Parker in 1835 beyond the Rocky Mountains." Oregon Historical Quarterly 28 (September 1927): 239-257.

5672. _____. "Whitman's Requests at Boston of American Board of Commissioners of Foreign Missions, April, 1834." Quarterly of the Oregon Historical Society 22 (December 1921): 357-359.

5673. Winston, E. T. "Father" Stuart and the Monroe Mission. Meridian, Mississippi: Press of Tell Farmer, 1927.

5674. Wright, Muriel H. "Notes on the Life

of Mrs. Hannah Worcester Hicks Hitchcock and the Park Hill Press." Chronicles of Oklahoma 19 (December 1941): 348-355.

5675. Wright, Muriel H., ed. "Samuel Austin Worcester: A Dedication." Chronicles of Oklahoma 37 (Spring 1959): 2-21.

QUAKER MISSIONS

The Society of Friends had a long history of cordial relations with the Indians, going back to William Penn. The Quakers maintained missions with the Indians and took an especially active part in the "peace policy" after the Civil War.

5676. Battey, Thomas C. The Life and Adventures of a Quaker among the Indians. Boston: Lee and Shepard, 1875.

5677. Brainerd, Ezra. "Jeremiah Hubbard, Hoosier Schoolmaster and Friends Missionary among the Indians." Chronicles of Oklahoma 29 (Spring 1951): 23-31.

5678. Carmony, Donald F., ed. "Message of Pennsylvania and New Jersey Quakers to Indians of the Old Northwest." Indiana Magazine of History 59 (March 1963): 51-58.

5679. Elkinton, Joseph. "The Quaker Mission among the Indians of New York State." Buffalo Historical Society Publications 18 (1914): 169-189.

5680. Elliott, Errol T. Quakers on the American Frontier: A History of the Westward Migrations, Settlements, and Developments of Friends on the American Continent. Richmond, Indiana: Friends United Press, 1969.

5681. Gibson, Arrell M. "Wyandotte Mission: The Early Years, 1871-1900." Chronicles of Oklahoma 36 (Summer 1958): 137-154.

5682. Harvey, Henry. History of the Shawnee Indians, from the Year 1681 to 1854, Inclusive. Cincinnati: Ephraim Morgan and Sons, 1855.

5683. Haygood, William Converse, ed. "A Mission to the Menominee: Alfred Cope's Green Bay Diary." Wisconsin Magazine of History 49 (Summer 1966): 302-323; 50 (Autumn 1966): 18-42; (Winter 1966): 120-144; (Spring 1967): 211-241.

5684. Hopkins, Gerard T. "A Quaker Pilgrimage: Being a Mission to the Indians from the Indian Committee of the Baltimore Yearly Meeting, to Fort Wayne, 1804," edited by William H. Love. Maryland Historical Magazine 4 (March 1909): 1-24. Originally published

in Philadelphia, 1862.

5685. "The Indians of Iowa in 1842." Iowa Journal of History and Politics 13 (April 1915): 250-263. Report by two members of the Society of Friends.

5686. Jackson, Halliday. Civilization of the Indian Natives; or, A Brief View of the Friendly Conduct of William Penn towards Them . . . ; the Subsequent Care of the Society of Friends . . . ; and a Concise Narrative of the Proceedings of the Yearly Meeting of Friends of Pennsylvania, New Jersey . . . since . . . 1795, in Promoting Their Improvement and Gradual Civilization. Philadelphia: Marcus T. C. Gould, 1830.

5687. Kelsey, Rayner Wickersham. "American Indians and the Inward Light." Bulletin of Friends' Historical Society of Philadelphia 8 (May 1918): 54-56.

5688. _____. Friends and the Indians, 1655-1917. Philadelphia: Associated Executive Committee of Friends on Indian Affairs, 1917.

5689. Knowles, David E. "Some Account of a Journey to the Cherokees, 1839-1840." Bulletin of Friends' Historical Society of Philadelphia 6 (November 1915): 70-78.

5690. Lindley, Harlow. "Friends and the Shawnee Indians at Wapakoneta." Ohio State Archaeological and Historical Quarterly 54 (January-March 1945): 33-39.

5691. Miller, Floyd E. "Hillside Mission." Chronicles of Oklahoma 4 (September 1926): 223-228.

5692. Nicholson, William. "A Tour of Indian Agencies in Kansas and the Indian Territory in 1870." Kansas Historical Quarterly 3 (August 1934): 289-326.

5693. Painter, Levinus K. "Jacob Taylor: Quaker Missionary Statesman." Bulletin of Friends' Historical Association 48 (Autumn 1959): 116-127.

5694. _____. "Jacob Taylor, Quaker Missionary Statesman." Niagara Frontier 6 (Summer 1959): 33-40.

5695. "Quakers and Nebraska Indians in 1869." Nebraska History 7 (April 1924): 59-61.

5696. Ragland, Hobert D. "Missions of the Society of Friends among the Indian Tribes of the Sac and Fox Agency." Chronicles of Oklahoma 33 (Summer 1955): 169-182.

5697. Snyderman, George S., ed. "Halliday Jackson's Journal of a Visit Paid to the Indians of New York (1806)." Proceedings of the American Philosophical

Society 101 (December 1957): 565-588.

5698. Some Account of the Conduct of the Religious Society of Friends towards the Indian Tribes in the Settlement of the Colonies of East and West Jersey and Pennsylvania. London: Edward March, 1844.

5699. Thomson, S. Carrie. "The Shawnee Friends Mission." Chronicles of Okla-homa 2 (December 1924): 392-394.

5700. Tolles, Frederick B. "Nonviolent Contact: The Quakers and the Indians." Proceedings of the American Philosophical Society 107 (April 15, 1963): 93-101.

See also the studies dealing with President Grant's "peace policy," for Quaker participation in it.

12
Legal Relations

The legal status and rights of Indians have been problems of long standing, but they have received much special attention in recent years.

REFERENCE WORKS AND PERIODICALS

Listed here are the standard handbooks on Indian legal matters, a recent case book, and a bibliography on Indian law.

5701. Cohen, Felix S. Handbook of Federal Indian Law, with Reference Tables and Index. Washington: Government Printing Office, 1942. Reprinted Albuquerque: University of New Mexico Press, 1972.

5702. Federal Indian Law. Washington: Government Printing Office, 1958. A revision of Cohen's Handbook of Federal Indian Law prepared by the Office of the Solicitor, Department of the Interior.

5703. Price, Monroe E. Law and the American Indian: Readings, Notes, and Cases. Indianapolis: Bobbs-Merrill Company, 1973.

5704. Sabatini, Joseph D. American Indian Law: A Bibliography of Books, Law Review Articles, and Indian Periodicals. Albuquerque: American Indian Law Center, School of Law, University of New Mexico, 1973.

Additional reference material can be found in the following articles.

5705. Becker, Roger. "American Indian Law: New Publications since 1970." North Dakota Law Review 51 (Fall 1974): 233-235.

5706. Merrill, M. H. "Introduction to the Function of a Journal of Indian Law." American Indian Law Review 1 (Winter 1973): 5-12.

5707. "Sources of American Indian Law." Law Library Journal 67 (November 1974): 494-527. A panel composed of George Grossman, Rennard Strickland, Hans Walker, Victoria S. Santana, and

Larry Levanthal.

Many periodical articles dealing with Indian legal matters can be located in the following general indexes.

5708. An Index to Legal Periodical Literature. 1791-1937. 6 volumes. Boston: Boston Book Company, 1888-1919, and later publishers.

5709. Index to Legal Periodicals. 1908--. New York: H. W. Wilson Company, 1909--.

The rise in interest in Indian legal status and rights has led to the publication of journals and newsletters devoted to Indian law.

5710. American Indian Law Newsletter. 1968--. Issued by American Indian Law Center, School of Law, University of New Mexico, Albuquerque.

5711. American Indian Law Review. 1973--. Published at University of Oklahoma Law School, Norman, Oklahoma.

5712. Education Journal. 1972--. Published by the Institute for the Development of Indian Law, Washington, D.C. Deals with other legal matters as well as with educational ones.

5713. Indian Law Reporter. 1974--. Published by the American Indian Lawyer Training Program, Washington, D.C.

5714. Legislative Review. 1971--. Issued by the Institute for the Development of Indian Law, Washington, D.C.

LEGAL STATUS: GENERAL AND MISCELLANEOUS STUDIES

The position of the Indians within the legal system of the United States is an anomalous one and has generated considerable writing. Listed here are chiefly general works, including a number of arguments from the 1880s on for bringing the Indians under United States laws.

5715. Abbott, Austin. "Indians and the Law." Harvard Law Review 2 (November 1888): 167-179.

5716. American Bar Association. "Report of Special Committee on Indian Legislation." Report of the Sixteenth Annual Meeting of the American Bar Association, 1893, pp. 351-363.

5717. "The American Indian--Tribal Sovereignty and Civil Rights." Iowa Law Review 51 (Spring 1966): 654-669.

5718. Associated Executive Committee of Friends on Indian Affairs. Need of Law on the Indian Reservations. Philadelphia: Sherman and Company, 1878.

5719. Bean, Jerry L. "The Limits of Indian Tribal Sovereignty: The Cornucopia of Inherent Powers." North Dakota Law Review 49 (Winter 1973): 303-331.

5720. Beatty, Donald R. History of the Legal Status of the American Indian with Particular Reference to California. San Francisco: R and E Research Associates, 1974.

5721. Brown, Ray A. "The Indian Problem and the Law." Yale Law Journal 39 (January 1930): 307-331.

5722. Bryan, George. The Imperialism of John Marshall: A Study in Expediency. Boston: Stratford Company, 1924. Discussion of Johnson and Graham's Lessee vs. McIntosh.

5723. Butte, George C. Legal Status of the American Indians: With Special Reference to the Tenure of Indian Lands. N.p., 1912.

5724. Canfield, George F. "The Legal Position of the Indian." American Law Review 15 (January 1881): 21-37.

5725. Cashman, Ben. "The American Indian--Standing in a Peculiar Legal Relation." Ph.D. dissertation, University of Washington, 1969.

5726. Chase, Hiram. "The Law and the American Indian in America." Ohio Law Reporter 9 (October 30, 1911): 345-349.

5727. Clute, James W. "The New York Indians' Right to Self-Determination." Buffalo Law Review 22 (Spring 1973): 985-1019.

5728. Cohen, Felix S. "The Erosion of Indian Rights, 1950-1953: A Case Study in Bureaucracy." Yale Law Journal 62 (February 1953): 348-390.

5729. _____. "Indian Rights and the Federal Courts." Minnesota Law Review 24 (January 1940): 145-200.

5730. _____. "Indian Wardship: The Twilight of a Myth." American Indian 6 (Summer 1953): 8-14.

5731. _____. "The Spanish Origin of Indian Rights in the Law of the United States." Georgetown Law Journal 31 (November 1942): 1-21.

5732. Flynn, Clinton R. "The Legal Status of the Indians in the United States." Central Law Journal 62 (May 25, 1906): 399-404.

5733. Foreman, Grant. "The Indian and the Law." Oklahoma Bar Association Journal 17 (January 19, 1946): 82-91.

5734. _____. "The U.S. Court and the Indian: Where the Red Man Gets a Square Deal." Overland Monthly 61 (June 1913): 573-579.

5735. Goodrich, Chauncey Shafter. "The Legal Status of the California Indian." California Law Review 14 (January 1926): 83-100; (March 1926): 157-187.

5736. Haas, Theodore H. The Indian and the Law. Tribal Relations Pamphlets, nos. 2 and 3. Washington: United States Indian Service, 1949.

5737. Harsha, William Justin. "Law for the Indian." North American Review 134 (March 1882): 272-292.

5738. Heimann, Robert K. "The Cherokee Tobacco Case." Chronicles of Oklahoma 41 (Autumn 1963): 299-322.

5739. Higgins, Frank B. "International Law Considerations of the American Indian Nations by the United States." Arizona Law Review 3 (Summer 1961): 74-85.

5740. Hoebel, E. Adamson. "To End Their Status." In The Indian in Modern America, edited by David A. Baerreis, pp. 1-15. Madison: State Historical Society of Wisconsin, 1956.

5741. Hornblower, William B. "The Legal Status of the Indian." Report of the Fourteenth Annual Meeting of the American Bar Association 14 (1891): 261-277.

5742. Houghton, N. D. "Wards of the United States"--Arizona Applications: A Study of the Legal Status of Indians. Tucson: University of Arizona, 1946.

5743. Indian Rights Association. The Helplessness of the Indians before the Law, with an Outline of Proposed Legislation. Philadelphia: Indian Rights Association, 1886. Report of the Law Committee.

5744. "Indians and the United States." Harvard Law Review 25 (June 1912): 733-734.

5745. Knoepfler, Karl J. "Legal Status of the American Indian and His Property." Iowa Law Bulletin 7 (May 1922): 232-249.

5746. Krieger, Heinrich. "Principles of the Indian Law and the Act of June 18, 1934." George Washington Law Review 3 (March 1935): 279-308.

5747. "The Lawless Indian." Independent 55 (March 5, 1903): 576-577.

5748. "Legal Status of the Indians-- Validity of Indian Marriages." Yale Law Journal 18 (March 1904): 250-252.

5749. Mundt, Karl E. "Indian Autonomy and Indian Legal Problems." Kansas Law Review 15 (1967): 505-511.

5750. Oliver, Robert W. "The Legal Status of American Indian Tribes." Oregon Law Review 38 (April 1959): 193-245.

5751. Pancoast, Henry S. The Indian before the Law. Philadelphia: Indian Rights Association, 1884.

5752. Pease, Gregory. "Constitutional Revision--Indians in the New Mexico Constitution." Natural Resources Journal 9 (July 1969): 466-470.

5753. Pound, Cuthbert W. "Nationals without a Nation: The New York State Tribal Indians." Columbia Law Review 22 (February 1922): 97-102.

5754. Price, Monroe. "The Indian and the White Man's Law." Art in America 60 (July-August 1972): 24-31.

5755. Rice, W. G. "The Position of the American Indian in the Law of the United States." Journal of Comparative Legislation and International Law, 3d series 16 (February 1934): 78-95.

5756. Russell, Isaac Franklin. "The Indian before the Law." Yale Law Journal 18 (March 1909): 328-337.

5757. Shinn, Preston A. "Chief Justice Marshall and the American Indian." Case and Comment 23 (March 1917): 842-843.

5758. Thayer, James Bradley. "A People without Law." Atlantic Monthly 68 (October 1891): 540-551; (November 1891): 676-687.

5759. W. F. C., Jr. "The Constitutional Rights of the American Tribal Indian." Virginia Law Review 51 (January 1965): 121-142.

5760. Weil, Robert. The Legal Status of the Indian. New York, 1888.

5761. Wise, Jennings C. "Indian Law and Needed Reforms." American Bar Association Journal 12 (January 1926): 37-40.

CITIZENSHIP

The acquisition of United States citizenship by the Indians was one of the objectives of reformers in the late nineteenth and early twentieth centuries, and by 1924 citizenship was granted to all Indians. Writings advocating citizenship and historical studies of the movement are listed here, together with a few more recent discussions of citizenship.

5762. Abbott, George W. "The American Indian, Federal Citizen and State Citizen." Federal Bar Journal 20 (Summer 1960): 248-254.

5763. Johnson, Kenneth W. "Sovereignty, Citizenship and the Indian." Arizona Law Review 15 (1973): 973-1003.

5764. Lee, R. Alton. "Indian Citizenship and the Fourteenth Amendment." South Dakota History 4 (Spring 1974): 198-221.

5765. Lembertson, G. M. "Indian Citizenship." American Law Review 20 (March-April 1886): 183-193.

5766. Lien, Arnold J. "The Acquisition of Citizenship by the Native American Indians." Washington University Studies 13 (October 1925): 121-179. Humanistic Series, no. 1.

5767. Smith, Michael T. "The History of Indian Citizenship." Great Plains Journal 10 (Fall 1970): 25-35.

5768. Stein, Gary C. "The Indian Citizenship Act of 1924." New Mexico Historical Review 47 (July 1972): 257-274.

5769. Walker, Francis A. "Indian Citizenship." International Review 1 (May-June 1874): 305-326. Reprinted in The Indian Question, Boston, 1874.

5770. Welsh, Herbert. How to Bring the Indian to Citizenship, and Citizenship to the Indian. Philadelphia: Indian Rights Association, 1892.

INDIAN RIGHTS

The rights of the Indians--civil rights, religious rights, and basic human rights-- are discussed in the recent writings listed here. Studies specifically on the Civil Rights Act of 1968 are listed below under a separate heading.

5771. Allen, John H. "Denial of Voting Rights to Reservation Indians." Utah

Law Review 5 (Fall 1956): 247-256.

5772. American Indian Civil Rights Handbook. Washington: United States Commission on Civil Rights, 1972.

5773. Bailin, Roxanne. "Ruiz v. Morton: BIA Welfare Extended to All American Indians." New York University Review of Law and Social Change 3 (Spring 1973): 201-212.

5774. Bean, Jerry L. "Native Americans and Discrimination in Kansas: Trails from Injustice." University of Kansas Law Review 20 (Spring 1972): 468-485.

5775. Black, Charles L., Jr. "Counsel of Their Own Choosing." American Indian 6 (Fall 1951): 3-17.

5776. Christman, Henry. "Southwestern Indians Win the Vote." American Indian 4, no. 4 (1948): 6-10.

5777. "Constitutional Law--Equal Protection of the Laws--Prohibition of Sale of Intoxicating Liquor to Indians." New York University Law Review 30 (November 1955): 1444-1447.

5778. "The Constitutional Rights of the American Tribal Indian." Virginia Law Review 51 (January 1965): 121-142.

5779. Crenshaw, Ronald W. "Jury Composition--the Purposeful Inclusion of American Indians." South Dakota Law Review 16 (Winter 1971): 214-221.

5780. "Federal Court Has Jurisdiction to Issue Writ of Habeas Corpus on Behalf of Indian Convicted by Tribal Court: Colliflower v. Garland." Harvard Law Review 79 (December 1965): 436-439.

5781. Fernandez, Ferdinand F. "Except a California Indian: A Study in Legal Discrimination." Southern California Quarterly 50 (June 1968): 161-175.

5782. Fretz, Burton D. "The Bill of Rights and American Indian Tribal Governments." Natural Resources Journal 6 (October 1966): 581-616.

5783. Houghton, N. D. "The Legal Status of Indian Suffrage in the United States." California Law Review 19 (July 1931): 507-520.

5784. "Indian Law: The Application of the One-Man, One-Vote Standard of Baker v. Carr to Tribal Elections." Minnesota Law Review 58 (March 1974): 668-676.

5785. "Indian Tribes and Civil Rights." Stanford Law Review 7 (March 1955): 285-292.

5786. Kane, Albert E. "The Negro and the

Indian: A Comparison of Their Constitutional Rights." Arizona Law Review 7 (Spring 1966): 244-251.

5787. Kelley, Dean M. "Guest Editorial: The Impairment of the Religious Liberty of the Taos Pueblo Indians by the United States Government." Journal of Church and State 9 (Spring 1967): 161-164.

5788. Kerr, James R. "Constitutional Rights, Tribal Justice, and the American Indian." Journal of Public Law 18 (1969): 311-338.

5789. La Barre, Weston. "Religious Freedom of Indians Again Upheld." American Anthropologist 67 (April 1965): 505.

5790. McCoy, Donald R., and Richard T. Ruetten. Quest and Response: Minority Rights and the Truman Administration. Lawrence: University Press of Kansas, 1973. Includes material on American Indians.

5791. Myhre, Russell J. "Indians--Protection of Personal Rights in General--the Right of Off-Reservation Indians to Receive General Welfare Assistance." North Dakota Law Review 49 (Winter 1973): 405-410.

5792. Ogborn, Michael J. "Constitutional Implications of an Indian Defendant's Right to a Lesser-Included Offense Instruction." South Dakota Law Review 16 (Spring 1971): 468-480.

5793. Pedersen, Alden. "Decision of Indian Tribal Court Held Reviewable through Federal District Court Habeas Corpus Proceeding: Colliflower v. Garland." Montana Law Review 26 (Spring 1965): 235-240.

5794. Sclar, Lee J. "Participation by Off-Reservation Indians in Programs of the Bureau of Indian Affairs and the Indian Health Service." Montana Law Review 33 (Summer 1972): 191-232.

5795. Sorensen, Stephen. "Ruiz v. Morton: Federal Welfare for Non-Reservation Indians." Utah Law Review, Summer 1973, pp. 328-334.

5796. Stevens, Carl. "Reapportionment: One Man, One Vote, As Applied to Tribal Government." American Indian Law Review 2 (Summer 1974): 137-146.

5797. "The Tobriner Decision." Indian Historian 6 (Fall 1973): 26-31. Constitutionality of peyote use in religious ceremonies.

5798. United States Commission on Civil Rights. The Southwest Indian Report. Washington: Government Printing Office, 1973.

5799. Ward, Edward J. "Minority Rights and American Indians." North Dakota Law Review 51 (Fall 1974): 137-190.

5800. Wheat, Douglas D. "Indian Law--Criminal Procedure--Instruction on Lesser Included Offenses under the Major Crimes Act." University of Kansas Law Review 22 (Spring 1974): 479-487.

5801. White, John R. "Civil Rights and the Native American." Integrated Education 11 (November-December 1973): 31-34.

CIVIL RIGHTS ACT 1968

Title II of the Civil Rights Act of 1968 extended the Bill of Rights to Indian tribes. The act and its implications are discussed in the studies listed here.

5802. Burnett, Donald L., Jr. "An Historical Analysis of the 1968 'Indian Civil Rights' Act." Harvard Journal of Legislation 9 (May 1972): 557-626.

5803. Coulter, Robert T. "Federal Law and Indian Tribal Law: The Right to Civil Counsel and the 1968 Indian Bill of Rights." Columbia Survey of Human Rights Law 3 (January 1971): 49-93.

5804. Davisson, Russell W. "Indian Law--Civil Rights--Federal Jurisdiction--When Tribal Remedies Effectively Exhausted Federal Courts Have Jurisdiction to Hear Claims Arising under Indian Civil Rights Act." University of Kansas Law Review 22 (Spring 1974): 461-470.

5805. Deloria, Vine, Jr. "Implications of the 1968 Civil Rights Act in Tribal Autonomy." In Indian Voices: The First Convocation of American Indian Scholars, pp. 85-92. San Francisco: Indian Historian Press, 1970.

5806. de Raismes, Joseph. "Indian Civil Rights Act of 1968 and the Pursuit of Responsible Tribal Self-Government." South Dakota Law Review 20 (Winter 1975): 59-106.

5807. Granen, Michael R., and Douglas E. Somers. "Indian Bill of Rights." Southwestern University Law Review 5 (Spring 1973): 139-164.

5808. "The Indian Bill of Rights and the Constitutional Status of Tribal Governments." Harvard Law Review 82 (April 1969): 1343-1373.

5809. "Indians--Criminal Procedure: Habeas Corpus as an Enforcement Procedure under the Indian Civil Rights Act of 1968." Washington Law Review 46 (May 1971): 541-554.

5810. Lazarus, Arthur, Jr. "Title II of the 1968 Civil Rights Act: An Indian Bill of Rights." North Dakota Law Review 45 (Spring 1969): 337-352.

5811. Muehlen, Mary L. "An Interpretation of the Due Process Clause of the Indian Bill of Rights." North Dakota Law Review 51 (Fall 1974): 191-204.

5812. Reiblich, G. Kenneth. "Indian Rights under the Civil Rights Act of 1968." Arizona Law Review 10 (Winter 1968): 617-648.

5813. Schusky, Ernest L. "American Indians and the 1968 Civil Rights Act." América Indígena 29 (April 1969): 369-376.

5814. Smith, Michael. "Tribal Sovereignty and the 1968 Indian Bill of Rights." Civil Rights Digest 3 (Summer 1970): 9-15.

5815. Warren, John S. "An Analysis of the Indian Bill of Rights." Montana Law Review 33 (Summer 1972): 255-265.

5816. Webb, Barbara J. Larson, and John R. Webb. "Equitable and Declaratory Relief under the Indian Civil Rights Act." North Dakota Law Review 48 (Summer 1972): 695-727.

5817. Ziontz, Alvin J. "In Defense of Tribal Sovereignty: An Analysis of Judicial Error in Construction of the Indian Civil Rights Act." South Dakota Law Review 20 (Winter 1975): 1-58.

JURISDICTION

One of the most difficult problems in Indian legal affairs is the precise line between federal, state, and tribal jurisdiction.

5818. Abourezk, James G. "South Dakota Indian Jurisdiction." South Dakota Law Review 11 (Winter 1966): 101-118.

5819. Angle, Jerry. Federal, State and Tribal Jurisdiction on Indian Reservations in Arizona. Bureau of Ethnic Research, American Indian Series, no. 2. Tucson: University of Arizona, 1959.

5820. Baldassin, William E., and John T. McDermott. "Jurisdiction over Non-Indians: An Opinion of the 'Opinion.'" American Indian Law Review 1 (Winter 1973): 13-22.

5821. Berger, Edward B., and William J. Mounce. "Applicability of State Conservation and Other Laws to Indian and Public Lands." Rocky Mountain Mineral

Law Institute Proceedings 16 (1971): 347-397.

5822. Canby, William C., Jr. "Civil Jurisdiction and the Indian Reservation." Utah Law Review, 1973, pp. 206-232.

5823. Carr, Allen Lane, and Stanley M. Johanson. "Extent of Washington Criminal Jurisdiction over Indians." Washington Law Review 33 (Autumn 1958): 289-302.

5824. Christoffel, Gregory J. "Indian Tribal Courts--Jurisdiction--Navajo Tribal Court Jurisdiction over Non-Indian Defendants." St. Louis University Law Journal 18 (Spring 1974): 461-473.

5825. Clayton, William F. "Indian Jurisdiction and Related Double Jeopardy Questions." South Dakota Law Review 17 (Spring 1972): 341-349.

5826. Cree, Linda. "The Extension of County Jurisdiction over Indian Reservations in California: Public Law 280 and the Ninth Circuit." Hastings Law Journal 25 (May 1974): 1451-1506.

5827. Crosse, Murray L. "Criminal and Civil Jurisdiction in Indian Country." Arizona Law Review 4 (Fall 1962): 57-64.

5828. Davis, Laurence. "Criminal Jurisdiction over Indian Country in Arizona." Arizona Law Review 1 (Spring 1959): 62-101.

5829. Dowling, Thomas F. "Criminal Jurisdiction over Indians and Post-Conviction Remedies." Montana Law Review 22 (Spring 1961): 165-175.

5830. DuMars, Charles T. "Indictment under the 'Major Crimes Act'--an Exercise in Unfairness and Unconstitutionality." Arizona Law Review 10 (Winter 1968): 691-705.

5831. Frizzell, Kent. "Evolution of Jurisdiction in Indian Country: Foreword." University of Kansas Law Review 22 (Spring 1974): 341-349.

5832. Gubler, Brent H. "A Constitutional Analysis of the Criminal Jurisdiction and Procedural Guarantees of the American Indian." D.S.S. dissertation, Syracuse University, 1963.

5833. Guthals, Joel E. "State Civil Jurisdiction over Tribal Indians--a Re-examination." Montana Law Review 35 (Summer 1974): 340-347.

5834. Hacker, Patrick E., Dennis C. Meier, and Dan J. Pauli. "State Jurisdiction over Indian Land Use: An Interpretation of the 'Encumbrance' Savings Clause of Public Law 280." Land and Water Law Review 9 (1974): 421-456.

5835. Hoebel, E. Adamson. "The Problem of Iroquois Law and Order." American Indian 2 (Spring 1945): 12-20.

5836. Johnson, Joel. "Courts--Jurisdiction--State Assumption of Jurisdiction over a Divorce Action between Enrolled Reservation Indians." North Dakota Law Review 51 (Fall 1974): 217-223.

5837. Kane, Albert E. "Jurisdiction over Indians and Indian Reservations." Arizona Law Review 6 (Spring 1965): 237-255.

5838. Koons, Melvin E., Jr., and Hans C. Walker, Jr. "Jurisdiction over Indian Country in North Dakota." North Dakota Law Review 36 (January 1960): 51-62.

5839. Kuswa, M. Wesley. "Criminal Law--Jurisdiction--Indians." Marquette Law Review 16 (November 1931): 57-59.

5840. LaFontaine, Frank S. "Criminal Jurisdiction over Non-Trust Lands within the Limits of Indian Reservations." Willamette Law Journal 9 (June 1973): 288-310.

5841. _____. "Indian Property and State Judgment Executions." Oregon Law Review 52 (Spring 1973): 313-324.

5842. McCrary, Henry T. "Indians--Jurisdiction--Federal or State Courts." Temple Law Quarterly 26 (Summer 1952): 93-96.

5843. MacMeekin, Daniel H. "Red, White, and Gray: Equal Protection and the American Indian." Stanford Law Review 21 (May 1969): 1236-1248.

5844. Matthews, M. A. "Indian Law: The Pre-emption Doctrine and Colonias de Santa Fe." Natural Resources Journal 13 (July 1973): 535-545. Rebuttal by Shirley Keith, 14 (April 1974): 283-292.

5845. Michaels, Lee S. "Courts--State Courts in New York May Not Inquire into Propriety of Indian Court Decisions." Syracuse Law Review 17 (Fall 1965): 87-89.

5846. Monro, James. "Constitutional Law: Cases: Indian Jurisdiction." South Dakota Law Review 13 (Spring 1968): 460-463.

5847. Mudd, John O. "Jurisdiction and the Indian Credit Problem: Considerations for a Solution." Montana Law Review 33 (Summer 1972): 307-316.

5848. Nash, Douglas. "Tribal Control of Extradition from Reservations." Natural Resources Journal 10 (July 1970): 626-634.

5849. O'Toole, Francis J., and Thomas N. Tureen. "State Power and the Passamaquoddy Tribe: 'A Gross National Hypocrisy?'" Maine Law Review 23 (1971): 1-39.

5850. Parker, Alan R. "Kennerly vs. District Court: A Memorandum." American Indian Culture Center Journal 3 (Fall-Winter 1971-1972): 12-15.

5851. _____. "State and Tribal Courts in Montana: The Jurisdictional Relationship." Montana Law Review 33 (Summer 1972): 277-290.

5852. Pritchett, L. Bow, Jr. "Problems of State Jurisdiction over Indian Reservations." DePaul Law Review 13 (Autumn-Winter 1963): 74-98.

5853. Ransom, Richard E., and William G. Gilstrap. "Indians--Civil Jurisdiction in New Mexico--State, Federal and Tribal Courts." New Mexico Law Review 1 (January 1971): 196-214.

5854. Reynolds, Osborne M. "Indians--Reservations--Federal Jurisdiction Ended Only by Express Provision of Congress." Arizona Law Review 5 (Fall 1963): 131-135.

5855. Richards, Clinton G. "Federal Jurisdiction over Criminal Matters Involving Indians." South Dakota Law Review 2 (Spring 1957): 48-58.

5856. Sonosky, Marvin J. "State Jurisdiction over Indians in Indian Country." North Dakota Law Review 48 (Summer 1972): 551-559.

5857. "State and Federal Jurisdiction in Indian Affairs--Habeas Corpus." Virginia Law Register, new series 11 (February 1926): 619-623.

5858. Sullivan, John F. "State Civil Power over Reservation Indians." Montana Law Review 33 (Summer 1972): 291-306.

5859. Taylor, Peter S., M. Frances Ayer, and Alan R. Parker. "Development of Tripartite Jurisdiction in Indian Country." University of Kansas Law Review 22 (Spring 1974): 351-385.

5860. Vollmann, Tim. "Criminal Jurisdiction in Indian Country: Tribal Sovereignty and Defendants' Rights in Conflict." University of Kansas Law Review 22 (Spring 1974): 387-412.

5861. Waters, James H. "State Lacks Jurisdiction over Abandoned Indian Minor--Federal Jurisdiction Exclusive." Utah Law Review 7 (Spring 1961): 417-421.

For jurisdictional problems concerning the power to tax, see the studies listed in the next section.

TAXATION

5862. Babbitt, Hattie. "State Taxation of Indian Income." Law and the Social Order, 1971, pp. 355-369.

5863. Brown, Robert C. "The Taxation of Indian Property." Minnesota Law Review 15 (January 1931): 182-209.

5864. Brunt, David. "Taxation and the American Indian." Indian Historian 6 (Spring 1973): 7-10, 42.

5865. Cuykendal, Clydia J. "State Taxation of Indians--Federal Preemption of Taxation against the Backdrop of Indian Sovereignty." Washington Law Review 49 (November 1973): 191-212.

5866. Davies, Glen E. "State Taxation on Indian Reservations." Utah Law Review, July 1966, pp. 132-151.

5867. Ellis, Hal William. "Federal Taxation: Exclusion of Earnings on Allotted Indian Land from Federal Income Taxation." American Indian Law Review 2 (Summer 1974): 119-124.

5868. Faulhaber, Dwight L. "The Power of a State to Impose an Income Tax on Reservation Indians." Willamette Law Journal 6 (December 1970): 515-524.

5869. Gainer, Phyllis Wilson. "Taxation--Indian Trust Property--State Inheritance Tax." St. Mary's Law Journal 5 (Spring 1973): 161-168.

5870. Hamlin, Thomas. "State Taxation on Sales to Reservation Indians: A Comment on the North Dakota Attorney General's Position." North Dakota Law Review 49 (Winter 1973): 343-358.

5871. Israel, Daniel H., and Thomas L. Smithson. "Indian Taxation, Tribal Sovereignty and Economic Development." North Dakota Law Review 49 (Winter 1973): 267-301.

5872. Johnson, David C. "State Taxation of Indians: Impact of the 1973 Supreme Court Decisions." American Indian Law Review 2 (Summer 1974): 1-27.

5873. Molloy, Donald W. "'Must the Paleface Pay to Puff?' Confederated Salish and Kootenai v. Moe." Montana Law Review 36 (Winter 1975): 93-102.

5874. Morrison, William E. "Taxation of a Possessory Interest in Restricted Indian Lands in Arizona." Law and the Social Order, 1972, pp. 467-475.

5875. Ott, Dennis G. "State Extension of Cigarette Sales Tax to Indians." Idaho Law Review 11 (Fall 1974): 101-111.

5876. Perez, Richard L. "Indian Taxation: Underlying Policies and Present Problems." California Law Review 59 (September 1971): 1261-1298.

5877. Putzi, Patrick. "Indians and Federal Income Taxation." New Mexico Law Review 2 (July 1972): 200-233.

5878. Sears, Kelley D. "Indian Law--Taxation--Reservation Indian's Income Not Taxable If Derived from Reservation Sources--State Power over Reservation Indians Is Limited." University of Kansas Law Review 22 (Spring 1974): 470-479.

5879. Sharum, Albert E. "Ad Valorem Taxation of Lands Affecting the Five Civilized Tribes." Oklahoma Bar Association Journal 18 (January 25, 1947): 94-111.

5880. White, Jay Vincent. Taxing Those They Found Here: An Examination of the Tax Exempt Status of the American Indian. Albuquerque: Institute for the Development of Indian Law, University of New Mexico, 1973.

5881. Zimmerman, William, Jr. "Some Problems Relating to Indian Treaties: Problems of Tax-Exemption." In Proceedings of the Conference on Indian Tribes and Treaties, pp. 58-67. Minneapolis: Center for Continuation Study, University of Minnesota, 1955.

WATER RIGHTS

Survival and development of Indian communities often depend on adequate water as well as on land. The erosion of Indian water rights and their reestablishment are the subject of the legal and historical studies listed here.

5882. Bloom, Paul L. "Indian 'Paramount' Rights to Water Use." Rocky Mountain Mineral Law Institute Proceedings 16 (1969): 669-693.

5883. Campbell, Susan Millington. "A Proposal for the Quantification of Reserved Indian Water Rights." Columbia Law Review 74 (November 1974): 1299-1321.

5884. Clark, Robert Emmet. "The Pueblo Rights Doctrine in New Mexico." New Mexico Historical Review 35 (October 1960): 265-283.

5885. Costo, Rupert. "Indian Water Rights: A Survival Issue." Indian Historian 5 (Fall 1972): 4-6.

5886. Dellwo, Robert D. "Indian Water Rights--the Winters Doctrine Updated." Gonzaga Law Review 6 (Spring 1971): 215-240.

5887. Haddon, Sam E. "Access and Wharfage Rights and the Territorial Extent of Indian Reservation Bordering on Navigable Water--Who Owns the Bed of Flathead Lake?" Montana Law Review 27 (Fall 1965): 55-75.

5888. Leaphart, Bill. "Sale and Lease of Indian Water Rights." Montana Law Review 33 (Summer 1972): 266-276.

5889. Martone, Rosalie. "The United States and the Betrayal of Indian Water Rights." Indian Historian 7 (Summer 1974): 3-11.

5890. Miller, Gerald R. "Indians, Water, and the Arid Western States--a Prelude to the Pelton Decision." Utah Law Review 5 (Fall 1957): 495-510.

5891. Ortiz, Alfonso. "The Gila River Piman Water Problem: An Ethnohistorical Account." In The Changing Ways of Southwestern Indians: A Historic Perspective, edited by Albert H. Schroeder, pp. 245-257. Glorieta, New Mexico: Rio Grande Press, 1973.

5892. Porter, Pat. "Indian Resources: Struggles over Water Rights." Christian Century 89 (February 16, 1972): 208-210.

5893. Patterson, John. "Extent of Indian Water Rights on Reservations in the West." Rocky Mountain Law Review 18 (June 1946): 427-430.

5894. Ranquist, Harold A. "Effect of Changes in Place and Nature of Use of Indian Rights to Water Reserved under the 'Winters Doctrine.'" Natural Resources Lawyer 5 (January 1972): 34-41.

5895. Sondheim, Harry B., and John R. Alexander. "Federal Indian Water Rights: A Retrogression to Quasi-Riparianism?" Southern California Law Review 34 (Fall 1960): 1-61.

5896. Veeder, William H. "Federal Encroachment on Indian Water Rights and the Impairment of Reservation Development." Toward Economic Development for Native American Communities. pp. 460-518. Washington: Government Printing Office, 1969.

5897. _____. "Indian Prior and Paramount Rights to the Use of Water." Rocky Mountain Mineral Law Institute Proceedings 16 (1971): 631-693.

5898. _____. "Indian Prior and Paramount Rights versus State Rights." North Dakota Law Review 51 (Fall 1974): 107-136.

5899. _____. "Indian Water Rights in the Upper Missouri River Basin." North Dakota Law Review 48 (Summer 1972): 617-637.

5900. _____. "Water Rights: Life or Death for the American Indian." Indian Historian 5 (Summer 1972): 4-21.

5901. _____. "Winters Doctrine Rights: Keystone of National Programs for Western Land and Water Conservation and Utilization." Montana Law Review 26 (Spring 1965): 149-172.

5902. Young, Ronald T. L. "Interagency Conflicts of Interest: The Peril to Indian Water Rights." Law and the Social Order, 1972, pp. 313-328.

HUNTING AND FISHING RIGHTS

An important area of legal controversy is that of hunting and fishing rights of Indians. These rights, frequently based on treaty stipulations, come in conflict with state laws.

5903. "Alaskan Natives Appeal to Court." American Indian 5, no. 1 (1949): 31-34.

5904. American Friends Service Committee. Uncommon Controversy: Fishing Rights of the Muckleshoot, Puyallup, and Nisqually Indians. Prepared by M. B. Isely and others. Seattle: University of Washington Press, 1970.

5905. Anderson, Owen L. "Indians--Hunting and Fishing Rights: State Law Must Yield to Federal Treaty." North Dakota Law Review 48 (Summer 1972): 729-737.

5906. Aschenbrenner, Peter J. "State Power and the Indian Treaty Right to Fish." California Law Review 59 (March 1971): 485-524.

5907. Bean, Jerry L. "Off-Reservation Hunting and Fishing Rights: Scales Tip in Favor of States and Sportsmen?" North Dakota Law Review 51 (Fall 1974): 11-30.

5908. Buchanan, Charles M. "Rights of the Puget Sound Indians to Game and Fish." Washington Historical Quarterly 6 (April 1915): 109-118.

5909. Burnett, Donald L., Jr. "Indian Hunting, Fishing and Trapping Rights: The Record and the Controversy." Idaho Law Review 7 (Spring 1970): 49-75.

5910. Hobbs, Charles A. "Indian Hunting and Fishing Rights." George Washington Law Review 32 (March 1964): 504-532.

5911. _____. "Indian Hunting and Fishing Rights II." George Washington Law Review 37 (July 1969): 1251-1273.

5912. J. J. D. "Indian Law--State Regula-tion--Hunting and Fishing Rights." New York Law Forum 18 (Fall 1972): 442-450. Reprinted in American Indian Law Review 1 (Winter 1973): 79-87.

5913. Johnson, Ralph W. "The States versus Indian Off-Reservation Fishing: A United States Supreme Court Error." Washington Law Review 47 (March 1972): 207-236.

5914. McLoone, John J. "Indian Hunting and Fishing Rights." Arizona Law Review 10 (Winter 1968): 725-739.

5915. Paulson, Michael I. "Indian Regulation of Non-Indian Hunting and Fishing." Wisconsin Law Review, 1974, pp. 499-523.

5916. Phillips, Richard G., Jr. "Indian Fishing Rights." Willamette Law Journal 8 (March 1972): 248-260.

5917. "Regulation of Treaty Indian Fishing." Washington Law Review 43 (March 1968): 670-683.

Reports of agitation over hunting and fishing rights can be found under Current Comment, especially since 1960.

LEGAL SERVICES

Studies on legal services and on training lawyers in Indian legal matters are listed here.

5918. Getches, David. "Difficult Beginnings for Indian Legal Services." NLADA Briefcase 30 (May 1972): 181-185.

5919. Gross, Michael Paul. "Reckoning for Legal Services: A Case Study of Legal Assistance in Indian Education." Notre Dame Lawyer 49 (October 1973): 78-104.

5920. Halverson, Lowell K. "Report on Legal Services to the Indians: A Study in Desperation." In Native Americans Today: Sociological Perspectives, edited by Howard M. Bahr and others, pp. 338-344. New York: Harper and Row, 1972.

5921. McDermott, John T. "The Indian Law Program at the University of Montana." Montana Law Review 33 (Summer 1972): 187-190.

5922. Price, Monroe E. "Lawyers on the Reservation: Some Implications for the Legal Profession." Law and the Social Order, 1969, pp. 161-206.

5923. Swan, Robert C. "Indian Legal Services Programs: The Key to Red Power?" Arizona Law Review 12 (Fall 1970): 594-626.

INDIAN DELINQUENCY AND CRIME

5924. Fisher, Carol Ann. "A Survey of Vandalism and Its Cultural Antecedents on Four New York State Indian Reservations." D.S.S. dissertation, Syracuse University, 1959

5925. Folsom, R. D. "American Indians Imprisoned in the Oklahoma Penitentiary: 'A Punishment More Primitive Than Torture.'" American Indian Law Review 2 (Summer 1974): 85-109.

5926. Forslund, Morris A., and Ralph E. Meyers. "Delinquency among Wind River Indian Reservation Youth." Criminology 12 (May 1974): 97-106.

5927. Hayner, Norman S. "Variability in the Criminal Behavior of American Indians." American Journal of Sociology 47 (January 1942): 602-613.

5928. Levy, Jerrold E., Stephen J. Kunitz, and Michael Everett. "Navaho Criminal Homicide." Southwestern Journal of Anthropology 25 (Summer 1969): 124-152.

5929. Luebben, Ralph A. "Anglo Law and Navajo Behavior." Kiva 29 (February 1964): 60-75.

5930. McCone, R. Clyde. "Cultural Factors in Crime among the Dakota Indians." Plains Anthropologist 11 (May 1966): 144-151.

5931. Minnis, Mhyra S. "The Relationship of the Social Structure of an Indian Community to Adult and Juvenile Delinquency." Social Forces 41 (May 1963): 395-403.

5932. Mudd, Joseph E. "Indian Juveniles and Legislative Delinquency in Montana." Montana Law Review 33 (Summer 1972): 233-254.

5933. Petterson, Jay R. "Education, Jurisdiction, and Inadequate Facilities as Causes of Juvenile Delinquency among Indians." North Dakota Law Review 48 (Summer 1972): 661-694.

5934. Reasons, Charles. "Crime and the American Indian." In Native Americans Today: Sociological Perspectives, edited by Howard M. Bahr and others, pp. 319-326. New York: Harper and Row, 1972.

5935. Riffenburgh, Arthur S. "Cultural Influences and Crime among Indian-Americans of the Southwest." Federal Probation 28 (September 1964): 38-46.

5936. Stewart, Omer C. "Questions Regarding American Indian Criminality." Human Organization 23 (Spring 1964): 61-66.

5937. Von Hentig, Hans. "The Delinquency of the American Indian." Journal of Criminal Law and Criminology 36 (July-August 1945): 75-84.

TRIBAL LAW AND GOVERNMENT

Publications on the laws of the Indian tribes are of various kinds--collections of laws passed by the Indian nations, present-day charters and constitutions of the tribes, studies of primitive tribal law, and accounts of tribal courts and other legal functions.

The following guides pertain to published Indian tribal laws.

5938. Anderson, Robert B., comp. "A Preliminary Check List of the Laws of the Indian Tribes." Law Library Journal 34 (July 1941): 126-148.

5939. Hargrett, Lester. A Bibliography of the Constitutions and Laws of the American Indians. Cambridge: Harvard University Press, 1947.

Many of the published Indian laws have been reprinted in a series called "The Constitutions and Laws of the American Indian Tribes," by Scholarly Resources, Wilmington, Delaware.

Under the Wheeler-Howard Act of 1934 Indian tribes were authorized to incorporate and establish tribal governments. The corporate charters, constitutions, and bylaws of the individual tribes have been published separately by the Bureau of Indian Affairs. Many of them have been transcribed in the following publication.

5940. Fay, George Emory, ed. Charters, Constitutions and By-Laws of the Indian Tribes of North America. Museum of Anthropology, Occasional Publications in Anthropology, Ethnology Series, volumes 1-15. Greeley: University of Northern Colorado, 1967-1972.

Listed below are general and miscellaneous studies dealing with primitive Indian law and with other aspects of law in the Indian tribes, past and present.

5941. Ballenger, T. L. "The Development of Law and Legal Institutions among the Cherokees." Ph.D. dissertation, University of Oklahoma, 1938.

5942. Beaglehole, Ernest. "Ownership and Inheritance in an American Indian Tribe." Iowa Law Review 20 (January 1935): 304-316.

5943. Benge, William B. "Law and Order on Indian Reservations." Federal Bar Journal 20 (Summer 1960): 223-229.

5944. Birkett, Peter W. "Indian Tribal Courts and Procedural Due Process: A Different Standard?" Indiana Law Journal 49 (Summer 1974): 721-739.

5945. Cohen, Felix S. "How Long Will Indian Constitutions Last?" Indians at Work 6 (June 1939): 40-43.

5946. Cox, Bruce Alden. "Law and Conflict Management among the Hopi." Ph.D. dissertation, University of California, 1968.

5947. Davis, Laurence. "Court Reform in the Navajo Nation." Journal of the American Judicature Society 43 (August 1959): 52-55.

5948. Duncan, James W. "Interesting Ante-Bellum Laws of the Cherokees, Now Oklahoma History." Chronicles of Oklahoma 6 (June 1928): 178-180.

5949. Haas, Theodore H. Ten Years of Tribal Government under I.R.A. Tribal Relations Pamphlets, no. 1. Chicago: United States Indian Service, 1947.

5950. Hagan, Horace H. "Tribal Law of the American Indian." Case and Comment 23 (February 1917): 735-738.

5951. Hoebel, E. Adamson. The Law of Primitive Man: A Study in Comparative Legal Dynamics. Cambridge: Harvard University Press, 1964.

5952. Humphrey, Norman D. "Police and Tribal Welfare in Plains Indian Cultures." Journal of Criminal Law and Criminology 33 (1942): 147-161.

5953. Knight, Oliver. "Fifty Years of Choctaw Law, 1834 to 1884." Chronicles of Oklahoma 31 (Spring 1953): 76-95.

5954. Lawrence, William J. "Tribal Injustice: The Red Lake Court of Indian Offenses." North Dakota Law Review 48 (Summer 1972): 639-659.

5955. Llewellyn, Karl N., and E. Adamson Hoebel. The Cheyenne Way: Conflict and Case Law in Primitive Jurisprudence. Norman: University of Oklahoma Press, 1941.

5956. Lowie, Robert H. "Property Rights and Coercive Powers of Plains Indian Military Societies." Journal of Legal and Political Sociology 1 (April 1943): 59-71.

5957. MacLachlan, Bruce B. "The Mescalero Apache Quest for Law and Order." Journal of the West 3 (October 1964): 441-458.

5958. _____. "The Mescalero Apache Tribal Court: A Study of the Manifestation of the Adjudicative Function in a Concrete Judicial Institution." Ph.D. dissertation, University of Chicago, 1962.

5959. MacLeod, William Christie. "Aspects of the Earlier Development of Law and Punishment." Journal of Criminal Law and Criminology 23 (1932): 169-190.

5960. _____. "Law, Procedure, and Punishment in Early Bureaucracies." Journal of Criminal Law and Criminology 25 (1934): 225-244.

5961. McNeil, Irving. "Indian Justice." New Mexico Historical Review 19 (October 1944): 261-270.

5962. Malinowski, Bronislaw. "A New Instrument for the Interpretation of Law--Especially Primitive: A Review of The Cheyenne Way." Lawyers Guild Review 2 (May 1942): 1-12.

5963. Parker, Alan. "Delinquents and Tribal Courts in Montana." American Indian Culture Center Journal 3 (Fall 1972): 3-6.

5964. Reid, John Phillip. "The Cherokee Thought: An Apparatus of Primitive Law." New York University Law Review 46 (April 1971): 281-302.

5965. _____. A Law of Blood: The Primitive Law of the Cherokee Nation. New York: New York University Press, 1970.

5966. Shepardson, Mary. "Problems of the Navajo Tribal Courts in Transition." Human Organization 24 (Fall 1965): 250-253.

5967. Strickland, Rennard. "Corpus of the Written Cherokee Laws." Law Library Journal 67 (February 1974): 110-119.

5968. _____. Fire and the Spirits: Cherokee Law from Clan to Court. Norman: University of Oklahoma Press, 1975.

5969. _____. "From Clan to Court: Development of Cherokee Law." Tennessee Historical Quarterly 31 (Winter 1972): 316-327.

5970. Thompson, Joseph J. "Law amongst the Aborigines of the Mississippi Valley." Illinois Law Quarterly 6 (April 1924): 204-223.

5971. Thompson, William P. "Courts of the Cherokee Nation." Chronicles of Oklahoma 2 (March 1924): 63-74.

13
Indian Education

Education was long considered the key means of acculturation and assimilation. Schools were provided by religious societies and by the federal government, and the curriculum was dominated by white ideas and ideals. Only in recent years has there been a move toward Indian control of Indian education.

REFERENCE GUIDES AND PERIODICALS

The following indexes and bibliographies are useful guides to Indian materials.

5972. Berry, Brewton. The Education of American Indians: A Survey of the Literature. Washington: Government Printing Office, 1969. A committee print, 91st Congress, 1st session, prepared for the Special Subcommittee on Indian Education of the Committee on Labor and Public Welfare, United States Senate. A bibliographical essay and list of articles, books, and theses and dissertations.

5973. Education Index. 1929--. New York: H. W. Wilson Company, 1932--.

5974. Educational Resources Information Center (ERIC). Research in Education. Washington: National Institute of Education, United States Department of Health, Education, and Welfare, 1967--. A monthly publication announcing recently completed research projects in education. Contains numerous Indian items, including bibliographies on Indian subjects. A preliminary volume covers the period 1956-1965.

5975. Current Index to Journals in Education (CIJE). New York: CCM Information Corporation, 1969--. A project of the Education Resources Information Center (ERIC).

5976. Martinez, Cecilia J., and James E. Heathman, comps. American Indian Education: A Selected Bibliography. University Park: ERIC Clearinghouse on Rural Education and Small Schools, New Mexico

State University, 1969. Supplement 1, compiled by Alyce J. Nafziger, 1970. Supplement 2, compiled by David M. Altus and Albert D. Link, 1971. Supplement 3, 1973. Supplement 4, 1973. Abstracts of documents from Research in Education and Current Index to Journals in Education.

5977. Findley, Charles A. "ERIC Reports: American Indians." Speech Teacher 22 (March 1973): 162-165.

The following periodicals are devoted to Indian education. Included here also are reprinted collections of articles from periodicals.

5978. Indian Education. 1936-1966. Published by the United States Bureau of Indian Affairs.

5979. Journal of American Indian Education. 1961--. Published by the Bureau of Educational Research and Services, Arizona State University, Tempe.

5980. Beatty, Willard W., and associates. Education for Action: Selected Articles from Indian Education, 1936-43. Washington: Education Division, United States Indian Service, 1944.

5981. _____. Education for Cultural Change: Selected Articles from Indian Education, 1944-51. Washington: United States Department of the Interior, Bureau of Indian Affairs, 1953.

5982. Thompson, Hildegard, and associates. Education for Cross-Cultural Enrichment: Selected Articles from Indian Education, 1952-64. Washington: United States Department of the Interior, Bureau of Indian Affairs, Branch of Education, 1964.

5983. Deever, R. Merwin, and others, eds. American Indian Education. Tempe: Bureau of Educational Research and Services, Arizona State University, 1974. Articles from Journal of American Indian Education.

5984. Henry, Jeannette, ed. The American

Indian Reader: Education. San Francisco: Indian Historian Press, 1972. Collection of articles on education from the Indian Historian.

See also education publications of the Bureau of Indian Affairs, such as the BIA Education Research Bulletin, and the IERC Bulletin, issued by the Indian Education Resources Center, Albuquerque, New Mexico.

HISTORY OF INDIAN EDUCATION

General Historical Studies

Despite the importance of Indian education, there have been few comprehensive histories of the subject.

5985. Adams, Evelyn C. American Indian Education: Government Schools and Economic Progress. New York: King's Crown Press, 1946.

5986. Fischbacher, Theodore. "A Study of the Role of the Federal Government in the Education of the American Indian." Ph.D. dissertation, Arizona State University, 1967.

5987. Layman, Martha Elizabeth. "A History of Indian Education in the United States." Ph.D. dissertation, University of Minnesota, 1942.

5988. Morris, Harold W. "A History of Indian Education in the United States." Ph.D. dissertation, Oregon State University, 1954.

Historical Studies: Special Topics

Indian education has been studied by chronological periods and by tribes or groups. These historical studies are listed here. Works dealing with particular schools and teachers are listed under a separate heading below. The educational work of missionaries, a considerable part of the history of Indian education, is for the most part included in the section on missions.

5989. Balyeat, Frank Allen. "Education in Indian Territory." Ph.D. dissertation, Stanford University, 1927.

5990. Beatty, Willard W. "History of Navajo Education." America Indigena 21 (January 1961): 7-31.

5991. Borden, Morton. "'To Educate the Natives.'" American History Illustrated 9 (January 1975): 20-27.

5992. Coates, Lawrence George. "A History of Indian Education by the Mormons, 1830-1900." Ed.D. dissertation, Ball State University, 1969.

5993. Davis, Caroline. "Education of the Chickasaw, 1856-1907." Chronicles of Oklahoma 15 (December 1937): 415-448.

5994. Davis, John Benjamin. "Public Education among the Cherokee Indians." Peabody Journal of Education 7 (November 1929): 168-173.

5995. Debo, Angie. "Education in the Choctaw Country after the Civil War." Chronicles of Oklahoma 10 (September 1932): 383-391.

5996. Ferris, Florence L. "Indian Schools in Colonial Days." Journal of American History 6 (1912): 141-158.

5997. Fletcher, Alice C. Indian Education and Civilization. Bureau of Education, Special Report, 1888. Washington: Government Printing Office, 1888. Senate Executive Document no. 95, 48th Congress, 2d session, serial 2264.

5998. Foreman, Carolyn Thomas. "Education among the Chickasaw Indians." Chronicles of Oklahoma 15 (June 1937): 139-165.

5999. _____. "Education among the Quapaws: 1829-1875." Chronicles of Oklahoma 25 (Spring 1947): 15-29.

6000. Friesen, John W., and Linda Moseson. "The Plains Indians and Educational Theory." Journal of American Indian Education 11 (October 1971): 19-26.

6001. Garrett, Kathleen. "Dartmouth Alumni in the Indian Territory." Chronicles of Oklahoma 32 (Summer 1954): 123-141.

6002. Hagan, Maxine Wakefield. "An Educational History of the Pima and Papago Peoples from the Mid-Seventeenth Century to the Mid-Twentieth Century." Ed.D. dissertation, University of Arizona, 1959.

6003. Harsha, William Justin. "Education and the 'Six Nations.'" Southern Workman 58 (December 1929): 562-566.

6004. _____. "Education and the So-Called 'Civilized Tribes.'" Southern Workman 59 (January 1930): 36-41.

6005. Hayes, Susanna Adella. "The Resistance to Education for Assimilation by the Colville Indians, 1872 to 1972." Ph.D. dissertation, University of Michigan, 1973.

6006. Hoopes, Alban W. "Indian Education, 1879-1939." Educational Outlook 14 (January 1940): 49-63.

6007. Hoyt, Milton. "Development of Education among the Southern Utes." Ed.D. dissertation, University of Colorado, 1967.

6008. Johnson, Ronald M. "Schooling the Savage: Andrew S. Draper and Indian Education." Phylon 35 (March 1974): 74-82.

6009. Keller, Robert H., Jr. "American Indian Education: An Historical Context." Journal of the West 13 (April 1974): 75-82. Puyallup Reservation.

6010. Kersey, Harry A., Jr. "Educating the Seminole Indians of Florida, 1879-1970." Florida Historical Quarterly 49 (July 1970): 16-35.

6011. Klingberg, Frank J. "Early Attempts at Indian Education in South Carolina, a Documentary." South Carolina Historical Magazine 61 (January 1960): 1-10.

6012. Knepler, Abraham E. "The Education of the Cherokee Indians." Ph.D. dissertation, Yale University, 1939.

6013. _____. "Education in the Cherokee Nation." Chronicles of Oklahoma 21 (December 1943): 378-401.

6014. _____. "Eighteenth Century Cherokee Educational Efforts." Chronicles of Oklahoma 20 (March 1942): 55-61.

6015. Kutzleb, Charles R. "Educating the Dakota Sioux, 1876-1890." North Dakota History 32 (October 1965): 197-215.

6016. McLaury, John Clark. "An Historical Outline of Efforts--Both Public and Private--towards the Education and Civilization of the Indian, and of His Present Status." Ped.D. dissertation, New York University, 1904.

6017. Reid, Leslie Sayne. "A History of the Education of the Ute Indians, 1847-1905." Ph.D. dissertation, University of Utah, 1972.

6018. Skelton, Robert Howard. "A History of the Educational System of the Cherokee Nation, 1801-1910." Ed.D. dissertation, University of Arkansas, 1970.

6019. Smith, Glenn. "Education for the Natives of Alaska: The Work of the United States Bureau of Education, 1884-1931." Journal of the West 6 (July 1967): 440-450.

6020. Szasz, Margaret. Education and the American Indian: The Road to Self-Determination, 1928-1973. Albuquerque: University of New Mexico Press, 1974.

6021. Tanis, Norman Earl. "Education in John Eliot's Indian Utopias, 1646-1675." History of Education Quarterly 10 (Fall 1970): 308-323.

6022. Wild, George Posey. "History of Education of the Plains Indians of Southwestern Oklahoma since the Civil War." Ph.D. dissertation, University of Oklahoma, 1941.

6023. Woerner, Davida. "Education among the Navajo: An Historical Study." Ph.D. dissertation, Columbia University, 1941.

6024. Wright, Muriel H. "Review of Chickasaw Education before the Civil War." Chronicles of Oklahoma 34 (Winter 1956-1957): 486-487.

Schools and Teachers

Listed here are studies of individual Indian schools and teachers, chiefly from the nineteenth century. Contemporary accounts of schools, especially for recent times, are found under Current Comment.

6025. Arnold, Oren. "Great White Mother." Collier's 126 (October 28, 1950): 24-25. Mrs. Lisbeth Bonnell Eubanks, teacher of Navajos.

6026. Baird, W. David. "Spencer Academy, Choctaw Nation, 1842-1900." Chronicles of Oklahoma 45 (Spring 1967): 25-43.

6027. Ballenger, T. L. "The Colored High School of the Cherokee Nation." Chronicles of Oklahoma 30 (Winter 1952-1953): 454-462.

6028. Balyeat, Frank A. "Arthur Grant Evans." Chronicles of Oklahoma 38 (Autumn 1960): 245-252. Teacher in Cherokee schools.

6029. _____. "Early Chickasaw Schools." Chronicles of Oklahoma 39 (Winter 1956-1957): 487-490.

6030. Blackmar, Frank W. "Haskell Institute As Illustrating Indian Progress." Review of Reviews 5 (June 1892): 557-561.

6031. Brown, Estelle A. Stubborn Fool: A Narrative. Caldwell, Idaho: Caxton Printers, 1952.

6032. Bryce, J. Y. "About Some of Our First Schools in Choctaw Nation." Chronicles of Oklahoma 6 (September 1928): 354-394.

6033. Butler, Josiah. "Pioneer School Teaching at the Comanche-Kiowa Agency School, 1870-3." Chronicles of Oklahoma 6 (December 1928): 483-528.

6034. Carr, Susan Jane. "Bloomfield Academy and Its Founder." Chronicles of

Oklahoma 2 (December 1924): 366-379.

6035. Conlan, Czarina Colbert. "Schools of the Five Civilized Tribes: Choctaw, Chickasaw, Seminole, Cherokee and Creek Indian Schools." Southern Magazine 3 (August-September 1936): 9-10, 48.

6036. Eastman, Elaine Goodale. "Mrs. Eastman's Reports from Dakota." South Dakota Historical Review 2 (July 1937): 185-196.

6037. Foreman, Carolyn Thomas. "Charity Hall: An Early Chickasaw School." Chronicles of Oklahoma 11 (September 1933): 912-926.

6038. _____. "Chickasaw Manual Labor Academy." Chronicles of Oklahoma 23 (Winter 1945-1946): 338-357.

6039. _____. "The Choctaw Academy." Chronicles of Oklahoma 6 (December 1928): 453-480.

6040. _____. "The Choctaw Academy." Chronicles of Oklahoma 9 (December 1931): 382-411; 10 (March 1932): 77-114.

6041. _____. "Miss Sophia Sawyer and Her School." Chronicles of Oklahoma 32 (Winter 1954-1955): 395-413.

6042. Gibson, Arrell M. "Joe Kagey: Indian Educator." Chronicles of Oklahoma 38 (Spring 1960): 12-19.

6043. Gilstrap, Harriet Patrick. "Memoirs of a Pioneer Teacher." Chronicles of Oklahoma 38 (Spring 1960): 20-34.

6044. Gold, Douglas. A Schoolmaster with the Blackfeet Indians. Caldwell, Idaho: Caxton Printers, 1963.

6045. Golden, Gertrude M. Red Moon Called Me: Memoirs of a Schoolteacher in the Government Indian Service. Edited by Cecil Dryden. San Antonio: Naylor Company, 1954.

6046. Guenther, Richard L. "The Santee Normal Training School." Nebraska History 51 (Fall 1970): 359-378.

6047. Halliburton, R., Jr. "Northeastern's Seminary Hall." Chronicles of Oklahoma 51 (Winter 1973-1974): 391-398.

6048. Hodge, Patt. "The History of Hammon and the Red Moon School." Chronicles of Oklahoma 44 (Summer 1966): 130-139.

6049. Hutchinson, E. Lillian. "Teacher in Navajo Land." Business Education World 27 (May 1947): 530-531.

6050. Jackson, Joe C. "Schools among the Minor Tribes in Indian Territory." Chronicles of Oklahoma 32 (Spring 1954): 58-69.

6051. _____. "Summer Normals in Indian Territory after 1898." Chronicles of Oklahoma 37 (Autumn 1959): 307-329.

6052. Johnson, N. B. "The Cherokee Orphan Asylum." Chronicles of Oklahoma 44 (Autumn 1966): 275-280.

6053. Johnson, Richard M. "Two Letters, 1828, Pertaining to Colonel Richard M. Johnson's Choctaw Indian School in Scott County." Filson Club Historical Quarterly 9 (October 1935): 244-247.

6054. McKinney, Lillie G. "History of the Albuquerque Indian School." New Mexico Historical Review 20 (April 1945): 109-138; (July 1945): 207-226; (October 1945): 310-335.

6055. McMillan, Ethel. "First National Indian School: The Choctaw Academy." Chronicles of Oklahoma 28 (Spring 1950): 52-62.

6056. Mahan, Bruce E. "The School on Yellow River." Palimpsest 5 (December 1924): 446-452.

6057. Marshall, J. F. B. "Montana Industrial School for Indians." Lend a Hand 2 (August 1887): 445-448.

6058. Mitchell, Irene B., and Ida Belle Renken. "The Golden Age of Bloomfield Academy in the Chickasaw Nation." Chronicles of Oklahoma 49 (Winter 1971-1972): 412-426.

6059. Parke, Frank E. "Some of Our Choctaw Neighborhood Schools." Chronicles of Oklahoma 4 (June 1926): 149-152.

6060. Platt, Elvira Gaston. "Reminiscences of a Teacher among the Nebraska Indians, 1843-1885." Transactions and Reports of the Nebraska State Historical Society 3 (1892): 125-143.

6061. _____. "Some Experiences as a Teacher among the Pawnees." Collections of the Kansas State Historical Society 14 (1915-1918): 784-794.

6062. Ragland, Hobert D. "Potawatomi Day Schools." Chronicles of Oklahoma 30 (Autumn 1952): 270-278.

6063. Rairdon, Jack T. "John Homer Seger: The Practical Indian Educator." Chronicles of Oklahoma 34 (Summer 1956): 203-216.

6064. Rosalita, Mary. "The Spring Hill Indian School Correspondence." Michigan Historical Magazine 14 (January 1930): 94-149.

6065. Rouse, Mrs. Shelley D. "Colonel Dick Johnson's Choctaw Academy: A Forgotten Educational Experiment." Ohio

Archaeological and Historical Quarterly 25 (January 1916): 88-117.

6066. Tinnin, Ida Wetzel. "Educational and Cultural Influences of the Cherokee Seminaries." *Chronicles of Oklahoma* 37 (Spring 1959): 59-67.

6067. Walker, Henry Pickering, ed. "Teacher to the Mojaves: The Experiences of George W. Nock, 1887-1889." *Arizona and the West* 9 (Summer 1967): 143-166; (Fall 1967): 259-280.

6068. Wright, Muriel H. "John D. Benedict: First United States Superintendent of Schools in the Indian Territory." *Chronicles of Oklahoma* 33 (Winter 1955-1956): 472-508.

6069. _____. "Wapanucka Academy, Chickasaw Nation." *Chronicles of Oklahoma* 12 (December 1934): 402-431.

Hampton and Carlisle Institutes

Two striking examples of white attempts to educate Indians for the white man's world were the industrial training schools at Hampton, Virginia, and Carlisle, Pennsylvania. Hampton, founded by Samuel C. Armstrong for Negro education after the Civil War, admitted Indians in 1878. Carlisle, founded specifically for Indians by Richard Henry Pratt in 1879, became the center for Pratt's assimilationist policies.

6070. Armstrong, Samuel C. *Concerning Indians: Extracts from the Annual Report of the Principal of the Hampton Normal and Agricultural Institute, for the School Year Ending June 30th, 1883*. Hampton, Virginia: Normal School Steam Press, 1883.

6071. _____. *Education for Life*. Hampton, Virginia: Press of the Institute, 1913.

6072. _____. *Indian Education at Hampton, Va.* New York: G. F. Nesbitt and Company, 1881.

6073. _____. *Indian Education in the East, at Hampton, Va., and Carlisle, Penna.* Hampton, Virginia: Normal School Steam Press, 1880.

6074. Brunhouse, Robert L. "Apprenticeship for Civilization: The Outing System at the Carlisle Indian School." *Educational Outlook* 13 (May 1939): 30-38.

6075. _____. "The Founding of the Carlisle Indian School." *Pennsylvania History* 6 (April 1939): 72-85.

6076. *Captain Pratt and His Work for Indian Education*. Philadelphia: Indian Rights Association, 1886. Includes essays by Helen W. Ludlow and Elaine Goodale.

6077. Chapman, Daniel T. "The Great White Father's Little Red Indian School." *American Heritage* 22 (December 1970): 48-53, 102.

6078. Eastman, Elaine Goodale. *Pratt: The Red Man's Moses*. Norman: University of Oklahoma Press, 1935.

6079. Gilcreast, Everett Arthur. "Richard Henry Pratt and American Indian Policy, 1877-1906: A Study of the Assimilation Movement." Ph.D. dissertation, Yale University, 1967.

6080. Gilles, Albert S., Sr. "The Lost Ones: Comanches on the School Trail." *Southwest Review* 51 (Winter 1966): 63-74.

6081. Gravatt, J. J. *The Record of Hampton's Returned Indian Pupils*. Philadelphia: Indian Rights Association, 1885.

6082. Grinnell, George Bird. "The Indians and the Outing System." *Outlook* 75 (September 19, 1903): 167-173.

6083. *Hampton Institute, 1868 to 1885: Its Work for Two Races*. Hampton, Virginia: Normal School Press, 1885. Contains essays by Mary Frances Armstrong, Helen W. Ludlow, and Elaine Goodale.

6084. *Hampton Normal and Agricultural Institute: Its Reply to a New Attack on Eastern Schools*. Hampton, Virginia, 1890.

6085. Johnson, John L. "Albert Andrew Exendine: Carlisle Coach and Teacher." *Chronicles of Oklahoma* 43 (Autumn 1965): 319-331.

6086. Jones, Mable Cronise. "The Indian School at Carlisle, Pennsylvania." *Leslie's Weekly* 86 (February 3, 1898): 75.

6087. Lippincott, J. A. "The Indian Training and Industrial School at Carlisle, Pa." *Education* 2 (May 1882): 482-489.

6088. Ludlow, Helen W. "Indian Education at Hampton and Carlisle." *Harper's New Monthly Magazine* 62 (April 1881): 659-675.

6089. Morton, Louis. "How the Indians Came to Carlisle." *Pennsylvania History* 29 (January 1962): 53-73.

6090. Peabody, Francis Greenwood. *Education for Life: The Story of Hampton Institute*. Garden City, New York: Doubleday, Page and Company, 1919.

6091. Pratt, Richard Henry. American Indians, Chained and Unchained. N.p., 1912.

6092. _____. Battlefield and Classroom: Four Decades with the American Indian, 1867-1904. Edited by Robert M. Utley. New Haven: Yale University Press, 1964.

6093. _____. "Education of Indians." Public Opinion 18 (June 27, 1895): 730.

6094. _____. How to Deal with the Indians: The Potency of Environment. N.p., n.d.

6095. _____. "Industrial Training as Applied to Indian Schools." Educational Review 10 (November 1895): 325-330.

6096. _____. "Industrial Training as Applied to Indian Schools." National Educational Association Journal of Proceedings and Addresses, 1895, pp. 759-764.

6097. _____. The Indian Industrial School, Carlisle, Pennsylvania: Its Origin, Purposes, Progress and the Difficulties Surmounted. Carlisle: Hamilton Library Association, 1908.

6098. Ryan, Carmelita S. "The Carlisle Indian Industrial School." Ph.D. dissertation, Georgetown University, 1962.

6099. Sellers, Charles Coleman. "'. . . There Is No Better Plan.'" In The Unforgettable Americans, edited by John A. Garraty, pp. 260-263. Great Neck, New York: Channel Press, 1960. On R. H. Pratt.

6100. Shaffner, Ruth. "Civilizing the American Indian." Chautauquan 23 (June 1896): 259-268.

6101. Start, Edwin A. "General Armstrong and the Hampton Institute." New England Magazine 12 (June 1892): 442-460.

6102. Super, O. B. "Indian Education at Carlisle." New England Magazine 18 (April 1895): 224-239.

6103. Ten Years' Work for Indians at Hampton Institute, Virginia, 1878-1888. Hampton, Virginia, 1888. Contains an essay by Helen W. Ludlow on the work of the school and a report on returned students by Cora M. Folsom.

6104. Tousey, Thomas G. Military History of Carlisle and Carlisle Barracks. Richmond: Dietz Press, 1939.

6105. Twenty-two Years' Work of the Hampton Normal and Agricultural Institute, at Hampton, Virginia: Records of Negro and Indian Graduates and Ex-Students.

Hampton, Virginia: Normal School Press, 1893.

6106. Welsh, Herbert. Are the Eastern Industrial Training Schools for Indian Children a Failure? Philadelphia: Indian Rights Association, 1886.

6107. Willard, Frances E. "The Carlisle Indian School." Chautauquan 9 (February 1889): 289-290.

Church-State Controversy

A controversy developed over the use of government funds to support mission schools (primarily Catholic schools). It raged strongest in the 1890s and in the early years of the twentieth century, and a good deal of comment on the question is found in religious journals.

6108. Casey, M. P. "Indian Contract Schools." Catholic World 71 (August 1902): 629-637.

6109. "Catholics and Indian Schools." Outlook 102 (October 5, 1912): 234-235.

6110. "Critics of Religious Garb in Indian Schools." Literary Digest 44 (March 2, 1912): 428.

6111. Dorchester, Daniel. "Government Schools and Contract Schools." Lend a Hand 10 (February 1893): 118-126.

6112. Elliott, Richard R. "Government Secularization of the Education of Catholic Indian Youth." American Catholic Quarterly Review 25 (January 1900): 148-168.

6113. "Indian Appropriations for Sectarian Schools." Outlook 79 (January 28, 1905): 221-222.

6114. "Indian Church Schools: The Way Out." Outlook 82 (February 3, 1906): 247-248.

6115. "Indian Funds for Sectarian Schools." Independent 63 (December 19, 1907): 1507-1508.

6116. "Indian Government Schools." Outlook 100 (March 30, 1912): 718-719.

6117. Indian Rights Association. Indian Trust Funds for Sectarian Schools. Philadelphia: Indian Rights Association, 1905.

6118. _____. Shall Public Funds Be Expended for the Support of Sectarian Indian Schools? Philadelphia: Indian Rights Association, 1914.

6119. "The Indian Schools." Independent 60 (April 12, 1906): 883-884.

6120. Indian Tribal Funds: The Case for the

Catholic Indians Stated. New York:
Marquette League, n.d.

6121. Leupp, Francis E. "Indian Funds
and Mission Schools." Outlook 83 (June
9, 1906): 315-319.

6122. Memorandum Relative to Commissioner
Morgan's Indian School Policy, and to the
Mission School System for the Education
of the Indians. N.p., n.d.

6123. Meredith, Howard. "Whirlwind: A
Study of Church-State Relationships."
Historical Magazine of the Protestant
Episcopal Church 43 (December 1974): 297-
304. An Episcopalian school.

6124. Mitchell, Fredric. "Church-State
Conflict: A Little-Known Part of the Con-
tinuing Church-State Conflict Found in
Early Indian Education." Journal of
American Indian Education 2 (May 1963):
7-14.

6125. Mitchell, Fredric, and James W.
Skelton. "The Church-State Conflict in
Early Indian Education." History of
Education Quarterly 6 (Spring 1966): 41-
51.

6126. Morgan, Thomas J. Roman Catholics
and Indian Education: An Address by Hon.
T. J. Morgan, Ex-Commissioner of Indian
Affairs, Delivered in Music Hall, Boston,
Mass., Sunday, April 16, 1893. Boston:
American Citizen Company, 1893.

6127. National League for the Protection of
American Institutions. A Petition Con-
cerning Sectarian Appropriations for
Indian Education. New York, 1892.

6128. "The Nuns'-Garb Question." Literary
Digest 45 (October 12, 1912): 626.

6129. Palladino, L. B. Education for the
Indian: Fancy and Reason on the Subject:
Contract Schools and Non-Sectarianism
in Indian Education. New York: Benziger
Brothers, 1892.

6130. "Public Money Diverted for Catholic
Schools." Christian Century 62 (January
24, 1945): 101. Discussion by Karl E.
Mundt and G. E. E. Lindquist, (February
21, 1945): 243; (March 14, 1945): 338.

6131. "Religious Garb in Indian Schools."
Independent 72 (February 15, 1912): 374-
375.

6132. "Religious Garb in Indian Schools."
Literary Digest 44 (February 24, 1912):
379-380.

6133. Sievers, Harry J. "The Catholic In-
dian School Issue and the Presidential
Election of 1892." Catholic Historical
Review 38 (July 1952): 129-155.

6134. "The State, the Church, and the In-

dian." Outlook 79 (February 11, 1905):
370-372.

6135. "Trust Funds for Catholic Schools."
Nation 80 (February 9, 1905): 106.

6136. The Two Sides of the School Question,
As Set Forth at the Annual Meeting of the
National Educational Association, Held at
Nashville, Tennessee, July, 1889, by
Cardinal Gibbons and Bishop Keane on the
One Hand, and Edwin D. Mead and Hon. John
Jay on the Other. Boston: Committee of
One Hundred, 1890.

6137. "Unfair Indian Fighting." Outlook
79 (February 4, 1905): 263-265.

Other material on church-state relations
in Indian affairs can be found under Missions and under Grant's Peace Policy.

Writings on Indian Education to 1900

Education of the Indians began to be of
great interest at the end of the nineteenth
century, as the federal policy of Americanization gained momentum. Representative
writings are listed here.

6138. Barrows, William. "The Education of
the Indian." Andover Review 16 (November
1891): 479-491.

6139. Blackmar, Frank W. "Indian Education." Annals of the American Academy
of Political and Social Science 2 (May
1892): 813-837.

6140. Collins, M. C. "The Indian on the
Reservation." Independent 44 (April 7,
1892): 472-473.

6141. Davenport, R. B. "Indian Education."
Pennsylvania School Journal 29 (November
1880): 207-209.

6142. Dawes, Anna L. "A Question of Pro-
portion." Independent 44 (April 7,
1892): 465-466.

6143. Dean, A. P. "Government Indian
Schools." Outlook 52 (October 5, 1895):
542-543.

6144. Dewey, Mary E. "Indian Schools Report." Lend a Hand 10 (April 1893): 229-
243.

6145. _____. "Training of Indians."
Lend a Hand 11 (September 1893): 163-167.

6146. Eastman, Elaine Goodale. "The Education of Indians." Arena 24 (October
1900): 412-414.

6147. _____. "A New Method of Indian
Education." Outlook 64 (January 27,
1900): 222-224. Carlisle "outing system."

6148. Frissell, H. B. "The Indian Problem."

National Education Association Journal of Proceedings and Addresses, 1900, pp. 682-692.

6149. Gates, Merrill E. "The Work for the Indians." Independent 44 (April 7, 1892): 465.

6150. Goodale, Elaine. "The Future Indian School System." Chautauquan 10 (October 1889): 51-55.

6151. _____. The Senator and the School-House. Philadelphia: Indian Rights Association, 1886.

6152. Hailmann, William N. "Educational Work for the Indians." Lend a Hand 13 (November 1894): 367-371.

6153. Harrison, J. B. Education for Indians. Philadelphia: Indian Rights Association, 1887.

6154. _____. "Education for Indians." Critic 11 (December 24, 1887): 321-322.

6155. "Indians as Workmen." Knowledge 2 (September 29, 1882): 288.

6156. "Indian Schools." Lend a Hand 14 (May 1895): 361-366.

6157. Jones, Calvin. "Account of the Cherokee Schools." Port Folio 26 (September 1821): 58-66.

6158. Kyle, James H. "How Shall the Indian Be Educated." North American Review 159 (November 1894): 434-447.

6159. "Lame Dancing-Masters: An Indian View of Government Schools." Land of Sunshine 12 (May 1900): 356-358.

6160. Lummis, Charles F. "My Brother's Keeper." Land of Sunshine 11 (August 1899): 139-147; (September 1899): 207-213; (October 1899): 263-267; (November 1899): 333-335; 12 (December 1899): 28-30 (January 1900): 90-94; (February 1900): 178-180.

6161. "The Montana Industrial School for Indians." Science 10 (August 5, 1887): 61-62.

6162. Morgan, Thomas J. "The Education of American Indians." Education 10 (December 1889): 246-254.

6163. _____. Indian Education. U.S. Bureau of Education, Bulletin no. 1, 1889. Washington: Government Printing Office, 1890.

6164. _____. A Plea for the Papoose: An Address at Albany, N.Y., by Gen. T. J. Morgan. N.p., n.d.

6165. Painter, Charles C. Extravagance, Waste and Failure of Indian Education.

Philadelphia: Indian Rights Association, 1892.

6166. Reynolds, Grindall. "The Education of Indian Children." Unitarian Review and Religious Magazine 17 (April 1882): 353-356.

6167. Richards, Josephine E. "The Training of the Indian Girl as the Uplifter of the Home." National Education Association Journal of Proceedings and Addresses, 1900, pp. 701-705.

6168. Ross, William P. "Public Education among the Cherokee Indians." American Journal of Education 1 (August 1855): 120-122.

6169. Seger, John. "Practical Methods in Indian Education." National Education Association Journal of Proceedings and Addresses, 1900, pp. 707-711.

6170. Sheldon, Henry D. "The Evolution of the Indian School System." Education 16 (September 1895): 7-15.

6171. Sparhawk, Frances C. "The English Language on an Indian Reservation." Education 12 (June 1892): 609-615.

6172. _____. "The Query Club: The Indian Question." Education 7 (September 1886): 50-57.

6173. "A Tour of Observation." Lend a Hand 14 (February 1895): 133-141.

6174. "Training of the Indian." Lend a Hand 17 (December 1896): 436-439.

6175. Welsh, Herbert. A Crisis in the Cause of Indian Education. Philadelphia: Indian Rights Association, 1892.

6176. Wilkins, Bertha S. "In a Government Indian School." Land of Sunshine 7 (November 1897): 242-247.

6177. Zitkala-Sa. "An Indian Teacher among Indians." Atlantic Monthly 85 (March 1900): 381-386.

The annual reports of the Lake Mohonk Conference and other writings of the Indian reformers make frequent mention of education.

Writings on Indian Education, 1901-1920

Concern of the reformers for Indian education continued into the twentieth century. An important forum for the expression of views on the subject was the annual meeting of the National Education Association.

6178. Baker, James H. "Our Educational Duties to the Indian." National Education Association Journal of Proceedings and Addresses, 1909, pp. 927-928.

6179. Cooper, Ella H. "How to Educate the Indians." Gunton's Magazine 22 (May 1902): 452-455.

6180. Covey, C. C. "Reservation Day School Should Be the Prime Factor in Indian Education." National Education Association Journal of Proceedings and Addresses, 1901, pp. 900-901.

6181. Creelman, G. C. "Indian Industrial Education." Outlook 67 (January 26, 1901): 234-236.

6182. Densmore, Frances. "Indian Education in Government Schools." Overland Monthly 46 (November 1905): 456-460.

6183. "The Failure of the Educated American Indian." American Monthly Review of Reviews 33 (May 1906): 629-630.

6184. Friedman, Moses. "Religious Work in Indian Schools." Missionary Review of the World 31 (July 1908): 535-536.

6185. Frissell, H. B. "To What Degree Has the Present System of Indian Schools Been Successful in Qualifying for Citizenship?" National Education Association Journal of Proceedings and Addresses, 1903, pp. 1049-1052.

6186. Hailmann, William N. Education of the Indian. Monographs on Education in the United States, no. 19. St. Louis: Department of Education, Universal Exposition, 1904.

6187. Hall, G. Stanley. "How Far Are the Principles of Education along Indigenous Lines Applicable to American Indians?" National Education Association Journal of Proceedings and Addresses, 1908, pp. 1161-1164.

6188. Harris, William T. "Civilization and Higher Education." National Education Association Journal of Proceedings and Addresses, 1901, pp. 896-899.

6189. "Indian Boarding Schools." Independent 63 (December 26, 1907): 1577-1578.

6190. Leupp, Francis E. "Indians and Their Education." National Education Association Journal of Proceedings and Addresses, 1907, pp. 70-74.

6191. McCormick, R. L. "Evolution of Indian Education." National Magazine 14 (June 1901): 259-264.

6192. Morgan, Thomas J. "Indian Education." Journal of Social Science 40 (December 1902): 165-180.

6193. Peairs, H. B. "Education of the American Indian." National Education Association Journal of Proceedings and

Addresses, 1911, pp. 252-255.

6194. _____. "Our Work: Its Progress and Needs." National Education Association Journal of Proceedings and Addresses, 1903, pp. 1044-1049.

6195. _____. "What Education Has Done for the Indian." National Education Association Journal of Proceedings and Addresses, 1909, pp. 938-939.

6196. Pierson, Arthur T. "The Indian Training-School, Tucson, Arizona." Missionary Review of the World 25 (August 1902): 561-564.

6197. Woodward, Calvin W. "What Shall Be Taught in an Indian School?" National Education Association Journal of Proceedings and Addresses, 1901, pp. 904-909.

MODERN INDIAN EDUCATION

Increasing attention has been paid to Indian education in the twentieth century. Reports such as those made by the Meriam survey (1640) and the Special Sub-Committee of the United States Senate (6632) have pointed up the problems and the needs. In addition to general studies, there are technical reports on numerous special topics. Works are listed here by rough subject categories.

General and Miscellaneous Studies

Indian education has been the subject of a large number of doctoral dissertations. Many are listed here, together with other similar studies.

6198. Allen, Ronald Lorraine. "A Study of the Characteristics of Successful and Unsuccessful Students Enrolled in the Adult Indian Training Program Conducted by the Adult Education Center of the University of Montana." Ed.D. dissertation, University of Montana, 1968.

6199. Anderson, Donald Howard. "Communication Linkages between Indian Communities and School Districts in Wisconsin." Ed.D. dissertation, University of Minnesota, 1972.

6200. Anderson, H. Dewey, and W. C. Eells. Alaska Natives: A Survey of Their Sociological and Educational Status. Palo Alto, California: Stanford University Press, 1935.

6201. Barney, Garold Dean. "A Descriptive Study of the Administration of Public Schools Attended by American Indian Youth Living on Federal Trust Lands in Kansas, Nebraska, and Iowa." Ed.D. dissertation, University of California, 1969.

6202. Bass, Willard P., and Henry G. Burger. American Indians and Educational Laboratories. Albuquerque: Southwest Cooperative Educational Laboratory, 1967.

6203. Benham, William Josephus, Jr. "Characteristics of Programs in Public Schools Serving Indian Students from Reservations in Five Western States." Ed.D. dissertation, University of Oklahoma, 1965.

6204. Bergman, Robert, and others. Problems of Cross-Cultural Educational Research and Evaluation: The Rough Rock Demonstration School. Edited by Arthur Harkins and Richard Woods. Minneapolis: Training Center for Community Programs, University of Minnesota, 1969.

6205. Berry, Ray M. Educating the People on the Fort Hill Indian Reservation. Moscow: Bureau of Business and Economic Research, University of Idaho, 1961.

6206. Billison, Samuel William. "School Administrators' Perceptions of American Indian Education." Ed.D. dissertation, University of Arizona, 1972.

6207. Breunig, Robert Glass. "Hopi Perspectives on Formal Education." Ph.D. dissertation, University of Kansas, 1973.

6208. Bryde, John F. The Indian Student: A Study of Scholastic Failure and Personality Conflict. 2d edition. Vermillion: University of South Dakota Press, 1970. First published in 1966.

6209. Calkins, Thomas Vincent. "Educating the Alaska Natives." Ph.D. dissertation, Yale University, 1931.

6210. Charles, Carol Morgan. "The Indian Child's Status in New Mexico's Public Elementary School Science Programs." Ph.D. dissertation, University of New Mexico, 1961.

6211. Coombs, L. Madison. Doorway toward the Light: The Story of the Special Navaho Education Program. Washington: U.S. Department of the Interior, Bureau of Indian Affairs, 1962.

6212. Coombs, L. Madison, and others. The Indian Child Goes to School: A Study of Interracial Differences. Washington: U.S. Department of the Interior, Bureau of Indian Affairs, 1958.

6213. Corrigan, Francis Vincent. "A Comparison of Self Concepts of American Indian Students from Public or Federal School Backgrounds." Ed.D. dissertation, George Washington University, 1970.

6214. Crump, Bonnie Lela Massey. "The Educability of Indian Children in Reservation Schools." Ph.D. dissertation, Columbia University, 1932.

6215. Dale, George Allan. Education for Better Living: A Study of the Effectiveness of the Pine Ridge Educational Program. Lawrence, Kansas: U.S. Department of the Interior, Bureau of Indian Affairs, 1955.

6216. Dale, Kenneth I. "Navajo Indian Educational Administration." Ph.D. dissertation, University of North Dakota, 1949.

6217. Grace, Cyril W. "A Study of the Problems of Indian-Caucasian Segregation in a South Dakota Community As Related to Integration in the Public School." Ed.D. dissertation, University of Virginia, 1959.

6218. Greenberg, Norman Charles. "Administrative Problems Related to Integration of Navajo Indians in Public Education." Ed.D. dissertation, University of Colorado, 1963.

6219. Griffiths, Kenneth Albert. "The Influence of an Intensive Pre-School Educational Experience on the Intellectual Functioning of Ute Indian Children." Ed.D. dissertation, University of Utah, 1967.

6220. Harkins, Arthur M. Public Education on a Minnesota Chippewa Reservation. 6 volumes. Washington: U.S. Office of Education, 1968.

6221. Havighurst, Robert J. "Education among American Indians: Individual and Cultural Aspects." Annals of the American Academy of Political and Social Science 311 (May 1957): 105-115.

6222. Howard, Homer H. In Step with the States: A Comparison of State and Indian Service Educational Objectives and Methods. Lawrence, Kansas: U.S. Indian Service, Haskell Institute, 1949.

6223. Hulsizer, Allan. Region and Culture in the Curriculum of the Navaho and the Dakota: A Technique and Its Development into an Educational Program. Federalsburg, Maryland: J. W. Stowell Company, 1940.

6224. Jackson, Curtis Emanuel. "Identification of Unique Features in Education at American Indian Schools." Ed.D. dissertation, University of Utah, 1965.

6225. Jurrens, James William. "The Music of the Sioux Indian of the Rosebud Reservation in South Dakota and Its Use in the Elementary School." Ed.D. dissertation, University of Northern Colorado, 1965.

6226. Kelly, William H. A Study of Southern Arizona School-Age Indian Children, 1966-67. Tucson: Bureau of Ethnic Research, University of Arizona, 1967.

6227. King, Alfred Richard. "A Case Study of an Indian Residential School." Ph.D. dissertation, Stanford University, 1964.

6228. Lane, Mary. "A Critical Study of the Contemporary Theory and Policy of the Indian Bureau with Regard to American Indian Education." Ph.D. dissertation, Catholic University of America, 1962.

6229. Lind, Marshall Lee. "Relationships between Work Attitudes, Perceived Needs Structures, and Type of Job Settings for Bureau of Indian Affairs Teachers in Alaska." Ph.D. dissertation, Northwestern University, 1969.

6230. Luhrs, Dorothy Louise. "An Anthropological Study of the Sources of Maladjustment among Eastern Pueblo Adolescents." Ph.D. dissertation, University of Southern California, 1945.

6231. Macgregor, Gordon. "Indian Education in Relation to the Social and Economic Background of the Reservation." In The Changing Indian, edited by Oliver La Farge, pp. 116-127. Norman: University of Oklahoma Press, 1942.

6232. Mestas, Leonard Joseph. "Administrators' Opinions and Attitudes Concerning the Bureau of Indian Affairs Navajo Schools' Responsibility in Providing Education for Navajo Exceptional Children." Ed.D. dissertation, University of Northern Colorado, 1970.

6233. Neff, Russell Charles. "Nez Perce Education: A Study of the Kamiah and Lapwai School Districts." Ed.D. dissertation, University of Idaho, 1969.

6234. Officer, James E. Indians in School: A Study of the Development of Educational Facilities for Arizona Indians. Tucson: Bureau of Ethnic Research, University of Arizona, 1956.

6235. Orata, Pedro T. Fundamental Education in an Amerindian Community. Washington: U.S. Department of the Interior, Bureau of Indian Affairs, 1953.

6236. Parmee, Edward A. Formal Education and Culture Change: A Modern Apache Indian Community and Government Education Programs. Tucson: University of Arizona Press, 1968.

6237. Randquist, Bobby Wayne. "An Investigation of the Educational Attainment and Opportunities of American Indian Students in the Anadarko Public School System." Ed.D. dissertation, University of Oklahoma, 1970.

6238. Roberts, Connell Bolton. "The Administration of Navaho Education." Ph.D. dissertation, University of California, 1958.

6239. Sanford, Gregory R. "The Study of Nez Perce Indian Education." Ph.D. dissertation, University of New Mexico, 1970.

6240. Smith, Anne M. Indian Education in New Mexico. Albuquerque: Institute for Social Research and Development, University of New Mexico, 1968.

6241. Smith, George Humphries. "High School Dropouts and Graduates among Pima Indians in Three Arizona High Schools." Ed.D. dissertation, Arizona State University, 1967.

6242. Spencer, Frank Clarence. "Education of the Pueblo Child: A Study of Arrested Development." Ph.D. dissertation, Columbia University, 1900.

6243. Stull, James Clyde. "Seminole Rejection of American Education." Ph.D. dissertation, University of Toledo, 1967.

6244. Thompson, Hildegard. "Education among American Indians: Institutional Aspects." Annals of the American Academy of Political and Social Science 311 (May 1957): 95-104.

6245. Ulibarri, Horacio. "Teacher Awareness of Socio-Cultural Differences in Multi-Cultural Classrooms." Ed.D. dissertation, University of New Mexico, 1960.

6246. Underwood, Jerald Ross. "An Investigation of Educational Opportunity for the Indian in Northeastern Oklahoma." Ed.D. dissertation, University of Oklahoma, 1966.

6247. Witherspoon, Younger T. "Cultural Influences on Ute Learning." Ph.D. dissertation, University of Utah, 1961.

6248. Zintz, Miles V. The Indian Research Study: The Adjustment of Indian and Non-Indian Children in the Public Schools of New Mexico. Albuquerque: College of Education, University of New Mexico, 1960.

For additional material see Research in Education (ERIC). Many particular studies are listed below under Writings on Indian Education.

Language and Communication Skills

Although English is no longer the sole

language in the instruction of Indian children, it is an essential tool, and there are many studies on teaching English to Indian children. Representative works on the subject are listed here, together with other studies on communication.

6249. Alexander, Rosemary. "Readers for Navajo Children." Instructor 79 (November 1969): 97.

6250. Alley, Robert D., Ronald G. Davison, Walter T. Kelley, and Raymond L. Kimble. "A Reading Improvement Strategy." Journal of American Indian Education 13 (January 1974): 14-20.

6251. Beatty, Willard W. "Forty Thousand 'First Americans' Who Can't Speak English." NEA Journal 36 (April 1947): 300-301.

6252. Beer, David F. "The Trouble with 'The.'" Journal of American Indian Education 4 (May 1965): 13-15.

6253. Bencenti, Maebali. "Children Who Speak Navajo." Young Children 25 (January 1970): 141-142.

6254. Blossom, Grace A. "Grammar and the Bilingual Student." Journal of American Indian Education 4 (January 1965): 14-16.

6255. _____. "A New Approach to an Old Problem." Journal of American Indian Education 1 (January 1962): 13-14.

6256. _____. "Teaching English as a Second Language." Journal of American Indian Education 2 (October 1962): 17-19.

6257. Briere, Eugene J. "Testing ESL among Navajo Children." Language Learning 18 (August 1968): 11-21.

6258. Brilhart, Barbara L. "Oral Communication for the Indian Student." English Journal 60 (May 1971): 629-632.

6259. "Cherokee Language Study." Intellect 101 (February 1973): 287-338.

6260. Condie, LeRoy. "An Experiment in Second-Language Instruction of Beginning Indian Children in New Mexico Public Schools." Ph.D. dissertation, University of New Mexico, 1961.

6261. Cook, Mary Jane, and Margaret Amy Sharp. "Problems of Navajo Speakers on Learning English." Language Learning 16 (1966): 21-29.

6262. Dundes, Alan, and C. Fayne Porter. "American Indian Student Slang." American Speech 38 (December 1963): 270-277.

6263. Eastman, Elaine Goodale. "On Learning to Speak." Education 59 (June 1939): 610-612.

6264. Fearn, Leif. "A Report of Three Pilot Studies into Initial Reading." Elementary English 48 (March 1971): 390-394. Navajo children.

6265. Fry, Maurine A., and Carol Schulte Johnson. "Oral Language Production and Reading Achievement among Selected Students." Journal of American Indian Education 13 (October 1973): 22-27.

6266. Gold, Douglas. "A Blackfeet Learns to Write His Name: Results of a Two Weeks Illiteracy School for Indians." Montana Education 7 (May 1931): 9-10.

6267. Gray, Lee Learner. "Rebus = Readability." American Education 8 (November 1972): back cover.

6268. Hill, Charles H. "Report: A Summer Reading Program with American Indians." Journal of American Indian Education 9 (May 1970): 10-14.

6269. Hoffman, Virginia. "Language Learning at Rough Rock." Childhood Education 46 (December 1969): 139-145.

6270. Holland, R. Fount. "School in Cherokee and English." Elementary School Journal 72 (May 1972): 412-418.

6271. Holm, Wayne. "Let It Never Be Said . . ." Journal of American Indian Education 4 (October 1964): 6-9.

6272. Hopkins, Thomas R. "Language Testing of North American Indians." Language Learning 18 (August 1968): 1-9.

6273. "IBM Computer for Navajo Language Textbooks." School and Society 99 (December 1971): 468-469.

6274. "The Indian Service Readers." Phi Delta Kappan 28 (March 1947): 305.

6275. "In Kirtland, N.M., English Is a Foreign Language." Grade Teacher 83 (May 1966): 94-97.

6276. Ivey, Lillian Patience. "Influence of Indian Language Background on Reading and Speech Development." Ed.D. dissertation, University of Oklahoma, 1968.

6277. Kennard, Edward A. "The Use of Native Languages and Cultures in Indian Education." In The Changing Indian, edited by Oliver La Farge, pp. 109-115. Norman: University of Oklahoma Press, 1942.

6278. Kersey, Harry A., and Rebecca Fadjo. "A Comparison of Seminole Reading Vocabulary and the Dolch Word Lists." Journal of American Indian Education 11 (October 1971): 16-18. Florida Atlantic University Project Report.

6279. Kersey, Harry A., Anne Keithley, and F. Ward Brunson. "Improving Reading Skills of Seminole Children." Journal of American Indian Education 10 (May 1971): 3-7. Florida Atlantic University Project Report.

6280. Kimble, Raymond L., and Ronald G. Davison. "Reading Improvement for Disadvantaged Indian Youth." Journal of Reading 15 (February 1972): 342-346.

6281. Kinkade, M. Dale. "Indian Languages at Haskell Institute." International Journal of American Linguistics 36 (January 1970): 46-52.

6282. Kuske, Irwin I., Jr. "Psycholinguistic Abilities of Sioux Indian Children." Ed.D. dissertation, University of South Dakota, 1969.

6283. Langley, Elizabeth G. "The Development of a Literacy Program among the Navaho Indians." Ed.D. dissertation, New York University, 1956.

6284. "Language Experiments of Indian Children." Progressive Education 9 (February 1932): 144-179.

6285. Lawhead, Helen E. "Teaching Navajo Children to Read." Progressive Education 9 (February 1932): 131-135.

6286. Lombardi, Thomas P. "Psycholinguistic Abilities of Papago Indian School Children." Exceptional Children 36 (March 1970): 485-493.

6287. Miller, D. D., and Gail Johnson. "What We've Learned about Teaching Reading to Navajo Indians." Reading Teacher 27 (March 1974): 550-554.

6288. Morris, Joyce. "An Investigation into Language-Concept Development of Primary School Pueblo Indian Children." Ph.D. dissertation, University of New Mexico, 1966.

6289. Mosser, Ann, and Susan Motylewski. "From Navajo to White Man's Tongue." Elementary English Review 16 (December 1939): 303-306.

6290. Narang, H. L. "Improving Reading Ability of Indian Children." Elementary English 51 (February 1974): 190-192.

6291. New, Lloyd H. "Using Cultural Difference as a Basis for Creative Expression." Journal of American Indian Education 4 (May 1965): 8-12.

6292. Olsen, Louise P. "The Problem of Language in the Indian Schools of Dakota Territory, 1885-88." North Dakota History 20 (January 1953): 47-57.

6293. Osborn, Lynn R. "Graduate Theses Concerning the Speech and Spoken Language of the North American Indian: An Index." Journal of American Indian Education 6 (October 1966): 25-33.

6294. _____. "The Indian Pupil in the High School Speech Class." Speech Teacher 16 (September 1967): 187-189.

6295. _____. "A Speaking and Listening Program." Journal of American Indian Education 7 (October 1967): 21-24.

6296. _____. "Speech Communication and the American Indian High School Student." Speech Teacher 17 (January 1968): 38-43.

6297. _____. "Teachers Tackle Speech Problem of Secondary Indian Pupils." Journal of American Indian Education 7 (October 1967): 19-21.

6298. _____. "Traditional Requisites of Indian Communication: Rhetoric, Repetition, Silence." Journal of American Indian Education 12 (January 1973): 15-21.

6299. Osborn, Lynn R., and C. Fayne Porter. "Programs of Speech and Drama Operated by the Bureau of Indian Affairs." Speech Teacher 14 (September 1965): 181-183.

6300. Philion, William L. E., and Charles G. Galloway. "Indian Children and the Reading Program." Journal of Reading 12 (April 1969): 553-560, 598-602.

6301. Philipsen, Gerry. "Navajo World View and Culture Patterns of Speech: A Case Study in Ethnorhetoric." Speech Monographs 39 (June 1972): 132-139.

6302. Ramstad, Vivian V., and Robert E. Potter. "Differences in Vocabulary and Syntax Usages between Nez Perce Indian and White Kindergarten Children." Journal of Learning Disabilities 7 (October 1974): 491-497.

6303. Salisbury, Lee H. "The Speech Education of the Alaskan Indian Students as Viewed by the Speech Educator." Journal of American Indian Education 4 (May 1965): 1-7.

6304. _____. "Teaching English to Alaska Natives." Journal of American Indian Education 6 (January 1967): 1-13.

6305. Sasaki, Tom T., and David L. Olmsted. "Navaho Acculturation and English-Language Skills." American Anthropologist 55 (January-March 1953): 89-99.

6306. Shears, Brian Thomas. "Attitude, Content and Method of Teaching Word Recognition with Young American Indian Children." Ph.D. dissertation, University of Minnesota, 1970. Red Lake Indian Reservation.

6307. Stafford, Kenneth. "Problem Solving by Navajo Children in Relation to Knowledge of English." Journal of American Indian Education 4 (January 1965): 23-25.

6308. Stuart, C. I. J. M. "American Indian Languages at Haskell Institute." International Journal of American Linguistics 28 (April 1962): 151.

6309. Tefft, Virginia. "Using Physical Education in English Language Practice." Journal of American Indian Education 11 (October 1971): 1-6.

6310. Thompson, Hildegard. "Teaching English to Indian Children." Elementary English 43 (April 1966): 333-340.

6311. Timmons, Barbara Joan. "An Exploratory Investigation of Attitudes toward Certain Speech Communication Variables Found among Male Post-High School Vocational Students at Haskell Indian Institute, Lawrence, Kansas." Ph.D. dissertation, University of Kansas, 1965.

6312. Tireman, L. S. "The Bilingual Child and His Reading Vocabulary." Elementary English 32 (January 1955): 33-35.

6313. Tireman, L. S., and Miles V. Zintz. "Factors Influencing Learning a Second Language." Education 81 (January 1961): 310-313.

6314. Townsend, Irving D. "Reading Achievement of Eleventh and Twelfth Grade Indian Students." Journal of American Indian Education 3 (October 1963): 9-10.

6315. _____. "The Reading Achievement of Eleventh and Twelfth Grade Indian Students and a Survey of Curricular Changes Indicated for the Improved Teaching of Reading in the Public High Schools in New Mexico." Ed.D. dissertation, University of New Mexico, 1962.

6316. Wall, Claude Leon. "Problems in Teaching English to Navajo Children." Ed.D. dissertation, Oklahoma State University, 1961.

6317. Weaver, Yvonne J. "Closer Look at TESL on the Reservation." Journal of American Indian Education 6 (January 1967): 26-31.

6318. Weaver, Yvonne J., and Evelyn C. Evvard. "Helping Navajo Children Change Pronunciation Habits." Journal of American Indian Education 5 (May 1966): 10-14.

6319. Werner, Ruth E. "An Oral English Experiment with Navajo Children." Elementary English 43 (November 1966): 777-784.

6320. Wilder, Virginia C. "Experiment in Remedial Reading with Indian Students." English Journal 31 (May 1942): 408-410.

6321. Willink, Elizabeth Wilhelmina. "A Comparison of Two Methods of Teaching English to Navajo Children." Ph.D. dissertation, University of Arizona, 1968.

Testing and Achievement Studies

The academic achievement of Indians has been the object of numerous studies. Representative ones are listed here, as well as studies on the use of various tests with Indian students.

6322. Anderson, Kenneth E., E. Gordon Collister, and Carl E. Ladd. The Educational Achievement of Indian Children: A Re-Examination of the Question: How Well Are Indian Children Educated? Lawrence, Kansas: Bureau of Indian Affairs, Department of the Interior, 1953.

6323. Arthur, Grace. "An Experience in Testing Indian School Children." Mental Hygiene 25 (April 1941): 188-195.

6324. Bebeau, Donald E. "Administration of a TOEFL Test to Sioux Indian High School Students." Journal of American Indian Education 9 (October 1969): 7-16.

6325. Bernardoni, Louis C. "Results of the TOGA with First Grade Indian Children." Journal of American Indian Education 1 (June 1961): 24-28.

6326. Cowen, Philip A. "Testing Indian School Pupils in the State of New York." Mental Hygiene 27 (January 1943): 80-82.

6327. Cress, Joseph N. "Cognitive and Personality Testing Use and Abuse." Journal of American Indian Education 13 (May 1974): 16-19.

6328. Cunningham, Juanita, Russell L. Connelley, and Mary Meighen. "Modern Objective Tests: History, Geography, and Money." Grade Teacher 56 (November 1938): 62-63, 70-71.

6329. Dankworth, Richard T. "Educational Achievement of Indian Students in Public Secondary Schools as Related to Eight Variables, Including Residential Environment." Ed.D. dissertation, Utah State University, 1969.

6330. Deissler, Kenneth L. "A Study of South Dakota Indian Achievement Problems." Journal of American Indian Education 1 (May 1962): 19-21.

6331. Dennis, Wayne. "The Performance of Hopi Children on the Goodenough Draw-A-Man Test." Journal of Comparative

Psychology 34 (October 1942): 341-348.

6332. Evvard, Evelyn. "Results of the Bender Gestalt Visual Motor Test Given in a Beginners' Class and First and Second Grades." Journal of American Indian Education 5 (May 1966): 6-10.

6333. Evvard, Evelyn, and Robert R. Weaver, Jr. "Testing--Some Implications of Counselors and Teachers." Journal of American Indian Education 5 (May 1966): 15-17.

6334. Fitzgerald, J. A., and W. W. Ludeman. "The Intelligence of Indian Children." Journal of Comparative Psychology 6 (August 1926): 319-328.

6335. Garth, Thomas R., and Owen D. Smith. "The Performance of Full-Blooded Indians on Language and Non-Language Intelligence Tests." Journal of Abnormal and Social Psychology 32 (October-December 1937): 376-381.

6336. Hansen, Harvey C. "Relationship between Sex and School Achievement of One Thousand Indian Children." Journal of Social Psychology 10 (August 1934): 399-406.

6337. _____. "Scholastic Achievement of Indian Pupils." Pedagogical Seminary and Journal of Genetic Psychology 50 (June 1937): 361-369.

6338. Haught, B. F. "Mental Growth of the Southwestern Indian." Journal of Applied Psychology 18 (1934): 137-142.

6339. Havighurst, Robert J., M. K. Gunther, and I. E. Pratt. "Environment and the Draw-A-Man Test: The Performance of Indian Children." Journal of Abnormal and Social Psychology 41 (January 1946): 50-63.

6340. Havighurst, Robert J., and Rhea R. Hilkevitch. "The Intelligence of Indian Children As Measured by a Performance Scale." Journal of Abnormal and Social Psychology 39 (October 1944): 419-433.

6341. Hunter, Walter S., and Eloise Sommermier. "The Relation of Degree of Indian Blood to Score on the Otis Intelligence Test." Journal of Comparative Psychology 2 (June 1922): 257-277.

6342. Johnson, Vandel Charles. "An Assessment of the Motivation Factor in the Estimation of Academic Achievement of Eleventh Grade Indian Students and the Factored Dimensions of the M-Scales: An Exploratory Study." Ph.D. dissertation, Michigan State University, 1963.

6343. Kayser, Joyce. "Scholastic Performance and Ethnicity: A Preliminary Study of Seven School Classes." Journal of American Indian Education 3 (October 1963): 27-30.

6344. Kersey, Harry A., Jr., and H. R. Greene. "Educational Achievement among Three Florida Seminole Reservations." School and Society 100 (January 1972): 25-28.

6345. Ladd, Carl E. "The Educational Growth of Indian Children in the Phoenix Area, 1951 to 1952, As Measured by Test Results." Ph.D. dissertation, University of Kansas, 1955.

6346. Melville, Robert S. "What Are the Factors Which Enhance or Retard Educational Achievement of Navajo Indian Students in the Sevier School District?" Ed.D. dissertation, Utah State University, 1966.

6347. Norman, Ralph D., and Katherine L. Midkiff. "Navajo Children on Raven Progressive Matrices and Goodenough Draw-A-Man Tests." Southwestern Journal of Anthropology 11 (Summer 1955): 129-136.

6348. Penoi, Charles Roderick. "Some Factors of Academic Achievement in High School Pupils Attending Selected Indian Boarding Schools in Oklahoma." Ed.D. dissertation, University of Oklahoma, 1956.

6349. Peters, Herbert D. "Performance of Hopi Children on Four Intelligence Tests." Journal of American Indian Education 2 (January 1963): 27-31.

6350. Peterson, Shailer. How Well Are Indian Children Educated? Summary of Results of a Three Year Program Testing the Achievement of Indian Children in Federal, Public and Mission Schools. Lawrence, Kansas: Haskell Printing Department, 1947.

6351. Rohrer, John H. "The Intelligence of Osage Indians." Journal of Social Psychology 16 (August 1942): 99-105.

6352. Snider, James G., and Arthur P. Coladarci. "Intelligence Test Performance of Acculturated Indian Children." California Journal of Educational Research 11 (January 1960): 34-46.

6353. Steggerda, Morris. "The McAdory Art Test Applied to Navajo Indian Children." Journal of Comparative Psychology 22 (October 1936): 283-285.

6354. Telford, C. W. "Test Performance of Full and Mixed-Blood North Dakota Indians." Journal of Comparative Psychology 14 (August 1932): 123-145.

6355. Witherspoon, Y. T. "The Measurement of Indian Children's Achievement in the Academic Tool Subjects." Journal of American Indian Education 1 (May 1962): 5-9.

Comparative Studies

Studies comparing Indian and non-Indian students in achievement or other characteristics are listed here.

6356. Armstrong, Robert L. "A Comparison of Student Activity Involvement." Journal of American Indian Education 9 (January 1970): 10-15.

6357. Boutwell, Richard C., and others. "Red Apples." Journal of American Indian Education 12 (January 1973): 11-14.

6358. Cassel, Russell N., and Richard A. Sanders. "A Comparative Analysis of Scores from Two Leadership Tests for Apache Indian and Anglo American Youth." Journal of Educational Research 55 (September 1961): 19-23.

6359. Downing, Lewis Jackson. "The Comparison-Reference Process As It Relates to Ninth Grade Indian and Non-Indian Boys of Low Socio-Economic Status." Ed.D. dissertation, University of Oklahoma, 1965.

6360. Havighurst, Robert J., and Bernice L. Neugarten. American Indian and White Children: A Sociopsychological Investigation. Chicago: University of Chicago Press, 1955.

6361. Hendra, Richard I. "An Assessment of the Motivation and Achievement of Michigan Reservation Indian High School Students and Michigan Caucasian High School Students." Ph.D. dissertation, Michigan State University, 1970.

6362. Johnson, Robert Severt. "Comparative Study of Educational Attainment of Warm Springs Indians and Non-Indians in the Madras Union High School for the Years 1956-1965 Inclusive." Ed.D. dissertation, Washington State University, 1967.

6363. Kennedy, Thomas G. "Crow--Northern Cheyenne Selected for Study." Journal of American Indian Education 11 (October 1971): 27-31. Personality differences between Indians and non-Indians.

6364. Kirk, Samuel A. "Ethnic Differences in Psycholinguistic Abilities." Exceptional Children 39 (October 1972): 112-118.

6365. Klineberg, Otto. "Racial Differences in Speed and Accuracy." Journal of Abnormal Social Psychology 22 (1928): 273-277.

6366. Lowry, Laura M. "Differences in Visual Perception and Auditory Discrimination between American Indian and White Kindergarten Children." Journal of Learning Disabilities 3 (July 1970): 359-363.

6367. Martig, Roger, and Richard De Blassie. "Self-Concept Comparisons of Anglo and Indian Children." Journal of American Indian Education 12 (May 1973): 9-16.

6368. Matthies, Bernard Dean. "Independence, Training, Hostility, and Values as Correlates of the Achievement of White and Indian Students." Ed.D. dissertation, University of Nebraska, 1965.

6369. Pecoraro, Joseph. "The Effect of a Series of Special Lessons on Indian History and Culture upon the Attitudes of Indian and Non-Indian Students." Journal of Education 154 (February 1972): 70-78.

6370. Reboussin, Roland, and Joel W. Goldstein. "Achievement Motivation in Navaho and White Students." American Anthropologist 68 (June 1966): 740-744.

6371. Rowe, E. C. "547 White and 268 Indian Children Tested by the Binet-Simon Tests." Pedagogical Seminary 21 (September 1914): 454-468.

6372. Rupiper, Omer John. "Multiple Factor Analysis of Academic Achievement: A Comparative Study of Full-Blooded Indian and White Children." Journal of Experimental Education 28 (March 1960): 177-205.

6373. Safar, Dwight. "An Exploratory Study of Mental Maturity, Achievement and Personality Test Results in Relation to the Academic Progress of Indians and Non-Indians in Grades Four through Eight in Six Public School Districts and One Parochial School in Fremont County, Wyoming." Ph.D. dissertation, University of Wyoming, 1964.

6374. Withycombe, Jeraldine S. "Relationships of Self-Concept, Social Status, and Self-Perceived Social Status and Racial Differences of Paiute Indian and White Elementary School Children." Journal of Social Psychology 91 (December 1973): 337-338.

Vocational Training

Training Indians to support themselves in white society has long been a preoccupation with educators. Listed here are writings specifically on vocational education, including home economics. Some of them come from the early twentieth century.

6375. Alexander, Arch B. "Conference for Teachers of Indians: No Words Minced." American Vocational Journal 47 (November 1972): 50, 52.

6376. Ayers, Solon G. "An Investigation of Terminal Vocational Education at Haskell Institute." Ph.D. dissertation, University of Kansas, 1952.

6377. Bakeless, O. H. "The Unification of Industrial and Academic Features of the Indian School." National Education Association Journal of Proceedings and Addresses 1901, pp. 902-904.

6378. Beatty, Willard W. "Education Offered by the U.S. Indian Service." Industrial Arts and Vocational Education 34 (March 1945): 134-135.

6379. Bernardoni, Louis Charles. "Critical Factors Influencing the Stated Vocational Preference of Male White Mountain Apache Students." Ph.D. dissertation, Arizona State University, 1962.

6380. Beyl, Doyle. "Remodeling on the Reservation." American Vocational Journal 49 (April 1974): 48.

6381. Blume, Paul Rountree. "An Evaluation of Institutional Vocational Training Received by American Indians through the Muskogee, Oklahoma Area Office of the Bureau of Indian Affairs." Ph.D. dissertation, Oklahoma State University, 1968.

6382. Clinton, Lawrence, Bruce A. Chadwick, and Howard M. Bahr. "Vocational Training for Indian Migrants: Correlates of 'Success' in a Federal Program." Human Organization 32 (Spring 1973): 17-27.

6383. Despain, Charles Ward, Jr. "Analysis of Male Navaho Students' Perception of Occupational Opportunities and Their Attitudes toward Development of Skills and Traits Necessary for Occupational Competence." Ed.D. dissertation, Washington State University, 1965.

6384. Edington, Everett D., and Darrell S. Willey. "Occupational Training for America's Forgotten Minority." Journal of American Indian Education 10 (January 1971): 15-20.

6385. Ellis, Dorothy G. "The Home Economics Program Adapted to Indian Home Life." Practical Home Economics 10 (December 1932): 375, 392.

6386. Friedman, M. "Manual Training in the Indian Schools." National Education Association Journal of Proceedings and Addresses, 1907, pp. 810-815.

6387. Grattan, H. W. "Zuni Day-School Shop." Industrial Arts and Vocational Education 27 (March 1938): 99-100.

6388. Hart, Virginia S. "Manpower Training in Navajo Land." School Life 45 (March 1963): 26-29.

6389. "Health Career Opportunities for American Indians." Journal of American Indian Education 12 (January 1973): 1-2.

6390. Keller, Leslie M. "Sioux Boys and Girls Learn Cattle Handling." Clearing House 20 (May 1946): 540-542.

6391. Kuyper, George A. "Home Economics in Indian Schools." Southern Workman 61 (March 1932): 110-112.

6392. McCaskill, Joseph C. "Occupational Orientation of Indian Students." Occupations 18 (January 1940): 257-261.

6393. McGinty, Doris Madeline. "An Analysis of the Effectiveness of the Secondary Home Economics Program in Meeting Needs of Young Married Papago Indian Homemakers." Ed.D. dissertation, University of Arizona, 1964.

6394. Minear, Leon P. "Some New Approaches in Meeting the Occupational Education Needs of the American Indian." Journal of American Indian Education 9 (October 1969): 18-22.

6395. "Navajo and Hopi Indians to Receive Industrial Training." Occupations 30 (March 1952): 450-451.

6396. O'Quinn, Jessie. "Training Future Indian Homemakers." Practical Home Economics 16 (August 1938): 308-309, 328.

6397. Peterson, John L., and Val Cordova. "Technical Skills for American Indians." American Vocational Journal 47 (November 1972): 47-49.

6398. Rogers, F. K. "The Teaching of Trades to the Indian." National Education Association Journal of Proceedings and Addresses, 1900, pp. 698-701.

6399. Ross, William T., and Golda Van Buskirk Ross. "Backgrounds of Vocational Choice: An Apache Study." Personnel and Guidance Journal 35 (January 1957): 270-275.

6400. Sanders, Margaret R. "A Family Centered Foods Course." Journal of Home Economics 44 (December 1952): 775-777.

6401. Schlick, Mary D. "Indian Community Forms Co-operative Kitchen." Journal of

Home Economics 57 (November 1965): 728.

6402. Schmieding, O. A., and Shirley F. Jensen. "American Indian Students: Vocational Development and Vocational Tenacity." Vocational Guidance Quarterly 17 (December 1968): 120-123.

6403. Scott, Loren Charles. "An Economic Evaluation of On-the-Job Training Conducted under the Auspices of the Bureau of Indian Affairs in Oklahoma." Ph.D. dissertation, Oklahoma State University, 1969.

6404. Sherry, S. Toledo. "Elementary Industrial Training in the Day School." National Education Association Journal of Proceedings and Addresses, 1909, pp. 950-952.

6405. Sipe, Susan B. "The Work of the Bureau of Plant Industry, United States Department of Agriculture, in Its Relation to Agricultural Instruction in Indian Schools." National Education Association Journal of Proceedings and Addresses, 1905, pp. 938-947.

6406. Standing, A. J. "The Proper Relation between Literary and Industrial Education in Indian Schools." National Education Association Journal of Proceedings and Addresses, 1900, pp. 692-695.

6407. Tanzman, Jack. "A New Approach to the World of Work." School Management 16 (November 1972): 30-32. Southwestern Indian Polytechnic Institute, Albuquerque.

6408. "Vocational Education for Indians." Manual Training Magazine 18 (January 1917): 207-208.

6409. Weber, Stanley, and Virginia S. Hart. "Vocational Programs for American Indians." School Shop 24 (May 1965): 17-18, 34.

6410. Wharton, H. J. "Cooperative Education in the Government's Indian Schools." School and Society 51 (March 23, 1940): 385-386.

Counseling

A few studies deal specifically with guidance and counseling of Indian students.

6411. Bryde, John F. Indian Students and Guidance. Boston: Houghton Mifflin Company, 1971.

6412. Charles, C. M. "A Tutoring-Counseling Program for Indian Students in College." Journal of American Indian Education 1 (May 1962): 10-12.

6413. Davis, Thomas, and Fred Sanderson. "Community Counselors and the Counseling Process." Journal of American Indian Education 14 (October 1974): 26-29.

6414. Hinckley, Edward Charles. "The Need for Student Records in the Counseling of Navaho Students." Journal of American Indian Education 2 (May 1963): 1-6.

6415. McMahon, Robert C., John D. Hartz, and Charles J. Pulvino. "The Counselor's Charge in the American Indian's Educational Dilemma." School Counselor 20 (March 1973): 270-274.

6416. Osborn, Harold Wesley, Jr. "Evaluation of Counseling with a Group of Southern Utah Paiute Indians." Ph.D. dissertation, University of Utah, 1959.

6417. Pelletieri, A. J. "Counseling Indian Youth." Occupations 20 (October 1941): 21-24.

6418. Prestwich, Sheldon G. "The Influence of Two Counseling Methods on the Physical and Verbal Aggression of Pre-School Indian Children." Ph.D. dissertation, Arizona State University, 1969.

6419. Ryan, Charles W. "Counseling the Culturally Encapsulated American Indian." Vocational Guidance Quarterly 18 (December 1969): 123-126.

6420. Spang, Alonzo. "Counseling the Indian." Journal of American Indian Education 5 (October 1965): 10-15.

6421. Youngman, Geraldine, and Margaret Sadonger. "Counseling the American Indian Child." Elementary School Guidance and Counseling 8 (May 1974): 273-277.

Higher Education

Indian students in higher education have increased in recent years. Studies of Indians in college and of Indian colleges are listed here.

6422. Abrahams, Ina. "Vocational Interest of Selected Indian College Students As Measured by the Kuder Preference Record." Journal of American Indian Education 2 (October 1962): 20-24.

6423. Artichoker, John, and Neil M. Palmer. The Sioux Indian Goes to College. Vermillion, South Dakota: Institute of Indian Studies and State Department of Public Instruction, 1959.

6424. "Challenge at Many Farms." Junior College Journal 39 (May 1969): 35-38. Navajo junior college.

6425. Clark, Richard O. "Higher Education

Programs for American Indians." Journal of American Indian Education 12 (October 1972): 16-20.

6426. Committee on Indian Education. "Indian Education at Arizona State University." Journal of American Indian Education 1 (January 1962): 24-27.

6427. Dolan, W. W. "Junior College for Indian Students." Junior College Journal 9 (November 1938): 63-67. Bacone College.

6428. "DQU: A New Breed." Saturday Review of Education 1 (March 1973): 64.

6429. Forbes, Jack D. "An American Indian University: A Proposal for Survival." Journal of American Indian Education 5 (January 1966): 1-7.

6430. Fuchs, Estelle. "The Navajos Build a College." Saturday Review 55 (March 4, 1974): 58-62.

6431. Henderson, Rose. "Indian Education at Bacone College." Southern Workman 63 (May 1934): 143-148.

6432. "Higher Education for Indians and Spanish-Speaking Americans." Intellect 101 (January 1973): 208-209.

6433. House, Lloyd Lynn. "The Historical Development of Navajo Community College." Ph.D. dissertation, Arizona State University, 1974.

6434. Jensen, Kenneth D., and Shirley Jensen. "Factors in College Education for Indian Students." Improving College and University Teaching 18 (Winter 1970): 52-54.

6435. Kleinfeld, J. S., and K. L. Kohout. "Increasing the College Success of Alaska Natives." Journal of American Indian Education 13 (May 1974): 27-31.

6436. Leighton, Elizabeth Roby. "The Nature of Cultural Factors Affecting the Success or Failure of Navajo College Students." Ph.D. dissertation, University of Arizona, 1964.

6437. Leonard, Leon, James Freim, and Jay Fein. "Introducing Engineering to the American Indian." Journal of American Indian Education 14 (January 1975): 6-11.

6438. Ludeman, W. W. "The Indian Student in College." Journal of Educational Sociology 33 (March 1960): 333-335.

6439. McGrath, G. D., and others. Higher Education of Southwestern Indians with Reference to Success and Failure. Tempe, Arizona: Arizona State University, 1962.

6440. Miller, Frank C. "Involvement in an Urban University." In The American Indian in Urban Society, edited by Jack O. Waddell and O. Michael Watson, pp. 312-340. Boston: Little, Brown and Company, 1971. Account of Department of American Indian Studies, University of Minnesota.

6441. Minton, Charles E. "The Place of the Indian Youth Council in Higher Education." Journal of American Indian Education 1 (June 1961): 29-32.

6442. Nix, Lonnie Elmer. "Promotion of Higher Education within Arizona Indian Groups." Ed.D. dissertation, Arizona State University, 1963.

6443. Overturf, Leonard L., Chris Cavender, Tillie Walker, and Pete Deluca. "Problems Faced in Higher Education by American Indians." College and University 47 (Summer 1972): 316-318.

6444. Patton, Walter, and Everett D. Edington. "Factors Related to the Persistence of Indian Students at College Level." Journal of American Indian Education 12 (May 1973): 19-23.

6445. Quimby, Robert Joseph. "American Indian Students in Arizona Colleges: A Discriminant Analysis of Select Variables That Contribute to Success and Failure." Ed.D. dissertation, Arizona State University, 1963.

6446. Roessel, Robert A., Jr. "A Light in the Night." Journal of American Indian Education 11 (May 1972): 26-29. Navajo community college.

6446a. Rosenthal, Elizabeth C. "Finding Ways to College." American Indian 7 (Spring 1956): 15-19.

6447. Shunatona, Gwen. "Indian Goals for Higher Education." Integrated Education 31 (September-October 1974): 30-31.

6448. Stuart, Jeanette. "No Dilemma--Just Challenge at Navajo Community College." Delta Kappa Gamma Bulletin 38 (Winter 1972): 13-20.

6449. Wright, Rolland Harry. "The American Indian College Student: A Study in Marginality." Ph.D. dissertation, Brandeis University, 1972.

Teacher Training

Listed here are works that deal with the training of teachers for Indian schools and students.

6450. Bayne, Stephen. "A Non-Answer to a Request for a Teacher's Guide to Indian Children." Journal of American Indian Education 10 (January 1971): 29-33.

6451. Bonnell, Louise S. "Teacher Orientation--Navajo Style." *Journal of American Indian Education* 11 (January 1972): 30-32.

6452. Faas, Larry A. "A Career Development Program for Indian Teachers." *Journal of American Indian Education* 11 (January 1972): 13-14.

6453. Greer, Dora Young. "Specialized Training Programs for Teachers of Navajo Students." Ed.D. dissertation, University of Arizona, 1969.

6454. Hedrick, Wiley O. "The Orientation of Teachers to the Cultural Differences of Navajo Children." Ed.D. dissertation, Utah State University, 1974.

6455. Kersey, Harry A. "Training Teachers in a Seminole Indian School--A Unique Experience with the Disadvantaged Child." *Journal of Teacher Education* 22 (Spring 1971): 25-28.

6456. Peterson, Kirk D. "Some Steps for a Beginning Teacher of Navajo Students." *Journal of American Indian Education* 10 (January 1971): 21-28.

6457. Powers, Joseph F. *Brotherhood through Education: A Guide for Teachers of American Indians.* Fayette: Upper Iowa University, 1965.

6458. Watson, Guy A. "Training for Cross-Cultural Teaching." *Audiovisual Instruction* 14 (January 1969): 50-54.

Writings on Indian Education, 1921-1932

The agitation for reform in Indian affairs in the 1920s also touched Indian education, especially after the Meriam Report appeared in 1928. The most important individual was W. Carson Ryan, Jr., who was a member of the Meriam survey staff, who was appointed Director of Education in the Bureau of Indian Affairs in 1929.

6459. "The Administration of Indian Schools." *School and Society* 29 (February 16, 1929): 217.

6460. Arnold, Frank P. "Gloomy Gray or Bright Red." *Sunset* 53 (November 1924): 34, 63.

6461. Bronson, Ruth Muskrat. "The Indians' Attitude toward Cooperation." *Proceedings of the National Conference of Social Work*, 1931, pp. 637-645.

6462. Burke, Charles H. "Indians Making Progress in Learning the White Man's Way." *School Life* 9 (June 1924): 239-242.

6463. Burnett, Floyd O. "A New Day in Indian Education." *Missionary Review of the World* 55 (July 1932): 405-408.

6464. Collier, John. "Mexico: A Challenge." *Progressive Education* 9 (February 1932): 95-98.

6465. "Conference of Indian School Supervisors." *School and Society* 30 (August 17, 1929): 225-226.

6466. Craig, Eugene. "Going to School in Death Valley." *American Childhood* 15 (November 1929): 17-20.

6467. "Educational Appointments in the Indian Service." *School and Society* 34 (November 14, 1931): 658-659.

6468. "An Educational Farce." *Educational Review* 67 (May 1924): 273-274. Indian education in the state of New York.

6469. "Education of Indian Children." *Elementary School Journal* 30 (November 1929): 171-173.

6470. "Federal Appropriations to Schools for Indian Children." *School and Society* 31 (May 24, 1930): 702-703.

6471. Heger, Nancy Irene. "Before Books in an Indian School." *Progressive Education* 9 (February 1932): 138-143.

6472. Hyde, Warren C. "New Type of Indian Schools." *National Republic* 19 (July 1931): 25, 41-42.

6473. "Indian Children and the Public Schools." *School and Society* 30 (September 21, 1929): 396-397.

6474. "Indian Children and the Public Schools." *School and Society* 33 (May 2, 1931): 582.

6475. "Indian Education in Oklahoma." *School and Society* 32 (November 8, 1930): 627-628.

6476. "Indian Woman Aids U.S. in Educating Race." *Journal of Education* 112 (December 29, 1930): 559. Ruth Muskrat of the Bureau of Indian Affairs.

6477. La Du, Blanche L. "What Minnesota Is Doing for the Indians." *Proceedings of the National Conference of Social Work*, 1931, pp. 626-636.

6478. La Farge, Oliver. "An Experimental School for Indians." *Progressive Education* 9 (February 1932): 87-94.

6479. Lindquist, G. E. E. "The Indian Problem Is an Educational Problem." *Southern Workman* 58 (April 1929): 170-181.

6480. Meriam, Lewis. "Indian Education Moves Ahead." *Survey* 66 (June 1, 1931): 253-257, 293.

6481. _____. "Statement of the Problem." Proceedings of the National Conference of Social Work, 1931, pp. 606-616.

6482. "Need for Additional Indian School Facilities." School and Society 16 (December 23, 1922): 715.

6483. Peairs, H. B. "Indians Trained to Compete on Even Terms with Other Races." School Life 11 (April 1926): 144-147.

6484. "The Plight of the Educated Indian." Literary Digest 102 (August 3, 1929): 23-24.

6485. Riggs, F. B. "In Indian Education What Might Have Been and What Still May Be." Missionary Review of the World 53 (April 1930): 284-287.

6486. Ryan, W. Carson, Jr. "Cooperation in Indian Education." Proceedings of the National Conference of Social Work, 1931, pp. 617-625.

6487. _____. "Educational Conferences of Indian Service Superintendents." School and Society 34 (December 5, 1931): 764-765.

6488. _____. "Federal-State Cooperation in Indian Education." School and Society 34 (September 26, 1931): 418-423.

6489. _____. "Indian Education in the 48 States." In U.S. Office of Education, Biennial Survey of Education, 1928-30, 1:593-598. Washington: Government Printing Office, 1932.

6490. _____. "The New Plan for Indian Education." School Life 16 (March 1931): 134-135.

6491. _____. "Special Capacities of American Indians." School and Society 36 (December 17, 1932): 777-780.

6492. Ryan, W. Carson, Jr., and Rose K. Brandt. "Indian Education Today." Progressive Education 9 (February 1932): 81-86.

6493. "School Facilities for Indian Children." School and Society 32 (October 18, 1930): 520.

6494. Seneca, Pauline L. "Indian Education in New York State." New York State Education 18 (October 1930): 165-167.

6495. "The Tragedy of the Indian Students." Missionary Review of the World 54 (April 1931): 266.

6496. "Unemployment and American Indian Education." School and Society 34 (October 3, 1931): 461.

Writings on Indian Education, 1933-1945

Developments in education were part of the Indian "New Deal." The chief spokesman was Willard W. Beatty, Director of Indian Education, who wrote widely on Indian education. Included here also are other comments and studies from the period.

6497. Adams, Lucy Wilcox. "Indians on the Peace Path." Journal of Adult Education 13 (June 1941): 243-248.

6498. _____. "Navajos Go to School." Journal of Adult Education 10 (April 1938): 149-153.

6499. "American Citizens in the Making: Boarding and Day Schools for Indians." Times Educational Supplement no. 1381 (October 18, 1941): 496.

6500. Beatty, Willard W. "The Federal Government and the Education of Indians and Eskimos." Journal of Negro Education 7 (July 1938): 267-272.

6501. _____. "The Government's Indian Schools: Revising Ideas about Indians." Clearing House 12 (January 1938): 268-271.

6502. _____. "Indian Education." National Parent-Teacher 32 (May 1938): 27-30.

6503. _____. "A Special Case of a World Education Problem." Educational Record 23 (January 1942, Supplement): 95-111.

6504. _____. "Uncle Sam Develops a New Kind of Rural School." Elementary School Journal 41 (November 1940): 185-194.

6505. Blauch, Lloyd E. Educational Service for Indians. Washington: Government Printing Office, 1939. Prepared for the Advisory Committee on Education.

6506. "Civilizing the Indian." Nation 138 (January 10, 1934): 33-34.

6507. "A Combined Effort to Solve the Indian Problem." School and Society 54 (December 20, 1941): 584.

6508. Conrad, Charles W. "Education of the Indian." Texas Outlook 23 (July 1939): 26.

6509. Dwight, B. H. "Relationships between Indian Homes and Schools." National Conference of Social Work, Proceedings, 1933, pp. 677-685.

6510. "Educational Loans for Indians."

Monthly Labor Review 43 (December 1936): 1460-1461.

6511. Erikson, Erik Homburger. "Observations on Sioux Education." Journal of Psychology 7 (January 1939): 101-156.

6512. Hulsizer, Allan. "Navajo Communities and Secondary Education." Junior-Senior High School Clearing House 9 (March 1935): 404-406.

6513. _____. "Selection of Experiences in the Curriculum for the Dakota." Curriculum Journal 12 (January 1941): 14-18.

6514. Ickes, Mrs. Harold L. "Educating the Child to Meet New Conditions." National Congress of Parents and Teachers, Proceedings 38 (1934): 23-31.

6515. "Indian Education." School Life 20 (February 1935): 127; (March 1935): 166; (April 1935): 191; (May 1935): 214; (June 1935): 238; 21 (September 1935): 17; (October 1935): 34; (November 1935): 68; (February 1936): 165.

6516. "Indian Education in the United States." School and Society 51 (June 29, 1940): 775-776.

6517. "In-Service Training for Indian Reservations." School and Society 44 (December 5, 1936): 727.

6518. John, Walton C. "Schools under the Federal Government: The Department of the Interior." School Life 25 (January 1940): 266-269.

6519. Johnson, Stanley W. "Tuscarora Indian School's Experiment." New York State Education 22 (June 1935): 696-697 +.

6520. Kramer, Max. "An Experiment in Indian Education." Progressive Education 12 (March 1935): 155-159.

6521. Larson, Roy H. "Education of Indian Children in Minnesota." Minnesota Journal of Education 26 (December 1945): 177.

6522. "The Las Vegas Conference on Indian Education." School and Society 39 (June 2, 1934): 696.

6523. Leroux, Loretta. "A Pueblo Day School." Childhood Education 18 (April 1942): 357-359.

6524. McCaskill, Joseph C. "Blazing New Indian Trails." Occupations 15 (March 1937): 508-512.

6525. Mekeel, Scudder. "An Anthropologist's Observations on Indian Education." Progressive Education 13

(March 1936): 151-159.

6526. _____. "Education, Child-Training and Culture." American Journal of Sociology 48 (May 1943): 676-681.

6527. Mundt, Karl E. "Let's Treat the Red Man White." Nation's Schools 32 (September 1943): 20-21.

6528. Orata, Pedro T., and others. "An Indian School Serves Its Community." Progressive Education 15 (February 1938): 152-155. Little Wound School on the Pine Ridge Reservation.

6529. Ricklefs, Robert U. "Project Development in an Indian School." Sierra Educational News 30 (April 1934): 41-43.

6530. Ryan, Carson V. "Science with the Eastern Cherokee Indians." Progressive Education 15 (February 1938): 143-146.

6531. "School Facilities for Indians." School and Society 37 (June 3, 1933): 706.

6532. Seymour, Flora Warren. "The Pedagogues Hunt Indians." American Mercury 29 (August 1933): 437-445.

6533. Seymour, Howard C. "Indian Youth Attend Boarding School." Harvard Educational Review 12 (October 1942): 405-415.

6534. Thompson, Samuel H. "The Indian Goes to School." Instructor 48 (October 1939): 6-7.

6535. Tisinger, R. M. "Civil Service in Indian Schools." Phi Delta Kappan 23 (December 1940): 133-134.

6536. Tyler, Ralph W. "Indian Education an Example for All Schools." Elementary School Journal 46 (October 1945): 68-69.

6537. Wharton, Howard. "Cooperative Education in the Government's Indian Schools." School and Society 51 (March 23, 1940): 385-386.

6538. White, Owen P. "Lo, the Poor Indian." Collier's 99 (February 6, 1937): 16-17, 40.

6539. "Why the Indian Boarding School Failed." Virginia Teacher 18 (January 1937): 11-13.

Writings on Indian Education, 1946-1960

Indians remained a concern of the educational press, which carried an increasing number of articles on Indian education. Included with the current comment are scientific articles dealing with aspects of the subject.

6540. Adair, Mildred Lee. "Finding a Common Denominator: Can Peoples Understand Each Other's Philosophies?" Arizona Teacher 45 (May 1957): 19, 22.

6541. "American Indians at School." Times Educational Supplement no. 2052 (August 27, 1954): 806.

6542. Beatty, Willard W. "Budget for Indian Education." Education Digest 13 (December 1947): 44-46.

6543. _____. "Education for Indian Children and Youth." Journal of Religious Thought 7 (Spring-Summer 1950): 121-127.

6544. _____. "Twenty Years of Indian Education." In The Indian in Modern America, edited by David A. Baerreis, pp. 16-49. Madison: State Historical Society of Wisconsin, 1956.

6545. _____. "U.S.A.: Indians and Eskimos." Year Book of Education, 1949, pp. 182-188.

6546. Bergan, K. W. "The Secondary School and the Acculturation of Indian People." Bulletin of the National Association of Secondary School Principals 43 (October 1959): 115-117.

6547. Boyce, George A. "Community Needs: U.S. Indian Schools Are Developing a Program Adapted to Local Cultures and Economic Levels." Clearing House 14 (March 1940): 397-399.

6548. Brodinsky, B. P. "Teaching Indian Children." Nation's Schools 50 (December 1952): 35-38.

6549. Brownlee, Aleta. "The American Indian Child." Children 5 (March-April 1958): 55-60.

6550. Cooper, Dan H. "Shameful Education for Indians." Elementary School Journal 48 (March 1948): 362-363.

6551. Coursen, Marshall. "Now I Thank You." Arizona Teacher-Parent 37 (March 1949): 10-11.

6552. "A Crying Need: Education for 15,000 Navaho Children." School Management: Administration, Equipment, Maintenance 17 (September 1947): 13.

6553. Dunne, George H. "The Indian's Dilemma." Commonweal 65 (January 4, 1957): 351-354.

6554. Eckel, Howard. "Boarding Schools for Indian Youth." School Executive 72 (September 1952): 82-84.

6555. "Education of Alaskan Natives: A Report on a Cooperative Research Project." School Life 42 (October 1959): 28-30.

6556. "Elementary-School Teachers Needed in the Indian Service." School and Society 73 (April 7, 1951): 219-220.

6557. First, Joan M. "Cultures in Crosscurrents." Michigan Education Journal 38 (November 1, 1960): 241-244, 281.

6558. Gilliland, Minnio. "Your Children Shall Learn Paper--a Report on Navajo Education." NEA Journal 45 (December 1956): 558-560.

6559. Gunther, Erna. "The Education of American Indians." Education Digest 14 (October 1948): 34-36.

6560. Gwilliam, Robert F. "Social Acceptance of Navajo Students." Educational Leadership 15 (May 1958): 496-500.

6561. Harper, Allan G. "Navajo Education." American Indian 5 (Fall 1950): 3-10.

6562. Hawley, Florence, and Donovan Senter. "The Grammar School as the Basic Acculturating Influence for Native New Mexicans." Social Forces 24 (May 1946): 398-407.

6563. Henry, Jules A. "A Cross-Cultural Outline of Education." Current Anthropology 1 (July 1960): 267-305.

6564. Hill, Clarence M., and Dorothy Pillsbury. "The P.T.A. in Navaho Land." National Parent-Teacher 52 (April 1958): 29-31.

6565. Johnson, Bert F. "Indian Children in Our Public Schools." Wisconsin Journal of Education 85 (November 1952): 3-4.

6566. Jones, Charles F. "Notes on Indian Education." Journal of Educational Sociology 27 (September 1953): 16-23.

6567. Lange, Charles H. "Education and Leadership in Rio Grande Pueblo Culture Change." American Indian 8 (Winter 1958-1959): 27-35.

6568. Neuberger, Richard L. "Sleep Well, Mr. Congressman." Education Digest 13 (December 1947): 46. Congressman Lowell Stockman and the closing of the Indian school at Chemawa, Oregon.

6569. Opler, Morris Edward. "Cultural Alternatives and Educational Theory." Harvard Educational Review 17 (Winter 1947): 28-44.

6570. Owens, John D. "New School for Navajos." School Executive 76 (October 1956): 61-62.

6571. Page, Marge. "Schoolhouse in the Desert." NEA Journal 42 (November 1953): 514.

6572. Podlich, William. "Adventure in Education: In the Land of the Hopi." Arizona Teacher 47 (March 1959): 14-16.

6573. Pratt, Wayne T. "Living beside Us--Worlds Apart." Childhood Education 34 (December 1957): 165-168.

6574. Ransom, Jay Ellis. "Education for Indian Life." Clearing House 22 (December 1947): 236-238.

6575. Rosenthal, Elizabeth C. "Advanced Education for Indians: A Preliminary Report." American Indian 5, no. 2 (1949): 29-34.

6576. Rothe, Aline. "Modern School for an Ancient Tribe." Texas Outlook 35 (August 1951): 12-13.

6577. Russell, Charles. "Centralizing New York Indian Schools: A Survey." American Indian 7 (Spring 1955): 45-53.

6578. Russell, Janet. "Indian Children Attend Public School." Minnesota Journal of Education 30 (September 1949): 19, 24.

6579. Sage, Janet Case. "Education or Starvation for Our Navahos?" National Parent-Teacher 42 (February 1948): 27-29.

6580. Tiffany, Warren I. "Federal Schools for Native Children in Alaska." School Life 40 (May 1958): 8-10.

6581. Wallis, Ruth Sawtell. "The Overt Fears of Dakota Indian Children." Child Development 25 (September 1954): 185-192.

6582. "We've Been Asked: Are Indian Schools Segregated?" U.S. News and World Report 43 (November 8, 1957): 116.

6583. Wilcox, Clare L. "With the Help of Nature." Progressive Education 23 (March 1946): 190-191, 199. Teaching retarded Indian children.

Writings on Indian Education, 1961-1970

Increased interest in Indian matters in the 1960s was reflected in the literature on Indian education. A great many technical studies appeared in addition to comment on the current state of Indian schools. Of special note was the searing condemnation of Indian education made by the Senate Sub-Committee on Indian Education in 1969 (6632).

6584. Allan, Ray A. "Whither Indian Education? A Conversation with Philleo Nash." School Review 79 (November 1970): 99-108.

6585. Anderson, James G., and Dwight Safar. "The Influence of Differential Community Perceptions on the Provision of Equal Educational Opportunities." Sociology of Education 40 (Summer 1967): 219-230.

6586. "Annual Indian Education Conference Covers Variety of Topics and 'Tools.'" Journal of American Indian Education 9 (May 1970): 24-27.

6587. Aurbach, Herbert A., ed. Proceedings of the National Research Conference on American Indian Education. Kalamazoo, Michigan: Society for the Study of Social Problems, 1967. An interim report to the U.S. Office of Education.

6588. Aurbach, Herbert A., and Estelle Fuchs, with Gordon Macgregor. The Status of American Indian Education. University Park: Pennsylvania State University, 1970. An interim report of the National Study of American Indian Education to the U.S. Office of Education.

6589. Bailey, Clarence W. "Bruce Lists Indian Youth Programs as Top Priority." Journal of American Indian Education 9 (January 1970): 31.

6590. Bayne, Stephen L. "Culture Materials in Schools' Programs for Indian Students." Journal of American Indian Education 9 (October 1969): 1-6.

6591. Bearking, Leonard. "Indian Education under Federal Domination." Indian Historian 2 (Spring 1969): 21-24.

6592. Beavan, Keith. "American Indians Are Still Called 'Filthy Savages.'" Times Educational Supplement no. 2834 (September 12, 1969): 20.

6593. Benham, William J. "Liaison: Key Word in School Program Completion." Journal of American Indian Education 5 (January 1966): 26-29.

6594. Bennett, Benjamin, Jr. "Seventh Grade Navaho Answer 'Why Education?'" Journal of American Indian Education 4 (October 1964): 17-19.

6595. Bennett, Robert L., and L. Madison Coombs. "Effective Education to Meet Special Needs of Native Children." Journal of American Indian Education 3 (May 1964): 21-25.

6596. Bernardoni, Louis C. "Apache Parents and Vocational Choice." Journal of American Indian Education 2

(January 1963)· 1-8.

6597. Brockmann, C. Thomas. "Social Class and Educational Level on the Flathead Reservation." Journal of American Indian Education 10 (October 1970): 23-31.

6598. Bryde, John F. "A New Approach to Indian Education." Integrated Education 6 (September-October 1968): 29-36.

6599. Burnett, Jacquetta H. "School Culture and Social Change in the City." Educational Leadership 26 (October 1968): 12-16.

6600. Clark, Erma. "A Nursery School on the Ute Indian Reservation." Childhood Education 41 (April 1965): 407-410.

6601. "A Commitment to Leadership: Report on All-Indian Upward Bound Project at Arizona State University." Journal of American Indian Education 10 (October 1970): 5-7.

6602. Conklin, Paul. "Good Day at Rough Rock: They're Giving Education Back to the Indians." American Education 3 (February 1967): 4-9.

6603. Coombs, L. Madison. "Indian Student Is Not Low Man on the Totem Pole." Journal of American Indian Education 9 (May 1970): 1-9.

6604. Cornelius, Elizabeth. "From Totems to Understanding." Instructor 80 (October 1970): 95-96, 98. Tlingit Indians.

6605. Crawford, Dean A. "Speaking of Indians . . . What's Your Problem?" Minnesota Journal of Education 49 (November 1968): 22-25.

6606. Crow, John. "Schools for the First Americans." American Education 1 (October 1965): 15-22.

6607. Dahlberg, Henry. "Community and School Service." Journal of American Indian Education 7 (May 1968): 15-19.

6608. Dumont, Robert V., Jr. "Cherokee Children and the Teacher." Social Education 33 (January 1969): 70-72.

6609. Emerson, Gloria J. "The Laughing Boy Syndrome." School Review 79 (November 1970): 94-98.

6610. Erickson, Donald A. "Custer Did Die for Our Sins!" School Review 79 (November 1970): 76-93.

6611. _____. "Failure in Navajo Schooling." Parents' Magazine 45 (September 1970): 66-68, 109-112.

6612. Erickson, Donald A., and Henrietta Schwartz. "What Rough Rock Demonstrates." Integrated Education 8 (March-April 1970): 21-34.

6613. Evvard, Evelyn, and George C. Mitchell. "Sally, Dick, and Jane at Lukachukai." Journal of American Indian Education 5 (May 1966): 2-6.

6614. Fannin, Paul J. "Indian Education: A Test for Democracy." Arizona Law Review 10 (Winter 1968): 661-673.

6615. Fearn, Leif. "The Education of Indian Children: Reflections." Journal of American Indian Education 7 (October 1967): 27-31.

6616. Fielding, Byron. "Federal Funds to Meet Local Needs." NEA Journal 55 (September 1966): 23-26.

6617. Fischer, George D., and Walter F. Mondale. "Indian Education--a National Disgrace." Today's Education 59 (March 1970): 24-27.

6618. Fisher, A. D. "White Rites versus Indian Rights." Trans-action 7 (November 1969): 29-33.

6619. Fuchs, Estelle. "American Indian Education: Time to Redeem an Old Promise." Saturday Review 53 (January 24, 1970): 54-57, 74-75.

6620. _____. "Learning to be Navaho-Americans: Innovation at Rough Rock." Saturday Review 50 (September 16, 1967): 82-84, 98-99.

6621. Gifford, Selene. "Educating the American Indian." School Life 47 (November 1964): 10-12.

6622. Gunsky, Frederic R. "School Problems of Indian Youth." California Education 3 (February 1966): 20-22.

6623. Havighurst, Robert J. The Education of Indian Children and Youth: Summary Report and Recommendations. National Study of American Indian Education, Final Report, series 4, no. 6. Minneapolis: Training Center for Community Progress, University of Minnesota, 1970.

6624. Helper, Malcolm M., and Sol L. Garfield. "Use of the Semantic Differential to Study Acculturation in American Indian Adolescents." Journal of Personality and Social Psychology 2 (December 1965): 817-822.

6625. Hillyard, Myrna. "Education on an Indian Reservation." Childhood Education 42 (October 1965): 97. Fort Apache Indian Reservation.

6626. Henninger, Daniel, and Nancy Esposito.

"Regimented Non-Education: Indian Schools." New Republic 160 (February 15, 1969): 18-21. Discussion (March 22, 1969): 31-33.

6627. Hofer, Barbara. "Still a Losing Battle." American Education 5 (November 1969): back cover. Brewton Berry's index to American Indian education.

6628. Hopkins, Tom R. "Leadership in Alaskan Native Education." Journal of American Indian Education 2 (October 1962): 1-5.

6629. Hoyt, Elizabeth E. "An Approach to the Mind of the Young Indian." Journal of American Indian Education 1 (June 1961): 17-23.

6630. _____. "Some Light on the Adjustment of Indian Children." Journal of American Indian Education 4 (January 1965): 26-29.

6631. Hurwitz, Al. "A Very Small Happening at Forty Mile Bend." NEA Journal 56 (September 1967): 71-72.

6632. Indian Education: A National Tragedy --a National Challenge. Report of the Special Sub-Committee on Indian Education, Committee on Labor and Public Welfare, U.S. Senate. Washington: Government Printing Office, 1969. Issued as Senate Report no. 501, 91st Congress, 1st session, serial 12836-1. Committee headed by Senator Robert Kennedy and later by Senator Edward Kennedy. The Committee also issued a number of committee prints dealing with Indian education.

6633. Johnson, Broderick H. Navaho Education at Rough Rock. Rough Rock, Arizona: Rough Rock Demonstration School, 1968.

6634. Johnston, Betty Kendall. "Gold Stars and Red Apples." Childhood Education 41 (May 1965): 466-468.

6635. Jose, Nelson. "Why We Need Our Education." Journal of American Indian Education 1 (May 1962): 22-25.

6636. Kennedy, Robert F. "America's Forgotten Children." Parents' Magazine 43 (June 1968): 30.

6637. Kersey, Harry A., Jr. "The Ahfachkee Day School." Teachers College Record 72 (September 1970): 93-103.

6638. Kersey, Harry A., Jr., and Neal E. Justin. "Florida Atlantic University Project: Big Cypress Seminoles Receive Three-Phase Program." Journal of American Indian Education 10 (October 1970): 20-22.

6639. Klein, Garry. "A Relevant Curriculum for Navajos." Southern Education Report 4 (April 1969): 2-5.

6640. Kutsche, Paul. "Cherokee High School Dropouts." Journal of American Indian Education 3 (January 1964): 22-30.

6641. Lee, Dorothy. "Education and Cultural Values." National Elementary Principal 42 (November 1962): 13-17.

6642. Lesser, Alexander. "Education and the Future of Tribalism in the United States: The Case of the American Indian." Social Service Review 35 (June 1961): 135-143.

6643. Lund, Betty Faye. "The Dilemma of the California Indian." CTA Journal 61 (October 1965): 20-23.

6644. McKenzie, Taylor. "What the Navajo Nation Needs." Integrated Education 8 (July-August 1970): 26-31.

6645. McNickle, D'Arcy. "The Sociocultural Setting of Indian Life." American Journal of Psychiatry 125 (August 1968): 219-223.

6646. Malan, Vernon D. "Factors Associated with Prejudice toward Indians." Journal of American Indian Education 2 (October 1962): 25-31.

6647. Mather, P. Boyd. "Tama Indians Fight for Their Own Schools." Christian Century 85 (October 2, 1968): 1251-1252.

6648. Meador, Bruce. "The Pupil as a Person." Journal of American Indian Education 4 (January 1965): 17-22.

6649. Menninger, Karl. "Dr. Karl Menninger Reflects on Rough Rock Demonstration School." Journal of American Indian Education 7 (May 1968): 42-43.

6650. Miller, Ethelyn. "American Indian Children and Merging Cultures." Childhood Education 44 (April 1968): 494-497.

6651. Miller, Frank C., and D. Douglas Caulkins. "Chippewa Adolescents: A Changing Generation." Human Organization 23 (Summer 1964): 150-159.

6652. Mittelholtz, Erwin F. "Minnesota's Plan for Indian Education." Minnesota Journal of Education 44 (December 1963): 9-10.

6653. Misiaszek, Lorraine. "The Cultural Dilemma of American Indians." Social Education 33 (April 1969): 438-439, 446.

6654. Moorefield, Story. "To Keep the Things We Love." American Education 6 (August-September 1970): 6-8.

6655. Muskrat, Joseph. "The Need for Cultural Empathy." School Review 79 (November 1970): 72-75.

6656. Nader, Ralph. "Ralph Nader Comments on Indian Education." Integrated Education 7 (November-December 1969): 3-13.

6657. Nash, Philleo. "The Education Mission of the Bureau of Indian Affairs." Journal of American Indian Education 3 (January 1964): 1-4.

6658. Nephew, Allen L. "Christian Education and the American Indian." Religious Education 62 (November-December 1967): 503-510.

6659. "Official Horror Story of Federally-Run Chilocco Indian School." Integrated Education 7 (July-August 1969): 48-51.

6660. Olsen, Donald A. "Administrative Service." Journal of American Indian Education 7 (May 1968): 20-23.

6661. Overby, H. D. "Tell It Like It Is, Only, How Is It?" Today's Education 58 (November 1969): 55-56.

6662. Padfield, Harland, Peter Hemingway, and Philip Greenfeld. "The Pima-Papago Education Population: A Census and Analysis." Journal of American Indian Education 6 (October 1966): 1-24.

6663. Penseno, William. "Nothing . . . But Death." Integrated Education 8 (September-October 1970): 17-25.

6664. Peterson, Ronald A. "Rehabilitation of the Culturally Different: A Model of the Individual in Cultural Change." Personnel and Guidance Journal 45 (June 1967): 1001-1007.

6665. Pfeiffer, Anna. "Educational Innovation." Journal of American Indian Education 7 (May 1968): 24-31.

6666. Platero, Dillon. "Let's Do It Ourselves!" School Review 79 (November 1970): 57-58.

6667. Polacca, Kathryn. "Ways of Working with the Navahos Who Have Not Learned the White Man's Ways." Journal of American Indian Education 2 (October 1962): 6-16.

6668. Pope, Allen. "An Educational Program for Adult American Indians." Adult Leadership 18 (November 1969): 143-144, 156.

6669. Renaud, Andre. "Acceleration of Socio-Cultural Adjustment and Change in Northern Communities." Journal of American Indian Education 3 (January 1964): 11-14.

6670. Reno, Thomas R. "A Demonstration in Navaho Education." Journal of American Indian Education 6 (May 1967): 1-5.

6671. Richardson, Bernard E. "A Wind Is Rising." Library Journal 95 (February 1, 1970): 463-467.

6672. Roessel, Robert A., Jr. "Indian Education in Arizona." Journal of American Indian Education 1 (June 1961): 33-38.

6673. _____. "An Overview of the Rough Rock Demonstration School." Journal of American Indian Education 7 (May 1968): 2-14.

6674. _____. "The Right to Be Wrong and the Right to Be Right." Journal of American Indian Education 7 (January 1968): 1-6.

6675. Roessel, Ruth. "Dormitory Living at Rough Rock." Journal of American Indian Education 7 (May 1968): 32-35.

6676. Ross, Richard M. "Cultural Integrity and American Indian Education." Arizona Law Review 11 (Winter 1969): 641-675.

6677. Roucek, Joseph S. "The Most Oppressed Race in the United States: The Indian." Educational Forum 29 (May 1965): 477-485.

6678. Saslow, Harry L., and May J. Harrover. "Research on Psychological Adjustment of Indian Youth." American Journal of Psychiatry 125 (August 1968): 224-231.

6679. "School for Community Pride." Instructor 80 (October 1970): 40-42. Grand Portage reservation school.

6680. Sheps, Efrain. "Indian Youth's Attitudes toward Non-Indian Patterns of Life." Journal of American Indian Education 9 (January 1970): 19-27.

6681. Shoen, Harriet H. "One Generation to Another." Saturday Review 49 (January 15, 1966): 68-70, 78-79.

6682. Sierksma, F., Murray Wax, Evelyn Wood, and Jules Henry. "More on Cross Cultural Education." Current Anthropology 2 (June 1961): 255-265.

6683. Sorkin, Alan. "Poverty and Dropouts: The Case of the American Indian." Growth and Change: A Journal of Regional Development 1 (July 1970): 14-18.

6684. Spang, Alonzo. "Eight Problems in Indian Education." Journal of American Indian Education 10 (October 1970): 1-4.

6685. Stark, Matthew. "Project Awareness: Minnesota Encourages the Chippewa Indians." Journal of American Indian Education 6 (May 1967): 6-13.

6686. Stillwell, Margaret P., and R. V. Allen. "Two Reports from Head Start." Teachers College Record 67 (March 1966): 443-447.

6687. Tefft, Stanton K. "Anomy, Values, and Culture Change among Teen-Age Indians: An Exploratory Study." Sociology of Education 40 (Spring 1967): 145-157.

6688. "Voice for Indians in Education Decisions." School and Society 98 (Summer 1970): 303-304.

6689. Wasson, Wilfred C. "Hindrances to Indian Education." Educational Leadership 28 (December 1970): 278-280.

6690. Waugh, Lynne, and John Waugh. "Renaissance of the Indian Spirit." American Education 6 (July 1970): 15-20.

6691. Wax, Murray L. "American Indian Education as a Cultural Transaction." Teachers College Record 64 (May 1963): 693-704.

6692. _____. "Gophers or Gadflies: Indian School Boards." School Review 79 (November 1970): 62-71.

6693. Wax, Murray L., and Rosalie H. Wax. "Cultural Deprivation as an Educational Ideology." Journal of American Indian Education 3 (January 1964): 15-18.

6694. Wax, Murray L., Rosalie H. Wax, and Robert V. Dumont. "Formal Education in an American Indian Community: Summary and Recommendations." Social Problems 2 Supplement (Spring 1964): 102-115.

6695. Wax, Rosalie H. "The Warrior Dropouts." Trans-action 4 (May 1967): 40-46.

6696. Wax, Rosalie H., and Murray L. Wax. "Indian Education for What?" In The American Indian Today, edited by Stuart Levine and Nancy Oestreich Lurie, pp. 163-169. Deland, Florida: Everett/Edwards, 1968. This appeared originally in Midcontinent American Studies Journal 6 (Fall 1965): 164-170.

6697. Wesley, Clarence. "Indian Education." Journal of American Indian Education 1 (June 1961): 4-7.

6698. "Which Way at Rough Rock." School Review 79 (November 1970): 59-61.

6699. Wilson, Jim. "Dormitory, Teacher Aides Are Big Help in South Dakota." Journal of American Indian Education 9 (January 1970): 3-9.

6700. Witherspoon, Gary. "Navajo Curriculum Center." Journal of American Indian Education 7 (May 1968): 36-41.

6702. Zintz, Miles V. "Problems of Classroom Adjustment of Indian Children in Public Elementary Schools in the Southwest." Science Education 46 (April 1962): 261-269.

Other material can be found listed in Education Index, in Research in Education (ERIC), and in Current Index to Journals in Education (CIJE).

Writings on Indian Education, 1971--

Numerous studies on Indian education appeared in the 1970s. Representative items are listed here--both technical studies and current comment. Of special note is the work of Fuchs and Havighurst (6741), which draws heavily on the National Study of American Indian Education.

6703. Adams, David. "Self-Determination and Indian Education." Journal of American Indian Education 13 (January 1974): 21-27.

6704. Allen, James R. "The Indian Adolescent: Psychosocial Tasks of the Plains Indians of Western Oklahoma." American Journal of Orthopsychiatry 43 (April 1973): 368-375.

6705. Alley, Robert D., and Ronald G. Davison. "Educating the American Indian: A School Joins the Twentieth Century." Clearing House 46 (February 1972): 347-351. Chilocco Indian School.

6706. Altman, S. Morton, and Robert Salmon. "A Service Program for Teenagers." Adolescence 6 (Winter 1971): 495-508.

6707. Antell, Will. "Education of the American Indians." Current History 67 (December 1974): 267-270, 279.

6708. Bass, Willard P. "Formal Education for American Indians." Journal of Research and Development in Education 4 (Summer 1971): 21-32.

6709. Benham, William J. "A Brief Overview of a Changing Era." Journal of American Indian Education 14 (October 1974): 1-3.

6710. _____. "In Albuquerque: An Indian Education Resources Center." Journal of American Indian Education 12 (October 1972): 21-24.

6711. Bigart, Robert. "Warriors in the Blackboard Jungle." Elementary School Journal 74 (April 1974): 408-421.

6712. Biglin, James E., and Jack Wilson. "Parental Attitudes towards Indian Education." Journal of American Indian Education 11 (May 1972): 1-6.

6713. Bodner, Bruce. "Indian Education: Tool of Cultural Politics." National Elementary Principal 50 (May 1971): 22-30.

6714. Boyer, Susan. "Blazing a New Trail." Saturday Review 54 (January 16, 1971): 53.

6715. Brightman, Lehman. "The Pictures on the Wall Are of White Men." Integrated Education 9 (May-June 1971): 37-42.

6716. "Building a Cultural Bridge." Instructor 82 (March 1973): 66-68. Sanostee Boarding School, New Mexico.

6717. "Candid Comments on Bureaucratic Education." Journal of American Indian Education 11 (May 1972): 15-19. Thirteenth Annual Indian Education Conference, Arizona State University.

6718. Case, C. C. "Navajo Education: Is There Hope?" Educational Forum 29 (November 1971): 129-132.

6719. Caspar, M. G. "Education of Menominee Youth in Wisconsin." Integrated Education 11 (January 1973): 45-51.

6720. Chadwick, Bruce A. "The Inedible Feast." In Native Americans Today: Sociological Perspectives, edited by Howard M. Bahr and others, pp. 131-145. New York: Harper and Row, 1972.

6721. Chavers, Dean. "Indian Education: Failure for the Future?" American Indian Law Review 2 (Summer 1974): 61-84.

6722. Collins, Lorraine. "Education and the American Indian: The Problems Aren't Simple." PTA Magazine 68 (December 1973): 30-32.

6723. Conn, Stephen. "At Ramah, New Mexico: Bilingual Legal Education." Journal of American Indian Education 12 (January 1973): 3-10.

6724. _____. "The Bicultural Legal Education Project at Ramah, New Mexico." Indian Historian 5 (Fall 1972): 36-39, 50.

6725. Deloria, Vine, Jr. "Integrity before Education." Integrated Education 12 (May-June 1974): 22-24. Discussion, pp. 24-28.

6726. De Vries, James, and Lee M. Swan. "In Great Lakes, Wisconsin, Adult Education for the Disadvantaged." Journal of American Indian Education 12 (October 1972): 27-32.

6727. Dickeman, Mildred. "The Integrity of the Cherokee Student." In The Culture of Poverty: A Critique, edited by Eleanor Burke Leacock, pp. 140-179. New York: Simon and Schuster, 1971.

6728. Dimock, Edmund, and Barbara Riegel. "Volunteering to Help Indians Help Themselves." Children 18 (January-February 1971): 23-27.

6729. Dlugokinski, Eric. "Review of an Old Stereotype." Journal of American Indian Education 11 (May 1972): 23-25. Riverside Indian Boarding School, Anadarko, Oklahoma.

6730. Dlugokinski, Eric, and Lyn Kramer. "A System of Neglect: Indian Boarding Schools." American Journal of Psychiatry 131 (June 1974): 670-673.

6731. Dodge, Marjorie T. "Should Values Be Taught in the Classroom?" Journal of American Indian Education 11 (January 1972): 15-17.

6732. Doherty, Matthew F. "Indian Education: Toward a Better Tomorrow." New York State Education 58 (April 1971): 16-17.

6733. "An Even Chance." Law and the Social Order, 1971, pp. 245-320.

6734. Fadden, John, and Louis Mofsie. "Student Reactions to Indian Teachers of Non-Indian Children." Social Education 36 (May 1972): 507-511.

6735. "Federal Funds for Indian Education." Intellect 102 (January 1974): 209-210.

6736. "First Model Preschool Program Developed at Tucson for Handicapped Indian Children." Journal of American Indian Education 10 (May 1971): 1-2.

6737. Fitzgerald, Paul, and Thomas Davis. "An Alternative to Failure." Journal of American Indian Education 13 (January 1974): 1-3. Menominee County community school.

6738. Foerster, Leona M., and Dale Little Soldier. "Open Education and Native American Values." Educational Leadership 32 (October 1974): 41-45.

6739. Forbes, Jack D. "Teaching Native American Values and Cultures." In Teaching Ethnic Studies: Concepts and Strategies, pp. 201-219. Washington: National Council for the Social Studies, 1973.

6740. Foster, Ashley. "Home Environment and Performance in School." School and

Society 100 (April 1972): 236-237.

6741. Fuchs, Estelle, and Robert J. Havighurst. To Live on This Earth: American Indian Education. Garden City, New York: Doubleday and Company, 1972. Based on the National Study of American Indian Education.

6742. Goldberg, Lazer. "Special Issue on the American Indian: Introduction." Science and Children 9 (March 1972): 9-10.

6743. Gover, Bill. "Serving the Needs of the Native American." Community and Junior College Journal 43 (May 1973): 32-33.

6744. Greene, Linda. "Justice in America: The Persistent Myth." Social Education 37 (November 1973): 637-638.

6745. Gregory, Jack, and Rennard Strickland. "You Didn't Have to Know English to Understand Funny Books." Journal of American Indian Education 11 (January 1972): 1-4.

6746. Gross, Michael Paul. "Indian Control for Quality Indian Education." North Dakota Law Review 49 (Winter 1973): 237-265.

6747. Haley, Bill. "Cross Culture Contact." Contemporary Education 43 (October 1971): 26-27.

6748. _____. "Cross over the Bridge." Journal of American Indian Education 10 (January 1971): 1-3.

6749. _____. "Synergizing." Journal of the National Association of Women Deans and Counselors 34 (Summer 1971): 151-152.

6750. Harris, Helen L. "On the Failure of Indian Education." Clearing House 48 (December 1973): 242-247.

6751. Harris, LaDonna. "Indian Education in New York State: Hope for the Future." New York State Education 58 (April 1971): 18-21.

6752. Havighurst, Robert J. "The American Indian: From Assimilation to Cultural Pluralism." Educational Leadership 31 (April 1974): 585-589.

6753. "The Havighurst National Study." Journal of American Indian Education 10 (May 1971): 26-27.

6754. "Head Start in the Grand Canyon." Saturday Review 55 (July 22, 1972): 34-37.

6755. Houlihan, Patrick T. "Museums and American Indian Education." Journal of American Indian Education 13 (October 1973): 20-21.

6756. "Indian Education." Inequality in Education, no. 7 (February 10, 1971). Entire issue.

6757. "Indian Participation in Public Schools." Social Education 35 (May 1971): 452-465.

6758. "In River Falls, Wisconsin: Indian Parents Begin Own Education." Journal of American Indian Education 14 (January 1975): 12-14.

6759. Jessen, Mariana. "An Early Childhood Education Program for American Indians." Contemporary Education 45 (Summer 1974): 278-281.

6760. Kalectaca, Milo, Gerald Knowles, and Robin Butterfield. "To Help--Not to Homogenize Native American Children." Educational Leadership 31 (April 1974): 590-592.

6761. Kaltsounis, Theodore. "The Need to Indianize Indian Schools." Phi Delta Kappan 53 (January 1972): 291-293.

6762. Kersey, Harry A., Jr. "An Adult Education Program for Seminole Indians in Florida." Adult Leadership 19 (March 1971): 281-282, 310.

6763. _____. "Concerning Indian Education." Educational Forum 36 (May 1972): 473-477.

6764. _____. "A Tale of Two Tribes." Educational Forum 38 (November 1973): 50.

6765. Kite, B. Alan. "Art of Ethnic Education." Urban Review 5 (May 1972): 13-22.

6766. Kleinfeld, J. S. "Regionalism in Indian Community Control." Journal of American Indian Education 11 (May 1972): 7-14.

6767. _____. "Sources of Parental Ambivalence toward Education in an Aleut Community." Journal of American Indian Education 10 (January 1971): 8-14.

6768. Kozoll, Charles E. "A Provocative Workshop in Indian Education." Integrated Education 9 (January-February 1971): 29-34.

6769. Kozoll, Charles E., and Edward H. Heneveld. "Shut Up, Teacher!" Journal of American Indian Education 10 (May 1971): 18-25.

6770. Krausen, Roland. "Indians Fight to Retain Cultural Identity." Times Educational Supplement no. 3001

(December 1, 1972): 12.

6771. Lefley, Harriet P. "Effects of a Cultural Heritage Program on the Self-Concept of Miccosukee Indian Children." Journal of Educational Research 67 (July-August 1974): 462-466.

6772. _____. "Social and Familial Correlates of Self-Esteem among American Indian Children." Child Development 45 (September 1974): 829-833.

6773. Leitka, Gene. "Search for Identity Creates Problems for Indian Students." Journal of American Indian Education 11 (October 1971): 7-10.

6774. Lewis, Rod. "Indian Education Legislation." Inequality in Education, no. 10 (December 1971): 19-21.

6775. Long, John, Lena Canyon, and David Churchman. "For Urban Los Angeles: A Tribal American Pre-School." Journal of American Indian Education 13 (October 1973): 7-13.

6776. Lukaczer, Moses. "National School Lunch Program and Indian School Children." Indian Historian 7 (Winter 1974): 17-23.

6777. Mackey, John E., ed. American Indian Task Force Report. New York: Council on Social Work Education, 1973.

6778. Martin, James C. "Self-Confidence of Selected Indian Students." Journal of American Indian Education 13 (May 1974): 32-34.

6779. Martin, Ken. "A Statistical Profile of the California Indian Population." Integrated Education 12 (September-October 1974): 31.

6780. "Menominee Indians." Instructor 81 (January 1972): 47-50.

6781. Meyer, D. Eugene. "We Continue to Massacre the Education of the American Indian." Journal of American Indian Education 11 (January 1972): 18-25.

6782. Moorefield, Story. "Indians in Charge Here." American Education 10 (October 1974): 6-10.

6783. Murphy, Elizabeth A. "The Classroom: Meeting the Needs of the Culturally Different Child—the Navajo Nation." Exceptional Children 40 (May 1974): 601-608.

6784. "Navajo School: A Study in Community Control." Architectural Forum 137 (September 1972): 54-57.

6785. "The NEA Resolution on American Indian Education." Science and

Children 9 (March 1972): 20.

6786. Nelson, Mary. "Problems Indian Students Face." Indian Historian 5 (Summer 1972): 22-24.

6787. "The Now Famous Soon to Be Forgotten." Integrated Education 10 (May-June 1972): 66-67. Havighurst report on Indian education.

6788. "Older Programs in Navajo Area Progressing, New Ones Promising." Journal of American Indian Education 11 (October 1971): 11-15.

6789. Onstad, Gwen, ed. "A Talk with Some Native Americans." Personnel and Guidance Journal 50 (October 1971): 103-108.

6790. Osborn, Lynn R. "The Teaching of Indian and Non-Indian Communication: A Curricular Innovation." Journal of American Indian Education 13 (May 1974): 20-26.

6791. Otis, Morgan. "Indian Education—a Cultural Dilemma." Indian Historian 4 (Fall 1971): 23-26.

6792. Parker, James R., and Martin Zanger. "Indian Children in White Western Wisconsin Schools: The Racial Abyss." Journal of American Indian Education 13 (May 1974): 9-15.

6793. Patch, Kenneth. "Leadership Training Program at Phoenix Indian High School." Journal of American Indian Education 10 (May 1971): 14-17.

6794. Payne, June P. "Pumpkins Are for Jack-o-Lanterns." Journal of American Indian Education 11 (January 1972): 28-29. Head Start Program at the Salt River Indian Reservation.

6795. Pearson, Elizabeth O. "Suggested Teaching Strategies." In Teaching Ethnic Studies: Concepts and Strategies, pp. 220-225. Washington: National Council for the Social Studies, 1973.

6796. Porter, Pat. "The Failure of Indian Education." Contemporary Education 45 (Fall 1973): 62-67.

6797. Redbird-Selam, Helen Marie, and Leroy B. Selam. "Cultural Conflict in the Classroom." Social Education 36 (May 1972): 512-519.

6798. Regan, Timothy F., and Jules Pagano. "The Place of Indian Culture in Adult Education." Adult Leadership 20 (June 1971): 53-55, 76.

6799. Ridley, Jack. "Current Trends in Indian Education." Indian Historian 6 (Fall 1973): 8-13.

6800. Ritzenthaler, Robert E. "Cultural Involution." Journal of American Indian Education 11 (May 1972): 20-22.

6801. Rosendorf, Sidney. "Pa-la-tee-sha: 'They Are Blooming.'" Children Today 3 (March-April 1974): 12-17.

6802. Rosenfelt, Daniel M. "Indian Schools and Community Control." Stanford Law Review 25 (April 1973): 489-550.

6803. _____. "New Regulations for Federal Indian Funds." Inequality in Education, no. 10 (December 1971): 22-26.

6804. Shunatona, Gwen. "Implementing Indian Culture in the Educational Program of BIA Boarding Schools." Indian Historian 5 (Fall 1972): 26-30.

6805. Silko, John R. "Beyond the Law--To Equal Educational Opportunities for Chicanos and Indians." New Mexico Law Review 1 (January 1971): 335-351.

6806. Snow, Albert J. "American Indian Ethno-Science: A Study of the Many Farms Science Project." Journal of American Indian Education 12 (October 1972): 5-11.

6807. _____. "Ethno-Science in American Indian Education." Science Teacher 39 (October 1972): 30-32.

6808. Spang, Alonzo T., Sr. "Understanding the Indian." Personnel and Guidance Journal 50 (October 1971): 96-102.

6809. Steif, William. "Give Us Our Schools." Nation's Schools 90 (July 1972): 32-35.

6810. "Strengthening Educational Opportunities for Indians." American Education 9 (October 1973): 32.

6811. Svensson, Frances E. "What about the First Americans?" Today's Education 62 (January 1973): 39-40, 60.

6812. Tunley, Roul. "Smooth Path at Rough Rock." American Education 7 (March 1971): 15-20.

6813. "Twelfth Annual Indian Education Conference: A Look at Indian Education in the 70's." Journal of American Indian Education 10 (May 1971): 8-9.

6814. Van Boven, Ella. "Rehoboth Mission Offers Retirees Navajo Knowledge." Delta Kappa Gamma Bulletin 37 (Spring 1971): 38-43.

6815. Wax, Murray L. "How Should Schools Be Held Accountable?" Urban Review 5 (January 1972): 11-15.

6816. Webster, Loraine. "Indian Studies with an Emphasis on Science." Science and Children. 9 (March 1972): 11-13.

6817. Weinman, Janice J. "Local Control over Formal Education in Two American-Indian Communities: A Preliminary Step toward Cultural Survival." Review of Educational Research 42 (Fall 1972): 533-539.

6818. White, John Rennardh. "An Experiment with Time: A Proposal for Positive Identity Reinforcement through Historical/Cultural Education for Native Americans." Indian Historian 5 (Winter 1972): 31-40.

6819. Wolcott, Harry F. "The Teacher as an Enemy." Practical Anthropology 19 (September-October 1972): 226-230.

6820. Woodward, Richard G. "Title VIII and the Oglala Sioux." Phi Delta Kappan 55 (December 1973): 249-251.

6821. Yaz, William [pseud.], "Teachers and Administrators in American Indian Education." Indian Historian 6 (Summer 1973): 18-22.

Other material can be found listed in *Education Index*, in *Research in Education* (ERIC), and in *Current Index to Journals in Education* (CIJE).

TEACHING ABOUT INDIANS

Concern has been expressed in recent years about how the Indian is portrayed in textbooks and in the school curriculum. Efforts have been made to correct the white bias and to present an accurate picture of Indian culture and history, and special courses and programs on Indians have been instituted. Writings on these topics are listed here.

6822. Abel, Midge B. "American Indian Life as Portrayed in Children's Literature." Elementary English 50 (February 1973): 202-208.

6823. Ballas, Donald J. "Geography and the American Indian." Journal of Geography 65 (April 1966): 156-168.

6824. Blanche, Jerry D. "Ignoring It Won't Make It Go Away." Journal of American Indian Education 12 (October 1973): 1-4.

6825. Bowker, Lee H. "Red and Black in Contemporary American History Texts: A Content Analysis." In Native Americans Today: Sociological Perspectives, edited by Howard M. Bahr and others, pp. 101-110. New York: Harper and Row, 1972.

6826. Brickman, Helen M. "Bringing

Students Up-to-Date on American Indians." *Missionary Review of the World* 53 (March 1930): 207-210.

6827. Buffalohead, W. Roger. "Review and Evaluation: Native American Studies Programs." In *Indian Voices: The First Convocation of American Indian Scholars*, pp. 161-167. San Francisco: Indian Historian Press, 1970.

6828. DiMino, Angelo V. "Stop Stereotyping Indian Studies: Filming Seneca History." *Instructor* 82 (November 1972): 100-103.

6829. Falkenhagen, Maria, Carole Johnson, and Michael A. Balasa. "The Treatment of Native Americans in Recent Children's Literature." *Integrated Education* 11 (July-October 1973): 58-59.

6830. Fisher, Frank L. "The Influences of Reading and Discussion on the Attitudes of Fifth Graders toward American Indians." Ed.D. dissertation, University of California, 1965.

6831. _____. "Influences of Reading and Discussion on the Attitudes of Fifth Graders toward American Indians." *Journal of Educational Research* 62 (November 1968): 130-134.

6832. Fisher, Laura. "All Chiefs, No Indians: What Children's Books Say about American Indians." *Elementary English* 51 (February 1974): 185-189.

6833. Gearing, Frederick O. "Why Indians?" *Social Education* 32 (February 1968): 128-131, 146.

6834. Gribskov, Margaret Elise T. H. "A Critical Analysis of Textbook Accounts of the Role of Indians in American History." Ph.D. dissertation, University of Oregon, 1973.

6835. Henderson, Earl E. "What Shall We Teach about the American Indians?" *Arizona Teacher* 51 (September 1962): 11, 22. Also published in *Wisconsin Journal of Education* 95 (November 1962): 17-18, and in other educational journals.

6836. Henry, Jeannette. "The American Indian in American History." In *Indian Voices: The First Convocation of American Indian Scholars*, pp. 105-117. San Francisco: Indian Historian Press, 1970.

6837. _____. "Native Americans in the Textbook Literature." In *Indian Voices: The First Convocation of American Indian Scholars*, pp. 365-373. San Francisco: Indian Historian Press, 1970.

6838. _____. "Our Inaccurate Textbooks." *Indian Historian* 1 (December 1967): 21-24.

6839. _____. "Textbook Distortion of the Indian." *Civil Rights Digest* 1 (Summer 1968): 4-8.

6840. _____. Textbooks and the American Indian. San Francisco: American Indian Historical Society, 1970.

6841. Hertzberg, Hazel W. "Issues in Teaching about American Indians." *Social Education* 36 (May 1972): 481-485.

6842. Hughes, J. Donald. "The De-racialization of Historical Atlases: A Modest Proposal." *Indian Historian* 7 (Summer 1974): 55-56.

6843. Keller, Robert H., Jr. "On Teaching Indian History: Legal Jurisdiction in Chippewa Treaties." *Ethnohistory* 19 (Summer 1972): 209-218.

6844. Lenarcic, R. J. "The Forgotten American--Remembered." *New York State Education* 58 (April 1971): 22-23.

6845. Lewis, Robert W. "English and American Indian Studies." *Indian Historian* 6 (Fall 1973): 32-37, 54.

6846. Lukes, Edward A. "Ethno-History of Indians in the U.S." *Indian Historian* 5 (Spring 1972): 23-25.

6847. McLaughlin, G. R. "High School History Course Highlights Indian Culture." *Montana Education* 44 (April 1968): 18.

6848. Mallam, R. Clark. "Academic Treatment of the Indian in Public School Texts and Literature." *Journal of American Indian Education* 13 (October 1973): 14-19.

6849. Medicine, Beatrice. "The Anthropologist and American Indian Studies Programs." *Indian Historian* 4 (Spring 1971): 15-19.

6850. Mickinock, Rey. "The Plight of the American Indian." *Library Journal* 96 (September 15, 1971): 2848-2851. Treatment of Indians in books for children and young adults.

6851. Morgan, James, and Marilyn Morgan. "About Textbooks." *Indian Historian* 2 (Spring 1969): 39-40.

6852. Napier, Georgia Pierce. "A Study of the North American Indian Character in Twenty Selected Children's Books." Ed.D. dissertation, University of Arkansas, 1970.

6853. Sprague, Arthur William, Jr. "Attitudinal Changes in Secondary School Students as a Result of Studying an Ethnohistory of the Kiowa Indians." Ph.D. dissertation, Ohio State University, 1972.

6854. Staniford, Edward F. "The California Indians: A Critique of Their Treatment by Historians." Ethnohistory 18 (Spring 1971): 119-125.

6855. Talbot, Steve. "Why the Native American Heritage Should Be Taught in College." Indian Historian 7 (Winter 1974): 42-44.

6856. Van Wie, Ethel K. "Understanding of Indian Life Leads to Mutual Respect." Delta Kappa Gamma Bulletin 38 (Winter 1972): 45-48.

6857. Vogel, Virgil J. The Indian in American History. Chicago: Integrated Education Associates, 1968.

6858. _____. "The Indian in American History." Social Education 33 (February 1969): 200-203.

6859. _____. "The Indian in American History Textbooks." Integrated Education 6 (May-June 1968): 16-32.

6860. Webb, B. G. "Teaching a Mini Course about the American Indian." School and Community 61 (October 1974): 32-34.

14
Indian Health

The health of the Indians has been of concern to whites, especially after 1900 when the progress of the Indians was seriously hindered by disease. A great many studies on Indian health, many of them technical, have been made in recent years. The following bibliographies indicate historical as well as technical studies.

6861. Barrow, Mark V., Jerry D. Niswander, and Robert Fortuine. Health and Disease of American Indians North of Mexico: A Bibliography, 1800-1969. Gainesville: University of Florida Press, 1972.

6862. Index Medicus. 1960--. Washington: National Library of Medicine, Public Health Service, 1960--. A monthly list of current articles. See also annual Cumulated Index Medicus, 1960--. The Index Medicus was preceded by other indexes to medical literature.

HEALTH OF THE INDIANS: GENERAL WORKS

The health of the Indians has been the subject of a number of general studies and articles of current comment. These works are arranged here by chronological periods.

Historical Studies and Accounts to 1900

6863. Allen, Virginia Ruth. "Health and Medical Care of the Southern Plains Indians, 1868-1892." Ph.D. dissertation, Oklahoma State University, 1973.

6864. Ashburn, P. M. "How Disease Came with the White Man: Stories of Early Medical Milestones in America." Hygeia 14 (March 1936): 205-207; (April 1936): 310-312; (May 1936): 438-440; (June 1936): 514-516; (July 1936): 636-637.

6865. Autry, Stephen, and R. Palmer Howard. "Health Care in the Cherokee Seminaries, Asylums and Prisons: 1851-1906." Journal of the Oklahoma State Medical Association 65 (December 1972): 495-502.

6866. Clinton, Fred S. "The First

Hospital and Training School for Nurses in the Indian Territory, Now Oklahoma." Chronicles of Oklahoma 25 (Autumn 1947): 218-228.

6867. Cobb, Carolus M. "Some Medical Practices among the New England Indians and Early Settlers." Boston Medical and Surgical Journal 177 (July 26, 1917): 97-105.

6868. Cook, Sherburne F. The Epidemic of 1830-1833 in California and Oregon. University of California Publications in American Archaeology and Ethnology, volume 43, no. 3. Berkeley: University of California Press, 1955.

6869. _____. "The Significance of Disease in the Extinction of the New England Indians." Human Biology 45 (September 1973): 485-508.

6870. Crockett, Bernice N. "Health Conditions in the Indian Territory from the Civil War to 1890." Chronicles of Oklahoma 36 (Spring 1958): 21-39.

6871. _____. "The Origin and Development of Public Health in Oklahoma, 1830-1930." Ph.D. dissertation, University of Oklahoma, 1953.

6872. Darling, Dr. "Indian Diseases and Remedies." Boston Medical and Surgical Journal 34 (February 4, 1846): 9-13.

6873. Duffy, John. "Smallpox and the Indians in the American Colonies." Bulletin of the History of Medicine 25 (July-August 1951): 324-341.

6874. Grinnell, Fordyce. "Indian Questions from a Medical Standpoint." Cincinnati Lancet and Observer 21 (February 1878): 157-169.

6875. Hunter, John D. "Remarks on Several Diseases Prevalent among the Western Indians, with Some Account of Their Remedies and Modes of Treatment." American Medical Recorder 5 (July 1822): 408-417.

6876. _____. "Remarks on the Diseases of the Females of Several Indian Tribes West of the Mississippi." New-York

Medical and Physical Journal 1 (July, August, and September 1822): 304-315.

6877. Jensen, Marguerite. "The Mandan Tragedy." Indian Historian 5 (Fall 1972): 18-22. Smallpox epidemic.

6878. Kneeland, Jonathan. "On Some Causes Tending to Promote the Extinction of the Aborigines of America." Transactions of the American Medical Association 15 (1864): 253-260.

6879. _____. "Remarks on the Social and Sanitary Condition of the Onondaga Indians." American Medical Times 9 (July 2, 1864): 4-6.

6880. Parrish, Joseph. "Account of a Fever Which Prevailed among the Indians on the Island of Nantucket, in 1763-4." Eclectic Repertory, and Analytical Review, Medical and Philosophical 1 (April 1811): 364-366.

6881. Pusey, William Allen. "The Smallpox Epidemic among the Mandan Indians in 1837." Journal of the American Medical Association 95 (December 27, 1930): 1992-1994.

6882. Quaife, Milo M., ed. "The Smallpox Epidemic on the Upper Missouri." Mississippi Valley Historical Review 17 (September 1930): 278-299. Journal of Francis Chardon, 1837.

6883. Scott, Leslie M. "Indian Diseases as Aids to Pacific Northwest Settlement." Oregon Historical Quarterly 29 (June 1928): 144-161.

6884. Simmons, James Stevens. "The Influence of Epidemic Diseases on the Early History of the Western Hemisphere." Military Surgeon 71 (August 1932): 133-143.

6885. Stearn, E. Wagner, and Allen E. Stearn. The Effect of Smallpox on the Destiny of the Amerindian. Boston: Bruce Humphries, 1945.

6886. Waldron, Martha M. "The Indian Health Question." Lend a Hand 5 (November 1890): 766-774.

6887. Williams, Herbert U. "The Epidemic of the Indians of New England, 1616-1620, with Remarks on Native American Infections." Johns Hopkins Hospital Bulletin 20 (November 1909): 340-349.

6888. Woodruff, Charles E. "Diseases of Northern California Indians." Medical Record 39 (January 24, 1891): 104-106.

Studies and Comments, 1901-1920

6889. Eastman, Charles A. "The Indian's Health Problem." American Indian Magazine 4 (April-June 1916): 139-145.

6890. _____. "The Indian's Health Problem." Popular Science Monthly 86 (January 1915): 49-54.

6891. Geare, R. I. "Some Diseases Prevalent among Indians of the Southwest and Their Treatment." Medical World 33 (August 1915): 305-310.

6892. "Government Health Work among the Indians." Outlook 114 (September 27, 1916): 168-169.

6893. Hrdlicka, Ales. "Diseases of the Indians, More Especially of the Southwest United States and Northern Mexico." Washington Medical Annals 4 (January 1906): 372-394.

6894. "Indians Medically Neglected." Survey 45 (December 25, 1920): 466.

6895. Lake, A. D. "The Civilized Indian, His Physical Characteristics and Some of His Diseases." New York Medical Journal 75 (March 8, 1902): 406-409.

6896. Murphy, Joseph A. "Health Problems of the Indians." Annals of the American Academy of Political and Social Science 37 (March 1911): 347-353.

Studies and Comments, 1921-1940

6897. Emerson, Haven. "Health of American Indians." Journal of the American Medical Association 88 (February 5, 1927): 424.

6898. Fleming, Henry Craig. "Medical Observations Made on the Zuñi Indians." Nation's Health 5 (August 15, 1923): 506-508, 580.

6899. Guthrie, M. C. "Health of American Indians." Journal of the American Medical Association 88 (April 9, 1927): 1198-1199.

6900. _____. "The Health of the American Indian." Public Health Reports 44 (April 19, 1929): 945-957.

6901. Hamlin, H. "A Health Survey of the Seminole Indians." Yale Journal of Biology and Medicine 6 (December 1933): 155-177.

6902. "Health of American Indians." Journal of the American Medical Association 88 (January 8, 1927): 104-105.

6903. Hoffman, Frederick L. "Are the Indians Dying Out?" American Journal of Public Health 20 (June 1930): 609-614.

6904. Jones, Howard. "Historical Medicine: Indian and White Man." Medical Journal and Record 134 (September 16, 1931): 297-298.

6905. Marshall, Louise R. "Health Studies

among the Indians." Trained Nurse and Hospital Review 97 (July 1936): 41-46.

6906. "Medical Needs of Our Indians." Literary Digest 85 (April 11, 1925): 23-24.

6907. Tillim, Sidney J. "Health among the Navajos." Southwestern Medicine 20 (July 1936): 273, 276-277; (August 1936): 310-313, 317-319; (September 1936): 355; (October 1936): 388-391; (November 1936): 432-433.

6908. Townsend, James G. "Disease and the Indian." Scientific Monthly 47 (December 1938): 479-495.

6909. _____. "Indian Health--Past, Present, and Future." In The Changing Indian, edited by Oliver La Farge, pp. 28-41. Norman: University of Oklahoma Press, 1942.

6910. Wissler, Clark. "Distribution of Deaths among American Indians." Human Biology 8 (May 1936): 223-231.

6911. _____. "The Effect of Civilization upon the Length of Life of the American Indian." Scientific Monthly 43 (July 1936): 5-13.

Studies and Comments, 1941-1960

6912. Adair, John, Kurt Deuschle, and Walsh McDermott. "Patterns of Health and Disease among the Navahos." Annals of the American Academy of Political and Social Science 311 (May 1957): 80-94.

6913. Braasch, W. F., B. J. Branton, and A. J. Chesley. "Survey of Medical Care among the Upper Midwest Indians." Journal of the American Medical Association 139 (January 22, 1949): 220-226.

6914. Cameron, Charles M., Jr. "Cherokee Indian Health Survey." Public Health Reports 71 (November 1956): 1086-1088.

6915. DeLien, H., and J. Nixon Hadley. "How to Recognize an Indian Health Problem." Human Organization 11 (Fall 1952): 29-33.

6916. Emerson, Haven. "Indian Health--Victim of Neglect." Survey 87 (May 1951): 219-221.

6917. Fleming, Arthur S. "Indian Health." Public Health Reports 74 (June 1959): 521-522.

6918. Foard, Fred T. "The Health of the American Indians." American Journal of Public Health 39 (November 1949): 1403-1406. Reprinted in American Indian 5 (Spring 1950): 47-52.

6919. French, Frank S., James R. Shaw, and Joseph O. Dean. "The Navajo Health Problem, Its Genesis, Proportions, and a Plan for Its Solution." Military Medicine 116 (June 1955): 451-454.

6920. Hadley, J. Nixon. "Health Conditions among Navajo Indians." Public Health Reports 70 (September 1955): 831-836.

6921. Haldeman, Jack C. "Problems of Alaskan Eskimos, Indians, Aleuts." Public Health Reports 66 (July 20, 1951): 912-917.

6922. "Indian Massacre--New Style." American Journal of Public Health and the Nation's Health 39 (November 1949): 1469-1470.

6923. "The Indians' Health and Public Health." American Journal of Public Health 44 (November 1954): 1461-1463.

6924. McKay, Raymond C. "Indian Health Needs and Services." American Indian 6 (Summer 1951): 29-32.

6925. Moorman, Lewis J. "Health of the Navajo-Hopi Indians: General Report of the American Medical Association Team." Journal of the American Medical Association 139 (February 5, 1949): 370-376.

6926. Salsbury, C. G. "Health and Tuberculosis Problems among Indians: Indian Health Problems." Transactions of the National Tuberculosis Association, 1953, pp. 484-487.

6927. _____. "White Medicine for the Red Man." Modern Hospital 74 (June 1950): 51-53.

6928. Shaw, James Raymond. "Meeting the Challenge of Indian Health." American Indian 7 (Winter 1956): 3-12.

6929. Spencer, Steven M. "They're Saving Lives in Navajo-Land." Saturday Evening Post 227 (April 23, 1955): 30-31 +.

6930. Stewart, Omer C. "Indian Health and Yours." Delphian Quarterly 34 (April 1951): 39-41.

6931. Watson, Editha L. "Giving Health Back to the Indians." Hygeia 24 (October 1946): 750-753, 790-791.

6932. "Will They Give It Back to the Indians?" Pennsylvania Medical Journal 44 (October 1940): 63-68.

6933. Winters, S. R. "Health for the Indians." Hygeia 22 (September 1944): 680-682, 694.

6934. Woods, Ozro T. "Health among the Navajo Indians." Journal of the American Medical Association 135 (December 13, 1947): 981-983.

Studies and Comments, 1961--

6935. Archibald, Charles W. "The Mainstream--Where Indians Drown." HSMHA

Health Reports 86 (June 1971): 489-494.

6936. Bean, L. J., and Corrine Wood. "The Crisis in Indian Health: A California Example." *Indian Historian* 2 (Fall 1969): 29-32, 36.

6937. *Biomedical Challenges Presented by the American Indian.* WHO, Pan American Health Organization, Scientific Publication 165. Washington: Pan American Health Organization, 1968.

6938. Bourgeois, Marie J. "The Present-Day Health and Illness Beliefs and Practices of the Seneca Indians." Ph.D. dissertation, Catholic University of America, 1968.

6939. "Committee on Indian Health." *Pediatrics* 48 (October 1971): 657-662.

6940. Fahy, Agnes, and Carl Muschenheim. "Third National Conference on American Indian Health." *Journal of the American Medical Association* 194 (December 6, 1965): 1093-1096.

6941. Findley, David. "Some Health Problems of the Navajo Indians." *Nebraska State Medical Journal* 49 (June 1964): 326-332.

6942. Hirschhorn, Norbert, and Gary H. Spivey. "Health and the White Mountain Apache." *Journal of Infectious Diseases* 126 (September 1972): 348-350.

6943. "Lo, the Poor Indian." *New England Journal of Medicine* 278 (January 4, 1968): 47-48.

6944. McCreary, Charles, Charles Deegan, Jr., and David Thompson. "Indian Health in Minnesota." *Minnesota Medicine* 56, Supplement 2 (October 1973): 87-90.

6945. Van Duzen, Jean L. "Medical Practice on the Navajo Reservation." *Journal of the American Medical Women's Association* 19 (July 1964): 558-560.

6946. Wallace, Helen M. "The Health of American Indian Children." *American Journal of Diseases of Children* 125 (March 1973): 449-454.

6947. _____. "The Health of American Indian Children." *Health Service Reports* 87 (November 1972): 867-876.

6948. _____. "The Health of American Indian Children: A Survey of Current Problems and Needs." *Clinical Pediatrics* 12 (February 1973): 83-87.

HEALTH SERVICES AND PROGRAMS

Health Services

Providing medical and dental care has been an important aspect of government re-

lations with the Indians. Reports and comments on these services and on the problems and needs that exist are listed here. Included are items about hospitals and about nursing.

6949. Abramowitz, Joseph. "The Implementation of a Program for Utilizing Auxiliaries: The Experience of the Indian Health Service." *Journal of Public Health Dentistry* 32 (Summer 1972): 142-148.

6950. Abramowitz, Joseph, and Robert E. Mecklenburg. "Quality of Care in Dental Practice: The Approach of the Indian Health Service." *Journal of Public Health Dentistry* 32 (Spring 1972): 90-99.

6951. Adair, John, and Kurt W. Deuschle. *The People's Health: Medicine and Anthropology in a Navajo Community.* New York: Appleton-Century-Crofts, 1970.

6952. _____. "Some Problems of the Physicians on the Navajo Reservation." *Human Organization* 16 (Winter 1958): 19-23.

6953. "American Indians Trained as Physician's Assistants." *HSMHA Health Reports* 86 (July 1971): 596.

6954. "APHA Supports the Indian Health Service." *American Journal of Public Health* 60 (July 1970): 1313.

6955. Arnold, Oren. "Sagebrush Surgeon." *Saturday Evening Post* 217 (November 18, 1944): 16-17, 67, 69-70. Dr. Clarence Salsbury and hospital for Navajos.

6956. Baggish, David Alan, and Chase Patterson Kimball. "The Problem of Transportation to Medical Facilities on an Indian Reservation." *Medical Care* 11 (November-December 1973): 501-508.

6957. Boggs, Donald C., and M. Anthony Schork. "Motivation and Retention of Dental Officers in the Indian Health Service." *Journal of Public Health Dentistry* 34 (Summer 1974): 146-160.

6958. Boynton, Ruth E., and Hortense Hilbert. "Government Medical Care Betters Health Conditions of Chippewa Indian Tribes." *Nation's Health* 8 (May 15, 1926): 306-307, 366.

6959. Bozof, Richard P. "Some Navajo Attitudes toward Available Medical Care." *American Journal of Public Health* 62 (December 1972): 1620-1624.

6960. Brodt, E. William. "Urbanization and Health Planning: Challenge and Opportunity for the American Indian Community." *American Journal of Public Health* 63 (August 1973): 694-701.

6961. Corry, R. Dan, and Louis F. Cannavale. "Expanded Functions Training for Dental Assistants in the Indian Health Service." Journal of the American Dental Association 85 (December 1972): 1343-1348.

6962. Crain, Kenneth C. "US Hospitals Bringing Health to Native Indians, Eskimos: Government Institutions Surmount Hardship to Achieve Great Work." Hospital Management 53 (April 1942): 18-19, 66, 68.

6963. Crockett, David C. "Medicine among the American Indians." HSMHA Health Reports 86 (May 1971): 399-407.

6964. Davis, Burnet M. "The Health Program of the Bureau of Indian Affairs." Military Surgeon 112 (March 1953): 171-174.

6965. DeGeyndt, Willy. "Health Behavior and Health Needs of Urban Indians in Minneapolis." Health Services Reports 88 (April 1973): 360-366.

6966. Deuschle, Kurt W. "Training and Use of Medical Auxiliaries in a Navajo Community." Public Health Reports 78 (June 1963): 461-469.

6967. Deuschle, Kurt, and John Adair. "An Interdisciplinary Approach to Public Health on the Navajo Reservation: Medical and Anthropological Aspects." Annals of the New York Academy of Sciences 84 (December 8, 1960): 887-905.

6968. Dorn, Christopher M. "Attitudes of 30 American Indian Women toward Birth Control." Health Services Reports 87 (August-September 1972): 658-663.

6969. Foard, Fred T. "The Federal Government and American Indians' Health." Journal of the American Medical Association 142 (February 4, 1950): 328-331.

6970. "For Healthier Little Indians." Today's Health 43 (July 1965): 12-14.

6971. Gerken, Edna A. "Influencing the Health Practices of Primitive People." Medical Woman's Journal 47 (January 1940): 25-30.

6972. Guidotti, Tee L. "Health Care for a Rural Minority: Lessons from the Modoc Indian Country in California." California Medicine 118 (April 1973): 98-104.

6973. Harple, Louise. "Snow in Navajoland." American Journal of Nursing 49 (September 1949): 554-556.

6974. Hoshiwara, Isao. "Ophthalmological Care for American Indians." Archives of Ophthalmology 86 (October 1971): 368.

6975. "Indian Health Services Transferred to PHS." Public Health Reports 69 (September 1954): 866.

6976. "Indian Medical Service to Public Health Service." American Journal of Public Health 44 (November 1954): 1449.

6977. Kane, Robert L. "Community Medicine on the Navajo Reservation." HSMHA Health Reports 86 (August 1971): 733-740.

6978. Kane, Robert L., and Rosalie Kane. "Determination of Health Care Expectations among Navajo Consumers: Consumers in a Federal Care System." Medical Care 10 (September-October 1972): 421-429.

6979. _____. Federal Health Care (with Reservations!). New York: Springer Publishing Company, 1972.

6980. Kemberling, Sidney R. "The Indian Health Service: Commentary on a Commentary." Pediatrics 51 (June 1973): 1066-1067.

6981. Kohen, Daniel P., Gerald Yost, and Jerry Lyle. "Letter: Indian Health Services, Continued." Pediatrics 52 (November 1973): 756.

6982. Kunstadter, Peter. "Culture Change, Social Structure, and Health Behavior: A Quantitative Study of Clinic Use among the Apaches of the Mescalero Reservation." Ph.D. dissertation, University of Michigan, 1961.

6983. Lathrop, Robert L. "Expanded Function from the Perspective of Dental Assistants of the Indian Health Service." Journal of the American Dental Association 82 (March 1971): 591-599.

6984. Layton, Jack. "The Community Health Medic Physician-Assistant Training Program." Arizona Medicine 28 (August 1971): 604.

6985. Loughlin, Bernice W. "Aide Training Reaches the Navajo Reservation." American Journal of Nursing 63 (July 1963): 106-109.

6986. McDermott, Walsh, Kurt Deuschle, John Adair, Hugh Fulmer, and Bernice Loughlin. "Introducing Modern Medicine in a Navajo Community." Science 131 (January 22, 1960): 197-205; (January 29, 1960): 280-287.

6987. McDermott, Walsh, Kurt W. Deuschle, and Clifford R. Barnett. "Health Care Experiment at Many Farms." Science 175 (January 7, 1972): 23-31.

6988. McGibony, J. R. "Health Center for 6000: White Man's Medicine Puts the 'Indian Sign' on Disease at the New Hospital of the Pima Agency." Modern Hospital 60 (January 1943): 60-61.

6989. Middleton, Arthur E. "Supplanting the Medicine Man." Modern Hospital 19 (July 1922): 41-44.

6990. Mortimer, Edward A., Jr. "Indian Health: An Unmet Problem." Pediatrics 51 (June 1973): 1065-1066.

6991. Mundt, Raymond. "Indian Medical Service." Military Surgeon 86 (February 1940): 103-106.

6992. Murphy, Joseph A. "The Work of the United States Medical Service." Survey 33 (January 23, 1915): 444-447.

6993. Old, H. Norman. "Sanitation Problems of the American Indians." American Journal of Public Health 43 (February 1953): 210-215.

6994. Owen, F. Carrington. "Improving Nursing Skills--a Program for Indian Women." Nursing Outlook 19 (April 1971): 258-259.

6995. Perrot, George St. J., and Margaret D. West. "Health Services for American Indians." Public Health Reports 72 (July 1957): 565-570.

6996. Peters, Joseph P. "Health Services to the American Indian: A Historical Summary." Westerners Brand Book (New York) 10 (1963): 51-55.

6997. Pijoan, Michel, and Charles S. McCammon. "The Problem of Medical Care for Navajo Indians." Journal of the American Medical Association 140 (July 23, 1949): 1013-1015.

6998. Posner, Michael Kagan. "Opportunities for Pediatric Training in the Indian Health Service." Pediatrics 49 (June 1972): 932.

6999. "Public Health Nursing for Montana Indians." Public Health Reports 74 (April 1959): 325-327.

7000. Rabeau, Erwin S., and Angel Reaud. "Evaluation of PHS Program Providing Family Planning Services for American Indians." American Journal of Public Health 59 (August 1969): 1331-1338.

7001. Rice, P. F. "The Indian Medical Service." Journal-Lancet 35 (August 15, 1915): 429-435.

7002. Riley, Harris D. "Indian Health Service." Pediatrics 50 (October 1972): 663-664.

7003. Rogers, Maria L., and Edward J. Fitzgerald. "New Medicine for the Sick Indian." Nation 138 (March 21, 1934): 326-327.

7004. "Rosebud Reveals the Responsiveness of the Indians: A Health Experiment That Won Permanence." Red Cross Courier 6 (March 1, 1927): 16-17.

7005. Salsbury, C. G. "Medical Work in Navajoland." American Journal of Nursing 32 (April 1932): 415-416.

7006. Sayre, Blaine M. "An Objective Look at PHS Doctors and Indian Patients." Medical Times 101 (May 1973): 48-51.

7007. Schlafman, Irving H. "Health Systems Research to Deliver Comprehensive Services to Indians." Public Health Reports 84 (August 1969): 697-704.

7008. Schnur, Leo. "Navajos Train Men to Counteract Medicine Men." Modern Hospital 59 (November 1942): 80.

7009. Schoenfeld, Lawrence S., R. Jeannine Lyerly, and Sheldon I. Miller. "We Like Us: The Attitudes of the Mental Health Staff toward Other Agencies on the Navajo Reservation." Mental Hygiene 55 (April 1971): 171-173.

7010. Shaw, James R. "Guarding the Health Care of Our Indian Citizens." Hospitals 31 (April 16, 1957): 38-44.

7011. Sievers, Maurice L. "The New Phoenix Indian Medical Center: A History of Its Predecessors." Arizona Medicine 28 (June 1971): 435-438.

7012. Sloan, Raymond P. "The White Man Becomes the Indian's Friend." Modern Hospital 43 (October 1934): 41-44.

7013. Sondheimer, Henry M. "Letter: Indian Health Services--by One Who Provides It." Pediatrics 53 (June 1974): 950.

7014. Stevenson, Albert H. "Sanitary Facilities Construction Program for Indians and Alaska Natives." Public Health Reports 76 (April 1961): 317-322.

7015. Taylor, Margaret S., Max Van Sandt, and Edward Terry. "Consultation by the 'Team' Method--an Experiment in Bureau of Indian Affairs Hospitals." Military Surgeon 113 (October 1953): 291-294.

7016. Tiber, Bertha M. "The Indian Service in Alaska." American Journal of Nursing 42 (October 1942): 1114-1118.

7017. _____. "Nursing among the Navajo Indians." American Journal of Nursing 49 (September 1949): 552-553.

7018. Tobey, James A. "Federal Health Work among the Indians: An Account of the Health Section of the Bureau of Indian Affairs." Nation's Health 4 (November 15, 1922): 687-689.

7019. Townsend, J. G. "Medical and Health Work among the North American Indians." Health Officer 2 (December 1937): 350-352.

7020. Uhrich, Richard B. "Tribal Community Health Representatives of the Indian Health Service." Public Health Reports 84 (November 1969): 965-970.

7021. Vincentia, Sister. "Our Students Learn from the Indians." Nursing Outlook 9 (June 1961): 356-358.

7022. Wagner, Carruth J. "Health Services for Indians and Alaskan Natives." Journal-Lancet 84 (September 1964): 289-292.

7023. Walker, Frances. "Bridging a Cultural Gap for Better Patient Care." Military Medicine 139 (January 1974): 26-29.

7024. Watson, Editha L. "Indian Hospital." Hygeia 17 (December 1939): 1110-1113, 1141.

7025. Westermeyer, Joseph, Richard Tanner, and Jean Smelker. "Change in Health Care Services for Indian Americans." Minnesota Medicine 57 (September 1974): 732-734.

7026. Wiens, Agnes A. "Nursing Service on a Chippewa Reservation." American Journal of Nursing 61 (April 1961): 92-93.

7027. Work, Hubert. "The Indian Medical Service." Military Surgeon 55 (October 1924): 425-428.

7028. Worley, J. F. "Indian Service Health Activities in Alaska." Health Officer 4 (October 1939): 192-201.

7029. Zinamon, J. Martin. "Indian Health Service." Pediatrics 50 (October 1972): 663.

Governmental agencies dealing with Indian health (Public Health Service, Indian Health Service) issue serial and other publications that contain important information on Indian health problems and programs. The names of the publications and of the issuing agencies vary. See, for example, various annual reports, Dental Services for American Indians and Alaska Natives, Indian Vital Statistics, Indian Health Trends and Services, and Report on Indian Health.

Diet and Nutrition

7030. Adams, Eleanor. "Upgrading Indian Nutrition--through Youth." Forecast for Home Economics 14 (October 1968): F44-F45.

7031. Bass, Mary A., and Lucille M. Wakefield. "Nutrient Intake and Food Patterns of Indians on Standing Rock Reservation." Journal of the American Dietetic Association 64 (January 1974): 36-41.

7032. Bosley, Bertlyn. "Nutrition in the Indian Health Program." Journal of the American Dietetic Association 35 (September 1959): 905-909.

7033. Carpenter, Thorne M., and Morris Steggerda. "The Food of the Present-Day Navajo Indians of New Mexico and Arizona." Journal of Nutrition 18 (September 1939): 297-305.

7034. Curry, Marie. "Hungry Land--Hungry People." Nursing Outlook 18 (July 1970): 32-35.

7035. Darby, William J., and others. "A Study of the Dietary Background and Nutriture of the Navajo." Journal of Nutrition 60, Supplement 2 (November 1956): 1-85.

7036. Hesse, Frank G. "A Dietary Study of the Pima Indian." American Journal of Clinical Nutrition 7 (September-October 1959): 532-537.

7037. Larkin, Frances A., and Anita M. Sandretto. "Dietary Patterns and the Use of Commodity Foods in a Potawatomi Indian Community." Journal of Home Economics 62 (June 1970): 385-388.

7038. Longman, Doris P. "Working with Pueblo Indians in New Mexico." Journal of the American Dietetic Association 47 (December 1965): 470-473.

7039. Mayberry, Ruben H. "A Survey of Chronic Disease and Diet in Seminole Indians in Oklahoma." American Journal of Clinical Nutrition 13 (September 1963): 127-134.

7040. Moore, William M., Marjorie Silverberg, and Merrill S. Read, eds. Nutrition, Growth and Development of North American Indian Children. Washington: Government Printing Office, 1972.

7041. Newman, Marshall T. "Adaptations in the Physique of American Aborigines to Nutritional Factors." Human Biology 32 (September 1960): 288-313.

7042. Payne, William. "Food for First Citizens." Civil Rights Digest 2 (Fall 1969): 1-4.

7043. Walter, John P. "Two Poverties Equal Many Hungry Indians: An Economic and Social Study of Nutrition." American Journal of Economics and Sociology 33 (January 1974): 33-44.

7044. Wenberg, Burness G., Margaret T. Boedeker, and Cecilia Shuck. "Nutritive Value of Diets in Indian Boarding Schools in the Dakotas: Observations on Growth and Development of Adolescent Sioux Indian Girls." Journal of the American Dietetic Association 46 (February 1965): 96-102.

Health Education

7045. Bailey, Flora L. "Suggested Techniques for Inducing Navajo Women to Accept Hospitalization during Childbirth and for Implementing Health Education." American Journal of Public Health 38 (October 1948): 1418-1423.

7046. Carl, Edward L. "Navajo Children

Learn Nutrition." School Executive 74
(November 1954): 60-61

7047. Chesley, A. J. "Is the Indian Susceptible to Health Education." American
Journal of Public Health 15 (February
1925): 133-136.

7048. Gerken, Edna A. "Development of a
Health Education Program: Navajo Indians."
American Journal of Public Health 30
(August 1940): 915-920.

7049. Jonz, Wallace W. "Staffing Health
Education Programs for American Indians."
Public Health Reports 81 (July 1966):
627-630.

7050. Mast, Elta Mae. "Ten Years of National Level Health Education Administration in Indian Health, 1951 to 1961."
Ph.D. dissertation, University of North
Carolina, 1966.

7051. Mico, Paul R. "A Task for Amerindian School Health Education." Journal
of School Health 32 (October 1962): 316-
320.

7052. Werden, Patricia. "Health Education
for Indian Students." Journal of School
Health 44 (June 1974): 319-323.

Doctors among the Indians

Some insight into health services can be
obtained from reminiscences and other accounts written by agency physicians or
other medical personnel. Some of those
listed here are from the nineteenth century.

7053. Crouch, Earl R., Jr. "Working with
the Cherokees and Creeks." Medical
Times 101 (May 1973): 52-56.

7054. Gregg, Elinor D. The Indians and
the Nurse. Norman: University of Oklahoma Press, 1965. Personal reminiscences.

7055. Grinnell, Fordyce. "Some Reminiscences of Indian Practice." California
State Journal of Medicine 7 (May 1909):
174-177.

7056. Karam, A. H. "Medicine Man from the
East." Southwest Review 52 (Autumn
1967): 393-403.

7057. Kartchner, Mark M. "Two Years with
American Indians." Resident Physician
11 (April 1965): 70-85.

7058. _____. "Two Years with the American Indians." Medical Times 93 (May
1965): 124a-142a.

7059. Mandell, Judith R. "A Wife's View
of Working with the Navajo." Medical
Times 101 (May 1973): 57-58.

7060. Michael, Lawrence F. "U.S. Indian
Service--Department of Medicine and

Surgery Cheyenne River Sioux Indians."
Journal-Lancet 51 (June 1, 1931): 363-
368; (June 15, 1931): 381-385.

7061. Moody, Charles S. "A Physician among
the Indians." American Journal of Clinical Medicine 14 (February 1907): 161-
167; (March 1907): 310-314.

7062. Neave, James L. "Medical Practice
among the Indians." American Journal of
Clinical Medicine 16 (December 1909):
1325-1330; 17 (January 1910): 25-32.

7063. _____. "Recollections of an
Agency Physician: A Doctor's Life among
Indians." American Journal of Clinical
Medicine 18 (December 1911): 1265-1271.
Fort Berthold Agency.

7064. Patterson, Frank D. "Medical Practice among the Indians." American
Journal of Clinical Medicine 16 (September 1909): 997-1000.

7065. _____. "The Physician's Work in
the Indian Service: A Field for the
Young Doctor." American Journal of
Clinical Medicine 17 (May 1910): 511-513.

7066. Sellers, James L., ed. "Diary of
Dr. Joseph A. Paxson, Physician to the
Winnebago Indians, 1869-1870." Nebraska
History Magazine 27 (July-September
1946): 143-204; (October-December 1946):
244-275.

7067. Titus, Willard H. "Observations on
the Menominee Indians." Wisconsin Magazine of History 14 (September 1930):
93-105; (December 1930): 121-132. Notes
written in 1875 by a government physician.

7068. Towsley, Alice C. "The Doctor's
Wife: Assignment, Indian Reservation."
Medical World News 8 (May 19, 1967): 138.

DISEASES AND MEDICAL PROBLEMS

The Indians fell prey to many diseases of
the white man and in some cases developed
special problems, which became the concern
of white society as well as of the Indian
communities. Included here are studies on
Indian disease in general, on two diseases
of special significance in Indian health
programs, trachoma and tuberculosis, and
on the serious problems of alcoholism and
suicide among Indians. For recent articles
on a great variety of diseases among Indians, consult the annual volumes of Index
Medicus (6862) and Barrow's bibliography
(6861).

Diseases among the Indians: General

7069. Bettman, Jerome W. "Eye Disease
among American Indians of the Southwest." Archives of Ophthalmology 88
(September 1972): 263-268.

7070. Emerson, Haven. "Morbidity of the American Indians." Science 63 (February 26, 1926): 229-231.

7071. Everett, Michael Wayne. "White Mountain Apache Health and Illness: An Ethnographic Study of Medical Decision-Making." Ph.D. dissertation, University of Arizona, 1971.

7072. Gies, William J., comp. "Some Causes for Changes in Susceptibility of Eskimos and Indians to Acute and Chronic Infections upon Contact with Modern Civilization." Journal of Dental Research 14 (June 1934): 230-231.

7073. Hill, Charles A., Jr., and Mozart I. Spector. "Natality and Mortality of American Indians Compared with U.S. Whites and Nonwhites." HSMHA Health Reports 86 (March 1971): 229-246.

7074. McGibony, J. R. "Indians and Selective Service." Public Health Reports 57 (January 2, 1942): 1-7.

7075. Porvaznik, John. "Surgical Problems of the Navajo and Hopi Indians." American Journal of Surgery 123 (May 1972): 545-548.

7076. Salsbury, C. G. "Disease Incidence among the Navajos." Southwestern Medicine 21 (July 1937): 230-233.

7077. Sievers, Maurice L. "Disease Patterns among Southwestern Indians." Public Health Reports 81 (December 1966): 1075-1083.

7078. Tyroler, H. A., and Ralph Patrick. "Epidemiologic Studies of Papago Indian Mortality." Human Organization 31 (Summer 1972): 163-170.

7079. Weaver, S. M. "Smallpox or Chickenpox: An Iroquoian Community's Reaction to Crisis, 1901-1902." Ethnohistory 18 (Fall 1971): 361-378.

7080. Woodville, Lucille. "Healthier Indian Mothers and Babies." Public Health Reports 79 (June 1964): 468.

Trachoma

7081. Bettman, Jerome W. "Eye Disease among American Indians of the Southwest: II, Trachoma." Archives of Ophthalmology 90 (December 1973): 440-446.

7082. Chesley, A. J. "Prevalence of Trachoma among the Indians of the Northwest." Eye, Ear, Nose and Throat Monthly 6 (August 1927): 395-396.

7083. Cobb, John C., and Chandler R. Dawson. "Trachoma among Southwestern Indians." Journal of the American Medical Association 175 (February 4, 1961): 405-406.

7084. Crouch, J. H. "A Trachoma Survey of 29 Public Schools on or near Indian Reservations in Montana." Public Health Reports 44 (March 1929): 637-645.

7085. Forster, Wesley G., and J. R. McGibony. "Trachoma." American Journal of Ophthalmology 27 (October 1944): 1107-1117.

7086. Foster, Stanley O. "Trachoma in an American Indian Village." Public Health Reports 80 (September 1965): 829-832.

7087. Fox, L. Webster. "The Indian and the Trachoma Problem." American Journal of Ophthalmology 12 (June 1929): 457-468.

7088. _____. "Trachoma among the North American Indians." Hygeia 4 (February 1926): 84-86.

7089. _____. "The Trachoma Problem among North American Indians." Journal of the American Medical Association 86 (February 6, 1926): 404-406.

7090. Guthrie, Marshall C. "Indian Service Part in Control of Trachoma." Eye, Ear, Nose and Throat Monthly 6 (August 1927): 399-401.

7091. Posey, William Campbell. "Observations of Trachoma among the Indians." Eye, Ear, Nose and Throat Monthly 6 (August 1927): 402-403.

7092. _____. "Trachoma among the Indians of the Southwest." Journal of the American Medical Association 88 (May 21, 1927): 1618-1619.

7093. "Sulfanilamide Aiding War against Trachoma Blindness." Science News Letter 36 (September 2, 1939): 150.

7094. Tillim, Sidney J. "Trachoma among American Indians." Sight-Saving Review 5 (September 1935): 176-186.

7095. Townsend, J. G. "Trachoma Control in the Indian Service." Sight-Saving Review 9 (December 1939): 280-289.

7096. "Trachoma Eradication." Science 90 (December 15, 1939): supplement, 10.

7097. Warner, H. J. "Notes on the Results of Trachoma Work by the Indian Service in Arizona and New Mexico." Public Health Reports 44 (November 29, 1929): 2913-2920.

Tuberculosis

7098. Alley, Ralph M. "Tuberculosis among Indians." Diseases of the Chest 6 (February 1940): 44-48.

7099. Brewer, Isaac W. "Tuberculosis among the Indians of Arizona and New Mexico." New York Medical Journal 84 (November 17, 1906): 981-983.

7100. Burns, Herbert A. "Tuberculosis in the Indian." American Review of Tuberculosis 26 (November 1932): 498-506.

7101. Crouch, J. H. "A Study of Tuberculosis among the Indians in Montana: A Preliminary Report." Public Health Reports 47 (September 16, 1932): 1907-1914.

7102. DeLien, Horace. "Continuity of Program--a Necessity in Tuberculosis Control among American Indians." Journal-Lancet 71 (April 1951): 136-137.

7103. DeLien, Horace, and Arthur W. Dahlstrom. "Tuberculosis Control among American Indians." Journal-Lancet 70 (April 1950): 131-134.

7104. Deuschle, Kurt W. "Tuberculosis among the Navajo: Research in Cross-Cultural Technologic Development in Health." American Review of· Respiratory Diseases 80 (August 1959): 200-206.

7105. _____. "Tuberculosis among the Navajo Indians." Pennsylvania Medical Journal 63 (February 1960): 304-305.

7106. Fellows, F. S. "Mortality in the Native Races of the Territory of Alaska, with Special Reference to Tuberculosis." Public Health Reports 49 (March 2, 1934): 289-298.

7107. Ferguson, R. G. "The Indian Tuberculosis Problem and Some Preventive Measures." Transactions of the National Tuberculosis Association, 1933, pp. 93-106.

7108. Foard, Fred T. "The Tuberculosis Problem among Indians." Transactions of the National Tuberculosis Association, 1952, pp. 787-794.

7109. Fox, Carroll. "Tuberculosis among the Indians of Southeast Alaska." Public Health Reports 16 (July 19, 1901): 1615-1616.

7110. Gillick, David W. "The Social and Community Aspects of the Indian Tuberculosis Problem." Transactions of the National Tuberculosis Association, 1932, pp. 208-212.

7111. Hrdlicka, Ales. "Tuberculosis in the Indian." Charities and the Commons 21 (November 7, 1908): 245-247.

7112. Jones, L. R. "Tuberculosis on a Small Thickly Populated Indian Reservation." American Review of Tuberculosis 42 (August 1940): 197-202. Turtle Mountain Indian Reservation, North Dakota.

7113. Koenig, Margaret W. Tuberculosis among the Nebraska Winnebago: A Social Study on an Indian Reservation. Lincoln: Nebraska State Historical Society, 1921.

7114. Long, Esmond R. "A Brief Comparison of Tuberculosis in the White, Indian, and Negro Races." American Review of Tuberculosis 35 (January 1937): 1-5.

7115. McGibony, J. R., and A. W. Dahlstrom. "Tuberculosis among Montana Indians." American Review of Tuberculosis 52 (August 1945): 104-121.

7116. Maher, Stephen J. "Tuberculosis among the American Indians." American Review of Tuberculosis 19 (April 1929): 407-411.

7117. Matthews, Washington. "Consumption among the Indians." New York Medical Journal 45 (January 1, 1887): 1-3.

7118. _____. "Consumption among the Indians." Transactions of the American Climatological Association, 1886, pp. 234-241.

7119. _____. "Further Contribution to the Study of Consumption among the Indians." Transactions of the American Climatological Association, 1888, pp. 136-155.

7120. Mays, Thomas J. "Does Pulmonary Consumption Tend to Exterminate the American Indian? A Reply to Dr. Washington Matthews, of the United States Army." New York Medical Journal 46 (September 3, 1887): 259-260.

7121. Montgomery, L. G. "Tuberculosis among Indian Children." Proceedings of the Staff Meetings of the Mayo Clinic 7 (May 4, 1932): 262-264.

7122. Murphy, Joseph F. "The Prevention of Tuberculosis in the Indian Schools." National Education Association Journal of Proceedings and Addresses, 1909, pp. 919-924.

7123. Myers, J. Arthur, and Virginia L. Dustin. "Albert Reifel and Tuberculosis among the American Indians." Hygeia 25 (April 1947): 272-273, 318-322.

7124. "Project to Combat Tuberculosis in Indians." Public Health Reports 71 (April 1956): 394.

7125. Reifel, Albert. "Tuberculosis among Indians of the United States." Diseases of the Chest 16 (August 1949): 234-247.

7126. Richards, W. G. "Tuberculosis among the Indians in Montana." American Review of Tuberculosis 26 (November 1932): 492-497.

7127. Rider, A. S. "Anti-Tuberculosis Work at the Flandreau Indian School." Journal-Lancet 58 (April 1938): 175-177.

7128. Robinson, Delorme W. "Tuberculosis among the Sioux Indians." American Monthly Review of Reviews 33 (March 1906): 340-341

7129. Townsend, James G. "Tuberculosis in the North American Indian." In Proceedings of the Eighth American Scientific Congress, Held in Washington, May 10-18, 1940. Volume 6: Public Health and Medicine, pp. 261-267. Washington: Department of State, 1942.

7130. Townsend, James G., Joseph D. Aronson, Robert Saylor, and Irma Parr. "Tuberculosis Control among the North American Indians." Transactions of the National Tuberculosis Association, 1941, pp. 66-76.

7131. "Tuberculosis among American Indians." Diseases of the Chest 16 (August 1949): 248-249.

7132. "Tuberculosis and the Indians." Charities and the Commons 17 (November 10, 1906): 277-278.

7133. Walker, James R. "Tuberculosis among the Oglala Sioux Indians." American Journal of the Medical Sciences 132 (October 1906): 600-605.

7134. Warner, H. J. "The Incidence of Tuberculous Infection among School-Children on Five Montana Indian Reservations." American Review of Tuberculosis 26 (November 1932): 507-515.

7135. Wauneka, Annie D. "Helping a People to Understand." American Journal of Nursing 62 (July 1962): 88-90.

Mental Health

7136. Anderson, Forrest N. "A Mental-Hygiene Survey of Problem Indian Children in Oklahoma." Mental Hygiene 20 (July 1936): 472-476.

7137. Beiser, Morton. "A Hazard to Mental Health: Indian Boarding Schools." American Journal of Psychiatry 131 (March 1974): 305-306.

7138. Bergman, Robert L. "A School for Medicine Men." American Journal of Psychiatry 130 (June 1973): 663-666.

7139. Denges, Norman, Myra L. Yazzie, and Gwen D. Tollefson. "Developmental Intervention for Navajo Family Mental Health." Personnel and Guidance Journal 52 (February 1974): 390-395.

7140. Devereux, George. "The Mental Hygiene of the American Indian." Mental Hygiene 26 (January 1942): 71-84.

7141. _____. Mohave Ethnopsychiatry and Suicide: The Psychiatric Knowledge and the Psychic Disturbances of an Indian Tribe. Bureau of American Ethnology Bulletin 175. Washington: Government Printing Office, 1961.

7142. Foulks, E. F., and S. Katz. "The Mental Health of Alaskan Natives." Acta

Psychiatrica Scandinavica 49 (1973): 91-96.

7143. Hendrie, Hugh C., and Diane Hanson. "A Comparative Study of the Psychiatric Care of Indian and Metis." American Journal of Orthopsychiatry 42 (April 1972): 480-489.

7144. Hoyt, Elizabeth E. "Young Indians: Some Problems and Issues of Mental Hygiene." Mental Hygiene 46 (January 1962): 41-47.

7145. Hummer, H. R. "Insanity among the Indians." American Journal of Insanity 69 (January 1913): 615-623.

7146. _____. "Insanity among the Indians." Proceedings of the American Medico-Psychological Association 19 (1912): 453-462.

7147. Kahn, Marvin W., and John L. Delk. "Developing a Community Mental Health Clinic on an Indian Reservation." International Journal of Social Psychiatry 19 (Autumn-Winter 1973): 299-306. Pagago Reservation.

7148. Kinzie, J. David, James H. Shore, and E. Mansell Pattison. "Anatomy of Psychiatric Consultation to Rural Indians." Community Mental Health Journal 8 (August 1972): 196-207.

7149. Krush, Thaddeus P., and John Bjork. "Mental Health Factors in an Indian Boarding School." Mental Hygiene 49 (January 1965): 94-103.

7150. Krush, Thaddeus P., John W. Bjork, Peter S. Sindell, and Joanna Nelle. "Some Thoughts on the Formation of Personality Disorder: Study of an Indian Boarding School Population." American Journal of Psychiatry 122 (February 1966): 868-876.

7151. La Barre, Weston. "Primitive Psychotherapy in Native American Cultures: Peyotism and Confession." Journal of Abnormal and Social Psychology 42 (1947): 294-309.

7152. Leighton, Alexander H. "The Mental Health of the American Indian." American Journal of Psychiatry 125 (August 1968): 217-218.

7153. Leighton, Alexander H., and Dorothea C. Leighton. "Elements of Psychotherapy in Navajo Religion." Psychiatry 4 (November 1941): 515-523.

7154. _____. "Some Types of Uneasiness and Fear in a Navajo Indian Community." American Anthropologist 44 (April-June 1942): 194-209.

7155. Martin, Harry W., Sara S. Sutker, Robert L. Leon, and William M. Hales. "Mental Health of Eastern Oklahoma

Indians: An Exploration." Human Organization 27 (Winter 1968): 308-315.

7156. Opler, Morris E. "Some Points of Comparison and Contrast between the Treatment of Functional Disorders by Apache Shamans and Modern Psychiatric Practice." American Journal of Psychiatry 92 (May 1936): 1371-1387.

7157. Robertson, G. G., and Michael Baizerman. "Psychiatric Consultation on Two Indian Reservations." Hospital and Community Psychiatry 20 (June 1969): 186.

7158. Stage, Thomas B., and Thomas J. Keast. "A Psychiatric Service for Plains Indians." Hospital and Community Psychiatry 17 (March 1966): 74-76.

Alcoholism

Scientific studies have been made of Indian alcoholism, and cultural as well as medical explanations have been offered.

7159. Baker, James L. "Indians, Alcohol and Homicide." Journal of Social Therapy 5 (1959): 270-275.

7160. Boyce, George A. Alcohol and American Indian Students. Washington: United States Department of the Interior, Bureau of Indian Affairs, Branch of Education, 1965.

7161. Curley, Richard T. "Drinking Patterns of the Mescalero Apache." Quarterly Journal of Studies on Alcohol 28 (March 1967): 116-131.

7162. Devereux, George. "The Function of Alcohol in Mohave Society." Quarterly Journal of Studies on Alcohol 9 (September 1958): 207-251.

7163. Dozier, Edward P. "Problem Drinking among American Indians: The Role of Sociocultural Deprivation." Quarterly Journal of Studies on Alcohol 27 (March 1966): 72-87.

7164. Fairbanks, Robert A. "The Cheyenne-Arapaho and Alcoholism: Does the Tribe Have a Legal Right to a Medical Remedy?" American Indian Law Review 1 (Winter 1973): 55-77.

7165. Ferguson, Frances Northend. "Navajo Drinking: Some Tentative Hypotheses." Human Organization 27 (Summer 1968): 159-167.

7166. _____. "A Treatment Program for Navaho Alcoholics: Results after Four Years." Quarterly Journal of Studies on Alcohol 31 (December 1970): 898-919.

7167. Graves, Theodore D. "Acculturation, Access, and Alcohol in a Tri-Ethnic Community." American Anthropologist 69 (June-August 1967): 306-321.

7168. _____. "Drinking and Drunkenness among Urban Indians." In The American Indian in Urban Society, edited by Jack O. Waddell and O. Michael Watson, pp. 274-311. Boston: Little Brown and Company, 1971.

7169. Hamer, John H. "Acculturation Stress and the Functions of Alcohol among the Forest Potawatomi." Quarterly Journal of Studies on Alcohol 26 (June 1965): 285-302.

7170. Hassrick, Royal B. "Alcohol and Indians." American Indian 4, no. 2 (1947): 19-26.

7171. Heath, Dwight B. "Prohibition and Post-Repeal Drinking Patterns among the Navajo." Quarterly Journal of Studies on Alcohol 25 (March 1964): 119-135.

7172. Hoffman, Helmut, and Douglas N. Jackson. "Comparison of Measured Psychopathology in Indian and Non-Indian Alcoholics." Psychological Reports 33 (December 1973): 793-794.

7173. Honigmann, John J., and Irma Honigmann. "Drinking in an Indian-White Community." Quarterly Journal of Studies on Alcohol 5 (March 1945): 575-619.

7174. Hurt, Wesley R., and Richard M. Brown. "Social Drinking Patterns of the Yankton Sioux." Human Organization 24 (Fall 1965): 222-230.

7175. Kline, James A., and Arthur C. Roberts. "A Residential Alcoholism Treatment Program for American Indians." Quarterly Journal of Studies on Alcohol 34 (September 1973): 860-868.

7176. Kunitz, Stephen J. "Navajo Drinking Patterns." Ph.D. dissertation, Yale University, 1970.

7177. Kunitz, Stephen J., and Jerrold E. Levy. "Changing Ideas of Alcohol Use among Navaho Indians." Quarterly Journal of Studies on Alcohol 35 (March 1974): 243-259.

7178. Kuttner, Robert E., and Albert B. Lorincz. "Alcoholism and Addiction in Urbanized Sioux Indians." Medical Times 51 (October 1967): 530-542.

7179. Lemert, Edwin M. "Alcohol and the Northwest Coast Indians." University of California Publications in Culture and Society 2 (1954): 303-406.

7180. _____. "On Alcoholism among the Northwest Coast Indians." American Anthropologist 58 (June 1956): 561.

7181. _____. "The Use of Alcohol in Three Salish Indian Tribes." Quarterly Journal of Studies on Alcohol 19 (March 1958): 90-107.

7182. Levy, Jerrold E., and Stephen J.

Kunitz. Indian Drinking: Navajo Practices and Anglo-American Theories. New
York: John Wiley and Sons, 1974.

7183. Littman, Gerard. "Alcoholism, Illness, and Social Pathology among American
Indians in Transition." American Journal
of Public Health 60 (September 1970):
1769-1787.

7184. Lunger, Harold L. "Seek Way to
Counter Indians' Drinking, Delinquency."
Christian Century 73 (May 2, 1956): 560.

7185. Lurie, Nancy Oestreich. "Indian
Drinking Patterns." American Journal of
Orthopsychiatry 42 (July 1972): 554.

7186. _____. "The World's Oldest On-
Going Protest Demonstration: North American Indian Drinking Patterns." Pacific
Historical Review 40 (August 1971): 311-
332.

7187. MacAndrew, Craig, and Robert B.
Edgerton. Drunken Comportment: A
Social Explanation. Chicago: Aldine
Publishing Company, 1969.

7188. Roy, Chunilal. "Indian Peyotists
and Alcohol." American Journal of Psychiatry 130 (March 1973): 329-330.

7189. Savard, Robert Joseph. "Cultural
Stress and Alcoholism: A Study of Their
Relationship among Navajo Alcoholic Men."
Ph.D. dissertation, University of Minne-
sota, 1968.

7190. _____. "Effects of Disulfiram
Therapy on Relationships within the
Navaho Drinking Group." Quarterly Journal of Studies on Alcohol 29 (December
1968): 909-916.

7191. Shore, James H., and Billie von
Fumetti. "Three Alcohol Programs for
American Indians." American Journal of
Psychiatry 128 (May 1972): 1450-1454.

7192. Sievers, Maurice L. "Cigarette and
Alcohol Usage by Southwestern American
Indians." American Journal of Public
Health 58 (January 1968): 71-82.

7193. Slater, Arthur D., and Stan L. Al-
brecht. "The Extent and Costs of Exces-
sive Drinking among the Uintah-Ouray
Indians." In Native Americans Today:
Sociological Perspectives, edited by
Howard M. Bahr and others, pp. 358-367.
New York: Harper and Row, 1972.

7194. Stratton, John. "Cops and Drunks:
Police Attitudes and Actions in Dealing
with Indian Drunks." International
Journal of the Addictions 8 (August
1973): 613-621.

7195. Trillin, Calvin. "U.S. Journal,
Gallup, New Mexico: Drunken Indians."
New Yorker, September 25, 1971, pp. 108-
114.

7196. Weast, Donald Ellsworth. "Patterns
of Drinking among Indian Youth: The
Case of a Wisconsin Tribe." Ph.D. dissertation, University of Wisconsin, 1969.
Oneida Indians.

7197. Westermeyer, Joseph J. "Alcohol-
Related Problems among Ojibway People in
Minnesota: A Social Psychiatry Study."
Ph.D. dissertation, University of
Minnesota, 1970.

7198. _____. "Chippewa and Majority
Alcoholism in the Twin Cities: A Com-
parison." Journal of Nervous and Mental
Disease 155 (November 1972): 322-327.

7199. _____. "Options Regarding Alcohol Use among the Chippewa." American
Journal of Orthopsychiatry 42 (April
1972): 398-403.

7200. Whittaker, James O. "Alcohol and
the Standing Rock Sioux Tribe: The Pattern of Drinking." Quarterly Journal of
Studies on Alcohol 23 (September 1962):
468-479.

7201. _____. "Alcohol and the Standing
Rock Sioux Tribe: Psychodynamic and
Cultural Factors in Drinking." Quarterly
Journal of Studies on Alcohol 24 (March
1963): 80-90.

For historical problems of Indian use of
alcohol, see the section on the liquor
trade (5008 to 5022).

Suicide

The high incidence of suicide among Indians has led to a number of studies.

7202. Bach, John L. "New Indian War--
against Suicide." Today's Health 48
(October 1970): 16-17.

7203. Bynum, Jack. "Suicide and the
American Indian: An Analysis of Recent
Trends." In Native Americans Today:
Sociological Perspectives, edited by
Howard M. Bahr and others, pp. 367-377.
New York: Harper and Row, 1972.

7204. Conrad, Rex D., and Marvin W. Kahn.
"An Epidemiological Study of Suicide and
Attempted Suicide among the Papago Indians." American Journal of Psychiatry
131 (January 1974): 69-72.

7205. Dizmang, Larry H. "Suicide among
the Cheyenne Indians." Bulletin of
Suicidology, July 1967, pp. 8-11.

7206. Dizmang, Larry H., Jane Watson,
Philip A. May, and John Bopp. "Adolescent Suicide at an Indian Reservation." American Journal of Orthopsychiatry 44 (January 1974): 43-49.

7207. Havighurst, Robert J. "The Extent
and Significance of Suicide among

American Indians Today." Mental Hygiene 55 (April 1971): 174-177.

7208. Levy, Jerrold E. "Navajo Suicide." Human Organization 24 (Winter 1965): 308-318.

7209. Resnik, H. L. P., and Larry H. Dizmang. "Observations on Suicidal Behavior among American Indians." American Journal of Psychiatry 127 (January 1971): 882-887.

7210. Shore, James H. "Suicide and Suicide Attempts among American Indians of the Pacific Northwest." International Journal of Social Psychiatry 18 (Summer 1972): 91-96.

7211. Shore, James H., and John F. Bopp, Thelma R. Waller, and James W. Dawes. "A Suicide Prevention Center on an In-dian Reservation." American Journal of Psychiatry 128 (March 1972): 1086-1091.

7212. Suicide among the American Indians. Public Health Service Publication no. 1903. Washington: National Institute of Mental Health, Indian Health Service, 1969.

7213. Westermeyer, Joseph J. "Disorganization: Its Role in Indian Suicide Rates." American Journal of Psychiatry 128 (July 1971): 123. Replies by H. L. P. Resnik and Larry H. Dizmang, pp. 123-124.

7214. Wyman, Leland C., and Betty Thorne. "Notes on Navajo Suicide." American Anthropologist 47 (April-June 1945): 278-288

15
Social and Economic Developments

The accommodation of Indian communities to white society has taken place on several fronts, which have been observed and studied by many writers. Entered here under separate classifications are works dealing with acculturation, urbanization, and economic development.

ACCULTURATION AND ASSIMILATION

All aspects of Indian-white relations touch on acculturation and assimilation. Singled out here are some theoretical studies on acculturation (or persistence of cultural traits) and a number of illustrative case studies. Many studies of acculturation dealing with individual tribes are listed under the tribe and can be located in the index.

7215. Barnett, H. G., and others. "Acculturation: An Exploratory Formulation." American Anthropologist 56 (December 1954): 973-1002.

7216. Blackmar, Frank Wilson. "The Socialization of the American Indian." American Journal of Sociology 34 (January 1929): 653-669.

7217. Bruner, Edward M. "Case Reports on Indian Assimilation: Assimilation among Fort Berthold Indians." American Indian 6 (Summer 1953): 21-29.

7218. _____. "Cultural Transmission and Cultural Change." Southwestern Journal of Anthropology 12 (Summer 1956): 191-199.

7219. _____. "Primary Group Experience and the Process of Acculturation." American Anthropologist 58 (August 1956): 605-623.

7220. Bushnell, John H. "From American Indian to Indian American: The Changing Identity of the Hupa." American Anthropologist 70 (December 1968): 1108-1116.

7221. Carman, J. Neale, and Karl S. Pond. "The Replacement of the Indian Languages of Kansas by English." Transactions of the Kansas Academy of Science 58 (Summer 1955): 131-150.

7222. Carter, E. Russell. "Case Reports on Indian Assimilation: Rapid City, South Dakota." American Indian 6 (Summer 1953): 29-38.

7223. Clemmer, Richard Ora. "Directed Resistance to Acculturation: A Comparative Study of the Effects of Non-Indian Jurisdiction on Hopi and Western Shoshone Communities." Ph.D. dissertation, University of Illinois, 1972.

7224. Colson, Elizabeth. "Assimilation of an American Indian Group." In Beyond the Frontier: Social Process and Cultural Change, edited by Paul Bohannan and Fred Plog, pp. 209-226. Garden City, New York: Natural History Press, 1967.

7225. Dimock, Janet. "The Effect of United States Land Allotment and Religious Policies on American Indian Culture." Historical Journal of Western Massachusetts 1 (Fall 1972): 18-33.

7226. Downs, James F. "The Cowboy and the Lady: Models as a Determinant of the Rate of Acculturation among the Piñon Navajo." Kroeber Anthropological Society Papers no. 29 (Fall 1963): 53-67.

7227. Dozier, Edward P. "Forced and Permissive Acculturation." American Indian 7 (Spring 1955): 38-44.

7228. Dozier, Edward P., George E. Simpson, and J. Milton Yinger. "The Integration of Americans of Indian Descent." Annals of the American Academy of Political and Social Science 311 (May 1957): 158-165.

7229. Edgerton, Robert B. "Some Dimensions of Disillusionment in Culture Contact." Southwestern Journal of Anthropology 21 (Autumn 1965): 231-243.

7230. Eggan, Fred. The American Indian: Perspectives for the Study of Social Change. Chicago: Aldine, 1966.

7231. Elkin, Henry. "The Northern Arapaho of Wyoming." In Acculturation in Seven American Indian Tribes, edited by Ralph

Linton, pp. 207-255. New York: D. Appleton-Century Company, 1940.

7232. Fontana, Bernard Lee. "Assimilative Change: A Papago Indian Case Study." Ph.D. dissertation, University of Arizona 1960.

7233. Fried, Morton H. "Land Tenure, Geography, and Ecology in the Contact of Cultures." American Journal of Economics and Sociology 11 (July 1952): 391-412.

7234. Graves, Theodore D. "Psychological Acculturation in a Tri-Ethnic Community." Southwestern Journal of Anthropology 23 (Winter 1967): 337-350.

7235. Hallowell, A. Irving. "American Indians, White and Black: The Phenomenon of Transculturalization." Current Anthropology 4 (December 1963): 519-531.

7236. Harris, Jack S. "The White Knife Shoshoni of Nevada." in Acculturation in Seven American Indian Tribes, edited by Ralph Linton, pp. 39-116. New York: D. Appleton-Century Company, 1940.

7237. "Institute on American Indian Assimilation: American Indian Viewpoints." American Indian 6 (Summer 1953): 15-21. Statements of Thomas A. Segundo and Clarence Wesley.

7238. Joffe, Natalie F. "The Fox of Iowa." In Acculturation in Seven American Indian Tribes, edited by Ralph Linton, pp. 259-331. New York: D. Appleton-Century Company, 1940.

7239. Kallen, Horace M. "On 'Americanizing' the American Indian." Social Research 25 (Winter 1958): 469-473.

7240. La Farge, Oliver. "Assimilation--the Indian View." New Mexico Quarterly 26 (Spring 1956): 5-13.

7241. Linton, Ralph, ed. Acculturation in Seven American Indian Tribes. New York: D. Appleton-Century Company, 1940. The editor contributed three final chapters, in which he discusses the acculturation process.

7242. McFee, Malcolm. "The 150% Man, a Product of Blackfeet Acculturation." American Anthropologist 70 (December 1968): 1096-1107.

7243. McKenzie, Fayette Avery. "The Assimilation of the American Indian." American Journal of Sociology 19 (May 1914): 761-772.

7244. McNickle, D'Arcy. The Indian Tribes of the United States: Ethnic and Cultural Survival. London: Oxford University Press, 1962.

7245. Malan, Vernon D. "Theories of Culture Change Relevant to the Study of the Dakota Indians." Plains Anthropologist 6 (February 1961): 13-20.

7246. Mead, Margaret. The Changing Culture of an Indian Tribe. New York: Columbia University Press, 1932.

7247. Mekeel, Scudder. "A Discussion of Culture Change As Illustrated by Material from a Teton-Dakota Community." American Anthropologist 34 (April-June 1932): 274-285.

7248. Mitchell, Michael Dan. "Acculturation Problems among the Plains Tribes of the Government Agencies in Western Indian Territory." Chronicles of Oklahoma 44 (Autumn 1966): 281-289.

7249. Muntz, E. E. "The Effect of Contact on the Social Organization of the American Indian." Scientific Monthly 24 (February 1927): 161-168.

7250. Officer, James E. "The Role of the United States Government in Indian Acculturation and Assimilation." Anuario Indigenista 25 (December 1965): 73-86.

7251. Opler, Marvin K. "The Southern Ute of Colorado." In Acculturation in Seven American Indian Tribes, edited by Ralph Linton, pp. 119-203. New York: D. Appleton-Century Company, 1940.

7252. Peretti, Peter O. "Enforced Acculturation and Indian-White Relations." Indian Historian 6 (Winter 1973): 38-52.

7253. Peterson, John H., Jr. "Assimilation, Separation, and Out-Migration in an American Indian Group." American Anthropologist 74 (October 1972): 1286-1295.

7254. Rodnick, David. "The Effect of Culture Change upon the Personalities of Second-Generation Reservation Indians." Yivo: Annual of Jewish Social Science 3 (1948): 252-261.

7255. Schultz, John Lawrence. "Acculturation and Religion on the Colville Indian Reservation." Ph.D. dissertation, Washington State University, 1971.

7256. Smith, Marian W. "The Puyallup of Washington." In Acculturation in Seven American Indian Tribes, edited by Ralph Linton, pp. 3-36. New York: D. Appleton-Century Company, 1940.

7257. Spicer, Edward H. "Persistent Cultural Systems: A Comparative Study of Identity Systems That Can Adapt to Contrasting Environments." Science 174 (November 19, 1971): 795-800.

7258. _____. "Types of Contact and Processes of Change." In Perspectives in American Indian Culture Change, edited by Edward H. Spicer, pp. 517-544. Chicago: University of Chicago Press, 1961.

7259. Spicer, Edward H., ed. Perspectives in American Indian Culture Change. Chicago: University of Chicago Press, 1961.

7260. Spoehr, Alexander. "Changing Kinship Systems: A Study in the Acculturation of the Creeks, Cherokee, and Choctaw." Field Museum of Natural History, Anthropological Series 33 (January 17, 1947): 153-235.

7261. Stipe, Claude Edwin. "Eastern Dakota Acculturation: The Role of Agents of Culture Change." Ph.D. dissertation, University of Minnesota, 1968.

7262. Tax, Sol. "Acculturation." In Men and Cultures: Selected Papers of the Fifth International Congress of Anthropological and Ethnological Sciences, Philadelphia, September 1-9, 1956, edited by Anthony F. C. Wallace, pp. 192-196. Philadelphia: University of Pennsylvania Press, 1960.

7263. _____. "The Importance of Preserving Indian Culture." América Indígena 26 (January 1966): 81-86.

7264. Tax, Sol. ed. Acculturation in the Americas: Proceedings and Selected Papers of the XXIXth International Congress of Americanists. Chicago: University of Chicago Press, 1952.

7265. Thompson, Laura, and Alice Joseph. "White Pressures on Indian Personality and Culture." American Journal of Sociology 53 (July 1947): 17-22. Mennonite mission influence on Hopi communities.

7266. Voget, Fred W. "The American Indian in Transition: Reformation and Accommodation." American Anthropologist 58 (April 1956): 249-263.

7267. _____. "The American Indian in Transition: Reformation and Status Innovations." American Journal of Sociology 62 (January 1957): 369-378.

7268. Vogt, Evon Z. "The Acculturation of American Indians." Annals of the American Academy of Political and Social Science 311 (May 1957): 137-146.

7269. Warne, William E. "The Public Share in Indian Assimilation." American Indian 4, no. 3 (1948): 3-11.

7270. "'Watch Out, You Might Assimilate.'" Natural History 80 (June 1971): 24-33.

7271. Whitman, William. "The San Ildefonso of New Mexico." In Acculturation in Seven American Indian Tribes, edited by Ralph Linton, pp. 390-460. New York: D. Appleton-Century Company, 1940.

URBANIZATION

One of the more striking phenomena of recent years is the large number of Indians living in cities. This migration and urbanization, stimulated to some extent by a government relocation program in the 1950s, has been studied under a number of aspects.

7272. Ablon, Joan. "American Indian Relocation: Problems of Dependency and Management in the City." Phylon 26 (Winter 1965): 362-371.

7273. _____. "Cultural Conflict in Urban Indians." Mental Hygiene 55 (April 1971): 199-205.

7274. _____. "Relocated American Indians in the San Francisco Bay Area: Concepts of Acculturation, Success, and Identity in the City." Ph.D. dissertation, University of Chicago, 1963.

7275. _____. "Relocated Americans in the San Francisco Bay Area: Social Interaction and Indian Identity." Human Organization 23 (Winter 1964): 296-304.

7276. Alfred, Braxton Marcellus. "Acculturative Stress among Navajo Migrants to Denver, Colorado." Ph.D. dissertation, University of Colorado, 1965.

7277. Amanullah, Mohammod. "The Lumbee Indians: Patterns of Adjustment." In Toward Economic Development for Native American Communities, pp. 277-298. Washington: Government Printing Office, 1969. Lumbee Indians in Baltimore.

7278. Bahr, Howard M. "An End to Invisibility." In Native Americans Today: Sociological Perspectives, edited by Howard M. Bahr and others, pp. 404-412. New York: Harper and Row, 1972.

7279. Bahr, Howard M., Bruce A. Chadwick, and Joseph H. Stauss. "Discrimination against Urban Indians in Seattle." Indian Historian 5 (Winter 1972): 4-11.

7280. Bigony, Beatrice Anne. "Migrants to the Cities: A Study of the Socio-Economic Status of Native Americans in Detroit and Michigan." Ph.D. dissertation, University of Michigan, 1974.

7281. Brinker, Paul A., and Benjamin J. Taylor. "Southern Plains Indian Relocation Returnees." Human Organization 33 (Summer 1974): 139-146.

7282. Brown, Lowell Edward. "A Study of Program Administration for Indians in the Urban Community." Ed.D. dissertation, University of Kansas, 1969.

7283. Chadwick, Bruce A., and Lynn C.

White. "Correlates of Length of Urban Residence among the Spokane Indians." Human Organization 32 (Spring, 1973): 9-16.

7284. Cohen, Fay G. "The Indian Patrol in Minneapolis: Social Control and Social Change in an Urban Context." Ph.D. dissertation, University of Minnesota, 1973.

7285. _____. "The Indian Patrol in Minneapolis: Social Control and Social Change in an Urban Context." Law and Society Review 7 (Summer 1973): 779-786.

7286. Cook, Sherburne F. "Migration and Urbanization of the Indians in California." Human Biology 15 (February 1943): 33-45.

7287. Dowling, John H. "A 'Rural' Indian Community in an Urban Setting." Human Organization 27 (Fall 1968): 236-240. Wisconsin Oneida Indians.

7288. Einhorn, Arthur. "The Indians of New York City." In American Indian Urbanization, edited by Jack O. Waddell and O. Michael Watson, pp. 90-100. Lafayette, Indiana: Institute for the Study of Social Change, Purdue University, 1973.

7289. Flad, Harvey Keyes. "The City and the Longhouse: A Social Geography of American Indians in Syracuse, New York." Ph.D. dissertation, Syracuse University, 1973.

7290. Fogleman, Billye Y. S. "Adaptive Mechanisms of the North American Indian to an Urban Setting." Ph.D. dissertation, Southern Methodist University, 1972.

7291. Gabourie, Fred W. "Justice and the Urban American Indian." California State Bar Journal 46 (January-February 1971): 36-49.

7292. Garbarino, Merwyn S. "The Chicago American Indian Center: Two Decades." In American Indian Urbanization, edited by Jack O. Waddell and O. Michael Watson, pp. 74-89. Lafayette, Indiana: Institute for the Study of Social Change, Purdue University, 1973.

7293. _____. "Life in the City: Chicago." In The American Indian in Urban Society, edited by Jack O. Waddell and O. Michael Watson, pp. 168-205. Boston: Little, Brown and Company, 1971.

7294. Graves, Theodore D. "Alternative Models for the Study of Urban Migration." Human Organization 25 (Winter 1966): 295-299.

7295. _____. "The Personal Adjustment of Navajo Indian Migrants to Denver, Colorado." American Anthropologist 72 (February 1970): 35-54.

7296. Graves, Theodore D., and Charles A. Lave. "Determinants of Urban Migrant Indian Wages." Human Organization 31 (Spring 1972): 47-61.

7297. Graves, Theodore D., and Minor Van Arsdale. "Values, Expectations and Relocation: The Navajo Migrant to Denver." Human Organization 25 (Winter 1966): 300-307.

7298. Haddad, Susan. "'I Can't Really Get Involved in Urban Indian Problems Because Anytime I May Go Home.'" NLADA Briefcase 30 (May 1972): 161-167.

7299. Hanson, Marshall Roy. "Plains Indians and Urbanization." Ph.D. dissertation, Stanford University, 1960.

7300. Harmer, Ruth Mulvey. "Uprooting the Indians." Atlantic Monthly 197 (March 1956): 54-57. Los Angeles Indian Center.

7301. Harris, Michael. "American Cities: The New Reservations." City 5 (March-April 1971): 44-48.

7302. Henning, Marilyn Jadene. "The Ethnography of an American Indian Protest System: A Symbolic Interaction View." Ph.D. dissertation, University of Kansas, 1972.

7303. Hodge, William H. The Albuquerque Navajos. University of Arizona Anthropological Papers, no. 11. Tucson: University of Arizona Press, 1969.

7304. _____. "Navajo Urban Migration: An Analysis from the Perspective of the Family." In The American Indian in Urban Society, edited by Jack O. Waddell and O. Michael Watson, pp. 346-391. Boston: Little, Brown and Company, 1971.

7305. Hurt, Wesley R., Jr. "The Urbanization of the Yankton Indians." Human Organization 20 (Winter 1961-1962): 226-231.

7306. Kemnitzer, Luis S. "Adjustment and Value Conflict in Urbanizing Dakota Indians Measured by Q-Sort Technique." American Anthropologist 75 (June 1973): 687-707.

7307. _____. "Familial and Extra-Familial Socialization in Urban Dakota Adolescents." In The Modern Sioux: Social Systems and Reservation Culture, edited by Ethel Nurge, pp. 246-267. Lincoln: University of Nebraska Press, 1970.

7308. Krutz, Gordon V. "Compartmentalization as a Factor in Urban Adjustment: The Kiowa Case." In American Indian Urbanization, edited by Jack O. Waddell and O. Michael Watson, pp. 101-116. Lafayette, Indiana: Institute for the Study of Social Change, Purdue University, 1973. Kiowas in the San Francisco Bay area.

7309. _____. "Transplanting and Revitalizing of Indian Cultures in the City." In American Indian Urbanization, edited by Jack O. Waddell and O. Michael Watson, pp. 130-139. Lafayette, Indiana: Institute for the Study of Social Change, Purdue University, 1973.

7310. Kunitz, Stephen J., Jerrold E. Levy, and Charles L. Odoroff. "A One Year Follow-up of Navajo Migrants to Flagstaff, Arizona." Plateau 42 (Winter 1970): 92-106.

7311. Kuttner, Robert E., and Albert B. Lorincz. "Promiscuity and Prostitution in Urbanized Indian Communities." Mental Hygiene 54 (January 1970): 79-91.

7312. Liberty, Margot Pringle. "The Urban Reservation." Ph.D. dissertation, University of Minnesota, 1973. Omaha Indians in Nebraska.

7313. McCracken, Robert Dale. "Urban Migration and the Changing Structure of Navajo Social Relations." Ph.D. dissertation, University of Colorado, 1968.

7314. Madigan, La Verne. The American Indian Relocation Program. New York: Association on American Indian Affairs, 1956.

7315. Makofsky, Abraham. "Tradition and Change in the Lumbee Indian Community of Baltimore." Ph.D. dissertation, Catholic University of America, 1971.

7316. Marriott, Alice, and Carol Rachlin. "Indians: 1966--Four Case Histories." Southwest Review 51 (Spring 1966): 149-160.

7317. Martin, Harry W. "Correlates of Adjustment among American Indians in an Urban Environment." Human Organization 23 (Winter 1964): 290-295.

7318. Metzler, William. "Relocation of the Displaced Worker." Human Organization 22 (Summer 1963): 142-145.

7319. Moke, Irene. "Role of Pueblo Indian Economy in Santa Fe." Economic Geography 22 (April 1946): 148-152.

7320. Nagata, Shuichi. "The Reservation Community and the Urban Community: Hopi Indians of Moenkopi." In The American Indian in Urban Society, edited by Jack O. Waddell and O. Michael Watson, pp. 114-159. Boston: Little, Brown and Company, 1971.

7321. _____. "Urbanization in a Reservation Community: The Hopi Indians of Moenkopi." In American Indian Urbanization, edited by Jack O. Waddell and O. Michael Watson, pp. 13-27. Lafayette, Indiana: Institute for the Study of Social Change, Purdue University, 1973.

7322. Neils, Elaine M. Reservation to City: Indian Migration and Federal Relocation. Chicago: University of Chicago, Department of Geography, 1971.

7323. Neog, Prafulla, Richard G. Woods, and Arthur M. Harkins. Chicago Indians: The Effects of Urban Migration. Minneapolis: Training Center for Community Programs, University of Minnesota, 1970.

7324. Officer, James E. "Federal Policy and the Urban Indian." In American Indian Urbanization, edited by Jack O. Waddell and O. Michael Watson, pp. 1-12. Lafayette, Indiana: Institute for the Study of Social Change, Purdue University, 1973.

7325. Olson, John W. "Epilogue: The Urban Indian as Viewed by an Indian Caseworker." In The American Indian in Urban Society, edited by Jack O. Waddell and O. Michael Watson, pp. 398-408. Boston: Little, Brown and Company, 1971.

7326. Paredes, J. Anthony. "Chippewa Townsmen: A Study in Small-Scale Urban Adaptation." Ph.D. dissertation, University of New Mexico, 1969.

7327. _____. "Interaction and Adaptation among Small City Chippewa." In American Indian Urbanization, edited by Jack O. Waddell and O. Michael Watson, pp. 51-73. Lafayette, Indiana: Institute for the Study of Social Change, Purdue University, 1973.

7328. _____. "Toward a Reconceptualization of American Indian Urbanization: A Chippewa Case." Anthropological Quarterly 44 (October 1971): 256-271.

7329. Patrick, Mary. "Indian Urbanization in Dallas: A Second Trail of Tears?" Oral History Review, 1973, pp. 48-65.

7330. "Placing Indians Who Live on Reservations: A Cooperative Program." Employment Security Review 26 (January 1959): 27-29.

7331. Price, John A. "The Migration and Adaptation of American Indians to Los Angeles." Human Organization 27 (Summer 1968): 168-175.

7332. Ritzenthaler, Robert, and Mary Sellers. "Indian in an Urban Situation." Wisconsin Archeologist, new series 36 (1955): 147-161.

7333. Shotwell, Louisa R. "Indian Off Reservation Seeks Acceptance." National Council Outlook 5 (September 1955): 21, 23.

7334. Snyder, Peter Z. "Kinship, Friendship and Enclave: The Problem of American Indian Urbanization." In American Indian

Urbanization, edited by Jack O. Waddell and O. Michael Watson, pp. 117-129. Lafayette, Indiana: Institute for the Study of Social Change, Purdue University, 1973.

7335. _____. "The Social Assimilation and Adjustment of Navajo Indian Migrants to Denver, Colorado." Ph.D. dissertation, University of Colorado, 1968.

7336. _____. "The Social Environment of the Urban Indian." In The American Indian in Urban Society, edited by Jack O. Waddell and O. Michael Watson, pp. 206-243. Boston: Little, Brown and Company, 1971.

7337. Sorkin, Alan L. "Some Aspects of American Indian Migration." Social Forces 48 (December 1969): 243-250.

7338. Steele, Charles Hoy. "American Indians and Urban Life: A Community Study." Ph.D. dissertation, University of Kansas, 1972.

7339. Stucki, Larry R. "Who Controls the Indians: Social Manipulation in an Ethnic Enclave." In American Indian Urbanization, edited by Jack O. Waddell and O. Michael Watson, pp. 28-50. Lafayette, Indiana: Institute for the Study of Social Change, Purdue University, 1973. Ajo, Arizona.

7340. Stull, Donald David. "Modernization and Symptoms of Stress: Attitudes, Accidents and Alcohol Use among Urban Papago Indians." Ph.D. dissertation, University of Colorado, 1973.

7341. Tyler, S. Lyman. "The Recent Urbanization of the American Indian." In Essays on the American West, 1973-1974, edited by Thomas G. Alexander, pp. 43-62. Charles Redd Monographs in Western History, no. 5. Provo, Utah: Brigham Young University Press, 1975.

7342. Waddell, Jack O., and O. Michael Watson, eds. The American Indian in Urban Society. Boston: Little, Brown and Company, 1971.

7343. _____. American Indian Urbanization. Lafayette, Indiana: Institute for the Study of Social Change, Purdue University, 1973.

7343a. Wagner, James R., and Richard Corrigan. "BIA Brings Indians to Cities, but Has Few Urban Services." National Journal 2 (July 11, 1970): 1493-1502.

7344. Weltfish, Gene. "When the Indian Comes to the City." American Indian 1 (Winter 1944): 6-10.

7345. Weppner, Robert S. "The Economic Absorption of Navajo Indian Migrants in Denver, Colorado." Ph.D. dissertation, University of Colorado, 1968.

7346. _____. "Urban Economic Opportunities: The Example of Denver." In The American Indian in Urban Society, edited by Jack O. Waddell and O. Michael Watson, pp. 244-273. Boston: Little, Brown and Company, 1971.

7347. Westerman, Joann. "The Urban Indian." Current History 67 (December 1974): 259-262, 275.

A bibliography and a number of reports and studies dealing with urban Indians have been prepared and circulated by the Training Center for Community Programs in coordination with the Office of Community Programs, Center for Urban and Regional Affairs, University of Minnesota, Minneapolis.

ECONOMIC DEVELOPMENT

The development of the economic resources of the Indians has received much attention. The following bibliography is a useful guide to recent studies.

7348. Snodgrass, Marjorie P. Economic Development of American Indians and Eskimos, 1930 through 1967: A Bibliography. Washington: United States Department of the Interior, 1968.

General and Miscellaneous Works

Listed here are general studies, current comment on economic development, and specialized studies, such as those on manpower or the rise of a tourist industry, which do not warrant separate classification.

7349. Aberle, David F. "A Plan for Navajo Economic Development." In Toward Economic Development for Native American Communities, pp. 223-276. Washington: Government Printing Office, 1969.

7350. "American Indians Come Nearer Mainstream." Business Week, June 7, 1969, pp. 118-120.

7351. Anderson, Edward J. "Conservation Practices Mark Indian Lands across Oklahoma." Soil Conservation 31 (April 1966): 202-203.

7352. Archerd, Mary Sawtell. "Broadening Work Opportunities for Indian Youth." Employment Security Review 28 (March 1961): 23-24.

7353. Ball, Ian Traquair. "Institution Building for Development: OEO Community Action Programs on Two North Dakota Indian Reservations." Ph.D. dissertation, Indiana University, 1968. Fort Berthold and Standing Rock.

7354. Ballas, Donald J. "The Livelihood of the Eastern Cherokees." Journal of Geography 61 (November 1962): 342-350.

7355. Barlow, Sarah W., and Martha W. Blue. "An Analysis of the Bureau of Indian Affairs General Assistance Program." North Dakota Law Review 51 (Fall 1974): 31-51.

7356. Beatty, Jerome, Jr. "American Indian Resorts." Redbook 142 (February 1974): 60-61

7357. Beatty, Willard W. "Training Indians for the Best Use of Their Own Resources." In The Changing Indian, edited by Oliver La Farge, pp. 128-138. Norman: University of Oklahoma Press, 1942.

7358. Bee, Robert L. "'Self-Help' at Fort Yuma: A Critique." Human Organization 29 (Fall 1970): 155-161.

7359. _____. "Tribal Leadership in the War on Poverty: A Case Study." Social Science Quarterly 50 (December 1969): 676-686.

7360. Bennett, Elmer F. "Federal Responsibility for Indian Resources." Federal Bar Journal 20 (Summer 1960): 255-262.

7361. Bennett, Robert L. "Building Indian Economies with Land Settlement Funds." Human Organization 20 (Winter 1961-1962): 159-163. Ute Indians.

7362. _____. "Economic Development as a Means of Overcoming Indian Poverty." In Toward Economic Development for Native American Communities, pp. 102-118. Washington: Government Printing Office, 1969.

7363. Berger, Edward B. "Negotiations for Acquiring Exploration Rights on Indian Lands." Rocky Mountain Mineral Law Institute Proceedings 19 (1974): 447-481.

7364. Blumenfeld, Ruth. "Mohawks: Round Trip to the High Steel." Trans-action 3 (November-December 1965): 19-21.

7365. Borton, Raymond Eugene. "Irrigation on the Crow Reservation: Tribal and Community Benefits of the Proposed Hardin Unit, Big Horn County, Montana." Ph.D. dissertation, Montana State University, 1964.

7366. Boyd, Harold J., and Shirley A. Allison. "Irrigation to the Navajo Tribe." Reclamation Era 51 (November 1965): 98-101.

7367. Brockmann, C. Thomas. "Reciprocity and Market Exchange on the Flathead Reservation." Northwest Anthropological Research Notes 5 (Spring 1971): 77-96.

7368. Cauthorn, Robert C. "Programming for Entrepreneurship among American Indians." Arizona Review 17 (May 1968): 11-15.

7369. Collins, Thomas William. "The Northern Ute Economic Development Program: Social and Cultural Dimensions." Ph.D. dissertation, University of Colorado, 1971.

7370. Conly, Robert L. "The Mohawks Scrape the Sky." National Geographic Magazine 102 (July 1952): 133-142.

7371. Connolly, Thomas E. "The Indian and the Poverty War." America 111 (September 12, 1964): 245, 260-261.

7372. Cook, Mrs. William R. "A Michigan Indian Project." Michigan History Magazine 27 (Summer 1943): 492-499.

7373. Cormack, Charles William. "Social Structure and Economic Production on an Arizona Indian Reservation." Ph.D. dissertation, University of Arizona, 1968. Gila River Reservation.

7374. "Development of American Indian Arts and Crafts." Monthly Labor Review 46 (March 1938): 655-658.

7375. d'Harnoncourt, René. "Indian Arts and Crafts and Their Place in the Modern World." In The Changing Indian, edited by Oliver La Farge, pp. 144-157. Norman: University of Oklahoma Press, 1942.

7376. Dobyns, Henry F. "Experiment in Conservation: Erosion Control and Forage Production on the Papago Indian Reservations in Arizona." In Human Problems in Technological Change, edited by Edward H. Spicer, pp. 209-223. New York: Russell Sage Foundation, 1952.

7377. Duin, Virginia Nolan. "The Problems of Indian Poverty: The Shrinking Land Base and Ineffective Education." Albany Law Review 36 (Fall 1971): 143-181.

7378. "Economic Development of the American Indian and His Lands." In Toward Economic Development for Native American Communities, pp. 410-417. Washington: Government Printing Office, 1969. A position paper of the National Congress of American Indians.

7379. Edwards, Newton. "Economic Development of Indian Reserves." Human Organization 20 (Winter 1961-1962): 197-202.

7380. Eicher, Carl K. "An Approach to Income Improvement on the Rosebud Sioux Indian Reservation." Human Organization 20 (Winter 1961-1962): 191-196.

7381. _____. "Constraints on Economic Progress on the Rosebud Sioux Indian Reservation." Ph.D. dissertation, Harvard University, 1961.

7382. Elder, Jim. "Life on the Reservation: American Indians Are Now in the Resort Business." Holiday 55 (March 1974): 48-49, 66.

7383. "The Emergency Employment Act on Indian Reservations." Monthly Labor Review 96 (November 1973): 62-63.

7384. "Employment Conditions among Indians." Monthly Labor Review 52 (April 1941): 872-874.

7385. Fitch, James Black. "Economic Development in a Minority Enclave: The Case of the Yakima Indian Nation, Washington." Ph.D. dissertation, Stanford University, 1974.

7386. "'Forgotten American' Is Aiding Himself." U.S. News and World Report 63 (October 2, 1967): 66-67. Rosebud Sioux Reservation.

7387. Franklin, Marvin L. "Payrolls: An Answer to the Indian Militants." Nation's Business 62 (June 1974): 54-58.

7388. Fryer, E. R. "Navajo Social Organization and Land Use Adjustment." Scientific Monthly 55 (November 1942): 408-422.

7389. Garbarino, Merwyn Stephens. "Economic Development and the Decision-Making Process on Big Cypress Indian Reservation, Florida." Ph.D. dissertation, Northwestern University, 1966.

7390. Gilbreath, Kent. Red Capitalism: An Analysis of the Navajo Economy. Norman: University of Oklahoma Press, 1973.

7391. Gold, Herbert. "How Rich Is a Rich Apache." New York Times Magazine, February 13, 1972, pp. 18-19 +.

7392. Gunther, Erna. "Indian Craft Enterprise in the Northwest." Human Organization 20 (Winter 1961-1962): 216-218.

7393. Hackett, Blanche. "Be My Guest!" Recreation 58 (March 1965): 115, 144.

7394. Harkin, Duncan Alfred. "Issues in Economic Development: The Menominee County, Wisconsin, Case." Ph.D. dissertation, University of Wisconsin, 1966.

7395. Hayden, William G. "Oklahomans for Indian Opportunity, Incorporated, and Economic Development for Non-Reservation Indian People." In Toward Economic Development for Native American Communities, pp. 418-441. Washington: Government Printing Office, 1969.

7396. Heyer, Claude Herbert. "American Indian Self-Sufficiency: A Study in Human and Natural Resource Development Policy." Ph.D. dissertation, University of Oklahoma, 1966.

7397. Hough, Henry W. Development of Indian Resources. Denver: World Press, 1967.

7398. Icenogle, John P. "Economic Development of Indian Reservations: Increasing Tribal Participation, Limiting Federal Control." Tulane Law Review 48 (April 1974): 649-664.

7399. "Increase in Job Opportunities for Indians." Monthly Labor Review 42 (April 1936): 942-944.

7400. Jenny, Albert II. "The American Indian: Needs and Problems." In Toward Economic Development for Native American Communities, pp. 46-60. Washington: Government Printing Office, 1969.

7401. Jett, Stephen Clinton. "Tourism in the Navajo Country: Resources and Planning." Ph.D. dissertation, Johns Hopkins University, 1964.

7402. Johnson, Helen W. "American Indians in Rural Poverty." In Toward Economic Development for Native American Communities, pp. 19-45. Washington: Government Printing Office, 1969.

7403. Jones, Gary T. "Enforcement Strategies for Indian Landlords." American Indian Law Review 2 (Summer 1974): 41-60.

7404. Jones, Paul. "Reclamation and the Indian." Utah Historical Quarterly 27 (January 1959): 51-56.

7405. Jorgensen, Joseph G. "Indians and the Metropolis." In The American Indian in Urban Society, edited by Jack O. Waddell and O. Michael Watson, pp. 66-113. Boston: Little, Brown and Company, 1971.

7406. Kelly, William H. "The Economic Basis of Indian Life." Annals of the American Academy of Political and Social Science 311 (May 1957): 71-79.

7407. Kent, Calvin A. "The Sioux: Their Dilemma of Economic Development." Science and Children 9 (March 1972): 18-19.

7408. King, Bill. "Some Thoughts on Reservation Economic Development." In Toward Economic Development for Native American Communities, pp. 66-74. Washington: Government Printing Office, 1969.

7409. King, Seth S. "Lo! The Rich Indian." New York Times Magazine, December 2, 1956, pp. 109-110, 112. Ute Indians.

7410. La Farge, Oliver. "Wampum Woes of the Navajos." Nation's Business 36 (July 1948): 32-34, 52.

7411. LaFontaine, Frank. "The Native American Credit Problem." American Indian Law Review 2 (Summer 1974): 29-40.

7412. Lang, Gottfried O. "Economic Development and Self-Determination: The Northern Ute Case." Human Organization 20 (Winter 1961-1962): 164-171.

7413. Lazarus, Arthur, Jr. "Indian Rights under the Federal Power Act." Federal Bar Journal 20 (Summer 1960): 217-222.

7414. Lindeborg, Karl Hartvig. Economic Analysis of Minimum-Size Farms for Various Levels of Income on the Fort Hall Indian Reservation. Moscow: Bureau of Business and Economic Research, University of Idaho, 1961.

7415. "A Long, Hard Trail for Operation Navajo." Business Week, May 19, 1973, pp. 104-105.

7416. Louviere, Vernon. "Tourism: A Feather in the Crow's Hat." Nation's Business 60 (December 1972): 13.

7417. McFeeley, Mark B. "Need for a Federal Policy in Indian Economic Development." New Mexico Law Review 2 (January 1972): 71-80.

7418. Macgregor, Gordon. "Barriers to Economic Development." In Toward Economic Development for Native American Communities, pp. 61-64. Washington: Government Printing Office, 1969.

7419. _____. "Community Development and Social Adaptation." Human Organization 20 (Winter 1961-1962): 238-242.

7420. McIntire, Elliot G. "Central Places on the Navajo Reservation: A Special Case." Yearbook of the Association of Pacific Coast Geographers 29 (1967): 91-96.

7421. Martin, John F. "The Organization of Land and Labor in a Marginal Economy." Human Organization 32 (Summer 1973): 153-162. Havasupai Indians.

7422. Mekeel, Scudder. The Economy of a Modern Teton Dakota Community. Yale University Publications in Anthropology, no. 6. New Haven: Yale University Press, 1936.

7423. Meyers, Harold B. "Let's Get the Indians into the Economy." Fortune 74 (September 1966): 104.

7424. "A Model City for Indian Lands." U.S. News and World Report 66 (June 23, 1969): 96-99. Four Corners region.

7425. Mooney, Prentice. "Indian Country Is a Frontier Again." Nation's Business 57 (September 1969): 76-78.

7426. Munsell, Marvin Robert. "Land and Labor at Salt River: Household Organization in a Changing Economy." Ph.D. dissertation, University of Oregon, 1967.

7427. Nagel, Gerald S. "Economics of the Reservation." Current History 67 (December 1974): 245-249, 278-279.

7428. Napier, Arch, and Tom Sasaki. "The Navajo in the Machine Age: Human Resources Are Important Too." New Mexico Business 11 (July 1958): 2-5.

7429. Nutten, Wesley L. III. "Probate Problems of the American Indian." Real Property, Probate and Trust Journal 7 (Fall 1972): 495-501.

7430. Nybroten, Norman, ed. Economy and Conditions of the Fort Hall Indian Reservation. Idaho Bureau of Business and Economic Research, Report no. 9. Moscow: University of Idaho, 1964.

7431. Oliver, Lester. "Indian Water Needs." American Forests 64 (December 1958): 28, 45-46.

7432. Olson, Thomas W. "Indians--State Jurisdiction over Real Estate Developments on Tribal Lands." New Mexico Law Review 2 (January 1972): 81-90.

7433. Padfield, Harland, and John van Willigen. "Work and Income Patterns in a Transitional Population: The Papago of Arizona." Human Organization 28 (Fall 1969): 208-216.

7434. Porter, Pat. "Indian Resources: Development and Land Depredations." Christian Century 89 (February 23, 1972): 225-226.

7435. "Progress of Indian Arts and Crafts." Monthly Labor Review 52 (April 1941): 874-876.

7436. Reese, Jim E., and Mary Fish. "Economic Genocide: A Study of the Comanche, Kiowa, Cheyenne, and Arapaho." Negro Educational Review 24 (January 1973): 86-103. Reply by Joseph M. Perry, pp. 104-105.

7437. "Research Firm Organized to Help Tribes with Contracts." Journal of American Indian Education 10 (May 1971): 28-29.

7438. Ritzenthaler, Robert E. "The Menominee Indian Sawmill: A Successful Community Project." Wisconsin Archeologist, new series 32 (June 1951): 39-44.

7439. Roberts, William O. "Successful Agriculture within the Reservation Framework." Applied Anthropology: Problems of Human Organization 2 (June 1943): 37-44.

7440. Rock, James Anthony. "A Theory of Economic Development at Warm Springs Indian Reservation, Oregon." Ph.D. dissertation, Oregon State University, 1962.

7441. Sasaki, Tom T., and Harry W. Basehart. "Sources of Income among Many Farms-- Rough Rock Navajo and Jicarilla Apache: Some Comparisons and Comments." Human Organization 20 (Winter 1961-1962): 187-190.

7442. Schifter, Richard. "Indian Reservation Development: Reality or Myth?" California Western Law Review 9 (Fall 1972): 38-56.

7443. Schurmacher, Emile C. "High Steel's for Indians." Nation's Business 40 (January 1952): 64-65.

7444. Schwechten, John L. "Epilogue: In Spite of the Law: A Social Comment on the Impact of Kennerly and Crow Tribe." Montana Law Review 33 (Summer 1972): 317-320.

7445. Scott, Loren C., and David W. Stevens. "An Economic Evaluation of On-the-Job Training Conducted under the Auspices of the Bureau of Indian Affairs: Concepts and Preliminary Findings." In Toward Economic Development for Native American Communities, pp. 171-190. Washington: Government Printing Office, 1969.

7446. Simpson, James R. "Uses of Cultural Anthropology in Economic Analysis: A Papago Indian Case." Human Organization 29 (Fall 1970): 162-168.

7447. Sorkin, Alan L. American Indians and Federal Aid. Washington: Brookings Institution, 1971.

7448. Stern, Theodore. "Livelihood and Tribal Government on the Klamath Indian Reservation." Human Organization 20 (Winter 1961-1962): 172-180.

7449. Sternberg, Arnold C., and Catherine M. Bishop. "Indian Housing: 1961-1971, a Decade of Continuing Crisis." North Dakota Law Review 48 (Summer 1972): 593-616.

7450. Stocker, Joseph. "Arizona's New Indian Uprising." Saturday Evening Post 224 (March 29, 1952): 32-33 +. Pima-Maricopa tribal farm.

7451. Streib, Gordon F. "An Attempt to Unionize a Semi-Literate Navajo Group." Human Organization 11 (Spring 1952): 23-31.

7452. Tax, Sol, and Sam Stanley. "Indian Identity and Economic Development." In Toward Economic Development for Native American Communities, pp. 75-76. Washington: Government Printing Office, 1969.

7453. Taylor, Benjamin J. "Indian Manpower Resources: The Experience of Five Southwestern Reservations." Arizona Law Review 10 (Winter 1968): 579-596.

7454. _____. "The Reservation Indian and Mainstream Economic Life." Arizona Business Bulletin 17 (December 1970): 12-22.

7455. Taylor, Benjamin J., and Dennis J. O'Connor. Indian Manpower Resources

in the Southwest: A Pilot Study. Tempe: Bureau of Business and Economic Research, Arizona State University, 1969.

7456. "Toward a New System for the Resolution of Indian Resource Claims." New York University Law Review 47 (December 1972): 1107-1149.

7457. Toward Economic Development for Native American Communities: A Compendium of Papers Submitted to the Subcommittee on Economy in Government of the Joint Economic Committee, Congress of the United States. 2 volumes. Washington: Government Printing Office, 1969. Reprinted as American Indians: Facts and Future. New York: Arno Press, 1970.

7458. "Tribal Consent and the Lease of Indian Lands for Federal Power Projects." Minnesota Law Review 59 (December 1974): 385-419.

7459. Tussig, Arlon R., and Douglas N. Jones. "Economic Development and Alaskan Natives." In Toward Economic Development for Native American Communities, pp. 313-330. Washington: Government Printing Office, 1969.

7460. Tuttle, Roger L. "Economic Development of Indian Lands." University of Richmond Law Review 5 (Spring 1971): 319-329.

7461. Uchendu, Victor Chikezie. "Seasonal Agricultural Labor among the Navaho Indians: A Study in Socio-Economic Transition." Ph.D. dissertation, Northwestern University, 1966.

7462. Udall, Stewart L. "Indian Development and the Development of Western Natural Resources." New Mexico Business 19 (July 1966): 1-5.

7463. United States Department of Labor. "Role of Manpower Programs in Assisting the American Indians." In Toward Economic Development for Native American Communities, pp. 119-170. Washington: Government Printing Office, 1969.

7464. Useem, Ruth Hill, and Carl K. Eicher. "Rosebud Reservation Economy." In The Modern Sioux: Social Systems and Reservation Culture, edited by Ethel Nurge, pp. 3-34. Lincoln: University of Nebraska Press, 1970.

7465. van Willigen, John. "Concrete Means and Abstract Goals: Papago Experiences in the Application of Development Resources." Human Organization 32 (Spring 1973): 1-8.

7466. Voget, Fred. "Introduction" and "Commentary" [to special issue on "American Indians and Their Economic Development"]. Human Organization 20 (Winter 1961-62): 157-158, 243-248.

7467. Waddell, Jack O. Papago Indians at Work. Anthropological Papers of the University of Arizona, no. 12. Tucson: University of Arizona Press, 1969.

7468. Wilson, James J. "The Role of Indian Tribes in Economic Development and the Efforts of the Indian Division of the Community Action Program of the Office of Economic Opportunity to Assist in Indian Reservation Economic Development." In Toward Economic Development for Native American Communities, pp. 370-374. Washington: Government Printing Office, 1969.

7469. Wilson, Paul Burns. "Farming and Ranching on the Wind River Indian Reservation, Wyoming." Ph.D. dissertation, University of Nebraska, 1972.

7470. Wojta, J. F. "Indian Farm Institutes in Wisconsin." Wisconsin Magazine of History 29 (June 1946): 423-434.

7471. Wolf, Roger C. "Needed: A System of Income Maintenance for Indians." Arizona Law Review 10 (Winter 1968): 597-616.

7472. Zimmerman, William, Jr. "Economic Status of Indians in the United States." Journal of Religious Thought 7 (Spring-Summer 1950): 108-120.

Industry

Listed here are studies and comments on the development of industries on Indian reservations.

7473. Bigart, Robert James. "Indian Culture and Industrialization." American Anthropologist 74 (October 1972): 1180-1188.

7474. "Firms Find Indian Reservation Is Good Place to Locate Plant." Industry Week 171 (October 18, 1971): 14-16.

7475. "Indian Reservations Prove Good Plant Sites." Industry Week 173 (April 24, 1972): 22-23.

7476. "Indian Wampum Builds an Electronics Plant." Business Week, May 23, 1964, pp. 74-76.

7477. "Industry Invades the Reservation." Business Week, April 4, 1970, pp. 72-73.

7478. Ritzenthaler, Robert E. "The Impact of Small Industry on an Indian Community." American Anthropologist 55 (January-March 1953): 143-148.

7479. Schaab, William C. "Indian Industrial Development and the Courts." Natural Resources Journal 8 (April 1968): 303-330.

7480. Sonnenberg, Maurice. "The Role of the Federal Government in Present-Day Indian Industrial and Commercial Development: A Discussion." In Toward Economic Development for Native American Communities, pp. 302-312. Washington: Government Printing Office, 1969.

7481. Sorkin, Alan L. "American Indians Industrialize to Combat Poverty." Monthly Labor Review 92 (March 1969): 19-25.

Forestry

7482. Carlson, Elmer J. "The Cherokee Indian Forest of the Appalachian Region." Journal of Forestry 51 (September 1953): 628-630.

7483. Collier, John, Ward Shepard, and Robert Marshall. "The Indians and Their Lands." Journal of Forestry 31 (December 1933): 905-910.

7484. Heritage, William. "Forest Accomplishments in the Indian Service in the Lake States." Journal of Forestry 37 (September 1939): 717-718.

7485. _____. "Forestry, Past and Future, on Indian Reservations in Minnesota." Journal of Forestry 34 (July 1936): 648-652.

7486. Kephart, George S. "Forestry on the Klamath Indian Reservation." Journal of Forestry 39 (November 1941): 896-899.

7487. Kinney, J. P., with Elwood R. Maunder and George T. Morgan, Jr. "Beginning Indian Lands Forestry: An Oral History Interview." Forest History 15 (July 1971): 6-15.

7488. "Navajos Manage Vast Stand." Forest Industries 89 (November 1962): 74-76.

7489. "Navajos Seek Sawmill Wampum from Pine Timberlands." Timberman 61 (April 1960): 80-81, 93.

7490. Neuberger, Richard L. "How Oregon Rescued a Forest." Harper's Magazine 218 (April 1959): 48-52. Klamath Indians.

7491. "NLMA Defense of P.L. 587." American Forests 64 (August 1958): 4, 50-53. National Lumber Manufacturers Association and Klamath timberlands.

7492. Petite, Irving. "Science and Mythology Manage a Forest." American Forests·62 (September 1956): 30-31, 54-56. Yakima Indian Reservation.

7493. Pomeroy, Kenneth B. "Terminating Federal Supervision over Indian Forests." Society of American Foresters Proceedings, 1957, pp. 83-85.

7494. "Sentiment Grows for Repeal of P.L. 587." American Forests 63 (December 1957): 25, 43.

7495. Watson, Editha L. "Giving the Forest Back to the Indians." *American Forests* 51 (December 1945): 590-591, 619.

7496. Woehlke, Walter V. "Success Story: Menominee Forest." *American Indian* 1 (Spring 1944): 13-17.

Livestock Industry

7497. Cooper, Charles. "New Hope for the Apache." *American Forests* 61 (September 1955): 24-26, 51.

7498. Downs, James F. *Animal Husbandry in Navajo Society and Culture.* University of California Publications in Anthropology, no. 1. Berkeley: University of California Press, 1964.

7499. _____. "The Effect of Animal Husbandry on Two North American Indian Tribes." Ph.D. dissertation, University of California, 1961. Washo and Navajo.

7500. Fonaroff, L. Schuyler. "Aid and the Indian: A Case Study in Faulty Communication." *California Geographer* 5 (1964): 57-68. Navajo livestock reduction program.

7501. _____. "Conservation and Stock Reduction on the Navajo Tribal Range." *Geographical Review* 53 (April 1963): 200-223.

7502. _____. "The Navajo Sheep Industry: A Study in Cross-Cultural Administration." Ph.D. dissertation, Johns Hopkins University, 1961.

7503. Getty, Harry T. *The San Carlos Indian Cattle Industry.* Anthropological Papers of the University of Arizona, no. 7. Tucson: University of Arizona Press, 1963.

7504. _____. "San Carlos Apache Cattle Industry." *Human Organization* 20 (Winter 1961-1962): 181-186.

7505. Kantor, Seth. "Indian Wool Makes the Grade." *Nation's Business* 60 (January 1972): 65-66.

7506. McCray, Ernest R. "The San Carlos Apache Is a Modern Cattleman." *American Cattle Producer* 23 (October 1941): 5-8.

7507. Schaus, Richard G. "San Carlos Apaches Advance with Herefords." *American Hereford Journal* 44 (July 1, 1953): 367-369 +.

Oil and Mineral Resources

Mineral rights on Indian lands have received renewed attention because of new development possibilities. Ecological and legal problems have been studied.

7508. Anderson, David H. "Strip Mining on Reservation Lands: Protecting the Environment and the Rights of Indian Allotment Owners." *Montana Law Review* 35 (Summer 1974): 209-226.

7509. Berger, Edward B. "Indian Mineral Interest--a Potential for Economic Advancement." *Arizona Law Review* 10 (Winter 1968): 675-689.

7510. Branam, James T. "Property Rights: Intertribal Mineral Rights in the Arkansas Riverbed." *American Indian Law Review* 2 (Summer 1974): 125-136.

7511. Brom, Thomas. "The Southwest: America's New Appalachia." *Ramparts* 13 (November 1974): 17-20.

7512. Budnik, Dan. "Black Mesa: Progress Report on Ecological Rape." *Art in America* 60 (July-August 1972): 98-105.

7513. Dalrymple, Dal. "Five Tribes' Income Average $3,000,000 Yearly from Oil." *Oil and Gas Journal* 35 (December 17, 1936): 15-16.

7514. _____. "Kiowas' Income from Petroleum on Ascending Scale." *Oil and Gas Journal* 36 (November 4, 1937): 11.

7515. Forbes, Gerald. "History of the Osage Blanket Lease." *Chronicles of Oklahoma* 19 (March 1941): 70-81.

7516. _____. "Oklahoma Oil and Indian Land Tenure." *Agricultural History* 15 (October 1941): 189-194.

7517. Gordon, Suzanne. *Black Mesa: The Angel of Death.* New York: John Day Company, 1973.

7518. Harris, Fred, and La Donna Harris. "Indians, Coal, and the Big Sky." *Progressive* 38 (November 1974): 22-26.

7519. Hilgendorf, Robert. "Black Mesa: Economic Development or Ecological Disaster for the Navajo." *NLADA Briefcase* 30 (May 1972): 171-175.

7520. Josephy, Alvin M., Jr. "Agony of the Northern Plains." *Audubon* 75 (July 1973): 68-88 +. Strip mining of Indian and other lands.

7521. Luebben, Ralph A. "A Study of Some Off-Reservation Navaho Miners." Ph.D. dissertation, Cornell University, 1955.

7522. McLane, Alfred E. *Oil and Gas Leasing on Indian Lands.* Denver: F. H. Gower, 1955.

7523. Miner, H. Craig. "The Cherokee Oil and Gas Co., 1889-1902: Indian Sovereignty and Economic Change." *Business History Review* 46 (Spring 1972): 45-66.

7524. Pohlmann, Henry Fred. "Dineh bi Keyah Lifts Navajo Spirits." *Oil and Gas Journal* 65 (October 9, 1967): 205-206, 208, 210-211.

7525. Radloff, Floyd E. "Survey after

Lease Issues--Federal and Indian Lands. Rocky Mountain Mineral Law Institute Proceedings 11 (1966): 473-501.

7526. Rees-Jones, Trevor. "Problems in the Development of Mineral Resources on Indian Lands." Rocky Mountain Mineral Law Institute Proceedings 7 (1962): 661-705.

7527. Roberts, W. R. "New Hope for the Hopi." Petroleum Today 6 (Winter 1965): 9-14.

7528. Sonosky, Marvin J. "Oil, Gas, and Other Minerals on Indian Reservations." Federal Bar Journal 20 (Summer 1960): 230-234.

16
Indians and Indian Groups

Although organization of this bibliographic guide is not primarily by tribal
groups, some studies are best classified by
tribe or region. This chapter is divided
by geographical areas and by tribes within
the areas. Included are general works
about Indians of each region or tribe and
specialized studies about the tribes that
did not fit into other classifications.
Biographical studies are also given here,
and a few special classifications are included after the tribal sections. See
also the numerous tribal studies presented
as expert testimony before the Indian
Claims Commission and listed under that
heading.

GENERAL ARCHEOLOGICAL AND ETHNOLOGICAL WORKS

Listed here are general works dealing
with Indian prehistory and with ethnological descriptions of the Indian tribes.
Some older studies are included. These
publications furnish background for the
history of Indian-white relations and some
of them have sections on white contacts.

7529. Brennan, Louis A. American Dawn:
A New Model of American Prehistory. New
York: Macmillan Company, 1970.

7530. Ceram, C. W. The First American:
A Story of North American Archaeology.
New York: Harcourt Brace Jovanovich,
1971.

7531. Dellenbaugh, Frederick S. The North-
Americans of Yesterday: A Comparative
Study of North-American Indian Life,
Customs, and Products, on the Theory of
the Ethnic Unity of the Race. New York:
G. P. Putnam's Sons, 1900.

7532. Driver, Harold E. Indians of North
America. 2d edition revised. Chicago:
University of Chicago Press, 1969.

7533. Embree, Edwin R. Indians of the
Americas: Historical Pageant. Boston:
Houghton Mifflin Company, 1939.

7534. Farb, Peter. Man's Rise to Civili-
zation Shown by the Indians of North
America from Primeval Times to the
Coming of the Industrial State. New
York: E. P. Dutton and Company, 1968.

7535. Farrand, Livingston. Basis of
American History, 1500-1900. New York:
Harper and Brothers, 1904.

7536. Hassrick, Royal B. The Colorful
Story of North American Indians. London:
Octopus Books, 1974. A pictorial account.

7537. Howard, James H. "The Culture-Area
Concept: Does It Diffract Anthropological
Light?" Indian Historian 8 (Spring
1975): 22-26.

7538. Josephy, Alvin M., Jr. The Indian
Heritage of America. New York: Alfred
A. Knopf, 1968.

7539. Kroeber, A. L. Cultural and Natural
Areas of Native North America. Berkeley:
University of California Press, 1939.

7540. McNickle, D'Arcy. "Americans Called
Indians." In North American Indians in
Historical Perspective, edited by
Eleanor Burke Leacock and Nancy Oestreich
Lurie, pp. 29-63. New York: Random House,
1971.

7541. Martin, Paul S., George I. Quimby,
and Donald Collier. Indians Before
Columbus: Twenty Thousand Years of North
American History Revealed by Archaeology.
Chicago: University of Chicago Press,
1947.

7542. Owen, Roger C., James J. F. Deetz,
and Anthony D. Fisher, eds. The North
American Indians: A Sourcebook. New
York: Macmillan Company, 1967. A collection of articles by various authors.

7543. Oswalt, Wendell H. This Land Was
Theirs: A Study of the North American
Indian. 2d edition. New York: John
Wiley and Sons, 1973.

7544. Radin, Paul. The Story of the
American Indian. Enlarged edition. New
York: Liveright Publishing Corporation,
1944. Originally published in 1927.

7545. Sanders, William T., and Joseph

Marino. New World Prehistory: Archaeology of the American Indian. Englewood Cliffs, New Jersey: Prentice-Hall, 1970.

7546. Schoolcraft, Henry R. Historical and Statistical Information Respecting the History, Conditions, and Prospects of the Indian Tribes of the United States. 6 volumes. Philadelphia: Lippincott, Grambo and Company, 1851-1857. An index to these volumes, compiled by Frances S. Nichols, appears in Bureau of American Ethnology Bulletin 152.

7547. Spencer, Robert F., Jesse D. Jennings, and others. The Native Americans: Prehistory and Ethnology of the North American Indians. New York: Harper and Row, 1965.

7548. Terrell, John Upton. American Indian Almanac. New York: World Publishing Company, 1971.

7549. Underhill, Ruth M. Red Man's America: A History of Indians in the United States. Chicago: University of Chicago Press, 1953.

7550. Verrill, A. Hyatt. The American Indian: North, South, and Central America. New York: D. Appleton and Company, 1927.

7551. _____. The Real Americans. New York: G. P. Putnam's Sons, 1954.

7552. Wax, Murray L. Indian Americans: Unity and Diversity. Englewood Cliffs, New Jersey: Prentice-Hall, 1971.

7553. Wissler, Clark. The American Indian: An Introduction to the Anthropology of the New World. 3d edition. New York: Oxford University Press, 1938.

7554. _____. Indians of the United States. Revised edition, prepared by Lucy Wales Kluckhohn. Garden City, New York: Doubleday and Company, 1966. First edition, 1940.

7555. The World of the American Indian. Washington: National Geographic Society, 1974.

INDIANS OF THE EAST AND NORTHEAST

General and Miscellaneous Studies

Listed here are general works on Indians of the East and Northeast, together with studies of particular tribes. Material on Delaware and Iroquois Indians is listed under separate headings below.

7556. Bennett, M. K. "The Food Economy of the New England Indians, 1605-75." Journal of Political Economy 63 (October 1955): 369-397.

7557. Boissevain, Ethel. "The Detribalization of the Narragansett Indians: A Case Study." Ethnohistory 3 (Summer 1956): 225-245.

7558. _____. "Narragansett Survival: A Study of Group Persistence through Adapted Traits." Ethnohistory 6 (Fall 1959): 347-362.

7559. Bolton, Reginald Pelham. Indian Life of Long Ago in the City of New York. New York: Joseph Graham, 1934.

7560. _____. "New York City in Indian Possession." Indian Notes and Monographs 2 (1920): 225-395.

7561. Bradshaw, Harold Clayton. The Indians of Connecticut: The Effect of English Colonization and of Missionary Activity on Indian Life in Connecticut. Deep River, Connecticut: New Era Press, 1935.

7562. Brasser, T. J. C. "The Coastal Algonkians: People of the First Frontiers." In North American Indians in Historical Perspective, edited by Eleanor Burke Leacock and Nancy Oestreich Lurie, pp. 64-91. New York: Random House, 1971.

7563. Brigham, Clarence S. "The Indians of Rhode Island." Apteryx 1 (April 1905): 29-36.

7564. Chapin, Howard M. Sachems of the Narragansetts. Providence: Rhode Island Historical Society, 1931.

7565. Cook, Sherburne F. "Interracial Warfare and Population Decline among the New England Indians." Ethnohistory 20 (Winter 1973): 1-24.

7566. Crane, John C. "The Nipmunks and Their Country." Proceedings of the Worcester Society of Antiquity 16 (1897): 101-117.

7567. De Forest, John W. History of the Indians of Connecticut from the Earliest Known Period to 1850. Hartford: William James Hammersley, 1851.

7568. Dorr, Henry C. "The Narragansetts." Collections of the Rhode Island Historical Society 7 (1885): 137-237.

7569. Gilbert, William Harlen, Jr. "Surviving Indian Groups of the Eastern United States." Annual Report of the Board of Regents of the Smithsonian Institution, 1948, pp. 407-438.

7570. Harling, Frederick F. "The Indians of Eastern Massachusetts, 1620-1645." Historical Journal of Western Massachusetts 1 (Spring 1972): 28-36.

7571. Hoffman, Bernard G. "Ancient Tribes Revisited: A Summary of Indian Distribution and Movement in the Northeastern United States from 1534 to 1779." *Ethnohistory* 14 (Winter-Spring 1967):1-46.

7572. Huden, John C. "Indian Groups in Vermont." *Vermont History* 26 (April 1958): 112-115.

7573. Kidder, Frederic. "The Abenaki Indians: Their Treaties of 1713 and 1717, and a Vocabulary, with a Historical Introduction." *Collections of the Maine Historical Society* 6 (1859): 229-263.

7574. Landis, D. H. *A Brief Description of the Indian Life and Indian Trade of the Susquehannock Indians*. Lancaster, Pennsylvania, 1929.

7575. Marten, Catherine. "The Wampanoags in the Seventeenth Century: An Ethnohistorical Study." *Occasional Papers in Old Colony Studies* 2 (December 1970): 3-40.

7576. Mochon, Marion Johnson. "Stockbridge-Munsee Cultural Adaptations: 'Assimilated Indians.'" *Proceedings of the American Philosophical Society* 112 (June 1968): 182-219.

7577. Mooney, James. *The Siouan Tribes of the East*. Bureau of American Ethnology Bulletin 22. Washington: Government Printing Office, 1894.

7578. Nelson, William. *The Indians of New Jersey: Their Origin and Development; Manners and Customs; Language, Religion and Government, with Notices of Some Indian Place Names*. Paterson, New Jersey: Press Printing and Publishing Company, 1894.

7579. Ruttenber, E. M. *History of the Indian Tribes of Hudson's River*. Albany, New York: J. Munsell, 1872.

7580. Skinner, Alanson. *The Indians of Greater New York*. Cedar Rapids, Iowa: Torch Press, 1915. New York City.

7581. Skinner, Vincent P. "The Children of the Forgotten: The Indians of Maine." *Contemporary Education* 42 (May 1971): 284-289.

7582. Speck, Frank G. "The Rappahannock Indians of Virginia." *Indian Notes and Monographs* 5 (1925): 25-83.

7583. _____. "Reflections upon the Past and Present of the Massachusetts Indians." *Bulletin of the Massachusetts Archaeological Society* 4 (April 1943): 33-38.

7584. Spiess, Mathias. *The Indians of Connecticut*. Tercentenary Commission of the State of Connecticut, Committee on Historical Publications, Pamphlet no. 19. New Haven: Yale University Press, 1933.

7585. Spingarn, Lawrence P. "Children of Uncas--the New England Indian Today."

American Indian 8 (Winter 1958-1959): 36-39.

7586. Sturtevant, William C., and Samuel Stanley. "Indian Communities in the Eastern States." *Indian Historian* 1 (June 1968): 15-19.

7587. Tamarin, Alfred H. *We Have Not Vanished: Eastern Indians of the United States*. Chicago: Follett Publishing Company, 1974.

7588. Tureen, Thomas N. "Remembering Eastern Indians." *Inequality in Education*, no. 10 (December 1971): 14-18.

7589. Vetromile, Eugene. *The Abnakis and Their History; or, Historical Notices on the Aborigines of Acadia*. New York: James B. Kirker, 1866.

7590. Wallace, Anthony F. C. "Political Organization and Land Tenure among the Northeastern Indians, 1600-1830." *Southwestern Journal of Anthropology* 13 (Winter 1957): 301-321.

7591. Wallace, Paul A. W. *Indians in Pennsylvania*. Harrisburg: Pennsylvania Historical and Museum Commission, 1961.

7592. Weeks, Alvin G. *Massasoit of the Wampanoags*. Fall River, Massachusetts: Plimpton Press, 1919.

7593. Weslager, C. A. *Delaware's Forgotten Folk: The Story of the Moors and Naticokes*. Philadelphia: University of Pennsylvania Press, 1943.

7594. Winsor, Justin. "The New England Indians, 1630-1700." *Proceedings of the Massachusetts Historical Society, 2d series* 10 (1895-1896): 327-359. Discussion of 17th century printed sources.

Delaware Indians

The Delawares were among the important groups of Indians met by the English colonists. Listed here are general accounts and biographical studies on the tribe.

7595. Brown, D. Alexander. "Black Beaver." *American History Illustrated* 2 (May 1967): 32-41.

7596. Farley, Alan W. *The Delaware Indians in Kansas, 1829-1867*. Kansas City, Kansas, 1955.

7597. Ferguson, Roger James. "The White River Indiana Delawares: An Ethnohistoric Synthesis, 1795-1867." Ed.D. dissertation, Ball State University, 1972.

7598. Harrington, M. R. "The Life of a Lenape Boy." *Pennsylvania Archaeologist* 3 (April 1933): 3-8.

7599. Hunter, Charles E. "The Delaware Nativist Revival of the Mid-Eighteenth Century. Ethnohistory 18 (Winter 1971): 39-49.

7600. Hunter, William A. "Moses (Tunda) Tatamy, Delaware Indian Diplomat." In A Delaware Indian Symposium, edited by Herbert C. Kraft, pp. 71-88. Harrisburg: Pennsylvania Historical and Museum Commission, 1974.

7601. Jennings, Francis. "The Delaware Indians in the Covenant Chain." In A Delaware Indian Symposium, edited by Herbert C. Kraft, pp. 89-101. Harrisburg: Pennsylvania Historical and Museum Commission, 1974.

7602. Kraft, Herbert C., ed. A Delaware Indian Symposium. Anthropological Series no 4. Harrisburg: Pennsylvania Historical and Museum Commission, 1974.

7603. MacLeod, William Christie. "The Family Hunting Territory and Lenápe Political Organization." American Anthropologist 24 (October-December 1922): 448-463.

7604. Newcomb, William W., Jr. "The Culture and Acculturation of the Delaware Indians." Ph.D. dissertation, University of Michigan, 1953.

7605. Penn, William. William Penn: His Own Account of the Lenni Lenape or Delaware Indians, 1683. Edited by Albert Cook Myers. Moylan, Pennsylvania, 1937.

7606. Speck, Frank G. "The Wapanáchki Delawares and the English: Their Past as Viewed by an Ethnologist." Pennsylvania Magazine of History and Biography 67 (October 1943): 319-344.

7607. Wallace, Anthony F. C. King of the Delawares: Teedyuscung 1700-1763. Philadelphia: University of Pennsylvania Press, 1949.

7608. Weslager, C. A. The Delaware Indians: A History. New Brunswick: Rutgers University Press, 1972.

Iroquois Indians

The following bibliography is an excellent guide to materials on the Iroquois.

7609. Weinman, Paul L. A Bibliography of the Iroquoian Literature, Partially Annotated. New York State Museum and Science Service, Bulletin no. 411. Albany: University of the State of New York, 1969. Topically arranged.

Works on the Iroquois Indians are divided here into general accounts and biographical studies.

General and Miscellaneous Accounts

7610. Abler, Thomas S. "Friends, Factions, and the Seneca Nation Revolution of 1848." Niagara Frontier 21 (Winter 1974): 74-79.

7611. Beauchamp, William M. A History of the New York Iroquois, Now Commonly Called the Six Nations. Bulletin 78. Albany: New York State Museum, 1905.

7612. Berkhofer, Robert F., Jr. "Faith and Factionalism among the Senecas: Theory and Ethnohistory." Ethnohistory 12 (Spring, 1965): 99-112.

7613. Blau, Harold. "Historical Factors in Onondaga Iroquois Cultural Stability." Ethnohistory 12 (Summer 1965): 250-258.

7614. Boyce, Douglas W. "Did a Tuscarora Confederacy Exist?" Indian Historian 6 (Summer 1973): 34-40.

7615. _____. "Did a Tuscarora Confederacy Exist?" In Four Centuries of Southern Indians, edited by Charles M. Hudson, pp. 28-45. Athens: University of Georgia Press, 1975.

7616. _____. "Tuscarora Political Organization, Ethnic Identity, and Sociohistorical Demography, 1711-1825." Ph.D. dissertation, University of North Carolina, 1973.

7617. Boyce, Douglas W., ed. "A Glimpse of Iroquois Culture History through the Eyes of Joseph Brant and John Norton." Proceedings of the American Philosophical Society 117 (August 1973): 286-294.

7618. Brown, Wallace. "Magnificent Were the Iroquois." American History Illustrated 8 (January 1974): 22-33.

7619. Brush, Edward Hale. Iroquois, Past and Present. Buffalo: Baker, Jones and Company, 1901.

7620. Colden, Cadwallader. The History of the Five Indian Nations Depending on the Province of New-York. Introduction and notes by John Gilmary Shea. New York: T. H. Morrell, 1866. First published in New York, 1727. Several editions.

7621. Collins, Helen. "The League of the Iroquois." Western Pennsylvania Historical Magazine 55 (April 1972): 171-178.

7622. Corwin, R. David. "Dilemma of the Iroquois." Natural History 76 (June-July 1967): 6-7, 60-66.

7623. Deardorff, Merle H., and George S. Snyderman, eds. "A Nineteenth-Century Journal of a Visit to the Indians of New York." Proceedings of the American Philosophical Society 100 (December

1956): 582-612. Journal of John Philips.

7624. Ewers, John C. "Iroquois Indians in the Far West." Montana, the Magazine of Western History 13 (April 1963): 2-10.

7625. Fenton, William N. "Collecting Materials for a Political History of the Six Nations." Proceedings of the American Philosophical Society 93 (June 10, 1949): 233-238.

7626. _____. "The Iroquois in History," In North American Indians in Historical Perspective, edited by Eleanor Burke Leacock and Nancy Oestreich Lurie, pp. 129-168. New York: Random House, 1971.

7627. _____. "Iroquois Studies at the Mid-Century." Proceedings of the American Philosophical Society 95 (June 12, 1951): 296-310.

7628. _____. "Problems Arising from the Historic Northeastern Position of the Iroquois." In Essays in Historical Anthropology of North America, pp. 159-251. Smithsonian Miscellaneous Collections, volume 100. Washington: Smithsonian Institution, 1940.

7629. Finigan, Elizabeth Moran. "The New York State Indians." United States Catholic Historical Society, Historical Records and Studies 15 (March 1921): 104-111.

7630. Freilich, Morris. "Cultural Persistence among the Modern Iroquois." Anthropos 53 (1958): 473-483. A study of Caughnawaga steel workers.

7631. Hatzan, A. Leon. The True Story of Hiawatha and History of the Six Nations Indians. Toronto: McClelland and Stewart, 1925.

7632. Hewitt, J. N. B. "Era of the Formation of the Historic League of the Iroquois." American Anthropologist 7 (January 1894): 61-67.

7633. Hill, Asa R. "The Historical Position of the Six Nations." Ontario Historical Society Papers and Records 19 (1922): 103-109.

7634. Hill, Esther V. "The Iroquois Indians and Their Lands since 1783." New York State Historical Association Quarterly Journal 11 (October 1930): 335-353.

7635. Hopkins, Vivian C. "De Witt Clinton and the Iroquois." Ethnohistory 8 (Spring 1961): 113-143; (Summer 1961): 213-241.

7636. Houghton, Frederick. The Migrations of the Seneca Nation." American Anthropologist 29 (April 1927): 241-250.

7637. Hunt, George T. The Wars of the Iroquois: A Study in Intertribal Trade

Relations. Madison: University of Wisconsin Press, 1940.

7638. Jennings, Francis. "The Constitutional Evolution of the Covenant Chain." Proceedings of the American Philosophical Society 115 (April 1971): 88-96.

7639. Johnston, Charles M. "Joseph Brant, the Grand River Lands and the Northwest Crisis." Ontario History 55 (December 1963): 267-282.

7640. Kimm, S. C. The Iroquois: A History of the Six Nations of New York. Middleburgh, New York: Pierre W. Danforth, 1900.

7641. Lankes, Frank James. The Senecas on Buffalo Creek Reservation. West Seneca, New York: West Seneca Historical Society, 1964.

7642. Leder, Lawrence H., ed. The Livingston Indian Records, 1666-1723. Gettysburg, Pennsylvania: Pennsylvania Historical Association, 1956.

7643. Morgan, Henry Lewis. League of the Ho-dé-no-sau-nee, or Iroquois. Rochester, New York: Sage and Brother, 1851. Several later editions.

7644. Otterbein, Keith F. "Why the Iroquois Won: An Analysis of Iroquois Military Tactics." Ethnohistory 11 (Winter 1964): 56-63.

7645. Painter, Levinus K. "The Seneca Nation and the Kinzua Dam." Niagara Frontier 17 (Summer 1970): 30-35.

7646. Parker, Arthur C. An Analytical History of the Seneca Indians. Researches and Transactions of the New York State Archeological Association, Lewis H. Morgan Chapter, volume 6. Rochester, New York, 1926.

7647. _____. "The Influence of the Iroquois on the History and Archaeology of the Wyoming Valley and the Adjacent Region." Proceedings and Collections of the Wyoming Historical and Geological Society 11 (1910): 65-102.

7648. _____. Parker on the Iroquois. Edited by William N. Fenton. Syracuse: Syracuse University Press, 1968.

7649. _____. "The Status of the New York Indians." New York State Museum Bulletin no. 253 (July 1924): 67-82.

7650. Ricciardelli, Alex F. "The Adoption of White Agriculture by the Oneida Indians." Ethnohistory 10 (Fall 1963): 309-328.

7651. Schoolcraft, Henry R. Notes on the Iroquois; or, Contributions to the Statistics, Aboriginal History, Antiquities and General Ethnology of Western New York. New York: Bartlett and Welford, 1846.

7652. Speck, Frank G. The Iroquois: A Study in Cultural Evolution. Bloomfield Hills, Michigan: Cranbrook Institute of Science, 1955.

7653. Stites, Sara Henry. Economics of the Iroquois. Lancaster, Pennsylvania: New Era Printing Company, 1905.

7654. Voget, Fred. "Acculturation at Caughnawaga: A Note on the Native-Modified Group." American Anthropologist 53 (April-June 1951): 220-231.

7655. Wallace, Anthony F. C. The Death and Rebirth of the Seneca. New York: Alfred A. Knopf, 1970.

7656. _____ . "The Tuscaroras: Sixth Nation of the Iroquois Confederacy." Proceedings of the American Philosophical Society 93 (May 1949): 159-165.

7657. Wallace, Paul A. W. "The Five Nations of New York and Pennsylvania." New-York Historical Society Quarterly 37 (July 1953): 228-250.

7658. _____ . "The Iroquois: A Brief Outline of Their History." Pennsylvania History 23 (January 1956): 15-28.

7659. Wilson, Edmund. Apologies to the Iroquois. New York: Farrar, Straus and Cudahy, 1960. Includes "A Study of the Mohawks in High Steel," by Joseph Mitchell.

Biographical Studies

7660. Bonham, Milledge L., Jr. "The Religious Side of Joseph Brant." Journal of Religion 9 (July 1929): 398-418.

7661. Chalmers, Harvey, in collaboration with Ethel Brant Monture. Joseph Brant: Mohawk. East Lansing: Michigan State University Press, 1955.

7662. Conover, George S. Sayenqueraghta, King of the Senecas. Waterloo, New York: Observer Steam Job Printing House, 1885.

7663. Eggleston, Edward, and Lillie Eggleston Seelye. Brant and Red Jacket, Including an Account of the Early Wars of the Six Nations, and the Border Warfare of the Revolution. New York: Dodd, Mead and Company, 1879.

7664. Godcharles, Frederic A. "Chief Cornplanter." Pennsylvania Archaeologist 5 (October 1935): 67-69.

7665. Gundy, H. Pearson. "Molly Brant--Loyalist." Ontario History 45 (Summer 1953): 97-108.

7666. Hale, Horatio. "Chief George H. M. Johnson--Onwanonsyshon: His Life and Work among the Six Nations." Magazine of American History 13 (February 1885): 131-142. Also published separately, New York: A. S. Barnes and Company, 1885.

7667. Hamilton, Milton W. "Joseph Brant--'the Most Painted Indian.'" New York History 39 (April 1958): 119-132.

7668. Hassler, William W. "The Real Hiawatha." American History Illustrated 1 (May 1966): 35-37, 53.

7669. Henry, Thomas Robert. Wilderness Messiah: The Story of Hiawatha and the Iroquois. New York: W. Sloane Associates, 1955.

7670. Howard, Helen Addison. "Hiawatha: Co-founder of an Indian United Nations." Journal of the West 10 (July 1971): 428-438.

7671. Hubbard, J. Niles. An Account of Sa-Go-Ye-Wat-Ha, or Red Jacket and His People, 1750-1830. Albany: Joel Munsell's Sons, 1886.

7672. Johnston, Jean. "Molly Brant: Mohawk Matron." Ontario History 56 (June 1964): 105-124.

7673. Kelsay, Isabel T. "Joseph Brant: The Legend and the Man, a Foreword." New York History 40 (October 1959): 368-379.

7674. Lecompte, Edouard. An Iroquois Virgin: Catherine Tekakwitha, Lily of the Mohawk and the St. Lawrence, 1656-1680. Edited by John J. Wynne; translated by Isabel Hamilton Melick. New York: Tekakwitha League, 1932.

7675. Manley, Henry S. "Red Jacket's Last Campaign, and an Extended Bibliographical and Biographical Note." New York History 31 (April 1950): 149-168.

7676. Mulkearn, Lois. "Half King, Seneca Diplomat of the Ohio Valley." Western Pennsylvania Historical Magazine 37 (Summer 1954): 65-81.

7677. Palmer, William E. Memoir of the Distinguished Mohawk Indian Chief, Sachem and Warrior, Capt. Joseph Brant. Brantford, Ontario: C. E. Stewart and Company, 1872.

7678. Parker, Arthur C. "Ely S. Parker, Last Grand Sachem." American Indian 1 (Winter 1944): 11-15.

7679. _____ . Red Jacket, Last of the Seneca. New York: McGraw-Hill Book Company, 1952.

7680. Rickard, Clinton. Fighting Tuscarora: The Autobiography of Chief Clinton Rickard. Edited by Barbara Graymont. Syracuse: Syracuse University Press, 1973.

7681. Smith, Marc J. "Joseph Brant, Mohawk Statesman." Ph.D. dissertation, University of Wisconsin, 1946.

7682. Stone, William L. The Life and Times

of Sa-Go-Ye-Wat-Ha, or Red Jacket. New York: Wiley and Putnam, 1841.

7683. _____. Life of Joseph Brant--Thayendanegea: Including the Border Wars of the Revolution, and Sketches of the Indian Campaigns of Generals Harmar, St. Clair, and Wayne. 2 volumes. New York: George Dearborn and Company, 1838.

INDIANS OF THE NORTH CENTRAL REGION

General and Miscellaneous Studies

Listed here are general works on the region and studies of particular tribes. Material on some tribes is listed under separate headings below.

7684. Anderson, Duane. "Ioway Ethnohistory: A Review." Annals of Iowa, 3d series 41 (Spring 1973): 1228-1241; 42 (Summer 1973): 41-59.

7685. Aumann, F. R. "The Ioway." Palimpsest 9 (October 1928): 38-41.

7686. Babcock, Willoughby M. "The Minnesota Indian and His History." Minnesota Archaeologist 19 (July 1954): 18-25.

7687. Black, Glenn A. "The Historic Indian of the Ohio Valley: An Archaeologist's View." Ohio State Archaeological and Historical Quarterly 63 (April 1954): 155-165.

7688. Blair, Emma Helen, ed. The Indian Tribes of the Upper Mississippi Valley and Region of the Great Lakes. 2 volumes. Cleveland: Arthur H. Clark Company, 1911-1912. Accounts by Nicholas Perrot, Bacqueville de la Potherie, Morrell Marston, and Thomas Forsyth.

7689. Blasingham, Emily J. "The Depopulation of the Illinois Indians." Ethnohistory 3 (Summer 1956): 193-224; (Fall 1956): 361-412.

7690. Clark, Charles A. "Indians of Iowa." Annals of Iowa 6 (July 1903): 81-106.

7691. Clark, Dan E. "The Indians of Iowa in 1842." Iowa Journal of History and Politics 13 (April 1915): 250-263.

7692. Dowling, John Hall. "The Impact of Poverty on a Wisconsin Oneida Indian Community." Ph.D. dissertation, University of Michigan, 1973.

7693. Erdman, Joyce M. Handbook on Wisconsin Indians. Madison: Governor's Commission on Human Rights, 1966.

7694. Force, M. F. Some Early Notices of the Indians of Ohio. Cincinnati: Robert Clarke and Company, 1879.

7695. Foreman, Grant. "Illinois and Her Indians." Papers in Illinois History, 1939, pp. 66-111.

7696. Greenman, Emerson F. "The Indians of Michigan." Michigan History 45 (March 1961): 1-33.

7697. Hauser, Raymond E. "An Ethnohistory of the Illinois Indian Tribe, 1673-1832." Ph.D. dissertation, Northern Illinois University, 1973.

7698. Hyde, George E. Indians of the Woodlands: From Prehistoric Times to 1725. Norman: University of Oklahoma Press, 1962.

7699. Johnston, John. "Account of the Present State of the Indian Tribes Inhabiting Ohio." Transactions and Collections of the American Antiquarian Society 1 (1820): 269-299.

7700. Kowalke, Otto L. "The Settlement of the Stockbridge Indians and the Survey of Land in Outagamie County, Wisconsin." Wisconsin Magazine of History 40 (Autumn 1956): 31-34.

7701. Larzelere, Claude S. "The Red Man in Michigan." Michigan History Magazine 17 (Summer and Autumn 1933): 344-376.

7702. League of Women Voters of Minnesota. Indians in Minnesota. St. Paul: League of Women Voters of Minnesota, 1971. An earlier edition appeared in 1962.

7703. Lurie, Nancy Oestreich. "Wisconsin: A Natural Laboratory for North American Indian Studies." Wisconsin Magazine of History 53 (Autumn 1969): 3-20.

7704. Mahan, Bruce E. "Winnebago and Pottawattamie." Palimpsest 9 (January 1928): 53-55.

7705. Merwin, Raymond E. "The Wyandot Indians." Transactions of the Kansas State Historical Society 9 (1905-1906): 73-88.

7706. Meyer, Roy W. "The Iowa Indians, 1836-1885." Kansas Historical Quarterly 28 (Autumn 1962): 273-300.

7707. Moorehead, Warren King. "The Indian Tribes of Ohio--Historically Considered." Ohio Archaeological and Historical Quarterly 7 (October 1898): 1-109.

7708. Peithmann, Irvin M. Indians of Southern Illinois. Springfield, Illinois: Charles C. Thomas, 1964.

7709. Richman, Irving B. "Indians of Iowa." Palimpsest 5 (October 1924): 357-362.

7710. Ritzenthaler, Robert E. "The Oneida Indians of Wisconsin." Bulletin of the Public Museum of the City of Milwaukee 19 (1950): 1-52.

7711. Shea, John Gilmary. "The Indian Tribes of Wisconsin." Annual Report and Collections of the State Historical Society of Wisconsin 3 (1856): 125-138.

7712. Smith, Dwight L. "The Problem of the Historic Indian in the Ohio Valley: The Historian's View." Ohio State Archaeological and Historical Quarterly 63 (April 1954): 172-180.

7713. Smith, Robert Emmett, Jr. "The Wyandot Indians, 1843-1876." Ph.D. dissertation, Oklahoma State University, 1973.

7714. Strong, William Duncan. The Indian Tribes of the Chicago Region, with Special Reference to the Illinois and the Potawatomi. Anthropology Leaflet 24. Chicago: Field Museum of Natural History, 1926.

7715. Taylor, E. L. "The Ohio Indians." Ohio Archaeological and Historical Quarterly 6 (January 1898): 72-94.

7716. Wakefield, Francis. "The Elusive Mascoutens." Michigan History 50 (September 1966): 228-234.

7717. Winchell, N. H. The Aborigines of Minnesota. St. Paul: Minnesota Historical Society, 1911.

Chippewa Indians

The following publication is a useful guide to materials on the Chippewa Indians.

7718. Chippewa and Dakota Indians: A Subject Catalog of Books, Pamphlets, Periodical Articles, and Manuscripts in the Minnesota Historical Society. St. Paul: Minnesota Historical Society, 1969.

Listed here are general and miscellaneous accounts of the Chippewa Indians.

7719. Armstrong, Benjamin G. "Reminiscences of Life among the Chippewa." Wisconsin Magazine of History 55 (Spring 1972): 175-196; (Summer 1972): 287-309; 56 (Autumn 1972): 37-58; (Winter 1972-1973): 140-161.

7720. Barnouw, Victor. Acculturation and Personality among the Wisconsin Chippewa. Memoir Series of the American Anthropological Association, no. 72. Menasha, Wisconsin, 1950.

7721. Bishop, Charles Aldrich. "The Northern Chippewa: An Ethnohistorical Study." Ph.D. dissertation, State University of New York at Buffalo, 1969.

7722. Brill, Charles. Indian and Free: A Contemporary Portrait of Life on a Chippewa Reservation. Minneapolis: University of Minnesota Press, 1971. Chiefly pictorial.

7723. Delorme, David P. "History of the Turtle Mountain Band of Chippewa Indians." North Dakota History 22 (July 1955): 121-134.

7724. _____. "A Socio-Economic Study of the Turtle Mountain Band of Chippewa Indians, and a Critical Evaluation of Proposals Designed to Terminate Their Federal Wardship Status." Ph.D. dissertation, University of Texas, 1955.

7725. Emmert, Darlene Gay. "The Indians of Shiawassee County." Michigan History 47 (June 1963): 127-155; (September 1963): 243-272.

7726. Friedl, Ernestine. "Persistence in Chippewa Culture and Personality." American Anthropologist 58 (October 1956): 814-825.

7727. Hesketh, John. "History of the Turtle Mountain Chippewa." Collections of the North Dakota State Historical Society 5 (1923): 85-154.

7728. Hickerson, Harold. The Chippewa and Their Neighbors: A Study in Ethnohistory. New York: Holt, Rinehart and Winston, 1970.

7729. _____. "The Chippewa of the Upper Great Lakes: A Study in Sociopolitical Change." In North American Indians in Historical Perspective, edited by Eleanor Burke Leacock and Nancy Oestreich Lurie, pp. 169-199. New York: Random House, 1971.

7730. _____. "The Genesis of a Trading Post Band: The Pembina Chippewa." Ethnohistory 3 (Fall 1956): 289-345.

7731. _____. The Southwestern Chippewa: An Ethnohistorical Study. American Anthropological Association, Memoir 92. Menasha, Wisconsin, 1962.

7732. Howard, James H. "The Turtle Mountain 'Chippewa.'" North Dakota Quarterly 26 (Spring 1958): 37-46.

7733. James, Bernard J. "Social-Psychological Dimensions of Ojibwa Acculturation." American Anthropologist 63 (August 1961): 721-746.

7734. Jones, Charles Frederick. "Social and Cultural Change in Three Minnesota Chippewa Indian Communities. Ph.D. dissertation, Yale University, 1962.

7735. Jones, Peter. History of the Ojebway Indians: With Especial Reference to Their Conversion to Christianity. London: A. W. Bennett, 1861. Reprinted, Freeport, New York: Books for Libraries, 1970.

7736. "Minnesota's Chippewas: Treaties and Trends." Minnesota Law Review 39 (June 1955): 853-872.

7737. Neill, Edward D. "History of the Ojibways, and Their Connection with Fur Traders, Based upon Official and Other Records." Collections of the Minnesota Historical Society 5 (1885): 395-510.

7738. Owl, Frell M. "Seven Chiefs Rule the Red Lake Band." American Indian 6 (Spring 1952): 3-12.

7739. Rogers, John. Red World and White: Memories of a Chippewa Boyhood. Norman: University of Oklahoma Press, 1974. First published in 1957 under the title, A Chippewa Speaks.

7740. Sherman, Merle. "A Geographic Study of the Red Lake Chippewa Indian Band of Minnesota." Proceedings of the Minnesota Academy of Science 30 (1962): 60-66.

7741. Vizenor, Gerald. "The Anishinabe." Indian Historian 4 (Winter 1971): 16-18.

7742. Warren, William W. History of the Ojibway Nation. Collections of the Minnesota Historical Society, volume 5. St. Paul, 1885.

7743. Weslager, C. A. "Enrollment List of Chippewa and Delaware-Munsies Living in Franklin County, Kansas, May 31, 1900." Kansas Historical Quarterly 40 (Summer 1974): 234-240.

Kickapoo Indians

Like other tribes from the north central region, the Kickapoos moved from their original homelands. Included here are studies of the tribe in Oklahoma and Mexico.

7744. Buntin, Martha. "The Mexican Kickapoos." Chronicles of Oklahoma 11 (March 1933): 691-708; (June 1933): 823-837.

7745. Dillingham, Betty Ann Wilder. "Oklahoma Kickapoo." Ph.D. dissertation, University of Michigan, 1963.

7746. "The Flight of the Kickapoos." Chronicles of Oklahoma 1 (October 1921): 150-156.

7747. Gibson, Arrell M. The Kickapoos: Lords of the Middle Border. Norman: University of Oklahoma Press, 1963.

7748. Goggin, John M. "The Mexican Kickapoo Indians." Southwestern Journal of Anthropology 7 (Autumn 1951): 314-327.

7749. Pope, Richard K. "The Withdrawal of the Kickapoo." American Indian 8 (Winter 1958-1959): 17-26.

7750. Silverberg, James. "The Kickapoo Indians: First One Hundred Years of White Contact in Wisconsin." Wisconsin Archeologist 38 (September 1957): 61-181.

7751. Wallace, Ben J. "Oklahoma Kickapoo Culture Change." Plains Anthropologist

14 (May 1969): 107-112.

Menominee Indians

Listed here are general and miscellaneous works dealing with the Menominees.

7752. Hart, Paxton. "The Making of Menominee County." Wisconsin Magazine of History 43 (Spring 1960): 181-189.

7753. Keesing, Felix M. The Menomini Indians of Wisconsin: A Study of Three Centuries of Cultural Contact and Change. Memoirs of the American Philosophical Society, volume 10. Philadelphia: American Philosophical Society, 1939.

7754. Ourada, Patricia Kathryn. "The Menominee Indians: A History." Ph.D. dissertation, University of Oklahoma, 1973.

7755. Raymer, Patricia. "Wisconsin's Menominees: Indians on a Seesaw." National Geographic 146 (August 1974): 228-251.

7756. Sady, Rachel Reese. "The Menominee: Transition from Trusteeship." Applied Anthropology 6 (Spring 1947): 1-14.

7757. Spindler, George D. Sociological and Psychological Processes in Menomini Acculturation. University of California Publications in Culture and Society, volume 5. Berkeley: University of California Press, 1955.

7758. Spindler, George, and Louise Spindler. Dreamers without Power: The Menomini Indians. New York: Holt, Rinehart and Winston, 1971.

7759. Spindler, Louise S. Menomini Women and Culture Change. American Anthropological Association, Memoir 91. Menasha, Wisconsin, 1962.

7760. Thwaites, Reuben Gold. "Oshkosh, Menominee Sachem." Proceedings of the State Historical Society of Wisconsin 59 (1911): 170-176.

For recent developments among the Menominees, see the section on termination.

Miami Indians

7761. Anson, Bert. The Miami Indians. Norman: University of Oklahoma Press, 1970.

7762. Blasingham, Emily J. "The Miami Prior to the French and Indian War." Ethnohistory 2 (Winter 1955): 1-10.

7763. Dillon, John B. "The National Decline of the Miami Indians." Indiana Historical Society Publications 1 (1897): 121-143.

7764. Faben, W. W. "Indians of the Tri-State Area: The Miamis, 1654-1752." Northwest Ohio Quarterly 41 (Fall 1969): 157-162.

7765. Young, Calvin M. Little Turtle (Me-she-kin-no-quah), The Great Chief of the Miami Indian Nation: Being a Sketch of His Life, Together with That of William Wells and Some Noted Descendants. Indianapolis: Sentinel Printing Company, 1917.

Potawatomi Indians

Listed here are general and miscellaneous works and biographical studies dealing with the Potawatomi Indians.

7766. Bourassa, J. N. "The Life of Wah-bahn-se: The Warrior Chief of the Pottawatamies." Kansas Historical Quarterly 38 (Summer 1972): 132-143.

7767. "The Career of Chief Waubunsee." Wisconsin Magazine of History 5 (June 1922): 410-411.

7768. Claspy, Everett. The Potawatomi Indians of Southwestern Michigan. Dowagiac, Michigan, 1966.

7769. Clifton, James A. "Chicago Was Theirs." Chicago History 1 (Spring 1970): 4-17.

7770. _____. "Factional Conflict and the Indian Community: The Prairie Pota-watomi Case." In The American Indian Today, edited by Stuart Levine and Nancy Oestreich Lurie, pp. 115-132. Deland, Florida: Everett/Edwards, 1968. This appeared originally in Midcontinent American Studies Journal 6 (Fall 1965): 101-123.

7771. Clifton, James A., and Barry Isaac. "The Kansas Prairie Potawatomi: On the Nature of a Contemporary Indian Community." Transactions of the Kansas Academy of Science 67 (Spring 1964): 1-24.

7772. Connelley, William Elsey. "The Prairie Band of Pottawatomi Indians (Reservation, Jackson County, Kansas)." Collections of the Kansas State Historical Society 14 (1915-1918): 488-570.

7773. Conway, Thomas G. "Potawatomi Politics." Journal of the Illinois State Historical Society 65 (Winter 1972): 395-418.

7774. Copley, A. B. "The Pottawatomies." Collections and Researches Made by the Michigan Pioneer and Historical Society 14 (1889): 256-267.

7775. Dickason, David H. "Chief Simon Pokagon: 'The Indian Longfellow.'" Indiana Magazine of History 57 (June 1961): 127-140.

7776. Edmunds, R. David. "A History of the Potawatomi Indians, 1615-1796." Ph.D. dissertation, University of Oklahoma, 1972.

7777. _____. "Potawatomis in the Platte Country: An Indian Removal Incomplete." Missouri Historical Review 48 (July 1974): 375-392.

7778. Faben, W. W. "Indians of the Tri-State Area: The Potowattamis." Northwest Ohio Quarterly 30 (Winter 1957-1958): 49-53; (Spring 1958): 100-105; 34 (Autumn 1962): 168-176.

7779. Francis, C. F. "Abram B. Burnett, Pottawatomie Chief." Collections of the Kansas State Historical Society 13 (1913-1914): 371-373.

7780. Jones, Dorothy V. "A Potawatomi Faces the Problem of Cultural Change: Joseph N. Bourassa in Kansas." Kansas Quarterly 3 (Fall 1971): 47-55.

7781. Lawson, Publius V. "The Potawatomi." Wisconsin Archeologist 19 (April 1920): 41-116.

7782. Mitchell, Kenneth S. "The Migrations of the Potawatami." Journal of American History 16 (October-December 1922): 353-360.

7783. Murphy, Joseph Francis. "Potawatomi Indians of the West: Origins of the Citizen Band." Ph.D. dissertation, University of Oklahoma, 1961.

7784. Rathke, William C. "Chief Waubonsie and the Pottawattamie Indians." Annals of Iowa 35 (Fall 1959): 81-100.

7785. Ritzenthaler, Robert E. "The Potawatomi Indians of Wisconsin." Bulletin of the Public Museum of the City of Milwaukee 19 (February 1953): 105-174.

7786. Smith, William E. "The Oregon Trail through Pottawatomie County." Collections of the Kansas State Historical Society 17 (1926-1928): 435-464.

7787. Winger, Otho. The Potawatomi Indians. Elgin, Illinois: Elgin Press, 1939.

Sac and Fox Indians

Listed here are general and miscellaneous accounts and biographical studies, especially those dealing with Black Hawk.

7788. Aumann, F. R., J. E. Briggs, and William J. Petersen. "Keokuk." Palimpsest 46 (May 1965): 225-272.

7789. Bicknell, A. D. "The Tama County Indians." Annals of Iowa, 3d series 4 (October 1899): 196-208.

7790. Black Hawk. <u>Black Hawk (Ma-Ka-Tai-Me-She-Kia-Kiak): An Autobiography</u>. Edited by Donald Jackson. Urbana: University of Illinois Press, 1955.

7791. _____. <u>Life of Black Hawk, Ma-Ka-Tai-Me-She-Kia-Kiak</u>. Edited by Milo M. Quaife. Chicago: R. R. Donnelley and Sons Company, 1916.

7792. _____. <u>Life of Ma-Ka-Tai-Me-She-Kia-Kiak, or Black Hawk</u>. Cincinnati, 1833. Written down by J. B. Patterson. Republished as <u>Autobiography of Ma-Ka-Tai-Me-She-Kia-Kiak, or Black Hawk</u>. St. Louis: Press of Continental Printing Company, 1882.

7793. "Black Hawk." <u>Annals of Iowa</u> 13 (October 1921): 126-131.

7794. Briggs, John Ely. "The Sacs and Foxes." <u>Palimpsest</u> 9 (February 1928): 45-48.

7795. Busby, Allie B. <u>Two Summers among the Musquakies, Relating to the Early History of the Sac and Fox Tribe</u>. Vinton, Iowa: Herald Book and Job Rooms, 1886.

7796. "Chief Poweshiek at Des Moines." <u>Annals of Iowa</u> 25 (July 1943): 58-60.

7797. Cole, Cyrenus. <u>I Am a Man--the Indian Black Hawk</u>. Iowa City: State Historical Society of Iowa, 1938.

7798. Drake, Benjamin. <u>The Life and Adventures of Black Hawk: With Sketches of Keokuk, the Sac and Fox Indians, and the Late Black Hawk War</u>. Seventh edition. Cincinnati: George Conclin, 1849.

7799. Ferris, Ida M. "The Sauks and Foxes in Franklin and Osage Counties, Kansas." <u>Collections of the Kansas State Historical Society</u> 11 (1909-1910): 333-395.

7800. Froncek, Thomas. "'I Was Once a Great Warrior.'" <u>American Heritage</u> 24 (December 1972): 16-21, 97-99. Chief Black Hawk.

7801. Gallaher, Ruth A. "The Tama Indians." <u>Palimpsest</u> 7 (February 1926): 44-53. Reprinted 38 (August 1957): 305-315; 48 (July 1967): 289-299.

7802. Gearing, Frederick O. <u>The Face of the Fox</u>. Chicago: Aldine Publishing Company, 1970.

7803. _____. "Today's Mesquakies." <u>American Indian</u> 7 (Spring 1955): 24-37.

7804. Green, C. R. <u>Sac and Fox Indians in Kansas</u>. Olathe, Kansas, 1914.

7805. Green, Michael D. "The Sac-Fox Annuity Crisis of 1840 in Iowa Territory." <u>Arizona and the West</u> 16 (Summer 1974): 141-156.

7806. Hagan, William T. <u>The Sac and Fox Indians</u>. Norman: University of Oklahoma Press, 1958.

7807. Jackson, Donald. "Black Hawk--the Man and His Times." <u>Palimpsest</u> 43 (February 1962): 65-79.

7808. Jones, William. "Notes on the Fox Indians." <u>Iowa Journal of History and Politics</u> 10 (January 1912): 70-112.

7809. Peck, Mrs. W. F. "Black Hawk: The Man--the Hero--the Patriot." <u>Annals of Iowa</u>, 3d series 2 (July 1896): 450-464.

7810. Petersen, William J. "The Tama Indians in 1967." <u>Palimpsest</u> 48 (July 1967): 320.

7811. Purcell, L. Edward. "The Mesquakie Indian Settlement in 1905." <u>Palimpsest</u> 55 (March-April 1974): 34-55.

7812. _____. "The Ward-Mesquakie Photograph Collection." <u>Palimpsest</u> 55 (March-April 1974): 56-64.

7813. Reising, Robert. "Jim Thorpe: Multi-Cultural Hero." <u>Indian Historian</u> 7 (Fall 1974): 14-16.

7814. Rideout, Henry Milner. <u>William Jones: Indian, Cowboy, American Scholar, and Anthropologist in the Field</u>. New York: Frederick A. Stokes Company, 1912.

7815. Swisher, J. A. "Chief of the Sauks." <u>Palimpsest</u> 13 (February 1932): 41-54. Black Hawk.

7816. Ward, Duren J. H. "Meskwakia." <u>Iowa Journal of History and Politics</u> 4 (April 1906): 178-189.

See also studies on the Black Hawk War (3483 to 3513).

Shawnee Indians

Many of the writings on the Shawnees have centered on Tecumseh. A number of biographies on him are listed here, together with other general and biographical works on the Shawnees.

7817. Alford, Thomas Wildcat, as told to Florence Drake. <u>Civilization</u>. Norman: University of Oklahoma Press, 1936.

7818. Bennett, John. <u>Blue Jacket, War Chief of the Shawnees, and His Part in Ohio's History</u>. Chillocothe: Ross County Historical Society Press, 1943.

7819. Drake, Benjamin. <u>Life of Tecumseh, and of His Brother the Prophet; with a Historical Sketch of the Shawanoe Indians</u>. Cincinnati: E. Morgan and Company, 1841.

7820. Eggleston, Edward, and Lillie Eggleston Seelye. <u>Tecumseh and the</u>

Shawnee Prophet. New York: Dodd, Mead and Company, 1878.

7821. Goltz, Herbert Charles Walter, Jr. "Tecumseh, the Prophet and the Rise of the Northwest Indian Confederation." Ph.D. dissertation, University of Western Ontario, 1973.

7822. Gurd, Norman S. The Story of Tecumseh. Toronto: W. Briggs, 1912.

7823. Harrington, Grant W. The Shawnees in Kansas. Kansas City, Kansas: Western Pioneer Press, 1937.

7824. Hinsdale, Wilbert B. "Tecumseh's Illusions." Papers of the Michigan Academy of Science, Arts and Letters 18 (1933): 31-52.

7825. Josephy, Alvin M., Jr. "'These Lands Are Ours. . . '" American Heritage 12 (August 1961): 14-25, 83-89. On Tecumseh.

7826. Klinck, Carl F., ed. Tecumseh: Fact and Fiction in Early Records: A Book of Primary Source Materials. Englewood Cliffs, New Jersey: Prentice-Hall, 1961.

7827. Moorehead, Warren K. "Logan, Tecumseh, the Shawano Indians." Ohio Archaeological and Historical Quarterly 36 (January 1927): 78-91.

7828. Oskison, John M. Tecumseh and His Times: The Story of a Great Indian. New York: G. P. Putnam's Sons, 1938.

7829. Raymond, Ethel T. Tecumseh: A Chronicle of the Last Great Leader of His People. Toronto: Brook and Company, 1915.

7830. Royce, Charles C. "An Inquiry into the Identity and History of the Shawnee Indians." American Antiquarian and Oriental Journal 3 (April 1881): 178-189.

7831. Siberell, Lloyd Emerson. Tecumseh: His Career, the Man, His Chillicothe Portrait. Chillicothe, Ohio: Ross County Historical Society, 1944.

7832. Tucker, Glenn. Tecumseh: Vision of Glory. Indianapolis: Bobbs-Merrill, 1956.

7833. Van Natter, Francis Marion. "Tecumseh, King of the Woods." National Republic 22 (May 1934): 5-6, 32; (June 1934): 19-20, 30.

7834. Whicker, J. Wesley. "Tecumseh and Pushmataha." Indiana Magazine of History 18 (December 1922): 315-331.

7835. Witthoft, John, and William A. Hunter. "The Seventeenth-Century Origins of the Shawnee." Ethnohistory 2 (Winter 1955): 42-57.

Winnebago Indians

Listed here are biographical studies as well as general and miscellaneous works on the Winnebago Indians.

7836. Clark, William Leslie, and Walker D. Wyman. Charles Round Low Cloud: Voice of the Winnebago. River Falls: University of Wisconsin-River Falls Press, 1973.

7837. Cloud, Henry Roe. "From Wigwam to Pulpit: A Red Man's Own Story of His Progress from Darkness to Light." Missionary Review of the World 38 (May 1915): 328-339.

7838. Lawson, Publius V. "Habitat of the Winnebago, 1632-1832." Proceedings of the State Historical Society of Wisconsin, 1906, pp. 144-166.

7839. Lurie, Nancy Oestreich. "The Winnebago Indians: A Study in Cultural Change." Ph.D. dissertation, Northwestern University, 1952.

7840. Mountain Wolf Woman. Mountain Wolf Woman, Sister of Crashing Thunder: The Autobiography of a Winnebago Indian. Edited by Nancy Oestreich Lurie. Ann Arbor: University of Michigan Press, 1961.

7841. Paquette, Moses. "The Wisconsin Winnebagoes." Collections of the State Historical Society of Wisconsin 12 (1892): 399-433. An interview with Rueben Gold Thwaites.

7842. Petersen, William J. "The Winnebago Indians." Palimpsest 41 (July 1960): 325-356.

7843. Radin, Paul. "The Influence of the Whites on Winnebago Culture." Proceedings of the State Historical Society of Wisconsin, 1913, pp. 137-145.

7844. _____. "Personal Reminiscences of a Winnebago Indian." Journal of American Folk-lore 26 (October-December 1913): 293-318.

7845. Radin, Paul, ed. Crashing Thunder: The Autobiography of an American Indian. New York: D. Appleton and Company, 1926.

7846. Steward, John D. II. "The Great Winnebago Chieftain: Simon Cameron's Rise to Power, 1860-1867." Pennsylvania History 39 (January 1972): 20-39.

INDIANS OF THE SOUTH AND SOUTHEAST

General and Miscellaneous Studies

Listed here are works on Indians in the region stretching from Virginia to Texas, including general studies and studies on particular groups and individuals. Material on the Five Civilized Tribes and on the Lumbee Indians is listed under separate headings below.

7847. Adair, James. The History of the American Indians: Particularly Those Adjoining to the Mississippi, East and West Florida, Georgia, South and North Carolina and Virginia. London: E. C. Dilly, 1775. Also later editions.

7848. Andrews, Charles M. "The Florida Indians in the Seventeenth Century." Tequesta 1 (July 1943): 36-48.

7849. Berlandier, Jean Louis. The Indians of Texas in 1830. Translated by Patricia Reading Leclercq. Edited by John C. Ewers. Washington: Smithsonian Institution, 1969.

7850. Bounds, John H. "The Alabama-Coushatta Indians of Texas." Journal of Geography 70 (March 1971): 175-182.

7851. Brown, Douglas S. The Catawba Indians: The People of the River. Columbia: University of South Carolina Press, 1966.

7852. Burch, Marvin C. "The Indigenous Indians of the Lower Trinity Area of Texas." Southwestern Historical Quarterly 60 (July 1956): 36-52.

7853. Burt, Jesse, and Robert B. Ferguson. Indians of the Southeast, Then and Now. Nashville: Abingdon Press, 1973.

7854. Calmes, Alan R. "Indian Cultural Traditions and European Conquest of the Georgia-South Carolina Coastal Plain, 3000 B.C.-1733 A.D.: A Combined Archaeological and Historical Investigation." Ph.D. dissertation, University of South Carolina, 1968.

7855. Coates, James R. "Native Indians of the Old Dominion State." American Indian 2 (Fall 1945): 22-25.

7856. Covington, James W. "Apalachee Indians, 1704-1763." Florida Historical Quarterly 50 (April 1972): 366-384.

7857. _____. "The Apalachee Indians Move West." Florida Anthropologist 17 (December 1964): 221-225.

7858. De Vorsey, Louis, Jr. "Early Maps as a Source in the Reconstruction of Southern Indian Landscapes." In Red, White, and Black: Symposium on Indians in the Old South, edited by Charles M. Hudson, pp. 12-30. Athens: University of Georgia Press, 1971.

7859. Ethridge, Adele Nash. "Indians of Grant Parish." Louisiana Historical Quarterly 23 (October 1940): 1107-1131.

7860. Fischer, Ann. "History and Current Status of the Houma Indians." In The American Indian Today, edited by Stuart Levine and Nancy Oestreich Lurie, pp. 133-147. Deland, Florida: Everett/Edwards, 1968. An earlier version appeared in Midcontinent American Studies Journal 6 (Fall 1965): 149-163. A small group in Louisiana.

7861. Goggin, John Mann. "The Tekesta Indians of Southern Florida." Florida Historical Quarterly 18 (April 1940): 274-284.

7862. Griffin, John W., ed. The Florida Indian and His Neighbors. Winter Park, Florida: Inter-American Center, Rollins College, 1949.

7863. Harrison, Benjamin. "Indian Races of Florida." Florida Historical Society Quarterly 3 (October 1924): 29-37.

7864. Hasdorff, James Curtis. "Four Indian Tribes in Texas, 1758-1858: A Reevaluation of Historical Sources." Ph.D. dissertation, University of New Mexico, 1971.

7865. Haywood, John. The Natural and Aboriginal History of Tennessee, up to the First Settlements Therein by the White People, in the Year 1768. Nashville, Tennessee: George Wilson, 1823.

7866. Hicks, George L. "Cultural Persistence versus Local Adaptation: Frank G. Speck's Catawba Indians." Ethnohistory 12 (Fall 1965): 343-354.

7867. Hudson, Charles M. The Catawba Nation. Athens: University of Georgia Press, 1970.

7868. Hudson, Charles M., ed. Four Centuries of Southern Indians. Athens: University of Georgia Press, 1975.

7869. _____. Red, White, and Black: Symposium on Indians in the Old South. Southern Anthropological Society Proceedings, no. 5. Athens: University of Georgia Press, 1971.

7870. Jacobson, Daniel. "The Origin of the Koasati Community of Louisiana." Ethnohistory 7 (Spring 1960): 97-120.

7871. Jones, Charles C., Jr. Antiquities of the Southern Indians, Particularly of the Georgia Tribes. New York: D. Appleton and Company, 1873.

7872. Juricek, John T. "The Westo Indians." Ethnohistory 11 (Spring 1964): 134-173.

7873. Milling, Chapman J. Red Carolinians. Chapel Hill: University of North Carolina Press, 1940.

7874. Mook, Maurice A. "The Aboriginal Population of Tidewater Virginia."

American Anthropologist 46 (April–June 1944): 193-208.

7875. _____. "Algonkian Ethnohistory of the Carolina Sound." *Journal of the Washington Academy of Sciences* 34 (June 15, 1944): 181-197; (July 15, 1944): 213-228.

7876. _____. "The Ethnological Significance of Tindall's Map of Virginia, 1608." *William and Mary College Quarterly Historical Magazine*, 2d series 23 (October 1943): 371-408.

7877. _____. "Virginia Ethnology from an Early Relation." *William and Mary College Quarterly Historical Magazine*, 2d series 23 (April 1943): 101-129.

7878. Newcomb, W. W., Jr. *The Indians of Texas, from Prehistoric to Modern Times*. Austin: University of Texas Press, 1961.

7879. Paredes, J. Anthony, and Kaye Lenihan. "Native American Population in the Southeastern States: 1960-70." *Florida Anthropologist* 26 (June 1973): 45-56.

7880. Peterson, John H., Jr. "The Indian in the Old South." In *Red, White, and Black: Symposium on Indians in the Old South*, edited by Charles M. Hudson, pp. 116-133. Athens: University of Georgia Press, 1971.

7881. Post, Lauren C. "Some Notes on the Attakapas Indians of Southwest Louisiana." *Louisiana History* 3 (Summer 1962): 221-242.

7882. Rights, Douglas L. *The American Indian in North Carolina*. Durham, North Carolina: Duke University Press, 1947.

7883. Rounds, Elizabeth W. *Lost Arrows: The Story of the Indians in the District of Columbia*. Washington, 1948.

7884. Scaife, H. Lewis. *History and Condition of the Catawba Indians of South Carolina*. Philadelphia: Indian Rights Association, 1896.

7885. Skeels, Lydia Lowndes Maury. *An Ethnohistorical Survey of Texas Indians*. Austin: Texas Historical Survey Committee, 1972.

7886. Smith, Hale G. "Florida Bibliography and Historiography: The Development of Knowledge Regarding the Florida Indians." *Florida Historical Quarterly* 37 (October 1958): 156-160.

7887. Speck, Frank G. "The Catawba Nation and Its Neighbors." *North Carolina Historical Review* 16 (October 1939): 404-417.

7888. Stern, Theodore. "Chickahominy: The Changing Culture of a Virginia Indian Community." *Proceedings of the American Philosophical Society* 96 (April 1952): 157-225.

7889. Swanton, John R. *The Indians of the Southeastern United States*. Bureau of American Ethnology Bulletin 137. Washington: Government Printing Office, 1946.

7890. _____. *Indian Tribes of the Lower Mississippi Valley and Adjacent Coast of the Gulf of Mexico*. Bureau of American Ethnology Bulletin 43. Washington: Government Printing Office, 1911.

7891. Vestal, Stanley. "The First Families of Oklahoma." *American Mercury* 5 (August 1925): 489-494.

7892. Watson, Virginia. *The Princess Pocahontas*. Philadelphia: Penn Publishing Company, 1916.

7893. Willey, Gordon R. "The Florida Indian and His Neighbors: A Summary." In *The Florida Indian and His Neighbors*, edited by John W. Griffin, pp. 139-167. Winter Park, Florida: Inter-American Center, Rollins College, 1949.

7894. Willoughby, Charles C. "The Virginia Indians in the Seventeenth Century." *American Anthropologist*, new series 9 (January-March 1907): 57-86.

7895. Winfrey, Dorman H., ed. *Texas Indian Papers, 1825-1916*. 5 volumes. Austin: Texas State Library, 1959-1966.

7896. Woodward, Grace Steele. *Pocahontas*. Norman: University of Oklahoma Press, 1969.

7897. Wright, Muriel H. *A Guide to the Indian Tribes of Oklahoma*. Norman: University of Oklahoma Press, 1951.

Cherokee Indians

Because of their long and active history of relations with the whites, the Cherokees have been the subject of many studies, including those on the Indians now in Oklahoma and on the Eastern Cherokees. The listing here is divided into general accounts and biographical studies.

General and Miscellaneous Accounts

7898. Ballas, Donald J. "Notes on the Population, Settlement, and Ecology of the Eastern Cherokee Indians." *Journal of Geography* 59 (September 1960): 258-267.

7899. Bloom, Leonard. "The Acculturation of the Eastern Cherokee." Ph.D. dissertation, Duke University, 1937.

7900. _____. "The Acculturation of the Eastern Cherokee: Historical Aspects." *North Carolina Historical Review* 19 (October 1942): 323-358.

7901. Britton, Wiley. "Some Reminiscences of the Cherokee People." Chronicles of Oklahoma 5 (June 1927): 180-184.

7902. Brown, John P. Old Frontiers: The Story of the Cherokee Indians from Earliest Times to the Date of Their Removal to the West, 1838. Kingsport, Tennessee: Southern Publishers, 1938.

7903. Buchanan, Robert Wayne. "Patterns of Organization and Leadership among Contemporary Oklahoma Cherokees." Ph.D. dissertation, University of Kansas, 1972.

7904. Clarke, Mary Whatley. Chief Bowles and the Texas Cherokees. Norman: University of Oklahoma Press, 1971.

7905. Collier, Peter. When Shall They Rest? The Cherokee's Long Struggle with America. New York: Holt, Rinehart and Winston, 1973.

7906. Coulter, E. Merton. "John Howard Payne's Visit to Georgia." Georgia Historical Quarterly 46 (December 1962): 333-376.

7907. Cunningham, Hugh T. "A History of the Cherokee Indians." Chronicles of Oklahoma 8 (September 1930): 291-314; (December 1930): 407-440.

7908. Dale, Edward Everett, and Gaston Litton, eds. Cherokee Cavaliers: Forty Years of Cherokee History As Told in the Correspondence of the Ridge-Watie-Boudinot Family. Norman: University of Oklahoma Press, 1939.

7909. Davis, Katharine Murdoch. "What Happened after They Got There?" Delphian Quarterly 35 (January 1952): 25-27.

7910. Dickson, John L. "The Judicial History of the Cherokee Nation from 1721 to 1835." Ph.D. dissertation, University of Oklahoma, 1964.

7911. The Eastern Cherokees: How They Live Today, Their History. Knoxville, Tennessee: J. L. Caton, 1937.

7912. Englund, Donald. "A Demographic Study of the Cherokee Nation." Ph.D. dissertation, University of Oklahoma, 1973.

7913. Foreman, Carolyn Thomas. Park Hill. Muskogee, Oklahoma: Press of the Star Printery, 1948.

7914. Foreman, Carolyn Thomas, ed. "An Early Account of the Cherokees." Chronicles of Oklahoma 34 (Summer 1956): 141-158. Account by George W. Featherstonhaugh.

7915. Foreman, Grant. "John Howard Payne and the Cherokee Indians." American Historical Review 37 (July 1932): 723-730.

7916. _____. "Some New Light on Houston's Life among the Cherokee Indians." Chronicles of Oklahoma 9 (June 1931): 139-152.

7917. Foreman, Grant, ed. "Captain John Stuart's Sketch of the Indians." Chronicles of Oklahoma 11 (March 1933): 667-672.

7918. _____. Indian Justice: A Cherokee Murder Trial at Tahlequah in 1840, as Reported by John Howard Payne. Oklahoma City: Harlow Publishing Company, 1934.

7919. Foster, George E. "Journalism among the Cherokee Indians." Magazine of American History 18 (July 1887): 65-70.

7920. Franks, Kenny A. "Political Intrigue in the Cherokee Nation, 1839." Journal of the West 13 (October 1974): 17-25.

7921. Gearing, Fred O. "Cherokee Political Organizations, 1730-1775." Ph.D. dissertation, University of Chicago, 1956.

7922. Gilbert, William H., Jr. "The Cherokees of North Carolina: Living Memorials of the Past." Annual Report of the Board of Regents of the Smithsonian Institution, 1956, pp. 529-555.

7923. Gregory, Jack, and Rennard Strickland. Sam Houston with the Cherokees, 1829-1833. Austin: University of Texas Press, 1967.

7924. Gulick, John. Cherokees at the Crossroads. Chapel Hill: Institute for Research in Social Science, University of North Carolina, 1960. Revised edition, 1973.

7925. _____. "Language and Passive Resistance among the Eastern Cherokees." Ethnohistory 5 (Winter 1958): 60-81.

7926. Hafen, LeRoy R. "Cherokee Gold-seekers in Colorado, 1849-50." Colorado Magazine 15 (May 1938): 101-109.

7927. Hagy, James William, and Stanley J. Folmsbee, eds. "The Lost Archives of the Cherokee Nation." East Tennessee Historical Society's Publications no. 43 (1971): 112-122; no. 44 (1972): 114-125; no. 45 (1973): 88-98.

7928. Hewes, Leslie. "Cherokee Occupance in the Oklahoma Ozarks and Prairie Plains." Chronicles of Oklahoma 22 (Autumn 1944): 324-337.

7929. _____. "Cultural Fault Line in the Cherokee Country." Economic Geography 19 (April 1943): 136-142.

7930. _____. "The Eastern Border of the Cherokee Country of Oklahoma as a Cultural 'Fault Line.'" Annals of the

Association of American Geographers 32 (March 1942): 120-121.

7931. _____. "The Geography of the Cherokee Country of Oklahoma." Ph.D. dissertation, University of California, 1940.

7932. _____. "Indian Land in the Cherokee Country of Oklahoma." Economic Geography 18 (October 1942): 401-412.

7933. _____. "The Oklahoma Ozarks as the Land of the Cherokees." Geographical Review 32 (April 1942): 269-281.

7934. Holland, Cullen Joe. "The Cherokee Indian Newspapers, 1828-1906: The Tribal Voice of a People in Transition." Ph.D. dissertation, University of Minnesota, 1956.

7935. Holland, Reid A. "Life in the Cherokee Nation, 1855-1860." Chronicles of Oklahoma 49 (Autumn 1971): 284-301.

7936. Howard, R. Palmer. "Cherokee History to 1840: A Medical View." Journal of the Oklahoma State Medical Association 63 (February 1970): 71-82.

7937. Jones, Robert L., and Pauline H. Jones. "Houston's Politics and the Cherokees, 1829-1833." Chronicles of Oklahoma 46 (Winter 1968-1969): 418-432.

7938. Kephart, Horace. "The Strange Story of the Eastern Cherokee." Outing 73 (March 1919): 312-315; 74 (April 1919): 28-31; (May 1919): 89-91.

7939. Kilpatrick, Jack Frederick. "An Adventure Story of the Arkansas Cherokees, 1829." Arkansas Historical Quarterly 26 (Spring 1967): 40-47.

7940. Kilpatrick, Jack Frederick, and Anna Gritts Kilpatrick, eds. New Echota Letters: Contributions of Samuel A. Worcester to the Cherokee Phoenix. Dallas: Southern Methodist University Press, 1968.

7941. _____. The Shadow of Sequoyah: Social Documents of the Cherokees, 1862-1964. Norman: University of Oklahoma Press, 1965.

7942. King, V. O. "The Cherokee Nation of Indians." Quarterly of the Texas State Historical Association 2 (July 1898): 58-72.

7943. Knight, Oliver. "History of the Cherokees, 1830-1846." Chronicles of Oklahoma 34 (Summer 1956): 159-182.

7944. Kupferer, Harriet J. "Cherokee Change: A Departure from Lineal Models of Acculturation." Anthropologica, new series 5 (1963): 187-198.

7945. _____. "Health Practices and Educational Aspirations as Indicators

of Acculturation and Social Class among the Eastern Cherokee." Social Forces 41 (December 1962): 154-163.

7946. _____. "The Isolated Eastern Cherokee." In The American Indian Today, edited by Stuart Levine and Nancy Oestreich Lurie, pp. 87-97. Deland, Florida: Everett/Edwards, 1968. This appeared originally in Midcontinent American Studies Journal 6 (Fall 1965): 124-134.

7947. _____. "The 'Principal People,' 1960: A Study of Cultural and Social Groups of the Eastern Cherokee." Ph.D. dissertation, University of North Carolina, 1961.

7948. Littlefield, Daniel F., Jr. "Utopian Dreams of the Cherokee Fullbloods: 1890-1934." Journal of the West 10 (July 1971): 404-427.

7949. Littlefield, Daniel F., Jr., and Lonnie E. Underhill. "Timber Depredations and Cherokee Legislation, 1869-1881." Journal of Forest History 18 (April 1974): 4-13.

7950. Litton, Gaston. "Enrollment Records of the Eastern Band of Cherokee Indians." North Carolina Historical Review 17 (July 1940): 199-231.

7951. Malone, Henry Thompson. "The Cherokee Phoenix: Supreme Expression of Cherokee Nationalism." Georgia Historical Quarterly 34 (September 1950): 163-188.

7952. _____. "The Cherokees as a Civilized Tribe." Emory University Quarterly 8 (December 1952): 225-232.

7953. _____. "The Cherokees Become a Civilized Tribe." Early Georgia 2 (Spring 1957): 12-15.

7954. _____. Cherokees of the Old South: A People in Transition. Athens: University of Georgia Press, 1956.

7955. _____. "Cherokee-White Relations on the Southern Frontier in the Early Nineteenth Century." North Carolina Historical Review 34 (January 1957): 1-14.

7956. _____. "New Echota--Capital of the Cherokee Nation, 1825-1830." Early Georgia 1 (Spring 1955): 6-13.

7957. Markman, Robert Paul. "The Arkansas Cherokees: 1817-1828." Ph.D. dissertation, University of Oklahoma, 1972.

7958. Martin, Robert G., Jr. "The Cherokee Phoenix: Pioneer of Indian Journalism." Chronicles of Oklahoma 25 (Summer 1947): 102-118.

7959. Milam, J. Bartley. "The Great Seal

of the Cherokee Nation." Chronicles of Oklahoma 21 (March 1943): 8-9.

7960. Mooney, James. Myths of the Cherokee. Annual Report of the Bureau of American Ethnology, 1897-1898, part 1. Washington: Government Printing Office, 1900.

7961. Moulton, Gary E. "Chief John Ross and Cherokee Removal Finances." Chronicles of Oklahoma 52 (Fall 1974): 342-359.

7962. Murchison, A. H., ed. "Intermarried-Whites in the Cherokee Nation between the Years 1865-1887." Chronicles of Oklahoma 6 (September 1928): 299-327.

7963. Painter, Charles C. The Eastern Cherokees. Philadelphia: Indian Rights Association, 1888.

7964. Parker, Thomas V. The Cherokee Indians, with Special Reference to Their Relations with the United States Government. New York: Grafton Press, 1907.

7965. Parris, John A. The Cherokee Story. Asheville, North Carolina: Stephens Press, 1950.

7966. Payne, John Howard. John Howard Payne to His Countrymen. Edited by Clemens De Baillou. Athens: University of Georgia Press, 1961.

7967. Pierce, Earl Boyd, and Rennard Strickland. The Cherokee People. Phoenix: Indian Tribal Series, 1973.

7968. Reagan, John H. "The Expulsion of the Cherokees from East Texas." Quarterly of the Texas State Historical Association 1 (July 1897): 38-46.

7969. Reed, Gerald A. "Financial Controversy in the Cherokee Nation, 1839-1846." Chronicles of Oklahoma 52 (Spring 1974): 82-98.

7970. _____. "The Ross-Watie Conflict: Factionalism in the Cherokee Nation, 1839-1865." Ph.D. dissertation, University of Oklahoma, 1967.

7971. Royce, Charles C. "The Cherokee Nation of Indians: A Narrative of Their Official Relations with the Colonial and Federal Governments." Annual Report of the Bureau of Ethnology, 1883-1884, pp. 121-378. Washington: Government Printing Office, 1887.

7972. Russell, Mattie U. "Devil in the Smokies: The White Man's Nature and the Indian's Fate." South Atlantic Quarterly 73 (Winter 1974): 53-69. William Holland Thomas, white leader of Eastern Cherokees in North Carolina.

7973. Smith, W. R. L. The Story of the Cherokees. Cleveland, Tennessee: Church of God Publishing House, 1928.

7974. Stambaugh, S. C., Amos Kendall, George W. Paschal, and M. St. Claire Clarke. A Faithful History of the Cherokee Tribe of Indians, from the Period of Our First Intercourse with Them, down to the Present Time. Washington: Jesse E. Dow, 1846.

7975. Starkey, Marion L. The Cherokee Nation. New York: Alfred A. Knopf, 1946.

7976. Starr, Emmet. History of the Cherokee Indians and Their Legands and Folk Lore. Oklahoma City: Warden Company, 1921.

7977. Strickland, Rennard. "Christian Gotelieb Priber: Utopian Precursor of the Cherokee Government." Chronicles of Oklahoma 48 (Autumn 1970): 264-279.

7978. Travis, V. A. "Life in the Cherokee Nation a Decade after the Civil War." Chronicles of Oklahoma 4 (March 1926): 16-30.

7979. Umberger, Wallace Randolph, Jr. "A History of Unto These Hills, 1941 to 1968." Ph.D. dissertation, Tulane University, 1970.

7980. Wahrhaftig, Albert L. "Institution Building among Oklahoma's Traditional Cherokees." In Four Centuries of Southern Indians, edited by Charles M. Hudson, pp. 132-147. Athens: University of Georgia Press, 1975.

7981. _____. "The Tribal Cherokee Population of Eastern Oklahoma." Current Anthropology 9 (December 1968): 510-518.

7982. Wahrhaftig, Albert L., and Robert K. Thomas. "Renaissance and Repression: The Oklahoma Cherokee." Trans-action 6 (February 1969): 42-48.

7983. Wardell, Morris L. A Political History of the Cherokee Nation, 1838-1907. Norman: University of Oklahoma Press, 1938.

7984. Winkler, Ernest William. "The Cherokee Indians in Texas." Quarterly of the Texas State Historical Association 7 (October 1903): 95-165.

7985. Woldert, Albert. "The Last of the Cherokees in Texas, and the Life and Death of Chief Bowles." Chronicles of Oklahoma 1 (June 1921): 179-226.

7986. Woodward, Grace Steele. The Cherokees. Norman: University of Oklahoma Press, 1963.

7987. Wright, Muriel H. "Seal of the Cherokee Nation." Chronicles of Oklahoma 34 (Summer 1956): 134-140.

Biographical Studies

7988. Anderson, Mabel Washbourne. "General

Stand Watie." Chronicles of Oklahoma 10 (December 1932): 540-548.

7989. _____. Life of General Stand Watie, the Only Indian Brigadier General of the Confederate Army and the Last General to Surrender. Pryor, Oklahoma: Mayes County Republican, 1915. Revised edition, 1931.

7990. Anderson, Rufus. Memoir of Catherine Brown, a Christian Indian of the Cherokee Nation. 3d edition. Boston: Crocker and Brewster, 1828. First published in 1825.

7991. Ballenger, T. L. "The Death and Burial of Major Ridge." Chronicles of Oklahoma 51 (Spring 1973): 100-105.

7992. _____. "Spring Frog." Chronicles of Oklahoma 44 (Spring 1966): 2-4.

7993. Bird, Traveller. Tell Them They Lie: The Sequoyah Myth. Los Angeles: Westernlore Publishers, 1971.

7994. Brown, John P. "Eastern Cherokee Chiefs." Chronicles of Oklahoma 16 (March 1938): 3-35.

7995. Corn, James F. "John Ross." Tennessee Valley Historical Review 2 (Fall 1973): 38-41.

7996. Dale, Edward Everett. "John Rollin Ridge." Chronicles of Oklahoma 4 (December 1926): 312-321.

7997. Dale, Edward Everett, ed. "Additional Letters of General Stand Watie." Chronicles of Oklahoma 1 (October 1921): 131-149.

7998. _____. "Letters of the Two Boudinots." Chronicles of Oklahoma 6 (September 1928): 328-347.

7999. _____. "Some Letters of General Stand Watie." Chronicles of Oklahoma 1 (January 1921): 30-59.

8000. Davis, John B. "The Life and Work of Sequoyah." Chronicles of Oklahoma 8 (June 1930): 149-180.

8001. De Baillou, Clemens. "James Vann, a Cherokee Chief." Georgia Review 17 (Fall 1963): 271-283.

8002. Eaton, Rachel Caroline. John Ross and the Cherokee Indians. Menasha, Wisconsin: George Banta Publishing Company, 1914.

8003. Forde, Lois Elizabeth. "Elias Cornelius Boudinot." Ph.D. dissertation, Columbia University, 1951.

8004. Foreman, Carolyn Thomas. "Aunt Eliza of Tahlequah." Chronicles of Oklahoma 9 (March 1931): 43-55.

8005. _____. "A Cherokee Pioneer, Ella Flora Coodey." Chronicles of Oklahoma 7 (December 1929): 364-374.

8006. _____. "Captain David McNair and His Descendants." Chronicles of Oklahoma 36 (Autumn 1958): 270-281.

8007. _____. "The Coodey Family of Indian Territory." Chronicles of Oklahoma 25 (Winter 1947-1948): 323-341.

8008. _____. "Edward W. Bushyhead and John Rollin Ridge, Cherokee Editors in California." Chronicles of Oklahoma 14 (September 1936): 295-311.

8009. Foreman, Grant. Sequoyah. Norman: University of Oklahoma Press, 1938.

8010. Foreman, Grant, ed. "The Murder of Elias Boudinot." Chronicles of Oklahoma 12 (March 1934): 19-24.

8011. _____. "The Story of Sequoyah's Last Days." Chronicles of Oklahoma 12 (March 1934): 25-41.

8012. _____. "The Trial of Stand Watie." Chronicles of Oklahoma 12 (September 1934): 305-339.

8013. Foster, George E. Se-Quo-Yah, the American Cadmus and Modern Moses. Philadelphia: Indian Rights Association, 1885.

8014. Franks, Kenny A. "Stand Watie and the Agony of the Cherokee Nation." Ph.D. dissertation, Oklahoma State University, 1973.

8015. Gabriel, Ralph Henry. Elias Boudinot, Cherokee, and His America. Norman: University of Oklahoma Press, 1941.

8016. Goodpasture, Albert V. "The Paternity of Sequoya, the Inventor of the Cherokee Alphabet." Chronicles of Oklahoma 1 (October 1921): 121-130.

8017. Hicks, J. C. "The Rhetoric of John Ross." Ph.D. dissertation, University of Oklahoma, 1971.

8018. Keith, Harold. "Memories of George W. Mayes." Chronicles of Oklahoma 24 (Spring 1946): 40-54.

8019. _____. "Problems of a Cherokee Principal Chief." Chronicles of Oklahoma 17 (September 1939): 296-308. Dennis Wolf Bushyhead.

8020. Ketchum, Richard M. Will Rogers: His Life and Times. New York: American Heritage Publishing Company, 1973.

8021. Kilpatrick, Jack Frederick, and Anna Gritts Kilpatrick, eds. "Letters from an Arkansas Cherokee Chief (1828-29)." Great Plains Journal 5 (Fall 1965): 26-34.

8022. Litton, Gaston L. "The Principal Chiefs of the Cherokee Nation." Chronicles of Oklahoma 15 (September 1937): 253-270.

8023. McClary, Ben Harris. "Nancy Ward: The Last Beloved Woman of the Cherokees." Tennessee Historical Quarterly 21 (December 1962): 352-364.

8024. Meserve, John Bartlett. "Cadmus of the Cherokees." National Republic 22 (July 1934): 4-5, 30. Biography of Sequoyah.

8025. _____. "The Cadmus of the Cherokees." Oklahoma State Bar Journal 5 (October 1934): 130-133. On Sequoyah.

8026. _____. "Chief Colonel Johnson Harris." Chronicles of Oklahoma 17 (March 1939): 17-21.

8027. _____. "Chief Dennis Wolfe Bushyhead." Chronicles of Oklahoma 14 (September 1936): 349-359.

8028. _____. "Chief John Ross." Chronicles of Oklahoma 13 (December 1935): 421-437.

8029. _____. "Chief Lewis Downing and Chief Charles Thompson (Oochalata)." Chronicles of Oklahoma 16 (September 1938): 315-325.

8030. _____. "Chief Thomas Mitchell Buffington and Chief William Charles Rogers." Chronicles of Oklahoma 17 (June 1939): 135-146.

8031. _____. "Chief William Potter Ross." Chronicles of Oklahoma 15 (March 1937): 21-29.

8032. Moore, Cherrie Adair. "William Penn Adair." Chronicles of Oklahoma 29 (Spring 1951): 32-41.

8033. Moulton, Gary E. "Chief John Ross during the Civil War." Civil War History 19 (December 1973): 314-333.

8034. _____. "John Ross, Cherokee Chief." Ph.D. dissertation, Oklahoma State University, 1974.

8035. Neet, J. Frederick, Jr. "Stand Watie, Confederate General in the Cherokee Nation." Great Plains Journal 6 (Fall 1966): 36-51.

8036. Robbins, Peggy. "Will Rogers: The Immortal Cherokee Kid." American History Illustrated 9 (July 1974): 4-11, 44-48.

8037. Ross, Mrs. William P., ed. The Life and Times of Hon. William P. Ross of the Cherokee Nation. Fort Smith, Arkansas: Weldon and Williams, 1893.

8038. Shadburn, Don L. "Cherokee Statesmen: The John Rogers Family of Chattahoochee." Chronicles of Oklahoma 50 (Spring 1972): 12-40.

8039. Tucker, Norma. "Nancy Ward, Ghighau of the Cherokees." Georgia Historical Quarterly 53 (June 1969): 192-200.

8040. Winfrey, Dorman H. "Chief Bowles of the Texas Cherokee." Chronicles of Oklahoma 32 (Spring 1954): 29-41. Reprinted Texana 2 (Fall 1964): 189-202.

8041. Wright, Muriel H. "Notes on Colonel Elias C. Boudinot." Chronicles of Oklahoma 41 (Winter 1963-1964): 382-407.

8042. Wright, Muriel H., ed. "The Journal of John Lowery Brown, of the Cherokee Nation, En Route to California in 1850." Chronicles of Oklahoma 12 (June 1934): 177-213.

See also studies on Indian removal, on the Indian Territory, and on the Five Civilized Tribes.

Chickasaw Indians

Biographical sketches of Chickasaw leaders and general and miscellaneous accounts dealing with the Chickasaws are included here.

8043. Baird, W. David. The Chickasaw People. Phoenix: Indian Tribal Series, 1974.

8044. Braden, Guy B. "The Colberts and the Chickasaw Nation." Tennessee Historical Quarterly 17 (September 1958): 222-249; (December 1958): 318-335.

8045. Carney, Champ Clark. "The Historical Geography of the Chickasaw Lands of Oklahoma." Ph.D. dissertation, Indiana University, 1961.

8046. Evans, W. A. "The Trial of Tishomingo." Journal of Mississippi History 2 (July 1940): 147-155.

8047. Gibson, Arrell M. The Chickasaws. Norman: University of Oklahoma Press, 1971.

8048. Jennings, Jesse D. "Chickasaw and Earlier Indian Cultures of Northeast Mississippi." Journal of Mississippi History 3 (July 1941): 155-226.

8049. Malone, James H. The Chickasaw Nation: A Short Sketch of a Noble People. Louisville, Kentucky: J. P. Morton and Company, 1922.

8050. Meserve, John Bartlett. "Governor Benjamin Franklin Overton and Governor Benjamin Crooks Burney." Chronicles of Oklahoma 16 (June 1938): 221-233.

8051. _____. "Governor Cyrus Harris." Chronicles of Oklahoma 15 (December 1937): 373-386.

8052. _____. "Governor Daugherty (Winchester) Colbert." Chronicles of Oklahoma 18 (December 1940): 348-356.

8053. _____. "Governor Jonas Wolf and

Governor Palmer Simeon Mosely." Chronicles of Oklahoma 18 (September 1940): 243-251.

8054. _____. "Governor Robert Maxwell Harris." Chronicles of Oklahoma 17 (December 1939): 361-363.

8055. _____. "Governor William Leander Byrd." Chronicles of Oklahoma 12 (December 1934): 432-443.

8056. _____. "Governor William Malcolm Guy." Chronicles of Oklahoma 19 (March 1941): 10-13.

8057. Phelps, Dawson A. "Colbert Ferry and Selected Documents." Alabama Historical Quarterly 25 (Fall-Winter 1963): 203-226.

8058. Roff, Joe T. "Reminiscences of Early Days in the Chickasaw Nation." Chronicles of Oklahoma 13 (June 1935): 169-190.

8059. Steacy, Stephen. "The Chickasaw Nation on the Eve of the Civil War." Chronicles of Oklahoma 49 (Spring 1971): 51-75.

8060. Sturdivant, Reita. "Francis, Chickawaw Nation, 1894." Chronicles of Oklahoma 45 (Summer 1967): 143-152. A Chickasaw town.

8061. Warren, Harry. "Chickasaw Traditions, Customs, etc." Publications of the Mississippi Historical Society 8 (1904): 543-553.

8062. _____. "Some Chickasaw Chiefs and Prominent Men." Publications of the Mississippi Historical Society 8 (1904): 555-570.

8063. Williams, Robert L. "Hindman H. Burris, 1862-1940." Chronicles of Oklahoma 20 (June 1942): 149-151.

8064. Wright, Muriel H. "The Great Seal of the Chickasaw Nation." Chronicles of Oklahoma 34 (Winter 1956-1957): 388-391.

8065. _____. "Jessie Elizabeth Randolph Moore of the Chickasaw Nation." Chronicles of Oklahoma 34 (Winter 1956-1957): 392-396.

See also studies on Indian removal, on the Indian Territory, and on the Five Civilized Tribes.

Choctaw Indians

General and miscellaneous accounts of Choctaw Indians as well as biographies of Choctaws are listed here.

8066. Baird, W. David. "Arkansas's Choctaw Boundary: A Study of Justice Delayed." Arkansas Historical Quarterly 28 (Autumn 1969): 203-222.

8067. _____. The Choctaw People. Phoenix: Indian Tribal Series, 1973.

8068. _____. Peter Pitchlynn: Chief of the Choctaws. Norman: University of Oklahoma Press, 1972.

8069. Bonnifield, Paul. "The Choctaw Nation on the Eve of the Civil War." Journal of the West 12 (July 1973): 386-402.

8070. Bushnell, David I., Jr. "The Choctaw of St. Tammany Parish." Louisiana Historical Quarterly 1 (January 1917): 11-20.

8071. Coker, William Sidney. "Pat Harrison's Efforts to Reopen the Choctaw Citizenship Rolls." Southern Quarterly 3 (October 1964): 36-61.

8072. Conlan, Czarina C. "David Folsom." Chronicles of Oklahoma 4 (December 1926): 340-355.

8073. _____. "Peter P. Pitchlynn: Chief of the Choctaws, 1864-66." Chronicles of Oklahoma 6 (June 1928): 215-224.

8074. Crossett, G. A. "A Vanishing Race." Chronicles of Oklahoma 4 (June 1926): 100-115.

8075. Culberson, James. "'Indian against Indian.'" Chronicles of Oklahoma 7 (June 1929): 164-167.

8076. Davis, Edward. "The Mississippi Choctaws." Chronicles of Oklahoma 10 (June 1932): 257-266.

8077. Debo, Angie. The Rise and Fall of the Choctaw Republic. Norman: University of Oklahoma Press, 1934.

8078. Edwards, John. "The Choctaw Indians in the Middle of the Nineteenth Century," edited by John R. Swanton. Chronicles of Oklahoma 10 (September 1932): 392-425.

8079. Egerton, John. "The Other Philadelphia Story." Southern Education Report 2 (September 1966): 24-28. Choctaw Indians surrounding Philadelphia, Mississippi.

8080. Fessler, W. Julian. "The Work of the Early Choctaw Legislature from 1869 to 1873." Chronicles of Oklahoma 6 (March 1928): 60-68.

8081. Fischer, LeRoy H. "Muriel H. Wright, Historian of Oklahoma." Chronicles of Oklahoma 52 (Spring 1974): 3-29.

8082. Foreman, Carolyn Thomas. "Notes of Interest Concerning Peter P. Pitchlynn." Chronicles of Oklahoma 7 (June 1929): 172-174.

8083. Henry, Delaura. "Traditions in the Choctaw Homeland." Historic Preservation

26 (January-March 1974): 28-31.

8084. Holmes, Jack D. L. "The Choctaws in 1795." Alabama Historical Quarterly 30 (Spring 1968): 33-49.

8085. Hudson, Peter James. "A Story of Choctaw Chiefs." Chronicles of Oklahoma 17 (March 1939): 7-16; (June 1939): 192-211.

8086. Langley, Mrs. Lee J. "Malmaison, Palace in a Wilderness, Home of General Leflore, Mississippi's Remarkable Indian Statesman." Chronicles of Oklahoma 5 (December 1927): 371-380.

8087. Lanman, Charles. "Peter Pitchlynn, Chief of the Choctaws." Atlantic Monthly 25 (April 1870): 486-497.

8088. Lewis, Anna. Chief Pushmataha, American Patriot: The Story of the Choctaws' Struggle for Survival. New York: Exposition Press, 1959.

8089. Lincecum, Gideon. "Life of Apushimataha." Mississippi Historical Society Publications 9 (1906): 415-485.

8090. McKee, Jesse O. "The Choctaw Indians: A Geographical Study in Cultural Change." Southern Quarterly 9 (January 1971): 107-141.

8091. Meserve, John Bartlett. "Chief Allen Wright." Chronicles of Oklahoma 19 (December 1941): 314-321.

8092. _____. "Chief Benjamin Franklin Smallwood and Chief Jefferson Gardner." Chronicles of Oklahoma 19 (September 1941): 213-220.

8093. _____. "Chief Coleman Cole." Chronicles of Oklahoma 14 (March 1936): 9-21.

8094. _____. "Chief George Hudson and Chief Samuel Garland." Chronicles of Oklahoma 20 (March 1942): 9-17.

8095. _____. "Chief Gilbert Wesley Dukes." Chronicles of Oklahoma 18 (March 1940): 53-59.

8096. _____. "Chief Wilson Nathaniel Jones." Chronicles of Oklahoma 14 (December 1936): 419-433.

8097. _____. "The McCurtains." Chronicles of Oklahoma 13 (September 1935): 297-312.

8098. Morrison, James D. "Problems in the Industrial Progress and Development of the Choctaw Nation, 1865 to 1907." Chronicles of Oklahoma 32 (Spring 1954): 70-91.

8099. _____. "Social History of the Choctaw, 1865-1907." Ph.D. dissertation, University of Oklahoma, 1951.

8100. Peterson, John H., Jr. "Louisiana

Choctaw Life at the End of the Nineteenth Century." In Four Centuries of Southern Indians, edited by Charles M. Hudson, pp. 101-112. Athens: University of Georgia Press, 1975.

8101. _____. "The Mississippi Band of Choctaw Indians: Their Recent History and Current Social Relations." Ph.D. dissertation, University of Georgia, 1970.

8102. Ray, Florence Rebecca. Chieftain Greenwood Leflore and the Choctaw Indians of the Mississippi Valley: Last Chief of Choctaws East of Mississippi River. 2d edition. Memphis: C. A. Davis Printing Company, 1936.

8103. Semple, W. F., and Winnie Lewis Gravitt. "Grady Lewis, Choctaw Attorney." Chronicles of Oklahoma 33 (Autumn 1955): 301-305.

8104. Tolbert, Charles Madden. "A Sociological Study of the Choctaw Indians in Mississippi." Ph.D. dissertation, Louisiana State University, 1958.

8105. West, Ruth Tenison. "Pushmataha's Travels." Chronicles of Oklahoma 37 (Summer 1959): 162-174.

8106. Whaley, Mrs. C. M. "Elizabeth Jacobs Quinton, Centenarian." Chronicles of Oklahoma 24 (Summer 1951): 126-136.

8107. Williams, R. L. "Peter James Hudson: 1861-1938." Chronicles of Oklahoma 17 (March 1939): 3-6.

8108. Wright, Muriel H. "A Brief Review of the Life of Doctor Eliphalet Nott Wright (1858-1932)." Chronicles of Oklahoma 10 (June 1932): 267-286.

8109. _____. "The Great Seal of the Choctaw Nation." Chronicles of Oklahoma 33 (Winter 1955-1956): 430-433.

8110. _____. "Lee F. Harkins, Choctaw." Chronicles of Oklahoma 37 (Autumn 1959): 285-287.

8111. _____. "Tewah Hokay." Chronicles of Oklahoma 33 (Winter 1955-1956): 434-439.

See also studies on Indian removal, on the Indian Territory, and on the Five Civilized Tribes.

Creek Indians

Listed here are both general and miscellaneous accounts and biographical studies dealing with the Creeks.

8112. Barnett, Leona G. "Este Cate Emunkv: Red Man Always." Chronicles of Oklahoma 46 (Spring 1968): 20-40. Alexander Posey.

8113. Caughey, John Walton. McGillivray of the Creeks. Norman: University of Oklahoma Press, 1938.

8114. Coulter, E. Merton. "Mary Musgove, 'Queen of the Creeks': A Chapter of Early Georgia Troubles." Georgia Historical Quarterly 11 (March 1927): 1-30.

8115. Crane, Verner W. "The Origin of the Name of the Creek Indians." Mississippi Valley Historical Review 5 (December 1918): 339-342.

8116. Dale, Edward Everett, ed. "The Journal of Alexander Lawrence Posey, January 1 to September 4, 1897." Chronicles of Oklahoma 45 (Winter 1967-1968): 393-432.

8117. Davis, T. Frederick. "Milly Francis and Duncan McKrimmon: An Authentic Florida Pocahontas." Florida Historical Quarterly 21 (January 1943): 254-265.

8118. Debo, Angie. The Road to Disappearance. Norman: University of Oklahoma Press, 1941.

8119. Douglass, Elisha P. "The Adventurer Bowles." William and Mary Quarterly 3d series 6 (January 1949): 3-23.

8120. Du Chateau, Andre Paul. "The Creek Nation on the Eve of the Civil War." Chronicles of Oklahoma 52 (Fall 1974): 290-315.

8121. Foreman, Carolyn Thomas. "Alexander McGillivray, Emperor of the Creeks." Chronicles of Oklahoma 7 (March 1929): 106-120.

8122. _____. "A Creek Pioneer: Notes Concerning 'Aunt Sue' Rogers and Her Family." Chronicles of Oklahoma 21 (September 1943): 271-279.

8123. _____. "Fishertown." Chronicles of Oklahoma 31 (Autumn 1953): 247-254. A Creek town.

8124. _____. "Lee Compere and the Creek Indians." Chronicles of Oklahoma 42 (Autumn 1964): 291-299.

8125. _____. "Marshalltown, Creek Nation." Chronicles of Oklahoma 32 (Spring 1954): 52-57.

8126. _____. "Two Notable Women of the Creek Nation." Chronicles of Oklahoma 35 (Autumn 1957): 315-337.

8127. _____. "The White Lieutenant of the Creek Nation." Chronicles of Oklahoma 38 (Winter 1960): 425-440.

8128. _____. "The Yuchi: Children of the Sun." Chronicles of Oklahoma 37 (Winter 1959-1960): 480-496.

8129. Foulke, William Dudley. "Despoiling a Nation." Outlook 91 (January 2, 1909): 40-44.

8130. Goodwin, Ralph William. "Pleasant Porter and the Decline of the Muskogee Nation." Ph.D. dissertation, Harvard University, 1960.

8131. Green, Donald E. The Creek People. Phoenix: Indian Tribal Series, 1973.

8132. Harriman, Helga H. "Economic Conditions in the Creek Nation, 1965-1871." Chronicles of Oklahoma 51 (Fall 1973): 325-334.

8133. Hodges, Bert. "Notes on the History of the Creek Nation and Some of Its Leaders." Chronicles of Oklahoma 43 (Spring 1965): 9-18.

8134. Jones, Charles C., Jr. Historical Sketch of Tomo-Chi-Chi, Mico of the Yamacraws. Albany: Joel Munsell, 1868.

8135. King, Jerlena. "Jackson Lewis, of the Confederate Creek Regiment." Chronicles of Oklahoma 41 (Spring 1963): 66-69.

8136. Knapp, David, Jr. "The Chickamaugas." Georgia Historical Quarterly 51 (June 1967): 194-196.

8137. Lambert, O. A. "Historical Sketch of Col. Samuel Checote, Once Chief of the Creek Nation." Chronicles of Oklahoma 4 (September 1926): 275-280.

8138. McAlister, Lyle N. "William Augustus Bowles and the State of Muskogee." Florida Historical Quarterly 40 (April 1962): 317-328.

8139. Meserve, John Bartlett. "Chief Isparhecher." Chronicles of Oklahoma 10 (March 1932): 52-76.

8140. _____. "Chief Opothleyahola." Chronicles of Oklahoma 9 (December 1931): 440-453.

8141. _____. "Chief Pleasant Porter." Chronicles of Oklahoma 9 (September 1931): 318-334.

8142. _____. "Chief Samuel Checote, with Sketches of Chiefs Locher Harjo and Ward Coachman." Chronicles of Oklahoma 16 (December 1938): 401-409.

8143. _____. "The MacIntoshes." Chronicles of Oklahoma 10 (September 1932): 310-325.

8144. Miller, Lou Whitfield. "Mallee." Tallahassee Historical Society Annual 3 (1937): 22-26.

8145. Morton, Ohland. "Early History of the Creek Indians." Chronicles of Oklahoma 11 (March 1931): 17-26.

8146. _____. "The Government of the Creek Indians." Chronicles of Oklahoma 8 (March 1930): 42-64; (June 1930): 189-225.

8147. O'Donnell, James H. "Alexander McGillivray: Training for Leadership, 1777-1783." Georgia Historical Quarterly 49 (June 1965): 172-186.

8148. Opler, Morris E. "The Creek Indian Towns of Oklahoma in 1937." Papers in Anthropology (University of Oklahoma) 13 (Spring 1972).

8149. Orrmont, Arthur. Diplomat in Warpaint: Chief Alexander McGillivray of the Creeks. London: Abelard-Schuman, 1967.

8150. Oskison, John M. "Walla Tenaka--Creek." Collier's 51 (July 12, 1913): 16-17, 32-33.

8151. Pickett, Albert J. "McGillivray and the Creeks." Alabama Historical Quarterly 1 (Summer 1930): 126-148.

8152. Rister, Carl Coke, and Bryan W. Lovelace, eds. "A Diary Account of a Creek Boundary Survey, 1850." Chronicles of Oklahoma 27 (Autumn 1949): 268-302.

8153. Robertson, Alice M. "The Creek Indian Council in Session." Chronicles of Oklahoma 11 (September 1933): 895-898.

8154. Russell, Orpha B. "Notes on Samuel William Brown, Jr., Yuchi Chief." Chronicles of Oklahoma 37 (Winter 1959-1960): 497-501.

8155. _____. "William G. Bruner, Member of the House of Kings, Creek Nation." Chronicles of Oklahoma 30 (Winter 1952-1953): 397-407.

8156. Swanton, John R. Early History of the Creek Indians and Their Neighbors. Bureau of American Ethnology Bulletin 73. Washington: Government Printing Office, 1922.

8157. Turner, C. W. "Events among the Muskogies during Sixty Years." Chronicles of Oklahoma 10 (March 1932): 21-34.

8158. Underhill, Lonnie E. "Hamlin Garland and the Final Council of the Creek Nation." Journal of the West 10 (July 1971): 511-520.

8159. Whitaker, Arthur Preston. "Alexander McGillivray, 1783-1789." North Carolina Historical Review 5 (April 1928): 181-203.

8160. _____. "Alexander McGillivray, 1789-1793." North Carolina Historical Review 5 (July 1928): 289-309.

8161. Wright, J. Leitch, Jr. William Augustus Bowles: Director General of the Creek Nation. Athens: University of Georgia Press, 1967.

8162. Wright, Muriel H. "The Great Seal of the Muscogee Nation." Chronicles of Oklahoma 34 (Spring 1956): 2-6.

8163. Woodward, Thomas Simpson. Woodward's Reminiscences of the Creek, or Muscogee Indians. Montgomery, Alabama: Barrett and Wimbish, 1859.

See also studies on Indian removal, on the Indian territory, and on the Five Civilized Tribes.

Five Civilized Tribes

Listed here are works that deal with two or more of the Five Civilized Tribes.

8164. Bartram, William. "Observations on the Creek and Cherokee Indians," edited by E. G. Squier. Transactions of the American Ethnological Society 3 (1853): 1-81.

8165. Cotterill, R. S. The Southern Indians: The Story of the Civilized Tribes before Removal. Norman: University of Oklahoma Press, 1954.

8166. Cushman, H. B. History of the Choctaw, Chickasaw and Natchez Indians. Greenville, Texas: Headlight Printing House, 1899. New edition, edited by Angie Debo. Stillwater, Oklahoma: Redlands Press, 1962.

8167. Davis, Edward. "Early Advancement among the Five Civilized Tribes." Chronicles of Oklahoma 14 (June 1936): 162-172.

8168. _____. "History of Federal Relations with the Five Civilized Tribes of Indians since 1865." Ph.D. dissertation, University of Texas, 1935.

8169. Debo, Angie. And Still the Waters Run. Princeton: Princeton University Press, 1940. New printing, 1972, with an addition to the Preface, "Thirty-Two Years After."

8170. _____. The Five Civilized Tribes of Oklahoma: Report on Social and Economic Conditions. Philadelphia: Indian Rights Association, 1951.

8171. Foreman, Grant. The Five Civilized Tribes. Norman: University of Oklahoma Press, 1934.

8172. Howard, R. Palmer. "A Historiography of the Five Civilized Tribes: A Chronological Approach." Chronicles of Oklahoma 47 (Autumn 1969): 312-331. Revised version printed separately, Oklahoma City: Oklahoma Historical Society, 1969.

8173. Marshall, Park. "Cushman's History of the Indians--Choctaws, Chickasaws and Natchez." Tennessee Historical Magazine 9 (April 1925): 59-65.

8174. Stuart, John. A Sketch of the Cherokee and Choctaw Indians. Little Rock, Arkansas: Woodruff and Pew, 1837.

8175. U.S. Census Office. Extra Census Bulletin: The Five Civilized Tribes in Indian Territory, the Cherokee, Chickasaw, Choctaw, Creek, and Seminole Nations. Washington: United States Census Printing Office, 1894.

8176. Winsor, Henry M. "Chickasaw-Choctaw Financial Relations with the United States, 1830-1880." Journal of the West 12 (July 1973): 356-371.

8177. Wright, Muriel H. "Official Seals of the Five Civilized Tribes." Chronicles of Oklahoma 18 (December 1940): 357-370.

8178. _____. "Organization of Counties in the Choctaw and Chickasaw Nations." Chronicles of Oklahoma 8 (September 1930): 315-334.

8179. _____. "Seals of the Five Civilized Tribes." Chronicles of Oklahoma 40 (Autumn 1962): 214-218.

8180. Wright, Muriel H., and Peter J. Hudson. "Brief Outline of the Choctaw and Chickasaw Nations in the Indian Territory, 1820-1860." Chronicles of Oklahoma 7 (December 1929): 388-418.

See also the sections on the individual tribes and on the Indian Territory.

Lumbee Indians

The Lumbee Indians have reasserted their identity as Indians. The following is a useful guide to literature on the group.

8181. Locklear, Janie Maynor, and Drenna J. Oxendine. "The Lumbee Indians: A Bibliography." Indian Historian 7 (Winter 1974): 52-54.

Listed here are recent general studies on the Lumbees.

8182. Blu, Karen I. "'We People': Understanding Lumbee Indian Identity in a Tri-Racial Situation." Ph.D. dissertation, University of Chicago, 1972.

8183. Dial, Adolph, and David K. Eliades. "The Lumbee Indians of North Carolina and Pembroke State University." Indian Historian 4 (Winter 1971): 20-24.

8184. _____. The Only Land I Know: A History of the Lumbee Indians. San Francisco: Indian Historian Press, 1975.

8185. Peck, John Gregory. "Urban Station: Migration Patterns of the Lumbee Indians." Ph.D. dissertation, University of North Carolina, 1972.

8186. Sider, Gerald Marc. "The Political History of the Lumbee Indians of Robeson County, North Carolina: A Case Study of Ethnic Political Affiliations." Ph.D.

dissertation, New School for Social Research, 1971.

Seminole Indians

The Seminoles have attracted considerable attention because of their late origin as a tribe and because they resisted total removal to the West. Works on the tribe are divided here into general accounts and biographical studies, the latter including material on Seminole Negroes.

General and Miscellaneous Accounts

8187. Blassingame, Wyatt. Seminoles of Florida. Tallahassee: Florida State Department of Agriculture, 1959.

8188. Burk, Jerry L. "Oklahoma Seminole Indians: Origin, History, and Pan-Indianism." Chronicles of Oklahoma 51 (Summer 1973): 211-223.

8189. Capron, Louis. "Florida's Emerging Seminoles." National Geographic Magazine 136 (November 1969): 716-734.

8190. Coe, Charles H. Red Patriots: The Story of the Seminoles. Cincinnati: Editor Publishing Company, 1898.

8191. Covington, James W. "Apalachicola Seminole Leadership: 1820-1933." Florida Anthropologist 16 (June 1963): 57-62.

8192. _____. "The Indian Scare of 1849." Tequesta 21 (1961): 53-63.

8193. _____. "Migration of the Seminoles into Florida: 1700-1820." Florida Historical Quarterly 46 (April 1968): 340-357.

8194. _____. "A Seminole Census: 1847." Florida Anthropologist 21 (December 1968): 120-122.

8195. _____. "White Control of Seminole Leadership." Florida Anthropologist 18 (September 1965): 137-146.

8196. Covington, James W., ed. "The Florida Seminoles in 1847." Tequesta 24 (1964): 49-57.

8197. Drew, Frank. "Notes on the Origin of the Seminole Indians of Florida." Florida Historical Society Quarterly 6 (July 1927): 21-24.

8198. Ellis, Leonora Beck. "The Seminoles of Florida." Gunton's Magazine 25 (December 1903): 495-505.

8199. Emerson, William Canfield. The Seminoles, Dwellers of the Everglades: The Land, History, and Culture of the Florida Indians. New York: Exposition Press, 1954.

8200. England, Ira Albert. "The Florida Seminole: A Study in Acculturation,

Culture Change and Curriculum." Ed.D. dissertation, University of Florida, 1957.

8201. Fairbanks, Charles Herron. The Florida Seminole People. Phoenix: Indian Tribal Series, 1973.

8202. Freeman, Ethel Cutler. "Culture Stability and Change among the Seminoles of Florida." In Men and Cultures: Selected Papers of the Fifth International Congress of Anthropological and Ethnological Sciences, Philadelphia, September 1-9, 1956, edited by Anthony F. C. Wallace, pp. 249-254. Philadelphia: University of Pennsylvania Press, 1960.

8203. _____. "Our Unique Indians, the Seminoles of Florida." American Indian 2 (Winter 1944-1945): 14-28.

8204. _____. "Two Types of Cultural Response to External Pressures among the Florida Seminoles." Anthropological Quarterly 38 (April 1965): 55-61.

8205. Garbarino, Merwyn S. Big Cypress: A Changing Seminole Community. New York: Holt, Rinehart and Winston, 1972.

8206. Griffin, John W., ed. "Some Comments on the Seminole in 1818." Florida Anthropologist 10 (November 1957): 41-49.

8207. Kersey, Harry A., Jr. "The Case of Tom Tiger's Horse: An Early Foray into Indian Rights." Florida Historical Quarterly 53 (January 1975): 306-318.

8208. Krogman, Wilton Marion. "The Racial Composition of the Seminole Indians of Florida and Oklahoma." Journal of Negro History 19 (October 1934): 412-430.

8209. _____. "Vital Data on the Population of the Seminole Indians of Florida and Oklahoma." Human Biology 7 (September 1935): 335-349.

8210. McReynolds, Edwin C. The Seminoles. Norman: University of Oklahoma Press, 1957.

8211. Moore-Willson, Minnie. "The Seminole Indians of Florida." Florida Historical Society Quarterly 7 (July 1928): 75-87.

8212. _____. The Seminoles of Florida. Philadelphia: American Printing House, 1896.

8213. Morris, John W. "The Agglomerated Settlements of the Greater Seminole Area." Ph.D. dissertation, George Peabody College for Teachers, 1941.

8214. Porter, Kenneth Wiggins. "Notes on the Seminole Negroes in the Bahamas." Florida Historical Quarterly 24 (July 1945): 56-60.

8215. _____. "Origins of the St. John's River Seminole: Were They Mikasuki?" Florida Anthropologist 4 (November 1951): 39-45.

8216. _____. "The Seminole in Mexico, 1850-1861." Hispanic American Historical Review 31 (February 1951): 1-36.

8217. The Seminole Indians of Florida. N.p., 1956. Assembled by the Seminole Agency staff, Bureau of Indian Affairs.

8218. Simmons, William Hayne. Notices of East Florida, with an Account of the Seminole Nation of Indians. Charleston, 1822. Facsimile edition, Gainesville: University of Florida Press, 1973.

8219. Skinner, Alanson. "Notes on the Florida Seminole." American Anthropologist 15 (January-March 1913): 63-77.

8220. Spoehr, Alexander. "Oklahoma Seminole Towns." Chronicles of Oklahoma 19 (December 1941): 377-380.

8221. Sturtevant, William C. "Creek into Seminole." In North American Indians in Historical Perspective, edited by Eleanor Burke Leacock and Nancy Oestreich Lurie, pp. 92-128. New York: Random House, 1971.

8222. Sturtevant, William C., ed. "R. H. Pratt's Report on the Seminole in 1879." Florida Anthropologist 9 (March 1956): 1-24.

8223. Webb, William S. "The Indian As I Knew Him." Ethnohistory 1 (November 1954): 181-198. Reminiscences from early 1900s.

8224. Work Projects Administration, Florida Writers' Project. The Seminole Indians in Florida. Tallahassee: Florida State Department of Agriculture, 1940.

8225. Wright, Muriel H. "Seal of the Seminole Nation." Chronicles of Oklahoma 34 (Autumn 1956): 262-271.

Biographical Studies

8226. Boyd, Mark F. "Asi-Yaholo or Osceola." Florida Historical Quarterly 33 (January-April 1955): 249-305.

8227. Coe, Charles H. "The Parentage and Birthplace of Osceola." Florida Historical Quarterly 17 (April 1939): 304-311.

8228. _____. "The Parentage of Osceola." Florida Historical Quarterly 33 (January-April 1955): 202-205.

8229. Cubberly, Fred. "Malee--Pocahontas of Florida." National Republic 21 (September 1933): 21-22, 32.

8230. Duke, Seymour R. Osceola; or, Fact and Fiction: A Tale of the Seminole War. New York: Harper and Brothers, 1838.

325

8231. Foreman, Carolyn Thomas. "John Jumper." Chronicles of Oklahoma 29 (Summer 1951): 137-152.

8232. _____. "The Jumper Family of the Seminole Nation." Chronicles of Oklahoma 34 (Autumn 1956): 272-285.

8233. Garbarino, Merwyn S. "Seminole Girl: The Autobiography of a Young Woman between Two Worlds." Trans-action 7 (February 1970): 40-46.

8234. Goggin, John M. "Osceola: Portraits, Features, and Dress." Florida Historical Quarterly 33 (January-April 1955): 161-192.

8235. Hartley, William, and Ellen Hartley. Osceola: The Unconquered Indian. New York: Hawthorn Books, 1973.

8236. Moore-Willson, Minnie. Osceola: Florida's Seminole War Chieftain. Palm Beach: Davies Publishing Company, 1931.

8237. "Old Tiger Tail Dead." Florida Historical Society Quarterly 4 (April 1926): 192-194.

8238. Porter, Kenneth Wiggins. "Abraham." Phylon 2 (1941): 105-116.

8239. _____. "Billy Bowlegs (Holata Micco) in the Civil War." Florida Historical Quarterly 45 (April 1967): 391-401.

8240. _____. "Billy Bowlegs (Holata Micco) in the Seminole Wars." Florida Historical Quarterly 45 (January 1967): 219-242.

8241. _____. "The Cowkeeper Dynasty of the Seminole Nation." Florida Historical Quarterly 30 (April 1952): 341-349.

8242. _____. "The Early Life of Luis Pacheco, Né Fatio." Negro History Bulletin 7 (December 1943): 52-53, 67-70.

8243. _____. "The Episode of Osceola's Wife: Fact or Fiction?" Florida Historical Quarterly 26 (July 1947): 92-98.

8244. _____. "Farewell to John Horse: An Episode of Seminole Negro Folk History." Phylon 8 (Third Quarter, 1947): 265-273.

8245. _____. "The Founder of the 'Seminole Nation': Secoffee or Cowkeeper." Florida Historical Quarterly 27 (April 1949): 362-384.

8246. _____. "John Caesar: Seminole Negro Partisan." Journal of Negro History 31 (April 1946): 190-207.

8247. _____. "The Negro Abraham." Florida Historical Quarterly 25 (July 1946): 1-43.

8248. _____. "Osceola and the Negroes."

Florida Historical Quarterly 33 (January-April 1955): 235-239.

8249. _____. "Three Fighters for Freedom." Journal of Negro History 28 (January 1943): 51-72. Seminole Negroes.

8250. _____. "Tiger Tail." Florida Historical Quarterly 24 (January 1946): 216-217.

8251. _____. "Wild Cat's Death and Burial." Chronicles of Oklahoma 21 (March 1943): 41-43.

8252. Rogers, George C. "A Description of Osceola." South Carolina Historical Magazine 65 (January 1964): 85-86.

8253. Sprague, Lynn Tew. "Osceola, Chief of the Seminoles." Outing 49 (February 1907): 644-652.

8254. Sturtevant, William C. "Notes on Modern Seminole Traditions of Osceola." Florida Historical Quarterly 33 (January-April 1955): 206-217.

8255. Ward, May McNeer. "The Disappearance of the Head of Osceola." Florida Historical Quarterly 33 (January-April 1955): 193-201.

8256. Williams, Isabella M. "The Truth Regarding 'Tiger Tail.'" Florida Historical Society Quarterly 4 (October 1925): 68-75.

See also studies on the Seminole wars, on the Indian Territory, and on the Five Civilized Tribes.

INDIANS OF THE PLAINS

General and Miscellaneous Studies

Listed here are studies dealing with the area as a whole or with individual tribes and persons. Materials on a number of particular tribes are listed under separate headings below.

8257. Brown, Dee. "Story of the Plains Indians." American History Illustrated 8 (August 1973): 3-50.

8258. Cash, Joseph H., and Gerald W. Wolff. The Three Affiliated Tribes (Mandan, Arikara, and Hidatsa). Phoenix: Indian Tribal Series, 1974.

8259. Denig, Edwin T. Five Indian Tribes of the Upper Missouri: Sioux, Arickaras, Assiniboines, Crees, Crows. Edited by John C. Ewers. Norman: University of Oklahoma Press, 1961. First published in 1930.

8260. Dusenberry, Verne. "The Rocky Boy Indians: Montana's Displaced Persons." Montana Magazine of History 4 (Winter 1954): 1-15.

8261. _____. "Waiting for a Day That Never Comes: The Tragic Story of the Dispossessed Metis of Montana." Montana, the Magazine of Western History 8 (April 1958): 26-39. Landless Cree and Chippewa Indians in Montana.

8262. Elam, Earl H. "The History of the Wichita Indian Confederacy to 1868." Ph.D. dissertation, Texas Technical University, 1971.

8263. _____. "The Origin and Identity of the Wichita." Kansas Quarterly 3 (Fall 1971): 13-20.

8264. Ewers, John C. Indian Life on the Upper Missouri. Norman: University of Oklahoma Press, 1968. Collection of previously published essays.

8265. Glover, William B. "A History of the Caddo Indians." Louisiana Historical Quarterly 18 (October 1935): 872-946.

8266. Goodbird the Indian: His Story. As told to Gilbert L. Wilson. New York: Fleming H. Revell Company, 1914. Biography of a Hidatsa Indian.

8267. Greenfield, Charles D. "Little Dog, Once-Fierce Piegan Warrior." Montana, the Magazine of Western History 14 (April 1964): 23-33.

8268. Grinnell, George Bird. Pawnee, Blackfoot and Cheyenne: History and Folklore of the Plains from the Writings of George Bird Grinnell. Edited by Dee Brown. New York: Charles Scribner's Sons, 1961.

8269. Haines, Francis, Sr. "Red Men of the Plains, 1500-1870." American West 10 (July 1973): 32-37.

8270. Howard, James H. "The Ponca Tribe." Ph.D. dissertation, University of Michigan, 1957.

8271. Hyde, George E. Indians of the High Plains: From the Prehistoric Period to the Coming of Europeans. Norman: University of Oklahoma Press, 1959.

8272. _____. "The Mystery of the Arikaras." North Dakota History 18 (October 1951): 187-218; 19 (January 1952): 25-58.

8273. Kenner, Charles L. A History of New Mexican-Plains Indian Relations. Norman: University of Oklahoma Press, 1969.

8274. King, Joseph B. "The Ottawa Indians in Kansas and Oklahoma." Kansas State Historical Society Collections 13 (1913-1914): 373-378.

8275. Long, James Larpenteur. The Assiniboines: From the Accounts of the Old Ones Told to First Boy. Edited by Michael Stephen Kennedy. Norman: University of Oklahoma Press, 1961.

8276. Lowie, Robert H. Indians of the Plains. New York: McGraw-Hill Book Company, 1954.

8277. Lyon, Owen. "The Quapaws and Little Rock." Arkansas Historical Quarterly 8 (Winter 1949): 336-342.

8278. _____. "The Trail of the Caddo." Arkansas Historical Quarterly 11 (Summer 1952): 124-130.

8279. _____. "The Trail of the Quapaw." Arkansas Historical Quarterly 9 (Autumn 1950): 205-213.

8280. McGinnis, Anthony R. "Economic Warfare on the Northern Plains, 1804-1877." Annals of Wyoming 44 (Spring 1972): 57-72.

8281. _____. "Intertribal Conflict on the Northern Plains, 1738-1889." Ph.D. dissertation, University of Colorado, 1974.

8282. Neighbours, Kenneth F. "Jose Maria: Anadarko Chief." Chronicles of Oklahoma 44 (Autumn 1966): 254-274.

8283. Nelson, Bruce. Land of the Dacotahs. Minneapolis: University of Minnesota Press, 1946.

8284. Rodnick, David. "The Present Day Life of the Assiniboine: A Study in Acculturation." Ph.D. dissertation, University of Pennsylvania, 1936.

8285. Schulenberg, Raymond F. "Indians of North Dakota." North Dakota History 23 (July-October 1956): 121-230.

8286. Taylor, Morris F. "Some Aspects of Historical Indian Occupation of Southeastern Colorado." Great Plains Journal 4 (Fall 1964): 17-28.

8287. Thompson, Vern E. "A History of the Quapaw." Chronicles of Oklahoma 33 (Autumn 1955): 360-383.

8288. Vandergriff, James H., ed. The Indians of Kansas. Emporia, Kansas: Teachers College Press, 1973.

8289. Weltfish, Gene. "The Plains Indians: Their Continuity in History and Their Indian Identity." In North American Indians in Historical Perspective, edited by Eleanor Burke Leacock and Nancy Oestreich Lurie, pp. 200-227. New York: Random House, 1971.

8290. Wissler, Clark. North American Indians of the Plains. 3d edition. New York: American Museum of Natural History, 1927. First published in 1912.

8291. _____. Population Changes among the Northern Plains Indians. Yale University Publications in Anthropology, no. 1. New Haven: Yale University Press, 1936.

8292. Wood, W. Raymond. "Notes on Ponca Ethnohistory, 1785-1804." Ethnohistory 6 (Winter 1959): 1-26.

8293. Wylie, Helen. "Omaha, Oto, and Missouri." Palimpsest 9 (January 1928): 42-44.

Arapaho Indians

8294. Bass, Althea. "Carl Sweezy, Arapaho Artist." Chronicles of Oklahoma 34 (Winter 1956-1957): 429-431.

8295. Fowler, Loretta Kay. "Political Process and Socio-Cultural Change among the Arapahoe Indians." Ph.D. dissertation, University of Illinois, 1970.

8296. Michelson, Truman. "Narrative of an Arapaho Woman." American Anthropologist 35 (October-December 1933): 595-610.

8297. Murphy, James C. "The Place of the Northern Arapahoes in the Relations between the United States and the Indians of the Plains, 1851-1879." Annals of Wyoming 41 (April 1969): 33-61; (October 1969): 203-259.

8298. Scott, Hugh Lenox. "The Early History and the Names of the Arapaho." American Anthropologist, new series 9 (July-September 1907): 545-560.

8299. Sweezy, Carl, as told to Althea Bass. "A Long Way from the Buffalo Road." American Heritage 17 (October 1966): 22-25, 92-98.

8300. Trenholm, Virginia Cole. "Arapahoes in Council." Annals of Wyoming 44 (Fall 1972): 235-236.

8301. _____. The Arapahoes, Our People. Norman: University of Oklahoma Press, 1970.

Blackfeet Indians

Both biographical material and general and miscellaneous accounts are listed here.

8302. Dempsey, Hugh A. Crowfoot, Chief of the Blackfeet. Norman: University of Oklahoma Press, 1972.

8303. Denman, Clayton C. "Cultural Change among the Blackfeet Indians of Montana." Ph.D. dissertation, University of California, 1968.

8304. Ewers, John C. The Blackfeet: Raiders on the Northwestern Plains. Norman: University of Oklahoma Press, 1958.

8305. _____. "The Last of the Buffalo Indians." American West 2 (Spring 1965): 26-31.

8306. Hyde, George E. The Early Blackfeet and Their Neighbors. Denver: John Van Male, 1933.

8307. Lone Wolf (Hart Merriam Schultz), as related to Paul Dyck. "Lone Wolf Returns . . . to That Long Ago Time." Montana, the Magazine of Western History 22 (January 1972): 18-41.

8308. McClintock, Walter. "The Tragedy of the Blackfoot." Southwest Museum Papers no. 3 (April 1930): 1-53.

8309. McFee, Malcolm. "Modern Blackfeet: Contrasting Patterns of Differential Acculturation." Ph.D. dissertation, Stanford University, 1962.

8310. _____. Modern Blackfeet: Montanans on a Reservation. New York: Holt, Rinehart and Winston, 1972.

8311. Mitchell, Jessie Lincoln. "Portal to the Past: The Blackfeet." Montana, the Magazine of Western History 14 (April 1964): 75-81.

8312. Sharp, Paul F. "Blackfeet of the Border: One People, Divided." Montana, the Magazine of Western History 20 (Winter 1970): 2-15.

8313. Sheridan, Clare. Redskin Interlude. London: Nicholson and Watson, 1938.

8314. West, Helen B. "Blackfoot Country." Montana, the Magazine of Western History 10 (Fall 1960): 34-44.

8315. _____. "Starvation Winter of the Blackfeet." Montana, the Magazine of Western History 9 (Winter 1959): 2-19.

Cheyenne Indians

Included here are works on both the Northern Cheyennes and the Southern Cheyennes--general accounts and biographical studies.

8316. Berthrong, Donald J. The Southern Cheyennes. Norman: University of Oklahoma Press, 1963.

8317. Brininstool, E. A. Dull Knife (a Cheyenne Napoleon). Hollywood, California, 1935.

8318. Campbell, Walter S. "The Cheyenne Dog Soldiers." Chronicles of Oklahoma 1 (January 1921): 90-97.

8319. Collings, Ellsworth. "Roman Nose: Chief of the Southern Cheyenne." Chronicles of Oklahoma 42 (Winter 1964-1965): 429-457.

8320. Dusenberry, Verne. "The Northern Cheyenne: All They Have Asked Is to Live in Montana." Montana Magazine of History 5 (Winter 1955): 23-40.

8321. Frink, Maurice. "Donald Hollow-

brest: Fighting Cheyenne Editor."
Montana, the Magazine of Western History
14 (October 1964): 27-30.

8322. Gage, Duane. "Black Kettle: A Noble
Savage?" Chronicles of Oklahoma 45
(Autumn 1967): 244-251.

8323. Garrard, Lewis H. "In the Lodge of
Vi-Po-Na: A Visit to the Cheyenne."
American West 5 (July 1968): 32-36.

8324. Grinnell, George Bird. The Cheyenne
Indians: Their History and Ways of Life.
2 volumes. New Haven: Yale University
Press, 1923.

8325. _____. The Fighting Cheyennes.
New York: Charles Scribner's Sons, 1915.

8326. Kias, Chief. "Chief Kias," edited by
Theodore A. Ediger. Chronicles of Oklahoma 18 (September 1940): 293-302.

8327. Liberty, Margot. "Suppression and
Survival of the Northern Cheyenne Sun
Dance." Minnesota Archaeologist 27
(1965): 121-143.

8328. Marquis, Thomas B. A Warrior Who
Fought Custer. Minneapolis: Midwest
Company, 1931. Wooden Leg.

8329. Mooney, James. "The Cheyenne Indians." Memoirs of the American Anthropological Association 1 (1905-1907):
357-442.

8330. Petersen, Karen D. Howling Wolf:
A Cheyenne Warrior's Graphic Interpretation of His People. Palo Alto, California: American West Publishing Company,
1968.

8331. _____. "The Writings of Henry
Roman Nose." Chronicles of Oklahoma 42
(Winter 1964-1965): 458-478.

8332. Powell, Peter J. "Journey to
Se'han." Montana, the Magazine of
Western History 18 (January 1968): 70-
75. The last days of John Stands in
Timber.

8333. _____. Sweet Medicine: The Con-
tinuing Role of the Sacred Arrows, the
Sun Dance, and the Sacred Buffalo Hat in
Northern Cheyenne History. 2 volumes.
Norman: University of Oklahoma Press,
1969.

8334. Powers, Ramon. "Why the Northern
Cheyenne Left Indian Territory in 1878:
A Cultural Analysis." Kansas Quarterly
3 (Fall 1971): 72-81.

8335. Sandoz, Mari. Cheyenne Autumn. New
York: McGraw-Hill Book Company, 1953.

8336. Schlesier, Karl H. "Action Anthropology and the Southern Cheyenne."
Current Anthropology 15 (September 1974):
277-283.

8337. Seger, John H. Early Days among the

Cheyenne and Arapahoe Indians. Edited
by Stanley Vestal. 2d edition. Norman:
University of Oklahoma Press, 1934.

8338. Stands in Timber, John, and Margot
Liberty. Cheyenne Memories. New Haven:
Yale University Press, 1967.

8339. Thornburgh, Luella. "Paul 'Flying
Eagle' Goodbear." New Mexico Historical
Review 36 (October 1961): 257-262.

8340. Weist, Katherine Morrett. "The
Northern Cheyennes: Diversity in a
Loosely Structured Society." Ph.D.
dissertation, University of California,
1970.

8341. Will, George F. "The Cheyenne
Indians in North Dakota." Proceedings
of the Mississippi Valley Historical
Association 7 (1913-1914): 67-78.

Comanche Indians

General accounts of the Comanches are
listed here as well as biographical studies.
Much attention has been paid to the Comanche
mixed-blood, Quanah Parker.

8342. Corwin, Hugh D. "Oscar Yellowwolf."
Great Plains Journal 1 (Spring 1962):
32-35.

8343. Day, James M. "Two Quanah Parker
Letters." Chronicles of Oklahoma 44
(Autumn 1966): 313-318.

8344. Debo, Angie. "Quanah Parker."
American Heritage 4 (Summer 1953): 30-
31, 63.

8345. Ewers, John C. "Jean Louis Berlandier: A French Scientist among the
Wild Comanches of Texas in 1828." In
Travelers on the Western Frontier,
edited by John Francis McDermott, pp.
290-300. Urbana: University of Illinois
Press, 1970.

8346. Faulk, Odie B. "The Comanche Invasion of Texas, 1743-1836." Great
Plains Journal 9 (Fall 1969): 10-50.

8347. Fehrenbach, T. R. Comanches: The
Destruction of a People. New York:
Alfred A. Knopf, 1974.

8348. Gilles, Albert S., Sr. "Wer-Que-
Yah, Jesus-Man Comanche." Southwest
Review 53 (Summer 1968): 277-291.

8349. Hagan, William T. "Quanah Parker,
Indian Judge." In Probing the American
West: Papers from the Santa Fe Conference,
edited by K. Ross Toole and others, pp.
71-78. Santa Fe: Museum of New Mexico
Press, 1962.

8350. Harston, J. Emmor. Comanche Land.
San Antonio: Naylor Company, 1963.

8351. Jackson, Clyde L., and Grace Jackson.
Quanah Parker, Last Chief of the

Comanches: A Study in Southwestern Frontier History. New York: Exposition Press, 1963.

8352. Smith, Ralph A. "The Comanche Bridge between Oklahoma and Mexico, 1834-1844." Chronicles of Oklahoma 39 (Spring 1961): 54-69.

8353. Tefft, Stanton Knight. "Cultural Adaptation: The Case of the Comanche Indians." Ph.D. dissertation, University of Minnesota, 1960.

8354. Tilghman, Zoe A. Quanah, the Eagle of the Comanches. Oklahoma City: Harlow Publishing Corporation, 1938.

8355. Tyler, Ronnie C. "Quanah Parker and the Lamp." American History Illustrated 9 (May 1974): 24-26.

8356. _____. "Quanah Parker's Narrow Escape." Chronicles of Oklahoma 46 (Summer 1968): 182-188.

8357. Wallace, Ernest. "The Comanches on the White Man's Road." West Texas Historical Association Year Book 29 (October 1953): 3-32.

8358. Wallace, Ernest, and E. Adamson Hoebel. The Comanches: Lords of the South Plains. Norman: University of Oklahoma Press, 1952.

8359. Wellman, Paul I. "Cynthia Ann Parker." Chronicles of Oklahoma 12 (June 1934): 163-170. White mother of Quanah Parker.

Crow Indians

Listed here are biographical studies and general works on the Crows.

8360. Beckwourth, James P. The Life and Adventures of James P. Beckwourth, Mountaineer, Scout, and Pioneer, and Chief of the Crow Nation of Indians. Written from his dictation by T. D. Bonner. New York: Harper and Brothers, 1856.

8361. Bradley, James H. "Arrapooash." Contributions to the Historical Society of Montana 9 (1923): 299-307.

8362. Castles, Jean I. "'Boxpotapesh' of the Crow Agency." Montana, the Magazine of Western History 21 (Summer 1971): 84-93.

8363. Krieg, Frederick C. "Chief Plenty Coups: His Final Dignity." Montana, the Magazine of Western History 16 (October 1966): 28-39.

8364. Leforge, Thomas H. Memoirs of a White Crow Indian (Thomas H. Leforge) As Told by Thomas B. Marquis. New York: Century Company, 1928.

8365. Linderman, Frank B. American: The Life Story of a Great Indian, Plenty-Coups, Chief of the Crows. New York: John Day Company, 1930.

8366. _____. Red Mother. New York: John Day Company, 1932. Republished as Pretty-Shield, Medicine Woman of the Crows. Lincoln: University of Nebraska Press, 1974.

8367. McGinnis, Dale K., and Floyd W. Sharrock. The Crow People. Phoenix: Indian Tribal Series, 1972.

8368. Nabokov, Peter. Two Leggings: The Making of a Crow Warrior. New York: Thomas Y. Crowell Company, 1967. Based on a field manuscript prepared by William Wildschut.

8369. Stafford, John Wade. "Crow Culture Change: A Geographical Analysis." Ph.D. dissertation, Michigan State University, 1972.

8370. Wiltsey, Norman B. "Plenty Coups: Statesman Chief of the Crows." Montana, the Magazine of Western History 13 (September 1963): 28-39.

Kansa Indians

Listed here are general works dealing with the Kansa Indians.

8371. Barry, Louise. "The Kansa Indians and the Census of 1843." Kansas Historical Quarterly 39 (Winter 1973): 478-490.

8372. Morehouse, George P. "History of the Kansa or Kaw Indians." Transactions of the Kansas State Historical Society 10 (1907-1908): 327-368.

8373. _____. The Kansa, or Kaw Indians, and Their History. Topeka: State Printing Office, 1908.

8374. Spencer, Joab. "The Kaw or Kansas Indians: Their Customs, Manners, and Folk-lore." Transactions of the Kansas State Historical Society 10 (1907-1908): 373-382.

8375. Unrau, William E. "The Depopulation of the Dheghia-Siouan Kansa Prior to Removal." New Mexico Historical Review 48 (October 1973): 313-328.

8376. _____. The Kansa Indians: A History of the Wind People, 1673-1873. Norman: University of Oklahoma Press, 1971.

8377. Wedel, Waldo R. "The Kansa Indians." Transactions of the Kansas Academy of Science 49 (June 1946): 1-35.

Kiowa Indians

General accounts and biographical studies

of the Kiowa and the Kiowa Apache Indians are listed here.

8378. Bittle, William E. "A Brief History of the Kiowa Apache." Papers in Anthropology (University of Oklahoma) 12 (Spring 1971): 1-34.

8379. Brant, Charles S. "The Kiowa Apache Indians: A Study in Ethnology and Acculturation." Ph.D. dissertation, Cornell University, 1951.

8380. _____. "White Contact and Cultural Disintegration among the Kiowa Apache." Plains Anthropologist 9 (February 1964): 8-13.

8381. Corry, John. "A Man Called Perry Horse." Harper's Magazine 241 (October 1970): 81-84.

8382. Corwin, Hugh D. "Delos K. Lonewolf, Kiowa." Chronicles of Oklahoma 39 (Winter 1961-1962): 433-436.

8383. _____. The Kiowa Indians: Their History and Life Stories. Lawton, Oklahoma, 1958.

8384. Crocchiola, Stanley Francis Louis [F. Stanley]. Satanta and the Kiowas. Borger, Texas: Jim Hess Printers, 1968.

8385. Debo, Angie. "History and Customs of the Kiowas." Panhandle-Plains Historical Review 7 (1934): 42-52.

8386. Levy, Jerrold E. "After Custer: Kiowa Political and Social Organization from the Reservation Period to the Present." Ph.D. dissertation, University of Chicago, 1959.

8387. Marriott, Alice. The Ten Grandmothers. Norman: University of Oklahoma Press, 1945.

8388. Mayhall, Mildred P. The Kiowas. Norman: University of Oklahoma Press, 1962.

8389. Methvin, J. J. "Ahpeahtone, Kiowa --a Bit of History." Chronicles of Oklahoma 9 (September 1931): 335-337.

8390. Monahan, Forrest D., Jr. "The Kiowas and New Mexico, 1800-1845." Journal of the West 8 (January 1969): 67-75.

8391. Nye, Wilbur Sturtevant. Bad Medicine and Good: Tales of the Kiowas. Norman: University of Oklahoma Press, 1962.

8392. Taylor, Morris F. "Kicking Bird: A Chief of the Kiowas." Kansas Historical Quarterly 38 (Autumn 1972): 295-319.

8393. Wharton, Clarence. Satanta, the Great Chief of the Kiowas and His People. Dallas: Banks Upshaw and Company, 1935.

8394. Whitewolf, Jim. Jim Whitewolf: The Life of a Kiowa Apache Indian. Edited by Charles S. Brant. New York: Dover Publications, 1969.

Mandan Indians

8395. Bruner, Edward M. "Mandan." In Perspectives in American Indian Culture Change, edited by Edward H. Spicer, pp. 187-277. Chicago: University of Chicago Press, 1961.

8396. Connolly, James B. "Four Bears." North Dakota History 25 (October 1958): 93-106.

8397. Glassner, Martin Ira. "The Mandan Migrations: Pre-Contact to 1876." Journal of the West 13 (January 1974): 25-46.

8398. _____. "The New Mandan Migrations: From Hunting Expeditions to Relocation." Journal of the West 13 (April 1974): 59-74.

8399. _____. "Population Figures for Mandan Indians." Indian Historian 7 (Spring 1974): 41-46.

8400. Goplen, Arnold O. "The Mandan Indians." North Dakota History 13 (October 1946): 153-175. Section of an article on "The Historical Significance of Fort Lincoln State Park."

Omaha Indians

Listed here are general studies of the tribe and biographical accounts by and about Omaha Indians.

8401. Crary, Margaret. Susette La Flesche: Voice of the Omaha Indians. New York: Hawthorn Books, 1973.

8402. Fletcher, Alice C. Historical Sketch of the Omaha Tribe of Indians in Nebraska. Washington: Judd and Detweiler, 1885.

8403. Fletcher, Alice C., and Francis La Flesche. The Omaha Tribe. Annual Report of the Bureau of American Ethnology, 1905-1906. Washington: Government Printing Office, 1911.

8404. Gilmore, Melvin Randolph. "The True Logan Fontenelle." Nebraska State Historical Society Publications 19 (1919): 64-71.

8405. Green, Norma Kidd. "Four Sisters: Daughters of Joseph La Flesche." Nebraska History 45 (June 1964): 165-176.

8406. _____. Iron Eye's Family: The Children of Joseph La Flesche. Sponsored by the Nebraska State Historical Society. Lincoln: Johnsen Publishing Company, 1969.

8407. La Flesche, Francis. The Middle Five: Indian Schoolboys of the Omaha Tribe. Foreword by David A. Baerreis. Madison: University of Wisconsin Press, 1963. First published in Boston, 1900.

8408. Smith, G. Hubert. "Notes on Omaha Ethnohistory, 1763-1820." Plains Anthropologist 18 (November 1973): 257-270.

8409. Wilson, Dorothy Clarke. Bright Eyes: The Story of Susette La Flesche, an Omaha Indian. New York: McGraw-Hill Book Company, 1974.

Osage Indians

Listed here are general and miscellaneous accounts and biographical studies dealing with the Osages.

8410. Bailey, Garrick A. "Changes in Osage Social Organization: 1673-1969." Ph.D. dissertation, University of Oregon, 1970.

8411. _____. "The Osage Roll: An Analysis." Indian Historian 5 (Spring 1972): 26-29.

8412. Baird, W. David. The Osage People. Phoenix: Indian Tribal Series, 1972.

8413. Burchardt, Bill. "Osage Oil." Chronicles of Oklahoma 41 (Autumn 1963): 253-269.

8414. Chapman, Berlin B. "Removal of the Osages from Kansas." Kansas Historical Quarterly 7 (August 1938): 287-305; (November 1938): 399-410.

8415. Chapman, Carl Haley. "The Origin of the Osage Indian Tribe: An Ethnographical, Historical and Archaeological Study." Ph.D. dissertation, University of Michigan, 1959.

8416. Christianson, James R. "A Study of Osage History Prior to 1876." Ph.D. dissertation, University of Kansas, 1968.

8417. Dickerson, Philip. History of the Osage Nation: Its People, Resources and Prospects. N.p., 1906.

8418. Finney, Frank F. "Maria Tallchief in History: Oklahoma's Own Ballerina." Chronicles of Oklahoma 38 (Spring 1960): 8-11.

8419. _____. "Progress in the Civilization of the Osage and Their Government." Chronicles of Oklahoma 40 (Spring 1962): 2-21.

8420. Griffis, Joseph K. (Chief Tahan). Tahan: Out of Savagery into Civilization. New York: George H. Doran Company, 1915.

8421. Mathews, John Joseph. The Osages: Children of the Middle Waters. Norman: University of Oklahoma Press, 1961.

8422. _____. Wah'kon-tah: The Osage and the White Man's Road. Norman: University of Oklahoma Press, 1932.

8423. Meserve, John Bartlett. "'Philip Nolan' of the Osages." National Republic 22 (December 1934): 5-7, 26.

8424. Parsons, David. "The Removal of the Osages from Kansas." Ph.D. dissertation, University of Oklahoma, 1940.

8425. Russell, Orpha B. "Chief James Bigheart of the Osages." Chronicles of Oklahoma 32 (Winter 1954-1955): 384-394.

Oto and Missouri Indians

8426. Berry, J. Brewton. "The Missouri Indians." Southwestern Social Science Quarterly 17 (September 1936): 113-124.

8427. Bray, Robert T. "The Missouri Indian Tribe in Archaeology and History." Missouri Historical Review 55 (April 1961): 213-225.

8428. Chapman, Berlin B. "The Barnes Family of Barneston." Nebraska History 47 (March 1966): 57-83.

8429. _____. The Otoes and Missourias: A Study of Indian Removal and the Legal Aftermath. Oklahoma City: Times Journal Publishing Company, 1965.

8430. Green, Albert L. "The Otoe Indians." Publications of the Nebraska State Historical Society 21 (1930): 175-209. Historical introduction by Addison E. Sheldon.

Pawnee Indians

8431. Chapin, Charles. "Removal of Pawnee and Peace with Their Neighbors." Nebraska History Magazine 26 (January-March 1945): 43-48.

8432. Dunbar, John B. "The Pawnee Indians: Their History and Ethnology." Magazine of American History with Notes and Queries 4 (April 1880): 241-281.

8433. Finney, Frank F. "William Pollock: Pawnee Indian Artist and Rough Rider." Chronicles of Oklahoma 33 (Winter 1955-1956): 509-511.

8434. Hodge, Frederick Webb. "Pitalesharu and His Medal." Masterkey 24 (July-August 1950): 111-119.

8435. Hyde, George E. Pawnee Indians. Denver: University of Denver Press, 1951. An earlier edition was published in 1934. New edition, Norman: University of Oklahoma Press, 1974.

8436. Irving, John Treat, Jr. Indian Sketches, Taken during an Expedition to the Pawnee Tribes. 2 volumes. Philadelphia: Carey, Lea and Blanchard,

1835. New edition, edited by John
Francis McDermott. Norman: University
of Oklahoma Press, 1955.

8437. "Lewis and Clark Description of
Pawnee Nation." Nebraska History Magazine 10 (July-September 1927): 195-200.

8438. Oehler, G. F., and D. Z. Smith.
"Description of a Journey and Visit to
the Pawnee Indians." Moravian Church
Miscellany 2 (August 1851): 217-225; 3
(February 1852): 55-69.

8439. Sanborn, Theo. A. "The Story of the
Pawnee Indian Village in Republic County,
Kansas." Kansas Historical Quarterly 39
(Spring 1973): 1-11.

8440. Smith, D. Z. "Description of the
Manners and Customs of the Pawnee
Indians." Moravian Church Miscellany 3
(March 1852): 86-94.

Sioux Indians

The Sioux, the most important of the
plains tribes, have received much attention from anthropologists and historians.
Works on the Sioux are divided here into
general accounts and biographical studies.
Some works of ethnology are included.

General and Miscellaneous Accounts

8441. Bad Heart Bull, Amos. A Pictographic
History of the Oglala Sioux. Lincoln:
University of Nebraska Press, 1967. Text
by Helen H. Blish.

8442. Borglum, Gutzon. "Memorials to the
Sioux Indians." Nebraska History 21
(October-December 1940): 253-255.

8443. Cash, Joseph H. The Sioux People.
Phoenix: Indian Tribal Series, 1971.

8444. Deloria, Ella C. Speaking of Indians.
New York: Friendship Press, 1944.

8445. Dollar, Clyde D. "Through the Looking Glass: History and the Modern Brule
Sioux." In Western American History in
the Seventies: Selected Papers Presented
to the First Western History Conference,
Colorado State University, August 10-12,
1972, edited by Daniel Tyler, pp. 38-45.
Fort Collins: Robinson Press for Educational Media and Information Systems,
1973.

8446. Ducheneaux, Frank. "The Cheyenne
River Sioux." American Indian 7 (Spring
1956): 20-30.

8447. Dyck, Paul. Brulé: The Sioux People
of the Rosebud. Flagstaff, Arizona:
Northland Press, 1971.

8448. Feraca, Stephen E., and James H.
Howard. "The Identity and Demography of
the Dakota or Sioux Tribes." Plains

Anthropologist 8 (May 1963): 80-84.

8449. Fiske, Frank. The Taming of the
Sioux. Bismarck: Bismarck Tribune,
1917.

8450. Goldfrank, Esther S. "Historic
Change and Social Character: A Study
of the Teton Dakota." American Anthropologist 45 (January-March 1943): 67-83.

8451. Hans, Fred M. The Great Sioux
Nation. Chicago: M. A. Donohue and
Company, 1907.

8452. Hassrick, Royal B. The Sioux: Life
and Customs of a Warrior Society.
Norman: University of Oklahoma Press,
1964.

8453. Holmgren, Philip S. "Sioux and
White Relations." Ph.D. dissertation,
University of Nebraska, 1950.

8454. Hyde, George E. Red Cloud's Folk:
A History of the Oglala Sioux Indians.
Norman: University of Oklahoma Press,
1937.

8455. _____. A Sioux Chronicle.
Norman: University of Oklahoma Press,
1956. History of the Sioux 1878-1890.

8456. _____. Spotted Tail's Folk: A
History of the Brule Sioux. Norman:
University of Oklahoma Press, 1961.

8457. Johnson, W. Fletcher. The Red Record
of the Sioux: Life of Sitting Bull and
History of the Indian War of 1890-'91.
Philadelphia: Edgewood Publishing Company, 1891.

8458. Jones, Douglas C. "Teresa Dean:
Lady Correspondent among the Sioux
Indians." Journalism Quarterly 49
(Winter 1972): 656-662.

8459. Landes, Ruth. The Mystic Lake
Sioux: Sociology of the Mdewakantonwan
Santee. Madison: University of Wiscon-
sin Press, 1968.

8460. Lass, William E. "The 'Moscow
Expedition.'" Minnesota History 39
(Summer 1965): 227-240. Attempt to
provision the Sioux, 1863.

8461. Macgregor, Gordon. "Changing Society:
The Teton Dakotas." In The Modern Sioux:
Social Systems and Reservation Culture,
edited by Ethel Nurge, pp. 92-106.
Lincoln: University of Nebraska Press,
1970.

8462. Macgregor, Gordon, with the col-
laboration of Royal B. Hassrick and
William E. Henry. Warriors without
Weapons: A Study of the Society and
Personality Development of the Pine
Ridge Sioux. Chicago: University of
Chicago Press, 1946.

8463. McNickle, D'Arcy. "Rescuing

Sisseton." American Indian 3 (Spring 1946): 21-27.

8464. Mails, Thomas E. The Mystic Warriors of the Plains. Garden City, New York: Doubleday, 1972.

8465. Mekeel, Scudder. "A Modern American Indian Community in the Light of Its Past: A Study of Culture Change." Ph.D. dissertation, Yale University, 1932.

8466. _____. "A Short History of the Teton-Dakota." North Dakota Historical Quarterly 10 (July 1943): 137-205.

8467. Meyer, Roy W. "The Canadian Sioux: Refugees from Minnesota." Minnesota History 41 (Spring 1968): 13-28.

8468. _____. History of the Santee Sioux: United States Indian Policy on Trial. Lincoln: University of Nebraska Press, 1967.

8469. _____. "The Prairie Island Community: A Remnant of Minnesota Sioux." Minnesota History 37 (September 1961): 271-282.

8470. Neill, Edward D. "Dakota Land and Dakota Life." Annals of the Minnesota Historical Society, 1853, pp. 45-64.

8471. Nurge, Ethel, ed. The Modern Sioux: Social Systems and Reservation Culture. Lincoln: University of Nebraska Press, 1970.

8472. Olden, Sarah Emilia. The People of Tipi Sapa. Milwaukee: Morehouse Publishing Company, 1918.

8473. Pennington, Robert. "An Analysis of the Political Structure of the Teton-Dakota Indian Tribe of North America." North Dakota History 20 (July 1953): 143-155.

8474. Relf, Francis H., ed. "Removal of the Sioux Indians from Minnesota." Minnesota History Bulletin 2 (May 1918): 420-425. Account of John P. Williamson.

8475. Robinson, Doane. The Sioux Indians --a History. Cedar Rapids: Torch Press, 1908. First published as "A History of the Dakota or Sioux Indians from the Earliest Traditions." South Dakota Historical Collections 2 (1904): 1-523.

8476. Rosenfelt, Willard E. The Last Buffalo: Cultural Views of the Plains Indians: The Sioux or Dakota Nation. Minneapolis: T. S. Denison and Company, 1973.

8477. Ruby, Robert H. The Oglala Sioux: Warriors in Transition. New York: Vantage Press, 1955.

8478. Schusky, Ernest L. "Contemporary Migration and Culture Change on Two Dakota Reservations." Plains Anthro-

pologist 7 (August 1962): 178-183.

8479. _____. "Cultural Change and Continuity in the Lower Brule Community." In The Modern Sioux: Social Systems and Reservation Culture, edited by Ethel Nurge, pp. 107-122. Lincoln: University of Nebraska Press, 1970.

8480. _____. The Forgotten Sioux: An Ethnohistory of the Lower Brule Reservation. Chicago: Nelson-Hall, 1975.

8481. _____. "The Lower Brule Sioux: The Description of a Distinct Community and the Processes Which Keep It Distinct." Ph.D. dissertation, University of Chicago, 1961.

8482. _____. Politics and Planning in a Dakota Indian Community: A Case Study of Views on Termination and Plans for Rehabilitation on the Lower Brule Reservation in South Dakota. Vermillion: Institute of Indian Studies, State University of South Dakota, 1959.

8483. Shunk, Harold W. "Reminiscing about the Dakota." Kansas Quarterly 3 (Fall 1971): 116-123.

8484. Standing Bear, Luther. Land of the Spotted Eagle. Boston: Houghton Mifflin Company, 1933.

8485. _____. My People, the Sioux. Edited by E. A. Brininstool. Boston: Houghton Mifflin Company, 1928.

8486. Swisher, J. A. "The Sioux." Palimpsest 9 (1928): 49-52. In Iowa.

8487. Terrell, John Upton. Sioux Trail. New York: McGraw-Hill Book Company, 1974.

8488. Useem, Ruth M. "The Aftermath of Defeat: A Study of Acculturation among the Rosebud Sioux of South Dakota." Ph.D. dissertation, University of Wisconsin, 1947.

8489. Utley, Robert M. The Last Days of the Sioux Nation. New Haven: Yale University Press, 1963.

8490. Vestal, Stanley, ed. New Sources of Indian History, 1850-1891. Norman: University of Oklahoma Press, 1934.

8491. White, Robert A. "Value Themes of the Native American Tribalistic Movement among the South Dakota Sioux." Current Anthropology 15 (September 1974): 284-289.

8492. Wilson, E. P. "The Story of the Oglala and Brule Sioux in the Pine Ridge Country of Northwest Nebraska in the Middle Seventies." Nebraska History 21 (October-December 1940): 259-274.

Biographical Studies

8493. Adams, Alexander B. Sitting Bull: An

Epic of the Plains. New York: G. P. Putnam's Sons, 1973.

8494. Allen, Charles W. "Red Cloud and the U.S. Flag." Nebraska History 21 (October-December 1940): 293-304.

8495. Allison, E. H. "Surrender of Sitting Bull," edited by Doane Robinson. South Dakota Historical Collections 6 (1910-1912): 231-270.

8496. Anderson, Harry H. The War Club of Sitting Bull: The Oglala." Nebraska History 42 (March 1961): 55-61.

8497. Brininstool, E. A., and others. "Chief Crazy Horse, His Career and Death." Nebraska History Magazine 12 (January-March 1929): 4-77.

8498. Burdick, Usher L. The Last Days of Sitting Bull, Sioux Medicine Chief. Baltimore: Wirth Brothers, 1941.

8499. Clough, Wilson C. "Mini-Aku, Daughter of Spotted Tail." Annals of Wyoming 39 (October 1967): 187-216.

8500. Collins, Dabney Otis. "The Fight for Sitting Bull's Bones." American West 3 (Winter 1966): 72-78.

8501. Cunninghame Graham, R. B. "Lone Wolf." Scribner's Magazine 69 (June 1921): 651-654.

8502. Deloria, Vine V., Sr. "The Standing Rock Reservation: A Personal Reminiscence." South Dakota Review 9 (Summer 1971): 169-195.

8503. Eastman, Charles A. "First Impressions of Civilization." Harper's Monthly Magazine 108 (March 1904): 587-592.

8504. _____. From Deep Woods to Civilization: Chapters in the Autobiography of an Indian. Boston: Little, Brown and Company, 1916.

8505. _____. Indian Boyhood. New York: McClure, Phillips and Company, 1902.

8506. _____. "Rain-in-the-Face." Outlook 84 (October 27, 1906): 507-512.

8507. _____. "The School Days of an Indian." Outlook 85 (April 13, 1907): 851-855; (April 20, 1907): 894-899.

8508. _____. The Soul of the Indian: An Interpretation. Boston: Houghton Mifflin Company, 1911.

8509. Fechet, E. G. "The True Story of the Death of Sitting Bull." Proceedings and Collections of the Nebraska State Historical Society, 2d series 2 (1898): 179-189.

8510. Fire, John (Lame Deer), and Richard Erdoes. Lame Deer: Seeker of Visions. New York: Simon and Shuster, 1972.

8511. Fiske, Frank Bennett. Life and

Death of Sitting Bull. Fort Yates, North Dakota: Pioneer-Arrow, 1933.

8512. Howard, James H., ed. The Warrior Who Killed Custer: The Personal Narrative of Chief Joseph White Bull. Lincoln: University of Nebraska Press, 1968.

8513. Hughes, Thomas. Indian Chiefs of Southern Minnesota. Mankato, Minnesota: Free Press Company, 1927.

8514. Johnson, Roy P. "Sitting Bull: Hero or Monster?" North Dakota History 29 (January-April 1962): 217-221.

8515. Miller, David Humphreys. "Sitting Bull's White Squaw." Montana, the Magazine of Western History 14 (April 1964): 55-71. Mrs. Catherine Weldon.

8516. Milroy, Thomas W. "A Physician by the Name of Ohiyesa: Charles Alexander Eastman, M.D." Minnesota Medicine 54 (July 1971): 569-572.

8517. Moorehead, Warren K. "The Passing of Red Cloud." Transactions of the Kansas State Historical Society 10 (1907-1908): 295-311.

8518. Neihardt, John G. Black Elk Speaks: Being the Life Story of a Holy Man of the Oglala Sioux. New York: William Morrow and Company, 1932.

8519. Olsen, Louise P. "Ben Brave." North Dakota History 18 (January 1951): 25-29.

8520. Ourada, Patricia K., ed. "The Hat Sitting Bull Wears." Annals of Wyoming 41 (October 1969): 272-274. Account by Andrew Fox.

8521. Pennanen, Gary. "Sitting Bull: Indian without a Country." Canadian Historical Review 51 (June 1970): 123-140.

8522. Pfaller, Louis. "'Enemies in '76, Friends in '85'--Sitting Bull and Buffalo Bill." Prologue: The Journal of the National Archives 1 (Fall 1969): 16-31.

8523. Riggs, Stephen R. "Dakota Portraits," edited by Willoughby M. Babcock, Jr. Minnesota History Bulletin 2 (November 1918): 481-568.

8524. Robinson, Doane. "The Education of Redcloud." South Dakota Historical Collections 12 (1924): 156-178.

8525. _____. "Some Sidelights on the Character of Sitting Bull." Collections of the Nebraska State Historical Society 16 (1911): 187-192.

8526. Rosenberg, Marvin, and Dorothy Rosenberg. "'There Are No Indians Left Now but Me.'" American Heritage 15

(June 1964): 18-23, 106-111. The last years of Sitting Bull.

8527. Sandoz, Mari. Crazy Horse, the Strange Man of the Oglalas: A Biography. New York: Alfred A. Knopf, 1942.

8528. Sibley, Henry Hastings. Iron Face: The Adventures of Jack Frazer, Frontier Warrior, Scout, and Hunter. Edited by Theodore C. Blegen and Sarah A. Davidson. Chicago: Caxton Club, 1950.

8529. Smitter, Wessel. "Red Warrior Who Licked Custer." Coronet 26 (August 1949): 117-120. Crazy Horse.

8530. Standing Bear, Luther. My Indian Boyhood. Boston: Houghton Mifflin Company, 1931.

8531. Taylor, Joseph Henry. "Inkpaduta and Sons." North Dakota Historical Quarterly 4 (April 1930): 153-164.

8532. Utley, Robert M. "The Ordeal of Plenty Horses." American Heritage 26 (December 1974): 15-19, 82-86.

8533. Vestal, Stanley. Sitting Bull, Champion of the Sioux: A Biography. Boston: Houghton Mifflin Company, 1932.

8534. _____. Warpath: The True Story of the Fighting Sioux Told in a Biography of Chief White Bull. Boston: Houghton Mifflin Company, 1934.

8535. _____. "The Works of Sitting Bull, Real and Imaginary." Southwest Review 19 (April 1934): 265-278.

8536. Worcester, Donald E. "Spotted Tail: Warrior, Diplomat." American West 1 (Fall 1964): 38-46, 87.

INDIANS OF THE SOUTHWEST

General and Miscellaneous Studies

Listed here are studies of particular tribes of the Southwest and other general and miscellaneous works. Materials on some tribes are listed separately below.

8537. Bartlett, Katherine. The Distribution of the Indians of Arizona in 1848." Plateau 17 (January 1945): 41-45.

8538. Bee, Robert Lawrence. "Sociocultural Change and Persistence in the Yuma Indian Reservation Community." Ph.D. dissertation, University of Kansas, 1967.

8539. Cain, H. T. "The Pima Indians: A Tribe in Transition." Medical and Biological Illustration 22 (April 1972): 82-84.

8540. Casanova, Frank E., ed. "General Crook Visits the Supais: As Reported by John G. Bourke." Arizona and the West

10 (Autumn 1968): 253-276.

8541. Crane, Leo. Indians of the Enchanted Desert. Boston: Little, Brown and Company, 1925. Navajo and Hopi.

8542. Cushing, Frank Hamilton. My Adventures in Zuni. Santa Fe: Peripatetic Press, 1941.

8543. Dale, Edward Everett. The Indians of the Southwest: A Century of Development under the United States. Norman: University of Oklahoma Press, 1949.

8544. Dobyns, Henry F., and Robert C. Euler. The Havasupai People. Phoenix: Indian Tribal Series, 1971.

8545. Dozier, Edward P. "The American Southwest." In North American Indians in Historical Perspective, edited by Eleanor Burke Leacock and Nancy Oestreich Lurie, pp. 228-256. New York: Random House, 1971.

8546. Dutton, Bertha Pauline. Friendly People: The Zuñi Indians. Santa Fe: Museum of New Mexico Press, 1963.

8547. Forbes, Jack D. "Nationalism, Tribalism, and Self-Determination: Yuman-Mexican Relations, 1821-1848." Indian Historian 6 (Spring 1973): 18-22, 42.

8548. _____. Warriors of the Colorado: The Yumas of the Quechan Nation and Their Neighbors. Norman: University of Oklahoma Press, 1965.

8549. Goddard, Pliny Earle. Indians of the Southwest. 3d edition. New York: American Museum of Natural History, 1927.

8550. Hackenberg, Robert Allan. "Indian Administration and Social Change." Ph.D. dissertation, Cornell University, 1961. Gila River Pima-Maricopa community.

8551. Hoover, J. W. "The Indian Country of Southern Arizona." Geographical Review 19 (January 1929): 38-60.

8552. _____. "Modern Canyon Dwellers of Arizona." Journal of Geography 28 (October 1929): 269-278. Havasupai Indians.

8553. Iliff, Flora Gregg. People of the Blue Water: My Adventures among the Walapai and Havasupai Indians. New York: Harper and Brothers, 1954.

8554. Jensen, Marguerite. "The Yaqui." Indian Historian 4 (Fall 1971): 41-43.

8555. Kelly, William H. Indians of the Southwest: A Survey of Indian Tribes and Indian Administration in Arizona. Tucson: Bureau of Ethnic Research, University of Arizona, 1953.

8556. Kennedy, Mary J. "Culture Contact and Acculturation of the Southwestern

Pomo." Ph.D. dissertation, University of California, 1955.

8557. Leighton, Dorothea C., and John Adair. People of the Middle Place: A Study of the Zuni Indians. New Haven: Human Relations Area Files Press, 1966.

8558. Manners, Robert A. "Tribe and Tribal Boundaries: The Walapai." Ethnohistory 4 (Winter 1957): 1-26.

8559. Meinig, D. W. Southwest: Three Peoples in Geographical Change, 1600-1970. New York: Oxford University Press, 1971.

8560. Quilliam, T. A. "A Pictorial Archive of a Vanishing Culture." Medical and Biological Illustration 22 (April 1972): 85-93. Pima Indians.

8561. Schroeder, Albert H. "Shifting for Survival in the Spanish Southwest." New Mexico Historical Review 43 (October 1968): 291-310.

8562. Schroeder, Albert H., ed. The Changing Ways of Southwestern Indians: A Historic Perspective. El Corral de Sante Fe Westerners Brand Book, 1973. Glorieta, New Mexico: Rio Grande Press, 1973.

8563. Shaw, Anna Moore. A Pima Past. Tucson: University of Arizona Press, 1974.

8564. Spicer, Edward H. Cycles of Conquest: The Impact of Spain, Mexico, and the United States on the Indians of the Southwest, 1533-1960. Tucson: University of Arizona Press, 1962.

8565. _____. "European Expansion and the Enclavement of Southwestern Indians." Arizona and the West 1 (Summer 1959): 132-145.

8566. _____. "Highlights of Yaqui History." Indian Historian 7 (Spring 1974): 2-9.

8567. _____. Pascua: A Yaqui Village in Arizona. Chicago: University of Chicago Press, 1940.

8568. _____. "Yaqui." In Perspectives in American Indian Culture Change, edited by Edward H. Spicer, pp. 7-93. Chicago: University of Chicago Press, 1961.

8569. Spier, Leslie. Yuman Tribes of the Gila River. Chicago: University of Chicago Press, 1933.

8570. Vroman, Adam Clark. "Zuni." American West 3 (Summer 1966): 42-55. Introduction by Ruth L. Mahood.

8571. Weaver, Thomas, ed. Indians of Arizona: A Contemporary Perspective. Tucson: University of Arizona Press, 1974.

8572. Webb, George. A Pima Remembers.

Tucson: University of Arizona Press, 1959.

8573. Wetzler, Lewis W. "A History of the Pima Indians." Ph.D. dissertation, University of California, 1949.

Apache Indians

Works on the several groups of Apache Indians are given here. The list is divided into general accounts and biographical studies.

General and Miscellaneous Accounts

8574. Basehart, Harry W., and Tom T. Sasaki. "Changing Political Organization in the Jicarilla Apache Reservation Community." Human Organization 23 (Winter 1964): 283-289.

8575. Borden, W. C. "The Vital Statistics of an Apache Indian Community." Boston Medical and Surgical Journal 129 (July 6, 1893): 5-10.

8576. Basso, Keith H. The Cibecue Apache. New York: Holt, Rinehart and Winston, 1970.

8577. Blount, Bertha. "The Apache in the Southwest, 1846-1886." Southwest Historical Quarterly 23 (July 1919): 20-38.

8578. Boyer, Ruth McDonald. "Social Structure and Socialization among Apaches of the Mescalero Reservation." Ph.D. dissertation, University of California, 1962.

8579. Brodhead, Michael J. "Elliott Coues and the Apaches." Journal of Arizona History 14 (Summer 1973): 87-94.

8580. Burlison, Irene. Yesterday and Today in the Life of the Apaches. Philadelphia: Dorrance and Company, 1973.

8581. Christiansen, Paige W. "The Apache Barrier." Rocky Mountain Social Science Journal 3 (October 1966): 93-108.

8582. Clum, John. "The Apaches." New Mexico Historical Review 9 (April 1929): 107-127.

8583. _____. "Apaches as Thespians in 1876." New Mexico Historical Review 6 (January 1931): 76-99.

8584. Crocchiola, Stanley Francis Louis [F. Stanley]. The Apaches of New Mexico, 1540-1940. Pampa, Texas: Pampa Print Shop, 1962.

8585. Davisson, Lori. "The Apaches at Home." Journal of Arizona History 14 (Summer 1973): 113-132. Photographic essay.

8586. Dobyns, Henry F. The Apache People. Phoenix: Indian Tribal Series, 1971.

8587. _____. The Mescalero Apache People. Phoenix: Indian Tribal Series, 1973.

8588. Ellis, Richard N. "Vincent Colyer and the New Mexico Press, 1871." In The Changing Ways of Southwestern Indians: A Historic Perspective, edited by Albert H. Schroeder, pp. 205-210. Glorieta, New Mexico: Rio Grande Press, 1973.

8589. Ellis, Richard N., ed. "'The Apache Chronicle.'" New Mexico Historical Review 47 (July 1972): 275-282.

8590. Federal Writer's Project, Arizona. The Apache. Flagstaff: Arizona State Teachers College, 1939.

8591. Fergusson, Erna. "Modern Apaches of New Mexico." American Indian 6 (Summer 1951): 3-14.

8592. Forbes, Jack D. Apache, Navaho, and Spaniard. Norman: University of Oklahoma Press, 1960.

8593. Goodwin, Grenville. Grenville Goodwin among the Western Apache: Letters from the Field. Edited by Morris E. Opler. Tucson: University of Arizona Press, 1973.

8594. Gunnerson, Dolores A. The Jicarilla Apaches: A Study in Survival. DeKalb: Northern Illinois University Press, 1974.

8595. Hoover, J. W. "The Jicarilla Indian Country of New Mexico." Bulletin of the Geographical Society of Philadelphia 34 (January 1936): 1-12.

8596. Jozhe, Benedict. "A Brief History of the Fort Sill Apache Tribe." Chronicles of Oklahoma 39 (Winter 1961-1962): 427-432.

8597. Levy, Jerrold E., and Stephen J. Kunitz. "Notes on Some White Mountain Apache Social Pathologies." Plateau 42 (Summer 1969): 11-19.

8598. Lockwood, Frank C. The Apache Indians. New York: Macmillan Company, 1938.

8599. Mails, Thomas E. The People Called Apache. Englewood Cliffs, New Jersey: Prentice-Hall, 1974.

8600. Miller, Peter Springer. "Secular Change among the Western Apache, 1940 to 1967." Ph.D. dissertation, University of Arizona, 1969.

8601. Ogle, Ralph H. Federal Control of the Western Apaches, 1848-1886. Albuquerque: University of New Mexico Press, 1970. Originally published in New Mexico Historical Review 14 (October 1939): 309-365; 15 (January 1940): 12-71; (April 1940): 188-248; (July 1940): 269-335.

8602. Opler, Morris E. "Jicarilla Apache Territory, Economy, and Society in 1850." Southwestern Journal of Anthropology 27 (Winter 1971): 309-329.

8603. Opler, Morris E., and Catherine H. Opler. "Mescalero Apache History in the Southwest." New Mexico Historical Review 25 (January 1950): 1-36.

8604. Perry, Richard John. "The Apache Continuum: An Analysis of Continuity through Change in San Carlos Apache Culture and Society." Ph.D. dissertation, Syracuse University, 1971.

8605. Reeve, Frank D. "The Apache Indians in Texas." Southwestern Historical Quarterly 50 (October 1946): 189-219.

8606. Simms, D. Harper. "Pawns of Conquest: The Jicarilla Apaches of New Mexico." In Troopers West: Military and Indian Affairs on the American Frontier, edited by Ray Brandes, pp. 63-75. San Diego: Frontier Heritage Press, 1970.

8607. Sonnichsen, C. L. The Mescalero Apaches. Norman: University of Oklahoma Press, 1958.

8608. Tate, Michael Lynn. "Apache Scouts, Police, and Judges as Agents of Acculturation, 1865-1920." Ph.D. dissertation, University of Toledo, 1974.

8609. Terrell, John Upton. Apache Chronicle. New York: World Publishing, 1972.

8610. Van Roekel, Gertrude B. Jicarilla Apaches. San Antonio: Naylor Company, 1971.

8611. Wilson, H. Clyde. Jicarilla Apache Political and Economic Structures. Berkeley: University of California Press, 1964.

8612. Worcester, Donald E. "The Apaches in the History of the Southwest." New Mexico Historical Review 50 (January 1975): 25-44.

8613. _____. "The Beginnings of the Apache Menace of the Southwest." New Mexico Historical Review 16 (January 1941): 1-14.

Biographical Studies

8614. Adams, Alexander B. Geronimo: A Biography. New York: G. P. Putnam's Sons, 1971.

8615. Arnold, Elliott. "Cochise--Greatest of the Apaches." Arizona Quarterly 7 (Spring 1951): 5-12.

8616. Arnold, Oren. "Apache Doctor Who Sparked a New Era for Indians." Today's Health 47 (October 1969): 30-33, 73-76. Carlos Montezuma.

8617. Ball, Eve. In the Days of Victorio:

Recollections of a Warm Springs Apache. Tucson: University of Arizona Press, 1970. Recollections of James Kaywaykla.

8618. Barrett, S. M., ed. Geronimo's Story of His Life. New York: Duffield and Company, 1906.

8619. Brandes, Ray. "Mangas Coloradas: King Philip of the Apache Nation." In Troopers West: Military and Indian Affairs on the American Frontier, edited by Ray Brandes, pp. 23-39. San Diego: Frontier Heritage Press, 1970.

8620. Clark, Neil M. "Dr. Montezuma, Apache: Warrior in Two Worlds." Montana, the Magazine of Western History 23 (Spring 1973): 56-65.

8621. Clum, John P. "Es-kim-in-zin." New Mexico Historical Review 3 (October 1928): 399-420; 4 (January 1929): 1-27. Also published in Arizona Historical Review 2 (April 1929): 53-72; (July 1929): 53-69.

8622. _____. "Geronimo." New Mexico Historical Review 3 (January 1928): 1-40; (April 1928): 121-144; (July 1928): 217-264.

8623. _____. "Victorio, Chief of the Warm Spring Apaches." Arizona Historical Review 2 (January 1930): 74-90.

8624. Cochise, Ciyé, as told to A. Kinney Griffith. The First Hundred Years of Niño Cochise: The Untold Story of an Apache Indian Chief. New York: Abelard-Schuman, 1971.

8625. Ellis, A. N. "Recollections of an Interview with Cochise, Chief of the Apaches." Collections of the Kansas State Historical Society 13 (1913-1914): 387-392.

8626. "Geronimo, a Relic of the Frontier." Outing 47 (January 1906): 478-480.

8627. Hayes, Jess G. Apache Vengeance: True Story of Apache Kid. Albuquerque: University of New Mexico Press, 1954.

8628. La Farge, Oliver. "Apache Chief--1949 Model." American Indian 5 (Spring 1950): 3-16.

8629. Myers, Lee. "The Enigma of Mangas Coloradas' Death." New Mexico Historical Review 41 (October 1966): 287-304.

8630. Opler, Morris E. Apache Odyssey: A Journey between Two Worlds. New York: Holt, Rinehart and Winston, 1969. Autobiography of Chris.

8631. Remington, Frederic. "Massai's Crooked Trail." Harper's New Monthly Magazine 96 (January 1898): 240-246.

8632. Salzman, M., Jr. "Geronimo: The Napoleon of Indians." Journal of

Arizona History 8 (Winter 1967): 215-247.

8633. Thrapp, Dan L. Juh: An Incredible Indian. El Paso: Texas Western Press, University of Texas at El Paso, 1973.

8634. _____. Victorio and the Mimbres Apaches. Norman: University of Oklahoma Press, 1974.

8635. Tyler, Barbara Ann. "Cochise: Apache War Leader, 1858-1861." Journal of Arizona History 6 (Spring 1965): 1-10.

See also the studies dealing with the Apache wars.

Hopi Indians

The Hopi Indians have attracted many scholars and other writers. Listed here are general works, a few more specialized studies, and some biographical accounts.

8636. Clemmer, Richard O. "The Fed-up Hopi: Resistance of the American Indian and the Silence of the Good Anthropologists." Journal of the Steward Anthropological Society 1 (Fall 1969): 18-40.

8637. Eggan, Dorothy. "The General Problem of Hopi Adjustment." American Anthropologist 45 (July-September 1943): 357-373.

8638. Euler, Robert C., and Henry F. Dobyns. The Hopi People. Phoenix: Indian Tribal Series, 1971.

8639. Fraps, Clara Lee. "Hopiland." Arizona Historical Review 6 (July 1935): 3-46.

8640. Hoover, J. W. "Tusayan: The Hopi Indian Country of Arizona." Geographical Review 20 (July 1930): 425-444.

8641. Hough, Walter. The Hopi Indians. Cedar Rapids, Iowa: Torch Press, 1915.

8642. James, Harry C. The Hopi Indians: Their History and Their Culture. Caldwell, Idaho: Caxton Printers, 1956.

8643. Josephy, Alvin M., Jr. "The Hopi Way." American Heritage 24 (February 1973): 49-55.

8644. McIntire, Elliot G. "Changing Patterns of Hopi Indian Settlement." Annals of the Association of American Geographers 61 (September 1971): 510-521.

8645. _____. "Hopi Colonization on the Colorado Reservation." California Geographer 10 (1969): 7-14.

8646. _____. "The Hopi Villages of Arizona: A Study in Changing Patterns." Proceedings of the Association of American Geographers 1 (1969): 95-99.

8647. _____. "The Impact of Cultural Change on the Land Use Patterns of the Hopi Indians." Ph.D. dissertation, University of Oregon, 1968.

8648. O'Kane, Walter Collins. The Hopis: Portrait of a Desert People. Norman: University of Oklahoma Press, 1953.

8649. _____. Sun in the Sky. Norman: University of Oklahoma Press, 1950.

8650. Sekaquaptewa, Helen, as told to Louise Udall. Me and Mine: The Life Story of Helen Sekaquaptewa. Tucson: University of Arizona Press, 1969.

8651. Talayesva, Don C. Sun Chief: The Autobiography of a Hopi Indian. Edited by Leo W. Simmons. New Haven: Yale University Press, 1942. Revised edition, 1963.

8652. Thompson, Laura. Culture in Crisis: A Study of the Hopi Indians. New York: Harper and Brothers, 1950.

8653. Thompson, Laura, and Alice Joseph. The Hopi Way. Chicago: University of Chicago Press, 1945.

8654. Titiev, Mischa. The Hopi Indians of Old Oraibi: Change and Continuity. Ann Arbor: University of Michigan Press, 1972.

8655. Waters, Frank. Book of the Hopi. New York: Viking Press, 1963.

8656. White, Elizabeth Q. (Polingaysi Qoyawayma), as told to Vada F. Carlson. No Turning Back: A True Account of a Hopi Indian Girl's Struggle to Bridge the Gap between the World of Her People and the World of the White Man. Albuquerque: University of New Mexico Press, 1964.

Navajo Indians

For the Navajos there are two extensive bibliographies, which will direct the student to numerous published works.

8657. Correll, J. Lee, Editha L. Watson, and David M. Brugge. Navajo Bibliography with Subject Index. Revised edition. Window Rock, Arizona: Research Section, Navajo Parks and Recreation, Navajo Tribe, 1969.

8658. Kluckhohn, Clyde, and Katherine Spencer. A Bibliography of the Navaho Indians. New York: J. J. Augustin Publisher, 1940. Reprint, New York: AMS Press, 1972.

Listed here are general and miscellaneous accounts and some biographical works dealing with the Navajos.

8659. Allen, T. D. [pseud.]. Navahos Have Five Fingers. Norman: University of Oklahoma Press, 1963.

8660. Blanchard, Kendall A. The Ramah Navajos: A Growing Sense of Community in Historical Perspective. Window Rock, Arizona: Research Section, Navajo Parks and Recreation, Navajo Tribe, 1971.

8661. _____. "Religious Change and Economic Behavior among the Ramah Navajo." Ph.D. dissertation, Southern Methodist University, 1971.

8662. Borgman, Francis. "Henry Chee Dodge, the Last Chief of the Navaho Indians." New Mexico Historical Review 23 (April 1948): 81-93.

8663. Boyce, George A. When Navajos Had Too Many Sheep: The 1940's. San Francisco: Indian Historian Press, 1974.

8664. Breed, Jack. "Better Days for the Navajos." National Geographic Magazine 114 (December 1958): 809-847.

8665. Burge, Moris. The Navajos and the Land, the Government, the Tribe and the Future. New York: American Indian Defense Association and National Association on Indian Affairs, 1937.

8666. Christian, Jane M. "The Navajo: A People in Transition." Southwestern Studies 2 (Fall 1964): 3-35; (Winter 1965): 39-69.

8667. Coolidge, Dane, and Mary Roberts Coolidge. The Navajo Indians. Boston: Houghton Mifflin Company, 1930.

8668. Crapanzano, Vincent. The Fifth World of Forster Bennett: Portrait of a Navaho. New York: Viking Press, 1972.

8669. Dietrich, Margretta S. "The Navajo in No-Man's Land." New Mexico Quarterly 20 (Winter 1950-1951): 439-450.

8670. Dobyns, Henry F., and Robert C. Euler. The Navajo People. Phoenix: Indian Tribal Series, 1972.

8671. Downs, James F. The Navajo. New York: Holt, Rinehart and Winston, 1972.

8672. Dyk, Walter, ed. A Navajo Autobiography. Viking Fund Publications in Anthropology, no. 8. New York: Viking Fund, 1947.

8673. Fonaroff, L. Schuyler. "Political Process and Culture Change among the Navajo." Geographical Review 61 (July 1971): 442-444.

8674. Frink, Maurice. Fort Defiance and the Navajos. Boulder, Colorado: Pruett Press, 1968.

8675. Gilpin, Laura. The Enduring Navaho. Austin: University of Texas Press, 1968.

8676. Henrikson, Craig Ernest. "Acculturation, Value Change, and Mental Health among the Navajo." Ph.D. dissertation, University of North Carolina, 1971.

8677. Hillery, George A., Jr., and Frank J. Essene. "Navajo Population: An Analysis of the 1960 Census." South-western Journal of Anthropology 19 (Autumn 1963): 297-313.

8678. Hoopes, Alban W. "The Indian Rights Association and the Navaho, 1890-1895." New Mexico Historical Review 11 (January 1946): 22-46.

8679. Hoover, J. W. "Navaho Land Problems." Economic Geography 13 (July 1937): 281-300.

8680. _____. "Navajo Nomadism." Geographical Review 21 (July 1931): 429-445.

8681. Hoskaninni-begay, as told to Charles Kelly. "Chief Hoskaninni." Utah Historical Quarterly 21 (July 1953): 219-226.

8682. Johnston, Bernice Eastman. Two Ways in the Desert: A Study of Modern Navajo-Anglo Relations. Pasadena, California: Socio-Technical Publications, 1972.

8683. Johnston, Denis Foster. "An Analysis of Sources of Information on the Population of the Navajo." Ph.D. dissertation, American University, 1961.

8684. Jones, Paul. "The Navajo Indians: Their Progress, Problems and Prospects." Arizona Business and Economic Review 6 (June 1957): 1-4.

8685. Kelly, Lawrence C. The Navajo Indians and Federal Indian Policy, 1900-1935. Tucson: University of Arizona Press, 1968.

8686. Kluckhohn, Clyde, and Dorothea Leighton. The Navaho. Cambridge: Harvard University Press, 1946. Revised edition by Lucy H. Wales and Richard Kluckhohn. Garden City, New York: Natural History Library, 1962.

8687. Kunitz, Stephen J. "Factors Influencing Recent Navajo and Hopi Population Changes." Human Organization 33 (Spring 1974): 7-16.

8688. Kunitz, Stephen J., and Jerrold E. Levy. "Navajo Voting Patterns." Plateau 43 (Summer 1970): 1-8.

8689. La Farge, Oliver. "The Navajos-- Most Hopeful Tribe of All." Natural History 57 (October 1948): 360-367.

9690. Leech, C. J. "The Navajos Today." Geographical Magazine 31 (February 1959): 479-492.

8691. Left Handed. Son of Old Man Hat: A Navaho Autobiography Recorded by Walter Dyk. New York: Harcourt Brace and Company, 1938.

8692. Leighton, Dorothea, and Clyde Kluckhohn. Children of the People: The Navaho Individual and His Development. Cambridge: Harvard University Press, 1947.

8693. Link, Martin A., ed. Navajo: A Century of Progress, 1868-1968. Window Rock, Arizona: Navajo Tribe, 1968.

8694. Lipps, Oscar H. The Navajos. Cedar Rapids, Iowa: Torch Press, 1909.

8695. Loh, Jules. Lords of the Earth: A History of the Navajo Indians. New York: Crowell-Collier Press, 1971.

8696. _____. "The Soul of the Navajo." Esquire 74 (November 1970): 162-167.

8697. Luebben, Ralph A. "Prejudice and Discrimination against Navahos in a Mining Community." Kiva 30 (October 1964): 1-17.

8698. McCombe, Leonard. Navaho Means People. Cambridge: Harvard University Press, 1951. Photographs by McCombe; text by Evon Z. Vogt and Clyde Kluckhohn.

8699. Mitchell, Emerson Blackhorse. Miracle Hill: The Story of a Navajo Boy. Edited by T. D. Allen [pseud.]. Norman: University of Oklahoma Press, 1967.

8700. Mitchell, Marie. The Navajo Peace Treaty, 1868. New York: Mason and Lipscomb Publishers, 1973.

8701. The Navajo Indian Problem: An Inquiry Sponsored by the Phelps Stokes Fund. New York, 1939.

8702. Newcomb, Franc Johnson. Hosteen Klah: Navaho Medicine Man and Sand Painter. Norman: University of Oklahoma Press, 1964.

8703. _____. Navaho Neighbors. Norman: University of Oklahoma Press, 1972.

8704. Parman, Donald L. "J. C. Morgan, Navajo Apostle of Assimilation." Prologue: The Journal of the National Archives 4 (Summer 1972): 83-98.

8705. Patzman, Stephen N. "Henry Chee Dodge: A Modern Chief of the Navajos." Arizoniana 5 (Spring 1964): 35-41.

8706. Pollock, Floyd Allen. "Navajo-Federal Relations as a Social-Cultural Problem." Ph.D. dissertation, University of Southern California, 1942.

8707. Reeve, Frank D. "Navaho Foreign Affairs, 1795-1846," edited by Eleanor B. Adams and John L. Kessell. New Mexico Historical Review 46 (April 1971): 101-132; (July 1971): 223-251.

8708. Reichard, Gladys A. Dezba: Woman of the Desert. New York: J. J. Augustin, 1939.

8709. Sasaki, Tom T. Fruitland, New Mexico: A Navaho Community in Transition. Ithaca: Cornell University Press, 1960.

8710. Shepardson, Mary. Navajo Ways in Government: A Study in Political Process. American Anthropological Association, Memoir 96. Menasha, Wisconsin, 1963.

8711. Shepardson, Mary, and Blowden Hammond. "Change and Persistence in an Isolated Navajo Community." American Anthropologist 66 (October 1964): 1029-1050.

8712. Spearman, Leonard H. O. "A Study of Values: The Navaho." Quarterly Review of Higher Education among Negroes 26 (January 1958): 15-21.

8713. Stucki, Larry R. "The Case against Population Control: The Probable Creation of the First American Indian State." Human Organization 30 (Winter 1971): 393-399.,

8714. Sullivan, Belle Shafer. The Unvanishing Navajos. Philadelphia: Dorrance and Company, 1938.

8715. Terrell, John Upton. The Navajos: The Past and Present of a Great People. New York: Weybright and Talley, 1970.

8716. Trafzer, Clifford E. "Anglos among the Navajos: The Day Family." In The Changing Ways of Southwestern Indians: A Historic Perspective, edited by Albert H. Schroeder, pp. 259-274. Glorieta, New Mexico: Rio Grande Press, 1973.

8717. _____. "Politicos and Navajos." Journal of the West 13 (October 1974): 3-16.

8718. Underhill, Lonnie E., and Daniel F. Littlefield, Jr. "Hamlin Garland and the Navajos." Journal of Arizona History 13 (Winter 1972): 275-285.

8719. Underhill, Ruth M. Here Come the Navaho! Edited by Willard W. Beatty. Lawrence, Kansas: Haskell Institute, 1953.

8720. _____. "The Navajo: Past, Present, and Future." Delta Kappa Gamma Bulletin 37 (Winter 1971): 23-31.

8721. _____. The Navajos. Norman: University of Oklahoma Press, 1956.

8722. Verplanck, James Delancey. A Country of Shepherds. Boston: Ruth Hill, 1938.

8723. Vogt, Evon Z. "The Automobile in Contemporary Navaho Culture." In Men and Cultures: Selected Papers of the Fifth International Congress of Anthropological and Ethnological Sciences, Philadelphia, September 1-9, 1956, edited by Anthony F. C. Wallace, pp. 359-363. Philadelphia: University of Pennsylvania Press, 1960.

8724. _____. "Navaho." In Perspectives in American Indian Culture Change, edited by Edward H. Spicer, pp. 278-336.

Chicago: University of Chicago Press, 1961.

8725. Worcester, Donald E. "Early History of the Navajo Indians." Ph.D. dissertation, University of California, 1947.

Papago Indians

8726. Burge, Moris. "Papago Self-Government." American Indian 5, no. 2 (1949): 23-28.

8727. Dobyns, Henry F. The Papago People. Phoenix: Indian Tribal Series, 1972.

8728. Hackenberg, Robert A., and others. "Modernization Research on the Papago Indians." Human Organization 31 (Summer 1972): 112-240. The entire issue is devoted to this topic, with separate articles by various authors.

8729. Joseph, Alice, Rosamond B. Spicer, and Jane Chesky. The Desert People: A Study of the Papago Indians. Chicago: University of Chicago Press, 1949.

8730. Patrick, Ralph, and H. A. Tyroler. "Papago Indian Modernization: A Community Scale for Health Research." Human Organization 31 (Summer 1972): 127-136.

8731. Stocker, Joseph. "Tom Segundo, Chief of the Papagos." American Indian 6 (Fall 1951): 18-25.

8732. van Willigen, John Gilbert. "The Role of the Community Level Worker in Papago Indian Development." Ph.D. dissertation, University of Arizona, 1971.

8733. Waddell, Jack O. "Resurgent Patronage and Lagging Bureaucracy in a Papago Off-Reservation Community." Human Organization 29 (Spring 1970): 37-42.

8734. Wilson, C. Roderick. "Papago Indian Population Movement: An Index of Culture Change." Rocky Mountain Social Science Journal 6 (April 1969): 23-32.

Pueblo Indians

Listed here are general works on the Pueblo Indians as well as studies of some particular pueblos.

8735. Aberle, Sophie B. The Pueblo Indians of New Mexico: Their Land, Economy and Civil Organization. Memoir Series of the American Anthropological Association, no. 70. Menasha, Wisconsin, 1948.

8736. Aberle, Sophie B., J. H. Watkins, and E. H. Pitney. "The Vital History of San Juan Pueblo." Human Biology 12 (May 1940): 141-187.

8737. Austin, Mary. "Social and Economic Organization of the New Mexico Pueblo."

Progressive Education 9 (February 1932): 117-121.

8738. Crane, Leo. Desert Drums: The Pueblo Indians of New Mexico, 1540-1928. Boston: Little, Brown and Company, 1928.

8739. Dozier, Edward P. Hano, a Tewa Indian Community in Arizona. New York: Holt, Rinehart and Winston, 1966.

8740. _____. The Hopi-Tewa of Arizona. Berkeley: University of California Press, 1954.

8741. _____. The Pueblo Indians of North America. New York: Holt, Rinehart and Winston, 1970.

8742. _____. "The Pueblo Indians of the Southwest: A Survey of the Anthropological Literature and a Review of Theory, Method, and Results." Current Anthropology 5 (April 1964): 79-97.

8743. _____. "Rio Grande Pueblos." In Perspectives in American Indian Culture Change, edited by Edward H. Spicer, pp. 94-186. Chicago: University of Chicago Press, 1961.

8744. Fynn, A. J. The American Indian as a Product of Environment, with Special Reference to the Pueblos. Boston: Little, Brown and Company, 1907.

8745. Gallenkamp, Charles. "The Pueblo Indians of New Mexico." Canadian Geographical Journal 50 (June 1955): 206-215.

8746. Gilpin, Laura. The Pueblos: A Camera Chronicle. New York: Hastings House, 1941.

8747. Griffith, Winthrop. "The Taos Indians Have a Small Generation Gap." New York Times Magazine, February 21, 1971, pp. 26-27, 93-97, 100.

8748. Hawley, Florence. "An Examination of Problems Basic to Acculturation in the Rio Grande Pueblos." American Anthropologist 50 (October-December 1948): 612-624.

8749. Houser, Nicholas P. "The Tigua Settlement of Ysleta del Sur." Kiva 36 (Winter 1970): 23-39.

8750. James, H. L. Acoma: The People of the White Rock. Glorieta, New Mexico: Rio Grande Press, 1970.

8751. Jenkins, Myra Ellen. "The Pueblo of Nambé and Its Lands." In The Changing Ways of Southwestern Indians: A Historic Perspective, edited by Albert H. Schroeder, pp. 91-105. Glorieta, New Mexico: Rio Grande Press, 1973.

8752. _____. "Taos Pueblo and Its Neighbors, 1540-1847." New Mexico Historical Review 41 (April 1966): 85-114.

8753. King, Scottie. "Pueblo Renaissance." Américas 24 (June-July 1972): 31-39.

8754. Lange, Charles H. Cochiti: A New Mexico Pueblo, Past and Present. Austin: University of Texas Press, 1959.

8755. _____. "The Role of Economics in Cochiti Pueblo Culture Change." American Anthropologist 55 (December 1953): 674-694.

8756. Law, George. "Laughing Eyes of Tesuque." Overland Monthly 78 (September 1921): 47-52.

8757. Morrill, Claire. A Taos Mosaic: Portrait of a New Mexico Village. Albuquerque: University of New Mexico Press, 1973.

8758. Nagata, Shuichi. Modern Transformations of Moenkopi Pueblo. Studies in Anthropology, no. 6. Urbana: University of Illinois Press, 1970.

8759. Ortiz, Alfonso, ed. New Perspectives on the Pueblos. Albuquerque: University of New Mexico Press, 1972.

8760. Ragsdale, Fred. "Cochiti Pueblo and the Seven-Day Weekend." American Indian Culture Center Journal 3 (Fall 1972): 7-14.

8761. Saunders, Charles Francis. The Indians of the Terraced Houses. New York: G. P. Putnam's Sons, 1912.

8762. Simons, Suzanne Lee. "Sandia Pueblo: Persistance and Change in a New Mexican Indian Community." Ph.D. dissertation, University of New Mexico, 1969.

8763. Underhill, Lonnie E., and Daniel F. Littlefield, Jr., eds. "Hamlin Garland at Isleta Pueblo." Southwestern Historical Quarterly 78 (July 1974): 45-68.

8764. Wadia, Maneck Sorabji. "Tesuque: A Community Study in Acculturation." Ph.D. dissertation, Indiana University, 1957.

8765. Watkins, J. H., E. H. Pitney, and S. B. Aberle. "Vital Statistics of the Pueblo Indians." American Journal of Public Health 29 (July 1939): 753-760.

8766. Zubrow, Ezra B. W. Population, Contact, and Climate in the New Mexican Pueblos. Tucson: University of Arizona Press, 1974.

CALIFORNIA AND BASIN-PLATEAU INDIANS

General and Miscellaneous Studies

Listed here are general works about the Indians of California, Nevada, and Utah. Materials on the Mojave, Paiute, Shoshoni, and Ute Indians are listed under separate headings below.

8767. Ainsworth, Ed. Golden Checkerboard. Palm Desert, California: Desert-Southwest, 1965. Cahuilla Indians.

8768. Allen, James Michael. Wi-ne-ma. New York: Vantage Press, 1956. Modoc Indian.

8769. American Friends Service Committee. Indians of California: Past and Present. Revised edition. San Francisco: American Friends Service Committee, 1957.

8770. Armsby, E. Raymond, and John G. Rockwell. "New Directions among Northern California Indians." American Indian 4, no. 3 (1948): 12-23.

8771. Azbill, Henry. "Maidu Indians of California: A Historical Note." Indian Historian 4 (Summer 1971): 21.

8772. Bean, Lowell John. Mukat's People: The Cahuilla Indians of Southern California. Berkeley: University of California Press, 1972.

8773. Browne, J. Ross. The Indians of California. San Francisco: Colt Press, 1944. Reprint of material originally published in 1864.

8774. Burrows, Jack. "The Vanished Miwoks of California." Montana, the Magazine of Western History 21 (January 1971): 28-39.

8775. Caughey, John Walton, ed. The Indians of Southern California in 1852: The B. D. Wilson Report and a Selection of Contemporary Comment. San Marino, California: Huntington Library, 1952.

8776. Conrotto, Eugene L. Miwok Means People: The Life and Fate of the Native Inhabitants of the California Gold Rush Country. Fresno, California: Valley Publishers, 1973.

8777. Cook, Sherburne F. "The Conflict between the California Indian and White Civilization: III, The American Invasion, 1848-1870." Ibero-Americana 23 (1943): 1-115.

8778. Downs, James F. "California." In North American Indians in Historical Perspective, edited by Eleanor Burke Leacock and Nancy Oestreich Lurie, pp. 289-316. New York: Random House, 1971.

8779. _____. The Two Worlds of the Washo: An Indian Tribe of California and Nevada. New York: Holt, Rinehart and Winston, 1966.

8780. Elkus, Charles de Y. "Whither the California Indians." American Indian 3 (Fall 1946): 7-14.

8781. Forbes, Jack D. "The Native American Experience in California History." California Historical Quarterly 50 (September 1971): 234-242.

8782. _____. Native Americans of California and Nevada. Healdsburg, California: Naturegraph Publishers, 1969.

8783. Forbes, Jack D., ed. Nevada Indians Speak. Reno: University of Nevada Press, 1967.

8784. Heizer, Robert F. Languages, Territories, and Names of California Indian Tribes. Berkeley: University of California Press, 1966.

8785. Heizer, Robert F., ed. The Destruction of California Indians: A Collection of Documents from the Period 1847 to 1865 in Which Are Described Some of the Things That Happened to Some of the Indians of California. Santa Barbara, California: Peregrine Smith, 1974.

8786. _____. They Were Only Diggers: A Collection of Articles from California Newspapers, 1851-1866, on Indian and White Relations. Ramona, California: Bellena Press, 1974.

8787. Heizer, Robert F., and Alan J. Almquist. The Other Californians: Prejudice and Discrimination under Spain, Mexico, and the United States to 1920. Berkeley: University of California Press, 1971.

8788. Heizer, Robert F., and M. A. Whipple, eds. The California Indians: A Source Book. 2d edition, revised and enlarged. Berkeley: University of California Press, 1971.

8789. Hill, Joseph J. The History of Warner's Ranch and Its Environs. Los Angeles, 1927.

8790. "Indians in California." Commonwealth 2 (June 8, 1926): 101-152. A series of articles by various authors.

8791. Jorgensen, Joseph G. The Sun Dance Religion: Power for the Powerless. Chicago: University of Chicago Press, 1972. Ute and Shoshone tribes.

8792. King, Tom. "New Views of California Indian Societies." Indian Historian 5 (Winter 1972): 12-17.

8793. Kroeber, A. L. "California Indian Population about 1910." University of California Publications in American Archaeology and Ethnology 47 (1957): 218-225.

8794. _____. Handbook of the Indians of California. Bureau of American Ethnology Bulletin 78. Washington: Government Printing Office, 1925.

8795. Kroeber, Theodora. Ishi in Two Worlds: A Biography of the Last Wild Indian in America. Berkeley: University of California Press, 1961.

8796. Kroeber, Theodora, and Robert F. Heizer. Almost Ancestors: The First Californians. San Francisco: Sierra Club, 1968.

8797. Leonard, Charles Berdan. "The Federal Indian Policy in the San Joaquin Valley: Its Application and Results." Ph.D. dissertation, University of California, 1928.

8798. Lipps, Oscar H. The Case of the California Indians. Chemawa, Oregon: U.S. Indian School Print Shop, 1932.

8799. Martin, Lucille J. "A History of the Modoc Indians: An Acculturation Study." Chronicles of Oklahoma 47 (Winter 1969-1970): 398-446.

8800. Merriam, C. Hart. "The Indian Population of California." American Anthropologist, new series 7 (October-December 1905): 594-606.

8801. Miller, Virginia Peek. "The Yuki: Culture Contact to Allotment." Ph.D. dissertation, University of California, Davis, 1973.

8802. Mitchell, Annie Rosalind. Jim Savage and the Tulareño Indians. Los Angeles: Westernlore Press, 1957.

8803. Palmer, William R. "Utah Indians Past and Present." Utah Historical Quarterly 1 (April 1928): 35-52.

8804. Phillips, George Harwood. Chiefs and Challengers: Indian Resistance and Cooperation in Southern California. Berkeley: University of California Press, 1975.

8805. Ray, Verne F. Primitive Pragmatists: The Modoc Indians of Northern California. Seattle: University of Washington Press, 1963.

8806. Robinson, W. W. The Indians of Los Angeles: Story of the Liquidation of a People. Los Angeles: Glen Dawson, 1952. Period 1769-1853.

8807. Stewart, Kenneth M. "A Brief History of the Chemehuevi Indians." Kiva 34 (October 1968): 9-27.

8808. Thomas, Richard Maxfield. "The Mission Indians: A Study of Leadership and Culture Change." Ed.D. dissertation, University of California, Los Angeles, 1964.

8809. Underhill, Ruth M. "Indians of California and the Southwest." In California and the Southwest, edited by Clifford M. Zierer, pp. 97-109. New York: John Wiley and Sons, 1956.

8810. Wright, Coulsen, and Geneva Wright. "Indian-White Relations in the Uintah Basin." Utah Humanities Review 2 (October 1948): 319-345.

Mojave Indians

8811. Kroeber, Clifton B. "The Mohave Nationalist, 1859-1874." Proceedings of the American Philosophical Society 109 (June 1965): 173-180.

8812. Sherer, Lorraine M. "Great Chieftains of the Mojave Indians." Southern California Quarterly 48 (March 1966): 1-35.

8813. _____. "The Name Mojave, Mohave: A History of Its Origin and Meaning." Southern California Quarterly 49 (March 1967): 1-36.

8814. _____. "The Name Mojave, Mohave: An Addendum." Southern California Quarterly 49 (December 1967): 455-458.

8815. Stewart, Kenneth M. "A Brief History of the Mohave Indians since 1850." Kiva 34 (April 1969): 219-236.

8816. Woodward, Arthur. "Irataba--'Chief of the Mohave.'" Plateau 25 (January 1953): 53-68.

Paiute Indians

8817. Brimlow, George F. "The Life of Sarah Winnemucca: The Formative Years." Oregon Historical Quarterly 53 (June 1952): 103-134.

8818. Brink, Pamela Jane. "The Pyramid Lake Paiute of Nevada." Ph.D. dissertation, Boston University, 1969.

8819. Euler, Robert C. The Paiute People. Phoenix: Indian Tribal Series, 1972.

8820. Fowler, Catherine S., and Don D. Fowler. "Notes on the History of the Southern Paiutes and Western Shoshonis." Utah Historical Quarterly 39 (Spring 1971): 95-113.

8821. Harnar, Nellie Shaw. The History of the Pyramid Lake Indians, 1843-1959 and Early Tribal History 1825-1834. Sparks, Nevada: Dave's Printing and Publishing, 1974.

8822. Hermann, Ruth. The Paiutes of Pyramid Lake: A Narrative Concerning a Western Nevada Indian Tribe. San Jose: Harlan-Young Press, 1972.

8823. Roberts, Bertram L. "Descendants of

the Numu." Masterkey 39 (January-
March 1965): 13-22; (April-June 1965):
66-76.

8824. Santee, J. F. "Egan of the Piutes."
Washington Historical Quarterly 26
(January 1935): 16-25.

8825. Stewart, Patricia. "Sarah Winnemucca." Nevada Historical Society
Quarterly 14 (Winter 1971): 23-38.

8826. Wheeler-Voegelin, Erminie. "The
Northern Paiute of Central Oregon: A
Chapter in Treaty-Making." Ethnohistory
2 (Spring 1955): 95-115; (Summer 1955):
241-272; 3 (Winter 1956): 1-10.

Shoshoni Indians

Listed here are general accounts and
biographical studies. Many of the items
deal with Sacajawea, who has attracted
much attention.

8827. Anderson, Irving W. "Probing the
Riddle of the Bird Woman." Montana, the
Magazine of Western History 23 (October
1973): 2-17.

8828. Chandler, Milford G. "Sidelights on
Sacajawea." Masterkey 43 (January-
March 1969): 58-66.

8829. Crawford, Helen. "Sakakawea." North
Dakota Historical Quarterly 1 (April
1927): 5-15.

8830. Crowder, David L. Tendoy, Chief of
the Lemhis. Caldwell, Idaho: Caxton
Printers, 1969.

8831. Dominick, David. "The Sheepeaters."
Annals of Wyoming 36 (October 1964):
131-168.

8832. Dorn, Edward. The Shoshoneans: The
People of the Basin-Plateau. New York:
William Morrow and Company, 1966. Photo-
graphs by LeRoy Lucas.

8833. Fowler, Donald D. "Cultural Ecology
and Culture History of the Eastern Shoshoni Indians." Ph.D. dissertation,
University of Pittsburgh, 1965.

8834. Fowler, Donald D., ed. "Notes on
the Early Life of Chief Washakie, Taken
Down by Captain Ray." Annals of Wyoming
36 (April 1964): 35-42.

8835. Hebard, Grace Raymond. Washakie: An
Account of Indian Resistance of the
Covered Wagon and Union Pacific Railroad
Invasions of Their Territory. Cleveland:
Arthur H. Clark Company, 1930.

8836. Howard, Harold P. Sacajawea.
Norman: University of Oklahoma Press,
1971.

8837. Howard, Helen Addison. "The Mystery
of Sacagawea's Death." Pacific North-

west Quarterly 58 (January 1967): 1-6.

8838. Hultkrantz, Ake. "The Shoshones in
the Rocky Mountain Area." Annals of
Wyoming 33 (April 1961): 19-41.

8839. Kingston, C. S. "Sacajawea as Guide:
The Evaluation of a Legend." Pacific
Northwest Quarterly 35 (January 1944):
3-18.

8840. Morgan, Dale L., ed. "Washakie and
the Shoshoni: A Selection of Documents
from the Records of the Utah Superintendency of Indian Affairs." Annals of
Wyoming 25 (July 1953): 141-189; 26
(January 1954): 65-80; (July 1954): 141-
190; 27 (April 1955): 61-88; (October
1955): 198-220; 28 (April 1956): 80-93;
(October 1956): 193-207; 29 (April 1957):
86-102; (October 1957): 195-227; 30
(April 1958): 53-89.

8841. Pence, Mary Lou. "Ellen Hereford
Washakie of the Shoshones." Annals of
Wyoming 22 (July 1950): 3-11.

8842. Rees, John E. "The Shoshoni Contribution to Lewis and Clark." Idaho
Yesterdays 2 (Summer 1958): 2-13.

8843. Reid, Russell. "Sakakawea." North
Dakota History 30 (April-July 1963):
101-113.

8844. "Sacajawea: A Symposium." Annals of
Wyoming 13 (July 1941): 163-194.

8845. Shaul, David L. "The Meaning of the
Name Sacajawea." Annals of Wyoming 44
(Fall 1972): 237-240.

8846. Stewart, Omer C. "The Shoshoni:
Their History and Social Organization."
Idaho Yesterdays 9 (Fall 1965): 2-5, 28.

8847. Swanson, Earl H. "Problems in Shoshone Chronology." Idaho Yesterdays
1 (Winter 1957-1958): 21-26.

8848. Taber, Ronald W. "Sacagawea and
the Suffragettes: An Interpretation of
a Myth." Pacific Northwest Quarterly 58
(January 1967): 7-13.

8849. Trenholm, Virginia Cole, and Maurine
Carley. The Shoshonis: Sentinels of the
Rockies. Norman: University of Oklahoma
Press, 1964.

8850. Williams, P. L. "Personal Recollections of Wash-a-kie, Chief of the Shoshones." Utah Historical Quarterly 1
(October 1928): 101-106.

Ute Indians

The following bibliographies are useful
guides to Ute material.

8851. Stewart, Omer C. Ethnohistorical
Bibliography of the Ute Indians of
Colorado. University of Colorado Studies,

Series in Anthropology, no. 18. Boulder: University of Colorado Press, 1971. Includes "Analysis of Records of the Southern Ute Agency, 1877 through 1952, National Archives RG 75, in the Federal Records Center, Denver, Colorado," by Frances L. Swadesh, and "Colorado and Out-of-State Newspaper Articles on Ute Indians," by Omer C. Stewart.

8852. Tyler, S. Lyman. The Ute People: A Bibliographical Checklist. Provo, Utah: Institute of American Indian Studies, Brigham Young University, 1964.

Listed here are both general and miscellaneous accounts and biographical studies dealing with the Utes.

8853. Allen, James B., and Ted J. Warner. "The Gosiute Indians in Pioneer Utah." Utah Historical Quarterly 39 (Spring 1971): 162-177.

8854. Bailey, Paul. The Claws of the Hawk: The Incredible Life of Wahker the Ute. Los Angeles: Westernlore Press, 1966. Earlier version published in 1950 under the title Walkara, Hawk of the Mountains.

8855. Benjamin, Peggy H. "The Last of Captain Jack." Montana, the Magazine of Western History 10 (April 1960): 22-30.

8856. Covington, James W. "Relations between the Ute Indians and the United States Government 1848-1900." Ph.D. dissertation, University of Oklahoma, 1950.

8857. Davis, H. L. "The Last Indian Outbreak: 1906." American Mercury 30 (September 1933): 50-57.

8858. Delaney, Robert W. "The Southern Utes a Century Ago." Utah Historical Quarterly 39 (Spring 1971): 115-128.

8859. Euler, Robert C., and Harry L. Naylor. "Southern Ute Rehabilitation Planning: A Study in Self-Determination." Human Organization 11 (Winter 1952): 27-32.

8860. Hafen, Ann Woodbury. "Efforts to Recover the Stolen Son of Chief Ouray." Colorado Magazine 16 (January 1939): 53-62.

8861. Jefferson, James, Robert W. Delaney, and Gregory C. Thompson. The Southern Utes: A Tribal History. Edited by Floyd A. O'Neil. Ignacio, Colorado: Southern Ute Tribe, 1972.

8862. Jorgensen, Joseph Gilbert. "The Ethnohistory and Acculturation of the Northern Ute." Ph.D. dissertation, Indiana University, 1965.

8863. King, Mrs. W. G. "Our Ute Indians." Colorado Magazine 37 (April 1960): 128-132.

8864. O'Neil, Floyd A. "An Anguished Odyssey: The Flight of the Utes, 1906-1908." Utah Historical Quarterly 36 (Fall 1968): 315-327.

8865. _____. "A History of the Ute Indians of Utah until 1890." Ph.D. dissertation, University of Utah, 1973.

8866. Opler, Marvin K. "The Ute and Paiute Indians of the Great Basin Southern Rim." In North American Indians in Historical Perspective, edited by Eleanor Burke Leacock and Nancy Oestreich Lurie, pp. 257-288. New York: Random House, 1971.

8867. Rockwell, Wilson. The Utes: A Forgotten People. Denver: Sage Books, 1956.

8868. Stacher, S. F. "The Indians of the Ute Mountain Reservation, 1906-9." Colorado Magazine 26 (January 1949): 52-61.

8869. _____. "Ouray and the Utes." Colorado Magazine 27 (April 1950): 134-140.

8870. Stewart, Omer C. "Ute Indians: Before and after White Contact." Utah Historical Quarterly 34 (Winter 1966): 38-61.

8871. Taylor, Morris F. "Ka-Ni-Ache." Colorado Magazine 43 (Fall 1966): 275-302; 44 (Spring 1967): 139-161.

8872. Ute People: An Historical Study. Compiled by June Lyman and Norman Denver and edited by Floyd A. O'Neil and John D. Sylvester. Salt Lake City: Uintah School District and the Western History Center, University of Utah, 1970.

8873. Weyrauch, Genevieve. "Ouray, Chief of the Utes." Southwestern Lore 4 (March 1939): 72-77.

8874. Willie, Gertrude Chapoose. "I Am an American." Utah Historical Quarterly 39 (Spring 1971): 194-195.

INDIANS OF THE PACIFIC NORTHWEST AND ALASKA

General and Miscellaneous Studies

Listed here are general accounts as well as studies of particular tribes and individuals of the area. Materials on Flathead, Nez Perce, and Spokane Indians are listed under separate headings below.

8875. Alaska Natives and the Land. Anchorage: Federal Field Committee for Development Planning in Alaska, 1968.

8876. Ames, Michael. "Indians of the Northwest Coast." American West 10 (July 1973): 12-17.

8877. Averkieva, Julia. "The Tlingit

Indians." In North American Indians in
Historical Perspective, edited by Eleanor
Burke Leacock and Nancy Oestreich Lurie,
pp. 317-342. New York: Random House,
1971.

8878. Bagley, Clarence B. "Chief Seattle
and Angeline." Washington Historical
Quarterly 22 (October 1931): 243-275.

8879. Bakken, Lavola J. Land of the North
Umpquas, Peaceful Indians of the West.
Grants Pass, Oregon: Te-Cum-Tom Publica-
tions, 1973.

8880. Beckham, Stephen Dow. Requiem for
a People: The Rogue Indians and the
Frontiersmen. Norman: University of
Oklahoma Press, 1971.

8881. Carriker, Robert C. The Kalispel
People. Phoenix: Indian Tribal Series,
1973.

8882. Codere, Helen. "Kwakiutl." In
Perspectives in American Indian Culture
Change, edited by Edward H. Spicer, pp.
431-516. Chicago: University of Chicago
Press, 1961.

8883. Collins, June M. "John Fornsby: The
Personal Document of a Coast Salish
Indian." In Indians of the Urban North-
west, edited by Marian W. Smith, pp.
287-341. New York: Columbia University
Press, 1949.

8884. _____. Valley of the Spirits:
The Upper Skagit Indians of Western Washington. Seattle: University of Washington Press, 1974.

8885. Colson, Elizabeth. The Makah Indians:
A Study of an Indian Tribe in Modern
American Society. Minneapolis: Uni-
versity of Minnesota Press, 1953.

8886. Daugherty, Richard D. The Yakima
People. Phoenix: Indian Tribal Series,
1973.

8887. De Menil, Adelaide, and William Reid.
Out of the Silence. New York: Outerbridge and Dienstfrey, 1971. Indians of
the Pacific Northwest: photographs and
text.

8888. Demmert, Dennis. "Alaska Indian
Culture." Historic Preservation 25
(January-March 1973): 31-34.

8889. Eliot, Samuel A. Report upon the
Conditions and Needs of the Indians of
the Northwest Coast. Washington, 1915.
Report by a member of the Board of
Indian Commissioners.

8890. Elliott, T. C. "The Murder of Peu-
Peu-Mox-Mox." Oregon Historical Quarterly 35 (June 1934): 123-130.

8891. Ervin, Alexander Mackay. "Civic
Capacity and Transculturation: The Rise
and Role of the Alaska Federation of

Natives." Ph.D. dissertation, University
of Illinois, 1974.

8892. French, David. "Wasco-Wishram." In
Perspectives in American Indian Culture
Change, edited by Edward H. Spicer, pp.
337-430. Chicago: University of Chicago
Press, 1961.

8893. French, Kathrine, and David French.
"The Warm Springs Indian Community: Will
It Be Destroyed?" American Indian 7
(Spring 1955): 3-17.

8894. Garrecht, Francis A. "An Indian
Chief." Washington Historical Quarterly
19 (July 1928): 165-180.

8895. Goddard, Pliny Earle. Indians of
the Northwest Coast. New York: American
Museum of Natural History, 1924.

8896. Gunther, Erna. Indian Life on the
Northwest Coast of North America as Seen
by the Early Explorers and Fur Traders
during the Last Decades of the Eighteenth
Century. Chicago: University of Chicago
Press, 1972.

8897. Hinckley, Ted C., ed. "'The Canoe
Rocks--We Do Not Know What Will Become
of Us': The Complete Transcript of a
Meeting between Governor John Green
Brady of Alaska and a Group of Tlingit
Chiefs, Juneau, December 14, 1898."
Western Historical Quarterly 1 (July
1970): 265-290.

8898. Liljeblad, Sven. The Idaho Indians
in Transition, 1805-1960. Pocatello:
Idaho State University Museum, 1972.

8899. _____. "The Indians of Idaho."
Idaho Yesterdays 4 (Fall 1960): 22-28.

8900. McWhorter, Lucullus V., ed. "Chief
Sluskin's True Narrative." Washington
Historical Quarterly 8 (April 1917):
96-101.

8901. Madsen, Brigham D. The Bannock of
Idaho. Caldwell, Idaho: Caxton Printers,
1958.

8902. Martin, Fredericka. "Three Years of
Pribilof Progress." American Indian 5
(Spring 1950): 17-26.

8903. Meany, Edmond S. "Chief Patkanim."
Washington Historical Quarterly 15
(July 1924): 187-198.

8904. Miller, Beatrice D. "Neah Bay: The
Makah in Transition." Pacific Northwest Quarterly 43 (October 1952): 262-
272.

8905. Minto, John. "The Number and Condition of the Native Race in Oregon
When First Seen by White Men." Quarterly
of the Oregon Historical Society 1
(September 1900): 296-315.

8906. O'Callaghan, Jerry A. "Klamath
Indians and the Oregon Wagon Road Grant,

1864-1938." Oregon Historical Quarterly 53 (March 1952): 23-28.

8907. Patty, Stanton H. "A Conference with the Tanana Chiefs." Alaska Journal 1 (Spring 1971): 2-18.

8908. Quimby, George I. "James Swan among the Indians: The Influence of a Pioneer from New England on Coastal Indian Art." Pacific Northwest Quarterly 61 (October 1970): 212-216.

8909. Ratcliff, James L. "What Happened to the Kalayuya? A Study of the Depletion of Their Economic Base." Indian Historian 6 (Summer 1973): 27-33.

8910. Ray, Verne F. "The Klamath Oppose Liquidation." American Indian 4 (1948): 15-22.

8911. Ruby, Robert H., and John A. Brown. The Cayuse Indians: Imperial Tribesmen of Old Oregon. Norman: University of Oklahoma Press, 1972.

8912. _____. Half-Sun on the Columbia: A Biography of Chief Moses. Norman: University of Oklahoma Press, 1965.

8913. St. John, Lewis H. "The Present Status and Probable Future of the Indians of Puget Sound." Washington Historical Quarterly 5 (January 1914): 12-21.

8914. Santee, J. F. "Pio-Pio-Mox-Mox." Oregon Historical Quarterly 34 (June 1933): 164-176.

8915. Smith, Marian W. "The Indians and Modern Society." In Indians of the Urban Northwest, edited by Marian W. Smith, pp. 3-18. New York: Columbia University Press, 1949. Coast Salish Indians.

8916. Smith, Marian W., ed. Indians of the Urban Northwest. New York: Columbia University Press, 1949.

8917. Spencer, Omar C. "Chief Cassino." Oregon Historical Quarterly 34 (March 1933): 19-30.

8918. Sperlin, O. B. "The Indian of the Northwest As Revealed by the Earliest Journals." Quarterly of the Oregon Historical Society 17 (March 1916): 1-43.

8919. Stern, Theodore. The Klamath Tribe: A People and Their Reservation. American Ethnological Society Monographs, no. 41. Seattle: University of Washington Press, 1965.

8920. Suttles, Wayne. "Post-Contact Culture Changes among the Lummi Indians." British Columbia Historical Quarterly 18 (January-April 1954): 29-102.

8921. Taylor, Herbert C., Jr. "Aboriginal Populations of the Lower Northwest Coast." Pacific Northwest Quarterly 54 (October 1963): 158-166.

8922. Upchurch, O. C. "The Swinomish People and Their State." Pacific Northwest Quarterly 27 (October 1936): 283-310.

8923. Van Stone, James W. "Ethnohistorical Research in Alaska." Alaska Review 3 (Fall-Winter 1967-1968): 51-59.

Flathead Indians

Listed here are general and miscellaneous works dealing with the Flathead Indians.

8924. Bigart, Robert James. "Patterns of Cultural Change in a Salish Flathead Community." Human Organization 30 (Fall 1971): 229-237.

8925. _____. "The Salish Flathead Indians during the Period of Adjustment, 1850-1891." Idaho Yesterdays 17 (Fall 1973): 18-28.

8926. Brockmann, C. Thomas. "Correlation of Social Class and Education on the Flathead Indian Reservation, Montana." Rocky Mountain Social Science Journal 8 (October 1971): 11-17.

8927. Carroll, James William. "Flatheads and Whites: A Study of Conflict." Ph.D. dissertation, University of California, 1959.

8928. Fahey, John. The Flathead Indians. Norman: University of Oklahoma Press, 1974.

8929. Harrison, Michael. "Chief Charlot's Battle with Bureaucracy." Montana, the Magazine of Western History 10 (October 1960): 27-33.

8930. Johnson, Olga Waydemeyer. Flathead and Kootenay: The Rivers, the Tribes, and the Region's Traders. Glendale, California: Arthur H. Clark Company, 1969.

8931. O'Connor, James. "The Flathead Indians." Records of the American Catholic Historical Society of Philadelphia 3 (1888-1891): 85-110.

8932. Ronan, Peter. Historical Sketch of the Flathead Indian Nation from the Year 1813 to 1890. Helena, Montana: Journal Publishing Company, 1890. Reprinted Minneapolis: Ross and Haines, 1965.

Nez Perce Indians

Listed here are general studies of the Nez Perces and biographical studies, particularly of Chief Joseph.

8933. Brown, Mark H. "Chief Joseph and the 'Lyin' Jack' Syndrome." Montana, the Magazine of Western History 22 (October 1972): 72-73.

8934. _____. "The Joseph Myth." Montana, the Magazine of Western History 22 (January 1972): 2-17.

8935. _____. "Yellowstone Tourists and the Nez Perce." Montana, the Magazine of Western History 16 (July 1966): 30-43.

8936. Chapman, Berlin B. "Nez Percés in Indian Territory: An Archival Study." Oregon Historical Quarterly 50 (June 1949): 98-121.

8937. Clark, J. Stanley. "The Nez Percés in Exile." Pacific Northwest Quarterly 36 (January 1945): 213-232.

8938. Coale, George L. "Ethnohistorical Sources for the Nez Percé Indians." Ethnohistory 3 (Summer 1956): 246-255; (Fall 1956): 346-360.

8939. Dozier, Jack. "1885: A Nez Perce Homecoming." Idaho Yesterdays 7 (Fall 1963): 22-25.

8940. Fee, Chester Anders. Chief Joseph: The Biography of a Great Indian. New York: Wilson-Erickson, 1936.

8941. Haines, Francis. The Nez Percés: Tribesmen of the Columbia Plateau. Norman: University of Oklahoma Press, 1955. A revision of Red Eagles of the Northwest: The Story of Chief Joseph and His People. Portland, Oregon: Scholastic Press, 1939.

8942. Howard, Helen Addison. War Chief Joseph. Caldwell, Idaho: Caxton Printers, 1941. Research assistance by Dan L. McGrath. Republished, 1965, as Saga of Chief Joseph.

8943. Howard, Oliver O. Nez Perce Joseph: An Account of His Ancestors, His Lands, His Confederates, His Enemies, His Murders, His War, His Pursuit and Capture. Boston: Lee and Shepard, 1881.

8944. Josephy, Alvin M., Jr. "The Naming of the Nez Perces." Montana, the Magazine of Western History 5 (October 1955): 1-18.

8945. _____. The Nez Perce Indians and the Opening of the Northwest. New Haven: Yale University Press, 1965.

8946. McBeth, Kate C. The Nez Perces since Lewis and Clark. New York: Fleming H. Revell Company, 1908.

8947. McWhorter, Lucullus Virgil. Hear Me, My Chiefs! Nez Perce History and Legend. Edited by Ruth Bordin. Caldwell, Idaho: Caxton Printers, 1952.

8948. McWhorter, Lucullus Virgil, ed. Yellow Wolf: His Own Story. Caldwell, Idaho: Caxton Printers, 1940.

8949. Moody, Charles Stuart. "The Nez Percés Indians." American Journal of Clinical Medicine 17 (October 1910): 1067-1072; (November 1910): 1180-1185; (December 1910): 1306-1312; 18 (February 1911): 184-188; (April 1911): 406-410; (May 1911): 507-512; (October 1911): 1036-1041; (November 1911): 1176-1181. Account of a physician who lived among the Indians.

8950. Morrill, Allen, and Eleanor Morrill. "Talmaks." Idaho Yesterdays 8 (Fall 1964): 2-15.

8951. Nieberding, Velma. "The Nez Perce in the Quapaw Agency, 1878-1879." Chronicles of Oklahoma 44 (Spring 1966): 22-30.

8952. Ruby, Robert H. "Return of the Nez Perce." Idaho Yesterdays 12 (Spring 1968): 12-15.

8953. Santee, J. F. "Lawyer of the Nez Perces." Washington Historical Quarterly 25 (January 1934): 37-48.

8954. Sass, Herbert Ravenel. "The Man Who Looked like Napoleon." Collier's 106 (September 21, 1940): 23, 60, 62. Chief Joseph.

8955. Slickpoo, Allen P., Sr. Noon Nee-Me-Poo (We, the Nez Perces): Culture and History of the Nez Perces. Deward E. Walker, Jr., Technical Advisor. Lapwai, Idaho: Nez Perce Tribe of Idaho, 1973.

8956. Walker, Deward E., Jr. Conflict and Schism in Nez Percé Acculturation: A Study of Religion and Politics. Pullman: Washington State University Press, 1968.

8957. _____. "Some Limitations of the Renascence Concept in Acculturation: The Nez Perce Case." In The American Indian Today, edited by Stuart Levine and Nancy Oestreich Lurie, pp. 149-162. Deland, Florida: Everett/Edwards, 1968. This appeared originally in Midcontinent American Studies Journal 6 (Fall 1965): 135-148.

8958. Wells, Donald N. "Farmers Forgotten: Nez Perce Suppliers of the North Idaho Gold Rush Days." Journal of the West 11 (July 1972): 488-496.

8959. _____. "Farmers Forgotten: Nez Perce Suppliers of the North Idaho Gold Ruch Days." Idaho Yesterdays 2 (Summer 1958): 28-32.

8960. Wood, C. E. S. "Chief Joseph, the Nez-Perce." Century Illustrated Monthly Magazine 28 (May 1884): 135-142.

Spokane Indians

8961. Jessett, Thomas E. Chief Spokan Garry, 1811-1892: Christian, Statesman, and Friend of the White Man. Minneapolis: T. S. Denison, 1960.

8962. Roy, Prodipto. "The Measurement of

Assimilation: The Spokane Indians."
American Journal of Sociology 67 (March
1962): 541-551.

8963. Roy, Prodipto, and Della M. Walker.
Assimilation of the Spokane Indians.
Pullman: Institute of Agricultural
Sciences, Washington State University,
1961.

8964. Ruby, Robert H., and John A. Brown.
The Spokane Indians: Children of the
Sun. Norman: University of Oklahoma
Press, 1970.

8965. White, Lynn C. "Assimilation of
the Spokane Indians: On-Reservation
versus Off-Reservation Residence." Ph.D.
dissertation, Washington State University,
1968.

8966. White, Lynn C., and Bruce A. Chadwick. "Urban Residence, Assimilation
and Identity of the Spokane Indian."
In Native Americans Today: Sociological
Perspectives, edited by Howard M. Bahr
and others, pp. 239-249. New York:
Harper and Row, 1972.

INDIAN BIOGRAPHY

Listed here are publications that provide biographies of more than one Indian.
Individual Indian biographies are listed
under appropriate tribes or regions.

8967. Andrews, Ralph W. Indian Leaders
Who Helped Shape America. Seattle:
Superior Publishing Company, 1971.

8968. Britt, Albert. Great Indian Chiefs:
A Study of Indian Leaders in the Two
Hundred Year Struggle to Stop the White
Advance. New York: McGraw-Hill Book
Company, 1938.

8969. Drake, Samuel G. Indian Biography,
Containing the Lives of More than Two
Hundred Indian Chiefs: Also Such Others
of That Race As Have Rendered Their
Names Conspicuous in the History of North
America, from Its First Being Known to
Europeans, to the Present Period.
Boston: Josiah Drake, 1832. Many re-
printings and revisions with variant
titles.

8970. Eastman, Charles A. Indian Heroes
and Great Chieftains. Boston: Little
Brown, and Company, 1918.

8971. Ewers, John C. "Deadlier than the
Male." American Heritage 16 (June 1965):
10-13. Sketches of four Indian women.

8972. Greenman, Emerson F. "Indian Chiefs
of Michigan." Michigan History Magazine
23 (Summer 1939): 220-249.

8973. Gridley, Marion E. American Indian
Women. New York: Hawthorn Books, 1974.

8974. _____. Contemporary American
Indian Leaders. New York: Dodd, Mead
and Company, 1972.

8975. _____. Indians of Today. 4th
edition. Chicago: Indian Council Fire
Publications, 1971. First edition, 1936.

8976. _____. Indians of Yesterday.
Chicago: M. A. Donohue and Company, 1940.

8977. Goodrich, Samuel G. Lives of
Celebrated American Indians. Boston:
Bradbury, Soden and Company, 1843.

8978. Johnston, Charles H. L. Famous
Indian Chiefs: Their Battles, Treaties,
Sieges, and Struggles with the Whites
for the Possession of America. Boston:
L. C. Page and Company, 1909.

8979. Josephy, Alvin M., Jr. The Patriot
Chiefs: A Chronicle of American Indian
Leadership. New York: Viking Press,
1961.

8980. Marquis, Thomas B., comp. Cheyenne
and Sioux: The Reminiscences of Four
Indians and a White Soldier. Edited by
Ronald H. Limbaugh. Stockton, California:
Pacific Center for Western Historical
Studies, University of the Pacific, 1973.
Includes accounts by Indian scouts.

8981. O'Beirne, H. F., comp. Leaders and
Leading Men of the Indian Territory,
with Interesting Biographical Sketches:
I, Choctaws and Chickasaws. Chicago:
American Publishers' Association, 1891.

8982. Porter, C. Fayne. Our Indian
Heritage: Profiles of 12 Great Leaders.
Philadelphia: Chilton Books, 1964.

8983. Sipe, C. Hale. The Indian Chiefs
of Pennsylvania. Butler, Pennsylvania:
Ziegler Printing Company, 1927.

8984. Stember, Sol. Heroes of the American Indian. New York: Fleet Press
Corporation, 1971.

8985. Stone, William L. Uncas and
Miantonomo. New York: Dayton and
Newman, 1842.

8986. Thatcher, B. B. Indian Biography;
or, An Historical Account of Those Individuals Who Have Been Distinguished
among the North American Natives as
Orators, Warriors, Statesmen, and Other
Remarkable Characters. 2 volumes. New
York: J. and J. Harper, 1832. Also
later editions.

See also Indian Tribes of North America,
by McKenney and Hall (9430).

OTHER TOPICS

Demography

Listed here are general studies or

comments on Indian population. The two works by Henry F. Dobyns provide extensive bibliographical material.

8987. Are the Indians Dying Out? Preliminary Observations Relating to Indian Civilization and Education. Washington, 1877.

8988. Dobyns, Henry F. "Estimating Aboriginal American Population: An Appraisal of Techniques with a New Hemispheric Estimate." Current Anthropology 7 (October 1966): 395-416.

8989. _____. Native American Historical Demography. Chicago: Newberry Library, forthcoming. A bibliographical essay.

8990. Driver, Harold E. "On the Population Nadir of Indians in the United States." Current Anthropology 9 (October 1968): 330.

8991. Hadley, J. Nixon. "The Demography of the American Indians." Annals of the American Academy of Political and Social Science 311 (May 1957): 23-30.

8992. Jacobs, Wilbur R. "The Tip of an Iceberg: Pre-Columbian Indian Demography and Some Implications for Revisionism." William and Mary Quarterly, 3d series 31 (January 1974): 123-132.

8993. Kroeber, A. L. "Native American Population." American Anthropologist 36 (January-March 1934): 1-25.

8994. Lorimer, Frank. "Observations on the Trend of Indian Population in the United States." In The Changing Indian, edited by Oliver La Farge, pp. 11-18. Norman: University of Oklahoma Press, 1942.

8995. Mallery, Garrick. "The Former and Present Number of Our Indians." Proceedings of the American Association for the Advancement of Science 26 (1877): 340-366.

8996. Mooney, James. The Aboriginal Population of America North of Mexico. Smithsonian Miscellaneous Collections, volume 80, no. 7. Washington: Government Printing Office, 1928.

8997. Pope, J. Worden. "The North American Indian--The Disappearance of the Race a Popular Fallacy." Arena 16 (November 1896): 945-959.

8998. Smith, Maurice G. "Notes on the Depopulation of Aboriginal America." American Anthropologist 30 (October-December 1928): 669-674.

8999. Spinden, H. J. "The Population of Ancient America." Geographical Review 18 (October 1928): 641-660.

Other population studies are listed under appropriate tribes or regions.

Mixed-Bloods

Although mixed-blooded Indians have played an important part in Indian-white relations, only a few writers have dealt specifically with the topic.

9000. Anderson, Harry H. "Fur Traders as Fathers: The Origins of the Mixed-Blooded Community among the Rosebud Sioux." South Dakota History 3 (Summer 1973): 233-270.

9001. Barrows, William. "The Half-Breed Indians of North America." Andover Review 12 (July 1889): 15-36.

9002. Berry, Brewton. Almost White. New York: Macmillan Company, 1963.

9003. Ewers, John C. "Mothers of the Mixed-Bloods: The Marginal Woman in the History of the Upper Missouri." In Probing the American West: Papers from the Santa Fe Conference, edited by K. Ross Toole and others, pp. 62-70. Santa Fe: Museum of New Mexico Press, 1962.

9004. Nagler, Mark. "North American Indians and Intermarriage." In Interracial Marriage: Expectations and Realities, edited by Irving R. Stuart and Lawrence Edwin Abt, pp. 279-291. New York: Grossman Publishers, 1973.

9005. Price, Edward T., Jr. "Mixed-Blood Populations of Eastern United States As to Origins, Localization, and Persistence." Ph.D. dissertation, University of California, 1950.

9006. Shapiro, H. L. "The Mixed-Blood Indian." In The Changing Indian, edited by Oliver La Farge, pp. 19-27. Norman: University of Oklahoma Press, 1942.

Indians and Blacks

The Indians could not escape contacts with blacks as well as whites. These relationships have been of varied kinds--from use of black slaves by Indians before the Civil War to joining in protests against white society in recent times. Listed here are studies that deal with aspects of Indian-black relations in the United States.

9007. Anderson, Robert L. "The End of an Idyll." Florida Historical Quarterly 42 (July 1963): 35-47. Negro slaves among the Florida Indians.

9008. Belton, Bill. "The Indian Heritage of Crispus Attucks." Negro History Bulletin 35 (November 1972): 149-152.

9009. Bennett, Lerone, Jr. "Red and Black: The Indians and the Africans." Ebony 26 (December 1970): 70-72 +.

9010. Bloom, Leonard. "Role of the Indian in the Race Relations Complex of the South." Social Forces 19 (December 1940): 268-273.

9011. Crowe, Charles. "Indians and Blacks in White America." In Four Centuries of Southern Indians, edited by Charles M. Hudson, pp. 148-169. Athens: University of Georgia Press, 1975.

9012. Davis, J. B. "Slavery in the Cherokee Nation." Chronicles of Oklahoma 11 (December 1933): 1056-1072.

9013. Duncan, Otis Durant. "The Fusion of White, Negro and Indian Cultures at the Converging of the New South and the West." Southwestern Social Science Quarterly 14 (March 1934): 357-369.

9014. Foster, Laurence. "Negro-Indian Relationships in the Southeast." Ph.D. dissertation, University of Pennsylvania, 1931.

9015. Halliburton, R., Jr. "Origins of Black Slavery among the Cherokees." Chronicles of Oklahoma 52 (Winter 1974-1975): 483-496.

9016. Jeltz, Wyatt F. "The Relations of Negroes and Choctaw and Chickasaw Indians." Journal of Negro History 33 (January 1948): 24-37.

9017. Johnson, Guy B. "Personality in a White-Indian-Negro Community." American Sociological Review 4 (August 1939): 516-523.

9018. Johnston, James Hugo. "Documentary Evidence of the Relations of Negroes and Indians." Journal of Negro History 14 (January 1929): 21-43.

9019. McLoughlin, William G. "Red Indians, Black Slavery and White Racism: America's Slaveholding Indians." American Quarterly 26 (October 1974): 367-385.

9020. "Negroes in Indian Service: Many Work in Sprawling Navajo Reservations to Alleviate Plight of Most Oppressed Minority." Ebony 6 (July 1951): 35-36, 38-39.

9021. Paschal, Andrew G. "History Shows Indians and Blacks Natural Allies in Battle against American Treachery." Muhammad Speaks 8 (November 22, 1968): 27, 30, 32.

9022. Porter, Kenneth Wiggins. "Negroes and Indians on the Texas Frontier, 1834-1874." Southwestern Historical Quarterly 53 (October 1949): 151-163.

9023. _____. "Negroes and Indians on the Texas Frontier, 1831-1876: A Study in Race and Culture." Journal of Negro History 41 (July 1956): 185-214; (October 1956): 285-310.

9024. _____. The Negro on the American Frontier. New York: Arno Press and the New York Times, 1971. Reprinting of earlier published essays.

9025. _____. "Notes Supplementary to 'Relations between Negroes and Indians.'" Journal of Negro History 18 (July 1933): 282-321.

9026. _____. "Relations between Negroes and Indians within the Present Limits of the United States." Journal of Negro History 17 (July 1932): 287-367.

9027. Price, Edward T. "A Geographic Analysis of White-Negro Indian Racial Mixtures in Eastern United States." Annals of the Association of American Geographers 43 (June 1953): 138-155.

9028. Roethler, Michael D. "Negro Slavery among the Cherokee Indians, 1540-1866." Ph.D. dissertation, Fordham University, 1964.

9029. Sefton, James E. "Black Slaves, Red Masters, White Middlemen: A Congressional Debate of 1852." Florida Historical Quarterly 51 (October 1972): 113-128.

9030. Speck, F. G. "Negroes and the Creek Nation." Southern Workman 37 (February 1908): 106-110.

9031. Troper, Harold Martin. "The Creek-Negroes of Oklahoma and Canadian Immigration, 1909-11." Canadian Historical Review 53 (September 1972): 272-288.

9032. Willis, William S. "Divide and Rule: Red, White, and Black in the Southeast." Journal of Negro History 48 (July 1963): 157-176.

9033. Wilson, Raleigh A. "Negro and Indian Relations in the Five Civilized Tribes from 1865 to 1907." Ph.D. dissertation, University of Iowa, 1949.

9034. Woodson, Carter G. "The Relations of Negroes and Indians in Massachusetts." Journal of Negro History 5 (January 1920): 45-57.

See also studies on the Second Seminole War and on the Civil War and Reconstruction in the Indian territory.

Indian Slavery

Distinct from the question of Indian use of black slaves was the enslavement of Indians by whites or by other Indians. Studies on that subject are listed here.

9035. Bailey, L. R. Indian Slave Trade in the Southwest: A Study of Slave-Taking and the Traffic of Indian Captives. Los Angeles: Westernlore Press, 1966.

9036. Creer, Leland Hargrave. "Spanish-

American Slave Trade in the Great Basin, 1800-1853." New Mexico Historical Review 24 (July 1949): 171-183.

9037. Dennis, Elsie F. "Indian Slavery in Pacific Northwest." Oregon Historical Quarterly 31 (March 1930): 69-81; (June 1930): 181-195; (September 1930): 285-296.

9038. Forbes, Gerald. "The Part Played by the Enslavement of the Indians in the Removal of the Tribes to Oklahoma." Chronicles of Oklahoma 16 (June 1938): 163-170.

9039. Hunt, H. F. "Slavery among the Indians of Northwest America." Washington Historical Quarterly 9 (October 1918): 277-283.

9040. Jones, Daniel W. "Brigham Young Opposes Indian Slavery." Utah Historical Quarterly 2 (July 1929): 81-82.

9041. Lauber, Almon Wheeler. Indian Slavery in Colonial Times within the Present Limits of the United States. New York: Columbia University, 1913.

9042. Magnaghi, Russell Mario. "The Indian Slave Trader: The Comanche, a Case Study." Ph.D. dissertation, Saint Louis University, 1970.

9043. Snell, William Robert. "Indian Slavery in Colonial South Carolina, 1671-1795." Ph.D. dissertation, University of Alabama, 1972.

9044. Sunrise, Alvin R. "The Indian Slave Trade in New Mexico, 1846-1861." Indian Historian 6 (Fall 1973): 20-22, 54.

9045. Winston, Sanford. "Indian Slavery in the Carolina Region." Journal of Negro History 19 (October 1934): 431-440.

For studies on black slavery among the Indians, see the section on Indians and Blacks.

Indians and the Horse

One of the most dramatic accommodations of the Indians to white patterns was the use of horses in Indian cultures. How the Indians got the horse and the diffusion of horses among the tribes have been studied by a number of writers.

9046. Alexander, H. B. "The Horse in American Indian Culture." In So Live the Works of Men: Seventieth Anniversary Volume Honoring Edgar Lee Hewitt, edited by Donald D. Brand and Fred E. Harvey, pp. 65-74. Albuquerque: University of New Mexico Press, 1939.

9047. Bonney, David. "The Indian and the Horse." American History Illustrated 1 (August 1966): 44-54.

9048. Clark, La Verne Harrell. "Early Horse Trappings of the Navajo and Apache Indians." Arizona and the West 5 (Autumn 1963): 233-248.

9049. _____. They Sang for Horses: The Impact of the Horse on Navajo and Apache Folklore. Tucson: University of Arizona Press, 1966.

9050. Dobie, James Frank. "The Comanches and Their Horses." Southwest Review 36 (Spring 1951): 99-103.

9051. _____. "Indian Horses and Horsemanship." Southwest Review 35 (Autumn 1950): 265-275.

9052. Ewers, John C. The Horse in Blackfoot Indian Culture, with Comparative Material from Other Western Tribes. Bureau of American Ethnology Bulletin 159. Washington: Government Printing Office, 1955.

9053. Haines, Francis. "Horses for Western Indians." American West 3 (Spring 1966): 4-15.

9054. _____. "How the Indian Got the Horse." American Heritage 15 (February 1964): 16-21, 78-81.

9055. _____. "Nez Perce Horses: How They Changed the Indian Way of Life." Idaho Yesterdays 4 (Spring 1960): 8-11.

9056. _____. "The Northward Spread of Horses among the Plains Indians." American Anthropologist 40 (July-September 1938): 429-437.

9057. _____. "Where Did the Plains Indians Get Their Horses?" American Anthropologist 40 (January-March 1938): 112-117.

9058. Moriarity, James Robert, and Walton Campbell. "The Indians Shall Have No Weapons or Horses." Western Explorer 4, no. 2 (1966): 1-8.

9059. Roe, Frank Gilbert. "From Dogs to Horses among the Western Indian Tribes." Transactions of the Royal Society of Canada, 3d series 33 (May 1939): 209-275.

9060. _____. The Indian and the Horse. Norman: University of Oklahoma Press, 1955.

9061. Schmidlin, Lois L. Nelsen. "The Role of the Horse in the Life of the Comanche." Journal of the West 13 (January 1974): 47-66.

9062. Sheffy, L. F. "The Spanish Horse on the Great Plains." Panhandle-Plains Historical Review 6 (1933): 80-101.

9063. Turney-High, Harry. "The Diffusion of the Horse to the Flatheads." Man 35 (December 1935): 183-185.

9064. Wissler, Clark. "The Diffusion of Horse Culture among the North American Indians." National Academy of Sciences Proceedings 1 (April 1915): 254-256.

9065. _____. "The Indian and the Horse." American Indian Magazine 7 (August 1920): 20-26.

9066. _____. "The Influence of the Horse in the Development of Plains Culture." American Anthropologist, new series 16 (January-March 1914): 1-25.

9067. _____. "Riding Gear of the North American Indians." Anthropological Papers of the American Museum of Natural History 17 (1915): 1-38.

9068. Worcester, Donald E. "Spanish Horses among the Plains Tribes." Pacific Historical Review 14 (December 1945): 409-417.

9069. _____. "The Spread of Spanish Horses in the Southwest." New Mexico Historical Review 19 (July 1944): 225-232.

9070. _____. "The Spread of Spanish Horses in the Southwest, 1700-1800." New Mexico Historical Review 20 (January 1945): 1-13.

9071. _____. "The Use of Saddles by American Indians." New Mexico Historical Review 20 (April 1945): 139-143.

Ghost Dance

The rise of a messiah can be seen as a response to white pressures upon the Indian cultures. The ghost dance is associated chiefly with the Sioux war of 1890-1891, but it had a wider impact. Listed here are a few works dealing with it.

9072. Aberle, David F. "The Prophet Dance and Reactions to White Contact." Southwestern Journal of Anthropology 15 (Spring 1959): 74-83.

9073. "Account of the Northern Cheyennes concerning the Messiah Superstition." Journal of American Folk-Lore 4 (January-March 1891): 61-69. Reprints accounts by George Bird Grinnell and Mrs. James A. Finley.

9074. Bailey, Paul Dayton. Wovoka, the Indian Messiah. Los Angeles: Westernlore Press, 1957.

9075. Brant, Charles S. "Indian-White Cultural Relations in Southwestern Oklahoma." Chronicles of Oklahoma 37 (Winter 1959-1960): 433-439.

9076. Brown, Donald N. "The Ghost Dance Religion among the Oklahoma Cheyenne." Chronicles of Oklahoma 30 (Winter 1952-1953): 408-416.

9077. Davis, H. L. "An American Apostle." American Mercury 30 (October 1933): 219-227.

9078. Dobyns, Henry F., and Robert C. Euler. The Ghost Dance of 1889 among the Pai Indians of Northwestern Arizona. Prescott College Studies in Anthropology, no. 1. Prescott, Arizona: Prescott College Press, 1967.

9079. Farb, Peter. "Ghost Dance and Cargo Cult." Horizon 11 (Spring 1969): 58-65.

9080. Fletcher, Alice C. "The Indian Messiah." Journal of American Folk-Lore 4 (January-March 1891): 57-60.

9081. Greenway, John. "The Ghost Dance: Some Reflections, with Evidence on a Cult of Despair among the Indians of North America." American West 6 (July 1969): 42-47.

9082. Moorehead, Warren K. "The Indian Messiah and the Ghost Dance." American Antiquarian and Oriental Journal 13 (May 1891): 161-167.

9083. Phister, Nat P. "The Indian Messiah." American Anthropologist 4 (April 1891): 105-108.

See also the works listed under Ghost Dance and Wounded Knee (4289 to 4333).

Pan-Indianism

Indians from diverse tribes have joined together in political, social, and religious ways. Studies of manifestations of this pan-Indianism are listed here.

9084. Deloria, Vine, Jr. "The Rise and Fall of the First Indian Movement." Historian 33 (August 1971): 656-664.

9085. Feagin, Joe R., and Randall Anderson. "Intertribal Attitudes among Native American Youth." Social Science Quarterly 54 (June 1973): 117-131.

9086. Hertzberg, Hazel W. The Search for an American Indian Identity: Modern Pan-Indian Movements. Syracuse: Syracuse University Press, 1971.

9087. Hirabayashi, James, William Willard, and Luis Kemnitzer. "Pan-Indianism in the Urban Setting." In The Anthropology of Urban Environments, edited by Thomas Weaver and Douglas White, pp. 77-87. Society for Applied Anthropology, Monograph no. 11. Washington: Society for Applied Anthropology, 1972.

9088. Howard, James H. "Pan-Indian Culture of Oklahoma." Scientific Monthly 81 (November 1955): 212-220.

9089. Hurt, Wesley R., Jr. "The Yankton Dakota Church: A Nationalistic Movement of Northern Plains Indians." In Essays in the Science of Culture in Honor of Leslie A. White, edited by Gertrude E. Dole and Robert L. Carneiro, pp. 269-287. New York: Thomas Y. Crowell Company, 1960.

9090. Johnson, N. B. "The National Congress of American Indians." American Indian 3 (Summer 1946): 1-4.

9091. _____. "The National Congress of American Indians." Chronicles of Oklahoma 30 (Summer 1952): 140-148.

9092. Kurath, Gertrude Prokosch. "Pan-Indianism in Great Lakes Tribal Festivals." Journal of American Folklore 70 (April-June 1957): 179-182.

9093. Laxson, Joan Dorothy. "Aspects of Acculturation among American Indians: Emphasis on Contemporary Pan-Indianism." Ph.D. dissertation, University of California, 1972.

9094. Newcomb, W. W., Jr. "A Note on Cherokee-Delaware Pan-Indianism." American Anthropologist 57 (October 1955): 1041-1045.

9095. Northrop, Gordon Douglas. "Pan-Indianism in the Metropolis: A Case Study of an Emergent Ethno-Syncretic Revitalization Movement." Ph.D. dissertation, Michigan State University, 1970.

9096. Powers, William K. "Contemporary Oglala Music and Dance: Pan-Indianism versus Pan-Tetonism." In The Modern Sioux: Social Systems and Reservation Culture, edited by Ethel Nurge, pp. 268-290. Lincoln: University of Nebraska Press, 1970.

9097. Rachlin, Carol K. "The Native American Church in Oklahoma." Chronicles of Oklahoma 42 (Autumn 1964): 262-272.

9098. Ridley, J. R. "Indian Organizations: A General Overall View." American Indian Culture Center Journal 4 (Winter 1973): 15-18.

9099. Sanford, Margaret. "Pan-Indianism, Acculturation, and the American Ideal." Plains Anthropologist 16 (August 1971): 222-227.

9100. Schusky, Ernest. "Pan-Indianism in the Eastern United States." Anthropology Tomorrow 6 (December 1957): 116-123.

9101. Stewart, Omer C. "The Native American Church and the Law with Description of Peyote Religious Services." Brand Book (Denver Westerners) 17 (1961): 3-47.

9102. Thomas, Robert K. "Pan-Indianism." In The American Indian Today, edited by Stuart Levine and Nancy Oestreich Lurie,

pp. 77-85. Deland, Florida: Everett/Edwards, 1968. This appeared originally in Midcontinent American Studies Journal 6 (Fall 1965): 75-83.

Activities of pan-Indian groups or organizations are sometimes treated under Current Comment.

Peyote

The use of peyote in religious ceremonies by Indians touches on Indian-white relations in several ways--Christian components in the cult, white opposition to the drug, and the legal questions involved in its use or suppression. A number of works which deal with these problems are listed here. A great many other studies, particularly those that concern the use of peyote within specific tribes, are omitted. See the extensive bibliographies in the works of Slotkin (9121) and La Barre (9109) and the bibliographical essay by La Barre (9110).

9103. Aberle, David F. The Peyote Religion among the Navaho. Viking Fund Publications in Anthropology, no. 42. New York: Wenner-Gren Foundation for Anthropological Research, 1966.

9104. Cairns, Huntington. "A Divine Intoxicant." Atlantic Monthly 144 (November 1929): 638-645.

9105. Dustin, C. Burton. Peyotism and New Mexico. Farmington, New Mexico, 1960.

9106. Easterlin, Malcolm. "Peyote--Indian Problem No. 1." Scribner's Commentator 11 (November 1941): 77-82.

9107. Jenkins, Hester Donaldson. "The Peyote Cult." World Outlook 4 (January 1918): 26.

9108. La Barre, Weston. "The 'Diabolic Root.'" New York Times Magazine, November 1, 1964, pp. 96, 98.

9109. _____. The Peyote Cult. New Haven: Yale University Press, 1938. Enlarged edition, Hamden, Connecticut: Shoestring Press, 1964.

9110. _____. "Twenty Years of Peyote Studies." Current Anthropology 1 (January 1960): 45-60.

9111. La Barre, Weston, David P. McAllester, J. S. Slotkin, Omer C. Stewart, and Sol Tax. "Statement on Peyote." Science 114 (November 30, 1951): 582-583.

9112. McNickle, D'Arcy. "Peyote and the Indian." Scientific Monthly 57 (September 1943): 220-229.

9113. Marriott, Alice, and Carol K. Rachlin. Peyote. New York: Thomas Y. Crowell Company, 1971.

9114. Newberne, Robert E. L. Peyote: An Abridged Compilation from the Files of the Bureau of Indian Affairs. Washington: Government Printing Office, 1922.

9115. Opler, Morris E. "The Influences of Aboriginal Pattern and White Contact in a Recently Introduced Ceremony, the Mescalero Peyote Rite." Journal of American Folk-Lore 49 (January-June 1936): 143-166.

9116. Peyote--an Insidious Evil. Philadelphia: Indian Rights Association, 1918.

9117. Pierson, Mrs. Delavan L. "American Indian Peyote Worship." Missionary Review of the World 38 (March 1915): 201-206.

9118. Schultes, Richard Evans. "Peyote and the American Indian." Nature Magazine 30 (September 1937): 155-157.

9119. Seymour, Gertrude. "Peyote Worship: An Indian Cult and a Powerful Drug." Survey 36 (May 13, 1916): 181-184.

9120. Simmons, Benjamin F. "Implications of Court Decisions on Peyote for the Users of LSD." Journal of Church and State 11 (Winter 1969): 83-91.

9121. Slotkin, J. S. The Peyote Religion: A Study in Indian-White Relations. Glencoe, Illinois: Free Press, 1956.

9122. Stenberg, Molly Peacock. "The Peyote Culture among Wyoming Indians: A Transitional Link between an Indigenous Culture and an Imposed Culture." University of Wyoming Publications 12 (September 15, 1946): 85-156.

9123. Stewart, Omer C. Washo-Northern Paiute Peyotism: A Study in Acculturation. University of California Publications in American Archaeology and Ethnology, no. 40. Berkeley: University of California Press, 1944.

9124. Underhill, Ruth M. "Peyote." Proceedings of the Thirtieth International Congress of Americanists, 1952, pp. 143-148.

Indians and the Environment

Listed here are articles dealing with Indian use of natural resources.

9125. Altboy, Anthony. "The Indian and the Forest." American Forests 60 (December 1954): 24-27, 63.

9126. Crawford, Cleo. "The First Ecologists." Science and Children 9 (March 1972): 21.

9127. Jacobs, Wilbur R. "Frontiersmen, Fur Traders, and Other Varmints: An Ecological Appraisal of the Frontier in American History." AHA Newsletter 8 (November 1970): 5-11. See discussion in later issues: 9 (March 1971): 37-40; (May 1971): 12-13; (September 1971): 31-34.

9128. Johnson, N. B. "The American Indian as Conservationist." Chronicles of Oklahoma 30 (Autumn 1952): 333-340.

9129. Smaby, Beverly P. "The Mormons and the Indians: Conflicting Ecological Systems in the Great Basin." American Studies 16 (Spring 1975): 35-48.

9130. Snow, Albert J. "The American Indian Knew a Better Way." American Biology Teacher 35 (January 1973): 20-22, 34.

9131. Strickland, Rennard. "The Idea of Environment and the Ideal of the Indian." Journal of American Indian Education 10 (October 1970): 8-15.

9132. Strong, Douglas Hillman. "The Indian and the Environment." Journal of Environmental Education 5 (Winter 1973): 49-51.

9133. Waters, Frank. "Two Views of Nature: White and Indian." South Dakota Review 1 (May 1964): 23-32.

17
Special Topics

This chapter includes a variety of miscellaneous topics dealing with Indian-white relations. Of special importance is the section on concepts and images of the Indian.

INDIAN CAPTIVITIES

Narratives of captivity among the Indians form a literary genre that began in early colonial days, and they have historical as well as literary significance. Individual works are too numerous to list here, but the following bibliographical aids are useful for finding them.

9134. Newberry Library. Narratives of Captivity among the Indians of North America: A List of Books and Manuscripts on This Subject in the Edward E. Ayer Collection of the Newberry Library. Chicago: Newberry Library, 1912. Supplement I, edited by Clara A. Smith. Chicago: Newberry Library, 1928.

9135. Vail, Robert W. G. "The Indians' Captives Relate Their Adventures." In The Voice of the Old Frontier, pp. 23-61. Philadelphia: University of Pennsylvania Press, 1949. A bibliographical essay.

The popularity of the narratives is indicated by the frequent reprinting of the accounts in collected form. The following are representative collections which reprint or retell the captives' stories.

9136. Drake, Samuel G., ed. Tragedies of the Wilderness; or, True and Authentic Narratives of Captives, Who Have Been Carried away by the Indians from the Various Frontier Settlements of the United States, from the Earliest to the Present Time. Boston: Antiquarian Bookstore and Institute, 1841.

9137. Drimmer, Frederick, ed. Scalps and Tomahawks: Narratives of Indian Captivity. New York: Coward-McCann, 1961.

9138. Peckham, Howard H. Captured by Indians: True Tales of Pioneer Survivors.

New Brunswick: Rutgers University Press, 1954.

9139. Van Der Beets, Richard. Held Captive by Indians: Selected Narratives, 1642-1836. Knoxville: University of Tennessee Press, 1973.

The narratives have been studied and analyzed for their literary and historical value. Listed here are works that offer commentary and interpretation.

9140. Ackerknecht, Erwin H. "'White Indians': Psychological and Physiological Peculiarities of White Children Abducted and Reared by North American Indians." Bulletin of the History of Medicine 15 (January 1944): 15-36.

9141. Axtell, James. "The White Indians of Colonial America." William and Mary Quarterly 32 (January 1975): 55-88.

9142. Barbeau, Marius. "Indian Captivities." Proceedings of the American Philosophical Society 94 (1950): 522-548.

9143. Behen, Dorothy M. F. "The Captivity Story in American Literature, 1577-1826: An Examination of Written Reports in English, Authentic and Fictitious, of the Experiences of White Men Captured by the Indians North of Mexico." Ph.D. dissertation, University of Chicago, 1951.

9144. Benson, Maxine. "Schoolcraft, James, and the 'White Indian.'" Michigan History 54 (Winter 1970): 311-328.

9145. Carleton, Phillips D. "The Indian Captivity." American Literature 15 (May 1943): 169-180.

9146. Coleman, Emma Lewis. New England Captives Carried to Canada between 1677 and 1760, during the French and Indian Wars. 2 volumes. Portland, Maine: Southworth Press, 1925.

9147. Dondore, Dorothy Anne. "White Captives among the Indians." New York History 13 (July 1932): 292-300.

358

9148. Drinnon, Richard. White Savage: The Case of John Dunn Hunter. New York: Schocken Books, 1972.

9149. Heard, J. Norman. White into Red: A Study of the Assimilation of White Persons Captured by Indians. Metuchen, New Jersey: Scarecrow Press, 1973.

9150. Knowles, Nathaniel. "The Torture of Captives by the Indians of Eastern North America." Proceedings of the American Philosophical Society 82 (March 22, 1940): 151-225.

9151. Meade, James Gordon. "The 'Westerns' of the East: Narratives of Indian Captivity from Jeremiad to Gothic Novel." Ph.D. dissertation, Northwestern University, 1971.

9152. Monical, David G. "Changes in American Attitudes toward the Indian As Evidenced by Captive Literature." Plains Anthropologist 14 (May 1969): 130-136.

9153. Pearce, Roy Harvey. "The Significance of the Captivity Narrative." American Literature 19 (March 1947): 1-20.

9154. Rister, Carl Coke. Border Captives: The Traffic in Prisoners by Southern Plains Indians, 1835-1875. Norman: University of Oklahoma Press, 1940.

9155. Russell, Jason Almus. "The Narratives of the Indian Captivities." Education 51 (October 1930): 84-88.

9156. Smith, Dwight L. "Shawnee Captivity Ethnography." Ethnohistory 2 (Winter 1955): 29-41.

9157. Swanton, John R. "Notes on the Mental Assimilation of Races." Journal of the Washington Academy of Sciences 16 (November 3, 1926): 493-502.

9158. Vail, Robert W. G. "Certain Indian Captives of New England." Proceedings of the Massachusetts Historical Society 68 (October 1944-May 1947): 113-131.

9159. Van Der Beets, Richard. "The Indian Captivity Narrative: An American Genre." Ph.D. dissertation, University of the Pacific, 1973.

9160. _____. "The Indian Captivity Narrative as Ritual." American Literature 43 (January 1972): 548-562.

9161. White, Lonnie J. "White Women Captives of the Southern Plains Indians, 1866-1875." Journal of the West 8 (July 1969): 327-354.

9162. Whitford, Kathryn. "Hannah Dustin: The Judgment of History." Essex Institute Historical Collections 108 (October 1972): 304-325.

See also the analysis of captivity nar-

ratives in Richard Slotkin, Regeneration through Violence (9252).

INDIAN PEACE MEDALS

The United States government, following the example of Great Britain, France, and Spain, presented silver medals to Indian chiefs as symbols of allegiance and peaceful relations. The chiefs expected to receive these marks of friendship, and the federal government took great pains to produce attractive medals and distribute them to appropriate Indian leaders. The medals carried a portrait of the President of the United States on the obverse and symbols of peace and friendship on the reverse. The full series of United States peace medals is described in the following works.

9163. Belden, Bauman L. Indian Peace Medals Issued in the United States. New York: American Numismatic Society, 1927. Reprinted, New Milford, Connecticut: N. Flayderman, 1966.

9164. Prucha, Francis Paul. Indian Peace Medals in American History. Madison: State Historical Society of Wisconsin, 1971.

There are a considerable number of studies on particular medals or groups of medals. Many of these works are numismatic in character, but they are nevertheless of value to historians. Included here also are a few items dealing with medals presented to Indians by European governments.

9165. Alfred, Lorraine C. "King George II Indian Peace Medal." Wisconsin Archeologist 16 (March 1935): 4-6.

9166. "American Indian Medals." American Journal of Numismatics 38 (April 1904): 98-103.

9167. Armstrong, William H. "Red Jacket's Medal: An American Badge of Nobility." Niagara Frontier 21 (Summer 1974): 26-36.

9168. Bentley, Esther Felt. "The Madison Medal and Chief Keokuk." Princeton University Library Chronicle 19 (Spring-Summer 1958): 153-158.

9169. Betts, Benjamin. "American Fur Company's Indian Medals." American Journal of Numismatics 32 (July 1897): 4-7.

9170. "British Indian Medals." American Journal of Numismatics 31 (July 1896): 7-11. Further notes appear 31 (January 1897): 78; 32 (October 1897): 55-56.

9171. Brown, Charles E. "Wisconsin Indian Medals." Wisconsin Archeologist 14 (April 1915): 28-36.

9172. Brown, Theodore T. "An Abraham Lincoln Medal." Wisconsin Archeologist 8 (April 1929): 103-105.

9173. Butler, James Davie. "The Hispano-Wisconsin Medal." Canadian Antiquarian and Numismatic Journal 11 (July 1882): 26.

9174. Chamberlain, Georgia Stamm. American Medals and Medalists. Annandale, Virginia, 1963. Reprints of articles on Indian peace medals and their artists.

9175. _____. "Chapman's Model of the President Polk Indian Peace Medal." Numismatist 70 (May 1957): 533-537.

9176. _____. "Ferdinand Pettrich, Sculptor of the President Tyler Indian Peace Medal." Numismatist 70 (April 1957): 387-390.

9177. _____. "President Zachary Taylor's Indian Peace Medal." Numismatist 72 (May 1959): 519-524.

9178. Cutright, Paul Russell. "Lewis and Clark Indian Peace Medals." Missouri Historical Society Bulletin 24 (January 1968): 160-167.

9179. Douglas, Damon G. "The First United States Indian Chief Peace Medal." Numismatist 58 (July 1945): 689-693.

9180. Eglit, Nathan N. "Indian Peace Medals and the Presidential Series." Numismatic Scrapbook Magazine 26 (April 1960): 929-950.

9181. Gillingham, Harrold E. "Early American Indian Medals." Antiques 6 (December 1924): 312-315.

9182. _____. "Indian Silver Ornaments." Pennsylvania Magazine of History and Biography 18 (April 1934): 97-126.

9183. Hilger, M. Inez. "A 'Peace and Friendship' Medal." Minnesota History 16 (September 1935): 321-323.

9184. Hodge, Frederick Webb. "Indian Peace and Other Medals." Masterkey 28 (May-June 1954): 109-110.

9185. Jamieson, Melvill Allan. Medals Awarded to North American Indian Chiefs, 1714-1922, and to Loyal African and Other Chiefs in Various Territories within the British Empire. London: Spink and Son, 1936. First half reprinted 1961.

9186. Jester, Margo. "Peace Medals." American Indian Tradition 7 (1961): 149-157.

9187. Julian, R. W. "Peace Medals Honor U S Presidents." Numismatic Scrapbook Magazine 35 (August 25, 1969): 1296-1299. First in a continuing series.

9188. Kannenberg, Arthur P. "Indian Medals in the Oshkosh Public Museum." Wisconsin Archeologist, new series 16 (1936): 97-99.

9189. "Medals Found in Pawnee Indian Graves." Numismatist 39 (March 1926): 139-140.

9190. Miller, Marianne F. "Indian Medals." Numismatic Scrapbook Magazine 19 (July 1953): 617-619.

9191. Morin, Victor. "Les Médailles décernées aux Indiens d'Amérique." Proceedings and Transactions of the Royal Society of Canada, 3d series 9 (December 1915): 277-353.

9192. "A New Variety of Washington Peace Medal." Numismatist 27 (June 1914): 300.

9193. Nute, Grace Lee. "Indian Medals and Certificates." Minnesota History 25 (September 1944): 265-270.

9194. Parish, Daniel, Jr. "Some New Light on the Washington Season Medals." American Numismatic and Archaeological Society of New York City, Proceedings and Papers, Thirty-Sixth, Seventh, and Eighth Annual Meetings, 1894-1895-1896, pp. 82-87.

9195. "A Presidential Medal Given to an Indian." American Journal of Numismatics 31 (July 1896): 20-21.

9196. Prucha, Francis Paul. "Early Indian Peace Medals." Wisconsin Magazine of History 45 (Summer 1962): 279-289.

9197. _____. "American Indian Peace Medals." Chicago History 2 (Fall 1972): 106-113.

9198. Porter, Mae Reed. "Indian Peace Medals." Antiques 46 (July 1944): 28-29.

9199. "Red Jacket Medals." American Journal of Numismatics 21 (January 1897): 84-85.

9200. Severance, Frank H. "The Red Jacket Relics." Publications of the Buffalo Historical Society 25 (1921): 233-242.

INDIAN DELEGATIONS

Groups of Indians often visited Washington and other cities in the East, called there to negotiate treaties or merely to be impressed with the works of the white man. A few studies treat specifically of these delegations or of delegations to Europe.

9201. Downing, Finis E. "With the Ute Peace Delegation of 1863, across the Plains and at Conejos." Colorado Magazine 22 (September 1945): 193-205.

9202. Ellis, Richard N., and Charlie R. Steen, eds. "An Indian Delegation in France, 1725." Journal of the Illinois

State Historical Society 67 (September 1974): 385-405. Translation by Charlie R. Steen of a French report.

9203. Ewers, John C. "'Chiefs from the Missouri and Mississippi,' and Peale's Silhouettes of 1806." Smithsonian Journal of History 1 (Spring 1966): 1-26.

9204. _____. "When the Light Shone in Washington." Montana, the Magazine of Western History 6 (October 1956): 2-11.

9205. Foreman, Carolyn Thomas. Indians Abroad, 1493-1938. Norman: University of Oklahoma Press, 1943.

9206. Foreman, Grant. "Our Indian Ambassadors to Europe." Missouri Historical Society Collections 5 (February 1928): 109-128.

9207. "Indians at Boston." Palimpsest 9 (September 1928): 338-346.

9208. Kellogg, Louise Phelps. "The Winnebago Visit to Washington in 1828." Transactions of the Wisconsin Academy of Sciences, Arts and Letters 29 (1935): 347-354.

9209. Kvasnicka, Robert M. "From the Wilderness to Washington--and Back Again: The Story of the Chippewa Delegation of 1855." Kansas Quarterly 3 (Fall 1971): 56-63.

9210. Raber, Jessie Melody. "An Indian Delegation Visits Europe." Colorado Magazine 26 (April 1949): 143-151.

9211. Turner, Katharine C. Red Men Calling on the Great White Father. Norman: University of Oklahoma Press, 1951.

9212. Viola, Herman J. "Invitation to Washington--a Bid for Peace." American West 9 (January 1972): 19-31.

9213. _____. "Portraits, Presents, and Peace Medals: Thomas L. McKenney and Indian Visitors to Washington." American Scene 11, no. 2 (1970).

9214. Wollon, Dorothy, ed. "Sir Augustus J. Foster and 'the Wild Natives of the Woods,' 1805-1807." William and Mary Quarterly 3d series 9 (April 1952): 191-214.

CONCEPTS AND IMAGES OF THE INDIAN

Images of the Indian

Whites dealt with Indians as they perceived them, and popular images and stereotypes greatly influenced Indian-white relations. Listed here are studies that deal with these images.

9215. Bidney, David. "The Idea of the Savage in North American Ethnohistory."

Journal of the History of Ideas 15 (April 1954): 322-327.

9216. Byler, Mary Gloyne. "The Image of American Indians Projected by Non-Indian Writers." Library Journal 99 (February 15, 1974): 546-549. Juvenile books.

9217. Cawelti, John G. "Cowboys, Indians, Outlaws: The West in Myth and Fantasy." American West 1 (Spring 1964): 28-35, 77-79.

9218. Crane, Fred Arthur. "The Noble Savage in America, 1815-1860: Concepts of the Indian, with Special Reference to the Writers of the Northeast." Ph.D. dissertation, Yale University, 1952.

9219. Dippie, Brian W. "This Bold but Wasting Race: Stereotypes and American Indian Policy." Montana, the Magazine of Western History 23 (January 1973): 2-13.

9220. _____. "The Vanishing American: Popular Attitudes and American Indian Policy in the Nineteenth Century." Ph.D. dissertation, University of Texas, 1970.

9221. Diket, A. L. "The Noble Savage Convention As Epitomized in John Lawson's 'A New Voyage to Carolina.'" North Carolina Historical Review 43 (October 1966): 413-429.

9222. Evans, James Leroy. "The Indian Savage, the Mexican Bandit, the Chinese Heathen--Three Popular Stereotypes." Ph.D. dissertation, University of Texas, 1967.

9223. Ewers, John C. "The Emergence of the Plains Indian as the Symbol of the North American Indian." Annual Report of the Board of Regents of the Smithsonian Institution, 1964, pp. 531-544.

9224. Fleming, E. McClung. "The American Image as Indian Princess, 1765-1783." Winterthur Portfolio 2 (1965): 65-81.

9225. _____. "From Indian Princess to Greek Goddess: The American Image, 1783-1815." Winterthur Portfolio 3 (1967): 37-66.

9226. Fontana, Bernard L. "Savage Anthropologists and Unvanishing Indians of American Southwest." Indian Historian 6 (Winter 1973): 5-10, 32.

9227. Green, Rayna Diane. "The Only Good Indian: The Image of the Indian in American Vernacular Culture." Ph.D. dissertation, Indiana University, 1973.

9228. Healy, George R. "The French Jesuits and the Idea of the Noble Savage." William and Mary Quarterly, 3d series 15 (April 1958): 143-167.

9229. Houts, Kathleen C., and Rosemary S. Bahr. "Stereotyping of Indians and Blacks in Magazine Cartoons." In Native Americans Today: Sociological Perspectives, edited by Howard M. Bahr and others, pp. 110-114. New York: Harper and Row, 1972.

9230. Kunitz, Stephen J. "Benjamin Rush on Savagism and Progress." Ethnohistory 17 (Spring 1970): 31-43.

9231. La Farge, Oliver. "Myths That Hide the American Indian." American Heritage 7 (October 1956): 4-19, 103-107.

9232. Lester, Joan. "The American Indian: A Museum's Eye View." Indian Historian 5 (Summer 1972): 25-31.

9233. McDermott, John Francis. "The Indian as Human Being." Nebraska History 52 (Spring 1971): 45-49.

9234. Mardock, Robert Winston. "Irresolvable Enigma?--Strange Concepts of the American Indian since the Civil War." Montana, the Magazine of Western History 7 (January 1957): 36-47.

9235. Martin, Calvin, and Steven Crain. "The Indian behind the Mask at the Boston Tea Party." Indian Historian 7 (Winter 1974): 45-47.

9236. Mays, John Bentley. "The Flying Serpent: Contemporary Imaginations of the American Indian." Canadian Review of American Studies 4 (Spring 1973): 32-47.

9237. Nash, Gary B. "The Image of the Indian in the Southern Colonial Mind." William and Mary Quarterly 29 (April 1972): 197-230.

9238. Nichols, Roger L. "Printer's Ink and Red Skins: Western Newspapermen and the Indians." Kansas Quarterly 3 (Fall 1971): 82-88.

9239. Nye, Russel B. "Parkman, Red Fate, and White Civilization." In Essays on American Literature in Honor of Jay B. Hubbell, edited by Clarence L. F. Gohdes, pp. 152-163. Durham, North Carolina: Duke University Press, 1967.

9240. Pearce, Roy Harvey. "The Metaphysics of Indian-Hating." Ethnohistory 4 (Winter 1957): 27-40.

9241. _____. "The 'Ruines of Mankind': The Indian and the Puritan Mind." Journal of the History of Ideas 13 (April 1952): 200-217.

9242. _____. The Savages of America: A Study of the Indian and the Idea of Civilization. Baltimore: Johns Hopkins Press, 1953. Paperback edition, Savagism and Civilization: A Study of the Indian and the American Mind. Baltimore: Johns Hopkins Press, 1967.

9243. Prucha, Francis Paul. "The Image of the Indian in Pre-Civil War America." In American Indian Policy: Indiana Historical Society Lectures 1970-1971, pp. 2-19. Indianapolis: Indiana Historical Society, 1971.

9244. Rutland, Robert. "The American Indian through English Spectacles, 1608-1791." Chronicles of Oklahoma 29 (Summer 1951): 169-172.

9245. Saum, Lewis O. "Frenchmen, Englishmen, and the Indian." American West 1 (Fall 1964): 4-11, 87-89.

9246. _____. The Fur Trader and the Indian. Seattle: University of Washington Press, 1965.

9247. _____. "The Fur Trader and the Noble Savage." American Quarterly 15 (Winter 1963): 554-571.

9248. Sheehan, Bernard W. "Paradise and the Noble Savage in Jeffersonian Thought." William and Mary Quarterly 26 (July 1969): 327-359.

9249. _____. "The Quest for Indian Origins in the Thought of the Jeffersonian Era." Midcontinent American Studies Journal 9 (Spring 1968): 34-51.

9250. Shulman, Robert. "Parkman's Indians and American Violence." Massachusetts Review 12 (Spring 1971): 221-239.

9251. Slate, Joseph. "A Climate Favorable to Darwinian Theories of Race: American Views of the Indian in Art and Literature, 1830-1860." In The Impact of Darwinian Thought on American Life and Culture: Papers Read at the Fourth Annual Meeting of the American Studies Association of Texas at Houston, Texas, December 5, 1959, pp. 73-83. Austin: University of Texas, 1959.

9252. Slotkin, Richard. Regeneration through Violence: The Mythology of the American Frontier, 1600-1860. Middletown, Connecticut: Wesleyan University Press, 1973.

9253. Sorber, Edna C. "The Noble Eloquent Savage." Ethnohistory 19 (Summer 1972): 227-236.

9254. Todd, Ruthven. "The Imaginary Indian in Europe." Art in America 60 (July-August 1972): 40-47.

9255. Vagts, Alfred. "The Germans and the Red Man." American-German Review 24 (October-November 1957): 13-17.

9256. Wasserman, Maurice Marc. "The American Indian As Seen by the Seventeenth Century Chroniclers." Ph.D. dissertation, University of Pennsylvania, 1954.

9257. Zolla, Elémire. The Writer and the Shaman: A Morphology of the American Indian. Translated by Raymond Rosenthal. New York: Harcourt Brace Jovanovich, 1973.

Since images are found largely in literature, in art, and in movies, see also the sections following which list works on these topics.

Indians in Literature

American Indians have entered deeply into literature written by whites. Novelists, dramatists, and an occasional poet have used Indian themes and have contributed significantly to the image of the Indian in the American mind.
A useful introduction to the subject is the following brief bibliography, which lists some works not found below.

9258. Peterson, Richard K. "Indians in American Literature." Bulletin of Bibliography 30 (January-March 1973): 42-44.

Studies which discuss the use of Indians and Indian themes in literature, both American and European, are given here. The literary works themselves are not listed.

9259. Adler, Joyce. "Melville on the White Man's War against the American Indian." Science and Society 36 (Winter 1972): 417-442.

9260. Aldridge, Alfred O. "Franklin's Deistical Indians." Proceedings of the American Philosophical Society 94 (August 1950): 398-410.

9261. _____. "Franklin's Letter on Indians and Germans." Proceedings of the American Philosophical Society 94 (August 1950): 391-395.

9262. Anderson, Marilyn Jeanne. "The Image of the American Indian in American Drama: From 1766 to 1845." Ph.D. dissertation, University of Minnesota, 1974.

9263. Ashliman, Dee L. "The American West in Nineteenth-Century German Literature." Ph.D. dissertation, Rutgers--The State University, 1969.

9264. Barba, Preston A. "The American Indian in German Fiction." German American Annals, new series 11 (May-August 1913): 143-174.

9265. Beaver, Harold. "Parkman's Crack-up: A Bostonian on the Oregon Trail." New England Quarterly 48 (March 1975): 84-103.

9266. Benson, Ronald M. "Ignoble Savage: Edward Eggleston and the American Indian." Illinois Quarterly 35 (February 1973): 41-51.

9267. Bissell, Benjamin. The American Indian in English Literature of the Eighteenth Century. New Haven: Yale University Press, 1925.

9268. Black, Albert. "The Pontiac Conspiracy in the Novel, 1833-1954." Michigan History 43 (March 1959): 115-119.

9269. Blegen, Theodore C. "A Note on Schiller's Indian Threnody." Minnesota History 39 (Spring 1965): 198-200.

9270. Boyd, Julian P. "Dr. Franklin: Friend of the Indians." Journal of the Franklin Institute 234 (October 1942): 311-330.

9271. Brenzo, Richard Allen. "Civilization against the Savage: The Destruction of Indians in American Novels, 1823-1854." Ph.D. dissertation, University of Wisconsin--Milwaukee, 1973.

9272. Brotherston, Gordon J. "An Indian Farewell in Prescott's The Conquest of Mexico." American Literature 45 (November 1973): 348-356.

9273. Buntin, Arthur R. "The Indian in American Literature, 1680-1760." Ph.D. dissertation, University of Washington, 1961.

9274. Campbell, Harry Modean. "A Note on Freneau's 'The Indian Burying Ground.'" Modern Language Notes 68 (December 1953): 551-552.

9275. Campbell, Walter S. "The Plains Indian in Literature--and in Life." In The Trans-Mississippi West: Papers Read at a Conference Held at the University of Colorado, June 18-June 21, 1929, edited by James F. Willard and Colin B. Goodykoontz, pp. 175-194. Boulder: University of Colorado, 1930.

9276. Clark, Harold Edward. "Fenimore Cooper's Leather-Stocking Tales: A Problem in Race." Ph.D. dissertation, Indiana University, 1955.

9277. Colby, Elbridge. "Chateaubriand and the American Indian." Catholic University Bulletin 20 (May 1914): 374-387.

9278. Collier, Gaylan Jane. "The Five Major Stereotypes in American Drama: An Analytical Survey of the Speech Delineation of the Stage Yankee, Frontiersman, Irishman, Negro, and Indian, as Depicted by Playwrights and Actors, 1766-1900." Ph.D. dissertation, University of Denver, 1958.

9279. Cox, Paul Ronald. "The Characterization of the American Indian in American Indian Plays 1800-1860 as a Reflection of the American Romantic Movement." Ph.D. dissertation, New York University, 1970.

9280. Cracroft, Richard H. "The American West of Karl May." American Quarterly 19 (Summer 1967): 249-258.

9281. Dabney, Lewis M. The Indians of Yoknapatawpha: A Study in Literature and History. Baton Rouge: Louisiana State University Press, 1974.

9282. Darnell, Donald. "Uncas as Hero: The ubi sunt Formula in The Last of the Mohicans." American Literature 37 (November 1965): 259-266.

9283. Davis, David Brion. "The Deerslayer, a Democratic Knight of the Wilderness." In Twelve Original Essays on Great American Novels, edited by Charles Shapiro, pp. 1-22. Detroit: Wayne State University Press, 1958.

9284. Davis, Rose M. "How Indian Is Hiawatha?" Midwest Folklore 7 (Spring 1957): 5-25.

9285. Denton, Lynn W. "Mark Twain and the American Indian." Mark Twain Journal 16 (Winter 1971-1972): 1-3.

9286. Dillon, Richard H. "Bound for Bashan." Papers of the Bibliographical Society of America 43 (Fourth Quarter 1963): 449-453.

9287. Dippie, Brian W. "'His Visage Wild, His Form Exotick': Indian Themes and Cultural Guilt in John Barth's The Sot-Weed Factor." American Quarterly 21 (Spring 1969): 113-121.

9288. _____. "Jack Crabb and the Sole Survivors of Custer's Last Stand." Western American Literature 4 (Fall 1969): 189-202.

9289. Duckett, Margaret. "Bret Harte and the Indians of Northern California." Huntington Library Quarterly 18 (November 1954): 59-83.

9290. _____. "Bret Harte's Portrayal of Half-Breeds." American Literature 25 (May 1953): 193-212.

9291. Eich, L. M. "The American Indian Plays." Quarterly Journal of Speech 30 (April 1944): 212-215.

9292. Fackler, Herbert V. "Cooper's Pawnees." American Notes and Queries 6 (October 1967): 21-22.

9293. Fairchild, Hoxie Neale. The Noble Savage: A Study in Romantic Naturalism. New York: Columbia University Press, 1928.

9294. Falkenhagen, Maria, and Inga K.

Kelly. "The Native American in Juvenile Fiction: Teacher Perception of Stereotypes." Journal of American Indian Education 13 (January 1974): 9-13.

9295. Fiedler, Leslie A. The Return of the Vanishing American. New York: Stein and Day, 1968.

9296. Frederick, John T. "Cooper's Eloquent Indians." Publications of the Modern Language Association of America 71 (December 1956): 1004-1017.

9297. Fussell, Edwin. "The Indian Summer of the Literary West." In Frontier: American Literature and the American West, pp. 327-396. Princeton: Princeton University Press, 1965.

9298. Gage, Duane. "William Faulkner's Indians." American Indian Quarterly 1 (Spring 1974): 27-33.

9299. Gill, Katharine Tracy. "Frontier Concepts and Characters in the Fiction of Fenimore Cooper." Ph.D. dissertation, University of Illinois, 1956.

9300. Gimlin, Joan Sherako. "Henry Thoreau and the American Indian." Ph.D. dissertation, George Washington University, 1974.

9301. Grigg, Quay. "The Kachina Characters of Frank Waters' Novels." South Dakota Review 11 (Spring 1973): 6-16.

9302. Gurian, Jay. "Style in the Literary Desert: Little Big Man." Western American Literature 3 (Winter 1969): 285-296.

9303. Hall, Joan Joffe. "Nick of the Woods: An Interpretation of the American Wilderness." American Literature 35 (May 1963): 173-182.

9304. Hamilton, Wynette L. "The Correlation between Societal Attitudes and Those of American Authors in the Depiction of American Indians, 1607-1860." American Indian Quarterly 1 (Spring 1974): 1-26.

9305. Hayne, Barrie. "Ossian, Scott, and Cooper's Indians." Journal of American Studies 3 (July 1969): 73-87.

9306. Hough, Robert L. "Washington Irving, Indians, and the West." South Dakota Review 6 (Winter 1968-1969): 27-39.

9307. Howell, Elmo. "The Chickasaw Queen: In William Faulkner's Story." Chronicles of Oklahoma 49 (Autumn 1971): 334-339.

9308. _____. "President Jackson and William Faulkner's Choctaws." Chronicles of Oklahoma 45 (Autumn 1967): 252-258.

9309. _____. "William Faulkner and the Chickasaw Funeral." American Literature 36 (January 1965): 523-525.

9310. _____. "William Faulkner and the Mississippi Indians." Georgia Review 21 (Fall 1967): 386-396.

9311. Hubbell, Jay B. "The Smith-Pocahontas Literary Legend." In South and Southwest: Literary Essays and Reminiscences, pp. 175-204. Durham: Duke University Press, 1965.

9312. _____. "The Smith-Pocahontas Story in Literature." Virginia Magazine of History and Biography 65 (July 1957): 275-300.

9313. Huddleston, Eugene L. "Indians and Literature of the Federalist Era: The Case of James Elliot." New England Quarterly 44 (June 1971): 221-237.

9314. Jennings, Francis P. "A Vanishing Indian: Francis Parkman versus His Sources." Pennsylvania Magazine of History and Biography 87 (July 1963): 306-323.

9315. Jones, George Elwood, Jr. "The American Indian in the American Novel (1875-1950)." Ph.D. dissertation, New York University, 1958.

9316. Jordan, Philip D. "The Source of Mrs. Sigourney's 'Indian Girl's Burial.'" American Literature 4 (November 1932): 300-305.

9317. Keiser, Albert. The Indian in American Literature. New York: Oxford University Press, 1933.

9318. _____. "Thoreau's Manuscripts on the Indians." Journal of English and Germanic Philology 27 (April 1928): 183-199.

9319. Kennedy, Brice Morris. "The Indian in Southwestern Fiction." Research (University of New Mexico) 1 (August 1937): 212-225.

9320. Kimball, Arthur G. "Savages and Savagism: Brockden Brown's Dramatic Irony." Studies in Romanticism 6 (Summer 1967): 214-225.

9321. Koppell, Kathleen Sunshine. "Early American Fiction and the Call of the Wild: Nature and the Indian in Novels before Cooper." Ph.D. dissertation, Harvard University, 1968.

9322. LaHood, Marvin J. "The Light in the Forest: History as Fiction." English Journal 55 (March 1966): 298-304.

9323. Leechman, Douglas. "The Indian in Literature." Queen's Quarterly 50 (Summer 1943): 155-163.

9324. _____. "John Rastell and the Indians." Queen's Quarterly 51 (Spring 1944): 73-78.

9325. _____. "Longfellow's Hiawatha." Queen's Quarterly 51 (Autumn 1944): 307-312.

9326. Lewis, Jay. "The Yamassee." In Other Men's Minds: The Critical Writings of Jay Lewis, edited by Phyllis Hanson, pp. 75-87. New York: G. P. Putnam's Sons, 1948.

9327. Marovitz, Sanford Earl. "Frontier Conflicts: Villains, Outlaws, and Indians in Selected 'Western' Fiction, 1799-1860." Ph.D. dissertation, Duke University, 1968.

9328. Marsh, Philip. "Indian Folklore in Freneau." Proceedings of the New Jersey Historical Society 71 (April 1953): 125-135.

9329. Meyer, Roy W. "Hamlin Garland and the American Indian." Western American Literature 2 (Summer 1967): 109-125.

9330. Miller, Mary Rita. "Attestations of American Indian Pidgin English in Fiction and Nonfiction." American Speech 42 (May 1967): 142-147.

9331. Moore, Jack Bailey. "Native Elements in American Magazine Short Fiction, 1741-1800." Ph.D. dissertation, University of North Carolina, 1963.

9332. Morris, Mabel. "Charles Brockden Brown and the American Indian." American Literature 18 (November 1946): 244-247.

9333. Morseberger, Robert E. "Edgar Rice Burroughs' Apache Epic." Journal of Popular Culture 7 (Fall 1973): 280-287.

9334. Moyne, Ernest J. "Manabozho, Tarenyawagon, and Hiawatha." Southern Folklore Quarterly 29 (September 1965): 195-203.

9335. Nigliazzo, Marc Anthony. "Faulkner's Indians." Ph.D. dissertation, University of New Mexico, 1973.

9336. O'Donnell, Thomas F. "More Apologies: The Indian in New York Fiction." New York Folklore Quarterly 23 (December 1967): 243-253.

9337. Oleson, Carole. "The Remembered Earth: Momaday's House Made of Dawn." South Dakota Review 11 (Spring 1973): 59-78.

9338. Oliva, Leo E. "Thomas Berger's Little Big Man as History." Western American Literature 8 (Spring-Summer 1973): 33-54.

9339. Orians, George Harrison. "The Indian Hater in Early American Fiction." Journal of American History 27 (1st Quarter 1933): 34-44.

9340. _____. "Pontiac in Literature." Northwest Ohio Quarterly 35 (Autumn

1963): 144-163; 36 (Winter 1964): 31-53.

9341. Paine, Gregory Lansing. "The Indians of the Leather-Stocking Tales." Studies in Philology 23 (January 1926): 16-39.

9342. Parker, Arthur C. "Sources and Range of Cooper's Indian Lore." New York History 35 (October 1954): 447-456.

9343. _____. "Who Was Hiawatha?" New York Folklore Quarterly 10 (Winter 1954): 285-288.

9344. Parker, Hershel. "The Metaphysics of Indian-Hating." Nineteenth Century Fiction 18 (September 1963): 165-173.

9345. Pearce, Roy Harvey. "Civilization and Savagism: The World of the Leather-stocking Tales." English Institute Essays, 1949, pp. 92-116.

9346. Peavy, Charles D. "The American Indian in the Drama of the United States." McNeese Review 10 (Winter 1958): 68-86.

9347. Pritchett, V. S. "Injun Mad." New Statesman 63 (April 27, 1962): 598-599. About Francis Parkman.

9348. Reamer, Owen J. "Garland and the Indians." New Mexico Quarterly 34 (Autumn 1964): 257-280.

9349. Redekop, Ernest. "The Redmen: Some Representations of Indians in American Literature before the Civil War." CAAS Bulletin 3 (Winter 1968): 1-44.

9350. Robinson, Linda Jane Rookwood. "Henry W. Longfellow's Hiawatha: An American Epic." Ph.D. dissertation, Tulane University, 1968.

9351. Russell, Jason Almus. "Cooper: Interpreter of the Real and the Historical Indian." Journal of American History 23 (First Quarter 1929): 41-71.

9352. _____. "Francis Parkman and the Real Indian." Journal of American History 22 (Second Quarter 1928): 121-129.

9353. _____. "Hawthorne and the Romantic Indian." Education 48 (February 1928): 381-386.

9354. _____. "The Indian in American Literature (1775-1875)." Ph.D. dissertation, Cornell University, 1929.

9355. _____. "Irving: Recorder of Indian Life." Journal of American History 25 (Fourth Quarter 1931): 185-195.

9356. _____. "Longfellow: Interpreter of the Historical and the Romantic Indian." Journal of American History 22 (Fourth Quarter 1928): 327-347.

9357. _____. "The Romantic Indian in Bryant's Poetry." Education 48 (June 1928): 642-649.

9358. _____. "The Southwestern Border Indian in the Writings of William Gilmore Simms." Education 51 (November 1930): 144-157.

9359. _____. "Thoreau: The Interpreter of the Real Indian." Queen's Quarterly 35 (August 1927): 37-48.

9360. Schmaier, Maurice D. "Conrad Richter's The Light in the Forest: An Ethnohistorical Approach to Fiction." Ethnohistory 7 (Fall 1960): 327-398.

9361. Schramm, Wilber Lang. "Hiawatha and Its Predecessors." Philological Quarterly 11 (October 1932): 321-343.

9362. Seyersted, Per. "The Indian in Knickerbocker's New Amsterdam." Indian Historian 7 (Summer 1974): 14-28.

9363. Shames, Priscilla. "The Long Hope: A Study of American Indian Stereotypes in American Popular Fiction, 1890-1950." Ph.D. dissertation, University of California, Los Angeles, 1969.

9364. Shapiro, Samuel. "Tashtego--the White Man's Victim." American Indian 8 (Winter 1958-1959): 40-43.

9365. Sitton, Fred. "The Indian Play in American Drama, 1750-1900." Ph.D. dissertation, Northwestern University, 1962.

9366. Slotkin, Richard Sidney. "Emergence of a Myth: John Filson's 'Daniel Boon Narrative' and the Literature of the Indian Wars, 1638-1848." Ph.D. dissertation, Brown University, 1967.

9367. Steuber, William. "The Novel as a Vehicle to Tell the Story of the Menominee Indians." Transactions of the Wisconsin Academy of Sciences, Arts and Letters 62 (1974): 51-55.

9368. Stockton, Edwin L., Jr. "The Influence of the Moravians upon the Leather-Stocking Tales." Ph.D. dissertation, Florida State University, 1960.

9369. Ten Kate, Herman F. C. "The Indian in Literature." Annual Report of the Board of Regents of the Smithsonian Institution, 1921, pp. 507-528.

9370. Thompson, Stith. "The Indian Legend of Hiawatha." Publications of the Modern Language Association of America 37 (March 1922): 128-140.

9371. Troy, Alice Anne. "The Indian in Adolescent Literature, 1930-1940 vs. 1960-1970." Ph.D. dissertation, University of Iowa, 1972.

9372. Underhill, Lonnie E. "Hamlin Garland and the Indian." American Indian Quarterly 1 (Summer 1974): 103-113.

9373. Walker, Warren S. "Cooper's Wooden

Indians." Chicago Jewish Forum 20 (Winter 1961-1962): 157-160.

9374. Wallace, Paul A. W. "Cooper's Indians." New York History 35 (October 1954): 423-446.

9375. _____. "John Heckewelder's Indians and the Fenimore Cooper Tradition." Proceedings of the American Philosophical Society 96 (August 1952): 496-504.

9376. Walser, Richard. "Senator Strange's Indian Novel." North Carolina Historical Review 26 (January 1949): 1-27.

9377. Willson, Lawrence. "From Thoreau's Indian Manuscripts." Emerson Society Quarterly no. 11 (1958): 52-55.

9378. _____. "Thoreau, Defender of the Savage." Emerson Society Quarterly no. 26 (1962): 1-8.

9379. _____. "Thoreau: Student of Anthropology." American Anthropologist 61 (April 1959): 279-289.

9380. Wylder, Delbert E. "Manfred's Indian Novel." South Dakota Review 7 (Winter 1969-1970): 100-109.

9381. _____. "Thomas Berger's Little Big Man as Literature." Western American Literature 3 (Winter 1969): 273-284.

9382. Young, Philip. "The Mother of Us All: Pocahontas Reconsidered." Kenyon Review 24 (Summer 1962): 391-415.

See also studies on images of the Indian and discussions of captivity narratives.

Indians in Painting and Sculpture

Artists were intrigued and inspired by Indians and Indian scenes and left an important historical as well as artistic record. Listed here are works by and about painters and sculptors who used Indian subjects. Photographs of Indians are treated in the section following.

9383. "The American Indian: A Pictorial Record." Chicago History 2 (Winter 1949): 53-58. Describes The Indian Tribes of North America by Thomas L. McKenney and James Hall.

9384. Beeler, Joe. "An Artist Looks at the American Indian." Montana, the Magazine of Western History 14 (April 1964): 83-90.

9385. Brinton, Ellen Starr. "Benjamin West's Painting of Penn's Treaty with the Indians." Bulletin of Friends' Historical Association 30 (Autumn 1941): 99-166.

9386. Brody, J. J. Indian Painters and White Patrons. Albuquerque: University of New Mexico Press, 1971.

9387. Bushnell, David I., Jr. Drawings by A. DeBatz in Louisiana, 1732-1735. Smithsonian Miscellaneous Collections, volume 80, no. 5. Washington: Smithsonian Institution, 1927.

9388. _____. "Friedrich Kurz, Artist-Explorer." Annual Report of the Board of Regents of the Smithsonian Institution, 1927, pp. 507-527.

9389. _____. Seth Eastman: The Master Painter of the North American Indian. Smithsonian Miscellaneous Collections, volume 87, no. 3. Washington: Smithsonian Institution, 1932.

9390. _____. Sketches by Paul Kane in the Indian Country, 1845-1848. Smithsonian Miscellaneous Collections, volume 99, no. 1. Washington: Smithsonian Institution, 1940.

9391. Catlin, George. Catlin's North American Indian Portfolio: Hunting Scenes and Amusements of the Rocky Mountains and Prairies of America, from Drawings and Notes of the Author, Made during Eight Years' Travel amongst Forty-eight of the Wildest and Most Remote Tribes of Savages in North America. New York: J. Ackermann, 1845.

9392. _____. Letters and Notes on the Manners, Customs, and Condition of the North American Indians. 2 volumes. London: Tosswill and Myers, 1841. Also later editions, with variant titles.

9393. Coen, Rena Neumann. "The Indian as the Noble Savage in Nineteenth Century American Art." Ph.D. dissertation, University of Minnesota, 1969.

9394. DeVoto, Bernard. "The First Illustrators of the West." In Across the Wide Missouri, appendix 2, pp. 391-415. Boston: Houghton Mifflin Company, 1947.

9395. Donaldson, Thomas C. The George Catlin Indian Gallery in the U.S. National Museum (Smithsonian Institution), with Memoir and Statistics. Washington: Government Printing Office, 1887.

9396. Erwin, Marie H. "Cheyenne Indian Portraits Painted by George Catlin." Annals of Wyoming 15 (July 1943): 234-241.

9397. Ewers, John C. "An Anthropologist Looks at Early Pictures of North American Indians." New-York Historical Society Quarterly 33 (October 1949): 222-234.

9398. _____. Artists of the Old West. Enlarged edition. Garden City, New York: Doubleday and Company, 1973. First published in 1965.

9399. _____. "Charles Bird King:

Painter of Indian Visitors to the Nation's Capital." Annual Report of the Board of Regents of the Smithsonian Institution, 1953, pp. 463-473.

9400. _____. "Cyrus E. Dallin, Master Sculptor of the Plains Indian." Montana, the Magazine of Western History 18 (January 1968): 34-43.

9401. _____. "George Catlin, Painter of Indians and the West." Annual Report of the Board of Regents of the Smithsonian Institution, 1955, pp. 483-528.

9402. _____. Gustavus Sohon's Portraits of Flathead and Pend d'Oreille Indians, 1854. Smithsonian Miscellaneous Collections, volume 110, no. 7. Washington: Smithsonian Institution, 1948.

9403. _____. "Winold Reiss: His Portraits and Protégés." Montana, the Magazine of Western History 21 (July 1971): 44-55. Painter of Blackfeet.

9404. Feest, Christian F. "The Virginia Indian in Pictures, 1612-1624." Smithsonian Journal of History 2 (Spring 1967): 1-30.

9405. Fenton, William N. "The Hyde De Neuville Portraits of New York Savages in 1807-1808." New-York Historical Society Quarterly 38 (April 1954): 118-137.

9406. Fundaburk, Emma Lila, ed. Southeastern Indians: Life Portraits, a Catalogue of Pictures, 1564-1860. Luverne, Alabama, 1958. Reprinted Metuchen, New Jersey: Scarecrow Reprint Corporation, 1969.

9407. Gaskin, L. J. P. "Catlin's 'North American Indian Portfolio.'" Man 36 (March 1936): 48-49.

9408. Gerdts, William H. "Marble Savage." Art in America 62 (July-August 1974): 64-70.

9409. Goosman, Mildred. "Maximilian-Bodmer Collection." Mountain-Plains Library Quarterly 9 (Spring 1964): 16-20, 32.

9410. Gridley, Marion E. America's Indian Statues. Chicago: Amerindian, 1966.

9411. Haberly, Loyd. Pursuit of the Horizon: A Life of George Catlin, Painter and Recorder of the American Indian. New York: Macmillan Company, 1948.

9412. Halpin, Marjorie. Catlin's Indian Gallery: The George Catlin Paintings in the United States National Museum. Washington: Smithsonian Institution, 1965.

9413. Harper, J. Russell. Paul Kane's Frontier. Austin: University of Texas Press, 1971. Includes Kane's Wanderings

of an Artist among the Indians of North America.

9414. Haverstock, Mary S. Indian Gallery: The Story of George Catlin. New York: Four Winds, 1973.

9415. Hodge, Frederick Webb. "The Origin and Destruction of a National Indian Portrait Gallery." In Holmes Anniversary Volume: Anthropological Essays Presented to William Henry Holmes, edited by F. W. Hodge, pp. 187-193. Washington: J. W. Bryan Press, 1916.

9416. Horan, James D. The McKenney-Hall Portrait Gallery of American Indians. New York: Crown Publishers, 1972.

9417. Hunter, H. Chadwick. "The American Indian in Painting." Art and Archaeology 8 (April 1919): 81-96.

9418. "Indian Tribe in Granite Is Next Plan of Gutzon Borglum, Sculptor of Mount Rushmore." Nebraska History 21 (October-December 1940): 291.

9419. Kane, Paul. Wanderings of an Artist among the Indians of North America. London, 1859.

9420. Kennedy, Michael S. "Portfolio of Paul Dyck: Indians of the Overland Trail." Montana, the Magazine of Western History 12 (July 1962): 56-66.

9421. Kinietz, W. Vernon. John Mix Stanley and His Indian Painting. Ann Arbor: University of Michigan Press, 1942.

9422. La Farge, Oliver. "George Catlin: Wild West Witness." Art News 52 (October 1953): 30-32, 66.

9423. Linderman, Frank B. Blackfeet Indians. St. Paul: Great Northern Railway, 1935. Pictures by Winold Reiss.

9424. Lockwood, Luke Vincent. "The St. Memin Indian Portraits." New-York Society Quarterly Bulletin 12 (April 1928): 3-26.

9425. Long, E. Waldo. "Dallin, Sculptor of Indians." World's Work 54 (September 1927): 563-568. Cyrus E. Dallin.

9426. Lorant, Stefan, ed. The New World: The First Pictures of America, Made by John White and Jacques Le Moyne and Engraved by Theodore De Bry, with Contemporary Narratives of the Huguenot Settlement in Florida, 1562-1565, and the English Colonies in Virginia, 1585-1590. New York: Duell, Sloan and Pearce, 1946.

9427. McCracken, Harold. George Catlin and the Old Frontier. New York: Dial Press, 1959.

9428. McDermott, John Francis. "The J. O. Lewis Port Folio." Minnesota History 33 (Spring 1952): 20-21.

9429. _____. Seth Eastman: Pictorial Historian of the Indian. Norman: University of Oklahoma Press, 1961.

9430. McKenney, Thomas L., and James Hall. History of the Indian Tribes of North America, with Biographical Sketches and Anecdotes of the Principal Chiefs. Philadelphia: Edward C. Biddle, and others, 1836-1844. Several later editions. The edition published in Edinburgh, 1933-1934, has an introduction by Frederick Webb Hodge.

9431. Miller, Alfred J. Braves and Buffalo: Plains Indian Life in 1837. Toronto: University of Toronto Press, 1973. Miller's water colors and descriptive notes.

9432. Monaghan, Jay. "The Hunter and the Artist: A Unique Partnership in the Documentation of the Mountain Man's West." American West 6 (November 1969): 4-13. William Drummond Stewart and Alfred Jacob Miller.

9433. Parry, Ellwood. The Image of the Indian and the Black Man in American Art, 1590-1900. New York: George Braziller, 1974.

9434. Peattie, Louise Redfield. "He Caught the Splendor of the First Americans." Reader's Digest 85 (October 1964): 257-262. George Catlin.

9435. Pipes, Nellie B. "John Mix Stanley, Indian Painter." Oregon Historical Quarterly 33 (September 1932): 250-258.

9436. Plate, Robert. Palette and Tomahawk: The Story of George Catlin, July 27, 1796--December 23, 1872. New York: D. McKay Company, 1962.

9437. Reinhard, Laura. "Indians on Stone." Antiques Journal 8 (August 1953): 14-15, 19.

9438. Scholder, Fritz, and Rudy H. Turk. "Indian Present: 'I Have Painted the Indian Real, Not Red.'" Intellectual Digest 3 (October 1972): 47-50.

9439. Sheldon, Addison E. "A Memorial to the Sioux Nation." Nebraska History 21 (October-December 1940): 281-285.

9440. Smith, Robert C. "The Noble Savage in Paintings and Prints." Antiques 74 (July 1958): 57-59.

9441. Stanley, John Mix. Portraits of North American Indians. Smithsonian Miscellaneous Collections, volume 2, no. 3. Washington: Smithsonian Institution, 1862.

9442. Sturtevant, William C. "Ethnographic Details in the American Drawings of John White, 1577-1590." Ethnohistory 12 (Winter 1965): 54-63.

9443. Tanner, Clara Lee. "The Influence of the White Man on Southwest Indian Art." Ethnohistory 7 (Spring 1960): 137-150.

9444. Thomas, Phillip Drennon. "Artists among the Indians, 1493-1850." Kansas Quarterly 3 (Fall 1971): 3-12.

9445. _____. "George Catlin: Pictorial Historian of Aboriginal America." Natural History 81 (December 1972): 30-43.

9446. "Two Views." American Scene 14, no. 4 (1973): 1-20. William de la Montagne Cary and Alfred Jacob Miller.

9447. Von Tungeln, Annie Laurie. "Catlin, Painter of Indians." Américas 26 (June-July 1974): 15-21.

9448. Wasserman, Emily. "The Artist-Explorers." Art in America 60 (July-August 1972): 48-57.

9449. Weitenkampf, Frank. "Cigar-Store Indians." Magazine of Art 41 (December 1948): 312-313.

9450. _____. "Early Pictures of North American Indians." Bulletin of the New York Public Library 53 (December 1949): 591-614.

9451. _____. "How Indians Were Pictured in Earlier Days." New-York Historical Society Quarterly 33 (October 1949): 212-221.

9452. "Winold Reiss Paints the Northern Indians." Survey 61 (January 1, 1929): 429-433.

9453. Winter, George. The Journals and Indian Paintings of George Winter, 1837-1839. Indianapolis: Indiana Historical Society, 1948. Includes articles on Winter by Howard H. Peckham, Wilbur D. Peat, and Gayle Thornbrough.

9454. Wright, Muriel H., and George H. Shirk. "Artist Möllhausen in Oklahoma, 1853." Chronicles of Oklahoma 31 (Winter 1953-1954): 392-441.

Photographs of Indians

There have been a number of photographers who worked with American Indian subjects. The most important was Edward S. Curtis, whose photographs have been frequently reproduced.

9455. Anderson, John A. The Sioux of the Rosebud: A History in Pictures. Norman: University of Oklahoma Press, 1971. Photographs by John A. Anderson; text by Henry W. Hamilton and Jean Tyree Hamilton.

9456. Andrews, Ralph W. "He Knew the Red Man." Montana, the Magazine of Western History 14 (April 1964): 2-12. Edward S. Curtis.

9457. _____. "The 'Vanishing Race' of Edward S. Curtis." Beaver 294 (Autumn 1963): 46-49.

9458. Belous, Russell E., and Robert A. Weinstein. Will Soule, Indian Photographer at Fort Sill, Oklahoma, 1869-74. Los Angeles: Ward Ritchie Press, 1969.

9459. Brown, Mark H., and W. R. Felton. "L. A. Huffman: Brady of the West." Montana, the Magazine of Western History 6 (January 1956): 29-37.

9460. Coleman, A. D., and T. C. McLuhan. Portraits from North American Indian Life. New York: Outerbridge and Lazard and the American Museum of Natural History, 1972. Photographs by Edward S. Curtis.

9461. Curtis, Edward S. The North American Indian: Being a Series of Volumes Picturing and Describing the Indians of the United States, and Alaska. Edited by Frederick Webb Hodge. 20 volumes. 20 portfolios of numbered plates. Seattle: E. S. Curtis, 1907-1930.

9462. _____. "Vanishing Indian Types." Scribner's Magazine 39 (May 1906): 513-529; (June 1906): 657-671.

9463. Ewers, John C. "Thomas M. Easterly's Pioneer Daguerreotypes of Plains Indians." Bulletin of the Missouri Historical Society 24 (July 1968): 329-339.

9464. Ewing, Douglas C. "North American Indian in Forty Volumes: E. S. Curtis' The North American Indian." Art in America 60 (July 1972): 84-88.

9465. Fowler, Don D. In a Sacred Manner We Live: Photographs of the North American Indian by Edward S. Curtis. Barre, Massachusetts: Barre Publishers, 1972.

9466. Grinnell, George Bird. "Portraits of Indian Types." Scribner's Magazine 37 (March 1905): 259-273. Photographs of Edward S. Curtis.

9467. Holm, Ed. "Gertrude Käsabier's Indian Portraits." American West 10 (July 1973): 38-41.

9468. Jerome, Ward. "Karl Moon's Photographic Record of the Indian of Today." Craftsman 20 (April 1911): 24-32.

9469. Josephy, Alvin M., Jr. "The Splendid Indians of Edward R. Curtis." American Heritage 25 (February 1974): 40-59, 96-97.

9470. Rinehart, Frank A. The Face of Courage: The Indian Photographs of Frank A. Rinehart. Fort Collins, Colorado: Old Army Press, 1972.

9471. Scherer, Joanna Cohan. Indian Images: Photographs of North American Indians 1847-1928 from the Smithsonian Institution National Anthropological Archives. Washington: Smithsonian Institution Press, 1970.

9472. Scherer, Joanna Cohan, with Jean Burton Walker. Indians: The Great Photographs That Reveal North American Indian Life, 1847-1929, from the Unique Collection of the Smithsonian Institution. New York: Crown Publishers, 1973.

9473. Steward, Julian H. Notes on Hillers' Photography of the Paiute and Ute Indians Taken on the Powell Expedition of 1873. Smithsonian Miscellaneous Collections, volume 98, no. 18. Washington: Smithsonian Institution, 1939.

9474. Vincent, John R. "Midwest Indians and Frontier Photography." Annals of Iowa, 3d series 38 (Summer 1965): 26-35.

9475. Watson, Elmo Scott. "The Photographs of Sitting Bull." Westerners Brand Book (Chicago) 6 (August 1949): 43, 47-48.

9476. Webb, William, and Robert A. Weinstein. Dwellers at the Source: Southwestern Indian Photographs of A. C. Vroman, 1895-1904. New York: Grossman, 1973.

9477. Weinstein, Robert A. "The Man Who Photographed Indians." In Troopers West: Military and Indian Affairs on the American Frontier, edited by Ray Brandes, pp. 93-103. San Diego: Frontier Heritage Press, 1970. William S. Soule.

9478. Weinstein, Robert A., and Russell B. Belous. "Indian Portraits: Fort Sill, 1869." American West 3 (Winter 1966): 50-63. Work of William S. Soule.

9479. Zucker, Harvey. "1898: The Year the Indians Came to Omaha to Have Their Portraits Taken." Popular Photography 71 (October 1972): 96-120. Photographs by Frank Rinehart.

Indians in Movies

Movie portrayal of Indians has influenced images and stereotypes of the Indian. Listed here are works that discuss the Indian in films.

9480. French, Philip. "The Indian in the Western Movie." Art in America 60 (July-August 1972): 32-39.

9481. Friar, Ralph E., and Natasha A. Friar. The Only Good Indian: The Hollywood Gospel. New York: Drama Book Specialists, 1972.

9482. Georgakas, Dan. "They Have Not Spoken: American Indians in Film." Film Quarterly 25 (Spring 1972): 26-32.

9483. Lacey, Richard. "Alternatives to

Cinema Rouge." Media and Methods 7 (April 1971): 45, 70-71.

9484. Mantell, Harold. "Counteracting the Stereotype." American Indian 5 (Fall 1950): 16-20.

9485. Price, John A. "The Stereotyping of North American Indians in Motion Pictures." Ethnohistory 20 (Spring 1973): 153-171.

9486. Rice, Susan. "And Afterwards Take Him to a Movie." Media and Methods 7 (April 1971): 43-44, 71-72.

9487. Talbot, Anne. "Prejudice: Thoughts Garnered among the Navajo." Media and Methods 9 (December 1972): 36-37.

9488. Vestal, Stanley. "The Hollywooden Indian." Southwest Review 21 (July 1936): 418-423.

IDEAS ON RACE

The following works contain useful information about racial ideas in America, including how they affected Indian-white relations.

9489. Berry, Brewton. Race and Ethnic Relations. 3d edition. Boston: Houghton Mifflin Company, 1965.

9490. Binder, Frederick M. The Color Problem in Early National America as Viewed by John Adams, Jefferson and Jackson. The Hague: Mouton, 1968.

9491. Curtis, Wardon Allan. "Race Reversion in America." Arena 27 (January 1902): 47-54.

9492. Gossett, Thomas Frank. Race: The History of an Idea in America. Dallas: Southern Methodist University Press, 1963.

9493. Haller, John S., Jr. Outcasts from Evolution: Scientific Attitudes of Racial Inferiority, 1859-1900. Urbana: University of Illinois Press, 1971.

9494. Hansen, Klaus J. "The Millennium, the West, and Race in the Antebellum American Mind." Western Historical Quarterly 3 (October 1972): 373-390.

9495. Horsman, Reginald. "Scientific Racism and the American Indian in the Mid-Nineteenth Century." American Quarterly 27 (May 1975): 152-168.

9496. McWilliams, Carey. Brothers under the Skin. Boston: Little, Brown and Company, 1943.

9497. Muntz, Earl Edward. Race Contact. New York: Century Company, 1927.

9498. Parker, James R. "Paternalism and Racism: Senator John C. Spooner and

American Minorities, 1897-1907." Wisconsin Magazine of History 57 (Spring 1974): 195-200.

9499. Sinkler, George. The Racial Attitudes of American Presidents, from Abraham Lincoln to Theodore Roosevelt. Garden City, New York: Doubleday and Company, 1971.

9500. Stanton, William R. The Leopard's Spots: Scientific Attitudes toward Race in America, 1815-59. Chicago: University of Chicago Press, 1960.

9501. Stocking, George W., Jr. Race, Culture, and Evolution: Essays in the History of Anthropology. New York: Free Press, 1968.

9502. Tingley, Donald F. "The Rise of Racialistic Thinking in the United States in the Nineteenth Century." Ph.D. dissertation, University of Illinois, 1952.

CONTRIBUTIONS OF INDIANS TO AMERICAN LIFE

The impact of Indians on white society has been studied under various aspects-- language, foods, and political institutions among others. Useful guides to such studies are the following bibliographies.

9503. Vogel, Virgil J. "The American Indian Impact on History and Culture." In This Country Was Ours: A Documentary History of the American Indian, pp. 433-451. New York: Harper and Row, 1972.

9504. _____. "Bibliography: A Selected Listing." Indian Historian 1 (Summer 1968): 36-38.

Listed here are a number of studies dealing with the contributions of the Indians. Works about Indian place names--one of the obvious ways that Indian culture has made an impression--are listed under a separate heading below.

9505. Barry, J. Neilson. "Indian Words in Our Language." Quarterly of the Oregon Historical Society 16 (December 1915): 338-342.

9506. Beatty, Willard W. "Some Indian Contributions to Our Culture." Childhood Education 18 (April 1942): 353-356.

9507. Bolton, Reginald Pelham. Indian Paths in the Great Metropolis. Indian Notes and Monographs no. 23. New York: Museum of the American Indian, Heye Foundation, 1922.

9508. Brooks, Harlow. "The Contributions of the Primitive American to Medicine." In Medicine and Mankind, edited by

Iago Galdston, pp. 79-102. New York: D. Appleton-Century Company, 1936.

9509. Capron, Marjorie. "An All-American Thanksgiving Dinner." World Review 3 (November 22, 1926): 151.

9510. Chamberlain, Alexander F. "Algonkian Words in American English: A Study in the Contact of the White Man and the Indian." Journal of American Folk-Lore 15 (October-December 1902): 240-267.

9511. _____. "The Contributions of the American Indian to Civilization." Proceedings of the American Antiquarian Society 16 (October 1903): 91-126.

9512. Cohen, Felix S. "Americanizing the White Man." American Scholar 21 (Spring 1952): 177-191.

9513. Colton, Amy Richards. "The Red Man's Contribution to Our Household Art." Garden and Home Builder 44 (September 1926): 31-32, 62, 74.

9514. Crofut, Doris Andrews. "Food for Thought." American Indian 1 (Summer 1944): 26-29.

9515. Crosby, Alfred W., Jr. The Columbian Exchange: Biological and Cultural Consequences of 1492. Westport, Connecticut: Greenwood Publishing Company, 1972.

9516. Driver, Harold E. "The Contributions of the Indians to Modern Life." In The Americas on the Eve of Discovery, edited by Harold E. Driver, pp. 165-174. Englewood Cliffs, New Jersey: Prentice-Hall, 1964.

9517. Eastman, Charles A. "The Indian's Gifts to the Nation." Quarterly Journal of the Society of American Indians 3 (January-March 1915): 17-23.

9518. _____. "'My People': The Indians' Contribution to the Art of America." Red Man 7 (December 1914): 133-140.

9519. Edwards, Everett E. "American Indian Contributions to Civilization." Minnesota History 15 (September 1934): 255-272.

9520. Estabrook, Emma Franklin. Givers of Life: The American Indians as Contributors to Civilization. Albuquerque: University of New Mexico Press, 1931. Pueblo Indians.

9521. Fenton, William N. "Contacts between Iroquois Herbalism and Colonial Medicine." Annual Report of the Board of Regents of the Smithsonian Institution, 1941, pp. 503-526.

9522. Frachtenberg, Leo J. "Our Indebtedness to the American Indian." Wisconsin Archeologist 14 (July 1915): 64-69.

9523. Haas, Theodore H. "The Impact of the American Indian on American Life." Mid-west Journal 3 (Winter 1950-1951): 115-125.

9524. Hallowell, Alfred Irving. "The Backwash of the Frontier: Impact of the Indian on American Culture." Annual Report of the Board of Regents of the Smithsonian Institution, 1958, pp. 447-472.

9525. _____. "The Backwash of the Frontier: The Impact of the Indian on American Culture." In The Frontier in Perspective, edited by Walker D. Wyman and Clifton B. Kroeber, pp. 229-258. Madison: University of Wisconsin Press, 1957.

9526. _____. "The Impact of the American Indian on American Culture." American Anthropologist 59 (April 1957): 201-217.

9527. Herndon, C. A. "A Dinner from the Indians." Mentor 12 (March 1924): 52.

9528. Herndon, G. Melvin. "Indian Agriculture in the Southern Colonies." North Carolina Historical Review 44 (July 1967): 283-297.

9529. Houghton, Louise Seymour. Our Debt to the Red Man: The French-Indians in the Development of the United States. Boston: Stratford Company, 1918.

9530. Hulbert, Archer Butler. Indian Thoroughfares. Cleveland: Arthur H. Clark Company, 1902.

9531. _____. "The Indian Thoroughfares of Ohio." Ohio Archaeological and Historical Quarterly 8 (January 1900): 263-295.

9532. James, George Wharton. The Indians' Secret of Health; or, What the White Race May Learn from the Indians. New and enlarged edition. Pasadena, California: Radiant Life Press, 1917.

9533. Jones, Howard. "Our Government Patterned after Iroquois Confederacy." American Indian 1 (September 1927): 8-9, 16.

9534. McCluney, Eugene B. "Lacrosse: The Combat of the Spirits." American Indian Quarterly 1 (Spring 1974): 34-42.

9535. Ogg, Frederic Austin. "Indian Money in the New England Colonies." New England Magazine 27 (February 1903): 749-760.

9536. Page, J. F. "Our Debt to the Iroquois." Chronicles of Oklahoma 29 (Winter 1951-1952): 415-418.

9537. Russell, Jason Almus. "The Influence of Indian Confederations on the Union of the American Colonies." Journal of American History 22 (1928): 53-57, 78-85.

9538. Safford, William E. "Foods Discovered with America." Scientific Monthly 21 (August 1925): 181-186.

9539. _____. "Our Heritage from the Indians." Annual Report of the Board of Regents of the Smithsonian Institution, 1926, pp. 405-410.

9540. Sears, Louis Martin. "The Puritan and His Indian Ward." American Journal of Sociology 22 (July 1916): 80-93.

9541. Spinden, Herbert J. "Thank the American Indian." Scientific American 138 (April 1928): 330-332.

9542. Stump, Sarain. "Who Said Buffalo and Land Are All They Stole from Us?" Indian Historian 7 (Winter 1974): 6-7. Indian music.

9543. Trumbull, J. Hammond. "Words Derived from Indian Languages of North America." Transactions of the American Philological Association 3 (1872): 19-32.

9544. Underhill, Ruth. "What Do Whites Owe to Indians?" American Teacher 33 (February 1949): 11-13.

9545. Verrill, A. Hyatt. Foods America Gave the World. Boston: L. C. Page and Company, 1937.

9546. Vogel, Virgil J. "American Indian Influence on Medicine and Pharmacology." Indian Historian 1 (December 1967): 12-15.

9547. _____. American Indian Medicine. Norman: University of Oklahoma Press, 1970.

9548. Walker, Edwin F. "League of the Iroquois--the Inspiration for the United States of America." Masterkey 22 (July 1948): 135-137.

9549. Waters, Frank. "Words." Western American Literature 3 (Fall 1968): 227-234.

9550. Wilcox, Howard G. "Redskin Remedies: Contributions of the American Indian to Patent Medicines." Rocky Mountain Medical Journal 71 (January 1974): 29-33.

9551. Wissler, Clark. "Some Permanent Influences of Aboriginal Cultivation." In Readings in the Economic History of American Agriculture, edited by Louis Bernard Schmidt and Earle Dudley Ross, pp. 49-52. New York: Macmillan Company, 1925.

9552. Wright, Muriel H. "Contributions of the Indian People to Oklahoma." Chronicles of Oklahoma 14 (June 1936): 156-161.

INDIAN PLACE NAMES

One obvious contribution of the Indians is place names; from coast to coast there are Indian names on the land. The following bibliography includes an extensive listing of studies on Indian place names. More recent materials can be found in Names: Journal of the American Name Society.

9553. Sealock, Richard B., and Pauline A. Seely. Bibliography of Place-Name Literature, United States and Canada. 2d edition. Chicago: American Library Association, 1967.

Listed here are a number of publications dealing with Indian place names. They indicate the scope of the literature.

9554. Beauchamp, William M. Aboriginal Place Names of New York. Bulletin 108. Albany: New York State Museum, 1907.

9555. Becker, Donald W. Indian Place-Names in New Jersey. Cedar Grove, New Jersey: Phillips-Campbell Publishing Company, 1964.

9556. Childears, Lucille. "Montana Place Names from Indian Myth and Legend." Western Folklore 9 (July 1950): 263-264.

9557. Dobyns, Henry F. "Southwestern Chronicle: The Case of Paint vs. Garlic." Arizona Quarterly 11 (Summer 1955): 156-160.

9558. Douglas-Lithgow, R. A. Dictionary of American-Indian Place and Proper Names in New England. Salem, Massachusetts: Salem Press, 1909.

9559. Drew, Frank. "Florida Place-Names of Indian Origin." Florida Historical Society Quarterly 6 (April 1928): 197-205.

9560. _____. "Some Florida Names of Indian Origin." Florida Historical Society Quarterly 4 (April 1926): 181-182.

9561. Dunlap, A. R., and C. A. Weslager. Indian Place-Names in Delaware. Wilmington: Archaeological Society of Delaware, 1950.

9562. Eckstorm, Fannie Hardy. Indian Place-Names of the Penobscot Valley and the Maine Coast. Orono, Maine: University Press, 1941.

9563. Halbert, Henry S. "Choctaw Indian Names in Alabama and Mississippi," edited by T. M. Owen. Transactions of the Alabama Historical Society 3 (1898-1899): 64-77.

9564. Heisey, M. Luther. "Indian Names of Local Interest with Their Origin and Meaning." *Journal of the Lancaster County Historical Society* 76 (Trinity 1972): 169-172.

9565. Hemperley, M. R., ed. "Indian Place Names in Georgia." *Georgia Historical Quarterly* 57 (Winter 1973): 562-579.

9566. Huden, John C. "Additional Indian Place-Names." *Vermont History* 24 (April 1956): 168-169.

9567. _____. *Indian Place Names of New England.* New York: Museum of the American Indian, Heye Foundation, 1962.

9568. _____. "Indian Place-Names in Vermont." *Vermont History* 23 (July 1955): 191-203.

9569. _____. "Iroquois Place-Names in Vermont." *Vermont History* 25 (January 1957): 66-80.

9570. Jett, Stephen C. "An Analysis of Navajo Place-Names." *Names* 18 (September 1970): 175-184.

9571. Kenny, Hamill. *The Origin and Meaning of the Indian Place Names of Maryland.* Baltimore: Waverly Press, 1961.

9572. Kroeber, A. L. "California Place Names of Indian Origin." *University of California Publications in American Archeology and Ethnology* 12 (June 15, 1916): 31-69.

9573. Kuhm, Herbert W. "Indian Place-Names in Wisconsin." *Wisconsin Archeologist* 33 (March-June 1952): 1-157.

9574. Leland, J. A. C. "Indian Names in Missouri." *Names* 1 (December 1953): 266-273.

9575. Lobdell, Jared C. "Some Indian Place Names in the Bergen-Passaic Area." *Proceedings of the New Jersey Historical Society* 84 (October 1966): 265-270.

9576. Mahr, August C. "Indian River and Place Names in Ohio." *Ohio Historical Quarterly* 66 (April 1957): 137-158.

9577. Parsons, Usher. *Indian Names of Places in Rhode-Island.* Providence: Knowles, Anthony and Company, 1861.

9578. Powell, J. V., William Penn, and others. "Place Names of the Quileute Indians." *Pacific Northwest Quarterly* 63 (July 1972): 105-112.

9579. Read, William A. *Florida Place-Names of Indian Origin and Seminole Personal Names.* University Studies no. 11. Baton Rouge: Louisiana State University Press, 1934.

9580. _____. *Indian Place-Names in Alabama.* University Studies no. 29 Baton Rouge: Louisiana State University Press, 1937.

9581. _____. *Louisiana Place-Names of Indian Origin.* University Bulletin, volume 19, no. 2. Baton Rouge: Louisiana State University, 1927.

9582. _____. "More Indian Place-Names in Louisiana." *Louisiana Historical Quarterly* 11 (July 1928): 445-462.

9583. Ruttenber, E. M. *Footprints of the Red Men: Indian Geographical Names in the Valley of Hudson's River, the Valley of the Mohawk, and on the Delaware, Their Location and the Probable Meaning of Some of Them.* Newburgh, New York: New York State Historical Association, 1906.

9584. Rydjord, John. *Indian Place-Names: Their Origin, Evolution, and Meanings, Collected in Kansas from the Siouan, Algonquian, Shoshonean, Caddoan, Iroquoian, and Other Tongues.* Norman: University of Oklahoma Press, 1968.

9585. Skinner, Alanson. "Some Menomini Indian Place Names in Wisconsin." *Wisconsin Archeologist* 18 (August 1919): 97-102.

9586. Sneve, Virginia Driving Hawk. *Dakota's Heritage: A Compilation of Indian Place Names in South Dakota.* Sioux Falls, South Dakota: Brevet Press, 1973.

9587. Swanton, John R. "Indian Place Names." *American Speech* 12 (October 1937): 212-215.

9588. Tooker, William Wallace. *The Indian Place-Names on Long Island and Islands Adjacent, with Their Probable Significations.* New York: G. P. Putnam's Sons, 1911.

9589. Trumbull, J. Hammond. "The Composition of Indian Geographical Names, Illustrated from the Algonkin Languages." *Collections of the Connecticut Historical Society* 2 (1870): 1-50.

9590. _____. *Indian Names of Places, etc., in and on the Borders of Connecticut: With Interpretations of Some of Them.* Hartford, Connecticut, 1881.

9591. Verwyst, Chrysostom. "Geographical Names in Wisconsin, Minnesota, and Michigan Having a Chippewa Origin." *Collections of the State Historical Society of Wisconsin* 12 (1892): 390-398.

9592. Vogel, Virgil J. *Indian Place Names in Illinois.* Springfield: Illinois State Historical Society, 1963.

9593. Walton, Ivan. "Indian Place Names in Michigan." *Midwest Folklore* 5 (Spring 1955): 23-34.

PERSONS INFLUENTIAL IN INDIAN AFFAIRS

Listed here are biographical studies of

persons who influenced Indian affairs, even though their careers may not have been devoted directly or fully to Indian-white relations. Included also are studies on the influence of anthropologists on Indians and on Indian-white relations. The listings are not meant to be exhaustive.

9594. Abbott, Lyman. Reminiscences. Boston: Houghton Mifflin Company, 1915. Member of Lake Mohonk Conferences.

9595. Barton, D. R. "Biographer of the Indian." Natural History 45 (April 1940): 246-249, 253-254. Anthropologist Clark Wissler.

9596. Berthrong, Donald J. "Walter Stanley Campbell: Plainsman." Arizona and the West 7 (Summer 1965): 91-104. Historian of Indians and Indian affairs who wrote under the name Stanley Vestal.

9597. Bieder, Robert Eugene. "The American Indian and the Development of Anthropological Thought in the United States, 1780-1851." Ph.D. dissertation, University of Minnesota, 1972.

9598. Bingham, Edwin R. Charles E. Lummis, Editor of the Southwest. San Marino, California: Huntington Library, 1955. Crusader for Indian rights in the Southwest.

9599. Brown, Ira V. Lyman Abbott, Christian Evolutionist: A Study in Religious Liberalism. Cambridge: Harvard University Press, 1953. A leading member of the Lake Mohonk Conference.

9600. Chandler, Joan Mary. "Anthropologists and United States Indians, 1928-1960." Ph.D. dissertation, University of Texas, 1972.

9601. Clark, Dan Elbert. Samuel Jordan Kirkwood. Iowa City: State Historical Society of Iowa, 1917. Senator from Iowa and Secretary of the Interior, 1881-1882.

9602. Clark, J. Stanley. "Carolyn Thomas Foreman." Chronicles of Oklahoma 45 (Winter 1967-1968): 368-375. Historian of Oklahoma Indian affairs.

9603. _____. "Grant Foreman." Chronicles of Oklahoma 31 (Autumn 1953): 226-242. Historian of Indian affairs. Includes a bibliography of his writings.

9604. Clark, LaVerne Harrell. "The Indian Writings of Mari Sandoz: 'A Lone One Left from the Old Times.'" American Indian Quarterly 1 (Autumn 1974): 183-192.

9605. Dale, Edward E. "A Dedication to the Memory of Grant Foreman, 1869-1953." Arizona and the West 6 (Winter 1964): 271-274. Historian of Indian affairs.

9606. Davidson, William C. "Sam Houston and the Indians: A Rhetorical Study of the Man and the Myth." Ph.D. dissertation, University of Kansas, 1971.

9607. Debo, Angie. "A Dedication to the Memory of Carolyn Thomas Foreman, 1872-1967." Arizona and the West 16 (Autumn 1974): 215-218. Historian of Indians of Oklahoma.

9608. Dodge, D. Stuart. Memorials of William E. Dodge. New York: Anson D. F. Randolph and Company, 1887. Member of the Board of Indian Commissioners.

9609. Eggan, Fred. "Lewis H. Morgan and the Future of the American Indian." Proceedings of the American Philosophical Society 109 (October 1965): 272-276. Pioneer anthropologist.

9610. Ellis, Elmer. Henry Moore Teller: Defender of the West. Caldwell, Idaho: Caxton Printers, 1941. Senator from Colorado and Secretary of the Interior.

9611. Fowler, Don D., and Catherine S. Fowler. "John Wesley Powell, Anthropologist." Utah Historical Quarterly 37 (Spring 1969): 152-172.

9612. Fuess, Claude Moore. Carl Schurz, Reformer. New York: Dodd, Mead and Company, 1932. Secretary of the Interior, 1877-1881.

9613. Goldman, Eric F. Charles J. Bonaparte, Patrician Reformer: His Earlier Career. Johns Hopkins University Studies in Historical and Political Science, series 61, no. 2. Baltimore: Johns Hopkins Press, 1943. Member of the Board of Indian Commissioners.

9614. Gordon, Dudley. Charles F. Lummis: Crusader in Corduroy. Los Angeles: Cultural Assets Press, 1972. Crusader for Indian rights.

9615. Grinnell, George Bird. The Passing of the Great West: Selected Papers of George Bird Grinnell. New York: Winchester Press, 1972.

9616. Harris, Wilmer C. Public Life of Zachariah Chandler, 1851-1875. Lansing: Michigan Historical Commission, 1917. Secretary of the Interior, 1875-1877.

9617. Hazard, Joseph T. Companion of Adventure: A Biography of Isaac Ingalls Stevens, First Governor of Washington Territory. Portland, Oregon: Binfords and Mort, 1952.

9618. Hopkins, Alphonso A. The Life of Clinton Bowen Fisk. New York: Funk and Wagnalls, 1888. Member of the Board of Indian Commissioners.

9619. Kelsey, Harry. "A Dedication to the Memory of Annie Heloise Abel-

Henderson, 1873-1947." Arizona and the West 15 (Spring 1973): 1-4. A noted historian of Indian policy.

9620. Kinney, J. P. My First Ninety-Five Years. Hartwick, New York, 1972. Lawyer in the Bureau of Indian Affairs, concerned with Indian forests.

9621. Lowery, Charles Douglas. "James Barbour: A Politician and Planter of Ante-Bellum Virginia." Ph.D. dissertation, University of Virginia, 1966. Secretary of War, 1825-1828.

9622. Lowitt, Richard. A Merchant Prince of the Nineteenth Century: William E. Dodge. New York: Columbia University Press, 1954. Member of the Board of Indian Commissioners.

9623. Lyon, Thomas J. Frank Waters. New York: Twayne Publishers, 1973. Writer on Southwest Indians.

9624. Lurie, Nancy Oestreich. "The Lady from Boston and the Omaha Indians." American West 3 (Fall 1966): 31-33, 80-85. Alice C. Fletcher, pioneer ethnologist.

9625. McNickle, D'Arcy. Indian Man: A Life of Oliver La Farge. Bloomington: Indiana University Press, 1971. Writer on Indians.

9626. Marden, David L. "Anthropologists and Federal Indian Policy Prior to 1940." Indian Historian 5 (Winter 1972): 19-26.

9627. Maynard, Eileen. "The Growing Negative Image of the Anthropologist among American Indians." Human Organization 33 (Winter 1974): 402-404.

9628. Merriam, Harold G. "Sign-Talker with Straight Tongue: Frank Bird Linderman." Montana, the Magazine of Western History 12 (July 1962): 2-20. Writer on Indian subjects.

9629. Merrill, Horace Samuel. William Freeman Vilas: Doctrinaire Democrat. Madison: State Historical Society of Wisconsin, 1954. Secretary of the Interior, 1888-1889.

9630. Moorman, Donald R. "A Political Biography of Holm O. Bursum, 1899-1924." Ph.D. dissertation, University of New Mexico, 1962. Senator from New Mexico and sponsor of the Bursum Bill.

9631. Resek, Carl. Lewis Henry Morgan: American Scholar. Chicago: University of Chicago Press, 1960. Anthropologist.

9632. Schmiel, Eugene David. "The Career of Jacob Dolson Cox, 1828-1900: Soldier, Scholar, Statesman." Ph.D. dissertation, Ohio State University, 1969. Secretary of the Interior, 1869-1870.

9633. Slattery, Charles Lewis. Felix Reville Brunot, 1820-1898: A Civilian in the War for the Union, President of the First Board of Indian Commissioners. New York: Longmans, Green, and Company, 1901.

9634. Stuart, George Hay. The Life of George Hay Stuart, Written by Himself. Edited by Robert Ellis Thompson. Philadelphia: J. M. Stoddart, 1890. Member of the Board of Indian Commissioners.

9635. Swain, Dwight V. "A Dedication to the Memory of Walter Stanley Campbell, 1887-1957." Arizona and the West 7 (Summer 1965): 87-90. Historian of Indians and Indian affairs who wrote under the name Stanley Vestal.

9636. Talbot, Edith Armstrong. Samuel Chapman Armstrong: A Biographical Study. New York: Doubleday, Page and Company, 1904. Head of Hampton Institute.

9637. Trani, Eugene. "Hubert Work and the Department of the Interior, 1923-28." Pacific Northwest Quarterly 61 (January 1970): 31-40.

9638. Weatherford, John W. "Warren King Moorehead and His Papers." Ohio Historical Quarterly 65 (April 1956): 179-190. Author and member of Board of Indian Commissioners.

9639. Welsh, Herbert. "Samuel Chapman Armstrong." Educational Review 6 (September 1893): 105-125. Head of Hampton Institute.

9640. Wilbur, Ray Lyman. The Memoirs of Ray Lyman Wilbur, 1875-1949. Edited by Edgar Eugene Robinson and Paul Carroll Edwards. Stanford, California: Stanford University Press, 1960. Secretary of the Interior in the Hoover administration.

See also the sections on Indian agents and superintendents and general works on Indian affairs.

INDIAN WRITINGS

Since the Indians had no written language, nearly all sources on Indian-white relations have been written by the whites. Recently, however, more attention has been paid to writing down oral tradition and to writings by contemporary Indians. Listed here are a number of collections of writings by Indians and some articles about Indian literature.

9641. Armstrong, Virginia Irving, ed. I Have Spoken: American History through the Voices of the Indians. Chicago: Swallow Press, 1971.

9642. Astrov, Margot, ed. The Winged
Serpent: An Anthology of American Indian
Prose and Poetry. New York: John Day
Company, 1946.

9643. Brandon, William. "American Indian
Literature." Indian Historian 4 (Summer
1971): 53-55.

9644. Dillinham, Peter. "The Literature
of the American Indian." English Journal
62 (January 1973): 37-41.

9645. Hamilton, Charles, ed. Cry of the
Thunderbird: The American Indian's Own
Story. Norman: University of Oklahoma
Press, 1972. Original publication, New
York: Macmillan Company, 1950.

9646. Haslam, Gerald. "The Light That
Fills the World: Native American Literature." South Dakota Review 11 (Spring
1973): 27-41.

9647. _____. "Literature of the People:
Native American Voices." CLA Journal 15
(December 1971): 153-170.

9648. McLuhan, T. C., ed. Touch the Earth:
A Self-Portrait of Indian Existence.
New York: Outerbridge and Dienstfrey,
distributed by E. P. Dutton and Company,
1971.

9649. Moquin, Wayne, and Charles Van Doren,
eds. Great Documents in American Indian
History. New York: Praeger Publishers,
1973.

9650. Sanders, Thomas E., and Walter W.
Peek, eds. Literature of the American
Indian. Beverly Hills, California:
Glencoe Press, 1973.

9651. Smith, William F., Jr. "American
Indian Literature." English Journal 63
(January 1974): 68-72.

9652. Turner, Frederick W. III, ed. The
Portable North American Indian Reader.
New York: Viking Press, 1974.

9653. Vanderwerth, W. C., ed. Indian
Oratory: Famous Speeches by Noted Indian
Chieftains. Norman: University of Okla-
homa Press, 1971.

9654. Witt, Shirley Hill, and Stan Steiner,
eds. The Way: An Anthology of American
Indian Literature. New York: Alfred A.
Knopf, 1972.

See also the bibliographies by Hirschfelder (256) and by Marken (266).

ON THE WRITING OF INDIAN HISTORY

The history of Indian-white relations has
stimulated theoretical and historiographical
writings about the field.

Historiography

Listed here are analytical articles,
reviews of the literature, and discussion
of sources.

9655. Berkhofer, Robert F., Jr. "Native
Americans and United States History."
In The Reinterpretation of American
History and Culture, edited by William
H. Cartwright and Richard L. Watson, Jr.,
pp. 37-52. Washington: National Council
for the Social Studies, 1973.

9656. _____. "The Political Context
of a New Indian History." Pacific
Historical Review 40 (August 1971):
357-382.

9657. Bolt, Christine. "Return of the
Native: Some Reflexions on the History
of American Indians." Journal of
American Studies 8 (August 1974): 247-
259.

9658. Brandon, William. "American Indians
and American History." American West
2 (Spring 1965): 14-25, 91-93.

9659. Cauthers, Janet Helen. "The North
American Indian As Portrayed by American
and Canadian Historians, 1830-1930."
Ph.D. dissertation, University of Washington, 1974.

9660. Edmunds, R. David. "The Indian in
the Mainstream: Indian Historiography
for Teachers of American History Surveys." History Teacher 8 (February
1975): 242-264.

9661. Ewers, John C. "When Red and White
Men Met." Western Historical Quarterly
2 (April 1971): 132-150. Excerpts
printed in American Heritage 23 (December 1971): 107-108.

9662. _____. "The White Man's Strongest Medicine." Bulletin of the Missouri
Historical Society 24 (October 1967):
36-46.

9663. Fenton, William N. "Indian and White
Relations in Eastern North America: A
Common Ground for History and Ethnology."
In American Indian and White Relations
to 1830: Needs and Opportunities for
Study, pp. 3-27. Chapel Hill: Uni-
versity of North Carolina Press, 1957.

9664. Forbes, Jack D. "Frontiers in
American History and the Role of the
Frontier Historian." Ethnohistory 15
(Spring 1968): 203-235.

9665. _____. "The Historian and the
Indian: Racial Bias in American History." Americas 19 (April 1963): 349-
362.

9666. _____. "The Indian in the West:

A Challenge for Historians." <u>Arizona and the West</u> 1 (Autumn 1959): 206-215.

9667. Gibson, Arrell M. "Sources for Research on the American Indian." <u>Ethnohistory</u> 7 (Spring 1960): 121-136.

9668. Gilbert, Arthur N. "The American Indian and United States Diplomatic History." <u>History Teacher</u> 8 (February 1975): 229-241.

9669. Haan, Richard L. "Another Example of Stereotypes on the Early American Frontier: The Imperialist Historians and the American Indian." <u>Ethnohistory</u> 20 (Spring 1973): 143-152.

9670. Hagan, William T. "On Writing the History of the American Indian." <u>Journal of Interdisciplinary History</u> 2 (Summer 1971): 149-154.

9671. Harmond, Richard. "The Maverick and the Red Man: Richard Hildreth Views the American Indian." <u>History Teacher</u> 7 (November 1973): 37-47.

9672. Hoopes, Alban W. "The Need for a History of the American Indian." <u>Social Studies</u> 29 (January 1938): 26-27.

9673. Jacobs, Wilbur R. "The Indian and the Frontier in American History--a Need for Revision." <u>Western Historical Quarterly</u> 4 (January 1973): 43-56.

9674. _____. "Native American History: How It Illuminates Our Past." <u>American Historical Review</u> 80 (June 1975): 595-609.

9675. Keefe, Harry L. "How Shall the Indian Be Treated Historically." <u>Collections of the Nebraska State Historical Society</u> 17 (1913): 263-277.

9676. Kluckhohn, Clyde. "The Personal Document in Anthropological Science." In <u>The Use of Personal Documents in History, Anthropology, and Sociology</u>, pp. 79-173. Bulletin 53. New York: Social Science Research Council, 1945.

9677. Magnaghi, Russell M. "Herbert E. Bolton and Sources for American Indian Studies." <u>Western Historical Quarterly</u> 6 (January 1975): 33-46.

9678. "The Newberry Library Conference on Indian Studies." <u>Newberry Library Bulletin</u> 3 (October 1952): 30-36.

9679. Nichols, David A. "Civilization over Savage: Frederick Jackson Turner and the Indian." <u>South Dakota History</u> 2 (Fall 1972): 383-405.

9680. Olson, James C. "Some Reflections on Historical Method and Indian History." <u>Ethnohistory</u> 5 (Winter 1958): 48-59.

9681. Pargellis, Stanley. "The Problem of American Indian History." <u>Ethnohistory</u> 4 (Spring 1957): 113-124.

9682. _____. "The Problem of American Indian History." <u>Newberry Library Bulletin</u> 4 (March 1957): 129-138.

9683. Peckham, Howard H. "Indian Relations in the United States." In <u>Research Opportunities in American Cultural History</u>, edited by John Francis McDermott, pp. 30-45. Lexington: University of Kentucky Press, 1961.

9684. Prucha, Francis Paul. "New Approaches to the Study of the Administration of Indian Policy." In <u>Research in the Administration of Public Policy</u>, edited by Frank B. Evans and Harold T. Pinkett, pp. 147-152. Washington: Howard University Press, 1975. Also printed in Prologue: The Journal of the <u>National Archives</u> 3 (Spring 1971): 15-19.

9685. Rogin, Michael Paul. "Indian Extinction, American Regeneration." <u>Journal of Ethnic Studies</u> 2 (Spring 1974): 93-104.

9686. Washburn, Wilcomb E. "A Moral History of Indian-White Relations: Needs and Opportunities for Study." <u>Ethnohistory</u> 4 (Winter 1957): 47-61.

9687. _____. "Philanthropy and the American Indian: The Need for a Model." <u>Ethnohistory</u> 15 (Winter 1968): 43-56.

9688. _____. "The Writing of American Indian History: A Status Report." <u>Pacific Historical Review</u> 40 (August 1971): 261-281.

9689. Wax, Murray L. "The Whiteman's Burdensome 'Business': A Review Essay on the Change and Constancy of Literature on the American Indians." <u>Social Problems</u> 16 (Summer 1968): 106-113.

Ethnohistory

Anthropologists and historians, largely because of cooperation in preparing testimony for the Indian Claims Commission, have developed a new awareness of a common ground of interest, which is called "ethnohistory." Listed here are essays that discuss this field of study.

9690. Baerreis, David A. "The Ethnohistoric Approach and Archaeology." <u>Ethnohistory</u> 8 (Winter 1961): 49-77.

9691. Dorson, Richard M. "Ethnohistory and Ethnic Folklore." <u>Ethnohistory</u> 8 (Winter 1961): 12-30.

9692. Euler, Robert C. "Ethnohistory in the United States." <u>Ethnohistory</u> 19 (Summer 1972): 201-207.

9693. Fenton, William N. "Ethnohistory and Its Problems." Ethnohistory 9 (Winter 1962): 1-23.

9694. _____. "Field Work, Museum Studies, and Ethnohistorical Research." Ethnohistory 13 (Winter-Spring 1966): 71-85.

9695. Fogelson, Raymond D. "On the Varieties of Indian History: Sequoyah and Traveller Bird." Journal of Ethnic Studies 2 (Spring 1974): 105-112.

9696. Forbes, Jack D. "The Ethnohistorian in the Southwest." Journal of the West 3 (October 1964): 430-436.

9697. Gould, Richard A. "Indian and White Versions of 'The Burnt Ranch Massacre': A Study in Comparative Ethnohistory." Journal of the Folklore Institute 3 (June 1966): 30-42.

9698. Hudson, Charles. "Folk History and Ethnohistory." Ethnohistory 13 (Winter-Spring 1966): 52-70.

9699. Lurie, Nancy Oestreich. "Ethnohistory: An Ethnological Point of View." Ethnohistory 8 (Winter 1961): 78-92.

9700. Pearce, Roy Harvey. "From the History of Ideas to Ethnohistory." Journal of Ethnic Studies 2 (Spring 1974): 86-92.

9701. Rodabaugh, James H. "American Indian Ethnohistorical Materials in Ohio." Ethnohistory 8 (Summer 1961): 242-255.

9702. Sturtevant, William C. "Anthropology, History, and Ethnohistory." Ethnohistory 13 (Winter-Spring 1966): 1-51.

9703. "Symposium on the Concept of Ethnohistory--Comment." Ethnohistory 8 (Summer 1961): 256-280. Comments by Eleanor Leacock, John C. Ewers, and Charles A. Valentine.

9704. Washburn, Wilcomb E. "Ethnohistory: History 'In the Round.'" Ethnohistory 8 (Winter 1961): 31-48.

9705. Wheeler-Voegelin, Erminie. "History and Ethnohistory, and a Case in Point." In Men and Cultures: Selected Papers of the Fifth International Congress of Anthropological and Ethnological Sciences, Philadelphia, September 1-9, 1956, edited by Anthony F. C. Wallace, pp. 364-367. Philadelphia: University of Pennsylvania Press, 1960.

Index

Reference is to the serial numbers of the items in the bibliography except where page is specifically designated.

Alcoholism, 7159-7201, 7340. *See also*
Liquor trade
Alcorn, Gordon D., 4132-4133
Alcorn, Rowena L., 4132-4133
Alden, John Richard, 217, 381, 479
Alden, Timothy, 5522
Alderson, William A., 1201
Aldrich, Vernice M., 5205, 5358
Aldridge, Alfred O., 9260-9261
Alcatraz Island, Indians on, 2381, 2391,
2416, 2464, 2555, 2558, 2755
Aleshire, Ruth Cory, 4353
Aleuts, 6767
Alexander, A., 834
Alexander, Arch B., 6375
Alexander, H. B., 9046
Alexander, John R., 5895
Alexander, Rosemary, 6249
Alexander, Thomas G., 2609
Alford, Thomas Wildcat, 7817
Alfred, Braxton Marcellus, 7276
Alfred, Lorraine C., 9165
Algonquian Indians, 439, 7562. *See also*
East, Indians of
Allan, Ray A., 6584
Allen, C. M., 1045
Allen, Charles W., 8494
Allen, James, 3638
Allen, James B., 8853
Allen, James Michael, 8768
Allen, James R., 6704
Allen, John H., 5771
Allen, Penelope Johnson, 5523
Allen, R. V., 6686
Allen, Ronald Lorraine, 6198
Allen, T. D. [pseud.], 8659
Allen, Virginia Ruth, 6863
Alley, Ralph M., 7098
Alley, Robert D., 6250, 6705
Allis, Samuel, 5524
Allison, E. H., 8495
Allison, Shirley A., 7366
Allotment of land, 831-832, 1160, 1163,
1372, 1447, 3117-3137, 7225. *See also*
Dawes Act
Allouez, Claude Jean, 5349
Allred, B. W., 4160
Almquist, Alan J., 8787
Altboy, Anthony, 9125
Alter, J. Cecil, 4902, 5505
Alternative Press Index, 155
Altman, S. Morton, 6706
Altus, David M., 5976
Alvord, Clarence Walworth, 382-383, 2867
Alvord, Henry E., 1125
Amanullah, Mohammod, 7277
America: History and Life, 158
American Baptist Foreign Mission Society,
5198
American Bar Association, 5716
American Board of Commissioners for
Foreign Missions, 238, 5529, 5533, 5582,
5618, 5626, 5630, 5649, 5656, 5672.
See also Presbyterian missions
American Friends Service Committee, 5904
American Fur Company, 224, 233, 4847,

4849, 4862, 4866-4867, 4875, 9169
American Geographical Society of New
York, 191
American Heritage Book of Indians, 307
American Historical Review, p. 18.
American Indian (1926-1931), 288
American Indian (1943-1959), 289
American Indian Chicago Conference,
2398, 2433, 2481a, 2483
American Indian Civil Rights Handbook,
5772
American Indian Culture and Research
Journal, 294
American Indian Culture Center Journal,
294
American Indian Defense Association, 290
American Indian Ethnohistory Series,
1897-2243
American Indian Exposition, Oklahoma,
2370
American Indian Law Center, University
of New Mexico, 5710
American Indian Law Newsletter, 5710
American Indian Law Review, 5711
American Indian Lawyer Training Pro-
gram, 5713
American Indian Life, 290
American Indian Magazine, 291
American Indian Mission Association,
5175
American Indian Quarterly, 295
American Indian Treaty Series, p. 10
American Indian scholars, 364-365
American Indian Studies programs, 6849
Americanization, of Indians, 1414, 1489,
1605, 1651. *See also* Acculturation
American-Mexican relations. *See* Mexican-
American relations
American Philosophical Society, 98-99,
227
Americans Before Columbus, 296
American State Papers, 39
Amerindian, 297
Amers, George Walcott, Jr., 3715
Ames, David W., 2244
Ames, John G., 23
Ames, Michael, 8876
Amherst, Jeffery, 3332-3333
Amsden, Charles, 2768
Anastasio, Angelo, 2225
Anderson, Adrian S., 3978
Anderson, Charles A., 5525-5528, 5580
Anderson, Clinton P., 3815
Anderson, David H., 7508
Anderson, Donald Howard, 6199
Anderson, Duane, 7684
Anderson, Edward J., 7351
Anderson, Forrest H., 7136
Anderson, H. Dewey, 6200
Anderson, Harry H., 2626, 2734, 2883-
2884, 3841, 3994, 4076-4078, 8496, 9000
Anderson, Hattie M., 3655
Anderson, Irving W., 8827
Anderson, James, 4411, 5404
Anderson, James G., 6585
Anderson, John A., 9455

Chase, Lew Allen, 4360
Chateaubriand, Francois Rene de, 9277
Chattahoochee River, 599
Chavano, Chief, 4944
Chavers, Dean, 6721
Cheadle, John Begg, 3028
Checklist of U.S. Public Documents, 25
Checote, Samuel, 8137, 8142
Chehalis Indians, 2199-2200
Chehaw Affair, 3471
Chelan Indians, 2229
Chemehuevi Indians, 2166, 8807
Cherokee Agency Reserve, 3054
Cherokee archives, 217
Cherokee Cases, 734, 736, 763, 790, 797, 821, 829, 867
Cherokee Commission, 1181-1191
Cherokee delegations. *See* Political pamphlets
Cherokee deputation, in Seminole War, 3534
Cherokee Indians, 219, 485, 498, 517, 546, 549, 584, 610, 620, 703, 728, 802, 904, 913-914, 917, 956, 960, 1058, 1060, 2397, 2635, 2880, 3553, 3595, 7260, 7898-7987, 9094; biography, 7988-8042; economic development, 7354, 7482; education, 5994, 6012-6014, 6018, 6027-6028, 6035, 6047, 6066, 6157, 6168, 6530, 6608, 6640, 6727; health, 6865, 6914, 7053; land claims, 1969-1971, 3070; language, 6259, 6270; law, 5941, 5948, 5964-5965, 5967-5969, 5971; missions, 5087, 5089, 5117, 5160, 5177, 5189, 5196, 5200, 5457, 5474, 5537, 5572, 5654, 5659, 5663, 5689, 5938; and railroads, 1106, 1124; removal of, 729-730, 733-734, 738, 741, 756, 759, 763, 774, 777, 780, 797, 804-807, 810, 827, 843-844, 850; in Revolution, 3358, 3360, 3364; slavery among, 9012, 9015, 9028; trade with, 4801-4802, 4827; treaties with, 2877, 2914, 2952. *See also* Cherokee Commission; Five Civilized Tribes; Indian Territory; Political pamphlets
Cherokee Nation v. Georgia, 763, 867
Cherokee Neutral Lands, 1106
Cherokee Oil and Gas Company, 7523
Cherokee Orphan Asylum, 6052
Cherokee Outlet, 1054, 1062-1063, 1189-1190, 2859. *See also* Cherokee Strip
Cherokee Phoenix, 7940, 7951, 7958
Cherokee Question, 952
Cherokee Strip, 1092, 1105, 1115-1116. *See also* Cherokee Outlet
Cherokee Strip Live Stock Association, 2852, 2857-2858
Cherokee Tobacco Case, 5738
Cherokee War, 3263
Chesky, Jane, 8729
Chesley, A. J., 6913, 7047, 7082
Chester, Peter, 511
Chesterman, A. de M., 5122
Chew, John, 3388
Cheyenne-Arapaho Reservation, 2791, 2796, 2849, 2853
Cheyenne Indians, 691, 967-969, 1471,

1984-1988, 2651-2652, 3128, 3633, 3994, 4116, 4160-4166, 4340-4341, 4951, 5399-5400, 7164, 7205, 7436, 8268, 8316-8341, 8980, 9073, 9076, 9396
Cheyenne Reservation, 1732
Cheyenne River Agency, 1436, 2734, 8446
Cheyenne Transporter, 1048
Chicago, Indians in, 7292-7293, 7323
Chicago Conference. *See* American Indian Chicago Conference
Chicago Massacre, 3453
Chicago region, Indians of, 7714
Chicago Treaty (1821), 2984
Chicago Treaty (1833), 2922, 2975
Chickahominy, 7888
Chickamauga Indians, 614, 8136
Chickasaw Agency, 2756
Chickasaw Cession, 3107
Chickasaw-Choctaw Agreement, 2957
Chickasaw Indians, 513, 1970, 2695, 3134, 3596, 8043-8065, 8981, 9016; education, 5993, 5998, 6024, 6029, 6035, 6037-6038, 6058, 6069; missions, 5216, 5583-5586, 5605, 5628, 5665; removal of, 795, 820; treaties, 2869, 2958, 2991, 2996. *See also* Five Civilized Tribes; Political pamphlets
Chickasaw Nation, 931, 1093
Chickenpox, 7079
Chilcott, Winona Hunter, 2638
Child, Lydia Maria, 1003, 1280
Child, Sargent B., 97
Childears, Lucille, 9556
Chilocco, Oklahoma, 1122
Chilocco Indian School, 6659, 6705
Chinook Indians, 2237
Chippewa Cree Tribe, 1915
Chippewa Indians, 624, 1566, 1889, 1899-1918, 1922, 1925, 1933, 1941, 2247, 2777, 2974, 3808, 4339, 6651, 7197-7199, 7326-7328, 7718-7743, 8261, 9209; bibliography, 7718; education, 6220, 6685; health, 6958, 7026; missions, 5096, 5173, 5246, 5385, 5393, 5573, 5582; treaties, 2903, 2929, 2959, 2987, 6843
Chiricahua Apache Indians, 2062
Chisholm, Johnnie Bishop, 5424
Chittenden, Hiram Martin, 4911, 5230
Chivington, John M., 3831, 3836-3837, 8360
Choctaw Academy, 6039-6040, 6053, 6055, 6065
Choctaw Agency, 2735, 2755
Choctaw-Chickasaw Treaty, 2958
Choctaw delegation. *See* Political pamphlets
Choctaw Indians, 713, 819, 932, 1083, 1166, 1181, 2695, 2702, 2957, 3134, 5033, 5616, 5953, 7260, 8066-8111, 8981, 9016; education, 5995, 6026, 6032, 6035, 6039-6040, 6059; missions, 5042, 5057, 5109, 5256, 5298, 5411, 5551-5552, 5583-5586, 5602-5604, 5609, 5618, 5629, 5657; removal of, 583, 742-747, 824, 830. *See also* Five Civilized Tribes; Political pamphlets

De Valinger, Leon, Jr., 452
Devereaux, George, 7140-7141, 7162
DeVorsey, Louis, Jr., 493-494, 7858
De Voto, Bernard, 4915, 9394
De Vries, James, 6726
Dewey, Mary E., 1212, 1394-1395, 6144-6145
De Witt, John H., 3439
DeWolf, James M., 4111
Dexter, Henry Martyn, 3306
Dexter, Horatio S., 2892
Dezba, 8708
d'Harnoncourt, Rene, 7375
Dhegiha-Siouan Kansa. *See* Kansa Indians
Dial, Adolph, 8183-8184
Diaz, Albert James, 121
Dickason, David H., 7775
Dickeman, Mildred, 6727
Dickerson, Philip, 8417
Dickinson, Mrs. J. B., 1213
Dickinson, William, 3144, 3757
Dickson, John L., 7910
Dickson, Robert, 4851, 4887-4888
Diet and nutrition, 7030-7044
Dietrich, Margretta S., 8669
Diffenderffer, F. R., 4797
Digested Index to Executive Documents, 43
"Digest of Indian Treaties," 64
Diket, A. L., 9221
Dillard, Anthony Winston, 2904
Dilley, Russell, 2536-2537
Dillingham, Betty Ann Wilder, 7745
Dillinham, Peter, 9644
Dillon, John B., 7763
Dillon, Lee A., 3853
Dillon, Richard H., 3933, 3936-3939, 9286
DiMino, Angelo V., 6828
Dimock, Edmund, 6728
Dimock, Janet, 7225
Dippie, Brian W., 4011-4014, 9219-9220, 9287-9288
Discrimination. *See* Rights, of Indians
Diseases. *See* Health
Dismounting, of Sioux Indians, 4088
Dissertations, 279-283
District of Columbia, Indians of, 7883
Dixon, James W., 3854
Dixon, Joseph K., 1541-1542
Dizmang, Larry H., 7205-7206, 7209, 7213
Dlugokinski, Eric, 6729-6730
Dobak, William A., 4090
Dobie, J. Frank, 1202, 9050-9051
Dobyns, Henry F., 1750-1751, 2090, 2098, 3035, 7376, 8544, 8586-8587, 8638, 8670, 8727, 8988-8989, 9078, 9557
Dockstader, Alice W., 281
Dockstader, Frederick J., 280-281
Doctors among the Indians, 7053-7068
Documents, collections of, 375-380
Dodd, Jack, 3703-3704
Doddridge, Joseph, 3259
Dodge, D. Stuart, 9608
Dodge, Henry, 3490, 3623, 3632, 3634
Dodge, Henry Chee, 8662, 8705
Dodge, Marjorie T., 6731
Dodge, Richard Irving, 1396-1397
Dodge, William E., 9608, 9622

Doerner, Rita, 4700
Doherty, Herbert J., Jr., 3532
Doherty, Matthew F., 6732
Doig, Ivan, 5364
Dolan, Thomas A., 2905
Dolan, W. W., 6427
Dole, William P., 883-884, 887
Dollar, Clyde D., 2538-2539, 8445
Domestic and Foreign Missionary Society
    of the Protestant Episcopal Church, 5365
Dominick, David, 8831
Donaldson, Thomas C., 9395
Dondore, Dorothy Anne, 9147
Donehoo, George P., 1543
Donnelly, James F., 2540
Donnelly, Joseph P., 4782, 5012, 5234-5237
Donnelly, Ralph W., 3165, 4101
Donnelly, William Patrick, 5238-5239
Donohue, Arthur Thomas, 5240
Doolittle, James R. 970-971, 985
Doolittle Report, 971, 985
Doolittle Survey, 970
Dorchester, Daniel, 6111
Doris Duke Oral History Collection, 186
Dorman, Isaiah, 4018, 4045
Dorn, Christopher M., 6968
Dorn, Edward, 8832
Dorner, Peter, 2408
Dorr, Henry C., 7568
Dorr, L. L., 4282a
Dorson, Richard M., 9691
Doster, Frank, 3855
Doster, James F., 1974-1975, 3440
Doty, James Duane, 4733
Dougherty, Dolorita Marie, 4916
Dougherty, John, 2682, 2717
Dougherty, Peter, 5526, 5667
Dougherty, W. E., 4295
Douglas, Damon G., 9179
Douglas, Ephriam, 616
Douglas-Lithgow, R. A., 9558
Douglass, Elisha P., 8119
Dove Creek, Battle of, 939
Downes, Randolph C., 528, 584-588, 1639, 1812, 1868, 3342, 3356, 4798
Downey, Fairfax, 3166-3169, 4701
Downing, A., 1060
Downing, Finis E., 9201
Downing, Lewis, 8029
Downing, Lewis Jackson, 6359
Dowling, John H., 7287, 7692
Dowling, Thomas F., 5829
Downs, James F., 7226, 7498-7499, 8671, 8778-8779
Doyle, Barrie, 2541
Doyle, Cornelius J., 3170
Dozier, Edward P., 7163, 7227-7228, 8545, 8739-8743
Dozier, Jack, 2795, 3118, 3705, 8939
DQU, 6428
Dragoo, Benjamin Crawford, 3644
Dragoons, 3480, 3589, 3592, 3598-3599, 3605, 3608, 3620, 3624, 3630-3631, 3636
Drake, Benjamin, 7798, 7819

Fort Larned, 4485
Fort Leavenworth, 4444, 4472-4473, 4487
Fort Leavenworth-Fort Gibson Military
  road, 3581
Fort Lewis, 4540
Fort Lincoln, 4511
Fort Loudoun, 3263
Fort McDowell Indian community, 2517
Fort McIntosh, 4352, 4373, 4398
Fort McKavett, 4505
Fort Mackinac, 4354
Fort McPherson, 4474
Fort Madison, 4381, 4407
Fort Marion, 3561, 3578, 4207, 4231, 4285
Fort Martin Scott, 4526
Fort Massac, 4358-4359
Fort Massachusetts, 3678, 4547
Fort Miami, 4355
Fort Miller, 4583-4584
Fort Mims, 3440
Fort Mims Massacre, 3459
Fort Missoula, 4418, 4475
Fort Mitchell (Alabama), 705
Fort Mitchell (Nebraska), 4456-4457
Fort Mojave, 4539
Fort Osage, 4411, 4436
Fort Peck Reservation, 2812
Fort Phantom Hill, 4517, 4530
Fort Phil Kearny, 3911, 3922, 4419, 4479
Fort Pueblo Massacre, 3666
Fort Randall, 4458, 4478
Fort Rawlins, 4452
Fort Reynolds, 4483
Fort Rive, 4460
Fort Richardson, 4501, 4510, 4537
Fort Riley, 4396
Fort Ripley, 4397, 4404
Fort Robinson, 3294, 4165, 4435, 4468
Forts. *See* Military posts; *and individ-
  ual forts*
Fort Saginaw, 4361-4362
Fort St. Clair, 4400
Fort Sanford, 4370
Fort Scott, 3581
Fort Sedgwick, 4425
Fort Selden, 4545
Fort Sidney, 4422
Fort Sill, 4496-4497, 4515, 4527, 4536,
  9458
Fort Sill Apache Indians, 8596
Fort Simcoe, 4580-4581, 4585
Fort Sisseton, 4443
Fort Smith, 1148, 2735, 4413, 4416-4417,
  4439
Fort Snelling, 4374, 4377-4380, 4383-4385
Fort Stanton, 4283, 4552
Fort Stanwix, 3365
Fort Stanwix, Treaty of (1768), 537, 2867-
  2868
Fort Stanwix, Treaty of (1784), 2966, 2976
Fort Stevens, 4483
Fort Stevenson, 4461
Fort Stockton, 4518
Fort Sully, 4441
Fort Sumner, 2834, 4563, 4572
Fort Supply, 4498
Fort Tejon, 4597

Fort Thorn, 4553
Fort Totten 4426, 4490
Fort Townsend, 4579
Fort Towson, 4523
Fort Tulerosa, 4554, 4559
Fort Umpqua, 4578
Fort Union (Dakota), 4968
Fort Union (New Mexico), 4555, 4557, 4573-
  4574, 4577
Fort Vasquez, 4933
Fort Wadsworth, 4430
Fort Wallace, 4445, 4463
Fort Walsh, 2884
Fort Washington, 4386
Fort Washita, 4524
Fort Wayne, 2666, 4376, 4410
Fort Wayne, Treaty of, 2889, 2932
Fort Webster, 4565
Fort Wilkins, 4360, 4363-4364
Fort Wingate, 4563
Fort Winnebago, 4405
Fort Wise, 4484
Fort Worth, 4520
Fort Yates, 2765
Fortuine, Robert, 6861
Foster, Ashley, 6740
Foster, Augustus J., 9214
Foster, Frank Hugh, 5573
Foster, George E., 7919, 8013
Foster, James Monroe, Jr., 4558
Foster, Laurence, 9014
Foster, Stanley O., 7086
Foster, William Amer, 2654
Fougera, Katherine Gibson, 4673
Foulke, William Dudley, 8129
Foulks, E. F., 7142
Fountain, Samuel W., 4238
Four Bears, 8396
Four Corners, 2602, 7424
Fourteenth Amendment, and Indian citizen-
  ship, 1162, 5764
Fowler, Arlen L., 3181
Fowler, Catherine S., 8820, 9611
Fowler, Don D., 8820, 8833-8834, 9465,
  9611
Fowler, Jo Ann V., 2550
Fowler, Loretta Kay, 8295
Fox, Andrew, 8520
Fox, Carroll, 7109
Fox, L. Webster, 7087-7089
Fox Indians. *See* Sac and Fox Indians
Frachtenberg, Leo J., 9522
Francis, C. F., 7779
Francis, Convers, 5127
Francis, Milly, 8117
Frank, Glenn, 1552
Franklin, Benjamin, 2866, 9260-9261, 9270
Franklin, J. L., 5015
Franklin, Marvin L., 7387
Franklin, W. Neil, 4800-4803
Franks, Kenny A., 920, 922-923, 1404,
  2917-2918, 7920, 8014
Fraps, Clara Lee, 8639
Frauds, 3092, 3137
Fray, John S., 4028
Frazer, Jack, 8528
Frazer, Robert W., 4345

Hawley, Florence, 6562, 8748. *See also* Ellis, Florence H.
Haworth, James M., 2672
Hawthorne, H. E., 4300
Hawthorne, Nathaniel, 9353
Hay, Thomas Robson, 4619
Hayden, Ralston, 2930
Hayden, Willard C., 3604
Hayden, William G., 7395
Hayes, E. M., 3646
Hayes, Jess G., 8627
Hayes, Rutherford B., 973
Hayes, Susanna Adella, 6005
Hayfield Fight, 3907, 3912
Haygood, William Converse, 5683
Hayne, Barrie, 9305
Hayner, Norman S., 5927
Hayter, Earl W., 1032
Haywood, John, 7865
Hazard, Joseph T., 9617
Hazen, William B., 4631-4632, 4645
Head, Frank H., 1293
Head, Sylvia, 764
Head, T. B., 852
Head Start, 6686, 6794
Health: alcoholism, 7159-7201; bibliographies, 6861-6862; diet and nutrition, 7030-7044, 7046; diseases, 7069-7080; doctors, 7053-7068, 8949; education, 7045-7052; general studies, 6863-6888; health services, 6866, 6949-7029; mental health, 7136-7158; studies and comments (1901-1920), 6889-6896; studies and comments (1921-1940), 6897-6911; studies and comments (1941-1960), 6912-6934; studies and comments (1961--), 6935-6948; suicide, 7202-7214; trachoma, 7081-7097; tuberculosis, 7098-7135
Health career opportunities, 6389
Health professions, 365
Healy, George R., 9228
Heard, Isaac V. C., 3777
Heard, J. Norman, 9149
Hearings, 48-51
Heart, Jonathan, 3384
Heaston, Michael D., 2670, 5017
Heath, Dwight B., 7171
Heath, G. Louis, 2555
Heath, Gary N., 928
Heath, Herschel, 3447
Heatherly Incident, 3609
Heathman, James E., 5976
Hebal, John James, 2617
Hebard, Grace Raymond, 3916, 8835
Heckewelder, John, 239, 457, 5481, 5500, 9375
Hedgepeth, William, 2416-2417
Hedrick, Wiley O., 6454
Hegemann, Elizabeth Compton, 4945
Heger, Nancy Irene, 6471
Heil, Anna Rose Octavia, 4047
Heilbron, Bertha L., 2931
Heimann, Robert K., 5738
Heineman, A. H., 1431
Heineman, John L., 2932
Heinzman, George M., 3872
Heirship problem, 3012, 3085

Heisey, M. Luther, 9564
Heizer, Robert F., 254, 2147, 8784-8788, 8796
Helderman, Leonard C., 3398
Hell Gate Treaty, 2898
Helper, Malcolm M., 6624
Hembree, Captain, 3691
Hembree, Waman C., 3713
Hemingway, Peter, 6662
Hemperly, Marion R., 2671, 9565
Henderson, Alice Corbin, 1698
Henderson, Archibald, 2871
Henderson, Earl E., 6835
Henderson, Harry McCorry, 3647
Henderson, Rose, 6431
Hendra, Richard I., 6361
Hendricks, Allen, 1089
Hendrie, Hugh C., 7143
Heneveld, Edward H., 6769
Henning, Dale R., 2023
Henning, Marilyn Jadene, 7302
Henninger, Daniel, 6626
Henningsen, Charles F., 4041
Henrichs, James R., 2171
Henrikson, Craig Ernest, 8676
Henry, Delaura, 8083
Henry, James D., 3490, 3506
Henry, Jane, 500
Henry, Jeannette, 261, 2418, 5984, 6836-6840
Henry, Jules A., 6563, 6682
Henry, Thomas Robert, 7669
Henry, William E., 8462
Henshaw, Henry W., 1561
Henslick, Harry, 2933
Heritage, William, 7484-7485
Hermilt, John, 1699
Hermann, Ruth, 8822
Herndon, C. A., 9527
Herndon, G. Melvin, 9528
Heron, Francis, 4963
Herriott, F. I., 3744
Hertzberg, Hazel W., 6841, 9086
Hesketh, John, 7727
Hesse, Frank G., 7036
Hester, Joseph A., Jr., 2145, 2160
Hetrick, Barbara, 2566
Hewes, Leslie, 7928-7933
Hewitt, J. N. B., 7632
Hewlett, Leroy, 255
Hey, Nigel S., 2419
Heyer, Claude Herbert, 7396
Heyman, Max L., Jr., 3822, 4620
Hiatt, Burritt M., 2672
Hiawatha, 7631, 7668-7670, 9284, 9343, 9370
Hibbetts, J. H., 1294
Hickerson, Harold, 1900, 1902, 1904, 1907, 2040, 4766, 5582, 7728-7731
Hicks, Elijah, 646
Hicks, George L., 7866
Hicks, J. C., 8017
Hidatsa Indians, 8258, 8266
Hieb, David L., 4440
Hiemstra, William L., 5583-5586
High Bull, 4119
Higher education, 6422-6449

Hopkins, Richard C., 3823
Hopkins, Thomas R., 6272, 6628
Hopkins, Vivian C., 7635
Hopper, W. L., 4518
Horan, James D., 9416
Horn, Stanley F., 3540
Hornblower, William B., 5741
Horr, David Agee, p. 86
Horse, John, 8244
Horses, and Indians, 9046-9071
Horseshoe Bend, Battle of, 3448-3449, 3455, 3470
Horsman, Reginald, 601-605, 767, 3399, 3450-3451, 9495
Horton, L. W., 930
Hoshiwara, Isao, 6974
Hoskaninni-begay, 8681
Hosmer, S. R., 4120
Hospitals. *See* Health, health services
Hosteen, Klah, 8702
Hough, Alfred L., 4079
Hough, Emerson, 1562
Hough, Franklin B., 606, 3312, 3329
Hough, Henry W., 7397
Hough, Robert L., 9306
Hough, Walter, 8641
Houghton, Frederick, 2806, 7636
Houghton, Louise Seymour, 9529
Houghton, N. D., 5742, 5783
Houghton, Ruth Edna Meserve, 2807
Houlihan, Patrick T., 6755
Houma Indians, 7860
House, Lloyd Lynn, 6433
House, R. Morton, 5182
Houser, Nicholas P., 8749
Housing, 7449
Houston, Sam, 7916, 7923, 7937
Houts, Kathleen C., 9229
Howard, Guy, 1297
Howard, Harold Charles, 5074
Howard, Harold P., 8836
Howard, Helen Addison, 2679, 3714, 7670, 8837, 8942
Howard, Homer H., 6222
Howard, James H., 1780, 7537, 7732, 8270, 8448, 8512, 9088
Howard, Oliver O., 4141, 4150, 4157, 4178-4179, 4267, 4302, 4602, 4623, 8943
Howard, R. Palmer, 6865, 7936, 8172
Howard-Neighbors controversy, 2684
Howe, George, 3313
Howe, George Frederick, 4102
Howe, M. A. DeWolfe, 5373-5374
Howe, Orlando C., 3745
Howell, Edgar M., 3874
Howell, Elmo, 9307
Howell, Erle, 5444
Howling Wolf, 8330
Hoyt, Elizabeth E., 6629-6630, 7144
Hoyt, Epaphras, 3266
Hoyt, Milton, 6007
Hoyt, William D., 3541
Hrdlicka, Ales, 1563, 6893, 7111
Hryniewicki, Richard J., 2935-2936
Hualapai Indians, 1521, 2097-2101, 8553, 8558
Hubach, Robert R., 201-202

Hubbard, J. Niles, 7671
Hubbard, Jeremiah, 5677
Hubbard, William, 3314, 3321
Hubbell, Jay B., 9311-9312
Hubbell, John Lorenzo, 4901
Huber, John P., 3400
Huck, Susan L. M., 2556
Huddleston, Eugene L., 9313
Huden, John C., 7572, 9566-9569
Hudson, Charles M., 7867-7869, 9698
Hudson, George, 8094
Hudson, Peter J., 5018, 8085, 8107, 8180
Hudson's Bay Company, 3684
Huffman, James, 5075
Huffman, L. A. 9459
Huggins, E. L., 1432
Huggins, Eli, 4100
Hughes, J. Donald, 6842
Hughes, Jack Thomas, 1999
Hughes, Robert P., 4103
Hughes, Thomas, 2937, 3746, 8513
Hughes, W. J., 3606
Hughes, William, 1818
Hughes, Willis B., 3607-3609
Hulbert, Archer Butler, 9530-9531
Hulbert, Winifred, 1700
Hull, Jacob, 813
Hull, Lewis Byram, 3917
Hull, Myra E., 3917
Hulsizer, Allan, 6223, 6512-6513
Hultkrantz, Ake, 2177-2178, 8838
Humitarian soldiers, 4612-4613
Humanities Index, 151
Hume, C. Ross, 2747, 5076
Hummel, Edward A., 4443
Hummer, H. R., 7145-7146
Humphrey, Heman, 853
Humphrey, Norman D., 5952
Humphrey, Seth K., 317, 1092
Humphreys, A. Glen, 2938
Humphreys, Mary Gay, 5077
Humphreys, R. A., 396-397
Hunnewell, James F., 5591
Hunnius, Ado, 1109
Hunt, Aurora, 4624
Hunt, Elizabeth H., 5592
Hunt, Elvid, 4444
Hunt, Frazier, 4030
Hunt, George T., 7637
Hunt, H. F., 9039
Hunt, Jack, 2808
Hunt, R. Douglas, 4445
Hunt, Robert, 4030
Hunt, Samuel F., 2939, 3401
Hunter, Charles E., 7599
Hunter, H. Chadwick, 9417
Hunter, J. D., 854
Hunter, J. Marvin, 3644
Hunter, John D., 6875-6876
Hunter, John Dunn, 9148
Hunter, Nathaniel Wyche, 3576
Hunter, Walter S., 6341
Hunter, William A., 458, 3267, 4810, 7600, 7835
Hunting and fishing rights, 2377, 5903-5917
Huntington, C. A., 1433

Savage, W. Sherman, 1121
Savage, William W., Jr., 1122-1123, 2857-2859
Savard, Robert Joseph, 7189-7190
Sawyer, Robert W., 2319
Sawyer, Sophia, 6041
Sawyer's Expedition, 3914
Sayenqueraghta, 7662
Saylor, Robert, 7130
Sayr, Hal, 3838
Sayre, Blaine M., 7006
Scaife, H. Lewis, 7884
Scalps, trade in, 693, 3676-3677
Scanlan, Peter L., 2710, 4401
Schaab, William C., 7479
Schaeffer, Claude E., 5106, 5331, 5464
Schafer, Joseph, 5257
Schaus, Richard G., 7507
Schellie, Don, 4270
Scherer, Joanna Cohan, 9471-9472
Schermerhorn, John Freeman, 823
Schermerhorn, R. A., 2356
Schifter, Richard, 354, 2982, 3072-3073, 7442
Schilling, Frank A., 4570
Schimberg, Albert P., 5332
Schlafman, Irving H., 7007
Schlesier, Karl H., 8336
Schlesinger, Sigmund, 3875
Schlick, Mary D., 6401
Schlup, Emil, 5465
Schmaier, Maurice D., 9360
Schmeckebier, Laurence F., 19, 2604
Schmidlin, Lois L. Nelsen, 9061
Schmidt, William F., 118
Schmieding, O. A., 6402
Schmiel, Eugene David, 9632
Schmitt, Karl, 3974
Schmitt, Martin, 130, 3218, 4606
Schnur, Leo, 7008
Schoenberg, Wilfred P., 5333-5336
Schoenberger, Dale T., 4058, 4271
Schoenfeld, Lawrence S., 7009
Schoenfuhs, Walter P., 5395
Schoenmakers, John, 5269
Scholder, Fritz, 9438
Schomburg, Arthur A., 5466
Schonbach, Samuel, 2580
Schoolcraft, Henry Rowe, 2692, 2711, 4733, 4751, 7546, 7651, 9144
Schools, Indian, 1460, 1495. *See also* Education
Schork, M. Anthony, 6957
Schramm, Wilber Lang, 9361
Schroeder, Albert H., 2051-2053, 2062-2063, 2141, 8561-8562
Schroeder, Louis C., 1839
Schroeder, Richard C., 2581
Schulenberg, Raymond F., 8285
Schulte, Marie Louise, 4059
Schultes, Richard Evans, 9118
Schultheis, Rose, 2983
Schultz, George A., 5197
Schultz, Hart Merriam, 8307
Schultz, John Lawrence, 7255
Schultz, Terri, 2582
Schultze, James Willard, 1721

Schulz, Larold K., 2472
Schurmacher, Emile C., 7443
Schurz, Carl, 1035-1037, 1039, 1377, 1468, 1497, 9612
Schusky, Ernest L., 18, 2473, 2747, 2759, 5107, 5813, 8478-8482, 9100
Schusky, Mary Sue, 18
Schwartz, Henrietta, 6612
Schwarze, Edmund, 5494
Schwechten, John L., 7444
Schwegmann, George A., 163
Sclar, Lee J., 5794
Scobee, Barry, 4534
Scott, Charles A., 3857
Scott, E. D., 4321
Scott, George W., 57
Scott, Hugh L., 1722, 8298
Scott, John Albert, 3365
Scott, Kenneth, 2875
Scott, Leslie M., 5645, 6883
Scott, Loren C., 6403, 7445
Scott, Nancy E., 5495
Scott, Walter, 9305
Scott, Winfield, 3488, 3562, 3727, 4608, 4649
Scouts, Indian, 4028, 4058, 4640, 4696-4723, 8608, 8980
Scoville, Annie Beecher, 1626
Scullin, Michael, 2475
Sculpture, Indians in. *See* Indians in painting and sculpture
Seabrook, S. L., 3633
Seagrove, James, 618
Sealock, Richard B., 9553
Searle, January, 3806
Sears, Kelley D., 5878
Sears, Louis Martin, 9540
Sears, Paul M., 4993
Seattle, 3692, 3709, 3723, 7279
Seattle, Chief, 8878
Seboyetanos, 3671
Sebring, F. M. 3733
Secessionists, Indians as, 892
Secondary school students, 273
Secondary school teachers, 268
Second Seminole War, 3514-3578
Secretary of the Interior, 75
Secretary of War, 74
Sectarian schools. *See* Church-state relations
Seely, Pauline A., 9553
Seelye, Lillie Eggleston, 7663, 7820
Sefton, James E., 9029
Seger, John Homer, 6063, 6169, 8337
Segundo, Thomas A., 7237, 8731
Seiber, Richard A., 5467
Seiler, Grace, 3300
Sekaquaptewa, Helen, 8650
Selam, Leroy B., 6797
Selander, Kenneth J., 1886
Selden, George B., Jr., 3285
Selective Service, 7074
Selenium, 4075
Self, Nancy Hope, 1124
Self, Zenobia, 4124
Self-determination, 2553. *See also* Legal status; Self-government

441

Smith, William Rudolph, 2987
Smithson, Thomas L., 5871
Smithsonian Institution, 117. *See also*
  Bureau of American Ethnology
Smitter, Wessel, 8529
Smoot, Joseph G., 5647
Smoyer, Stanley C., 3287
Snake Indians, 2172
Snake Mountain, Battle of, 4121
Snana, 3807
Sneed, R. A., 4996
Snell, William Robert, 9043
Sneve, Virginia Driving Hawk, 9586
Snider, James G., 6352
Sniffen, Matthew K., 1234, 1630-1632,
  1654, 1729
Snodgrass, Marjorie P., 7348
Snohomish Indians, 2195
Snook, George A., 3324
Snow, Albert J., 6806-6807, 9130
Snow, C. O., 2835
Snow, D. Rebecca, 2410
Snow, Fred, 3988
Snyder, Peter Z., 7334-7336
Snyderman, George S., 235-236, 3288,
  5697, 7623
Socialization. *See* Acculturation
Social Sciences and Humanities Index, 151
Social Sciences Index, 151
Social workers, 1707
Society for Promoting and Propagating
  the Gospel in New England, 5124
Society for Propagating the Gospel among
  the Indians and Others in North Amer-
  ica, 5591
Society for the Propagation of the Gospel
  in Foreign Parts, 5136, 5139-5140
Society of American Indians, 291
Society of Friends. *See* Quakers
Sociological perspectives, 361
Sociologists, and Indians, 2594
Socolofsky, Homer E., 3111
Socwell, Clarence P., 4997
Sohon, Gustavus, 9402
Soldier and Brave, 3201
Soldiers, 3148-3149, 3160, 3212-3213,
  3225, 3386-3387; Indians as, 1484,
  3173, 3177, 3215, 3220
Somers, Douglas E., 5807
Sommermier, Eloise, 6341
Sommers, Richard J., 136
Sonderegger, Richard P., 521
Sondheim, Harry B., 5895
Sondheimer, Henry M., 7013
Sonnenberg, Maurice, 7480
Sonnichsen, C. L., 8607
Sonosky, Marvin J., 5856, 7528
Sooners, 1053
Sorber, Edna C., 9253
Sorkin, Alan L., 3018, 6683, 7337, 7447,
  7481
Sosin, Jack M., 418, 564, 3347, 3367
Soule, William S., 9458, 9477-9478
South, Charles E., 4
South, Indians of, 558, 580-581, 595,
  600, 7847-8256

South Carolina, colonial Indian affairs,
  505, 507-508
Southern Apache Agency, 2750
Southern Boundary Commission, 599
Southern Cheyenne Indians. *See* Cheyenne
  Indians
Southern colonies, Indian affairs in, 479-
  524
Southern Historical Collection, 126
Southern Plains Indians, 687, 998
Southwest, Indians of, 686, 8537-8766
Southwest, Old. *See* Old Southwest
Southwestern American Indian Society, 295
Southwestern Indian Polytechnic Institute,
  6407
Southwest Indian Report, 5798
Southwest Indian wars, 3655-3681. *See
  also* Apache Indians, wars; Navajo
  Indians, wars
Southwest Territory, Indian affairs in,
  588
Sovereignty, tribal. *See* Legal status;
  Self-government
Spaid, Stanley S., 2716
Spalding, Arminta Scott, 5109
Spalding, Henry H., 5554, 5557, 5606,
  5623, 5633
Spang, Alonzo, 6420, 6684, 6808
Spangler, John W., 3591
Spain, and Indian affairs, 522, 574, 600,
  620, 1956, 2872
Sparhawk, Frances C., 1501, 1633, 6171-
  6172
Sparks, Joe P., 2477
Spear, Elsa, 4479
Spearman, Leonard H. O., 8712
Special collections, 217-240
Special Sub-Committee on Indian Educa-
  tion, 6632
Speck, Frank G., 3077, 7582-7583, 7606,
  7652, 7866, 7887, 9030
Spector, Mozart I., 7073
Speeches on the Removal Bill, 752, 871
Spence, Mary Lee, 4745
Spencer, Frank Clarence, 6242
Spencer, Joab, 8374
Spencer, Katherine, 8658
Spencer, Milton, 3775
Spencer, Omar C., 8917
Spencer, Robert F., 7547
Spencer, Steven M., 6929
Spencer Academy, 6026
Sperlin, O. B., 4998, 8918
Splitlog, Chief, 5297
Spicer, Edward H., 330, 356, 2478, 7257-
  7259, 8564-8568
Spicer, Rosamond B., 8729
Spier, Leslie, 8569
Spiess, Mathias, 7584
Spiker, LaRue, 2479
Spinden, Herbert J., 1730, 8999, 9541
Spindler, George D., 7757-7758
Spindler, Louise S., 7758-7759
Spindler, Will H., 4325
Spingarn, Lawrence P., 7585
Spirit Lake Massacre, 3742-3751
Spivey, Gary H., 6942

Index

Thompson, Joseph J., 5970
Thompson, Laura, 7265, 8652-8653
Thompson, Peter, 4046
Thompson, Ray, 3113
Thompson, Robert Ellis, 5497
Thompson, Samuel H., 6534
Thompson, Stith, 9370
Thompson, Vern E., 8287
Thompson, William P., 5971
Thomson, Charles, 419
Thomson, Louise, 5652
Thomson, S. Carrie, 5699
Thoreau, Henry, 9300, 9318, 9359, 9377-9379
Thornbrough, Gayle, 3428-3429, 9453
Thornburgh, Luella, 8339
Thornburgh, Thomas T., 4187
Thorne, Betty, 7214
Thorp, Willard, 5157
Thorpe, Jim, 7813
Thrapp, Dan L., 4220, 4276-4278, 4716, 8633-8634
Throne, Mildred, 3811
Thwaites, Reuben Gold, 142, 215, 566-567, 3114, 3349, 3508, 4753, 4884-4886, 5343-5344, 5384, 5653, 7760, 7841
Tibbles, Susette, 1508. See also La Flesche, Susette
Tibbles, Thomas Henry, 1040-1042, 1509
Tiber, Bertha M., 7016-7017
Tidwell, H. M., 2763
Tiffany, Warren I., 6580
Tigua Indians, 2058-2059
Tigua settlement, 8749
Tiger Tail, 8237, 8250, 8256
Tilghman, Zoe A., 8354
Tillamook Indians, 2236
Tilley, Nannie M., 104
Tillim, Sidney J., 6907, 7094
Tillis, James Dallas, 3740
Tilsen, Kenneth E., 2589
Timber, sale of, 1351
Timmons, Barbara Joan, 6311
Tingley, Donald F., 9502
Tinnin, Eda Wetzel, 6066
Tippecanoe, Battle of, 3413, 3428
Tipton, John, 2659
Tireman, L. S., 6312-6313
Tishomingo, 8046
Tisinger, R. M., 6535
Titiev, Mischa, 8654
Titus, Nelson C., 4158
Titus, Willard H., 7067
Tlingit Indians, 6604, 8877, 8897
Tobey, James A., 7018
Tobriner Decision, 5797
Todd, John B. S., 3614
Todd, Ronald, 695
Todd, Ruthven, 9254
Tohill, Louis Arthur, 4887-4888
Tohopeka, Battle of. See Horseshoe Bend, Battle of
Tolbert, Charles Madden, 8104
Toler, Sally F., 1127
Tollefson, Gwen D., 7139
Tolles, Frederick B., 5700
Tomahawks, 4762

Tomo-Chi-Chi, 8134
Tonto Apache Indians, 2063, 2066
Tooker, William Wallace, 9588
Too-Qua-Stee. See Duncan, DeWitt Clinton
Tootle, James Roger, 420
Torbet, Robert G., 5198
Torrans, Thomas, 275
Torrey, Charles Cutler, 5654
Tortugas, New Mexico, 2056
Torture of captives, 9150
Tourism, 7356, 7382, 7393, 7401, 7416
Tousey, Thomas G., 6104
Toward Economic Development for Native American Communities, 7457
Town life, in Indian Territory, 1070
Townsend, Irving D., 6314-6315
Townsend, James G., 6908-6909, 7019, 7095, 7129-7130
Towsley, Alice C., 7068
Trachoma, 7081-7097
Tracy, E. C., 5655
Tracy, Joseph, 5656
Tracy, Valerie, 2764
Trade: bibliographies, 4757-4758; colonial, 479, 509, 4782-4839; East and Mississippi Valley, 4840-4899, 7737; general studies, 3462, 4759-4781, 9246-9247; Mexican-American, 693; Trans-Mississippi West, 4900-5007, 9000. See also Factory system
Trade and Intercourse Acts, 681
Traders, 2721, 2946. See also Trade
Trading houses. See Factory system
Trafzer, Clifford E., 4974, 8716-8717
Trail of Tears, 740, 766, 786, 807. See also Indian removal
Train, Percy, 2171
Trani, Eugene, 9637
Transculturalization. See Acculturation
Transfer issue, 974, 1152, 1169, 1298, 1411
Trans-Mississippi Exposition. See Omaha Exposition
Trans-Pecos region, 3223
Trant, William, 1510
Trask, J. N., 1344
Trask, William Blake, 443
Traub, Peter E., 4327
Travelers, 198-216, 612, 815, 5021
Traverse des Sioux, Treaty of, 2885, 2937
Travis, V. A., 7978
Treacy, Kenneth W., 821
Treaties, 16, 59-65, 634, 1166, 1467, 1997, 2865-2996, 3510, 5881, 8700. See also American Indian Ethnohistory Series; and individual treaties
Treaty of Chicago, 1922, 2922, 2975, 2984
Treaty of Coweta, 1978
Treaty of Dancing Rabbit Creek, 2904, 2920, 2927
Treaty of Fort Gibson, 2964
Treaty of Fort Harmar, 2906
Treaty of Fort Laramie, 2883
Treaty of Fort Stanwix (1768), 573, 2867-2868
Treaty of Fort Stanwix (1784), 2966, 2976
Treaty of Fort Wayne, 2889, 2932

447

United States Mounted Ranger Battalion, 3641
United States Statutes at Large, 52, 60
Universal Peace Union, 1016
Unrau, William E., 698, 2729-2730, 2766, 2990, 3892, 4485, 5005, 8375-8376
"Unto These Hills," 7979
Upchurch, O. C., 8922
Upham, Warren, 4892
Upper Missouri Agency, 2743
Upper Missouri River, Indian affairs on, 889
Upper Platte Agency, 2676, 2727
Upton, Richard, 4486
Upward Bound project, 6601
Urbanization, 2353, 6965, 7272-7347, 7405, 8966
Ursulines, 5333
Useem, John, 1789
Useem, Ruth Hill, 1789, 7464, 8488
Utah, Indian affairs in, 673, 2839, 3184, 8803
Utah State University, 138
Ute Indians, 876, 1346, 1373, 1446, 1894, 2180-2187, 2643, 3098, 4944, 7251, 7409, 8791, 8853-8874, 9201, 9473; bibliography, 8851-8852; economic development, 7369, 7412; education, 6007, 6017, 6219, 6247, 6600; removal of, 1406, 1472, 1476; wars, 3660, 3666, 4186-4206, 4336
Ute Reservation, 2805, 2830
Ute Treaty, 2953
Utley, Henry M., 4893
Utley, Robert M., 1023, 3225-3228, 3681, 3893-3894, 4070-4073, 4128, 4281, 4573-4574, 4693, 8489, 8532

Vagts, Alfred, 9255
Vail, Robert W. G., 276, 9135, 9158
Valentine, Robert G., 1608, 1636
Valpulic, Marian E., 4282a
Van Arsdale, Minor, 7297
Van Boven, Ella, 6814
Vance, John T., 1895
Vance, Z. B., 3229
Van Cleve, Banjamin, 3432
Van de Mark, Dorothy, 2363
Van den Broek, Father, 5332
Vandenbusche, Duane, 4576
Van Der Beets, Richard, 9139, 9159-9160
Vandergriff, James H., 8288
Van der Heyden, J., 5347
Vanderwerth, W. C., 9653
Van der Zee, Jacob, 2842, 3115, 3509-3510, 3637-3638, 4406-4407, 4894
Van de Water, Frederick F., 4694
Vandiveer, Clarence A., 4780
Van Doren, Carl, 2866
Van Duzen, Jean L., 6945
Van Every, Dale, 822, 3433
Van Hoeven, James William, 823
Vanishing Indians, 1837, 2260
Van Loon, L. G., 2878
Vann, James, 8001
Van Natter, Francis Marion, 7833
Van Ness, W. P., 3570
Van Roekel, Gertrude B., 8610

Van Sandt, Max, 7015
Van Stone, James W., 8923
Van Valkenburgh, Richard F., 2108-2109
Van Wie, Ethel K., 6856
van Willigen, John, 7433, 7465, 8732
Vatican Library, 223
Vaughan, Alden T., 444-445, 3301
Vaughn, J. W., 3130, 3932, 4129-4130
Veeder, William H., 5896-5901
Vermont, Indians of, 7572
Vernon, Walter N., 5470
Verplanck, James Delancey, 8722
Verrill, A. Hyatt, 7550-7551, 9545
Verwyst, Chrysostom, 5348-5349, 9591
Vestal, Stanley, 1007, 1790, 4074, 7891, 8337, 8490, 8533-8534, 9488. *See also* Campbell, Walter Stanley
Vetromile, Eugene, 7589
Victor, Frances Fuller, 3736
Victorio, 4284, 8617, 8623, 8634
Victory dance, 1556, 1780
Vigness, David M., 3654
Vilas, William Freeman, 9629
Villard, Oswald Garrison, 1731, 1850
Vincent, John R., 9474
Vincent, Philip, 3302
Vincentia, Sister, 7021
Vinegar Hill, Battle of, 4183
Viola, Herman J., 699, 2622, 9212-9213
Virginia: colonial Indian affairs, 491, 2877 (*see also* Southern colonies); Indians of, 7855, 7874-7877, 7894
Virginia-Chickasaw Treaty of 1783, 2869
Virginia Gazette Index, 168
Virtue, Ethel B., 5666
Vitry, Father, 5275
Vivian, James F., 568
Vivian, Jean H., 568
Vizenor, Gerald, 7741
Vocational training, 6375-6410
Voegelin, Erminie Wheeler. *See* Wheeler-Voegelin, Erminie
Vogel, Virgil J., 378, 2490, 5667, 6857-6859, 9503-9504, 9546-9547, 9592
Voget, Fred W., 2014, 2843, 7266-7267, 7466, 7654
Vogt, Evon Z., 1777, 1791, 7268, 8698, 8723-8724
Vollmann, Tim, 5860
Vollmar, E. R., 5350
Volunteer soldiers, 3858
Volwiler, Albert T., 4831
von Fumetti, Billie, 7191
Von Hentig, Hans, 5937
Von Hoeffern, Antoinette, 5306
Von Tungeln, Annie Laurie, 9447
Voting rights, 5771, 5776, 5783
Vreeland Bill, 1606
Vroman, Adam Clark, 8570, 9476

Waddell, Jack O., 7342-7343, 7467, 8733
Wade, John Williams, 824
Wadia, Maneck Sorabji, 8764
Wagner, Carruth J., 7022
Wagner, Henry R., 204
Wagner, James R., 7343a
Wagner, Oswald F., 5398